VIRAGO
⊃ NON-FICTION

Vera Brittain

Vera Brittain (1893–1970) grew up in provincial comfort in the north of England. In 1914 she won an exhibition to Somerville College, Oxford, but a year later abandoned her studies to enlist as a VAD nurse. She served throughout the war, working in London, Malta and close to the Front in France.

At the end of the war, with all those closest to her dead, Vera Brittain returned to Oxford. There she met Winifred Holtby – author of *South Riding* – and this friendship, which was to last until Winifred Holtby's untimely death in 1935, sustained her in those difficult post-war years.

Vera Brittain was a convinced pacifist, a prolific speaker, lecturer, journalist and writer, she devoted much of her energy to the causes of peace and feminism. She wrote 29 books in all, novels, poetry, biography and autobiography, and other non-fiction, but it was *Testament of Youth* which established her reputation and made her one of the best loved writers of her time. The authorised biography, *Vera Brittain: A Life* (1995) by Paul Berry and Mark Bostridge, is published by Virago Press.

Vera Brittain married in 1925 and had two children, one of whom, Shirley Williams, writes the preface to this edition of her mother's most famous work.

TESTAMENT OF YOUTH

An Autobiographical Study of the Years
1900–1925

Vera Brittain

With a new Introduction by Mark Bostridge
and a Preface by Shirley Williams

virago

VIRAGO

First published by Virago Press in 1978
This edition published by Virago Press in 2018

3 5 7 9 10 8 6 4 2

First published by Victor Gollancz Limited in 1933

A CIP catalogue record for this book
is available from the British Library.

ISBN 978-0-349-01027-4

Typeset by Palimpsest Book Production Limited, Falkirk, Stirlingshire
Printed and bound in Great Britain by Clays Ltd, Elcograf S.p.A.

Papers used by Virago are from well-managed forests
and other responsible sources.

MIX
Paper from
responsible sources
FSC
www.fsc.org   FSC® C104740

Virago Press
An imprint of
Little, Brown Book Group
Carmelite House
50 Victoria Embankment
London EC4Y 0DZ

An Hachette UK Company
www.hachette.co.uk

www.virago.co.uk

To
R.A.L. and E.H.B.
In Memory

'And some there be, which have no memorial; who are perished, as though they had never been; and are become as though they had never been born; and their children after them. But these were merciful men, whose righteousness hath not been forgotten . . . Their bodies are buried in peace; but their name liveth for evermore. The people will tell of their wisdom, and the congregation will shew forth their praise.'

ECCLESIASTICUS XLIV

Contents

Introduction   ix
Preface   xxv
Author's Acknowledgments   xxvii
Foreword   xxix

PART I

Chapter	I	Forward from Newcastle	*page*	3
	II	Provincial Young-Ladyhood		34
	III	Oxford *versus* War		75
	IV	Learning *versus* Life		114
	V	Camberwell *versus* Death		181

PART II

VI	"When the Vision Dies . . ."	213
VII	Tawny Island	262
VIII	Between the Sandhills and the Sea	329
IX	"This Loneliest Hour"	390

PART III

X	Survivors Not Wanted	427
XI	Piping for Peace	490
XII	"Another Stranger"	557

August · 664 pages · 8/6

VERA BRITTAIN'S

TESTAMENT OF YOUTH:

AN AUTOBIOGRAPHICAL STUDY OF THE YEARS 1900-1925

Some advance opinions:

Sarah Gertrude Millin:

"It was my first impulse to write that 'Testament of Youth' is the loveliest book of its kind I know. But, really, it is the only book of its kind I know."

Phyllis Bentley:

"A particularly fascinating autobiography : a personal record of great beauty, insight and courage."

Storm Jameson:

"Its mere pressure on mind and senses makes it unforgettable."

Naomi Royde-Smith:

"I am still a little shaken by it."

Described overleaf ☞

71

Gollancz's catalogue announcement of *Testament of Youth*, 1933
(William Ready Division of Archives and Research Collections,
McMaster University Library, Hamilton, Canada)

Introduction

For more than eight decades now, Vera Brittain's *Testament of Youth* has spoken to successive generations of readers about the horrors of the First World War, and the scale of human suffering, sacrifice and loss that resulted from four years of intensive fighting.

Originally published by Gollancz in 1933, Vera Brittain's autobiographical account of the cataclysmic impact of the conflict on young men and women who were just reaching maturity in August 1914 immediately became a bestseller on both sides of the Atlantic. Arriving at the tail-end of the boom in memoirs and novels about the Great War, the book served a dual purpose. It reminded those old enough to remember them of the years 1914–18; and, appearing only months after Adolf Hitler was installed as Chancellor of Germany, it also issued a powerful warning about the threat of another world war. Pressing this message home still further in the weeks following publication would be the news that Hitler's Germany had withdrawn from the League of Nations, the internationalist body for which Vera Brittain had campaigned and on which she had pinned her hopes for peace since coming down from Oxford in 1921.

One of Brittain's specific aims in writing her memoir was to try to influence the youth of another generation against succumbing to the 'false glamour' of war. The attractions of militarism and of 'heroism in the abstract', she believed, had played a crucial role in sending her own male contemporaries to their deaths. 'The causes of war are always falsely represented,' she wrote in chapter VII; 'its honour is dishonest and its glory meretricious, but the challenge to spiritual endurance, the intense sharpening

of all the senses . . . remain to allure those boys and girls who
have . . . reached the age when love and friendship and adventure call more persistently than at any later time.'

In Britain, in the years to 1939, *Testament of Youth* sold 120,000
copies. After the Second World War the book continued to sell
steadily. But by the early fifties sales had stalled, and when at the
end of that decade Brittain attempted to find a publisher to reissue
the book in paperback she was told that its commercial prospects
were limited. In 1960 an abridged paperback of *Testament of Youth*
was published by Arrow Books, in an edition prepared by the
author herself, but its impact, as predicted, was minimal.

Even the renewal of interest in the First World War, heralded
by BBC Television's landmark documentary series *The Great War*,
broadcast in 1964 to commemorate the fiftieth anniversary of the
outbreak of the war, failed to bring new readers to the book. This
was despite an article in *The Times* on 'The Writers' War', in which
Sir William Haley, the paper's editor (writing as Oliver Edwards),
hailed *Testament of Youth* as 'the real war book of the Women of
England'. Understandably enough, the emphasis of the BBC series,
first shown on the newly launched BBC2, was on military history
and the memories of surviving male combatants. Indeed, what
remains memorable about the series today is the interviews with
sober-suited veterans, most of them speaking publicly for the first
time about their wartime experiences. Nevertheless, it now seems
extraordinary that *The Great War* devoted only minutes of its
running time of more than seventeen hours to exploring the contribution of women to the war effort.

In her final years, before her death in 1970, Vera Brittain was
disappointed at the lack of recognition given to *Testament of Youth*,
but she put her faith in the judgement of posterity. 'Some day in
the distant future,' she wrote, 'when the First World War has really
passed into history and all of us who remember it are gone, it
may well be that a new type of interest in it will arise.'

In the event, the revival of interest arrived much quicker than
that, and when it did so its success far exceeded anyone's expectations. In April 1978, Virago Press, a new feminist publishing
house that had gained a reputation for reprinting neglected

women's classics, reissued *Testament of Youth* with a simple, but bold, cover design: a red poppy on a black background. Carmen Callil, the company's founder, had been given a copy of the book by Rosalind Delmar, a member of Virago's advisory group, and had determined to republish it after a first reading reduced her to tears. The following year, in the autumn of 1979, the broadcast of BBC Television's award-winning adaptation of the book, scripted in five parts by Elaine Morgan, with a luminous performance by Cheryl Campbell in the central role, helped to put *Testament of Youth* back at the top of the bestseller lists. It has never been out of print since.

Forty years on from Virago's republication, Vera Brittain's autobiography is secure in its position at the heart of the canon of First World War literature. In 2015, another adaptation of *Testament of Youth*, this time on the big screen in James Kent's film version, helped to make the book a bestseller once again. The film, like the television series before it, was defined by a no less remarkable performance, with the Swedish actress Alicia Vikander taking the part of Vera Brittain.

One hundred years on from 1918 and the Armistice that finally silenced the guns, *Testament of Youth* is the most widely read British autobiography of the First World War. Ironically, it is probably more familiar to readers today than the famous memoirs by men that inspired it and which caught the imagination of the reading public in the late twenties. It remains the most moving and eloquent account of the suffering and bereavement inflicted by the 1914–18 war, while offering a variety of windows onto different perspectives of the conflict: from that of the volunteer nurse, serving with the British armies at home and abroad; to the young subalterns in the trenches of Flanders, France and Italy; and to the English middle-classes at home, encountering unexpected and unwelcome social changes arising from wartime. Significantly for the book's popularity, its overarching narrative, from war enthusiasm to war disillusionment, and ultimately to a conviction of the war's 'futility', fits closely the popular image of the First World War that has been predominant in Britain since the mid-sixties. (This view of a futile war was certainly not held by the majority of the British population in 1914, determined to fight German militarism, nor by Brittain herself at the outbreak of war.)

In this centenary year, one other development in the book's publishing history should be noted. For Vera Brittain, who nursed German prisoners of war at Étaples in northern France in 1917, and travelled in Germany in 1924 to witness post-war conditions there, it would have been especially welcome: in 2018, *Testament of Youth* will be published in a German translation for the first time.

THE LONG GESTATION

The seed of the idea behind *Testament of Youth* may be traced to as far back as March 1916, three months after the death in France of her fiancé Roland Leighton, when Vera Brittain wrote to her brother Edward, who had himself recently departed for the Front, that 'if the War spares me, it will be my one aim to immortalise in a book the story of us four . . .' (her friendship with Geoffrey Thurlow, the fifth member of their wartime circle, still lay in the future). By that time she had already written a short story, which no longer survives, about her relationship with Roland Leighton. However, the constraints of her work as a Voluntary Aid Detachment nurse (VAD) meant that Brittain had little time to write anything beyond poetry during the war. In August 1918, soon after her return from nursing in France, she published a slim volume of her *Verses of a V.A.D.*, the first of twenty-nine books she would publish in a fifty-year career as a writer. Predominantly documentary and elegiac in tone, the collection included many of the poems that were later to appear in *Testament of Youth*, including 'Perhaps', written in Roland Leighton's memory, and 'To My Brother', completed only days before Edward Brittain's death in June 1918. Two poems, 'The Sisters Buried at Lemnos' and 'Vengeance is Mine', commemorating the nursing sisters killed in the German air raid on Étaples in May 1918, anticipate one of the major themes of her autobiography: a concern that feats of wartime female heroism should not go unrecorded.

In the final months of the war, Vera Brittain was also close to completing her first novel based on her war experiences. Entitled 'The Pawn of Fate', and later revised as 'Folly's Vineyard', this was drawn from her time as a VAD at the 24 General Hospital at Étaples. It included moving descriptions of nursing German prisoners, but the novel's lurid plot centred on an eccentric nursing sister, based on Faith Moulson ('Hope Milroy', the same name she was later given in *Testament of Youth*), who had been in charge of the German ward where Brittain nursed in 1917. Fears of a potential libel action led Brittain to put this novel aside.

In 1922, while sharing a flat with Winifred Holtby at 52 Doughty Street in Bloomsbury, Vera Brittain submitted typed selections from the diary she had kept between 1913 and 1917 for a publisher's competition offering a prize for a personal diary or autobiography. She called her selections 'A Chronicle of Youth' and reduced the diary's length by almost a half. She also gave the characters pseudonyms and cut the text short at April 1916, shaping the narrative as a tragic love story that ends with the death of 'Vincent Farringdon' (Roland Leighton) and her consuming grief for him. In a preface Brittain wrote that '[c]ould we have but a few more records like these to aid the imagination of the militarist and the sceptic, I believe that there would be few left who would be willing to condemn another generation to endure what this one has endured'.

The diary was not chosen, but reading it may have prompted Brittain's enquiry of her publisher Grant Richards – who published her first two works of fiction, *The Dark Tide* (1923) and *Not Without Honour* (1924) – about the possibility of publishing a war novel. Richards was as encouraging as he could be given the publishing world's uncertain attitude to books about the war, but it was not until early 1926, following her marriage to George Catlin and temporary relocation to the United States, that concrete proposals for Brittain's novel surfaced. It was to be called 'The Incidental Adam', she told Winifred Holtby, and she intended to write it 'very quickly, without having to look up anything except my letters and diaries'. She was 'aching, at long last, to write about the war', she wrote again to Holtby, later that year, 'all the grieving and the struggle and the loss'.

'The Incidental Adam' was broadly conceived as a narrative of a woman's development over the course of a decade. In discarded drafts of other novels from this time – preserved in the Brittain archive at McMaster University in Hamilton, Ontario – the war theme is much more central. 'The Stranger Son' focuses on the 'Problem of Pacifism' and dramatises the clash 'between the desire to serve one's country and the belief that war is wrong' through the story of Vincent Harlow, who declares his pacifist beliefs on the outbreak of war in 1914. Here Brittain appears to be deliberately attempting to write away from her own experience. By contrast, 'The Kingdom of Endurance' or 'Youth's Calvary', is much closer to fictionalised autobiography. Indeed, at the outset it bears a very close resemblance to the early chapters of *Testament of Youth*. Virginia Dennison, Brittain's fictional alter ego, is the daughter of Robert, a hard-headed businessman, director of the 'famous Dennison china firm', and his wife Mildred, who originates from 'the poverty-stricken family of an obscure professional singer'.

Structurally and narratively, 'The Two Islands', an incomplete novel about the wartime relationship of a brother and sister, Gabriel and Ruth Barrington, is the most coherent of all Brittain's fictional versions of her war experiences. The book juxtaposes the sombreness of 'the Grey Island' (Britain) with 'the brightness of the Gold' (Malta), but portrays the deepening shadow that the war casts over both of them. Ruth is in love with Lawrence Sinclair, a brilliant young journalist, who volunteers immediately on the outbreak of war and is killed at Loos. With his death, Gabriel 'becomes the only hope of [Ruth's] future'. Significantly, the focus of 'The Two Islands', on the close bond between Ruth and Gabriel, rather than on the Roland character, Lawrence Sinclair, is undoubtedly a reflection of the fact that, of all Vera Brittain's wartime losses, her brother Edward's was by the far the most painful and the one which time could do the least to heal. Ruth volunteers for foreign service and is sent to Malta. Gabriel, meanwhile, is awarded the Military Cross for his bravery on the Somme and is posted to Salonika, where he is seriously wounded. He arrives at Ruth's hospital, but dies after an unsuccessful operation. The final scene of the novel, planned but never written, was to have depicted Ruth leaning over the ship's rail, sailing out of Valletta Harbour on her way home, watching as 'the tawny island' disappeared below the horizon.

What finally brought an end to this protracted search for the form best suited to her war book was a change in the literary climate. The successful publication of works by such writers as Edmund Blunden and Siegfried Sassoon, beginning in 1928, suddenly guaranteed the war literature of disillusionment a new popularity. The following year, the spate of war books reached its numerical peak: twenty-nine were published in Britain, including the English translation of Erich Maria Remarque's *In Westen nichts Neues* as *All Quiet on the Western Front*, which sold 250,000 copies in its first year; Robert Graves's *Goodbye to All That*; and Richard Aldington's *Death of a Hero*. The decade since the Armistice had allowed writers a period of emotional detachment in which to make their considered responses to the memory of the war, while the public appetite for a disillusioned picture may have been in part a product of disillusionment, not with the war itself, but with the condition of Britain at the end of the twenties. Expectations of post-war prosperity – 'a land fit for heroes' – had been sorely disappointed, and a new era beckoned of even higher unemployment and hunger marches.

Vera Brittain made a close study of the war books of Blunden, Sassoon and Graves, and they influenced her decision to write not a novel, but an autobiography of her war experiences. She read Blunden's *Undertones of War* at Christmas 1928. She found it 'grave, dignified, but perfectly simple and straightforward: why shouldn't I write one like that?' Accompanied by Winifred Holtby, she attended a performance early in 1929 of the theatrical hit of the season, R. C. Sherriff's trench drama, *Journey's End*; and towards the end of the year, she reviewed *Death of a Hero* in *Time and Tide*, finding it to be 'a devastating indictment of pre-war civilization, with its ignorance, its idiocies, and its values even falser than those of today'.

Brittain described Aldington's novel as 'one of the greatest war books that I have so far read'. Its 'through-going embodiment of disillusion' very much chimed with her own view of the war. But she also objected to Aldington's misogyny and to the way in which his book poured a 'cynical fury of scorn' on the wartime suffering of women. In an article in the *Nation and Athenaeum* at the beginning of 1931, Brittain stated that women's experience in the war had obviously differed vastly from men's, and that she made 'no puerile claim to equality of suffering and service'. Nevertheless, she maintained 'that any picture of the war years is incomplete which omits those aspects that mainly concern women . . . The woman is still silent, who by presenting the war in its true perspective in her own life, will illuminate its meaning afresh for its own generation.' By the time she wrote those words she had embarked on *Testament of Youth*, and clearly intended to be that woman.

There had of course already been a large number and variety of books by women about their wartime experiences, published both during the war and afterwards. Brittain expressed warm words of commendation for Mary Lee's 1929 novel *It's a Great War*, while pointing out that since the book was American, it dealt with the war only from 1917 onwards. She admired Mary Borden's *The Forbidden Zone* (1929), derived from Borden's time nursing in a mobile hospital attached to the French army at the Front. Later she would read, 'with deep interest and sympathy', Irene Rathbone's novel *We That Were Young* (1932), based on Rathbone's experiences at the First London General in Camberwell, where Brittain had nursed in 1915–16.

However, to read even the best of the other war books by women is to appreciate the scope and depth of Vera Brittain's approach in *Testament of Youth*. In writing 'an autobiographical study of the years 1900–1925' she saw herself as contributing a chapter to the wider history of women's emancipation in Britain. Two chapters of almost a hundred pages precede her narrative of the war, which describe Brittain's attempts to escape from her 'provincial young-ladyhood' and her struggles to gain a university education. Rebecca West, an early reviewer, saw this as 'an interesting piece of social history, in its picture of the peculiarly unsatisfying position of women in England before the war'. And in the book's final section, after the declaration of the Armistice in November 1918, and following the granting of the vote to women over thirty in February that year (an event that passed unnoticed by Brittain at the time because of her absorption in her nursing work in France), *Testament of Youth* returns to feminist themes: to Brittain's involvement in equal-rights feminism, to her working partnership with her great friend Winifred Holtby and, finally, to her engagement to a survivor of the war generation, and the promise of a marriage that will be defined in feminist terms.

Testament of Youth needs also to be seen in the context of the large number of women's autobiographies and biographical histories published in the twenties and thirties that attempted to reconstruct and reassess the pre-war period, as well as the years between 1914 and 1918. Works like Beatrice Webb's *My Apprenticeship* (1926), Ray Strachey's *The Cause* (1928), Sylvia Pankhurst's *The Suffragette Movement* (1931) and Helena Swanwick's *I Have Been Young* (1935) adopted what had been hitherto a predominantly masculine form of writing in order to celebrate the achievements of women's public lives. In common with these women, Brittain understood that the story of a woman's life could no longer be defined in terms of the purely personal. In light of the campaigns for the vote, and their experience of the war years, women could now see themselves as representatives of the times, and their lives as a mirror of vast social change.

WRITING AND PUBLICATION

The writing of *Testament of Youth* was plagued with problems. At the beginning of December 1929, after only a few weeks' work on the book, Vera Brittain discovered that she was pregnant with her second child. Her ability to write in the year following her daughter Shirley's birth in July 1930 was considerably reduced. She had resolved on quoting from the letters of the four young men in her story, convinced that these would give the book a special authenticity. Subsequently, though, she found that the restrictions of copyright required her to resort to paraphrase at points, necessitating some rewriting. Then, in the final stages before publication, she was forced to deal with the objections of her husband, George Catlin, to his appearance in the book. Believing that Brittain's frank discussion of their courtship and engagement would hold him up to ridicule from his academic colleagues, he insisted that she cut certain passages. She complied by reducing him in the final draft to the shadowy figure of 'G.', bitterly regretting that the symbolism of her post-war resurrection, represented by this relationship, had been weakened.

The novelist Phyllis Bentley, with whom Brittain had a difficult, not to say rivalrous, relationship in the early thirties, later remembered how *Testament of Youth* was written 'through every kind of harassment and interruption'. At times, domestic and professional pressures on Brittain were intense. She relied as always on the loving support of Winifred Holtby, though Holtby was far from well, diagnosed in the course of 1932 with the illness that would eventually kill her. In mid-February 1933 Brittain finally completed the revision of her typescript and Victor Gollancz accepted it immediately for publication. Gollancz, who was to employ his considerable flair in promoting and selling the book, confessed to Brittain that, in places, her story had moved him 'intolerably'.

Testament of Youth was published on 28 August, selling out its first printing on publication day. 'Oh what a head-cracking week . . .', Brittain recorded in her diary, after reading the early reviews. 'Never did I imagine that the *Testament* would inspire such praise at length, or provoke – in smaller doses – so much abuse.' Lavish praise came from, among others, Pamela Hinkson, Compton Mackenzie and John Brophy, while in the *Sunday Times* Storm Jameson concluded that 'Miss Brittain has written a book which stands alone among books written by women about the war'. In the United States, where Macmillan published the book in October, and where Brittain would be fêted on a triumphant lecture-tour in 1934, it enjoyed similar success. R. L. Duffus in the *New York Times* commented that 'of all the personal narratives covering the World War period there can surely have been none more honest, more revealing . . . or more heartbreakingly beautiful than this of Vera Brittain's'.

Some detractors were unnerved by the book's frankness. James Agate struck a blow for misogyny when he wrote that it reminded him of a woman crying in the street. Virginia Woolf saw *Testament of Youth* as a 'new sort' of book, 'the hard anguished sort' that exposed the writer to public gaze. In her diary she admitted that it had kept her out of bed until she had finished reading it. She wrote later to Brittain about how much *Testament of Youth* had interested her, particularly the connections the book had 'lit up' for her between feminism and pacifism, which were to leave their strongest impress on *Three Guineas* (1938) and Woolf's analysis of the links between patriarchy and militarism.

Letters flowed in from readers. The writer St John Ervine thought it 'a superb account of what the War did to our generation', and felt that '[t]he futility of the War becomes clearer and clearer as your tale of young men dying unfolds itself'. One woman, only eighteen months old in 1914, who had taken part in the February 1933 'King and Country' debate at the Oxford Union – in which the motion 'that this House will in no circumstances fight for its King and Country' was carried by 275 votes to 153 – told Brittain that 'the whole of my generation owes you a great debt, & I hope very sincerely that we shall repay you by the fulfilment shown at the . . . debate, at which I was present'. On the other hand, A. H. Jolliffe, who had been in the same house at Uppingham School as Roland Leighton, Edward Brittain and Victor Richardson, admired *Testament of Youth* but none the less made a significant criticism when he suggested to Brittain that she had allowed her own tragic experiences 'to colour your picture of war time'. Jolliffe implied that her perspective on the war was a reflection of the disillusionment of the post-war years rather than of the war itself, when, he wrote, '[t]he majority of fighting men . . . were prepared to devote their energies to winning it'.

Approaching forty, Vera Brittain had at last passed from relative obscurity to the literary fame she had dreamed of since childhood, when as a girl she had written five 'novels' on waste-cuts from her father's paper-mill. In the process she had exorcised her 'brutal, poignant, insistent' memories of the war, releasing her deeply felt obligations to her war dead: to Roland and Edward, to Victor and Geoffrey.

But amidst all the lionisation, one letter from a reader brought with it a distressing shock. In the summer of 1934, Charles Hudson,

Edward's commanding officer in the 11th Sherwood Foresters, contacted Brittain to inform her that, as she had suspected in 1918, he had withheld certain essential details from her about the circumstances of her brother's death. Hudson had felt traduced by the account in chapter ix of *Testament of Youth* of his wartime meetings with Brittain and had decided to put the record straight. On the eve of the battle on the Asiago Plateau in which he was killed, Edward was warned that one of his letters, which made it 'unmistakeably plain' that he had been involved in homosexual relations with men in his company, had been intercepted by the military police. In all likelihood, had he survived the offensive on 15 June, he would have faced a court-martial, and Hudson wondered whether Edward had deliberately sought death to avoid the inevitable disgrace.

Vera Brittain was not surprised by what Colonel Hudson had told her about Edward's sexuality, but she did find 'almost unendurable the thought of how bitter his last days must have been'. After a century, much about Edward's death remains a mystery.

AUTOBIOGRAPHY VERSUS HISTORY

In 1960 Vera Brittain gave a lecture in London at the Royal Society of Literature, entitled 'Literary Testaments', and jokingly alluded to a previous talk given by Edmund Blunden, in which he had described dreaming of looking up the word 'autobiography' in a dictionary. In his dream Blunden had found the words '*See* fiction' under the entry. But when he looked up 'fiction', he was presented with the cross-reference, '*See* autobiography'.

In *Testament of Youth*, Brittain had made a conscious attempt to make her story 'as truthful as history, but as readable as fiction'. She carefully researched the background to the war in historical records like the *Annual Register* and in the collections of the British Red Cross and the Imperial War Museum. She also employed a patchwork of quotations from her diary and wartime letters, her own and those of her male friends, to contribute to the documentary effect and to bring the protagonists alive. But she was fearful of 'numerous inaccuracies through queer tricks of memory'. For her highly inaccurate account of the Étaples mutiny, which had occurred in September 1917 while she was at the camp and which was still not widely acknowledged or written about, she was forced to rely on little more than the memory of Harry Pearson, an ex-soldier and friend of Winifred Holtby, who had had no direct involvement in the events either.

Inevitably, though, in her efforts to construct a readable narrative Brittain sometimes used novelistic devices to heighten reality. These in turn distorted biographical truth. The posthumous publication of Brittain's diary (in 1981) and her correspondence from the war (in 1998) has revealed the extent to which, in her treatment of her relationship with Roland Leighton, for instance, she creates a conventional love story instead of dealing with the complex web of emotions that were a product of all the stresses and strains associated with a wartime love affair. Her description of getting into Oxford University overstates the singlemindedness of her pursuit of that goal, while exaggerating her bleak isolation from the rest of the Buxton household, studying for her exams 'in a chilly little north-west room'. It ignores the considerable assistance, both practical and financial, that Brittain received from her parents, especially from her mother Edith.

More seriously for the historical picture, *Testament of Youth* contains very little of Brittain's own enthusiasm about the war, at times amounting to jingoistic euphoria, which is present in her contemporary records. The opening sentence of the book, explaining that 'the Great War . . . came to me not as a superlative tragedy, but as an interruption of the most exasperating kind to my personal plans', hardly tallies with her diary entries from the outbreak of war in which she follows the international crisis closely, is buoyed up by patriotic excitement and echoes the bombastic rhetoric in the press.

Other differences between Brittain's perspectives of 1914–18 and 1933 are starker still. In her autobiography she reveals nothing of the part she had played at the beginning of the war in persuading Edward to volunteer, in opposition to their father's wishes, and she seems reluctant overall to confront her own susceptibility as a young woman to the glamour and idealism of war. Her account of the period she spent as a VAD at the 24 General at Étaples, from August 1917 to April 1918, does not possess the reliability of chronology and detail of earlier parts of the book. In part this is due to the fact that she had ceased to keep a diary after returning from Malta in 1917, and had to depend on a few letters and rushed notes, and a sometimes hazy recollection of events some fifteen years after they had taken place. However, her description of nursing German prisoners of war in chapter VIII highlights something more significant: the extent to which *Testament of Youth* is coloured by the spirit of internationalism and pacifism that Vera Brittain developed only in the years after the war (she did not formally become a pacifist until 1937, but the writing of her auto-biography undoubtedly hastened her conversion). Contrary to Brittain's account of German prisoners dying in vast numbers at the 24 General, the official records for the hospital in the National Archives show a very low mortality rate – as low as 2 per cent for the prisoner-patients during the time Brittain nursed there. Her chilling picture of the plight of her German patients is there-fore largely fictional, but fits with the overarching anti-war, war-disillusionment theme of *Testament of Youth*.

Vera Brittain presented her own experiences of the war as 'fairly typical'. But of course they are not. *Testament of Youth* stands as a portrait of the war as experienced by the volunteer nurse and the volunteer soldier. The young men in the story are representative of the subalterns who went straight from their public schools or Oxbridge to the killing fields of France and Flanders. As a demo-graphic class, these junior officers show mortality rates that are signif-icantly higher than those of other officers, or of the British army as a whole. Uppingham School lost about one in five of every old boy that served. The Bishop of Worcester, dedicating the war memorial at another public school, Malvern College, observed that the loss of former pupils in the war 'can only be described as the wiping out of a generation'. The existence of a lost generation is not literally true, and is entirely unsupported by the statistical evidence. But given the disproportionate death rate among junior officers, and the weight of her personal losses, it is perhaps no wonder that Brittain believed, as she wrote in *Testament of Youth*, that 'the finest flowers of English manhood had been plucked from a whole generation'.

'WHAT YOU HAVE STRIVEN FOR WILL NOT END IN NOTHING'
Vera Brittain to Roland Leighton, 26 September 1915

Vera Brittain died at the age of seventy-six on 29 March 1970, after a writing and campaigning life devoted to the causes of feminism and peace. In accordance with her wishes, her ashes were scattered on Edward Brittain's grave at Granezza in northern Italy. 'For nearly fifty years much of my heart has been in that Italian village cemetery,' she had told her daughter Shirley in 1967.

The military cemetery at Granezza, four thousand feet up on the Asiago Plateau, is still a remote destination today. More accessible is Roland Leighton's grave at Louvencourt, on the Somme, a short drive along the road to Doullens from Albert. On the south-east side of the village, a large stone cross dominates the skyline, surrounded by acres of tranquil farmland. It is a small cemetery, designed by Sir Reginald Blomfield, of 151 Commonwealth and seventy-six French graves, beautifully cared for, as are all the military cemeteries of the First World War, by the Commonwealth Graves Commission.

In the summer of 2017 I paid a visit to Louvencourt in the company of Vera Brittain's daughter Shirley Williams, her granddaughter Rebecca and Rebecca's sons, two of Brittain's great-grandchildren. We visited the Maison de Louvencourt, deserted, with its windows locked and shuttered, but its garden immaculately maintained, where Roland died, after an unsuccessful operation, on 23 December 1915. We saw the village church where his funeral was held, and walked along the lane by the side of the cemetery, renamed *Allée Roland Leighton* to mark the centenary of Roland's death in 2015. Later we drove to Hébuterne, and just beyond the courtyard and outer buildings of New Toutvent Farm identified the British position where Roland received his mortal wound. We also saw the track along which the ambulance conveyed him, on a slow and agonising drive, to Louvencourt.

At the cemetery, Roland's grave is in the middle, not far from the memorial cross and cenotaph, and its inscription includes the closing line from one of his and Vera Brittain's favourite poems, W. E. Henley's 'Echoes: XLII', 'Never Goodbye' (though Roland's age at death is mistakenly given as nineteen instead of twenty on the gravestone).

On our 2017 visit, a large wreath of poppies from the pupils of a girls' school at Bramley in Surrey had recently been laid on the grave. In the visitors' book in a little cupboard in the wall I counted, as on earlier visits, numerous messages from visitors from around the world honouring the memory of Roland Leighton – paying tribute to him because they had read about his brief life and early death in *Testament of Youth*. To echo the words of Shirley Williams in her preface, it is a precious sort of immortality.

One hundred years after the end of the First World War, *Testament of Youth*'s power to disturb and to move remains undiminished. Vera Brittain's 'passionate plea for peace', which attempts to show 'without any polite disguise, the agony of the war to the individual and its destructiveness to the human race', is one that, tragically, still resonates in our world today.

Mark Bostridge
2018

FURTHER READING

Paul Berry and Mark Bostridge, *Vera Brittain: A Life* (1995)

Mark Bostridge, *Vera Brittain and the First World War. The Story of Testament of Youth* (2014)

Vera Brittain, *Chronicle of Youth. Vera Brittain's War Diary 1913–1917*, edited by Alan Bishop with Terry Smart (1981)

Vera Brittain *et al.*, *Letters from a Lost Generation: First World War Letters of Vera Brittain and Four Friends*, edited by Alan Bishop and Mark Bostridge (1998)

Vera Brittain, *Because You Died. Poetry and Prose of the First World War and After*, edited and introduced by Mark Bostridge (2008)

Preface

Shirley Williams is Vera Brittain's daughter. She is a former Labour cabinet minister, the co-founder of the Social Democratic Party, and was until 2004 the Leader of the Liberal Democrats in the House of Lords.

It is now sixty years since the First World War ended, and few are still alive who survived that fearful experience at first hand. The War should now be a part of history; the weapons, the uniforms, the static horror of battles fought in trenches are all obsolete now. Yet the First World War refuses to fade away. It has marked all of us who were in any way associated with it, even at one generation's remove through our parents. The books, the poetry, the artefacts of those four and a half years still speak to young men and women who were not even born when the Second World War ended.

Why are we so haunted? I think it is because of the terrible irony of the War; the idealism and high-mindedness that led boys and men in their hundreds of thousands to volunteer to fight and, often, to die; the obscenity of the square miles of mud, barbed wire, broken trees and shattered bodies into which they were flung, battalion after battalion; and the total imbalance between the causes for which the war was fought on both sides, as against the scale of the human sacrifice. As Wilfred Owen put it in 'The Send-Off',

> Shall they return to beatings of great bells
> In wild train-loads?
> A few, a few, too few for drums and yells

There is another reason, too. The First World War was the culmination of personal war; men saw the other human being they had killed, visibly dead. Men fought with bayonets, with knives or even their bare hands. The guns themselves were on the battlefields, thick with smoke, the gunners sweaty and mudbound. War had not yet become a pitting of scientist against scientist or technologist against technologist. Death was not, on either side, elimination through pressing a button, but something seen and experienced personally, bloody, pathetic and foul.

My own picture of the War was gleaned from my mother. Her life, like that of so many of her contemporaries who were actually in the fighting or dealing with its consequences, was shaped by it and shadowed by it. It was hard for her to laugh unconstrainedly; at the back of her mind, the row upon row of wooden crosses were planted too deeply. Through her, I learned how much courage it took to live on in service to the world when all those one loved best were gone: her fiancé first, her best friend, her beloved only brother. The only salvation was work, particularly the work of patching and repairing those who were still alive. After the War, the work went on – writing, campaigning, organising against war. My mother became a lifelong pacifist. I still remember her in her seventies, determinedly sitting in a CND demonstration, and being gently removed by the police.

Testament of Youth is, I think, the undisputed classic book about the First World War written by a woman, and indeed a woman whose childhood had been a very sheltered one. It is an autobiography and also an elegy for a generation. For many men and women, it described movingly how they themselves felt. Time and again, in small Welsh towns and in big Northern cities, someone has come up to me after a meeting to ask if my mother was indeed the author of *Testament of Youth*, and to say how much it meant to them. It is a precious sort of immortality.

I hope now that a new generation, more distant from the First World War, will discover the anguish and pain in the lives of those young people sixty years ago; and in discovering will understand.

Shirley Williams
August 1977

Author's Acknowledgments

My very warm and grateful thanks are due to Roland Leighton's family for their generosity in allowing me to publish his poems and quote from his letters; to my parents for permitting me to reproduce E. H. B.'s letters and his song 'L'Envoi,' as well as for their untiring assistance in the tracing of war letters and documents; to B. B. for the extracts from my uncle's letters which appear in Chapter VII; to my husband for the letters quoted in Chapter XII and for much valuable criticism; and to Winifred Holtby, whose unstinted services no words can adequately acknowledge or describe, for the use of her letters and the poem 'Trains in France,' for her help in correcting the proofs, and for the unfailing co-operation of her constant advice and her vivid memory. I am, in addition, greatly indebted to Madame Smeterlin for correcting proof of the song 'L'Envoi'; to Mr H. H. Price, of Trinity College, Oxford, for verifying the quotation from Cicero at the beginning of Part III; and to the officials of the Imperial War Museum for their courtesy and kindness on several occasions. I should also like to thank Miss Phyllis Bentley very gratefully indeed for much generous help and encouragement during the final year of this book's vicissitudes.

Acknowledgments and thanks are due to the following for kindly permitting the use of copyright poems or long quotations: Miss May Wedderburn Cannan, for 'When The Vision Dies'; Mr Rudyard Kipling for the quotation from 'Dirge of Dead Sisters' out of *The Five Nations* (copyright 1903 by Rudyard Kipling and reprinted by permission from Messrs A. P. Watt & Son, agents, Messrs Methuen & Co., Ltd., London, the Macmillan Company, Toronto, and Messrs Doubleday, Doran & Company, Inc., New York, Publishers); Miss Rose Macaulay, for 'Picnic, July, 1917'; Mr

Walter de la Mare for 'The Ghost,' out of *The Listeners*; Mr Wilfred
Meynell for 'Renouncement,' by Alice Meynell; Sir Owen Seaman
for '"The Soul of a Nation"'; Mr Basil Blackwell for the poems
from *Oxford Poetry, 1920* and quotations from two numbers of
the *Oxford Outlook*; Messrs Macmillan & Co., Ltd., London, and
Messrs Charles Scribner's Sons, New York, for quotations from
the poems of W. E. Henley; Messrs John Murray, for 'The Death
of Youth,' from *Verse and Prose in Peace and War*, by William Noel
Hodgson; the literary executor, Messrs Sidgwick & Jackson, Ltd.,
and Messrs Dodd, Mead & Co., New York (copyright, 1915, by
Dodd, Mead & Company, Inc.), for the sonnet ('Suggested by
Some of the Proceedings of the Society for Psychical Research')
by Rupert Brooke. I also want to express my gratitude to the
authors of the poems quoted on pp. 127–8 (from *London Opinion*)
and p. 163 (from the *Westminster Gazette*), as well as my regret
that I was unable to approach them personally, because in the one
case the poem was signed only by initials and in the other the
long-ago date of publication was unknown.

Finally, I am much indebted to the editors of *The Times*, the
Observer, *Time and Tide*, the *Daily Mail*, the *Star*, and the *Oxford
Chronicle* for the valuable assistance of their columns in the recon-
struction of recent history.

V. B.
May, 1933

Foreword

For nearly a decade I have wanted, with a growing sense of urgency, to write something which would show what the whole War and post-war period – roughly, from the years leading up to 1914 until about 1925 – has meant to the men and women of my generation, the generation of those boys and girls who grew up just before the War broke out. I wanted to give too, if I could, an impression of the changes which that period brought about in the minds and lives of very different groups of individuals belonging to the large section of middle-class society from which my own family comes.

Only, I felt, by some such attempt to write history in terms of personal life could I rescue something that might be of value, some element of truth and hope and usefulness, from the smashing up of my own youth by the War. It is true that to do it meant looking back into a past of which many of us, preferring to contemplate to-morrow rather than yesterday, believe ourselves to be tired. But it is only in the light of that past that we, the depleted generation now coming into the control of public affairs, the generation which has to make the present and endeavour to mould the future, can understand ourselves or hope to be understood by our successors. I knew that until I had tried to contribute to this understanding, I could never write anything in the least worth while.

The way to set about it at first appeared obvious; it meant drawing a picture of middle-class England – its interests, its morals, its social ideals, its politics – as it was from the time of my earliest conscious memory, and then telling some kind of personal story against this changing background. My original idea was that of a long novel, and I started to plan it. To my dismay it turned out a hopeless failure; I never got much further than the planning, for I found that the people and the events about which I was writing were still too near and too real to be made the subjects of an imaginative, detached reconstruction.

Then I tried the effect of reproducing parts of the long diary which I kept from 1913 to 1918, with fictitious names substituted for all the real ones out of consideration for the many persons still alive who were mentioned in it with a youthful and sometimes rather cruel candour. This too was a failure. Apart from the fact that the diary ended too soon to give a complete picture, the fictitious names created a false atmosphere and made the whole thing seem spurious.

There was only one possible course left – to tell my own fairly typical story as truthfully as I could against the larger background, and take the risk of offending all those who believe that a personal story should be kept private, however great its public significance and however wide its general application. In no other fashion, it seemed, could I carry out my endeavour to put the life of an ordinary individual into its niche in contemporary history, and thus illustrate the influence of world-wide events and movements upon the personal destinies of men and women.

I have tried to write the exact truth as I saw and see it about both myself and other people, since a book of this kind has no value unless it is honest. I have also made as much use as possible of old letters and diaries, because it seemed to me that the contemporary opinions, however crude and ingenuous, of youth in the period under review were at least as important a part of its testament as retrospective reflections heavy with knowledge. I make no apology for the fact that some of these documents renew with fierce vividness the stark agonies of my generation in its early twenties. The mature proprieties of 'emotion remembered in tranquillity' have not been my object, which, at least in part, is to challenge that too easy, too comfortable relapse into forgetfulness which is responsible for history's most grievous repetitions. It is not by accident that what I have written constitutes, in effect, the indictment of a civilisation.

The task of creating a matrix for these records has not been easy, for it is almost impossible to see ourselves and our friends and lovers as we really were seven, fifteen or even twenty years ago. Many of our contemporaries of equal age, in spite of their differences of environment and inheritance, appear to resemble us more closely than we resemble ourselves two decades back in time, since the same prodigious happenings and the same profound changes of opinion which have moulded us have also moulded them. As Charles Morgan so truly says in *The Fountain*: 'In each instant of their lives men die to that instant. It is not time that passes away from them, but they who recede from the constancy, the immutability of time, so that when afterwards they look back upon themselves it is not themselves they see, not even – as it is customary to say – themselves as they formerly were, but strange ghosts made in their image, with whom they have no communication.'

It is because of these difficulties of perspective that this book has been so long delayed; even to be wise in my generation and take advantage of the boom in War literature, I could not hurry it. Now, late in the field and already old enough for life's most formative events to seem very far away, I have done my best to put on record a personal impression of those incomparable changes which coincided with my first thirty years.

Vera Brittain
November 1929–March 1933

PART I

'Long ago there lived a rich merchant who, besides possessing more treasures than any king in the world, had in his great hall three chairs, one of silver, one of gold, and one of diamonds. But his greatest treasure of all was his only daughter, who was called Catherine.

'One day Catherine was sitting in her own room when suddenly the door flew open, and in came a tall and beautiful woman, holding in her hands a little wheel.

'"Catherine," she said, going up to the girl, "which would you rather have – a happy youth or a happy old age?"

'Catherine was so taken by surprise that she did not know what to answer, and the lady repeated again: "Which would you rather have – a happy youth or a happy old age?"

'Then Catherine thought to herself: "If I say a happy youth, then I shall have to suffer all the rest of my life. No, I will bear trouble now, and have something better to look forward to." So she looked up and said: "Give me a happy old age."

'"So be it," said the lady, and turned her wheel as she spoke, vanishing the next moment as suddenly as she had come.

'Now this beautiful lady was the Destiny of poor Catherine.'

Sicilianische Märchen, by Laura Gonzenbach.
(Included in *The Pink Fairy Book*, edited
by Andrew Lang.)

CHAPTER I

Forward from Newcastle

THE WAR GENERATION: AVE

In cities and in hamlets we were born,
    And little towns behind the van of time;
A closing era mocked our guileless dawn
    With jingles of a military rhyme.
But in that song we heard no warning chime,
    Nor visualised in hours benign and sweet
The threatening woe that our adventurous feet
    Would starkly meet.

Thus we began, amid the echoes blown
    Across our childhood from an earlier war,
Too dim, too soon forgotten, to dethrone
    Those dreams of happiness we thought secure;
While, imminent and fierce outside the door,
    Watching a generation grow to flower,
The fate that held our youth within its power
    Waited its hour.

V.B.

1932.

1

When the Great War broke out, it came to me not as a superlative tragedy, but as an interruption of the most exasperating
kind to my personal plans.

To explain the reason for this egotistical view of history's
greatest disaster, it is necessary to go back a little – to go back,
though only for a moment, as far as the decadent 'nineties, in

which I opened my eyes upon the none-too-promising day. I have, indeed, the honour of sharing with Robert Graves the subject of my earliest recollection, which is that of watching, as a tiny child, the flags flying in the streets of Macclesfield for Queen Victoria's Diamond Jubilee.

Fortunately there is no need to emulate my contemporary's *Good-bye to All That* in travelling still further back into the ponderous Victorianism of the nineteenth century, for no set of ancestors could have been less conspicuous or more robustly 'low-brow' than mine. Although I was born in the 'Mauve Decade', the heyday of the Yellow Book and the Green Carnation, I would confidently bet that none of my relatives had ever heard of Max Beerbohm or Aubrey Beardsley, and if indeed the name of Oscar Wilde awakened any response in their minds, it was not admiration of his works, but disapproval of his morals.

My father's family came from Staffordshire; the first place-names bound up with my childish memories are those of the 'Five Towns' and their surrounding villages – Stoke, Hanley, Burslem, Newcastle, Longport, Trentham, Barlaston and Stone – and I still remember seeing, at a very early age, alarming glimpses through a train window of the pot-bank furnaces flaming angrily against a black winter sky. At an old house in Barlaston – then, as now, associated with the large and dominant Wedgwood family – my father and most of his eleven brothers and sisters were born.

The records of my more distant predecessors are few, but they appear to have been composed of that mixture of local business men and country gentlemen of independent means which is not uncommon in the Midland counties. They had lived in the neighbourhood of the Pottery towns for several generations, and estimated themselves somewhat highly in consequence, though there is no evidence that any of them did anything of more than local importance. The only ancestor of whom our scanty family documents record any achievement is a certain Richard Brittain, who was Mayor of Newcastle-under-Lyme in 1741. The others were mostly small bankers, land agents, and manufacturers on a family scale.

In 1855, when Victorian prosperity was flourishing on the

pinnacle represented by the Great Exhibition of 1851, my great-grandfather gave up his work at a private bank in Newcastle, and purchased a little paper mill in the Potteries from a Huguenot family of paper-machine inventors. Towards the end of the century, his growing firm, in which my father was now a junior partner, acquired another small mill in the neighbourhood of Leek. From this business – of which, in 1889, the weekly wages bill was under £12 – the greater part of the family income has since been derived. My father was one of the four chief directors until his retirement during the War, and even I am a capitalist to the extent of owning a few shares.

Out of my great-grandfather's experiment has now grown a large and flourishing concern which produces some exquisite fine papers from the most up-to-date plant and machinery, though the outlook of its directors – honourable, efficient business men, like the shrewd North-country manufacturers in a Phyllis Bentley novel – is still tinged with the benevolent commercial feudalism of the later nineteenth century. The collective psychology of the neighbourhood in my childhood may be deduced from a saying once proverbial in Staffordshire: 'Let us go to Leek out of the noise.' In those days my father, who even now regards my membership of the Labour Party as a strange highbrow foible, used often to boast to chance visitors that his firm 'had never had a Trade Union man on the place'.

When my father, who was the best-looking and the most reasonable of a large and somewhat obstinate family, married my mother in 1891, his relatives disapproved, since she was without money or pedigree, and had nothing but her shy and wistful prettiness to recommend her. Instead of being the prospective heiress of 'county' rank which my prospering grand-parents doubtless thought appropriate for their eldest son, she was merely the second of four daughters of a struggling musician who had come from Wales to take the post of organist at a church in Stoke-on-Trent. Since the remuneration brought in by this appointment was quite insufficient for the support of a wife and six growing children, he gave music and singing lessons, which paid a little, and composed songs and organ voluntaries, which did not pay at all.

As a young man my father fancied his voice and so took a few singing lessons from the kindly organist; thus he met my mother, then a graceful and exceptionally gentle girl of twenty-one, dominated by her more positive mother and sisters. After they were married – rather quickly and quietly at Southport, owing to the sudden premature death of my charming but impecunious grandfather – my father's family showed no disposition, beyond a formal visit on the part of his mother to hers, to see any more of these modest in-laws, and for some years the two families continued to live within a few miles of each other, but hardly ever to meet.

When I reached an age of comparative intelligence, I deduced from various anecdotes related by my young and pretty mother the existence of this attitude of initial disdain on the part of my father's people towards her own. For some years it puzzled me, since to my hypercritical youth the majority of my paternal relatives, with their austere garments and their Staffordshire speech, appeared uncongenial and alarming, while my mother's sisters, all of whom made their way in the world long before independence was expected of middle-class women, were good-looking and agreeable, with charming musical voices and a pleasant taste in clothes. But after I left school, I soon learnt from my brief experience of the fashionable 'set' in Buxton that a family's estimate of its intrinsic importance is not always associated with qualifications which immediately convert the outsider to the same point of view.

2

During the early years of their marriage, my parents lived at Newcastle-under-Lyme.

They began their life together with a series of misfortunes, for their first child, a boy, was still-born, and shortly afterwards my father developed appendicitis, which proved a baffling mystery to the rough-and-ready provincial surgeons of the time, and left him prostrate for nearly twelve months. Eventually, however, I made my appearance at the decorous little villa in Sidmouth Road, arriving precipitately but safely during my father's absence at a pantomime in Hanley.

In the early stages of that urge towards metropolitanism which I developed with adolescence, I used to believe that such a typically provincial suburb as Newcastle could never have produced any man or woman of the smallest eminence, and with the youthful confidence that characteristically prefers to dwell on the fruits of success rather than to calculate their cost, I made up my mind as quickly as possible to repair that omission. But a few years ago I strangely discovered, through a chance meeting in a *wagon-lit* on the way to Geneva, that the small Staffordshire town – or rather, an adjacent village known as Silverdale – was at least the birthplace of Sir Joseph Cook, a former High Commissioner for Australia, who during our brief acquaintance at the League that summer habitually addressed me as 'Little Newcastle'.

I must have been about eighteen months old when my family moved to Macclesfield, which was a reasonable though none too convenient railway journey from the Potteries. Here, in the small garden and field belonging to our house, and in the smooth, pretty Cheshire lanes with their kindly hedges and benign wild flowers, I and my brother Edward, less than two years my junior, passed through a childhood which was, to all appearances, as serene and uneventful as any childhood could be.

The first memories of my generation are inevitably of an experience which we all share in common, for they belong to dramatic national events, to the songs, the battles and the sudden terminations of suspense in a struggle more distant and more restricted than that which was destined to engulf us. Like the rest of my contemporaries, I began to distinguish real occurrences from fables and fancies about the time that the South African War broke out at the end of 1899. Before 1900, though animate and assertive, I could hardly have been described as a conscious observer of my background.

From the unrolling mists of oblivious babyhood, the strains drift back to me of 'We're Soldiers of the Queen, me lads!' and 'Good-bye, Dolly, I must leave you'. An organ was triumphantly playing the first of these tunes in a Macclesfield street one cold spring morning when I noticed that banners and gay streamers were hanging from all the windows.

'It's because of the Relief of Ladysmith,' my mother explained in response to my excited questioning; 'Now Uncle Frank will be coming home.'

But Uncle Frank – a younger brother of my father's who had been farming in South Africa when the War began and had joined the Queen's forces as a trooper – never came home after all, for he died of enteric in Ladysmith half an hour before the relief of the town.

I had quite forgotten him on a grey January afternoon nearly a year later, when I sat snugly in our warm kitchen, drawing birds and dragons and princesses with very long hair, while the old lady whose Diamond Jubilee had made such an impression upon my three-year-old consciousness sank solemnly into her grave. In front of the fire, the little plump cook read the evening paper aloud to the housemaid.

'"The Queen is now asleep,"' she quoted in sepulchral tones, while I, absorbed with my crayons, remained busily unaware that so much more than a reign was ending, and that the long age of effulgent prosperity into which I had been born was to break up in thirteen years' time with an explosion which would reverberate through my personal life to the end of my days.

It seemed only a few weeks afterwards, though it was actually eighteen months, and peace with South Africa had already been signed, that Edward and I were assiduously decorating with flags the railing which divided the lower lawn from the hayfield, when my father came hurriedly up the drive with an anxious face and a newspaper in his hand.

'You can take down your decorations,' he announced gloomily. 'There'll be no Coronation. The King's ill!'

That night I prayed earnestly to God to make the dear King better and let him live. The fact that he actually did recover established in me a touching faith in the efficacy of prayer, which superstitiously survived until the Great War proved to me, once for all, that there was nothing in it. To those who were twenty or more at the time of Victoria's death, the brief reign of Edward – to whatever extent that indefatigable visitor to Paris and Biarritz may have been a factor in the coming of the deluge when it did

– must have seemed merely a breathing space between the Victorian age and the German invasion of Belgium. To us, the War generation, it was much more than that, for in those nine years we grew from children into adolescents or adults. Yet of the King himself I remember nothing between his untimely attack of appendicitis, and the pious elegy in the best Victorian manner which I produced at school when my form was told to write a poem in memory of his passing.

3

Not only in its name, Glen Bank, and its white-painted semi-detachment, but in its hunting pictures and Marcus Stone engravings, its plush curtains, its mahogany furniture and its scarcity of books, our Macclesfield house represented all that was essentially middle-class in that Edwardian decade.

Following the long-established example of my father's parents, we even had prayers before breakfast, during which performance everybody – from my mother, who perturbedly watched the boiling coffee-machine on the table, to the maids who shuffled uneasily in their chairs while the postman banged at the front door and the milkman thundered at the back – presented an aspect of inattentive agitation. The ceremony frequently ended in a tempestuous explosion on the part of my father, since Edward was almost always late, and could never say the Lord's Prayer as rapidly as the others. As a rule he was still patiently pleading with the Deity to lead him not into 'tation, while the rest of us were thankfully vociferating 'Amen'.

Although my father, as a self-willed young man in his thirties, was somewhat liable to these outbursts of irritation, they never really alarmed me, for he was always my champion in childhood, and could be relied upon as a safe bulwark against the bewildering onslaughts of his practical-joke-loving younger brothers and sisters, who regarded a small girl as fair game for their riotous ingenuity. Far more disturbing to my peace of mind was the strange medley of irrational fears which were always waiting to torment me – fears of thunder, of sunsets, of the full moon, of the dark, of standing under railway arches or crossing bridges over noisy streams, of the end of the world and of the devil waiting to catch me round the corner (this last being due to a nursemaid who overheard me, at the age of five or six, calling Edward 'Little fool!' and immediately commented: 'There, you've done it! *Now* you'll go to hell!').

Parents and nurses had by that time outgrown the stage of putting children into dark cupboards as a 'cure' for this type of 'tiresomeness' – an atrocity once perpetrated on my mother which adversely affected her psychology for ever afterwards – but such terrors did appear to them to have no other origin than a perverse unreasonableness, and I was expostulated with and even scolded for thus 'giving way'. There seemed to be no one to whom I could appeal for understanding of such humiliating cowardice, nobody whom I instinctively felt to be on my side against the mysterious phenomena which so alarmed me. Since I thus grew up without having my fears rationalised by explanation, I carried them with me, thrust inward but very little transformed, into adulthood, and was later to have only too good reason to regret that I never learnt to conquer them while still a child.

On the whole, in spite of these intermittent terrors, the years in which life is taken for granted were pleasant enough, if not conspicuously reassuring. For as long as I could remember, our house had always been full of music, never first-rate, but tuneful, and strangely persistent in its ability to survive more significant recollections. To the perturbation of my father, who never really cared for music in spite of the early singing lessons, there was always much practising of songs, or pianoforte solos, and later of violin exercises, and in Macclesfield my mother gave periodic 'musical evenings', for which Edward and I, at the ages of about seven and nine, used to sit up in order to play tinkling duets together, or innocuous trios with our governess.

My mother, who had an agreeable soprano voice, took singing lessons in Manchester; at musical parties, she sang 'When the Heart is Young', 'Whisper and I Shall Hear' or 'The Distant Shore' – a typical example of Victorian pathos which always reduced me to tears at the point where 'the mai-den – drooped – and – DIED'.

I was much more stimulated by 'Robert the Devil', and whenever my mother, her back safely turned towards me, trilled 'Mercy! Mercy! Mer-russy!' in her ardent soprano, I flung myself up and down upon the hearthrug in an ecstasy of masochistic fervour.

My first acquaintance with literature was less inspiring, for in Macclesfield the parental library consisted solely of a few yellow-back novels, two or three manuals on paper-making, and a large tome entitled *Household Medicine*, in which the instructions were moral rather than hygienic. Lest anyone should suspect the family of being literary, these volumes were concealed beneath a heavy curtain in the chill, gloomy dining-room. My father was once told by a publisher's traveller that the Pottery towns held the lowest record for book-buying in England. Being a true son of his district, which has an immense respect for 'brass' but none whatever for the uncommercial products of a poetic imagination, he remained faithful in Cheshire as in Staffordshire to his neighbourhood's reputation.

When I had exhausted my own nursery literature – a few volumes of Andrew Lang's fairy-tales, one of which was punctiliously presented to me on each birthday, and some of the more saccharine children's stories of L. T. Meade – I turned surreptitiously to the yellow-back novels. These were mostly by Wilkie Collins, Desant and Rice, and Mrs Henry Wood, and many were the maudlin tears that I wept over the sorrows of Poor Miss Finch and Lady Isabel Vane.

It was not till later, at the age of ten, that I discovered the manifold attractions of *Household Medicine*. The treatment of infectious diseases left me cold, but I was secretly excited at the prospect of menstruation; I also found the details of a confinement quite enthralling, though I had never shown that devotion to dolls which is supposed to indicate a strong maternal instinct. The whole subject of child-birth was completely dissociated in my mind from that of sex, about which I knew little and cared less. I was particularly impressed at the time by the instructions given to the child-bearing woman in the final stage of labour, though I can now only remember that she was advised to braid her hair in two plaits, and to wear an old flannel petticoat under her nightgown.

I must have been about eight when two solitary classics – probably neglected Christmas presents – found their way on to a whist table in the drawing-room. One was *Longfellow's Complete Poems*, bound in a bilious mustard-brown leather, and the other a copy of Matthew Arnold's *Sohrab and Rustum*. I soon had Longfellow's poems – including 'Tales of a Wayside Inn' and 'The New England Tragedies' – almost by heart, and even now, when I am searching through my memory for an appropriate quotation, 'Life is real, life is earnest', and 'Hadst thou stayed I must have fled!' will insist upon ousting A. E. Housman and Siegfried Sassoon. But I found *Sohrab and Rustum* even more entrancing than Longfellow, and over and over again, when I was sure of having the drawing-room to myself, I indulged the histrionic instinct which had derived so much satisfaction from 'Robert the Devil' by imitating in dumb show the throes of the unfortunate Sohrab,

> *Lovely in death, upon the common sand.*

My mother did her conscientious best to remedy the deficiencies of our literary education by reading Dickens aloud to us on Sunday afternoons. We ploughed through *David Copperfield* and *Nicholas Nickleby* in this manner, which perhaps explains why I have never been able to finish anything else by Dickens except *A Tale of Two Cities*. Far more effective as compensations for the lack of external stimulus were the five 'novels' that I wrote before I was eleven, on special books patiently constructed for me by a devoted and intelligent governess out of thick waste paper from the mills, and the exciting legends of a mythical community called 'The Dicks', which from my bed in the night nursery I used to relate to Edward across the passage in the day nursery after we were both supposed to be asleep. I was always the inventor and he the recipient of these enthralling communications, which must have begun when I was about six, and continued until I reached the mature age of eleven and went to school.

Edward was always a good listener, since his own form of self-expression then consisted in making unearthly and to me quite meaningless sounds on his small violin. I remember him, at the age of seven, as a rather solemn, brown-eyed little boy, with beautiful arched eyebrows which lately, to my infinite satisfaction, have begun to reproduce themselves, a pair of delicate question-marks, above the dark eyes of my five-year-old son. Even in childhood we seldom quarrelled, and by the time that we both went away to boarding-school he had already become the dearest companion of those brief years of unshadowed adolescence permitted to our condemned generation.

4

When I was eleven our adored governess departed, and my family moved from Macclesfield to a tall grey stone house in Buxton, the Derbyshire 'mountain spa', in order that Edward and I might be sent to 'good' day-schools. His was a small preparatory school of which a vigorous Buxton man was then headmaster; mine inevitably described itself as 'a school for the daughters of gentlemen'. My brother's school, which certainly gave him a better grounding than I received from mine, will always be associated in my recollection with one significant experience.

Soon after Edward went there I happened, on my way to the town, to pass the school playground at a time when the boys were uproariously enjoying an afternoon break. Seeing Edward, I stopped; he called several of his newly made cronies, and we spent a few moments of pleasant 'ragging' across the low wall. I felt no consciousness of guilt, and was unaware that I had been seen, on their return home along an adjacent road, by my mother and an aunt who was staying with us. At tea-time a heavy and to me inexplicable atmosphere of disapproval hung over the table; shortly afterwards the storm exploded, and I was severely reprimanded for my naughtiness in thus publicly conversing with Edward's companions. (I think it was the same aunt who afterwards informed me that the reason why our letters had to be left open at my school was 'in case any of the girls should be so wicked as to write to boys'. Probably this was true of most girls' schools before the War.)

The small incident was my first intimation that, in the eyes of the older generation, free and unself-conscious association between boys and girls was more improper than a prudish suspicion of the opposite sex. It aroused in me a rebellious resentment that I have never forgotten. I had not heard, in those days, of co-educational schools, but had I been aware of their experimental existence and been able to foresee my far-distant parenthood, I should probably have decided, then and there, that my own son and daughter should attend them.

I do not remember much about my day-school except that when I first went there I was badly bullied by two unpleasant little girls, who soon tired of the easy physical advantage given them by their superior age and stature, and instead endeavoured to torment my immature mind by forcing upon it items of sexual information in their most revolting form. My parents, who had suffered such qualms of apprehension over my entirely whole-some friendliness with Edward's riotous companions, remained completely unaware of this real threat to my decency and my peace. I never mentioned it to them owing to a bitter sense of shame, which was not, however, aroused by my schoolfellows' unæsthetic communications, but by my inability to restrain my tears during their physical assaults. So ambitious was I already, and so indifferent to sex in all its manifestations, that their attempts to corrupt my mind left it as innocent as they found it, and I resented only the pinchings and wrist-twistings which always accompanied my efforts to escape.

Though my school took a few boarders, most of its pupils were local; in consequence the class-room competition was practically non-existent. At the age of twelve I was already preening the gay feathers of my youthful conceit in one of the top forms, where the dull, coltish girls of sixteen and seventeen so persistently treated me as a prodigy that I soon lost such small ability as I had possessed to estimate my modest achievements at their true and limited worth.

When I first went to the school, it was in charge of an ancient mistress who was typical of the genteel and uncertificated past, but soon afterwards a new Principal was appointed with an unim-peachable Degree acquired from Cheltenham. In Buxton this was regarded as quite a remarkable qualification for a headmistress, and in those days my parents' standards of scholarship were almost as unexacting. They had never, indeed, had much opportunity to become otherwise, for my mother had received a very spasmodic and unorthodox education, while my father, after reacting with characteristic if pardonable obstinacy against the rigours of Malvern in the eighteen-seventies, had been sent to the High School at Newcastle-under-Lyme, where the boys' only consistent occupation was a perpetual baiting of the much-enduring masters.

During my father's uproarious days at Newcastle High School, a Hanley boy, two or three years his junior, named Enoch Arnold Bennett, was more profitably pursuing his studies at the Middle School in the same town. There was, needless to say, very little communication between the pupils from the Middle School, and the domineering young tyrants at the High School. Even after the author of *The Old Wives' Tale* had won his lasting place in English literature, my relatives still thought nothing much of the Bennetts, whom they characteristically described as 'very ordinary people'.

The education given to my parents, in both quality and quantity, was of a type at that time shared, and considered quite adequate, by almost the whole of the provincial middle-classes. Its shortcomings were in no way compensated by the superior attainments of their friends, for throughout my childhood in Macclesfield and Buxton, I cannot remember that anyone ever came to the house of more interest to me than relatives, or mentally restricted local residents with their even more limited wives.

These families were typical of the kind that still inhabit small country towns; the wives 'kept house', and the husbands occupied themselves as branch bank-managers, cautious and unenterprising solicitors, modest business men who preferred safety to experiment, and 'family' doctors whose bedside manner camouflaged their diagnostical uncertainties. Schoolmasters were not encouraged, as my father found their conversation tedious. Always a staunch Free-Trader, he was ready to join issue against any supporter of Joseph Chamberlain in the topical controversy of

Free Trade *versus* Tariff Reform, but he did object to being diverted from the enthralling discussion of paper manufacture to subjects of such remote interest as the bombardment of Port Arthur, the Turkish atrocities in Macedonia, or the policy of the Russian revolutionary party which was bloodily agitating for the establishment of a Duma.

To my own immature ears, hardly an echo of these or other far-off and rather more divine events ever succeeded in penetrating; even the elements of fiscal argument, though respectable enough, were regarded as beyond a schoolgirl's understanding. I suppose it was the very completeness with which all doors and windows to the more adventurous and colourful world, the world of literature, of scholarship, of art, of politics, of travel, were closed to me, that kept my childhood so relatively contented a time. Once I went away to school, and learnt − even though from a distance that filled me with dismay − what far countries of loveliness, and learning, and discovery, and social relationship based upon enduring values, lay beyond those solid provincial walls which enclosed the stuffiness of complacent bourgeoisdom so securely within themselves, my discontent kindled until I determined somehow to break through them to the paradise of sweetness and light which I firmly believed awaited me in the south.

I often wonder how many of my present-day friends were themselves limited by a horizon as circumscribed as that which bounded my first thirteen years. Up to the time, indeed, that I was twenty-one, my sole contacts with life outside England were confined to a Cook's tour to Lucerne, where I developed mumps immediately on arrival and spent the rest of the fortnight in a sanatorium, and a brief visit to Paris, during which my father was knocked down by a taxicab and promptly insisted upon all of us returning to Buxton.

I believe that it is Albert Edward Wiggam, the American author of *The Fruit of the Family Tree*, who has calculated that half the world's distinguished men and women are produced by only one per cent of its population, and that all the teeming mediocre millions of the rest of mankind are required to contribute the other half of its leaders. But when I consider − and in my later teens I often used to consider – the incalculable advantages of heredity and early environment that are involved in merely being born a member of such families as the Huxleys, the Haldanes, the Frys, the Darwins or the Arnolds, what really seems remarkable is not that the undistinguished residue produces only half the sum of human talent, but that those who belong to it ever emerge at all from the blackest obscurity.

5

At the age of thirteen, small for my years and still very much of a child in spite of my mature Fifth Form associates, I was sent away to school at the recently founded St Monica's, at Kingswood in Surrey – a safe choice, because the eldest and ablest of my mother's sisters was one of the two Principals. Her partner, Louise Heath Jones, a brilliant, dynamic woman who had been educated at Cheltenham and Newnham, alternately inspired and intimidated both girls and mistresses by her religious idealism and the strongly individual quality of her teaching. The *tempo* at which her ardent spirit caused her to live wore out too quickly her fragile constitution; a premature breakdown led to her early retirement soon after I left the school, and she died in 1931 after many years of illness.

My aunt, level-headed and self-reliant, remained in charge from 1914 until the end of 1930, and though she possessed neither college degree nor technical training in education, her personal dignity and her natural gift for organisation soon raised St Monica's to a high position, with a refreshingly enlightened and broad-minded régime among girls' private schools. It has recently passed out of this category into the hands of an exclusively masculine committee, and now ranks as a public school.

When, a few years before the War, I first went to St Monica's, the young school had not yet reached the high educational standards of its later days, and though my budding ambition to go to college – which developed as soon as I discovered that such places as women's colleges existed, and learnt what they stood for – met with real sympathy from both Principals and staff, it received no practical preparation for the necessary examinations, which were not then taken as a matter of normal routine. No doubt my father's persistent determination throughout my schooldays that I should be turned into an entirely ornamental young lady deterred both my aunt and Miss Heath Jones from the efforts that they would otherwise have made on my behalf; the most benevolent and aspiring headmistresses are, after all, singularly helpless in the hands of misguided but resolute parents.

My classroom contemporaries regarded my ambitions, not unnaturally, with no particular interest or sympathy. Many of them were fashionable young women to whom universities represented a quite unnecessary prolongation of useless and distasteful studies, and they looked upon my efforts to reach the top of a form, and my naïve anxiety to remain there, as satisfactorily exonerating them from the troublesome endeavour to win that position for themselves.

Socially, of course, I was quite without standing among these wealthy girls, designed by their parents for London or Edinburgh society, with their town addresses in Mayfair or Belgravia, and their country houses of which the name 'Hall' or 'Park' was frequently a part. My parents could not afford the numerous theatres and concerts to which many of them were taken by request of their families; my 'best' clothes were home-made or purchased from undistinguished shops in Buxton or Manchester; and the presents that I received at Christmas or on birthdays did not bear comparison with the many elegant gifts that my class-mates displayed for the admiration of contemporaries on returning to school after the holidays.

It is hardly surprising that few of the girls coveted the reputation unenthusiastically conceded to me for 'brains', or even envied my comparative freedom from refused lessons, but regarded these assets as mere second-rate compensations for my obvious inferiority in the advantages that they valued most. In those days as in these, girls' private schools attracted but few parents possessed of more than a half-hearted intention to train their daughters for exacting careers or even for useful occupations. Both for the young women and their mothers, the potential occurrence that loomed largest upon the horizon was marriage, and in spite of the undaunted persistence with which both the Principals upheld their own progressive ideals of public service, almost every girl left school with only two ambitions – to return at the first possible moment to impress her school-fellows with the glory of a grown-up *toilette*, and to get engaged before everybody else.

Although I was then more deeply concerned about universities than engagements, I shared the general hankering after an adult wardrobe which would be at least partly self-chosen, since all girls' clothing of the period appeared to be designed by their elders on the assumption that decency consisted in leaving exposed to the sun and air no part of the human body that could possibly be covered with flannel. In these later days, when I lie lazily sunning myself in a mere gesture of a bathing-suit on the gay *plage* of some small Riviera town – or even, during a clement summer, on the ultra-respectable shores of southern England – and watch the lean brown bodies of girl-children, almost naked and completely unashamed, leaping in and out of the water, I am seized with an angry resentment against the conventions of twenty years ago, which wrapped up my comely adolescent body in woollen combinations, black cashmere stockings, 'liberty' bodice, dark stockinette knickers, flannel petticoat and often, in addition, a long-sleeved, high-necked, knitted woollen 'spencer'.

At school, on the top of this conglomeration of drapery, we wore green flannel blouses in the winter and white flannel blouses in the summer, with long navy-blue skirts, linked to the blouses by elastic belts which continually slipped up or down, leaving exposed an unsightly hiatus of blouse-tape or safety-pinned shirt-band. Green and white blouses alike had long sleeves ending in buttoned cuffs at the wrist, and high collars covering the neck almost to the chin, and fastening tightly at the throat with stiff green ties. For cricket and tennis matches, even in the baking summer of 1911, we still wore the flowing skirts and high-necked blouses, with our heavy hair braided into pigtails; it was not until after the War that the school went into sleeveless white linens for summer games. Only in the gymnasium class did our handicapped limbs acquire freedom, and even then the tight, long-sleeved blouses were worn under our weighty pleated tunics. In spite of these impediments, the games and drill did make us lithe and hard, and during the War I had reason to thank them for the powers of endurance of which they laid the foundation.

The only intimate friends that I made at Kingswood were a small, dark, half-foreign girl and a pretty, fair, sweet-natured Anglo-Saxon, whose names might very suitably have been Mina and Betty. Mina, a younger daughter in a large and wealthy family, displayed at school a real artistic talent, while Betty possessed intellectual possibilities which she was never sufficiently interested to explore, owing to a quite frankly acknowledged desire to marry and have children. In neither case did the intimacy long survive our departure from school.

Mina, during the War, developed under the stress of a perturbing love-affair a strong disapproval of my character, which led her to conclude that I had never been worthy of her friendship. When I was nursing in London in the early part of 1916, and she was cultivating her considerable gift for drawing at an art school, she made an appointment with me at − of all appropriate places for a moral condemnation − the Albert Memorial, in order to inform me that I was selfish, insincere, ambitious, and therefore no longer deserving of her affection. I can see her sturdy little figure now, conspicuous in a coat and skirt of strange pink cloth against the solid stone basis of the immaculate Albert, as she arraigned me for the harsh, unmelting bitterness into which I had been frozen by the first real tragedy of my experience.

'You never really cared for Roland; you only wanted to marry him out of ambition! If you'd really loved him you couldn't possibly have behaved in the way you've done the past few weeks!'

It was, of course, typical of the average well-to-do girl of the period to assume that the desire for power, which is as universal among women as among men, could only be fulfilled by the acquisition of a brilliant husband. I do not recall the mood in which I spent the long 'bus ride back to Camberwell, but I probably minded dreadfully at the time. At any rate, we parted for good, and I cannot recollect that I have ever encountered Mina since that morning.

With Betty the association lasted longer and I owe far more to it; for nearly two years during the War we served by arrangement in the same military hospitals, and even after it was over kept up the kind of friendship that renews itself at Old Girls' Association meetings and exchanges of annual Christmas cards. But real intimacy between us became difficult as soon as we left school, for our homes were in different parts of England, our parents cherished different social aspirations, and our personal ambitions were not the same. Betty had no desire for a university education or the independence of a professional woman. The War, which frustrated individual as well as national hopes, caused her future to remain uncertain until 1922, when she married a man considerably her senior who soon afterwards became a Conservative Member of Parliament. To-day her two pretty children, a little older than my own, still provide a point of contact between lives which in other respects could hardly differ more widely.

6

I remember Kingswood very clearly as it looked twenty years ago, with the inviolate Downs stretching away to Smitham, and the thick woods unbroken by the pink and grey eruption of suburban villas which has now torn them ruthlessly into sections. On summer evenings one of our favourite rambles took us across the sloping fields, sweet with clover and thyme and wild roses, between Kingswood and Chipstead; there as twilight descended we looked a little nervously at the darkening sky for indications of Halley's Comet which was said to herald such prodigious disasters, or listened more serenely to the nightingales in a stillness broken only at long intervals by the lazy, infrequent little trains which ambled down the toy railway line in the valley. The thyme and the roses still blossom bravely about those doomed meadows, but I have never heard the nightingales there since the War, and the once uninterrupted walks have long been spoilt by barbed-wire barriers and notices drawn up for the intimidation of stray trespassers.

In the months before I went up to Oxford, when I had to

plough, solitary and unaided, through the tedious intricacies of examination syllabuses, I often privately condemned my parents for not sending me to Cheltenham, or Roedean, or even to an ordinary High School, where practised authorities would have saved me from the fret of wrestling with academic mysteries. But of late years I have realised that St Monica's, although it did not then possess certain routine advantages of a public school, is very far from being a matter for regret. No doubt it did not provide that prolonged and exacting type of education which is now the inevitable preliminary to any professional career; but such training was then mainly obtainable in schools which sterilised the sexual charm out of their pupils, and turned them into hockey-playing hoydens with *gauche* manners and an armoury of inhibitions.

St Monica's did not, of course, prepare me either for the strain and stress of a very few years later, but I question if the artificial atmosphere of hockey matches and High School examinations would have done this any better, or whether, indeed, the early development of a more critical and less idealistic spirit would have proved, in the long run, an effective weapon against annihilating calamity. A dozen years' periodic observation of Oxford dons has led me to doubt whether, even for those misguided dupes the boys and girls of the War generation, an over-development of the critical faculty would not have been at least as dangerous as its under-development. The latter, at any rate, does nothing to destroy that vitality which is more important than any other quality in combating the obstacles, the set-backs and the obtuse ridicule which are more often encountered in early youth than at any other time.

We were too young to have had power to divert the remorseless impetus of history; we should probably have gone – have had to go – to the War whatever our psychology, and it is arguable that our early months of illumined faith were a factor in the ultimate return of some of us to life. At least the unexacting demands of the easy lessons at St Monica's, the mildness of the intellectual competition – a little more substantial than that of the Buxton school only because the girls were drawn from a wider area – and the lovely peace of the rich, undisturbed country, left scope for much reading of Dante and Shakespeare, of Shelley and Browning and Swinburne, and gave opportunity for dreams of which many, in the strangest ways and against all probability, have since materialised.

Only the other day a fellow-journalist, half rueful and half amused, told me that I had made a better thing out of sex equality than she had ever thought possible for such a portentous topic until I began to scatter articles on equal pay and married women's careers through the pages of the daily and weekly Press. If that is so, I can only reply that I have written nothing on the various aspects of feminism which has not been based upon genuine conviction, and that the foundations of that conviction were first laid, strangely enough, at a school which was apparently regarded by many of the parents who patronised it as a means of equipping girls to be men's decorative and contented inferiors.

Miss Heath Jones, who from my knowledge of her temperament I now suspect to have been secretly in sympathy with the militant suffrage raids and demonstrations which began after the foundation of the Women's Social and Political Union in 1905, was an ardent though always discreet feminist. She often spoke to me of Dorothea Beale and Emily Davies, lent me books on the woman's movement, and even took me with one or two of the other senior girls in 1911 to what must have been a very mild and constitutional suffrage meeting in Tadworth village. This practical introduction to feminism was to be for ever afterwards associated in my mind with the great heat, the railway strikes, the Parliament Bill debates and the international crises of that hectic summer, which provided such wealth of topical detail for my passionate editorial in the 1911 School Magazine.

To this day I can remember some of the lessons which Miss Heath Jones gave us in History and Scripture – lessons which raced backwards and forwards in the same five minutes from the French Revolution to the Liberal Victory in the 1910 General Elections, from the prophecies of Isaiah to the 1911 Italian invasion of Tripoli. From the unimaginative standpoint of pre-war examinations they were quite unpractical, but as teaching in the real sense of the word – the creation in immature minds of the power to think, to visualise, to perceive analogies – they could hardly have been surpassed. In 1908, after Austria-Hungary's annexation of Bosnia and Herzegovina, she set us drawing maps of the Balkan Peninsula, and in 1911 she arranged a school debate on the Morocco crisis – about which I held forth with vague but patriotic fervour – when Germany sent the *Panther* to Agadir.

Her encouragement even prevailed upon us to read the newspapers, which were then quite unusual adjuncts to teaching in girls' private schools. We were never, of course, allowed to have the papers themselves – our innocent eyes might have strayed from foreign affairs to the evidence being taken by the Royal Commission on Marriage and Divorce or the Report of the International Paris Conference for the suppression of the White Slave Traffic – and the carefully selected cuttings invariably came from *The Times* or the *Observer* unmodified by contrary political opinions, but the fact that we had them at all testified to a recognition of the importance of current events far from customary at a time when politics and economics were still thought by most headmistresses to be no part of the education of marriageable young females.

Among the girls Miss Heath Jones's lessons were not always appreciated, for most of the sheltered young women in that era displayed no particular anxiety to have the capacity for thought developed within them. Even now I recall the struggles of some of my contemporaries to avoid facing some of the less agreeable lessons of 1914. There is still, I think, not enough recognition by teachers of the fact that the desire to think – which is fundamentally a moral problem – must be induced before the power is developed. Most people, whether men or women, wish above all else to be comfortable, and thought is a pre-eminently uncomfortable process; it brings to the individual far more suffering than happiness in a semi-civilised world which still goes to war, still encourages the production of unwanted C3 children by exhausted mothers, and still compels married partners who hate one another to live together in the name of morality.

Out of the desultory and miscellaneous reading in which, under Miss Heath Jones's inspired and unconventional tuition, I indulged between the ages of fifteen and eighteen, a poem, a novel and a challenging triumph of propaganda especially determined the direction in which I was moving. During Preparation one wild autumn evening in St Monica's gymnasium, when the wind shook the unsubstantial walls and a tiny crescent of moon, glimpsed through a skylight in the roof, scudded in and out of the flying clouds, I first read Shelley's 'Adonais', which taught me in the most startling and impressive fashion of my childhood's experience to perceive beauty embodied in literature, and made me finally determine to become the writer that I had dreamed of being ever since I was seven years old. I still defy anyone, however 'highbrow', to better the thrill of reading, for the first time and at sixteen, the too-familiar lines:

> *The One remains, the many change and pass;*
> *Heaven's light forever shines, Earth's shadows fly;*
> *Life, like a dome of many-coloured glass,*
> *Stains the white radiance of Eternity . . .*

The novel, strangely enough, was Mrs Humphry Ward's deistic tract, *Robert Elsmere*. Had I realised when I read it that its author was even then portentously engaged in rallying the anti-suffrage forces, it might have influenced me less, but I remained ignorant until some years later of Mrs Ward's political machinations, and her book converted me from an unquestioning if somewhat indifferent church-goer into an anxiously interrogative agnostic.

To Olive Schreiner's *Woman and Labour* – that 'Bible of the Woman's Movement' which sounded to the world of 1911 as insistent and inspiring as a trumpet-call summoning the faithful to a vital crusade – was due my final acceptance of feminism. Miss Heath Jones lent me the book soon after its publication, and I can still tingle with the excitement of the passage which re-inforced me, brought up as were nearly all middle-class girls of that period to believe myself predestined to a perpetual, distasteful but inescapable tutelage, in my determination to go to college and at least prepare for a type of life more independent than that of a Buxton young lady:

'"*We take all labour for our province!*"

'From the judge's seat to the legislator's chair; from the statesman's closet to the merchant's office; from the chemist's laboratory to the astronomer's tower, there is no post or form of toil for which it is not our intention to attempt to fit ourselves; and there is no closed door we do not intend to force open; and there is no fruit in the garden of knowledge it is not our determination to eat.'

Thus it was in St Monica's garden, beside a little over-grown pool where the plump goldfish slid idly in and out of the shadows, and the feathered grasses drooped their heavy heads to the water's edge, that I first visualised in rapt childish ecstasy a world in which women would no longer be the second-rate, unimportant creatures that they were now considered, but the equal and respected companions of men. Indeed, that school garden, now trimly beautiful in its twenty-year-old mellowness, but then recently hewn from the rough surface of the Downs and golden-hedged with tangled gorse and broom, has been for me somehow associated with every past phase of life.

There, at the age of sixteen, I first began to dream how the men and women of my generation – with myself, of course, conspicuous among that galaxy of Leonardos – would inaugurate a new Renaissance on a colossal scale, and incidentally redeem all the foolish mistakes of our forefathers. There, more realistically, I planned my long-desired and constantly postponed career, there sought refuge after the anxiety of college examinations, there waited for news from the War, and felt the sinister shudder of the guns from the Belgian coast shake the Caterham Valley like a subterranean earthquake. There, too, when the War was over, I wandered about after taking the older girls for classes in history and international relations, thinking about relations quite other than international, and wondering whether or not to get married.

But I anticipate. In my last term, as head-girl, I did no examinations and very little work, except for special history and literature classes with a visiting mistress, Miss F., one of those rare teachers who, like Miss Heath Jones, possessed originality and a real talent for inspiring ideas. Her gifts may be judged from the fact that she succeeded in filling me with a tremendous enthusiasm for the works of Carlyle and Ruskin. 'The most important of all terms so far – as it marked the rising of my Star,' begins an earnest fragment of sixteen-year-old diary recorded during the holidays after Miss F. first went to Kingswood – though fortunately the reference was not to herself, but to the impetus given by her teaching to the growth of those sentiments which, under the influence of *Past and Present*, I should then have described as my Ideals.

An elegant, introspective, temperamental creature, Miss F. once spent a few days in Buxton with me and my family – who mildly disapproved of her – and told our fortunes on a dull afternoon. Over Edward, who was then sixteen, she appeared indefinite and uncommunicative, but to me she remarked: 'I think you'll be married all right' (the phrase implying acceptance even on her part of what was still supposed to be the major preoccupation of an intelligent girl), 'but if you're not married at twenty-one, you'll have to wait till you're thirty. By that time you'll have some kind of a career; I don't know quite what it will be, but it will turn out well and your marriage won't interfere with it.'

Just before I left St Monica's I played the part of the Madonna in *Eager Heart*, Miss Buckton's Christmas mystery play, which gave a peculiarly memorable and emotional quality to my last weeks at school. Temperamentally, at least, I was thoroughly well adapted to the rôle, and this fact, to anyone who knows the play, with its half-sentimental, half-mystical detachment from the pedestrian demands of everyday life, will perhaps give a better idea than anything else of the state of mind in which, before I had turned eighteen, I left school to 'come out' into the alien atmosphere of Buxton 'society'.

7

It would not, I think, be possible for any present-day girl of the same age even to imagine how abysmally ignorant, how romantically idealistic and how utterly unsophisticated my more sensitive contemporaries and I were at that time. The naïveties of the diary which I began to write consistently soon after leaving school, and kept up until more than half way through the War, must be read in order to be believed. My 'Reflective Record, 1913', is endorsed on its title page with the following comprehensive aspirations:

'To extend love, to promote thought, to lighten suffering, to combat indifference, to inspire activity.'

'To know everything of something and something of everything.'

The same page contains a favourite quotation from Rostand's '*Princesse Lointaine*':

> *Ah! l'inertie est le seul vice, Maître Erasme,*
> *Et le seul vertu, c'est . . . l'enthousiasme.*

One entry, made on December 20th, 1913, after a local dance, runs as follows: 'It leaves me with a very unsatisfied feeling to have met so many stupid and superficial men with whom all the girls are obviously so pleased. How I wish I could meet a good strong splendid man, full of force and enthusiasm, and in earnest about his life! There must *be* such!'

I have never shown this expression of my emotional aspirations to my husband, so I do not know whether or not he would regard himself as fulfilling the description.

By 1916, the optimistic ideals of earlier years had all disappeared from the title-page of my ingenuous journal; they were replaced by a four-line verse from the writings of Paul Verlaine which has always seemed to me to represent more precisely than any other poem the heavy sense of having lived so long and been through so much that descended upon the boys and girls of my generation after a year or two of war:

> *Oh, qu'as tu fait, toi que voilà*
> *Pleurant sans cesse?*

Dis, qu'as tu fait, toi que voilà
De ta jeunesse?

William Noel Hodgson, who when only twenty was killed on the Somme, similarly lamented this lost youth which we had barely known in one of the saddest little songs that the War produced. It brought me near to weeping, I remember, when after four years of hospitals, and last leaves, and farewells, I heard it sung by Topliss Green at the Albert Hall about 1919:

> *Take my Youth that died to-day,*
> *Lay him on a rose-leaf bed,—*
> *He so gallant was and gay,—*
> *Let them hide his tumbled head,*
> *Roses passionate and red*
> *That so swiftly fade away.*
>
> *Let the little grave be set*
> *Where my eyes shall never see;*
> *Raise no stone, make no regret*
> *Lest my sad heart break, — and yet,*
> *For my weakness, let there be*
> *Sprigs of rue and rosemary.*

But again I anticipate. The naïve quotations from my youthful diary which I have used, and intend to use, are included in this book in order to give some idea of the effect of the War, with its stark disillusionments, its miseries unmitigated by polite disguise, upon the unsophisticated *ingénue* who 'grew up' (in a purely social sense) just before it broke out. The annihilating future Armageddon, of which the terrors are so often portrayed in vivid language by League of Nations Union prophets, could not possibly, I think, cause the Bright Young People of to-day, with their imperturbable realism, their casual, intimate knowledge of sexual facts, their familiarity with the accumulated experiences of us their foredoomed predecessors, one-tenth of the physical and psychological shock that the Great War caused to the Modern Girl of 1914.

It is, of course, conceivable that young women brought up, like myself, in the provinces, were more childishly and idealistically ignorant than their London contemporaries; yet, looking back upon the London girls with whom I went to school, I do not think that the difference was very great. One of them I well remember saying to me, just after she 'came out', that she was always afraid of going too far with men, because she really didn't know what 'too far' was. I was quite unable to enlighten her, though an incident that had happened to me two or three years earlier made me certain that the vague peril was something extremely embarrassing and profoundly uncomfortable.

At the end of one school term, I had been as usual shepherded by a mistress into the train at St Pancras for the long journey to Buxton. Carefully observing the rule, which originated in contemporary White Slave Traffic alarms, that we were never to travel in carriages alone with men, she selected a compartment in which the one male passenger was safely accompanied by a respectable elderly female. Unfortunately at Kettering, the first stop after we left St Pancras, the elderly female got out, and immediately the train started again the strange man, a swarthy, black-haired individual of the commercial-traveller class, with rolling eyes and large hairy hands, came over from his corner and sat down beside me.

'I was waiting for that old cat to get out so that we could have a nice little talk,' he promisingly began.

More alarmed than I allowed myself to appear, I looked helplessly at the closed door leading to the corridor, but though its very existence protected me better than I realised, it was completely cut off by my companion's insinuating bulk.

'I see you're going to Buxton,' he continued, looking at my initialled suitcase. 'How I wish I hadn't got to get out at Leicester! Now won't you just tell me your name?'

Encouraged by the mention of Leicester, which was only another half-hour's journey, I responded inventively that my name was Violet Brown and that I didn't live in Buxton but was only going there for a week to stay with friends – a fabrication inspired by the nightmarish fear that this apparition might suddenly appear in search of me on our own front doorstep.

'And how old are you?' he inquired, pressing closer, and looked disappointed when I answered truthfully that I was fourteen.

'Why,' he exclaimed, 'you're such a pretty little girl – I thought you must be quite seventeen! When you get home you must send me your photograph—' and he squeezed me still further into the corner.

It was then that I realised that the train, upon which I was depending to convey me to Leicester and salvation, had suddenly come to a standstill. Some shouts were raised along the line; my enemy heard them, and informed me with satisfaction that we had broken down, and could not possibly get to Leicester for over an hour.

'Now what a lucky thing we're together!' he said softly, and took my hand – a grubby enough schoolgirl's fist, with ink-stained nails chipped by games and amateur gardening. 'Pretty little girls like you shouldn't bite their nails,' he murmured playfully, examining my fingers. 'You'll stop biting them to please me, won't you? – and give me a kiss to show that we're pals?'

The leering black eyes, the pawing hands and the alcoholic breath combined with the train's delay to drive me into a panic. Suddenly desperate, and probably more muscular than my tormentor had anticipated, I flung myself with an immense effort out of his encroaching arms, and dashed frantically into the corridor. The subdued middle-aged woman into whose compartment I blindly stumbled, flushed and hatless, regarded me with amazement, but she accepted my incoherent tale of an 'awful man', and pacified my agitation by giving me a share of her luncheon sandwiches. When, after quite an hour's breakdown, we did at last pass Leicester, she went with me to retrieve my suitcase from the compartment in which I still feared to see my swarthy assailant, but he had gone.

I never related this incident to my family – the thought of the hullabaloo that would follow, of the fuss that would be made both at home and at school whenever I had to travel alone, filled me with too great a distaste – but so deep was the repugnance aroused in me that I remember it as clearly as though it had happened last week. It was not, however, until the summer of 1922, when from an open-air platform in Hyde Park I supported the Six Point Group in urging the passage of the Criminal Law Amendment Bill by the House of Commons, that I realised the existence, as legal conceptions, of indecent assault and the age of consent.

So far as I can now judge, at eighteen I was at least as interested in social problems and in what were then always referred to as 'the facts of life' as most of my contemporaries, though my sexual curiosity was always a bad second to my literary ambition. Yet when the War broke out, I did not clearly understand what was meant by homosexuality, incest or sodomy, and was puzzled by the shadow that clung to the name of Oscar Wilde, whose plays I discovered in 1913 and read with a rapturous delight in their epigrams.

Nearly all the older girls with whom I went to school had been addicted to surreptitious conversations about the advent of babies; periodic discovery by parents or teachers thrust these intriguing speculations still further underground, and led to that intensive searching for obstetrical details through the Bible and such school-library novels as *David Copperfield* and *Adam Bede* which appears to have been customary almost everywhere among the adolescents of my generation. Thanks to this composite enlightenment in addition to the decorous elucidations of *Household Medicine*, I had a fairly comprehensive though somewhat Victorian idea of the primitive fashion in which the offspring of even the most civilised parents make their appearance, but of how to rear infants and train small children I had not the slightest notion either in theory or in practice, since the influence of married women in the education of girls mostly destined for wifehood and maternity was then considered even less desirable than it is to-day. I was also, despite my stock of physiological information, still extremely hazy with regard to the precise nature of the sexual act.

This half-knowledge engendered in me so fierce an antipathy to the idea of physical relationship in so far as this happened to be separable from romance, that when, soon after I left school, I was proposed to by a neighbour of ours – a large, athletic young man with limited brains and evangelical principles, who strongly disapproved of my 'unwomanly' ambitions, and could not possibly have been attracted by anything more substantial than my childish pretty-prettiness – my immediate and only reaction was a sense of intolerable humiliation and disgust.

When first I had to nurse a case of venereal disease – which I had hitherto seen referred to in the Press only under the mysterious title of 'the hidden plague' – I did not know exactly what it was; I was fully enlightened only in 1917, when in a Malta hospital I watched a syphilitic orderly die in convulsions after an injection of salvarsan. Finally, my pre-war knowledge of Army doctors and nurses was derived entirely from the more idealistic poems of Kipling, which by no means helped me to understand the suggestive words and movements, the desperate secret manœuvrings, of men and women tormented by unnecessary segregation.

It should now be clear that – easy victims as I and the boys and girls similarly reared provided, with our naïve, uninformed generosities and enthusiasms, for the war propagandist in a non-conscription country – few young women could have been less forewarned and forearmed than I was against war in general, and Army Hospital Service in particular.

CHAPTER II

Provincial Young-Ladyhood

IN THE ROSE-GARDEN

Dew on the pink-flushed petals,
Roseate wings unfurled;
What can, I thought, be fairer
In all the world?

Steps that were fain but faltered
(What could she else have done?)
Passed from the arbour's shadow
Into the sun.

Noon and a scented glory,
Golden and pink and red;
'What after all are roses
To me?' I said.

R. A. L.
July 11th, 1914.

1

But when I became, in 1912, a provincial débutante, decked out in London-bought garments that I did not know how to wear, the War was still two years away and my hospital service more than three. That unparalleled age of rich materialism and tranquil comfort, which we who grew up at its close will never see again, appeared to us to have gone on from time immemorial, and to be securely destined to continue for ever.

At my first dance, the High Peak Hunt Ball, I appeared modestly attired in the conventional white satin and pearls; this ingenuous uniform entitled me to spend the greater part of the next few weeks gyrating to the strains of 'Dreaming' and 'The Vision of Salome' in the arms of physically boisterous and conversationally inept young men. Those dances were by no means the mere gay functions that they seemed; they were supposed to test out the marriageable qualities of the young women on the basis of their popularity as dancing partners, and were therefore attended by numerous competitive chaperones who watched the proceedings with every symptom of apprehension and anxiety. Judging from the inferiority-complex permanently implanted in one or two of my contemporaries who did not come out of the test with flying colours, I am inclined to believe that provincial dances are responsible for more misery than any other commonplace experience.

Three years afterwards, as I was clearing my desk before going as a V.A.D. to London – I was quitting Buxton for ever, though I did not then realise it – I came across a ribbon-tied heap of my early dance-programmes carefully put away in a drawer. By that time so many of the fatuous young men had acquired dignity through death in France and the Dardanelles, that these records of my dances with them seemed like the incongruous souvenirs of a long-vanished and half-forgotten world – a world in which only the sinking of the *Titanic* had suddenly but quite temporarily reminded its inhabitants of the vanity of human calculations. I put the programmes back with the half-sorrowful, half-scornful indulgence that a middle-aged woman might feel when coming upon the relics of some youthful folly.

For the rest of 1912 and the first half of 1913, I went to more dances, paid calls, skated and tobogganed, played a good deal of Bridge and a great deal of tennis and golf, had music lessons and acted in amateur theatricals; in fact I passed my days in all those conventional pursuits with which the leisured young woman of every generation has endeavoured to fill the time that she is not qualified to use. Even my persevering attempts to follow, in accordance with St Monican tradition, the intricacies of Home Rule and Welsh Disestablishment through the columns of *The Times* gradually slackened and ceased for lack of external encouragement. My only concession to the social conscience uncomfortably developed in me at school consisted of reluctant visits to my mother's 'district' in the village of Burbage, near the limekilns below the sickle-like curve of Axe Edge. Here I made myself 'useful' by distributing copies of *Mothers in Council*, the official organ of that curious Union which believes the compulsory association of antagonistic partners to be somehow conducive to the sanctity of marriage.

My desultory and totally unorganised reading of George Eliot, Thackeray, Mrs Gaskell, Carlyle, Emerson and Merejkowski made little impression upon this routine, though their writings offered occasional compensation for its utter futility. 'The reading of *Romola*,' enthusiastically records my diary for April 27th, 1913, 'has left me in a state of exultation! It is wonderful to be able to purchase so much rapture for 2*s*. 6*d*. ! . . . It makes me wonder when in my life will come the moments of supreme emotion in which all lesser feelings are merged, and which leave one's spirit different for evermore.'

Throughout those months which witnessed the outbreak of the first Balkan War, the renewal of the Triple Alliance, and a great deal of intermittent agitation over German spies, I never ceased – though often now with a failing heart, since the possibilities had begun to seem so small and the obstacles to be overcome so great – to pester my parents to send me to college. These importunities were invariably received by my father with the statement that he had already spent quite as much on my education as was necessary, and that 'little girls' must allow their elders to know what was best for them. I found this attitude of good-natured scepticism peculiarly exasperating, since in my own eyes I was not, of course, a 'little girl' at all, but a twentieth-century evangelist entrusted with the task of leading a benighted universe from darkness to light.

The apparent objects of my upbringing being what they were, some of my acquaintances have been surprised that I was never sent to Paris to be 'finished' – i.e. to be shaped yet more defi-nitely in the trivial feminine mould which every youthful instinct and ambition prompted me to repudiate. Despairing of Oxford, and defensively smitten with the idea of postponing the dreaded isolation of Buxton, I had even, in my last term at school, misguid-edly pleaded for a few months in Paris or Brussels. But my father was almost as much opposed to Paris as to college, on the ground that as soon as I got over there I should probably be seized with appendicitis – a not unnatural fear on his part, though I had never been threatened with the disease, and up to the present have escaped it.

Baulked of the minor alleviation, I returned again and again to the major attack; the desire for a more eventful existence and a less restricted horizon had become an obsession, and it never occurred to me to count on marriage as a possible road to freedom. From what I already knew of men, it seemed only too probable that a husband would yet further limit my opportunities – a conclusion fully warranted by the fact that nearly all the men I knew not only lived in Buxton, but regarded it as the most desirable place of residence in England.

Each fresh refusal to spend another penny on my education (though the cost of my music lessons, and of the expensive new piano which was ungrudgingly bought for me to practise on, would have paid for nearly a year at Oxford) plunged me into further depths of gloom; I felt trammelled and trapped, and after a few months at home I hated Buxton, in spite of the austere beauty of its peaks and dales and the health-giving air which induced so many rheumatic invalids to live hopefully in its hotels and take its waters, with a detestation that I have never since felt for any set of circumstances. Nearly two hundred miles from London, and therefore completely cut off – in days when a conscientious provincial mother would almost as soon have submitted her adolescent daughter to seduction as allow her to spend a few unaccompanied hours in town or entrust her with the Baby Austin type of freedom – from the groups of ambitious, intelligent boys and girls who naturally gravitate together in university towns and capital cities, I was wholly at the mercy of local conditions and family standards. I had nothing to do and no one to talk to; Edward for most of the year was at Uppingham, and with Mina and Betty I became more and more out of touch as the months went by.

Even at eighteen, a mentally voracious young woman cannot live entirely upon scenery. Two things alone prevented me, during Edward's school terms, from dying of spontaneous combustion –

my diary, which I kept in a voluminous detail that now makes me marvel at the amount of time I must have had on my hands, and the appearance in a neighbouring village of a rationalistic curate, whose unorthodox dissertations on the Higher Criticism I took for the profoundest learning, and whose florid, dramatic sermons, to which every Sunday I walked three miles to listen, seemed to me the most inspired eloquence. The holidays were more bearable, for Edward's return from Uppingham always brought with it a fresh outburst of music, which lent, if only vicariously, some object to life. I was never more than a second-rate pianist, for my hands were too small to stretch an octave easily, but Edward – already a skilled and passionate violinist – depended upon me to accompany him in the complicated sonatas and concertos that he brought home from school. So at Christmas and Easter and midsummer I went round with him to local At Homes, amateur concerts and musical evenings, ploughing strenuously after him through the *prestissimos* and *rallentandos*, the *arpeggios*, *tremolos* and accidentals, of the Beethoven No. 1 Sonata, the Mendelssohn and Spohr Concertos, and the rippling seventeenth-century melodies of Alessandro Scarlatti and Pietro Nardini.

Those two pre-war years in Buxton left me deeply imbued with a form of snobbishness which I do not suppose that I shall ever outgrow, and which is, perhaps, the only one in which I was not deliberately educated. The universal middle-class snobberies of birth and wealth and Anglicanism I soon repudiated and took a naïve delight in so doing; I even believe that I have set myself free, though only within recent years, from the more insidious snobbery of puritan respectability, which causes women of my class and generation to regard the sexual lives of their husbands as a species of personal property, and to treat with sour disapproval or self-conscious patronage any female acquaintance who happens at any time to have indulged in extra-marital relations. But from the snobbery of metropolitanism, the superiority of the Londoner towards the small-town dweller, I do not think I am likely to recover, even though the calm voice of reason – so irritatingly disdainful of our dearest prejudices – tells me that the wireless and the cinema and the long-distance motor 'bus have probably transformed the provinces out of all recognition since 1915.

To me provincialism stood, and stands, for the sum-total of all false values; it is the estimation of people for what they have, or pretend to have, and not for what they are. Artificial classifications, rigid lines of demarcation that bear no relation whatsoever to intrinsic merit, seem to belong to its very essence, while contempt for intelligence, suspicion and fear of independent thought, appear to be necessary passports to provincial popularity. Its mean, censorious spirit is typified for me by the local bank-manager's querulous little wife who took my mother, as a young married woman giving her first small dinner-party in Macclesfield, severely to task for having 'mixed her sets'.

In some of the larger provincial cities a rich and enterprising life does seem possible which is free from this carping pettiness; I am thinking especially of Manchester, where we often used to go for a day's shopping. The home of such remarkable families as the Pankhursts and the Laskis and the Simons, Manchester seems to have escaped the stigma of provincialism – perhaps on account of the national standing of the *Manchester Guardian* (which in Buxton we never saw, the household preferring the Manchester edition of the *Daily Mail*), perhaps even more because the hard-working *habitués* of the city keep the leisured members of their families out of the way in the surrounding suburbs. Social snobbery and unreal values seem to reach their height in towns with between ten and twenty thousand inhabitants. Buxton, which my father used to describe as 'a little box of social strife lying at the bottom of a basin', must have had a population of about twelve thousand apart from the visitors who came to take the waters.

I am not, I think, a naturally vindictive person, but in those years when the beautiful heather-covered hills surrounding Buxton represented for me the walls of a prison, I used to swear to Edward that one day I would take my revenge in a novel – and I did. None of my books have had large sales and the least successful of them all was my second novel, *Not Without Honour*, but I have never enjoyed any experience more than the process of decanting my hatred into that story of the social life of a small provincial town.

2

Sometimes, during Edward's holidays, I used to relate to him incidents destined to appear in this book in much the same way as, during our childhood, I had kept him awake at night with tales of the fabulous 'Dicks'. He was still as good a listener as ever, since the chief interest of his life and the exclusive object of his ambition was, as in earlier years, his violin.

It is, and always has been, difficult to estimate what manner of person Edward really was at the close of his Uppingham years, and it becomes harder as time marches on. He came, soon after the War broke out, to mean so much to me, and I to him, that I sometimes wonder whether either of us troubled completely to understand the other apart from our very close mutual relationship. Undoubtedly he was handsome; in incongruous contrast to my five-foot-three, he grew to be well over six feet in height, and had dark, velvety, rather sombre brown eyes beneath long thick lashes and almost black arched eyebrows, which gave some substance to my mother's theory that there had been French or Spanish blood in her family a little distance back. At sixteen he was inclined to be rather priggish and self-righteous – not such bad qualities in adolescence after all, since most of us have to be self-righteous before we can be righteous.

By the time that Edward reached nineteen, he had acquired a charming, easy-going manner (another inheritance, perhaps, from our musical grandfather) which won him a good deal of popularity and was particularly effective in interviews with senior officers and War Office officials; but beneath the agreeable surface I and others who knew him well continually came up against something adamant and rigid through which we could not penetrate – 'like a vein of flint in a soft rock', as I described it in my diary in 1914. Mentally, I suppose, he was intelligent rather than intellectual; his taste in literature was limited to plays, short stories and a few poems, most of which had some practical significance, and though he won a good many prizes as a small schoolboy, he continually missed them as he grew older. At Uppingham he was invariably second or third in his form; his school reports, apart from those of his music-masters, were never brilliant and never unsatisfactory.

His one absorbing passion was music, to which he added the persistent determination that our unlucky grandfather had so conspicuously lacked. At seventeen he had already begun to compose songs and concertos; as soon as a sheet of music paper was in his hand he became a different creature, irritable, alert, absorbed. On instruments other than the violin – the organ, the piano, the viola – he became a tolerable performer after a very few lessons. How gifted he really was as a violinist, how promising as a composer, I cannot now tell, though it is perhaps significant that both Mr R. Sterndale Bennett at Uppingham and Sir Hugh (then Dr) Allen at Oxford were keenly interested in his possibilities.

My father's plans for him varied between the successorship to himself at the paper-mills – an occupation to which I should have been better adapted than Edward, who had no business ambitions and no interest whatever in commercial processes – and the Indian Civil Service, for which his form-master declared that he would never pass the necessary examinations. In his private dreams Edward always visualised himself as a famous conductor-composer, a kind of junior Sir Henry Wood, but he had too much discretion to press the claims of his talent upon my father, who regarded music (for a man) as one of life's non-essentials, and always explosively objected to the sounds of violin-practising.

Edward's whole nature led him to prefer round-about methods of persuasion to the challenging directness with which I was wont to stir up parental opposition. 'Dear child! So *worried!*' he used to remark with laconic amusement whenever I emerged, breathless and angry, from one of my belligerent encounters with the family. Secretly he determined to read Music as well as Greats at Oxford, and to let his future be dictated by the result. He was, I think, inwardly relieved when he failed to win a scholarship for New College in 1914, but passed in easily as a Commoner on his papers; he was thus freed from the obligation to work for a high Honours Degree which would have interfered considerably with the time available for music.

In spite of his limited qualities of scholarship and his fitful interest in all non-musical subjects, the idea of refusing Edward a university education never so much as crossed my father's mind. I loved him too dearly even while he was still at school to be jealous of him personally, particularly as he was always my gallant supporter, but I should have been far more patient and docile than I ever showed any symptom of becoming if I had not resented his privileged position as a boy. The most flattering of my school reports had never, I knew, been regarded more seriously than my inconvenient thirst for knowledge and opportunities; in our family, to adapt a famous present-day phrase, what mattered was not the quality of the work, but the sex of the worker.

The constant and to me enraging evidences of this difference of attitude towards Edward and myself violently reinforced the feminist tendencies which I had first acquired at school, and which were being indirectly but surely developed by the clamorous drama of the suffragette movement far away in London.

'It feels sad to be a woman!' I wrote in March 1913 – the very month in which the 'Cat and Mouse' Act was first introduced for the ingenious torment of the militants. 'Men seem to have so much more choice as to what they are intended for.'

The passage of time – or so, at least, I fondly believe – has changed my furious Buxton resentments into mellower and more balanced opinions, but probably no ambitious girl who has lived in a family which regards the subservience of women as part of the natural order of creation ever completely recovers from the bitterness of her early emotions. Perhaps it is just as well; women have still a long way to travel before their achievements are likely to be assessed without irrelevant sex considerations entering in to bias the judgment of the critic, and even their recent political successes are not yet so secure that those who profit by them can afford to dispense with the few acknowledged feminists who are still vigilant, and still walk warily along once forbidden paths.

3

Early in 1913, when my hopes of ever escaping from provincial young-ladyhood were almost abandoned, came the first unexpected intimations of eventual release.

One spring evening a Staffordshire acquaintance – an old family lawyer – came to spend the night at our house. Judiciously prompted by my mother, who was now beginning – perhaps because my refusal to adapt myself to Buxton had now convinced her – secretly to sympathise with the idea of college, he began at dinner to talk about Oxford, and I learnt that his elder son, who had won a scholarship there, had only just gone down after taking a brilliant degree.

My father, not to be outdone in parental self-congratulation, thereupon not only mentioned his determination to send Edward to Oxford, but threw in my own continual requests to go to college to make up the balance. To his surprise, our visitor took this expression of feminine ambition entirely as a matter of course, and even mentioned one or two of his son's acquaintances among the women students. Like many men who have been brought up without academic contacts, my father was at first more ready to listen to family cronies without any special title to their opinions, than to unfamiliar experts with every qualification for offering advice. The fact that his highly respected old friend regarded the presence of women at Oxford as in no way remarkable undoubtedly caused him to revise his opinion on the whole subject of the higher education of daughters. This transformation process was completed by a course of University Extension Lectures given by Mr J. A. R. Marriott – now Sir John – in Buxton Town Hall during the spring of 1913.

Of recent years I have sometimes heard criticisms of Sir John Marriott by his political opponents both at Oxford and elsewhere. These party criticisms usually imply, more or less directly, that long experience as a university teacher does not adapt a man or woman to political life, and that it was probably owing to his academic qualities that Sir John lost the supposedly safe Conservative seats of Oxford and York.

In this country, apart from university constituencies, there is certainly a rigid line, difficult to cross, between the political and the academic worlds – a line which in parts of America is becoming indistinct, with advantages to both sides. Judging from my experience as a graduate of one university and the wife of a professor attached to another, it does seem to me that academic life in any country tends to make both men and women narrow, censorious and self-important. My husband I believe to be among the exceptions, but one or two of his young donnish contemporaries have been responsible for some of the worst exhibitions of bad manners that I have ever encountered. Apparently most dons grow out of this contemptuous brusqueness as the years go by; elderly professors, though often disapproving, are almost always punctilious. On the whole I have found American dons politer than English, and those from provincial universities more courteous than the Oxford and Cambridge variety.

To attribute, however, to Sir John Marriott the brusquer characteristics of academic Oxford seems to me to argue precisely that lack of perspicacity that Party opponents so often encourage in themselves. (I write this without rancour, since I belong myself to that Party whose programme is anathema to Sir John and his colleagues. To-day I can agree with few of his political opinions, but if he believed every clause of the Versailles Treaty to be divinely inspired I think I should forgive him, so deep still is my thankfulness for his breezy and uncalculating intervention in my obscure affairs.) No man could have had less contempt for unfamiliar ways of living, or more interest in the by-paths of experience. On the only occasion that they met I remember how skilfully he persuaded my father – with whom he can have had next to nothing in common – to discourse with lively enthusiasm on the technique of paper-making, and to relate the modest history of our mill.

For me Sir John remains and always will remain the kindly, stimulating teacher in whose genial presence obstacles hitherto insuperable melted away like snow in April. He represents the *deus ex machina* of my unsophisticated youth, the Olympian who listened without a hint of patronage or amusement to the halting account of a callow girl's vaunting, ingenuous ambitions. To him I owe my final victory over family opposition, my escape from the alien atmosphere of Buxton, and the university education which for all its omissions did at long last equip me for the kind of life that I wanted to lead. It is a debt that I acknowledge with humble gratitude, and can never hope to repay.

The most optimistic enthusiast for adult education could hardly have described that Buxton course of Extension Lectures on the Problems of Wealth and Poverty as a conspicuous success. I stayed away from the first to go to a dance (this far had I already fallen from grace!) but I attended and wrote – the sole regular essayist out of the whole town – for all the five others.

Sir John gave of his vigorous and popular best, but a prophet from heaven could not have impressed his listless and dwindling audience, of which the older and somnolent half had come out of consideration for the feelings of the local secretary, and the younger and fidgety half under compulsion from its parents. It was, I think, at the fourth or fifth lecture that he was moved to tell his yawning listeners that Buxton did not strike him as *particularly* inquisitive – a remark which led to a good deal of adverse criticism of the lectures at subsequent tea-parties. I even heard one voluminous lady (whose husband had launched out upon an essay answering all three alternative questions, instead of selecting one as he had been told to do) remark to sympathetic acquaintances that she never *had* liked 'the man's' manner, and that she had heard he only came to Buxton because they wouldn't have him in Oxford!

My own persevering essays on the Industrial Revolution, the Problem of Distribution, the History of Trade Unionism and the Rise of the Socialist Movement must have been crude and superficial in the extreme, since neither the local Free Library nor the little collection of schoolbooks on my bedroom shelves contained any relevant works on either history or economics, but the reports that they received from Sir John were sufficiently encouraging to be described by my father as 'a great honour from an Oxford man'.

No doubt – as indeed I have since discovered when lecturing myself – one wheat-ear of enthusiasm was worth a good many tares of indifference. I signed my first tentative effort with initials only, and when I nervously went up to claim it Sir John showed considerable surprise – as well indeed he might have done, for no one could have looked more immature, or less capable of formulating a coherent idea, than I did in those days. For all my long skirts and elaborate Empire curls, I never succeeded up to the time that the War broke out in appearing older than an unfledged fifteen.

At the request of the local secretary – a cultured woman who was, needless to say, only on the fringe of 'the set' – my family agreed to put Sir John up for his last Buxton lecture. On this occasion he returned my weekly essay at home after we came back from the now almost empty Town Hall. His praise moved me to speak, in my parents' presence, of my longing to go to Oxford, and I asked his advice with regard to the first steps to be taken. The genial matter-of-factness with which he gave it seemed to dispel all doubts, and made the customary objections look so trivial that they were hardly ever mentioned again.

The next morning he departed, leaving a singular feeling of emptiness where his stimulating presence, his tweed coat and his golf clubs had been. I do not suppose that he ever thought again of our household, or realised in the least how completely his flying visit had altered the atmosphere.

4

After Sir John had gone changes seemed, in comparison with the utter stagnation of the previous year, to happen very quickly. I went in for, and won, an essay competition which he had advised me to attempt in connection with that year's Oxford Summer Meeting; I also received, and accepted, an invitation to stay at St Hilda's Hall for the meeting itself with my aunt and Miss Heath Jones.

The result of the essay competition further gratified the dawning pride in my modest achievements which Sir John's encouragement had aroused in my father. Before I went to the Summer School he told me that he had decided to send me to Oxford for a year, and did not seem unduly disconcerted when I returned home with the information – then as much news to me as to him – that if I wanted a Degree I must remain at college not merely for one year but for three.

I went to St Hilda's in a state of ecstactic entrancement which I do not now know whether to regard as funny or pathetic or incredible; I only wish that I were still capable of feeling it about anything. 'Oh, when I think of it all,' I had written in my diary with ingenuous rapture after accepting my aunt's invitation, 'I feel as though I were in a dream from which I am afraid to awaken. Oxford! What doesn't it call up to the mind! The greatest romance of England – the mellowed beauty of time and association, the finest lectures the world can produce, wonderful libraries and fascinating old bookshops, the society of Miss H. J. and Miss B. the best I could desire on earth and the meeting all the interesting intellectual people Miss H. J. knows – oh God, have pity on my fierce excitement and grant that it may come to pass and be even better than I dream!'

When I did arrive at this Earthly Paradise I was not, strangely enough, in the least disappointed. Even the lectures 'the finest the world can produce', came up to my expectations – a fact which seems to indicate that few of the usual term-time lecturers can have been included in the Summer School programme. There was a light on my path and a dizzy intoxication in the air; the old buildings in the August sunshine seemed crowned with a golden glory, and I tripped up and down the High Street between St Hilda's and the Examination Schools on gay feet as airy as my soaring aspirations.

My fellow 'thirsters' were the usual Summer Meeting collection of unoccupied spinsters, schoolmistresses on holiday, fatherly chapel-goers and earnest young men in sweaters and soft collars, but I thought them all extremely talented and enormously important. Had anyone told me that less than a decade afterwards I should myself be lecturing to similar gatherings, I should blankly have refused to believe him, for if I was in awe of the audiences, the lecturers seemed to me to be at least on a level with Angels and Archangels and all the company of heaven. And perhaps, since they included not only Sir John Marriott on the Monarchy of France, but Dean Inge, grave, scholarly and a little alarming on Old Testament Eschatology, I had some excuse for thinking that I had strayed by accident into the most exclusive circle of a celestial hierarchy.

The fact that Sir John had asked me to dine with him one evening while I was attending the School added the final drop to my cup of excitement. Palpitating with awe and amazement, I presented myself at his house in Northmoor Road, where I met his beautiful wife and elegant, clever daughter, who afterwards became, rather surprisingly, absorbed in the Girls' Diocesan Association. So remarkably had my prospects changed since the spring, that we talked of my university future as a foregone conclusion. Sir John, no doubt bearing in mind the sheltered life of a Buxton young lady, took for granted that I should try to enter Lady Margaret Hall, for this has always been the politest of the four Oxford women's colleges, and in those days it invariably wore, like my Buxton academy, 'a school for the daughters of gentlemen' air. (Strictly Anglican gentlemen, of course.)

Trembling but determined, in spite of the gratitude and admiration which almost unnerved me, I contradicted his assumption. I had already talked over the four colleges with a business associate of my father's, Mr Horace Hart, then Controller of the Oxford University Press, who told me that Somerville was undenominational and that it had become, owing to its high examination standards, by far the most difficult of the women's colleges to enter.

From the University Press windows Mr Hart and I had looked across Walton Street at the terra-cotta walls of Somerville drowsing in the afternoon sun. I had found irresistibly fascinating both its closed garden and the idea of its arrogant, intellectual impregnability, but perhaps what chiefly attracted me – still theologically dominated by *Robert Elsmere* and the rationalistic Buxton curate – was its religious toleration. So I told Sir John that it was not the socially safe Head of Lady Margaret Hall whom I had arranged to see, but the scholarly and intimidating Principal of Somerville.

My appointment with her was fixed for eight o'clock one evening after dinner. I felt indescribably elated, yet definitely insecure about the legs, when I found myself for the first time within the walled garden, and saw the wide lawn and the heavy, drooping elms and sycamores in the fast-vanishing light. I came upon the Principal – 'who is just like a tigercat', I noted afterwards in my diary – before I expected to see her, sitting over her after-dinner coffee with the History tutor on the narrow stretch of grass outside the Senior Common Room.

As I followed the scout across the garden, the Principal got up to greet me. Her immensely tall, angular figure seemed to go on unfolding for several minutes before my apprehensive eyes, and the vast gulf of lawn between us made me even more conscious than usual of my insignificant stature. Being quite ignorant of the plain-Jane-and-no-nonsense conventions of Oxford women dons, I had carefully changed, in accordance with the sartorial habits of Buxton, into evening dress, and was wearing a flimsy lace frock under a pale blue and grey reversible satin cloak, and an unsubstantial little pair of high-heeled white suède shoes. So unlike the customary felt hat and mackintosh of the average 1913 woman student was this provincially modish attire, that the Principal actually referred to it when she interviewed me during the Scholarship examinations in the following March. 'I remember you,' she said immediately, 'you're the girl who came across the lawn in a blue evening cloak.'

But on this first occasion my frivolous appearance, combined with my complete lack of examination certificates and my deplorable ignorance of even the Greek alphabet, obviously convinced her that I was a singularly unpromising candidate. Nevertheless she patiently described to my appalled ears the barbed-wire fence of examinations that had to be scaled before an ambitious but totally unqualified young woman could hope to enter Somerville, and, incredible as it must have appeared to her that I did not know it, endeavoured to make me understand the difference between University Responsions and the College Entrance Examination.

In conclusion, she advised me to take English (then, as now, the 'woman's subject' at Oxford), to exempt myself from Responsions (since I knew no Greek) by means of the Oxford Senior Local, and on no account to try for a scholarship. Finally she left me at the gate with a sheaf of printed regulations in my hands and returned to her companion, probably calculating with some satisfaction that she was never likely to see me again.

For the greater part of an anguished night, I sat up in my little room at St Hilda's and puzzled over those documents. My aunt and Miss Heath Jones had already departed; the maiden ladies in whose charge I had been left were, I knew, even more ignorant than myself about women's colleges, while I was only too well aware that no one either at home or in Buxton would regard those lists of bewildering alternatives with any sentiment more helpful than mystified impatience. More than once I dissolved into angry tears of baffled despair. No one familiar with examination rules has any idea what Arabic and Sanscrit they can appear to an anxious, unsophisticated young candidate whose very chance of success may depend upon her correct interpretation of their complex intricacies.

As it was, I never grasped from the Somerville data the fact that if I wanted a Degree in some distant and improbable future when Degrees for women were attained, the Oxford Senior would not exempt me from Responsions Greek, and that I would still have to take the subject after I went up. So instead of tackling the easy rudiments of Greek grammar, I set myself the unnecessarily difficult task of reaching a high standard in mathematics – always a weak point – and in Latin, with which I had the merest nodding acquaintance, since it was not included in the regular curriculum at St Monica's before 1914.

When at last I went to bed with the dawn, sleep was effectually banished by a return of the black despair that had so often overwhelmed me in Buxton. Why, I wonder, do people who at one time or another have all been young themselves, and who ought therefore to know better, generalise so suavely and so mendaciously about the golden hours of youth – that period of life when every sorrow seems permanent, and every set-back insuperable?

During that miserable night I fully believed that I had overcome the psychological objections to the life that I so much desired, only to be frustrated by inexperience and academic shortcomings. My slowly relenting father, I felt, must not be asked to finance two sets of coaching for two separate examinations, and even if he could be persuaded to do so, who was there in Buxton capable of preparing me for College Entrance papers?

These difficulties, and my weakness in Latin and mathematics, meant that it was the dreary Oxford Senior for which I must be coached. Somehow or other I should have to do my best with the Somerville English unaided, although I had no books, no notion of the standard that I ought to reach, no knowledge – since public and High School girls were quite outside the range of my experience – of the probable attainments of my competitors, and no one – for I feared to trouble the magnificent Sir John any further – to whom to turn for advice. Apprehensively I quailed at the prospect of simultaneously preparing, in the Bridge-and-dance dominated atmosphere of Buxton, for two examinations, the Somerville Entrance to be taken in March, and the Oxford Senior in the following July.

Not until I returned to Buxton, and encountered the cheerful equanimity of Edward, home for the holidays, did I finally resolve, not only to take my chance of success despite unfavourable appearances, but to adopt an even bolder policy than I really thought feasible.

'Why not take the Somerville Schol.?' demanded Edward, as we were practising tennis strokes against a brick wall in our circumscribed back yard one afternoon. 'Why stick at the Entrance? You've got far more brains than most girls.'

'How do I know I have?' I inquired, with some reason.

'Oh, I'm sure you have! Most of the chaps' sisters are such idiots . . . Besides, old Marriott wouldn't have made all that up about your essays. I'd try for the Schol. if I were you, I would really. You won't get one, of course, but you'll have a much better chance of getting in than if you take the potty Entrance papers.'

So at length I decided, in the teeth of the Principal's sagacious advice, to shoulder the additional burden of the Scholarship examination, partly to spite her obvious and pardonable assumption that I was a complete fool, partly in order to keep Edward's respect, which I valued, and partly because in those days the difficult thing had a will-o'-the-wisp fascination, luring me, in spite of a great deal of natural timidity, down unfamiliar and alarming roads of experience. I had been rash enough to select the college with the highest standard of scholarship; I might as well be a little more foolish, and attempt to enter it by the most resistant of doors.

5

The next few months were an uphill grind enough, but I thoroughly enjoyed them. No longer did my conscience prick me because I omitted to read about gun-running in Ulster, or to study those tentative treaties in the too-inflammable Balkans which so nearly coincided with that curiously ironic ceremony, the opening of the Palace of Peace at the Hague. Even the suffragette movement in which I was so deeply interested became for the time being a mere far-away fable of window-smashings and bomb explosions and damaged pictures in public galleries. To have some real work to do after more than a year of purposeless pottering was like a bracing visit to a cliff-bound coast after lethargic existence on a marshy lowland.

The mornings I gave to the Scholarship examination, getting up every day at six o'clock and working steadily till lunch-time in a chilly little north-west room, known as 'the sewing room', at the back of the house. It was on the ground floor and dark as well as cold, but I was not allowed a fire out of consideration for the maids, though we then kept three and a garden-boy. But I gladly endured my frozen hands and feet in order to obtain the privacy and quiet which none of the living-rooms in ordinary use would have given me.

Books were as usual a problem. The Free Library appeared to stock nothing that had been published since 1880, and the local circulating libraries, justified by the exclusive demands of their customers, supplied little else but fiction. So I spent the greater part of that autumn's tiny dress-allowance on the necessary volumes of Fielding and Goldsmith, Wordsworth and the *Cambridge History of English Literature*. Friends and relatives helped at Christmas with haphazard volumes of criticism, chosen entirely at random but with the best of intentions, on the Lakeland Poets and the Romantic Revival. After luncheon the energetic twitching of my athletic limbs drove me, fortunately for my health, out of doors to an afternoon's golf or tennis. From this I returned to tussle, often lacrimoniously, with mathematics and Latin for the rest of the day.

At first the complications of finding tuition for these two nightmare subjects had appeared almost insuperable. Help was naturally not to be expected from establishments founded for the creation, out of very raw material, of matrimonially eligible young ladies. The lackadaisical and self-conscious young masters from the local boys' preparatory schools were approached in vain. My rationalistic curate might have proved adequate, but his days were already overcrowded, and the numerous remaining clerics understood the social gradations of Anglican unctuousness better than the scientific pitfalls of mathematics.

I had already begun to contemplate a tedious journey two or three times weekly into Manchester, which would greatly have interfered with my work for the Scholarship, when the problem was solved by a neighbour of ours who ran a small institution for pushing backward boys by force into Sandhurst or Woolwich. Financially this coaching school was always on the rocks – it did not, in fact, survive my need of it by many weeks – and any apprehensions which its owner may have felt about the occasional presence of a young female among his feather-brained students was swallowed up in his relief at the prospect of some unexpected fees. The ages of the youths in his charge varied from seventeen to about twenty-three. As the whole dozen had between them barely enough intelligence to fill the head of a normal Sixth Form schoolboy, it can well be imagined that the coaching obtainable there was not of a very remarkable order.

The owner of the school, a social acquaintance of ours, took me himself for mathematics. He was patient and benevolent, but not very resourceful in coaching devices, and could only repeat helplessly, 'Oh yes, you do, you know!' in response to my frequent and quite honest asseverations that I did not understand almost all the algebraical propositions that he put before me. For him his rowdy pupils had some rudiments of respect – which was not, however, accorded to his elderly classical assistant, who wore a beard, spoke with a lisp, and owned a singularly infelicitous cognomen which cannot have helped him to manage the ruthless young adolescents who came under his charge.

The tedious hours which I spent in listening to this unattractive individual's elucidations of the Æneid appeared to the young gentlemen to be humorous in the extreme. A sudden enthusiasm for the reference-books on the shelves of my classroom was apt to seize them as soon as my coachings began, and one after another would come in at intervals to borrow a dictionary or return an encyclopædia. Strange phenomena invariably followed these periodic visitations. Piles of books would fall with a crash to the floor; pieces of furniture would mysteriously collapse, and on one occasion a gramophone concealed behind the window-curtain burst forth zestfully into 'Stop yer ticklin', Jock!'

After each of these *poltergeisterisch* disturbances my teacher would look suspiciously round like a puzzled old dog, but it never seemed to occur to him to connect them with the boys.

6

Any reader who has succeeded in following up to this point my warfare against Buxton young-ladyhood will probably feel that I have given far too much time and space to the adolescent subject of examinations. Readers, as almost all my editors have informed me at one time or another, are apt to remain quite untouched by any topic that is not well saturated with 'human interest' (i.e. love-affairs, sex crises and maternal self-indulgences, irreverently familiar in journalistic terminology under the comprehensive abbreviation of 'H.I.').

Unfortunately, the persevering introduction of 'H.I.' at this stage of my development would not in the least represent the true situation. Between August 1913 and April 1914, examinations did in fact occupy not only all my time but both my waking and sleeping thoughts. It must have been shortly after my visit to St Hilda's that I received the proposal of marriage already mentioned, but after the first shock of instinctive revulsion, sex and its concomitant emotions were completely obliterated by the *Cambridge History of English Literature* and the elusive secrets of quadratic equations. Marriage, to any man that I then knew, would merely have rooted me the more firmly among the detested hills and dales of Derbyshire; the Somerville Scholarship and the Oxford Senior Local appeared to provide the only road that would eventually lead me southward. I did not dream that the War Offices of France and Germany were busily preparing another.

To the inhabitants of Buxton, my preoccupation with Goldsmith and Wordsworth and Unseen Translations seemed quite as unnatural as it could possibly appear to any present-day reader. No sooner had the bare mention of Oxford penetrated, at third or fourth remove, the astonished and affronted ears of my mother's calling acquaintances, than rumour began to run wildly round the town.

'Have you heard? Vera Brittain's going to be a lecturer!'

Doubtful as I was even of my ability to fulfil with success the humble rôle of student that I had chosen, I found these extravagant inaccuracies of gossip both ludicrous and exasperating. Strange as it now seems, I was then far more deeply impressed by the superb remoteness, the godlike superiority of lecturers, than by the achievements of even the most famous of authors. I was accustomed to regard myself as destined – dimly, of course, and very distantly – to play some kind of star-turn in a paradisiacal Fleet Street, entirely vague in its details though splendidly Elysian in its glamour; but to stand on a platform like Sir John Marriott and harangue a breathlessly expectant audience seemed to me an utterly unattainable height of courage and power. Had I been able to look into the future and see myself finding platforms accessible long before editors and publishers ceased to be impervious, I should have believed myself destined to die in the interval and waken again to quite another life. And such a fate was perhaps, after all, not so different from the one that actually befell me.

Whatever their respective merits in the eyes of Omniscience, writers and lecturers and university women were all equally unnatural to the censorious Buxton ladies, and equally obnoxious. Had I possessed a gift for drawing and wanted to study in Paris; had I been, like Edward, a potential musician, and contemplated a career beginning at the Royal College of Music and continuing in Dresden or Leipzig, my parents' acquaintances would probably have thought me interesting and even wonderful. But so unpopular at that time was the blue-stocking tradition, and so fathomless the depth of provincial self-satisfaction, that my decision to go to an English town to study the literature of my own language caused me to be labelled 'ridiculous', 'eccentric', and 'a strongminded woman'.

For a few weeks my mother had quite a bad time at the G.F.S. teas and Mothers' Union meetings which she was then accustomed to attend. On these occasions she was invariably tackled by one or two stalwart middle-class mothers who did not hesitate to tell her how deplorable they thought my future plans, and to identify her acquiescence in them with her abandonment of all hope of finding me a husband. 'How *can* you send your daughter to college, Mrs Brittain!' moaned one lugubrious lady. 'Don't you want her ever to get *married*?'

But as soon as the initial ferment had died down, our feminine neighbours promptly ceased to take my examinations seriously at all. For the rest of that winter I was bombarded as usual with infuriating requests to help with jumble sales, 'wait' at bazaar teas, play in amateur theatricals, and take the place of tiresome individuals who had fallen out at Bridge. Girls who now, as a matter of course, prepare themselves for college in the comparatively peaceful seclusion of school, have no idea how strenuously each uninterrupted hour had to be fought for in the restless, critical, busy-busy atmosphere of a pre-war provincial town.

The month of the Somerville examination, March 1914, came far too quickly for the progress of my much-disturbed solitary studies. The journey to Oxford and the four hectic days that I spent there represented, I know, an immense experience at the time, but all that I can now remember of them is my alarmed impression of the imperturbable brilliance of my fellow-competitors – roughly a hundred for about twenty vacancies – and the bitter, paralysing cold of the little ground-floor room assigned to me in the west wing of the college.

I know of no place where the wind can be so icy and the damp so penetrating as in Oxford round about Easter-time. On my first intimidating night, the longing to thaw my stiff fingers tempted me to abandon even a frantic last-minute revision for that prolonged struggle to light a fire with which every Somerville student is familiar. My efforts were, of course, unavailing; the Oxford women's colleges have never had the means to afford the best drawing-room nuggets, and my previous experience with good Midland coal had not endowed me with the skill that I later acquired in wresting warmth out of a mass of dust, a few damp sticks, and some nobbly chunks of slate.

As Somerville did not then run to a large supply of hot baths – though I should have been too shy to appropriate one if it had – I spent the night in a shivering stupor, kept wretchedly awake by the misery of my frozen feet and the periodic clamour of unfamiliar bells. Consequently my first paper the next morning plunged me at once into panic, in which condition I sat for an hour without writing a word, desperately clasping and unclasping my hands under the table, and inwardly resolving that the moment we were permitted to leave the room, I would tell the Principal that I was returning home at once.

The subsequent course of my entire future probably depended upon the mere chance that something – perhaps my guardian angel, perhaps nothing more romantic than the warmth gradually restored to my icy limbs by the stuffiness of the lecture-room in which we were working – suddenly made me decide to 'stick out' the ordeal for which I had prepared at such cost of combat and exasperation, and to make the best of the job that had begun so badly. So, frantically seizing my pen, I started to write; any nonsense, I felt, was better than the blank sheets that would so forlornly typify my failure of imagination and courage.

All through the days of the examination, in spite of the three or four quickly-made friends with whom between papers I ate large teas in the town, I felt an unadapted alien to an extent that privately filled me with shame, and remember still the ludicrous shock from which I suffered after first meeting two or three of my terrifying competitors from East End or north-country High Schools. Probably no other girl who came up to take the Somerville Scholarship papers in 1914 had been reared to be quite such a sensitive plant as myself, or so securely sheltered in the greenhouse warmth of bourgeois comfort and provincial elegance. My mother's conscientious standards of cooking and cleanliness were, and are, about the most exacting that I have ever encountered, while at St Monica's, with its tasteful decorations and gracious garden, its appetising meals and large staff of servants, its limited number of fashionable pupils from homes far wealthier than my own, a still higher level of luxury had been taken for granted.

Until I spent those four days at Somerville in that freezing March, I had unthinkingly assumed that women's colleges were much the same as men's; Virginia Woolf had not then written *A Room of One's Own* to emphasise the sad difference between iced pudding and prunes and custard. It had never consciously occurred to me that, in nine households out of ten, linen sheets and hot and cold water and thickly carpeted floors were unattainable ambitions rather than the accepted facts of everyday life, nor that, by much more than half mankind, gristly mutton, boiled potatoes and tepid rice pudding would be considered an ample and even a luxurious diet. Still less had I realised that girls from homes far more genuinely cultured than mine could speak in accents as thick as a London fog, or wear ill-fitting, shabby clothes which compared unfavourably with the maids' Sunday reach-me-downs purchased from the pegs of the Buxton drapers.

When, on my first evening at Somerville, I stood timidly at the door of the big dining-hall, heard the shrill clamour of feminine accents from every geographical area, noticed the long-sleeved dowdiness of dinner frocks, and shuddered to see the homely food and piles of emptied soup-plates in the hatches, a suddenly sinking heart threatened me with the fear that even if I succeeded in getting to college, I should never be able to endure it. It required all my ambition, and all my touching belief that I was a natural democrat filled with an overwhelming love of humanity, to persuade me that I had never really felt the snobbish revulsion against rough-and-readiness which my specialised upbringing had made inevitable.

There is an unduly optimistic proverb which declares that God tempers the wind to the shorn lamb. My subsequent history was hardly to justify such naïve faith in the Deity, but on this first occasion Providence at least let me down gently by giving me a year at college before pitchforking me, a willing victim, into the crudities of Army service.

I had hardly been at home for a week when a letter from the Principal informed me that I had been awarded a college exhibition, to take effect the following autumn if I passed the Oxford Senior in July. Neither I nor my astonished parents, who had never seriously believed that my inconvenient eccentricities could possibly have any sound cash value, took in the contents of her brief note until we had each read it several times. Even now I do not really understand how it happened that my amateur, untutored efforts, in competition with the carefully trained sophistication of a hundred other young women from High Schools and provincial universities, succeeded in winning one of the few prizes that the college had to offer. I can only conclude that a sudden weariness of Sixth Form cocksureness must have seized the Somerville judges, or that some hopeful quality in my wild essay (on the well-worn theme that 'History is the Biography of Great Men') atoned by its unexpectedness for the obvious lack of information displayed in the subjects that I was supposed to have prepared.

Overwhelmed though I was by the exciting relief of the news, amazement rather than jubilation remained my prevailing emotion. The gate to liberty was not yet completely open, for the Oxford Senior, to me far more formidable, still barred my way into Somerville. But before I resumed my work for that intimidating final test which awaited me in the summer, something occurred that was destined – at any rate for the next few years – to affect me far more deeply than success in examinations.

7

Late one night the previous holidays, my mother, noticing the light still burning in Edward's room, had gone up to see if anything was the matter. She found Edward, flushed and absorbed, sitting on the bed in his pyjamas surrounded by loose sheets of ruled manuscript. He was setting to music, he told her, a poem called '*L'Envoi*', which the captain of his House had written for last summer's school magazine in honour of the boys who were leaving Uppingham.

A day or two later Edward showed me both the setting and the poem. I have the setting still; I know nothing of its musical merits, but it was melodious and memorable, and well suited to the words:

L'ENVOI

Words by R.A.Leighton

Music by E.H.Brittain

Larghetto con expressione

On-ly a turn of head, A Good-bye light-ly said, And you set out to tread Your man-lier road.

But our youth's paths once met, And

In April 1914, Edward invited the author of the poem to Buxton to stay with us for part of the Easter holidays. He looked forward to his friend's coming with definite pleasure but also with a little trepidation, for Roland, besides being captain of their House, was considerably Edward's senior, and had an enormous school reputation for brilliance and unapproachableness; he was head of Uppingham in work, and editor of the school magazine. Like Edward, he was destined for Oxford in the autumn, and had recently won the Senior Open Classical Postmastership at Merton College. I had seen him for a brief interval at the Uppingham function known as 'Old Boys' the previous summer, but could not remember him at all clearly.

Armed with my Somerville exhibition and my few months' seniority, I refused to be prospectively impressed by this person, but such equanimity was difficult to achieve, for to Roland's family attached the glamour which Bohemia always possesses for aspiring provincials. His father, a popular writer of stories for boys, who had been on the literary staff of a great daily newspaper, and his mother, the celebrated author of many romantic novels and *feuilletons*, had once lived amid a famous circle of writers and artists in St John's Wood, but now they had moved to a pleasant house on the coast at Lowestoft. In those days neither Roland nor his parents as yet realised the full potentialities of his gifted schoolgirl sister Clare, who was to be known seventeen years later as one of the best of young woodcut artists.

Although my interest threatened effervescence, I managed to be out of the house when Roland arrived. Coming in purposely late for dinner, I greeted with a lofty assumption of indifference the unknown young man who rose hastily from his chair as I opened the door. But I had not been with him for ten minutes before I realised that in maturity and sophistication he was infinitely the superior of both Edward and myself.

At nineteen, Roland looked twenty-four and behaved with the assurance of thirty. Physically he belonged to a type which is impressive rather than handsome; though he was not so tall as slim six-foot Edward, his powerful frame and big head with its stiff, thick hair gave him the appearance of a very large person.

In strange contrast with his fair head and pale face, his large dark eyes looked contemplatively at the world from beneath black, strongly marked eyebrows.

I hardly saw him that evening, for after dinner I had to hurry off to Higher Buxton to attend some amateur theatricals which I had been asked to criticise for the *Buxton Advertiser*, whose limited staff of reporters all happened to be otherwise engaged. Not being as well acquainted as I am now with the expedients of newspapers in search of free 'copy', I felt very proud of this job. It can hardly have impressed Roland, whose mother had for many years been paid a retaining salary by the Northcliffe Press and who was himself intended for a post on some dignified newspaper such as *The Times*, but the next day, when I was anxiously composing the criticism, I found him beside me unobtrusively suggesting words and phrases.

My diary reminds me that, for the rest of the day, 'Roland and I discussed various matters such as literature and religion'; that I washed my hair that evening and carried on our conversation in the process of drying it, and that the next morning, on a long walk to a neighbouring village (where the rationalist curate preached and Edward had organ lessons) we 'had a most interesting conversation, a good deal of which was about our ideas of immortality'.

Modern parents, of course, need hardly to be reminded that if they do not want a serious-natured boy and girl to be mutually attracted, immortality is one of the topics on to which they must not permit them to drift. Another is the intimate analysis of the one's character by the other – an occupation with which I amused myself and tormented Roland during the course of a ten-mile Sunday walk between hills and moors through the famous Goyt Valley and back to Buxton down the steep Manchester Road. He became very silent under my animadversions on his 'conceit' and that manner of expressing it which I called 'the Quiet Voice' – a superior tone in speaking which is known to present-day Americans as 'the Oxford accent'.

Only one fragment of our conversation drifts back to me through the medium of a letter written to Edward during the War:

'But what *is* God, then?'

'Well, of course, if we're going to discuss the nature of the Deity . . .'

But that he had not resented anything I said nor the way in which I said it, I discovered long afterwards from a poem – one of the very few that he did not consign to the waste-paper basket – which he had called '*Nachklang*', and dated April 19th, 1914:

> *Down the long white road we walked together,*
> *Down between the grey hills and the heather,*
> *Where the tawny-crested*
> *Plover cries.*
>
> *You seemed all brown and soft, just like a linnet,*
> *Your errant hair had shadowed sunbeams in it,*
> *And there shone all April*
> *In your eyes.*
>
> *With your golden voice of tears and laughter*
> *Softened into song: 'Does aught come after*
> *Life,' you asked, 'When life is*
> *Laboured through?*
>
> *What is God, and all for which we're striving?'*
> *'Sweetest sceptic, we were born for living.*
> *Life is Love, and Love is—*
> *You, dear, you.'*

When at last we came in for Sunday night supper, which our elders had left for us, Roland and I were seized with remorse at our mutual neglect of Edward – who was, however, mentally composing a piano-and-violin sonata, and did not appear to object – and the three of us sat late over the supper-table, discussing psychical research, and dreams, and premonitions. Roland told us that he had recently gone with his mother to have his hand read by Cheiro, the celebrated palmist, who had warned him that in a year or two he would run considerable risk of 'assassination'.

'As if anyone would want to assassinate me!' he laughed gaily, and we agreed that, despite his quite remarkable likeness to ex-King Manoel of Portugal, the possibility seemed remote.

Before Roland returned home I had to leave Buxton for a long-arranged visit to some relatives in the Lake District. I had been looking forward immensely to this holiday, and could not understand why, when the time came, I suddenly felt so unwilling to go. While I was away a small parcel came for me, addressed in Roland's handwriting; it contained Olive Schreiner's *The Story of an African Farm*, which we had discussed in one of our serial conversations about immortality. During the next few weeks I spent a good many troubled, speculative, exciting hours with the little volume clasped in my hands.

'It is for love's sake yet more than for any other,' I read with sudden amazed understanding, 'that we look for that new time . . . Then when that time comes . . . when love is no more bought or sold, when it is not a means of making bread, when each woman's life is filled with earnest, independent labour, then love will come to her, a strange sudden sweetness breaking in upon her earnest work; not sought for, but found.'

I cannot remember whether it was before or after the sending of this gift that Roland told me how he had himself been a feminist ever since he discovered that his mother's work as well as his father's had paid for his education and their household expenses. A few days later, at any rate, another letter came; its purport was to persuade me to go to Uppingham Speech Day in the summer, and to enclose two more of his poems for which I had asked, 'Triolet', and 'Lines on a Picture by Herbert Schmaltz'.

Latin and mathematics seemed duller and more elusive than ever when I returned to them after my few days in the Lakes. That Easter meeting with Roland had stirred a spring ferment in my blood, which made Latin proses far less congenial than prolonged contemplation of the garden through the window.

'The birds and the flowers and the sunshine seemed to call me so, I could not keep my mind on what I was doing,' I wrote in my diary on May 18th. 'I could only gaze outside and long for someone strong and loving, a man in preference to a woman as most women annoy me, who would be intimate and understanding, so that I should not be any more alone. I long for this,' I continued sententiously, 'though I know all the time that strong souls retain and increase their strength best by solitude. Surely though periods of solitude and not solitude always are all that is necessary. I so desire a sympathetic companionship, I do so want as Lyndall did in Olive Schreiner's book, "something to worship".'

Tentatively I broached the subject of Uppingham, and found my mother perfectly willing to take me with her to Edward's last Speech Day; no doubt she welcomed anything that would deflect my attention — to say nothing of my conversation — from the imminent Oxford Senior. The fact that this ordeal would follow immediately after the Speech Day lost, for the moment, its importance, and I settled down to work and to wait with as much patience as juvenile adulthood could muster.

Somehow, the time passed more quickly than I had expected. Absorbed in Unseen Translations and the Binomial Theorem, eagerly looking forward to seeing Roland once more at Uppingham, and mitigating the interval by a heartless retrospective flirtation with my would be suitor of the previous summer, I entirely failed to notice in the daily papers of June 29th an account of the assassination, on the previous morning, of a European potentate whose name was unknown to me, in a Balkan town of which I had never heard.

8

I have not seen Uppingham since 1914, and probably should not recognise to-day the five-mile road winding up to the village from Manton, nor the grey school buildings and the tiny cramped rooms of the Waterworks Cottage where we stayed. But for ever in my mind's eye remains a scene which in fact no longer exists, since its background vanished when Edward's House was pulled down to make room for the Uppingham War Memorial.

It is late evening on a hot July day. My mother has gone to talk to the housemaster, and Edward and I are standing in a dark quadrangle outside the lighted windows of the prefects' studies. 'There are boys about in various stages of undress, so we can't go inside with you here,' Edward informs me.

I am waiting, as I admit afterwards in my diary, 'to get a glimpse of the person on whose account, even more than on Edward's, I must confess I have come' – and whose Uppingham nickname, I have already gathered, is 'the Lord' or, alternatively, 'Monseigneur'. But naturally, when his shy, eager face appears at the open window, I give no indication of my anxiety to see him; I just laugh, and mock, and tease him for having broken the Uppingham record for prizes.

'I shall look out for every atom of conceit when you get them to-morrow,' I tell him, 'and as soon as I see the least symptom, I mean to squash it flat.'

He caps my criticism without hesitation.

'Well,' he replies, 'you won't be so very original, after all. One of the housemaster's wives was asked the other day what she thought of the boy who was taking so many prizes, and she said she knew nothing about him except that he was the biggest mass of conceit in the whole of Uppingham. I wanted to tell her,' he adds, 'that I perfectly agreed with her, only I didn't ask her to say it out loud in front of so many people.'

When, however, I saw Roland – who like Edward was in the Officers' Training Corps – wearing his colour-sergeant's uniform at the corps review on the Middle Field next morning, I did not feel inclined to tease him any more. On his mother's side he had military ancestors, and took the O.T.C. very seriously. He and Edward and their mutual friend Victor, the third member of the devoted trio whom Roland's mother had christened 'the Three Musketeers', were going into camp together near Aldershot for a fortnight after the end of the term.

Some of the masters, perhaps, were more prescient, but I do not believe that any of the gaily clad visitors who watched the corps carrying out its manœuvres and afterwards marching so impressively into the Chapel for the Speech Day service, in the least realised how close at hand was the fate for which it had prepared itself, or how many of those deep and strangely thrilling boys' voices were to be silent in death before another Speech Day. Looking back upon those three radiant days of July 1914, it seems to me that an ominous stillness, an atmosphere of brooding expectation, must surely have hung about the sunlit flower gardens and the shining green fields. But actually I noticed nothing more serious than the deliberate solemnity of the headmaster's speech at the prize-giving after the service.

At that time the Headmaster of Uppingham was habitually referred to by the boys as 'the Man'. A stern and intimidating figure, he had a wide reputation for tact with parents both male and female, and whenever he met my mother – who went to Uppingham much oftener than my father – he never failed to recognise her or to make some discreet comment on Edward's progress. In this respect he was wiser and more modern-minded than some of his scholastic and clerical contemporaries, who tended to regard women as 'irrelevant', and even to-day occasionally combine to write letters to the Press on family life without the collaboration of those who are responsible for the family's continuation. At least one famous pre-war headmaster, who afterwards became a bishop, was widely regarded as a woman-hater – a reputation hardly guaranteed to inculcate respect for their mothers and their future wives in the impressionable adolescents who came under his influence.

Since the noblest and profoundest emotions that men experience – the emotions of love, of marriage, of fatherhood – come to them, and can come to them, only through women, it seems curious and not a little disturbing that so many schoolmasters appear to regard contempt for the female sex as a necessary part of their educational equipment. I often wonder how many male homosexuals, actual and potential, owe their hatred and fear of women to the warped minds of the men who taught them at school.

At Uppingham Speech Day, however, I had no personal grounds for deploring the attitude of the older boys towards their feminine contemporaries. As the Headmaster strode, berobed and majestic, on to the platform of the School Hall, I was in the midst of examining with appreciation my Speech Day programme, and especially the page headed 'Prizemen, July, 1914', of which the first seven items ran as follows:

Nettleship Prize for English Essay	R. A. Leighton
Holden Prize for Latin Prose	1st, R. A. Leighton
	2nd, C. R. B. Wrenford
Greek Prose Composition	R. A. Leighton
Latin Hexameters	R. A. Leighton
Greek Iambics	R. P. Garrod
Greek Epigram – 'γνῶθι σεαυτόν'	R. A. Leighton
Captain in Classics	R. A. Leighton

But, still automatically responsive to school discipline, I hastily put down the programme as the Headmaster began, with enormous dignity, to address the audience.

I do not recall much of the speech, which ended with a list of the precepts laid down for boys by a famous Japanese general – a monument of civilisation whose name I forget, but whose qualities were evidently considered entirely suitable for emulation by young English gentlemen. I shall always, however, remember the final prophetic precept, and the breathless silence which followed the Headmaster's slow, religious emphasis upon the words:

'If a man cannot be useful to his country, he is better dead.'

For a moment their solemnity disturbed with a queer, inde-scribable foreboding the complacent mood in which I watched Roland, pale but composed, go up to receive his prizes.

As Roland had no relatives there of his own – his mother was finishing a book, and in any case took her son's triumphs for granted with a serenity which seemed to my own inconspicuous family almost reprehensible – he sat with me after luncheon at the school concert. This function gave Edward, who had as usual been second or third in every subject, the opportunity to atone for his lack of prizes by playing a violin solo, Dvořák's 'Ballade'. Apart from his performance, I was less interested in the music than in the various contemporaries of Edward and himself whom Roland pointed out to me in the choir and orchestra.

Of these I recall only one, Ivan Dyer, son of the general of Amritzar notoriety, but I missed an acquaintance of Edward's whom I had seen at the Old Boys' cricket match the previous summer, and Roland told me that this boy, Henry Maxwell Andrews – now the husband of Rebecca West – had left Uppingham in 1913. Henry Andrews, a slim, serious, very tall boy with dark, spectacled eyes, reappeared in my life ten years afterwards as a friend and New College contemporary of my husband. He seemed to me then to have altered very little since I saw him at Uppingham, and four years in Ruhleben – he had gone to Germany for the 1914 summer vacation, and was interned when war broke out – had developed in him a measure of kindness and tolerant wisdom considerably beyond the unexacting standards of the average Englishman.

The afternoon was so hot, and our desire for conversation so great, that Roland and I were relieved when the concert ended, and we could lose ourselves in the crowd at the Headmaster's garden-party. I remember to-day how perfectly my dress – a frilled pink ninon with a tiny pattern, worn beneath a rose-trimmed lace hat – seemed to have been made for our chosen corner of the garden, where roses with velvet petals softly shading from orange through pink to crimson foamed exuberantly over the lattice-work of an old wooden trellis. But even if I had forgotten, I should still have Roland's verses, 'In the Rose-Garden', to renew the fading colours of a far-away dream.

We were not long left in peace to resume our perpetual discussion of Olive Schreiner and immortality. Roland was deeply engrossed in explaining to me Immanuel Kant's theory of survival, when our seclusion was suddenly invaded by his and Edward's housemaster, who remarked, with the peculiar smile reserved by the middle-aged for very young couples who are obviously growing interested in one another, 'Ha! I *thought* I should find you here,' and bore us off triumphantly to tea. But we continued the conversation next day both before and after Sunday chapel, and leaving Edward and my mother to entertain each other, walked up and down a wooded park known as Fairfield Gardens in spite of long intervals of slow, quiet rain.

Two years afterwards Victor, a handsome, reticent boy even

taller than Edward, who was alternatively known to him and to Roland as 'Tah' and 'the Father Confessor', spoke to me of this day.

'I can't of course remember,' he told me in effect, 'exactly what he said to me on that Sunday. It's difficult to summarise the intangible. Do you remember the two Karg-Elert pieces that Sterndale Bennett played at the beginning of the service that afternoon? One of them, "*Clair de Lune*", seemed to move him deeply. He said it reminded him of you in its coldness and the sense of aloofness from the world. He said that after talking with you in Fairfield it seemed very strange to go and mix with the others in the chapel . . . I told him that he loved you then. He said he didn't, but I could see that that was merely a conventional answer. I said, "Very well, we'll meet here again on Speech Day 1924 and see who is right." I think he agreed to this.'

If Victor reported the conversation correctly, Roland at that time was certainly more courageously self-analytical and more articulate than I – though the latter quality may merely have been due to the fortunate possession of a friend with whom articulateness was easy. Not having any such confidant – since Edward was already too much depressed at the prospect of separation from Roland, who was going to another Oxford college, and from Victor, who had qualified for Cambridge, to be further burdened by a sister's emotions which would then have seemed to him absurdly premature – I was thrust back as usual upon an inner turmoil for which there seemed no prospect of relief.

After bidding good-bye to Roland at the lodge gates that evening, I was conscious of nothing more definite than intense exasperation, which lasted without intermission for several days. All through the journey back to Buxton next morning I was indescribably cross; I answered my mother's conversational efforts in surly monosyllables, and couldn't find a polite word to say.

9

I have written so much of Uppingham Speech Day because it was the one perfect summer idyll that I ever experienced, as well as my last care-free entertainment before the Flood. The lovely legacy of a vanished world, it is etched with minute precision on the tablets of my memory. Never again, for me and for my generation, was there to be any festival the joy of which no cloud would darken and no remembrance invalidate.

To my last week of mathematics and Latin I returned apprehensively enough – the more so since Oxford had begun, dimly and for the first time, to represent something more than the object of unmitigated ambition. I even permitted myself, at the close of a long day's work, to visualise a pair of dark, intent eyes examining with me the Joshua Reynolds windows in New College Chapel, and to picture a scholar's gown swinging up St Giles's on its way to Somerville.

On July 20th, exactly a fortnight before the world as I had known it crashed into chaos, I went to Leek to take my Oxford Senior. As in the case of the earlier examination, I had been obliged to ascertain for myself the various regulations and the localities at which the papers could be taken, and had chosen Leek because my father, who motored every day from Buxton into Staffordshire, could put me down there on his way to the mills.

After two years of having been (so to speak) 'grown-up', it felt strange and a little humiliating to be examined in the airless atmosphere of Leek Technical School, surrounded by rough-looking and distinctly odoriferous sixteen-year-olds of both sexes. It was not a heroic setting for the final stage of my prolonged battle with persons and circumstances, and I left Leek with a depressed sense that I had certainly failed.

War had already broken out, and the map of Europe was undergoing daily transformation, when I learnt, in the last week of August, that my papers had reached the 'required standard'. But instead of arousing congratulations, this news, coming when it did, provoked one of those breakfast-table scenes which were once common in our household, though they have long become legendary. No sooner had I, for the moment completely forgetting the state of Europe, begun proudly to announce this final triumph, when my father – though he soon relented – gave way to an outburst of fury. It was useless for me, he thundered, to think of going to Oxford now this War was on; in a few months' time we should probably all find ourselves in the Workhouse!

An unexpected scolding seemed a hard reward for a year's steady work. For some moments a sharp family altercation ensued, I, fortified by my full share of the ancestral explosiveness, hotly pointing out how many obstacles I had surmounted, and my father – violent in speech though always generous in action when once convinced of its necessity – fulminating furiously against the Government, the Germans, the financial situation at the mills, and the trouble and expense that we were all causing him. The controversy ended, none too satisfactorily, with Edward remarking, placidly but firmly, that if I could not be sent to Oxford he wouldn't go either.

For the time being I simmered wrathfully in anger and hopeless resentment. By means of what then appeared to have been a very long struggle, I had made for myself a way of escape from my hated provincial prison – and now the hardly-won road to freedom was to be closed for me by a Serbian bomb hurled from the other end of Europe at an Austrian archduke.

It is not, perhaps, so very surprising that the War at first seemed to me an infuriating personal interruption rather than a worldwide catastrophe.

CHAPTER III

Oxford versus War

AUGUST, 1914

God said: 'Men have forgotten Me;
The souls that sleep shall wake again,
And blinded eyes be taught to see.'

So, since redemption comes through pain,
He smote the earth with chastening rod,
And brought destruction's lurid reign;

But where His desolation trod,
The people in their agony
Despairing cried: 'There is no God!'

V. B. 1914.

From *Verses of a V.A.D.*

1

My diary for August 3rd, 1914, contains a most incongruous mixture of war and tennis.

The day was Bank Holiday, and a tennis tournament had been arranged at the Buxton Club. I had promised to play with my discouraged but still faithful suitor, and did not in the least want to forgo the amusement that I knew this partnership would afford me – particularly as the events reported in the newspapers seemed too incredible to be taken quite seriously.

'I do not know,' I wrote in my diary, 'how we all managed to play tennis so calmly and take quite an interest in the result. I suppose it is because we all know so little of the real meaning of war that we are so indifferent. B. and I had to owe 30. It was good handicapping as we had a very close game with everybody.'

In spite of my vague memories of the South African campaigns, Spion Kop and Magersfontein were hardly more real to me than the battles between giants and mortals in the Andrew Lang fairy-books that I began to read soon afterwards. My father had taken Edward and myself round Macclesfield in a cab on Mafeking Night, and I had a confused recollection of fireworks and bonfires and excited shouting which were never clearly distinguished in my mind from the celebrations for Edward the Seventh's post-poned coronation.

Throughout July, and especially after the failure of the Home Rule Conference and the agitation over the Dublin shooting, there had been prayers in all the churches for salvation from the danger of civil war in Ireland, and to those of us who, wrapped up in our careers or our games or our love-affairs, had paid no attention to the newspapers, the direction from which the storm was rolling was quite unexpected. At St Monica's, Miss Heath Jones, with the accurate foresight of the vigilant, had endeavoured to prepare our sceptical minds for disasters that she believed to be very near; I remembered her gravity in 1911 at the time of the Agadir crisis, and the determination with which, when she and my aunt were visiting Buxton a year or two earlier, she had made me accompany her to the local theatre to see a play that I had thought crude and ridiculous, called *An Englishman's Home*. At school we had treated her obsession with the idea of a European War as one of those adult preoccupations to which the young feel so superior. 'She's got her old German mania again,' we said.

But when I arrived home warm and excited from the amusing stimulus of the tournament, the War was brought nearer than it had yet been by the unexpected appearance of Edward – whom I had supposed to be at Aldershot – still wearing his O.T.C. uniform.

The previous midnight, he told me, they had had orders from the War Office to disband and vanish as quickly as possible; the cooks and military apparatus were required for purposes more urgent than schoolboy manœuvres. He had made his way home between southern trains congested and disorganised by troops hastening to join their regiments, leaving a few seniors – such as Roland – to clear up the camp.

A sudden chill momentarily banished my self-satisfaction as I saw him looking so handsome and fit and efficient; that brief misgiving was my first realisation that a war of the size which was said to be impending was unlikely to remain excitingly but securely confined to the columns of newspapers. So I made myself face what seemed the worst that could possibly happen to us.

'I was glad to see him back,' I wrote of Edward that evening, 'though if matters become extreme it is not impossible that he being a member of the O.T.C. may be called up for home defence.'

After that events moved, even in Buxton, very quickly. The German cousins of some local acquaintances left the town in a panic. My parents rushed over in the car to familiar shops in Macclesfield and Leek, where they laid in stores of cheese, bacon and butter under the generally shared impression that by next week we might all be besieged by the Germans. Wild rumours circulated from mouth to mouth; they were more plentiful than the newspapers, over which a free fight broke out on the station platform every time a batch came by train from London or Manchester. Our elderly cook, who had three Reservist sons, dissolved into continuous tears and was too much upset to prepare the meals with her usual competence; her young daughter-in-law, who had had a baby only the previous Friday, became hysterical and had to be forcibly restrained from getting up and following her husband to the station. One or two Buxton girls were hurriedly married to officers summoned to unknown destinations. Pandemonium swept over the town. Holiday trippers wrestled with one another for the *Daily Mail*; habitually quiet and respectable citizens struggled like wolves for the provisions in the food-shops, and vented upon the distracted assistants their dismay at learning that all prices had suddenly gone up.

My diary for those few days reflects *The Times* in its most pontifical mood. 'Germany has broken treaty after treaty, and disregarded every honourable tie with other nations . . . Germany has destroyed the tottering hopes of peace . . . The great fear is that our bungling Government will declare England's neutrality . . . If we at this critical juncture refuse to help our friend France, we should be guilty of the grossest treachery.'

I prefer to think that my real sentiments were more truly represented by an entry written nearly a month later after the fabulously optimistic reports of the Battle of Le Cateau. I had been over to Newcastle-under-Lyme to visit the family dentist, and afterwards sat for an hour in a tree-shadowed walk called The Brampton and meditated on the War. It was one of those shimmering autumn days when every leaf and flower seems to scintillate with light, and I found it 'very hard to believe that not far away men were being slain ruthlessly, and their poor disfigured bodies heaped together and crowded in ghastly indiscrimination into quickly provided common graves as though they were nameless vermin . . . It is impossible,' I concluded, 'to find any satisfaction in the thought of 25,000 slaughtered Germans, left to mutilation and decay; the destruction of men as though beasts, whether they be English, French, German or anything else, seems a crime to the whole march of civilisation.'

Only that day I had heard from my dentist that a hundred thousand Russians had been landed in England; 'a whole trainful of them,' I reported, 'is said to have passed through Stoke, so that is why the Staffordshire people are so wise.' But when I returned to Buxton I learnt that a similar contingent had been seen in Manchester, and for a few days the astonishing ubiquitousness of the invisible Russians formed a topic of absorbing interest at every tea-table throughout the country.

By the time, however, that we started believing in Russians, England had become almost accustomed to the War. On the night that the British ultimatum to Germany expired, I went up to Higher Buxton for a meeting of the University Extension Committee, to which I had recently been elected; we took only a moment to decide to do nothing until the never very ardent local zest for learning re-emerged from its total eclipse by the European deluge, so I spent the rest of the evening in wandering round the town. I read, with a feeling that I had been transported back into an uglier century, the mobilisation order on the door of the Town Hall; I joined the excited little group round the Post

Office to watch a number of local worthies who had suddenly donned their Territorial uniforms and were driving importantly about in motor-cars with their wives or their chauffeurs at the wheel. Later, on my way home, I found the Pavilion Gardens deserted, and a depressed and very much diminished band playing lugubriously to rows of empty chairs.

My feet ached, and my head whirled dizzily from the vain endeavour to take in what was happening. To me and my contemporaries, with our cheerful confidence in the benignity of fate, War was something remote, unimaginable, its monstrous destructions and distresses safely shut up, like the Black Death and the Great Fire, between the covers of history books. In spite of the efforts of Miss Heath Jones and other intelligent teachers, 'current events' had remained for us unimportant precisely because they were national; they represented something that must be followed in the newspapers but would never, conceivably, have to be lived. What really mattered were not these public affairs, but the absorbing incidents of our own private lives – and now, suddenly, the one had impinged upon the other, and public events and private lives had become inseparable . . . Uneasily I recalled a passage from *Daniel Deronda* that I had read in comfortable detachment the year before:

'There comes a terrible moment to many souls when the great movements of the world, the larger destinies of mankind, which have lain aloof in newspapers and other neglected reading, enter like an earthquake into their own lives – when the slow urgency of growing generations turns into the tread of an invading army or the dire clash of civil war . . . Then it is that the submission of the soul to the Highest is tested and . . . life looks out from the scene of human struggle with the awful face of duty.'

Edward, whose risks, whatever happened, were likely to be greater than mine, took the whole situation more calmly, as he always took everything. On that evening of August 4th he had gone serenely to the local Hippodrome with a Buxton friend, Maurice Ellinger, who had been with him at school. Maurice was a cousin of the musical comedy actress, Desirée Ellinger, who in those days often stayed in Buxton, a tiny dark doll of a girl about my own age. Her real name was Dorothy; she seemed very childish and often came to our house to sing, in the lovely young voice which she then intended for Grand Opera, Elizabeth's Prayer from *Tannhäuser* or the Jewel Song from *Faust* to my capricious accompaniment.

Already the two boys were discussing, though quite vaguely, the possibilities of enlisting. When they returned from the Hippodrome they brought back a 'Late Special' which told us that no answer had been received from Germany, and Edward related, with much amusement, how he had seen a German waiter thrown over the wall of the Palace Hotel.

For the next few weeks we all suffered from the epidemic of wandering about that had seized everyone in the town. After the tearing-up of the 'scrap of paper', the *Daily Mail* had a heart-ravishing leader called 'The Agony of Belgium' which made us feel guilty and miserable. At home the atmosphere was electric with family rows, owing to Edward's expressed wish to 'do some-thing'. The suggestions put forward with such authoritarian impressiveness by the Headmaster of Uppingham and the O.T.C. organisers had already served their purpose in the national exploitation of youth by its elders; the 'Three Musketeers', like so many others, were not only willing but anxious to risk their lives in order to save the face of a Foreign Secretary who had committed his country to an armed policy without consulting it beforehand.

My father vehemently forbade Edward, who was still under military age, to join anything whatsoever. Having himself escaped immersion in the public-school tradition, which stood for militaristic heroism unimpaired by the damping exercise of reason, he withheld his permission for any kind of military training, and ended by taking Edward daily to the mills to divert his mind from the War. Needless to say, these uncongenial expeditions entirely failed of their desired effect, and constant explosions – to which, having inherited so many of my father's characteristics, I seemed only to add by my presence – made our house quite intolerable. A new one boiled up after each of Edward's tentative efforts at defiance, and these were numerous, for his enforced subservience seemed to him synonymous with everlasting disgrace. One vague application for a commission which he sent to a Notts and Derby regiment actually was forwarded to the War Office – 'from which,' I related with ingenuous optimism, 'we are expecting to hear every post.'

When my father discovered this exercise of initiative, his wrath and anxiety reached the point of effervescence. Work of any kind was quite impossible in the midst of so much chaos and apprehension, and letters to Edward from Roland, describing his endeavours to get a commission in a Norfolk regiment, did nothing to ease the perpetual tension. Even after the result of my Oxford Senior came through, I abandoned in despair the Greek textbooks that Roland had lent me. I even took to knitting for the soldiers, though only for a very short time; utterly incompetent at all forms of needlework, I found the simplest bed-socks and sleeping-helmets altogether beyond me. 'Oh, how I wish I could wake up in the morning,' concludes one typical day's entry describing these commotions, 'to find this terrible war the dream it seems to me to be!'

2

Few of humanity's characteristics are more disconcerting than its ability to reduce world-events to its own level, wherever this may happen to lie. By the end of August, when Liège and Namur had fallen, and the misfortunes of the British Army were extending into the Retreat from Mons, the ladies of the Buxton élite had already set to work to provincialise the War.

At the First Aid and Home Nursing classes they cluttered about the presiding doctor like hens round a barnyard cock, and one or two representatives of 'the set', who never learnt any of the bandages correctly themselves, went about showing everybody else how to do them. In order to have something to take me away from the stormy atmosphere at home, I went in for and passed both of these elementary examinations, at which stout 'patients', sitting on the floor with flushed and worried faces, were treated for various catastrophies by palpitating and still stouter 'nurses'.

An hotel in the main street, Spring Gardens, was turned into a Red Cross Supply Depôt, where 'helpers' went to listen to the gossip that would otherwise have been carried on more privately over tea-tables. They wasted so much material in the amateur cutting-out of monstrous shirts and pyjamas, that in the end a humble local dressmaker whom my mother employed for our summer cottons had to be called in to do the real work, while the polite female society of Buxton stalked up and down the hotel rooms, rolled a few bandages, and talked about the inspiration of helping one's country to win the War. One or two would-be leaders of fashion paraded continually through the town in new Red Cross uniforms. Dressed in their most elaborate lace under-clothing, they offered themselves as patients to would-be bandagers and bed-makers, and one of them disliked me intensely because, in a zestful burst of vigour, I crumpled the long frills of her knickers by tucking them firmly into the bed.

Already my link with Oxford had given me the ability to regard local scrambles and squabbles over the Home Nursing classes, and the Supply Depôt, and the newly-opened Red Cross convales-cent hospital, with an amused detachment of which I had not been capable so long as Buxton had seemed to me a Nazareth whence no good thing and no worth-while person was ever likely to emerge. This sense of release from the strain of the first shat-tering weeks increased considerably after I had received another letter from Roland, who wrote that his application for a commis-sion had been refused on account of imperfect eyesight – a defect which his youthful vanity had hitherto concealed from me. He had tried in vain the infantry, the artillery, and the Army Service Corps, and though he was still endeavouring to get the objec-tion to his eyesight removed, the possibility that he would be at Oxford with me after all came once more into the foreground.

'Come what may,' he told me in sudden enthusiasm after hearing that I was safely through my Oxford Senior, 'I *will* go now. And I look forward to facing a hedge of chaperons and Principals with perfect equanimity if I may be allowed to see something of you on the other side.'

My heart rejoiced absurdly, but I made one of my spasmodic resolutions to be sceptical.

'I don't think I am ever likely to marry as I am too hard to please . . .' I informed my diary after going to one of the numerous local weddings that followed the outbreak of War. 'I would be satisfied with nothing less than a mutually comprehensive loving companionship. I could not endure to be constantly propitiating any man, or to have a large range of subjects on which it was quite impossible to talk to him.'

In the early autumn, Edward and I went to stay for a week at St Monica's, for I wanted to buy some new clothes in London – where the numerous flags fluttering above the river made me childishly pleased that we had so many Allies – and Edward, after what seemed like an eternity of perturbation but was really only a few weeks after the outbreak of War, had at last been given reluctant permission by my father to apply to the Senior O.T.C. at Oxford for training as an officer.

It was a very bright, clear September in which the British and French Armies won their decisive victories on the Marne and the Aisne. 'ALLIES ADVANCING!' triumphantly announced the placards which told us that Paris had been saved, but though the news sent a shudder of relief through London, the air was thicker than ever with dramatic and improbable rumours. Stories of atrocities mingled with assertions that in ten days' time the Austrian Emperor would be suing for peace and in fourteen the Kaiser fleeing from his people. Edward, while waiting vainly for news from Oxford, composed a violin ballade; he and I were plunged into gloom by a fresh though inaccurate rumour that Fritz Kreisler, his favourite violinist, had been killed on the Austrian front, but his anxiety lasted longer than mine, for I found St Monica's garden a most peaceful and appropriate place in which to soliloquise about Roland. He was, I told myself, 'a unique experience in my existence; I never think definitely of him as man or boy, as older or younger, taller or shorter than I am, but always of him as a mind in tune with mine, in which many of the notes are quite different from mine but are all in the same key.'

Whether it was really true at that time that Roland represented to me only a congenial mind, I cannot now determine. If it was, it did not remain so for very much longer. One afternoon during a game of golf when we had returned to Buxton, Edward and I discovered a fairy ring; I stood in it, and quite suddenly found myself wishing that Roland and I might become lovers, and marry. Edward asked me to tell him my wish. I replied: 'I'll tell you if you ask me again in five years' time, for by then the wish will have come true or be about to come true, or it will never come true at all.'

Although we had examined, only a day or two before, some Press photographs of the damage done by the German bombardment of Rheims, we still talked as though our life-long security had not been annihilated and time would go on always for those whom we loved. And it was just then that Roland wrote that he had, after all, some chance of a commission in a Norfolk regiment.

'Anyhow,' he told me, 'I don't think in the circumstances I could easily bring myself to endure a secluded life of scholastic vegetation. It would seem a somewhat cowardly shirking of my obvious duty . . . I feel that I am meant to take an active part in this War. It is to me a very fascinating thing – something, if often horrible, yet very ennobling and very beautiful, something whose elemental reality raises it above the reach of all cold theorising. You will call me a militarist. You may be right.'

'Scholastic vegetation', hurt just a little; it seemed so definitely to put me outside everything that now counted in life, as well as outside his own interests, and his own career. I felt it altogether contrary to his professed feminism – but then, so was the War; its effect on the women's cause was quite dismaying.

'Women get all the dreariness of war, and none of its exhilaration,' I wrote in reply. 'This, which you say is the only thing that counts at present, is the one field in which women have made no progress – perhaps never will (though Olive Schreiner thinks differently). I sometimes feel that work at Oxford, which will only bear fruit in the future and lacks the stimulus of direct connection with the War, will require a restraint I am scarcely capable of. It is strange how what we both so worked for should now seem worth so little.'

Obviously I was suffering, like so many women in 1914, from an inferiority complex. I did not know that only a week or two before his letter, he had written one of his curiously prophetic poems, 'I walk alone', which certainly did not suggest that I and my work no longer counted. It bears, I think, only one interpretation – that he visualised me as having fulfilled those ambitions of which we were always talking and writing, but pictured himself as dead.

Actually, he went to Norwich about a fortnight later and was gazetted to the Norfolks shortly afterwards. But at the beginning of October, when I was getting ready to go to Somerville, neither Edward nor Roland nor Victor, who lived at Hove and had periodically tackled various battalions of the Royal Sussex Regiment, seemed much nearer commissions than they had been in August. Though all three had definitely decided not to go up to their various colleges, the prospect, which at moments had come near, of the War affecting me personally, seemed once again to become quite remote.

3

So I went up to Oxford, and tried to forget the War. At first, though Edward should have gone up the day that I did and Roland the day after, I succeeded pretty well.

'This is an important step I am taking, the biggest since I left school, perhaps the biggest I have ever taken,' I reflected with the consoling priggishness that then sustained me through the initial stages of every new experience: 'But it does not do to dwell overmuch on the responsibilities such a decision as I made a year ago will now begin to involve, but rather to take them up as they come, and throughout them all remain true to myself and my ideals.'

As soon as I arrived at Somerville, I was dismayed to learn that I had to take Responsions Greek in December and Pass Moderations the following June, instead of embarking, as I had fondly imagined, straight away upon English. The unwelcome discovery was made the more bitter by the fact that my Classical tutor obviously attributed my lack of Greek to laziness, instead of to a complete inability to understand why the Principal, after learning the result of my Oxford Senior, had advised me to study it.

'Oh, how many better ways I might have chosen to get into Oxford than the ones I did in my ignorance choose!' I lamented to my diary; 'How much better prepared I might easily have been!'

But my perturbation quickly evaporated as soon as I emerged from the first confusion of newness, and drifted into the company of Norah H., a first-year student from Winchester, who had come up to college chiefly because she was bored by the Cathedral set. Our mutual detestation of small-town snobberies made us friends for the time being, and together we observed and discussed the more interesting personalities of the different Years.

'There are,' I observed, 'two classes of second- and third-year people, (1) those who thoroughly examine every atom of you, (2) those who do not look at you at all; and appear perfectly oblivious of your presence even if you get in their way. Of the two I prefer the former.'

Several potentially interesting young women were then in their last year at Somerville. They included Charis Ursula Barnett, now Mrs Sidney Frankenburg and the author of numerous books and articles on birth-control and the rearing of children; Margaret Chubb, who soon afterwards became Mrs Geoffrey Pyke and is now Secretary of the National Birth Control Association; Muriel Jaegar, subsequently the writer of several intelligent novels; Jeannie Petrie, daughter of the celebrated Egyptologist, and Dorothy L. Sayers, who dominated her group at college, and does so still by the fame of her vigorous detective stories.

I took an immediate liking to Dorothy Sayers, who was affable to freshers and belonged to the 'examine-every-atom-of-you' type. A bouncing, exuberant young female who always seemed to be preparing for tea-parties, she could be seen at almost any hour of the day or night scuttling about the top floor of the new Maitland building with a kettle in her hand and a little checked apron fastened over her skirt. She belonged to the Bach Choir, which I too had joined, and her unconcealed passion for Sir Hugh – then Doctor – Allen was a standing joke in college. During the practices of the Verdi Requiem, which we were preparing to sing in the Easter term, she sat among the mezzo-contraltos and gazed at him with wide, adoring eyes as though she were in church worshipping her only God. But a realistic sense of humour always saved her from becoming ridiculous, and at the Going-Down Play given by her Year the following summer, she caricatured her idol with triumphant accuracy and zest.

Against one of these Third-Years, a plain, mature-looking girl with penetrating eyes, who wore high-collared blouses and knew how to put freshers in their places, I conceived the strong prejudice natural to the snubbed after meeting her at a tea-party to which I had been invited by a friendly senior. Ten minutes after the introduction, she suddenly turned to me and inquired witheringly: '*What* is your name? I wasn't paying any attention when it was told me.' Infatuated still by the glamour of Oxford, I did not remark as I might have done how closely the manners of Third-Years to First-Years resembled those of the Buxton élite to persons outside 'the set'. But I noted in my diary that evening that the Principal was 'not nearly so condescending as one or two of the third-year people'.

I soon found that a far more persistent and disturbing centre of interest than any third-year student was Agnes Elizabeth Murray, Professor Gilbert Murray's beautiful daughter, whose presence relegated her second-year contemporaries to impersonal mediocrity. Wildly brilliant and fiercely in love with life, she did not in the least suggest her mournful fate of early death. At college she had not yet acquired the lovely elegance which for a short time after the War caused her to shine like a bright meteor amid the constellation of humbler stars at the League of Nations Union. Her eccentric clothes were untidy, and her straight black hair was often unkempt, but she strode like a young goddess through the Somerville students and condescended to notice very few of them outside a small group which included her devoted friend, Phyllis Siepmann. They were a tragically predestined couple, for Phyllis died before Elizabeth, in 1920 – as the result, I believe, of an illness due to war-work.

Norah and I blinked our eyes with proper reverence at these radiant lights, but we discussed with less respectful frankness the members of our own first year, and particularly a trio which later co-opted me as a fourth – an English scholar whom we all knew as 'E. F.', Marjorie B., afterwards a teacher, and Theresa S., a fair, gay, half-Belgian girl, who developed into my one real friend amongst these 1914 contemporaries. 'E. F.' was subsequently to fulfil in appropriate fashion her early promise, for she became a don at a famous women's college and a distinguished authority on Marlowe, but, like many other successful academics, she was the source in her student days of a good deal of secret amusement.

A slight girl with fine, clear-cut features, smooth dark hair and dreamy, humourless eyes, she bore a strong resemblance to Gwen Ffrangçon-Davies, the actress, and went about the corridors with an expression of earnest pursuit. Her attitude towards Marlowe was mystical, and though she never quite reached the point of putting it into words, we suspected her of a private belief in herself as his reincarnation. A more incongruous embodiment of that roystering taverner it would be difficult to imagine, for 'E. F.' then possessed a soft, precise voice and a deferential manner to conspicuous seniors. Her special goddesses belonged to an eclectic little group known as M.A.S. (Mutual Admiration Society), the members of which had made a corner in literary aspirations. They took themselves very seriously, and apparently do so still, for only a year or two ago one of them wrote to me to protest that in a popular article on Somerville novelists I had underestimated their subsequent achievements.

4

In spite of the prosaic demands of Greek verbs and the tedium of ploughing with a 'crib' through the *Alkestis* of Euripides almost before I knew the Greek alphabet, I spent my first few weeks at Somerville in a state of exhilaration, 'half-delightful, half-disturbing, wholly exciting'. I had never known anything so consistently stimulating as that urgent, hectic atmosphere, in which a number of highly strung young women became more neurotic and *exaltées* than ever through over-work and insufficient sleep.

Like the half dozen freshers with whom I consorted, I rarely
went to bed before 2 a.m. through the whole of that term. Having
hitherto been thrown for speculative companionship chiefly upon
my own society, I found cocoa-parties and discussions on religion, genius, dons and Third-Years far too enthralling to be abandoned merely for the sake of a good night's rest. After years of
regular ten-o'clock bedtime in Buxton, the short nights told on
me very quickly, but I never dreamed of attributing my excitement to fatigue.

Early in the term, with a heart swelling with pride, I learnt
from Norah that I was considered one of the 'lions' of my year.
This information inspired me with a pleasant sense of mental and
moral superiority, of which I was particularly aware at a certain
tea-party where, as I recorded in my diary, 'we talked religion
most of the time. Miss G. and Miss P. were there too – two simple
souls who evidently had not thought much for themselves, and
who cannot – yet, at any rate – stand alone, or ever conceive the
idea of doing so.

'It is so vastly different from me, who think one has no right
to have great and intimate friends unless one can stand alone first,'
I reflected with satisfaction. 'The time may come – in fact does
come to everyone – when we have to decide something important on our own, be responsible perhaps not only for our own
lives and fortunes, but those of other people. And if when the
momentous decision must be made by us alone, if we have been
accustomed to depend on others, to refer all resolutions to others,
and never to be sufficient unto ourselves – what then? We may
fall,' I concluded tragically, 'never more to rise.'

My elated consciousness of growing prominence soon drove
me vigorously into action. I joined the Oxford Society for Woman
Suffrage; I joined the Bach Choir; I joined the War and Peace
Society; I reviewed *Sinister Street* for the women's intercollegiate
magazine, the *Fritillary*; I did not, despite much persuasion, join
the Christian Union. For the choir, Dr Allen, who enjoyed living
up to his Oxford reputation of *enfant-terrible* eccentricity, tested my
voice and asked me if I thought I had a good one. When I replied
that I imagined I was a soprano though I really wanted to sing

alto, he remarked: 'I see. You're one of those cantankerous people. I suppose if you'd been an alto you'd have wanted to sing soprano.'

To the War and Peace Society I paid my two-and-sixpenny subscription 'chiefly to see Gilbert Murray. He was not at all like what I expected but the impression was not at all disappointing. He is a tall, slight man, not at all past middle age, with brown hair scarcely grey anywhere, and a curious shaped head just going bald. He has a rather penetrating but very kindly glance and wears spectacles, and also has an unassuming undidactic way of talking which appealed to me very much, especially as it was unexpected. His daughter hardly gives the impression of having anything unpretentious about her.'

It was all so thrilling that for the time being the neglected War, with its Siege of Antwerp, its First Battle of Ypres and the *Sydney's* prolonged pursuit of the *Emden*, seemed quite out of the picture. Although Roland had now become a Territorial second-lieutenant, and Edward had appeared in Oxford only a week later than myself in order to begin his O.T.C. training under the auspices of New College, I wondered why I had ever been so much concerned about the troubles of Europe. After all, I told myself, they could never really touch me very closely, whereas the activities of college did and must. Somerville seemed at the moment so enormously important that I endeavoured to cheer Roland's spiritual isolation among the subalterns at Norwich by telling him – of course from a very lofty standpoint – all that I thought about it.

'I like it very well indeed,' I informed him, 'but I am never likely to fall into the typical college woman's blind infatuation with everybody and everything, or to think this place the only place, or these ideas the only ideas. It is an immense advantage to have been at home for a while and have seen other points of view besides this one. At present I am almost equally aware of its limitations and its advantages. It is a delightful change to me to be in surroundings where work is expected of you, instead of where you are thought a fool for wanting to do it, and of course the whole atmosphere of Oxford is ideal if you want to study or think or prepare to be. The last "if" however points to one of the limitations here, as already I have come across several people who seem to regard their residence here as an end in itself, instead of a mere preparation for better and wider things in the future.'

In the intervals snatched from cocoa, Greek and religion, I saw something of Edward. On account of the strict chaperonage regulations of those days (always disrespectfully referred to as 'chap. rules') I was not allowed to go to his rooms in Oriel Street lest I should encounter the seductive gaze of some other undergraduate, but I met him in cafés and at the practices of the Bach Choir and Orchestra, for which Dr Allen had chosen him to be a first violin. If ever he dropped in unexpectedly to tea with me at Somerville, I was obliged hastily to eject any friends who might be sitting in my room, for fear his tabooed sex might contaminate their girlish integrity.

Towards the end of November he was gazetted to the 11th Sherwood Foresters, and the next day he left Oxford for Sandgate. With his tall figure, his long beautiful hands, and the dark arched eyebrows which almost met above his half-sad, half-amused eyes, he looked so handsome in his new second-lieutenant's uniform that the fear which I had felt when he returned from Aldershot on the eve of the War suddenly clutched me again. Reluctantly I said good-bye to him in the Woodstock Road at the entrance to Little Clarendon Street, almost opposite the place where the Oxford War Memorial was to be erected ten years afterwards 'In memory of those who fought and those who fell'.

I often thought of him in camp as the November rain deluged the city and churned the Oxfordshire roads into mud, and once again the War crept forward a little from its retreat in the back of my mind. One student in my Year had a brother who was actually at the front; I contemplated her with awe and discomfort, and carefully avoided her for the rest of the term.

5

The second week in December brought Responsions Greek, which I passed easily enough. The fact that this was done on six weeks' study of that lovely language, which is totally unsuited to such disrespectful treatment, testifies to the simplicity of

Responsions as an examination, and to the unnecessary circum-ambulation of the alternative with which I had burdened myself. I returned home to find Buxton almost a military centre, with the enormous Empire Hotel just below our gates turned into a depôt for Territorials.

At first I tried to communicate my enthusiasm for Oxford to the family circle, for Edward's absence had left a depressing blank in the household, and after the congenial companionships of Oxford I felt lonely and almost a stranger. I did not, however, find my parents susceptible to infection. My father had an *idée fixe* about university dons, all of whom he believed to be 'dried up' and 'cold-blooded', while my long-suffering mother, who must have endured indescribable *ennui* during the months in which I was immersed in examinations, could only reiterate her thank-fulness that I had done Responsions away from Buxton, as she 'would have got so bored hearing about it always'.

After describing this lamentable failure to impress my family, my diary records that on December 15th, 1914, I went with my mother for a day's shopping in Manchester. While I was there, I saw on placards carried by vociferous paper-boys the news of that morning's raid by German ships on Scarborough, Hartlepool and Whitby, but no telepathic vision had shown me through the early mists of that winter's day the individual with whom my future was to be so closely bound, marching with her fellow-schoolgirls from Queen Margaret's, Scarborough, beneath the falling shells. In her second novel, *The Crowded Street*, she has given a dramatic account of the bombardment, but five dark and adventurous years were to pass before I met Winifred Holtby. That afternoon the news of the raid impressed me less than my purchase of a little black moiré and velvet hat trimmed with red roses. It was one of the prettiest hats that I have ever had, and also one of the most memorable, for I was to be indescribably happy while wearing it, yet in the end to tear off the roses in a gesture of impotent despair.

That first wartime Christmas seemed a strange and chilling experience to us who had always been accustomed to the exuberant house-decorating and present-giving of the prosperous pre-war years.

'A good many people,' I observed, 'have decided that they are both too poor and too miserable to remember their friends, particularly the rich people who have no one at all in any danger. The poorer ones, and those who are in anxiety about something or other, have all made an effort to do the same as usual. At St John's . . . we had the inevitable sermon dwelling on the obvious incongruity of celebrating the birth of the Prince of Peace while the world was at war.'

Edward, who had succeeded in getting Christmas leave, was with us in Buxton. It was the last Christmas that we spent together as a family, and the unspoken but haunting consciousness in all our minds that perhaps it might be, somewhat subdued the pride with which we displayed him to acquaintances in the Pavilion Gardens. He endeavoured to cheer us up by telling us that the British and French armies could drive the Germans back whenever they chose and would have done so weeks ago had they not preferred to wait for the New Armies to come out in the spring and turn the action into a decisive victory. Better authenticated than this optimistic information was the news that Roland – who had sent me his photograph in exchange for one of mine, together with five books, *Tess of the D'Urbervilles*, *Pêcheur D'Islande*, *The Seven Seas*, Maeterlinck's *Monna Vanna* and Turgenev's *On the Eve* – was spending Christmas in London at a flat temporarily taken by his mother near Regent's Park.

It had already been arranged that at the end of the year I was to stay for two or three days in my maternal grandmother's small house at Purley, and be taken into town by an aunt to buy clothes and college furniture. The coincidence seemed to have been specially designed by a benevolent destiny. When I thanked Roland for the books, I told him that I was coming up to town, and by return of post he had planned a series of meetings.

6

Incredible as it may seem to modern youth, it was then considered correct and inevitable that my aunt should cling to me like a limpet throughout the precious hours that I spent with Roland.

But she was benevolent and enormously interested in our mutual attraction, and after we had all lunched and shopped together, she and Edward, who was going back to his battalion, tactfully walked towards Charing Cross while Roland and I loitered down Regent Street.

I longed to look at him closely and yet was too shy: his uniform and little moustache had changed him from a boy into a man, and one so large and powerful that even in the splendour of the rose-trimmed hat and a new squirrel coat given me by my father, I felt like a midget beside him. Months of intimate correspondence had bound us together, and yet between us was this physical barrier of the too conscious, too sensitive flesh. It was getting dark and all the streets were dim, for the first German air raid had occurred just before Christmas, and the period of Darkest London had begun. In the sky the searchlight, a faint, detached glimmer, quivered at the edges of the clouds, or slowly crawled, a luminous pencil, across the deep indigo spaces between. Roland, who had worked one himself, was immensely amused at my naïve absorption, and for the first time tentatively took my arm to guide me across the darkening streets. In those days people's emotions, for all the War's challenge, still marched deliberately and circumspectly to their logical conclusion.

As I undressed some hours later in the tiny bedroom of my grandmother's house, I no longer wondered what I really thought of him. Glowing with a warmth that defied the bitter cold of the fireless hearth, I hardly waited to throw my woollen dressing-gown over my nightdress before seizing the familiar black book and my friendly fountain pen.

'O Roland,' I wrote, in the religious ecstasy of young love sharpened by the War to a poignancy beyond expression, 'Brilliant, reserved, extravagant personality – I wonder if I shall have found you only to lose you again, or if Time will spare us till it may come about that the greatest word in the world – of which now I can only think and dare not name – shall be used between us. God knows, and will answer.'

In spite of the War, the next day was heaven.

At the Florence Restaurant, still aunt-chaperoned, I lunched with Roland and was quite unable – and indeed did not try very hard – to shake him off at my dressmaker's or my milliner's, or even in the underclothing department at D. H. Evans. I hardly knew what I was buying; the garments and the furniture which had interested me so intensely had somehow lost their fascination, and I chose Leonardo da Vinci prints for my room with my judgment blinded by the dazzling but disturbing fact that in half an hour's time I was to meet Roland's mother and sister at the Criterion for tea.

In the end we were late, and drove there in a taxi. Roland's mother was waiting for us in the lounge. Picturesquely dressed in rich furs and velvets, she appeared to my rapturous eyes as the individual embodiment of that distant Eldorado, the world of letters. I knew that I was in for a critical inspection, for to Roland, who had told her 'all about me', including the fact that I was at Somerville, she had said: 'Why does she want to go to Oxford? It's no use to a writer – except of treatises.' I was, therefore, pleased and relieved when she turned to him and remarked: 'Why, she's quite human, after all! I thought she might be very academic and learned.'

The mutual devotion between herself and Roland was very pleasant to see. It was her pride and delight that she understood him as few mothers understand sons or daughters, and their instinctive knowledge of each other's moods was certainly remarkable. A little apart from that magic circle of intimacy sat the fifth member of the party, Roland's sister Clare, who was then a jolly, vivacious girl of sixteen, with two long thick plaits and a disarming naïveté of manner which made her seem very young for her age. If any disconcerting prophet had whispered to Roland and me how successful she was destined to become, we should then have treated him, I think, with amused incredulity.

I remember little more of that Criterion tea, but it left me with the agreeable impression that Roland's mother, whose generous temperament predisposed her favourably towards youthful love-affairs, definitely approved of my friendship with Roland. She disliked, I gathered, the strident type of girl who boasted of being 'modern', and I was too much the pretty-pretty type ever to seem aggressively up to date. As one Army Sister remarked of me three years later to another with whom I had become close friends: 'That V.A.D. of yours is a pretty little thing, but she's got a vacant face − very vacant!'

7

At dinner that evening − once again at the Florence − Roland gave me a bunch of tall pink roses with a touch of orange in their colouring and the sweetest scent in the world. He watched me fasten them, in the fashion of the moment, just above my waist against the dark blue silk of my dress, and murmured 'Yes!' under his breath. In the warm atmosphere of the restaurant, their wistful, tender perfume clung about us like a benediction.

Incongruously we talked, that dinner-time, about the way we should like to be buried. I thought I should prefer to be burnt on a pyre, like Achilles, but Roland wanted to be put Viking-wise in a flaming boat, and left to drift out to sea. I asked him quite suddenly: 'If you could choose your death, would you like to be killed in action?' My aunt was horrified at this inconsiderate directness. 'My dear girl, why do you talk about such things?' she exclaimed, but Roland replied quite quietly: 'Yes, I should. I don't want to die, but if I must I should like to die that way. Anyhow I should hate to go all through this War without being wounded at all; I should want something to prove that I had been in action.'

Long afterwards, Victor told me that Roland had once remarked, with the dramatic emphasis inherited from his family, that he could wish for no better end than to be found dead in a trench at dawn.

After dinner he took us to His Majesty's Theatre to see Sir Herbert Tree's production of *David Copperfield*. No doubt this performance was most spectacular, but though I apparently witnessed the whole of it, I was hardly conscious even of the changes of scene. In one interval, I whispered to Roland how much I had liked his mother.

'She thought you the most charming girl she had ever met!' he told me enthusiastically.

'Oh, I'm *so* relieved!' I exclaimed. 'You don't know *what* I should have felt like if she'd disliked me!'

'I knew she wouldn't,' he observed reassuringly. 'I knew just what she would think – her tastes are very much the same as mine . . .'

'Sh-h—!' reprimanded our unsympathetic neighbours as the curtain went up.

At Charing Cross, with half an hour to wait for the last train to Purley, we walked together up and down the platform. It was New Year's Eve, a bright night with infinities of stars and a cold, brilliant moon; the station was crowded with soldiers and their friends who had gathered there to greet the New Year. What would it bring, that menacing 1915?

Neither Roland nor I was able to continue the ardent conversation that had been so easy in the theatre. After two unforgettable days which seemed to relegate the whole of our previous experience into a dim and entirely insignificant past, we had to leave one another just as everything was beginning, and we did not know – as in those days no one for whom France loomed in the distance ever could know – when or even whether we should meet again. Just before the train was due to leave I got into the carriage, but it did not actually go for another ten minutes, and we gazed at one another submerged in complete, melancholy silence.

My aunt, intending, I suppose, to relieve the strain – which must certainly have made the atmosphere uncomfortable for a third party – asked us jokingly: 'Why don't you say something? Is it too deep for words?'

We laughed rather constrainedly and said that we hoped it wasn't as bad as all that, but in our hearts we knew that it was just as bad and a great deal worse. The previous night I had become ecstatically conscious that I loved him; on that New Year's Eve I realised that he, too, loved me, and the knowledge that had been an unutterable joy so long as any part of the evening remained became an anguish that no words could describe as soon as we had to say good-bye.

The New Year came in as I sat in the train, trying to picture the dark, uncertain future, and watching the dim railway lights in a blurred mist go swiftly by. When at last I was alone in my bedroom, the tears that had blurred the lights fell unrestrainedly upon the black book to which I had confided so much repressed bitterness, so many private aspirations. It was now to receive a secret of a more primitive kind, for I wrote in it that I would gladly give all that I had lived and hoped for during my few years of conscious ambition, not, for the first time, to astonish the world by some brilliant achievement, but one day to call a child of Roland's my own.

8

After all, I saw him again quite soon.

But first there came a letter telling me that he too had witnessed, not without emotion, the coming of 1915.

'When I left you I stood by the fountain in Piccadilly Circus to see the New Year in. It was a glorious night, with a full moon so brightly white as to seem blue slung like an arc-lamp directly overhead. I had that feeling of extreme loneliness one is so often conscious of in a large crowd. There was very little demonstration; two Frenchmen standing up in a cab singing the "Marseillaise"; a few women and some soldiers behind me holding hands and softly humming "Auld Lang Syne". When twelve o'clock struck there was only a little shudder among the crowd and a distant muffled cheer and then everyone seemed to melt away again, leaving me standing there with tears in my eyes and feeling absolutely wretched.'

The letter ended with half a dozen little words which, for all their gentle restraint, once more transformed speculation into bright, sorrowful certainty.

'You are a dear, you know.'

The next day, in church, Cowper's hymn, 'God moves in a mysterious way', so often sung during the War by a nation growing ever more desperately anxious to be reassured and consoled, almost started me weeping; as I listened with swimming eyes to its gentle, melodious verses, I wondered whether I should ever have sufficient understanding of the world's ironic pattern to be able to accept the comfort that they offered:

> *Ye fearful saints, fresh courage take;*
> *The clouds ye so much dread*
> *Are big with mercy, and shall break*
> *In blessings on your head.*
>
> *Judge not the Lord by feeble sense,*
> *But trust Him for His grace;*
> *Behind a frowning providence*
> *He hides a smiling face.*
>
> *Blind unbelief is sure to err,*
> *And scan His work in vain;*
> *God is His own interpreter,*
> *And He will make it plain.*

For the first time, too, I began to realise that love, in addition to its heights and depths, had also its inconveniences. Thoughts of Roland were certainly not conducive to solid work for Pass Mods.; 'I may write the better novels some day for a little passionate experience,' I observed ruefully, 'but I do not think the inspiration will run in the direction of Latin proses.'

The prospects of the proses were not improved when there came, in almost his next letter, the exciting suggestion that if I could go back to Oxford for the Easter term *via* London or Leicester, he would invent an excuse to get a day's leave from Peterborough and meet me. Instead of giving my mind to Pliny and Plato, I spent the best part of a week in carefully arranging to carry out this plan without arousing suspicion at home.

Sophisticated present-day girls, free immediately after leaving school to come and go as they wish, or living, as independent professional women, in their own rooms or flats, have no conception of the difficulties under which courtships were conducted by provincial young ladies in 1915. There was no privacy for a boy and girl whose mutual feelings had reached their most delicate and bewildering stage; the whole series of complicated relationships leading from acquaintance to engagement had to be conducted in public or not at all.

Before the War, the occupations, interests and most private emotions of a young woman living in a small town were supervised from each day's beginning to its end, and openly discussed in the family circle. Letters were observed and commented on with a lack of compunction only to be prevented by lying in wait for the postman with an assiduity that could not be permanently maintained under a system of four posts a day. The parental habit – then almost universally accepted as 'correct' where daughters were concerned – of inquisition into each day's proceedings made private encounters, even with young men in the same town, almost impossible without a whole series of intrigues and subterfuges which robbed love of all its dignity.

With men living in other places, unobserved meetings were hardly feasible at all. The shortest railway journey to an unspecified destination for an unrevealed purpose was outside the bounds of possibility. Before I went up to Oxford I had never even spent a day in Manchester without being accompanied by my mother or a reliable Buxton resident. On all my longer journeys I was seen off at the station, had my ticket purchased for me, and was expected to send a telegram home immediately on arrival, the time of which was carefully looked up beforehand. In these requirements my parents were not exceptional; they merely subscribed to a universal middle-class tradition.

At the beginning of 1915 I was more deeply and ardently in love than I have ever been or am ever likely to be, yet at that time Roland and I had hardly been alone together, and never at all without the constant possibility of observation and interruption. In Buxton our occasional walks had always been taken either through the town in full view of my family's inquisitive acquaintances, or as one half of a quartette whose other members kept us continually in sight. At Uppingham every conversation that we had was exposed to inspection and facetious remark by schoolmasters or relatives. In London we could only meet under the benevolent but embarrassingly interested eyes of an aunt. Consequently, by the middle of that January, our desire to see one another alone had passed beyond the bounds of toleration.

In my closely supervised life, a secret visit to London was impossible even *en route* for Oxford; I knew that I should be seen off by a train which had been discussed for days and, as usual, have my ticket taken for me. But Leicester was a conceivable *rendez-vous*, for I had been that way before, even though from Buxton the obvious route was *via* Birmingham. So for my family's benefit, I invented some objectionable students, likely to travel by Birmingham, whom I wanted to avoid. Roland, in similar mood, wrote that if he could not get leave he would come without it.

When the morning arrived, my mother decided that I seemed what she called 'nervy', and insisted upon accompanying me to Miller's Dale, the junction at which travellers from Buxton change to the main line. I began in despair to wonder whether she would elect to come with me all the way to Oxford, but I finally escaped without her suspecting that I had any intention other than that of catching the first available train from Leicester. The usual telegram was demanded, but I protested that at Oxford station there was always such a rush for a cab that I couldn't possibly find time to telegraph until after tea.

At Leicester, Roland, who had started from Peterborough soon after dawn, was waiting for me with another sheaf of pale pink roses. He looked tired, and said he had had a cold; actually, it was incipient influenza and he ought to have been in bed, but I did not discover this till afterwards.

To be alone with one another after so much observation was quite overwhelming, and for a time conversation in the Grand Hotel lounge moved somewhat spasmodically. But constraint disappeared when he told me with obvious pride that he had asked his own colonel for permission to interview the colonel of the 5th Norfolks, who were stationed some distance away and were shortly going to the front, with a view to getting a transfer.

'Next time I see the C.O.,' he announced, 'I shall tell him the colonel of the 5th was away. I shall say I spent the whole day looking for him – so after lunch I'm coming with you to Oxford.'

I tried to subdue my leaping joy by a protest about his cold, but as we both knew this to be insincere it was quite ineffective. I only stipulated that when we arrived he must lose me at the station; 'chap. rules', even more Victorian than the social code of Buxton, made it inexpedient for a woman student to be seen in Oxford with a young man who was not her brother.

So we found an empty first-class carriage and travelled together from Leicester to Oxford. It was a queer journey; the memory of its profound unsatisfactoriness remains with me still. I had not realised before that to be alone together would bring, all too quickly, the knowledge that being alone together was not enough. It was an intolerable realisation, for I knew too that death might so easily overtake us before there could be anything more. I was dependent, he had only his pay, and we were both so distressingly young.

Thus a new constraint arose between us which again made it difficult to talk. We tried to discuss impersonally the places that we wanted to see when it was possible to travel once more; we'd go to Florence together, he said, directly the War was over.

'But,' I objected – my age-perspective being somewhat different from that of to-day – 'it wouldn't be proper until I'm at least thirty.'

'Don't worry,' he replied persuasively. 'I'm sure I can arrange for it to be "proper" before you get to that age!'

And then, somehow, we found ourselves suddenly admitting that each had kept the other's letters right from the beginning. We were now only a few miles from Oxford, and it was the first real thing that we had said. As we sat together silently watching the crimson sun set over the flooded land, some quality in his nearness became so unbearable that, all unsophisticated as I was, I felt afraid. I tried to explain it to myself afterwards by a familiar quotation: 'There is no beauty that hath not some strangeness in the proportion.'

When the grey towers slid into view, unsuitably accompanied by the gas-works and the cemetery, I put out my hand to say good-bye. With sudden vehemence he pressed it against his lips, and kept it there until the train stopped. I could not speak any more, but at the station I looked back at him walking forlornly down the platform; as a final irony I had allowed him to send off the telegram saying that I had arrived safely. Later he told me that he had followed me in a hansom to Somerville and had walked up and down outside the circumspect red walls until it was time for his train to leave. He did not say how he had retraced the tedious journey to Peterborough, but he admitted that the prolonged travelling had cost him three days in bed. '"Do I still think it was all worth while?" Can you ask?'

9

To be once again at college, hearing the Principal congratulate me with unwonted cordiality upon my 'brilliant performance' in getting through Responsions Greek in record time, brought me back with a jerk out of my dream to the realisation that examinations still existed and some people still thought they mattered. So I joined the Pass Mods. class and studied the *Cyropædia* and Livy's *Wars* with a resentful feeling that there was quite enough war in the world without having to read about it in Latin. My real life was lived in my letters to Roland, which I began to write the next day as soon as I had unpacked.

'One of the chief joys of college is that the sun sets behind a tall tree opposite my window. I am watching it now and feeling less inclined to make the inevitable plunge into proses and unseens than ever. I feel that with dead yesterday I left reality behind and that unborn to-morrow will only bring concerns of superficial importance. To-day is the aimless intermediate when I cannot think of anything I want to do that is not impossible. I do wonder how I am going to get through this eight weeks.'

In the end it turned out to be a happier term than the one before. I was no longer working alone, and Roland's letters came even more frequently, in beautiful handwriting on extremely expensive notepaper, which after eighteen years has neither curled nor yellowed. How curious it seems that letters are so much less vulnerable than their writers! His, even at that stage, were invariably punctilious, and the enforced use of two halfpenny stamps instead of a penny one always perturbed him.

One day in the early spring, he and Edward simultaneously wrote in great distress to tell me that Victor, who had become a second-lieutenant in a Royal Sussex regiment, was ill – they feared fatally – with cerebro-spinal meningitis. They both got leave and met in Hove, but they were not allowed to see him. Ultimately he recovered, but with much diminished chances of ever going to the front. For some days I shared their suspense. The love between these three was a genuine emotion which the War had deepened, and I tried to drown my grief for their anxiety in a long discussion into which Norah H. and 'E. F.' and Theresa and I, labelling ourselves 'Young Oxford', plunged one evening on twentieth-century poetry and the spirit of the age.

We were very much in earnest, and our conclusions, which I wrote down afterwards, may be interesting, for reasons of comparison, to our successors who discuss similar topics, and congratulate themselves on their vast differences from 'the pre-war girl':

'(1) The age is intensely introspective, and the younger generation is beginning to protest that supreme interest in one's self is not sin or self-conscious weakness or to be overcome, but is the essence of progress.

'(2) The trend of the age is towards an abandonment of specialisation and the attainment of versatility – a second Renaissance in fact.

'(3) The age is in great doubt as to what it really wants, but it is abandoning props and using self as the medium of development.

'(4) The poetry of this age lies in its prose – and in much else that I have no time to put down since it is nearly 2 a.m.'

When my perturbations over Victor were ended, a fresh series arose from the renewal of Roland's efforts to go to the front. Because of his eyesight, I did not believe that he would succeed, but my cold fear that he might do so made something twist cruelly inside me every time I found a letter from him in my pigeon-hole. He was now stationed at Lowestoft, but seemed to spend more time in the Royal Norfolk and Suffolk Yacht Club writing letters, than in visiting his family.

'Everything here is always the same,' he told me on February 25th. 'The same khaki-clad civilians do the same uninspiring things as complacently as ever. They are still surprised that anyone should be mad enough to want to go from this comfort to an unknown discomfort – to a place where men are and do not merely play at being soldiers. I am writing this in front of an open casement window overlooking the sea. The sky is cloudless, and the russet sails of the fishing smacks flame in the sun. It is summer – but it is not war; and I dare not look at it. It only makes me angry with myself for being here – and with the others for being content to be here. When men whom I have once despised as effeminate are being sent back wounded from the front, when nearly everyone I know is either going or has gone, can I think of this with anything but rage and shame?'

The warm beauty of that early spring, which in France was hastening the preparations for Neuve Chapelle, made me less ready than ever to accept the possibility of his going. I felt, too, vaguely disturbed and irritated by the tranquillity with which elderly Oxford appeared to view the prospect of spring-time death for its young men. The city, like the rest of England, was now plastered with recruiting posters –

REMEMBER BELGIUM
———

OFFER

YOUR SERVICES

NOW
———

THERE'S STILL A PLACE IN THE LINE
FOR YOU
———

IF YOU   /   TRY AND

  CANNOT   /   GET A

    JOIN THE   /   RECRUIT

     ARMY
                 ———

– and dons and clerics were still doing their best to justify the War and turn it into England's Holy Crusade. A pamphlet by Professor Gilbert Murray, called 'How Can War Ever Be Right?', had a good sale and was discussed with approval, but the pacifist bias which modified its conclusion that war is occasionally justified was far from appearing in the belligerent utterances of some of his colleagues.

'I think it is harder now the spring days are beginning to come,' I wrote in reply to Roland's letter, 'to keep the thought of war before one's mind – especially here, where there is always a kind of dreamy spell which makes one feel that nothing poignant and terrible can ever come near. Winter departs so early here' (I was comparing Oxford with Buxton, where it lasts until May) 'and during the calm and beautiful days we have had lately it seems so much more appropriate to imagine that you and Edward are actually here enjoying the spring than to think that before long you may be in the trenches fighting men you do not really hate. In the churches in Oxford, where so many of the congregation are soldiers, we are always having it impressed upon us that "the call of our country is the call of God". Is it? I wish I could feel sure that it was. At this time of the year it seems that everything ought to be creative, not destructive, and that we should encourage things to live and not die.'

At the end of the term, just when I was least expecting it, the blow descended abruptly. During the last week, I had been really ill with a sharp attack of influenza, which the amenities then obtainable at college were not calculated to cure with exceptional speed. At that time, illness among women students was regarded with surprise, and the provisions made for nursing were somewhat elementary. (It was partly owing to the suggestions of Winifred Holtby and myself at a college meeting after the War that a visiting nurse came to be attached to the Somerville staff.) Except in serious cases, the patient was usually isolated from her friends – who could at least have contributed to her comfort – and left to the care of the domestic staff.

After several days of existing for meal after meal upon the monotonous slops which constituted 'invalid diet', and of getting up to wash in a chilly room with a temperature of 103 degrees, I began to feel very weak, and my mother, who was in Folkestone with my father visiting Edward, hurried up to Oxford in alarm. I was thankful to see her, and to be carried off home, three days before the official date for going down, after acting with immense effort the part of the child Victoria in the First Year Play, Stanley Houghton's *The Dear Departed.*

As my temperature was now normal, and I needed only rest and home amenities to compensate for the depressing after-effects of my illness, my mother left me in Buxton and returned to London to join my father. Lying luxuriously in my comfortable bed after a pleasant breakfast, with a sense of agreeable indiffer-ence to Press descriptions of the Allied Fleet in the Dardanelles and the more recent incidents of the new submarine blockade, I lazily opened a letter from Roland which had been forwarded from Somerville. Ten minutes after reading it I was dressed and staggering dizzily but frantically about the room, for it told me that he had successfully manœuvred a transfer to the 7th Worcestershire Regiment and was off to the front in ten days' time. Assuming that I was going down from Oxford at the offi-cial end of term, he had asked me to meet him in London, where he was staying for his final leave, to say good-bye.

As the letter had taken three days to reach me, I fell into a panic of fear that I should miss him altogether. After spending the whole day in writing, telephoning, and tottering down to the town through a sudden spell of bitter cold to send off telegrams, I did endeavour in the few lines that I wrote him that evening to restrain my desperation.

'I was expecting something like it of course but it is none the less of a shock for all that. It is still difficult to realise that the moment has actually come at last when I shall have no peace of mind any more until the War is over. I cannot pretend any longer that I am glad even for your sake, but I suppose I must try to write as calmly as you do – though if it were my own life that were going to be in danger I think I could face the future with more equanimity.'

My parents returned the next day to find me still feverish and excited. As it would have been 'incorrect' for me to go alone to London, and as I was, in any case, still hardly fit to do so, they agreed that Roland, who had telephoned that he could manage it, should come to Buxton for the night. My father, however, did inquire from my mother with well-assumed indignation 'why on earth Vera was making all this fuss of that youth without a farthing to his name?'

10

When he had driven up in the taxi with me from the station, and we were left together in the morning-room, which looked across the snow-covered town to the sad hills beyond, the sudden effect of seeing him in my semi-invalid weakness after such agitation of mind brought me so near to crying that I couldn't prevent him from noticing it.

Fighting angrily with the tears, I asked him: 'Well, are you satisfied at last?'

He replied that he hardly knew. He certainly had no wish to die, and now that he had got what he wanted, a dust-and-ashes feeling had come. He neither hated the Germans nor loved the Belgians; the only possible motive for going was 'heroism in the abstract', and that didn't seem a very logical reason for risking one's life.

Mournfully we sat there recapitulating the brief and happy past; the future was too uncertain to attract speculation. I had begun, I confessed to him, to pray again, not because I believed that it did any good, but so as to leave no remote possibility unexplored. The War, we decided, came hardest of all upon us who were young. The middle-aged and the old had known their period of joy, whereas upon us catastrophe had descended just in time to deprive us of that youthful happiness to which we had believed ourselves entitled.

'Sometimes,' I told him, 'I've wished I'd never met you – that you hadn't come to take away my impersonal attitude towards the War and make it a cause of suffering to me as it is to thousands of others. But if I could choose not to have met you, I wouldn't do it – even though my future had always to be darkened by the shadow of death.'

'Ah, don't say that!' he said. 'Don't say it will all be spoilt; when I return things may be just the same.'

'*If* you return,' I emphasised, determined to face up to things for both of us, and when he insisted: '"When", not "if",' I said that I didn't imagine he was going to France without fully realising all that it might involve. He answered gravely that he had thought many times of the issue, but had a settled conviction that he was coming back, though perhaps not quite whole.

'Would you like me any less if I was, say, minus an arm?'

My reply need not be recorded. It brought the tears so near to the surface again that I picked up the coat which I had thrown off, and abruptly said I would take it upstairs – which I did the more promptly when I suddenly realised that he was nearly crying too.

After tea we walked steeply uphill along the wide road which leads over lonely, undulating moors through Whaley Bridge to Manchester, twenty miles away. This was 'the long white road' of Roland's poems, where nearly a year before we had walked between 'the grey hills and the heather', and the plover had cried in the awakening warmth of the spring. There were no plover there that afternoon; heavy snow had fallen, and a rough blizzard drove sleet and rain in our faces.

It was a mournfully appropriate setting for a discussion on death and the alternative between annihilation and an unknown hereafter. We could not honestly admit that we thought we should survive, though we would have given anything in the world to believe in a life to come, but he promised me that if he died in France he would try to come back and tell me that the grave was not the end of our love. As we walked down the hill towards Buxton the snow ceased and the evening light began faintly to shine in the sky, but somehow it only showed us the more clearly how grey and sorrowful the world had become.

Time, so desperately brief, so immeasurably precious, suddenly seemed to be racing. At dinner that night I wore my prettiest frock, a deep blue ninon over grey satin, with a wide *chiné* sash, and afterwards, though my father kept Roland smoking and talking in the dining-room too long for my impatience, we were left to ourselves in the dim, lamplit drawing-room.

Still too much bewildered and distressed by the love that had descended upon us with such young intensity to make any coherent plans for the future – even supposing that the War allowed us to have one – we nevertheless mentioned, for the first time, the subject of marriage.

'Mother says that people like me just become intellectual old maids,' I told him.

'I don't see why,' he protested.

'Oh, well, it's probably true!' I said, rather sharply, for misery had as usual made me irritable. 'After the War there'll be no one for me to marry.'

'Not even me?' he asked very softly.

'How do I know I *shall* want to marry you when that time comes?'

'You know you wouldn't be happy unless you married an odd sort of person.'

'That rather narrows the field of choice, doesn't it?'

'Well – do you need it to be so very wide?'

The rest was fragmentary. We sat on the sofa till midnight, talking very quietly. The stillness, heavy-laden with the dull oppression of the snowy night, became so electric with emotion that we were frightened of one another, and dared not let even our fingers touch for fear that the love between us should render what we both believed to be decent behaviour suddenly unendurable.

I was still incredibly ignorant. I had read, by then, too much to have failed to acquire a vague and substantially correct idea of the meaning of marriage, but I did not yet understand the precise nature of the act of union. My ignorance, however, was incapable of disturbing my romantic adoration, for I knew now for certain that whatever marriage might involve in addition to my idea of it, I could not find it other than desirable. I realised as clearly as he did that a hereafter in which we should both be deprived of our physical qualities could mean very little to either of us; he would not be Roland without his broad shoulders, his long-lashed dark eyes, and above all the singularly attractive voice which I could never recall when he was absent.

'"I want no angel, only she,"' Olive Schreiner had written in the strange little novel which had become our Bible: '"No holier and no better, with all her sins upon her, so give her me or give me nothing." . . . For the soul's fierce cry for immortality is this – only this: Return to me after death the thing as it was before. Leave me in the Hereafter the being that I am to-day. Rob me of the thoughts, the feelings, the desires that are my life, and you have left nothing to take. Your immortality is annihilation, your Hereafter is a lie.'

So I, too, wanted to find no angel after the War, after the Flood, after the grave; I wanted the arrogant, egotistic, vital young man that I loved.

The next day I saw him off, although he had said that he would rather I didn't come.

In the early morning we walked to the station beneath a dazzling sun, but the platform from which his train went out was dark and very cold. In the railway carriage we sat hand in hand until the whistle blew. We never kissed and never said a word. I got down from the carriage still clasping his hand, and held it until the gathering speed of the train made me let go. He leaned through the window looking at me with sad, heavy eyes, and I watched the train wind out of the station and swing round the curve until there was nothing left but the snowy distance, and the sun shining harshly on the bright, empty rails.

When I got back to the house, where everyone mercifully left me to myself, I realised that my hands were nearly frozen. Vaguely resenting the physical discomfort, I crouched beside the morning-room fire for almost an hour, unable to believe that I could ever again suffer such acute and conscious agony of mind. On every side there seemed to be cause for despair and no way out of it. I tried not to think because thought was intolerable, yet every effort to stop my mind from working only led to a fresh outburst of miserable speculation. I tried to read; I tried to look at the gaunt white hills across the valley, but nothing was any good, so in the end I just stayed huddled by the fire, immersed in a mood of blank hopelessness in which years seemed to have passed since the morning.

At last I fell asleep for some moments, and awoke feeling better; I was, I suppose, too young for hope to be extinguished for very long. Perhaps, I thought, Wordsworth or Browning or Shelley would have some consolation to offer; all through the War poetry was the only form of literature that I could read for comfort, and the only kind that I ever attempted to write. So I turned at once to Shelley's 'Adonais', only to be provoked to new anguish by the words:

> *O gentle child, beautiful as thou wert,*
> *Why didst thou leave the trodden paths of men*
> *Too soon, and with weak hands though mighty heart*
> *Dare the unpastured dragon in his den?*

But the lovely cadences stirred me at last to articulateness; there was no one to whom I wanted to talk, but at least I could tell my diary a good deal of the sorrow that seemed so fathomless.

'I can scarcely bear to think of him,' I wrote, 'and yet I cannot bear to think of anything else. For the time being all people, all ideas, all interests have set, and sunk below the horizon of my mind; he alone I can contemplate, whom of all things in heaven and earth it hurts to think about most.'

Certainly the War was already beginning to overshadow scholarship and ambition. But I was not ready, yet, to give in to it; I wanted very badly to be heroic – or at any rate to seem heroic to myself – so I tried hard to rationalise my grief.

'I felt,' I endeavoured subsequently to assure myself, 'a weak and cowardly person . . . to shrink from my share in the Universal Sorrow. After all it was only right that I should have to suffer too, that I had no longer an impersonal indifference to set me apart from the thousands of breaking hearts in England to-day. It was my part to face the possibility of a ruined future with the same courage that he is going to face death.'

So I finished up the miserable morning by looking through some of the short verses that he had left with me, and especially one in which – as in two or three of his poems – some prophetic instinct led him to a truer knowledge of the future than the strong, dominant consciousness that felt certain of survival:

> *Good-bye, sweet friend. What matters it that you*
> *Have found Love's death in joy and I in sorrow?*
> *For hand in hand, just as we used to do,*
> *We two shall live our passionate poem through*
> *On God's serene to-morrow.*

CHAPTER IV

Learning versus Life

VILLANELLE

Violets from Plug Street Wood,
Sweet, I send you oversea.
(It is strange they should be blue,
Blue, when his soaked blood was red,
For they grew around his head;
It is strange they should be blue.)

Violets from Plug Street Wood—
Think what they have meant to me—
Life and Hope and Love and You
(And you did not see them grow
Where his mangled body lay,
Hiding horror from the day;
Sweetest, it was better so.)

Violets from oversea,
To your dear, far, forgetting land
These I send in memory,
Knowing You will understand.

R. A. L.

Ploegsteert Wood, April 1915.

1

Roland went to the front on March 31st, 1915. For those who cared to remember such things, it was Wednesday in Passion Week. *'Je suis fiancé; c'est la guerre!'* he announced before leaving to his mother, who accepted the news, which cannot altogether have astonished her, with commendable toleration.

In the interval between his leaving me and his crossing over to France, there was time for each of us to reinforce the other's courage with letters; time, too, for me to receive a large amethyst set as a brooch, and sent with a tiny card inscribed: 'In Memoriam. March 18th, 1915.' I held it up in front of the fire; the red glow reflected in its surface made it shine like a great drop of blood.

'All that is left is to wait and work and hope,' he had written to me from Maldon on the evening of the day that we said good-bye. 'But I *am* coming back, dear. Let it always be "when" and not "if". As yet everything is incomplete, but last night, unreal as it seems to be, must have some consummation. The day will come when we shall live our roseate poem through – as we have dreamt it.'

Determinedly I responded in the same confident strain: 'It is hard that on that difficult path I can do nothing to help you face the Death you will meet with so often. But when you are fighting the fear of it – bravely, as I know you will – I too shall be facing that fear, and can at least be with you in spirit then . . . Sometime after you had gone, I began again to dream of all that may still be after the War – *when* you return, and to plan out work to make me worthier of the future and to fill up the hours until the sorrowful time is past . . . It would not be right for us to be given a vision of the Promised Land only to be told we were never to enter it. We shall dwell in it in the end, and it will seem all the fairer because we have wandered in the desert between then and now . . . Good-bye, my dear, and as much love as you wish.'

Confidence, however, was difficult just then, for immediately after Roland left me, the casualties began to come through from Neuve Chapelle. As usual the Press had given no hint of that tragedy's dimensions, and it was only through the long casualty lists, and the persistent demoralising rumour that owing to a miscalculation in time thousands of our men had been shot down by our own guns, that the world was gradually coming to realise something of what the engagement had been. The 6th Sherwood Foresters, which included many of the Buxton young men, had left for France three weeks earlier; they were incorrectly reported

to have been involved in the battle, and rumours of death and
wounds were already abroad. It was not an encouraging moment
for bidding farewell to a lover, and, as often happened in periods
of absorbing stress, a quotation from Longfellow slipped, unim-
peded by literary eclecticism, into my diary:

> *The air is full of farewells to the dying,*
> *And mournings for the dead;*
> *The heart of Rachel for her children crying*
> *Will not be comforted.*

The determination to work hard and to plan out the days so
that each moment would be occupied became singularly hard to
fulfil, for I could not open a book without finding some subject
that I had discussed with Roland or seeing words which reminded
me of his characteristic phrases; I could not even seek solitude
in a favourite refuge beyond the town without passing some road
along which I had walked with him, or thinking that perhaps
some day we should walk there again. Latin and Greek became
even more irksome than before, and I began to feel that some
kind of vigorous, practical toil would be better adapted to a
chaotic wartime world. Rather lamely I tried – as the majority
of Oxford dons, had I but known it, were trying also – to find
some compelling reason for continuing the former when the
latter seemed so much more appropriate.

'I suppose he is right,' I argued with myself, 'and the only thing,
which is the hardest thing, is to work and wait – and certainly
to hope, which one must do or die.'

How fortunate we were who still had hope, I did not then
realise; I could not know how soon the time would come when
we should have no more hope, and yet be unable to die. Roland's
letters – the sensitive letters of the newly baptised young soldier,
so soon to be hardened by the protective iron of remorseless indifference to horror and pain – made the struggle to concentrate
no easier, for they drove me to a feverish searching into fundamental questions to which no immediate answers were forthcoming.

'It seems delightfully incongruous,' he wrote from Armentières, 'that there should be good shops and fine buildings and comfortable beds less than half an hour's walk from the trenches . . . A bullet whizzed uncomfortably near my head on the way in last night. I myself cannot yet realise that each little singing thing that flies near me holds latent in it the power of death for someone. Soon perhaps I may see death come to someone near and realise it and be afraid. I have not yet been afraid . . . There are three German graves a little further down along the trench. There is no name on them, but merely a piece of board with "German Grave – R.I.P." scrawled on it. And yet somebody once loved the man lying there.'

Torn by inward conflict and continually keyed up to the highest pitch by the constant reading and writing of letters, I spent the rest of the vacation in riding my bicycle about the hills and dales, feverishly inventing analogies and distinctions between life and death, soul and intellect, spirit and immortality. Certain Derbyshire names – Ashwood Dale, Topley Pike, Chee Tor, Miller's Dale, King Sterndale – always bring back to me those desperate struggles after a philosophy of life.

'Sorrow, and the higher joy that is not mere happiness, and you, all seem to be the same thing just now,' I explained haltingly to Roland. 'Is it really all for nothing – for an empty name – an ideal? Last time I saw you it was I who said that and you who denied it. Was I really right, and will the issue not be worth one of the lives that have been sacrificed for it? Or did we need this gigantic catastrophe to wake up all that was dead within us? . . . In the light of all that you have seen, tell me what you think . . . Surely, surely it is a worthy ideal – to fight that you may save your country's freedom from falling into the hands of this terrible and ruthless foe. It is awful to think that the very progress of civilisation has made this war what it is . . . Just to think that we have got to the stage of motors, aeroplanes, telephones, and 17-inch shells, and yet have not passed the stage of killing one another. . . . For me I think the days are over of sheltered physical comfort and unruffled peace of mind. I don't think they will ever come again.'

I thought rightly, for they never did; and the profound shock of their initial departure left me as helpless and bewildered as a child abandoned on the alien shores of some illimitable sea. My diary for March and April 1915 is full of impossible, excruciating attempts to work out gigantic problems, which were apt to conclude – when they concluded at all, which was seldom – in a kind of vague pantheism. The spasmodic study of Plato, whose *Apologia* and *Meno* I was reading for Pass Mods., certainly did nothing to discourage my hysterical pursuit of elusive definitions. Wearily I wrote of myself as 'trying to determine what that is of which intellect is only the instrument – trying to give a name to that vague but certain element and meditating as to whether it is deathless' – and again of 'often sitting motionless and seeing nothing beneath the oppression of my struggling thought'.

Sometimes, by way of variety, a bout of vague Olive Schreiner-ish philosophising mingled incongruously with records of banal domestic vexations. A typical entry runs as follows: 'To know that the soul of man – God in him – is the source of strength, that by growing it causes suffering, yet through suffering it grows – this at least is Light. Daddy was in bed all day with an inflamed eye. Mother went to Manchester too so I had to look after him a good deal. What with that and thinking I did not get through much work.'

Just at this time a group of super-patriotic Buxton women, who were busily engaged in forming a women's volunteer corps, provided yet another source of disturbance and interruption. Proudly they drilled and marched about the town in uniform, though none of them know what precisely was the object of all this activity. They were, however, most assiduous in telling me that I ought to join this, or that, or the other, the idea of course being that college was a pleasant and idle occupation which led nowhere. Thoroughly exasperated, I avoided their society, and it was not until two acquaintances outside the volunteer corps left Buxton to join a hospital under the French Red Cross, that the idea occurred to me of combining some nursing with my work for Oxford.

'I remember once at the beginning of the War,' I wrote enthusiastically to Roland, 'you described college as "a secluded life of scholastic vegetation". That is just what it is. It is, for me at least, too soft a job . . . I want physical endurance; I should welcome the most wearying kinds of bodily toil.'

So closely, at this stage, was active war-work of every type associated in the public mind with the patriotic impulse which sent men into the Army that I never dreamed, amid all my analytical speculations, of inquiring whether 'joining up' would not be, for me, a mere emotional antidote involving no real sacrifice. At the time my preoccupation with possible methods of following the persistently beating drum merely provided a blessed temporary relief from philosophical flounderings.

On Easter Sunday I noticed in church the Matron of the Devonshire Hospital, a local institution for the treatment of rheumatic complaints, which now took a number of soldiers. Impulsively I tackled her and asked if she had any work to offer which I could undertake in the intervals of reading. She looked at me sceptically and replied rather drily that if I knew how to darn there were always plenty of socks to be mended. As this happened to be the only form of elementary needlework that I had ever mastered, I gratefully accepted the somewhat prosaic alternative to my heroic visions; and when, a few days later, I sat surrounded by coloured wools in the hospital's vaccine-room and attacked the colossal holes, I felt that I had advanced at least one step nearer to Roland and the War.

2

On April 17th, 1915, when the British were gruesomely capturing Hill 60, the first mention of Zeppelin raids appears in my diary. Newcastle-upon-Tyne, Maldon and Shorncliffe were the places attacked, and Edward, whose battalion was still in Folkestone, wrote that the raiders had caused a refreshing outbreak of activity to interrupt the daily routine. Another raid, on Lowestoft, gave me some anxious hours, but it need not have done so, for Roland's mother, who was naturally courageous, merely regarded the upset as profitable 'copy'.

Two days later, meditations on the air-raids had given way to a dissertation on the controversial topic of 'war-babies' as treated by various newspapers. My own comments on this engrossing subject combined a limited number of independent opinions with inherited remnants of ancestral morality:

'One set of people who write letters are most unmorally moral, want to disgrace the poor girls as much as possible and enlarge the offence out of all proportion . . . The other, the hysterical party, absolutely excuses the offence on the score of abnormal conditions (though true morality is supreme over circumstances), hold forth about "the children of the heroes of Mons and the Marne" (which they are not), and even make suggestions of compensation so extremely favourable to the offenders as to encourage others to repeat the sin, and thus undermine our whole social and moral structure.'

A leading article in *The Times*, dealing 'with both sides of the question', I condescendingly described as 'very sensible'. It remarked, I recorded, that 'this is a case for sense and charity . . . while we must not condone the offence, we must not make its results worse by harsh and narrow treatment . . . we must condemn the sin and the sinners while yet remarking that the results of it can be made the useful citizens of to-morrow.'

How warmly the leader-writer of that 'sensible' article must have congratulated himself on his skilful Primrose Day compromise! What, I wonder, if he is still living to-day, would be his editorial reactions to 'peace-babies' with a similar unorthodox origin?

That morning I left the reassuring study of *The Times* to take part in one of the first national 'flag-days' organised during the War. As I wandered with my basket of primroses up and down the Buxton streets, blindingly white as they always became in the midday sunshine, my thoughts swung dizzily between the conviction that Roland would return and the certainty that he could never possibly come back. I had little patience to spare for my mother's middle-aged acquaintances, who patronised me as they bought my primroses, and congratulated me on putting aside my 'studies' to 'do my bit in this terrible War'. I took their pennies with scant ceremony, and one by one thrust them with a noisy clatter into my tin.

'Those who are old and think this War so terrible do not know what it means to us who are young,' I soliloquised angrily. 'When I think how suddenly, instantly, a chance bullet may put an end to that brilliant life, may cut it off in its youth and mighty promise, faith in the "increasing purpose" of the ages grows dim.'

The fight around Hill 60 which was gradually developing, assisted by the unfamiliar horror of gas attacks, into the Second Battle of Ypres, did nothing to restore my faith in the benevolent intentions of Providence. With that Easter vacation began the wearing anxiety of waiting for letters which for me was to last, with only brief intervals, for more than three years, and which, I think, made all non-combatants feel more distracted than anything else in the War. Even when the letters came they were four days old, and the writer since sending them had had time to die over and over again. My diary, with its long-drawn-out record of days upon days of miserable speculation, still gives a melancholy impression of that nerve-racking suspense.

'Morning,' it observes, 'creeps on into afternoon, and afternoon passes into evening, while I go from one occupation to another, in apparent unconcern – but all the time this gnawing anxiety beneath it all.'

Ordinary household sounds became a torment. The clock, marking off each hour of dread, struck into the immobility of tension with the shattering effect of a thunderclap. Every ring at the door suggested a telegram, every telephone call a long-distance message giving bad news. With some of us the effect of this prolonged apprehension still lingers on; even now I cannot work comfortably in a room from which it is possible to hear the front-door bell.

'I dare not think too vividly of him just now,' I wrote one black evening after several days without a letter; 'I can scarcely bear to look at the photograph taken at Uppingham . . . I have been trying to picture to myself what I should feel if I heard he was dead. It would be impossible to realise; life would seem so utterly empty and purposeless without him that it is almost inconceivable . . . I only know that such an anguish could never be conquered in a life of scholastic endeavour . . . never among those indifferent, unperceiving college women for the majority of whom war and love and grief might not exist. The ability to endure these things would come back in time, but only after some drastic change.'

To this constant anxiety for Roland's life was added, as the end of the fighting moved ever further into an incalculable future, a new fear that the War would come between us – as indeed, with time, the War always did, putting a barrier of indescribable experience between men and the women whom they loved, thrusting horror deeper and deeper inward, linking the dread of spiritual death to the apprehension of physical disaster. Quite early I realised this possibility of a permanent impediment to understanding. 'Sometimes,' I wrote, 'I have feared that even if he gets through, what he has experienced out there may change his ideas and tastes utterly.'

In desperation I began to look carefully through his letters for every vivid word-picture, every characteristic tenderness of phrase, which suggested that not merely the body but the spirit that I desired was still in process of survival. To begin with, the tender phrases came often enough, blinding my eyes with sharp tears after I had read, with determined equanimity, his half-gay, half-wistful descriptions of danger or fatigue.

'I have just picked you these violets,' he wrote one April day from 'Plug Street Wood', enclosing four little blue flowers gathered from the roof of his dug-out. I have them still; the blue is brown now, and crinkled, but the flower shapes remain unspoilt. With the violets he had intended to send a villanelle that he had written to accompany them, but, dissatisfied as always with his work, he kept back the poem for revision, and did not give it to me until some weeks afterwards.

The letters that he wrote me were happy and very typical so long as they remained in that 'thick wood of tall thin trees'. A rich brewer from Armentières, he told me, owned Ploegsteert Wood; it had been his pheasant ground. Sometimes I wonder if he and the pheasants are back there again, and whether he has the heart to shoot them where so much more than pheasants was destroyed. In Roland's day there was a grave in the wood with a carefully made wooden cross inscribed with the words: 'Here lie two gallant German officers.' The men who put up the cross congratulated themselves a little on their British magnanimity, but when, later, they pushed the enemy out of the trenches in front of the wood, they found another grave as carefully tended, and inscribed: 'Here lie five brave English officers.'

How earnestly I wished, as I sat, gloomily critical, at the last hospital working party which I was able to attend before going back to Somerville, that something of that generous dignity could be reflected at home!

'Mrs W. and Miss A. got together,' I related intolerantly, 'and after discussing various people they knew who were nursing, they talked at length of cooks, and then entered on a long and deep conversation on the subject of combinations and pyjamas. Finally Sister J. came in and told us all about some very bad cases of wounded from Neuve Chapelle she had seen in a hospital in the south of England. After that the ladies seemed to try and outdo one another in telling stories of war horrors. I don't think they could have known or loved anyone in the trenches. They made me feel absolutely cold.'

In those days I knew, of course, nothing of psychology, that beneficent science which has begun to make men and women more merciful to each other than they used to be in earlier generations. I was still too young to realise how much vicarious excitement the War provided for frustrated women cut off from vision and opportunity in small provincial towns, or to understand that the deliberate contemplation of horror and agony might strangely compensate a thwarted nature for the very real grief of having no one at the front for whom to grieve.

As we left the hospital we spoke to a wounded Tommy – a small elderly man who had been, the Sister told us, through Neuve Chapelle. He looked, I noticed, regarding him with awe – for at that time I had seen very few men back from the front – 'not unnerved or even painfully ill – but very, very sad.' Would Roland, I wondered, look as sad as that if I ever saw him again?

3

The day after Rupert Brooke's death in the Ægean, and a few hours before the Allied landing at Cape Helles on April 25th, I returned for the last term of my first year to an Oxford that now seemed infinitely remote from everything that counted. During the vacation, Somerville College, adjacent as it was to the Radcliffe Infirmary, had been commandeered by the War Office for conversion into a military hospital. Since Oxford was now almost empty of undergraduates except for the Cadet Corps and a few of the permanently disabled, the St Mary Hall Quadrangle of Oriel had been offered to Somerville for the duration of the War, and the students were distributed between this hall and various ex-masculine lodging-houses.

But my thoughts were far less concerned with these changes than with the Second Battle of Ypres and the direction in which it might be spreading. 'I would have given anything not to have had to come back,' I confessed in my diary. 'If it had not been for P. Mods. I could have started nursing at once' – for to become a nurse was now my intention. It was not, perhaps, an obvious choice for a Somerville exhibitioner, but I was then in no mood for the routine Civil Service posts which represented the only type of 'intellectual' war-work offered to uncertificated young women. I never even dreamed of patiently putting in the two remaining years of self-qualification before taking part in the War. Even had I not believed – as everyone except Lord Kitchener then believed – that it could not possibly last for more than another year, I should still have been anxious to get as far as I could from intellect and its torment; I longed intensely for hard physical labour which would give me discomfort to endure and weariness to put mental speculation to sleep.

I left to my mother the task of completing my arrangements with the Devonshire Hospital, where I had planned to begin my nursing. After a few weeks of training there I hoped, if I could get a year's leave of absence from Somerville, somehow to join up in a London hospital and thus be on the spot when Roland came home wounded or on leave. My mother co-operated willingly in these schemes, for she was sorry for me, and kind. She perhaps found love, even for a suitor whose brains were his capital, a more comprehensible emotion than harsh and baffling ambition; having come from a hard-working family herself, she had none of my father's practical distrust of the unendowed professional classes. Thanks, however, to the noble Edward, with whom he had been staying at Folkestone, even his instinctive prejudice against 'Bohemians' was gradually undergoing modification, for Edward had tactfully told him, in the best public-school manner, that 'Roland was of a most honourable nature, and there was no one he would rather see Vera married to.'

Preoccupied as I was, the excitement of the Somerville students over their altered circumstances seemed at first as remote as the soundless clamour of a dream. At an ancient panelled lodging-house known as Micklem Hall, in Brewer Street off St Aldate's, I found myself separated from almost all my little group of friends. Theresa, 'E. F.', and Norah H. were in Oriel; only Marjorie went with me to Micklem to alleviate the noisy mediocrity of a type of student which we were snobbishly accustomed to designate 'the lower millstone'. At meal-times the close proximity of the English tutor, who was in charge of the Micklem party, overwhelmed 'the lower millstone' into palpitating silence.

'It's just like a perpetual "High",' Marjorie and I complained to one another over cocoa in my room after we had exhaustingly maintained the conversation for several meals on end. Compared with the small, bright study which had looked on to the sunset from the Maitland building, my new room did not appear very attractive; it was old and dingy, with oak beams, a crooked floor, and innumerable dark corners and crevices partially concealed by fatigued draperies suggestive of spiders, blackbeetles, and similar abominations. But the garden, with its heavy, drooping trees, at least promised a refuge, and I was glad to be spared the chattering, pervasive femininity which had already taken possession of St Mary Hall.

I should not have to bear it very long, I reflected, as I stood in the Cathedral a week later and listened, indescribably uplifted by my new determination to play some active part in the glorious Allied fight against militarism, to a large contingent of the Oxford and Bucks Light Infantry singing, in their vigorous young voices, 'The Son of God goes forth to war!' In my coat pocket lay a letter that had come that morning from Roland – another of the dear and tender letters written in Ploegsteert Wood.

'A little poem of W. E. Henley's came into my head last night as I came across the fields in the starlight. Do you know it?

> *A wink from Hesper, falling*
> *Fast in the wintry sky,*
> *Comes through the even blue,*
> *Dear, like a word from you . . .*
> *Is it good-bye?*
>
> *Across the miles between us*
> *I send you sigh for sigh.*
> *Good night, sweet friend, good night:*
> *Till life and all take flight,*
> *Never good-bye.*

'You can listen,' he went on after a purely personal interlude, 'to the undulating artillery bombardment from the direction of Ypres, not with equanimity but with a certain tremulous gratitude that it is no nearer. Someone is getting hell, but it isn't you – yet . . . It was a glorious morning, and from where we were on the hill we could see the country for miles around. It looked rather like the clear-cut landscape in a child's painting-book. The basis was deep green with an occasional flame-coloured patch in the valley where a red-roofed farm-house had escaped the guns. Just below the horizon and again immediately at our feet was a brilliant yellow mustard-field.'

Enclosed in the letter was a 'souvenir', which I examined with deep interest after I had crossed St Aldate's to go back to my room. It consisted of a few pages torn from a child's exercise-book that he had found in a ruined house, and appeared to contain some stumbling translations from Flemish into French. The first exercise that caught my eye, in infantile writing and with many erasures, ran as follows:

'Avelghem le 27/4/12.
'Description.
'Les Vacances.
'Les vacances précedentes, que j'allongeais depuis longtemps
étaient enfin dej enfin arrivées.'

It seemed an eloqent comment on the situation. Where, I
wondered, was the child spending his prolonged *vacances* now?

In my reply I told Roland of my intention to nurse, and
described how much I had been moved by the Cathedral service.

'At such times I worship Oxford. One is able then to forget
that there are dusty old dons and proctors who exact the same
from women as from men and yet treat us sometimes as if we
were strangers in a strange land. They have criticised Oriel exceedingly for taking us in! One realises at such times the value of men
who have sufficient imagination and far-sightedness to be feminists. On the day we come into our own the dons and proctors
won't be shown much mercy!'

That evening, in her Sunday 'sermon', the Principal delivered
an impressive discourse on the conduct required of us as temporary inhabitants of St Mary Hall. We must be careful, she said, 'to
avoid conspicuousness and exercise self-restraint'. Conspicuousness, however, was by no means easy to avoid, for to the Press
our anomalous position seemed a fruitful subject for mirth.
Thankful to find a new source of comic relief amid the growing
gloom engendered by the *communiqués* from Flanders, *London
Opinion* came out with the following lively production:

> *A hundred wounded soldiers fill*
> *(In days like these one might have feared it)*
> *The pleasant haunts of Somerville*
> *For Kitchener has commandeered it!*
>
> *But, driven from their loved abodes,*
> *The learned ladies find a corner*
> *Where once was sheltered Cecil Rhodes,*
> *Clough, Matthew Arnold, P. F. Warner!*

> *The quads adorned by Newman, Froude,*
> > *Keble, and other grave professors,*
> *Are thronging with a multitude*
> > *Of ardent feminine successors!*
>
> *The Common Room, which saw contend*
> > *Logician with acute logician,*
> *Is proving in the latter end*
> > *The home of merest intuition!*
>
> *O Oriel, centuries ago*
> > *To flowing-vested monks devoted,*
> *To think that thou again canst show*
> > *A horde of scholars petticoated!*
>
> *And when thy gallant sons return,*
> > *Of whom the cruel wars bereave thee,*
> *Will not thy fair alumnæ spurn*
> > *Suggestions that it's time to leave thee?*

Before the term was very old, the few remaining undergraduates in the still masculine section of Oriel not unnaturally concluded that it would be a first-rate 'rag' to break down the wall which divided them from the carefully guarded young females in St Mary Hall. Great perturbation filled the souls of the Somerville dons when they came down to breakfast one morning to find that a large gap had suddenly appeared in the protecting masonry, through which had been thrust a hilarious placard:

''OO MADE THIS 'ERE 'OLE?'
'MICE!!!'

Throughout that day and the following night the Senior Common Room, from the Principal downwards, took it in turns to sit on guard beside the hole, for fear any unruly spirit should escape through it to the forbidden adventurous males on the other side. Long after the War, I discovered that the graduates of New

College still cherished a ribald legend of this incident, based upon the report that part of the historic nocturnal vigil had been shared by the Somerville dons with the Provost of Oriel.

4

I remember that summer term much as a traveller might recall a tranquil hour spent securely in a sunny garden before setting out on a harsh and dangerous journey. In spite of the dread that darkened its calm, golden evenings, the memories that survive are fragrant and serene.

Since the others had all done Pass Mods. the previous term, I was relegated to solitary coachings with the Classical tutor, who accompanied me patiently through Pliny and Plato and Homer. The trial and death of Socrates, the lovely lines from the *Iliad* which describe Andromache holding out the child Astyanax to Hector before Troy and 'smiling through her tears', will be for ever associated for me with those poignant early days of the War. My tutor, I think, realised that I was in love, for she was always very kind to my evident distress over each new catastrophe – the more so, perhaps, because she herself was beginning to desire some occupation less detached from the War than the coaching of immature females. A year or so afterwards she escaped from Oxford to war-work in Serbia and Salonika.

I still recall the quiet hour spent in her panelled room at Oriel on the warm May evening that the news came through of the sinking of the *Lusitania*. It appropriately closed a day of disasters which included the recapture of Hill 60 by the Germans and a melancholy letter from Roland to say that he had been under shell-fire and it was 'a nerve-racking job' – 'horror piled on horror till one feels that the world can scarcely go on any longer,' I recorded miserably. By the time that my coaching came I was almost in tears, though I knew no one on the *Lusitania* and should not even have recognised among the survivors the names of the future Food-Controller and his daughter, Lady Mackworth, afterwards Viscountess Rhondda, to whose weekly review, *Time and Tide*, I was to contribute many years later. There was no escape from these stormy preoccupations except in the small successive events of everyday life – May Morning, the Somerville tennis team, uncensored letters from Roland in green envelopes, services at the Cathedral or New College Chapel, and invalid cookery classes which the Classical tutor also joined, working with real vigour in a voluminous overall, and tersely commenting on the disconcerting number of facets possessed by a potato.

On May Morning at sunrise, I went to Magdalen Bridge with the usual trio to hear the Magdalen choir sing their annual hymn, '*Te Deum Patrem colimus*', from the summit of the tower. The song gave me a choked feeling; I could only think how Roland and Edward ought to have been there, and were not. When it was over we rode off on our bicycles and breakfasted in a copse beyond Marston, at the edge of a field already golden with cowslips. Vivid green grass covered the ground in the copse, thick as a carpet and patterned gaily with half-opened bluebells and yellow primroses rooted in the red sandy soil. Above our heads the rooks cawed softly, and through the delicate network of branches we could see glimpses of milk-blue sky.

Much of my time that term was passed – for to pass it quickly had become my chief object – in an apparently light-hearted absorption in tennis. Without much difficulty I got into the Somerville six – for which I sometimes played first couple but usually second – because one of its senior members had encountered me the previous year in a match between Buxton and a Manchester club. Thanks chiefly to the long-limbed and devoted B., who was as usual my partner, we had put up a terrific fight against a really first-class team, and the Somervillian, who had been playing for the Manchester club, had left the courts with the impression that I was B.'s feminine equivalent at volleys and rallies.

I could not help enjoying the college matches – my limbs were too muscular, my love of strenuous activity in the sun and air too keen – but beneath the pleasure lay a miserable feeling of guilt. 'Tennis now is like Nero fiddling while Rome was burning,' I solemnly decided after the *Lusitania* disaster. During one very hard match, when grave reports and long casualty lists had come for

days from Festubert, the rhythm of the balls resolved itself into a
sentence from one of Roland's letters: 'Some-one – is get-ting
hell – but – it – isn't you – yet.' Exhausted by the long-drawn-
out play, and tormented almost to desperation by the ceaseless
beat of the sinister phrase, I flung myself on my bed afterwards
and tried to get some comfort from the volume of Wordsworth
which had been the delight of my scholarship work in that long-
ago that was already beginning to be labelled 'pre-war'. But I
opened the page straight away at the sonnet:

> *Surprised by joy – impatient as the Wind*
> *I turned to share the transport – Oh! with whom,*
> *But Thee, deep buried in the silent tomb,*
> *That spot which no vicissitude can find? . . .*

At the moment it seemed prophetic, and I hid my face in the
pillow and cried.

New College Chapel and the Cathedral services, with the
haunting beauty of their organ melodies, really provided better
consolation than tennis-matches; they kept one's mind face to
face with the poignant facts, instead of creating a diversion
inevitably followed by the sharp shock of recollection. Habitually,
on Sunday evenings, I sat with 'E. F.' or Marjorie in the Cathedral,
gazing at the grey walls stained crimson and purple by the light
shining through the coloured glass of the windows, and winking
back the tears that came whenever the organ rolled suddenly
through the building, in the endeavour to prevent my companion
from discovering the existence of an emotion of which she was
already well aware. Oxford that term was full of music, which
brought continually thoughts of Roland and the War, tear-
making, unbearable – and yet from which I could never keep
away. Like a lost soul I haunted New College and Christ Church,
cherishing my sorrow.

It drove me quite early in the term to open the question of
provisional notice with the Principal, for the decision to nurse
was already growing into a determination to remain away from
Oxford until the War was over, although I knew that – in those

early days before the W.A.A.C., the W.R.N.S. and the W.R.A.F. existed – the obstacles to worth-while service for girls under twenty-three were only to be overcome by consistent prevarication. The Principal listened patiently to my aspirations after Red Cross experience, and characteristically replied that, although my Exhibition might complicate matters a little, everyone must decide such a question for themselves. When I wrote later from Buxton to tell her that I had definitely decided to go down for a year, she answered with generous kindness, wishing me luck in my undertakings, and feeling sure that in the end my work would benefit greatly from this experience of the deeper and more serious side of life.

The time had not yet come when the fear of a feminine stampede into war-work inspired numerous authoritative proclamations to women students, bidding them – as women before and after Joan of Arc have so often been bidden – to stay where they were. Three years later, when Winifred Holtby, in spite of academic pronouncements, went down after a distracted year at Somerville to join the W.A.A.C., her inconvenient gesture inspired a Sunday-night address from the Principal on the duty of remaining at college. But in 1915 neither the demand for war-workers nor the response to it had reached its alarming stage, and I was left, uncriticised, to make such arrangements as I chose.

So I wrote off at once, outlining a nursing shceme, to Mina and Betty, who had both recently expressed to me their anxiety to 'do something'. Betty seemed favourable, but Mina became tentative, and asked me if I quite understood what a probationer's work in hospital really meant.

'Of course I know,' I told her indignantly; 'I shall hate it, but I will be all the more ready to do it on that account.' To my diary I gave my reason more explicitly: 'He has to face far worse things than any sight or act I could come across; he can bear it – and so can I.'

Truly the War had made masochists of us all.

5

One chilly May evening the English tutor invited Marjorie and myself into her room at Micklem to see her Milton manuscripts. When we had looked at them we moved closer to the fire and she showed us her latest acquisition from Blackwell's – the newly published first edition of Rupert Brooke's *1914*. Those famous sonnets, brought into prominence by the poet's death on the eve of the Dardanelles campaign, were then only just beginning to take the world's breath away, and I asked our tutor if she would read us one or two.

For the young to whom Rupert Brooke's poems are now familiar as classics, it must be impossible to imagine how it felt to hear them for the first time just after they were written. With my grief and anxiety then so new, I found the experience so moving that I should not have sought it had I realised how hard composure would be to maintain. Silently I struggled for it as I listened to the English tutor's grave, deliberate voice reading the sonnets, unhackneyed, courageous, and almost shattering in their passionate, relevant idealism:

> *Glad from a world grown old and cold and weary,*
> *Leave the sick hearts that honour could not move,*
> *And half-men, and their dirty songs and dreary—*

But not, oh, surely not,

> *all the little emptiness of love?*

Was that really what Rupert Brooke had felt? Was it what Roland would come to feel? Almost more bearable was the sonnet on 'The Dead', with what might become its terribly personal application:

> *These laid the world away; poured out the red*
> *Sweet wine of youth; gave up the years to be*
> *Of work and joy . . .*

How would Rupert Brooke have written, I wonder, had he lived until 1933? Would the world of 1914 really have seemed to him old and cold and weary, compared with the grey and tragic present? Would he still have thought that Holiness and Nobleness and Honour described the causes for which those sacrifices of youth and work and immortality were offered? His poems made all too realistic a letter that came the next day from Roland.

'One of my men has just been killed – the first . . . I did not actually see it – thank heaven. I only found him lying very still at the bottom of the trench with a tiny stream of blood trickling down his cheek into his coat . . . I do not quite know how I felt at that moment. It was not anger – even now I have no feeling of animosity against the man who shot him – only a great pity, and a sudden feeling of impotence. It is cruel of me to tell you this . . . Try not to remember; as I do.'

A few days afterwards the Liberal Government of the Parliament Act and the ultimatum to Germany vanished into history, and its place was taken by a Coalition which suffered from the delusion that victory depended mainly upon an increased output of shells. 'There is a political crisis now,' I noted on May 20th; 'a national non-Party Government is to be formed for the duration of the War.' The entry for May 24th contained yet further impersonal items of information: 'There were 316 officers in the casualty list. Italy has formally declared war' – an event which was to affect me so personally, so deeply, but which at the time, with my mind on the Western Front, I barely noticed in passing. By May 28th I had become entirely egotistical again, owing to the humiliating fact that my tutor had reproached me for going out to dinner without her permission.

'It is a queer, incongruous feeling,' I protested in my diary, with an indignant disregard of grammar hardly appropriate to the holder of an exhibition in English Language and Literature, 'for I who know and think only of the one big thing in my life to be corrected on account of something small and unimportant by someone who does not know!'

This high-souled indifference to 'small and unimportant' college regulations evidently became something of a problem to my

English tutor that summer term, for my diary, after describing the excitement at Oxford on May 31st over a big Zeppelin raid on London, again records the necessity for reproof – followed, of course, by typical outbursts of righteous indignation – on at least two subsequent occasions. But Roland, writing at the beginning of June, recalled the larger issues to my mind by describing an incident which was, perhaps, one of the minor results of the 'political crisis':

'The Prime Minister, of all persons, was responsible for the abrupt ending of my last letter. He was brought along to have an informal look at us, and it was arranged that he should see the men while they were having a bath in the vats. We only had about half an hour's notice and had to rush off and make arrangements for the "accidental" visit. I and two other subalterns being at the moment in a mischievous mood decided to have a bath at the same time and successfully timed it so that we all three welcomed Asquith dressed only in an identity disc. I still don't quite know what he was doing over here when he is wanted so much in England; but perhaps the shell question had something to do with it. He looked old and rather haggard, I thought.'

A week or two before the end of term it was a relief to see Edward, who had been stationed all that summer in the south, and get once more into close contact with the things that mattered. He came from Maidstone on his motorcycle to spend the weekend with me, and we sat and talked in the garden at Micklem. Since we had last been together, many of our Buxton contemporaries had been killed on the Aubers Ridge and in the Dardanelles, where Edward warned me that his regiment might be going. Several acquaintances had disappeared during one engagement of the Manchesters in Gallipoli, including a broad, smiling young man who had squeezed my hand behind the scenes at the Buxton Opera House during a performance of *Raffles* in which we had both been acting. The idea of Frank as part of the Dardanelles tragedy seemed so incongruous as almost to be fantastic.

'Somehow,' I told Roland, 'death always seems further removed from one's "summer friends" – from the kind of people with whom one dances and plays games and perhaps flirts a little – even than from the beloved people who are part of one's very existence. These latter belong to the whole – to the dark shadows as well as the sunlit patches, but it gives one the shock of incongruity to imagine the Angel of Death brooding over one's light and pleasant acquaintances, and to think of them with all their lightness and pleasantness shed away.'

By the time that Edward and I had accustomed ourselves to face death, as it were from a distance, through the medium of these 'summer friends', the long-postponed darkness of a June evening shrouded the quiet garden. When the light had gone it somehow became easier to stand up to our own future and confront the end of things for ourselves, though I listened with chill misery to his confirmation of my dread that Roland could not help but come back changed. 'They're all changed,' he said, 'after two or three months out there.' Nevertheless, he felt convinced of Roland's safe return.

'Tonius'll get through all right,' he insisted, and quoted a sentence from a letter that Roland, with typical arrogant confidence, had written to Victor a few days before: 'I wanted to get into the Army and I got there; I wanted to go to the front, and I went to the front; now I want to come back and I shall come back.'

Of himself, Edward told me, he felt less certain; with a sad wistfulness reminiscent of Maeterlinck's *Prédestinés*, he visualised the early close of his little tale of years in a world rendered too dear and lovely by its rich undertones of music, its soaring pinnacles of sound.

'It would be just part of the irony of life if I don't come back, because I'm such a lover of peace,' he declared, 'but I can never imagine the end of the War or what it'll be like; I believe now it'll last for years and I've no notion what I would do if it were ended.'

That night I sat long and sorrowfully over my diary. 'If it is really to go on for years, what shall we do?' I asked it. 'I wonder if courage and endurance will bear the strain?'

At least, I thought, Roland hasn't changed yet. On my table lay the letter in which he had mentioned Asquith – a letter which showed that he still loved me, and still cherished those memories of twelve months ago that seemed like a thousand years.

'Do you remember the Sunday that we walked up and down Fairfield Gardens together and wouldn't come in out of the rain? And I couldn't keep the tears out of my eyes afterwards when Sterndale Bennett played Karg-Elert's "*Clair de Lune*" in the chapel. You were sitting at the back near the door and I couldn't see you without looking round, I remember. It all seems so far away now. I sometimes think I must have exchanged my life for someone else's.'

6

Two days before Pass Mods., Norah and I took a punt up the river as far as Water Eaton. After that term I never saw her again; she went down to join a motor-cycle corps, and subsequently married a Serbian artist without returning to Somerville.

We took our dinner with us and stayed out till twilight. I felt that I liked her, and Oxford, more than – apart from the ignorant dreams of 1913 – I had ever cared for either before; I realised then how precious individuals and places become the moment that the possibility of leaving them turns into fact. No evening on the river had held a glamour equal to that one, which might so well be the last of all such enchanted evenings. How beautiful they seemed – the feathery bend with its short, stumpy willows, the deep green shadows in the water under the bank, the blue, brilliant mayflies which somersaulted in the air and fell dying into the water, gleaming like strange, exotic jewels in the mellow light of the setting sun.

Lying on our backs in the sunshine, we talked of our literary ambitions, of the War, of nursing, of going down for a time and never, perhaps, coming back. The lovely Oxford summer filled me with regret. I had meant to do such wonderful things that year, to astonish my fellows by unprecedented triumphs, to lay the foundations of a reputation that would grow ever greater and last me through life; and instead the War and love had intervened, and between them were forcing me away with all my confident dreams unfulfilled. For me, as for Roland, all that I had worked so hard to win had been turned by 1914 into dust and ashes. Should I ever return to Oxford, I wondered – ever really belong there? The water, still almost as metal, shone like molten gold as we punted homewards.

On the 17th of June, my four friends accompanied me, for luck, to the gates of All Souls. As the Examination Schools had been transformed into a hospital, the Codrington Library was temporarily dedicated to the baser uses of Pass Moderations – for which, in spite of the War, fifty men and only four women had entered. At one time its vicissitudes would have filled pages of my diary, but since this was now almost entirely occupied with Roland and his letters, my luck in the examination was relegated to a few hasty lines at the close of each day's entry.

'I can't help thinking all this week,' I wrote to him, 'how charming you would have been to me over Pass Mods., and how tactfully condescending. You would have left your level of forty-eight books of Homer to talk to me about my five without even relapsing into the Quiet Voice. And I should have felt that it wasn't quite so absurd as I thought to try and do Pass Mods. on nine months' Greek. But now you are not here to show me the condescension which I once so teased you about and now would give anything to meet with again, face to face, even in its most blatant form, and it matters little enough whether it is absurd to do Pass Mods. or not.'

By way of compensating him for my heretical indifference to the loveliness of Greek – a loveliness that came back to me in quieter days, more potent than life, more permanent than war – I enclosed with my letter the cutting of a recent *Times* leader which had encouraged me to hope for the future resurrection of pre-war literary values. It was called 'The Unsubmerged City', and began as follows:

'A medieval fancy that still lingers, ghost-like, on the more lonely sea-shores, such as that Breton one so tenderly described by Renan, is the legend of the submerged city. It lies out there barely hidden under the waves, and on a still summer eve they say you may hear the music of its Cathedral bells. One day the waters will recede and the city in all its old beauty be revealed again. Might this not serve to figure the actual conditions of literature, in the nobler sense of the term, submerged as that seems to many to be by the high tide of war? Thus submerged it seemed, at any rate, to the most delicate of our literary artists, who was lately accounting for his disused pen to an aggrieved friend. 'I have no heart,' he said, 'for literature in this war; we can only have faith that it is still there under the waters, and will some day re-emerge.' . . . There is fortunately no truth in the idea of a sunken literature. A function of the spirit, it can never be submerged, or, indeed, as much as touched by war or any other external thing. It is an inalienable possession and incorruptible part of man.'

Somehow, during the rest of that week, I did give my mind to Logic and Latin, to Proses and Unseens, to Homer's *Iliad* and Plato's *Apologia*. To keep my thoughts on the examination at all seemed something of an achievement, for in the middle of it came a letter from Roland, which after beginning: 'I am feeling somewhat *ennuyé* and very far from bellicose at the moment. One never seems to get much forrarder, and I never was a very patient individual, as you may have found out by now – too ardent an admirer of the meteoric, with an innate abhorrence of gathering moss,' concluded with a small, significant postscript: 'It is just possible that I may get six days' leave in the near future.'

If only it can be soon, I thought, absorbed by realistic visions of our meeting instead of revising the *Meno*; if only it can really happen! 'Sometimes I have felt that I would forgive the future if it would only bring him to me once again . . . At other times I have thought I couldn't bear to see him till the War is over, that though I am out for hard things there is just one I could not endure, and that is to live over again the early morning of March 19th on Buxton station. But now that there is a chance I may have to do it, I know it is worth while.'

The last week-end, which I had dreaded for its sadness, vanished away in rapt anticipations and a frantic round of farewells. Alone, since nearly all my friends had already departed, discreetly wishing me good luck in a relationship of which I had never actually spoken, I spent a final hour in New College Garden, visited Merton Chapel as an act of piety to Roland, and went to yet one more Cathedral service, where I tried to find an omen of hope in the closing words of the anthem:

And sorrow — and sorrow — shall flee away.

At St Monica's, the obvious refuge for the two days between my last paper and the Viva Voce, my mother's delicate and charming brother, known to the family as 'Uncle Bill', endeavoured to encourage me with reassuring news about the progress of the War. To his sorrow and secret shame, for it prevented him from enlisting, he held a 'key' position at the head office of the National Provincial Bank in Bishopsgate, and was believed by all of us to have secret access to official sources of information. Lemberg, he told me cheerfully, was about to fall; the French would have the Germans 'on the run' as soon as they had taken Souchez; *The Times*'s attack on Kitchener and its perturbation over munitions were only a 'put-up job' to persuade our men into making armaments for the Russians; a steel net stretched across the Channel north of all the Continental routes enabled our ships to run between England and France in absolute safety.

They sound ludicrous enough now, these rumours, these optimisms, these assurances, to us who still wonder why, in spite of all our incompetence, we managed to 'win' the War. But at the time they helped us to live. I cannot, indeed, imagine how long we should have succeeded in living without them.

'It seems years and years since I was here — more like thirteen than three,' I wrote to Roland, sitting at one of the windows from which as a child I had meditated over the dark outline of the Surrey Downs, curving serenely beneath the pale night skies of far-off care-free summers. 'Everything before the War seems centuries ago; I told my headmistress that I felt about thirty, and

she said that the War did have that effect on anyone who realised
it at all, but how very glad I should be when the War was over
and I woke up from the nightmare to find that I was only twenty-
three or twenty-four after all. Shall I ever, my dear, shall I ever?
It is not I myself that can bring me that awakening.'

The next day, after the Viva, I soon learnt that I was safely
through Pass Mods., and with a sigh of relief at having satisfactorily rounded off a phase of life, I caught the last train to Buxton.
Had I failed to pass the examination my entire post-war future
would certainly have been different, but at the time the significant
little success seemed less important than a letter which I found at
home from Roland's mother, telling me how strongly she approved
of my decision to become a nurse. Roland had told her that I
hoped after a time to get out to France, and she felt sure I knew
as well as she did that if one had an original mind and something
of ambition, it was not by poring over books that one grew and
developed. One's intellect, she said, could always take care of itself.
It was one's personality that counted, and that could be better
nourished sometimes in active life than in halls of learning.

It was a point of view that I was ready most enthusiastically
to endorse. Learning, for the moment, had certainly been pushed
into the background by life.

7

On Sunday morning, June 27th, 1915, I began my nursing at the
Devonshire Hospital. The same date, exactly ten years afterwards,
was to be, for me, equally memorable. Between the one day and
the other lies the rest of this book.

From our house above the town I ran eagerly downhill to my
first morning's work, not knowing, fortunately for myself, that my
servitude would last for nearly four years. The hospital had originally been used as a riding-school, but a certain Duke of Devonshire,
with exemplary concern for the welfare of the sick but none whatever for the feet of the nursing staff, had caused it to be converted
to its present charitable purpose. The main part of the building
consisted of a huge dome, with two stone corridors running one

above the other round its quarter-mile circumference. The nurses were not allowed to cross its diameter, which contained an inner circle reserved for convalescent patients, so that everything forgotten or newly required meant a run round the circumference. As kitchens, sink-rooms and wards all led off the circular corridors and appeared to have been built as far from one another as possible, the continuous walking along the unresistant stone floors must have amounted, apart from the work itself, to several miles a day.

My hours there ran from 7.45 a.m. until 1 p.m., and again from 5.0 p.m. until 9.15 p.m. – a longer day, as I afterwards discovered, than that normally required in many Army hospitals. No doubt the staff was not unwilling to make the utmost use of so enthusiastic and unsophisticated a probationer. Meals, for all of which I was expected to go home, were not included in these hours. As our house was nearly half a mile from the hospital on the slope of a steep hill, I never completely overcame the aching of my back and the soreness of my feet throughout the time that I worked there, and felt perpetually as if I had just returned from a series of long route marches.

I never minded these aches and pains, which appeared to me solely as satisfactory tributes to my love for Roland. What did profoundly trouble and humiliate me was my colossal ignorance of the simplest domestic operations. Among other 'facts of life', my expensive education had omitted to teach me the prosaic but important essentials of egg-boiling, and the Oxford cookery classes had triumphantly failed to repair the omission. I imagined that I had to bring the saucepan to the boil, then turn off the gas and allow the egg to lie for three minutes in the cooling water. The remarks of a lance-corporal to whom I presented an egg 'boiled' in this fashion led me to make shamefaced inquiries of my superiors, from whom I learnt, in those first few days, how numerous and devastating were the errors that it was possible to commit in carrying out the most ordinary functions of everyday life. To me, for whom meals had hitherto appeared as though by clockwork and the routine of a house had seemed to be worked by some invisible mechanism, the complications of sheer existence were nothing short of a revelation.

Despite my culinary shortcomings, the men appeared to like me; none of them were very ill, and no doubt my youth, my naïve eagerness and the clean freshness of my new uniform meant more to them than any amount of common sense and efficiency. Perhaps, too, the warm and profoundly surprising comfort that I derived from their presence produced a tenderness which was able to communicate back to them, in turn, something of their own rich consolation.

Throughout my two decades of life, I had never looked upon the nude body of an adult male; I had never even seen a naked boy-child since the nursery days when, at the age of four or five, I used to share my evening baths with Edward. I had therefore expected, when I first started nursing, to be overcome with nervousness and embarrassment, but, to my infinite relief, I was conscious of neither. Towards the men I came to feel an almost adoring gratitude for their simple and natural acceptance of my ministrations. Short of actually going to bed with them, there was hardly an intimate service that I did not perform for one or another in the course of four years, and I still have reason to be thankful for the knowledge of masculine functioning which the care of them gave me, and for my early release from the sex-inhibitions that even to-day – thanks to the Victorian tradition which up to 1914 dictated that a young woman should know nothing of men but their faces and their clothes until marriage pitchforked her into an incompletely visualised and highly disconcerting intimacy – beset many of my female contemporaries, both married and single.

In the early days of the War the majority of soldier-patients belonged to a first-rate physical type which neither wounds nor sickness, unless mortal, could permanently impair, and from the constant handling of their lean, muscular bodies, I came to understand the essential cleanliness, the innate nobility, of sexual love on its physical side. Although there was much to shock in Army hospital service, much to terrify, much, even, to disgust, this day-by-day contact with male anatomy was never part of the shame. Since it was always Roland whom I was nursing by proxy, my attitude towards him imperceptibly changed; it became less romantic and more realistic, and thus a new depth was added to my love.

In addition to the patients, I managed to extract approval from most of the nurses – no doubt because, my one desire being to emulate Roland's endurance, I seized with avidity upon all the unpleasant tasks of which they were only too glad to be relieved, and took a masochistic delight in emptying bed-pans, washing greasy cups and spoons, and disposing of odoriferous dressings in the sink-room. The Matron – described as 'a slave-driver' by one of the elegant lady V.A.D.s who intermittently trotted in to 'help' in the evenings after the bulk of the work was done – treated me with especial kindness, and often let me out through her private gate in order to save me a few yards of the interminable miles upon my feet.

My particular brand of enthusiasm, the nurses told me later, was rare among the local V.A.D.s, most of whom came to the hospital expecting to hold the patients' hands and smooth their pillows while the regular nurses fetched and carried everything that looked or smelt disagreeable. Probably this was true, for my diary records of one Buxton girl a month later: 'Nancy thinks she would like to take up Red Cross work but does not want to go where she would have to dust wards and clean up as she does not think she would like that.'

On my first day at the hospital, a Scottish sergeant produced a comment of which the stark truth came finally home to me three summers afterwards.

'We shall beat them,' he said, 'but they'll break our hearts first!'

This same man told me a story – later guaranteed as true by Roland – which once again convinced me of the futility of war between men who (as I was beginning to realise even amid the bloodthirsty armchair patriotism so rampant in England just then) bore no grudge against one another.

Once, he said, when they were opposite the Saxons near Ypres, they and the enemy made a mutual agreement not to shoot one another. In order to appear active they continued to use their rifles, but fired into the air. Occasionally they met and talked in the space between the trenches, and when, finally, the Saxons had to change places with the Prussian Guards, they promised to fire a volley as warning. This promise they faithfully observed.

A few weeks afterwards I was given a variant on this story by a neighbour, who had heard it from a Buxton officer home on sick-leave. A similar truce, he related, had been in progress in another part of the line, where the occupants of the trenches on both sides would take it in turns to work in No Man's Land quite unmolested. In the midst of this truce, the British company commander went sick, and a fire-eating patriot took his place. On the first occasion after his arrival that a group of Saxons left their trenches and placidly began their wire-mending, the fire-eater ordered his company's machine guns to be turned on them. The men had no choice but to obey, and a large number of benevolent Saxons were ignominiously wiped out.

Four out of the five men, said my informant, to whom the young officer told this tale, roared with laughter and called the company commander's action 'a smart piece of work'. So much, I thought, for 'Hun atrocities' – for I was already beginning to suspect, as all my generation now knows, that neither side in wartime has a monopoly of butchers and traitors.

Perhaps it was a subconscious brooding on this story, perhaps a letter from Roland to say that all leave was temporarily cancelled, which gave me a few nights later one of the vividest dreams that I have ever had in my life.

I thought that I was standing, in a large room which looked like a schoolroom, before a table covered with green baize and littered with papers. A crowd of vague men and women pressed in upon me, but I never saw any of them clearly. I knew that I was in grave suspense, and had come there to hear news of some kind. I had not waited long when another shadowy individual came up to the table and said: 'He is dead; he has died of wounds in France.'

Somehow I realised that the people in the room were speaking of Roland; that while they did not know him personally nor even by name, they were aware of his existence and of the relation in which I stood to him. When I heard their messenger's words I was paralysed with the shock that comes when something happens that one has dreaded yet half expected – often a worse shock than that produced by the unforeseen. But I managed to ask my informant: 'How do you know?'

'It's written down,' he told me. 'The name is here,' and he handed me a folded slip of paper. I opened it quickly and there saw, written in unfamiliar but ordinary characters, the name 'Donald Neale'. I knew this to be the name of the man who had died, and almost fainted in the revulsion of feeling. In an agony of relief I cried: 'This isn't his name! It's all a mistake! It isn't true!'

At that moment the alarm-clock that roused me early went off. I awoke feeling very limp, staring at the window and repeating to myself in a kind of ecstasy: 'That wasn't his name! It's all a mistake! It isn't true – thank God!'

8

The excitement of really beginning at last to nurse drove me into a fresh outburst of correspondence with Mina and Betty on the subject of joining up together in an Army hospital in London. Our objective was the 1st London General Hospital in Camberwell, where Mina was supposed to have a friend among the Sisters. Betty's efforts to go there, though serene and amiable, were genuine and consistent, but Mina, whose dawning love-affair with an artist not in the Army had an effect upon her precisely contrary to the fervour for service produced by mine, was unexpectedly elusive when pinned down to the taking of any precise step, and in the end was deterred by an attack of minor illness from nursing at all.

The responses wrested from Red Cross Headquarters at Devonshire House, which I also bombarded with letters, were hardly more illuminating than Mina's distracted replies to requests for first-hand information from London.

'I had an unsatisfactory sort of letter from the Red Cross,' I noted one evening, 'talking vaguely of delays and numerous interviews. British authorities and their red tape are distinctly depressing. Strange that they should plead for volunteers and then make it as unpleasant as possible for you when you have volunteered.'

Ultimately I had to get a day's leave to go up to London, for I knew that the Buxton Red Cross Society, which believed its little convalescent hospital in Higher Buxton to provide the only kind of nursing that any polite young woman could wish for, would never do anything drastic or send me anywhere. So, as the first step towards getting into a London hospital, I went to Paddington to join Mina's Voluntary Aid Detachment, London 128, and, as I had already passed my First Aid and Home Nursing examinations, was enrolled as a full-fledged member of the British Red Cross.

In July, when I seemed already to have been nursing for months, my peaceful relations with the Devonshire Hospital staff were disturbed by the arrival of a new Sister-in-Charge. No doubt ideal nurses were difficult to obtain at that time by civilian hospitals, even with their complement of soldiers, for the new arrival was not precisely an example of the Nightingale tradition at its best. A weather-beaten, dry little woman, with hard brown eyes and a fussy manner, she had a habit of tight-lacing which made her appear aggressively out of proportion. Her aitches, though right numerically, were wrongly distributed, and I had difficulty in maintaining the correct expression of disciplined composure when she forcibly inquired, as she did every evening: 'Narse! Have you given 'Ibbert his haspirin?'

When she wanted to address me she always shouted 'Narse!' except when she tried to use my name. This she invariably got wrong, although it seemed to me simple enough to remember – particularly in wartime, when we were all so patriotic. Her distrust of V.A.D. probationers was evident from the first, but was counterbalanced by a determination even greater than my own to make me maid-of-all-work.

'I've been a narse for seventeen yahs and a Sistah for twelve,' she informed me ominously when I protested at being told for the second time to dust a ward which, as part of the ordinary morning's routine, had been finished hours before.

'Really,' I wrote to Roland, 'if feminism gains a hearing after this War is over, the leaders of the movement will have to be picked and chosen, I think the kind that shout and order about and find fault will have to be eliminated.'

For a few days – since I not unnaturally evaded the new Sister as much as possible – the hospital rang with cries of 'Narse! Narse! Where's that little V.A. narse! Why can't *she* sweep this floor – or make this bed – or empty this bucket?' – or whatever the particular job happened to be. Whenever my morning's work was unusually heavy, I would hear her pattering after me.

'Narse! Have you a minute to spah?'

'I'm sorry, Sister,' I would reply, looking as busy as possible, 'but I've an awful lot to get through this morning.'

'Oh, *nevah* mind!' would come her affronted response; 'I'll get one of the othah narses to do it!'

Fortunately for my peace, she and the house-surgeon – a dapper little man with bandy legs and a serious long-nosed countenance – gradually became sworn enemies, and the faster their mutual antipathy increased, the longer they appeared to spend in frantically looking for one another.

From the Sister as from other incidental irritations, I sought, as usual, refuge in my letters to Roland.

'Reminiscences again!' I reproached myself on the anniversary of Speech Day. 'These are the prerogative of the old, aren't they, not of the young! But one lives so much in the past when the future is all blank and dim. Recollection is the privilege of the aged rather than of youth because when one is young one is supposed to have definite things to look forward to all the time. Sometimes I feel as if I were anticipating the point of view I may have when, if I live, I shall be old. The future of old age must look something like this, and that is why it delights them so to remember . . .

'You will be amused to hear,' I continued more cheerfully, 'that I am making myself quite hardened to blackbeetles – of which there are batches in various places in hospital.' (There had also been a number at Micklem Hall, and about these I was not at all brave.) 'Last night when I was washing up cups in the surgical kitchen they were running about the floor and tumbling over one another in the sink. I didn't run away, I just fastened my skirt up and went on washing the cups. I consider that as quite the most heroic thing I have done since the War started. To-night I raced round after them with the inevitable Keatings. To switch off on to quite a different subject, have you ever read Stephen Phillip's *Christ in Hades*?'

From trenches in which blackbeetles must have appeared an extremely desirable alternative to their most numerous inhabitants, he replied with one of those letters which I specially treasured for their vivid evidence that the Roland I loved was still very much alive.

'The sky was wonderful as we came along an hour ago – deep blue with mackerel spots of light gold clouds in the west meshed like chain armour on a blue ground, and below in the horizon a long bar of cloud so dark as to look purple against the sun. Why are sunsets more beautiful normally than sunrise?'

I remembered, as I read his description, the melancholy, colourful fragment of a poem which he had written just before the War.

> *And so, farewell. All our sweet songs are sung,*
> *Our red rose-garlands withered;*
> *The sun-bright day—*
> *Silver and blue and gold*
> *Wearied to sleep.*
>
> *The shimmering evening, like a grey, soft bird,*
> *Barred with the blood of sunset,*
> *Has flown to rest*
> *Under the scented wings*
> *Of the dark-blue Night.*

Would he ever write any more such poems, I wondered, a little uncertain whether it had not been cruel of me to send him the volume of Rupert Brooke on which he now commented with so bitter a sense of achievement postponed.

'It makes me ... want to sit down and write things myself instead of doing what I have to do here. It stirs up the old forgotten things,

and makes me so, so angry and impatient with most of the soulless
nonentities one finds around one here. I used to talk of the Beauty
of War; but it is only War in the abstract that is beautiful. Modern
warfare is merely a trade, and it is only a matter of taste whether
one is a soldier or a greengrocer, as far as I can see. Sometimes by
dint of an opportunity a single man may rise from the sordidness
to a deed of beauty; that is all.'

Anxiously I endeavoured to restore his confidence in the ultimate survival of the 'old forgotten things'.

'It is Europe's fault, not ours, that we have grown to a preco-
cious bitterness, and learnt that glamour fades, and that behind
that glamour grim realities lie . . . But don't despair – dear child!
Even War must end some time, and perhaps if we are alive in
three or four years' time, we may recover the hidden childhood
again and find that after all the dust and ashes which covered it
haven't spoilt it much.'

9

In spite of periodic encounters with the Sister, my new life brought
me tranquillity to exactly the extent that it diverted my mind
from the letter that had not come or the telegram that might be
coming. Going home in the warm dusk one evening I asked
myself rather naïvely: 'What *do* I think about when I am doing
my work at the hospital?' and came to the conclusion that the
answer was: 'Nothing whatever, except the thing that I am going
to do next.' Such mental quiescence, I told Roland, was more
than worth the fatigue involved.

'I thought to myself as I was wandering round with ten pints
of milk and sixteen cups on a heavy wooden tray, "You're nothing
but a thing that work is squeezed out of – a drudge, a time-
machine, toiling by the clock along a stereotyped routine." . . .
Nevertheless, sometimes when I am making extremely untidy
beds in the morning, or boiling water for Bovril in the dim little
kitchen in the evening . . . I see it all in a kind of golden glow
and I feel strangely thrilled inside and whisper to myself exult-
ingly: "War knows no power."'

When a fortnight passed in which no letter came from Roland at all, I was glad to have attached myself so securely to the hospital.

'If it were not for the nursing I do not know how I could bear this,' I confessed. 'I feel as if I couldn't go on much longer without news of some sort, and yet it is no good feeling like that because one *has* to go on, come what may . . . I often wonder just how I should take it if I heard he was dead. Sometimes my heart feels very tumultuous, full of passion and fierce desire; at others it is possessed by a sort of blank and despairing resignation to what one feels must be inevitable. And – when I think of all that brilliant life could do and be, I scarcely know how to contain my bitter and anguished feelings.'

The only way to contain them was by work, and I flung myself into the more sordid and tedious obligations of nursing with the fervour of a religious devotee. Never had I worked so furiously even before the Somerville scholarship; my days gave me a new insight into the lives of women who had always to toil in this way for mere maintenance, and at night I was often so tired that the entries in my diary are almost indecipherable. But for Roland I reserved half-hours of tranquillity from the hard, monotonous days; even when I did not hear from him for a long, anxious period, I endeavoured, as I believed he was endeavouring for me, to preserve the integrity of the self that he had loved

'Like no one else,' I told him in a letter written at the end of July, 'you share that part of my mind that associates itself mostly with ideal things and places . . . The impression thinking about you gives me is very closely linked with that given me by a lonely hillside or a sunny afternoon or wind on the moorlands or rich music . . . or books that have meant more to me than I can explain, or the smell of the earth after a shower or the calmness of the sky at sunset . . . This is grand, but still it isn't enough for this world, whatever it may be like "when we're beyond the sun". The earthly and obvious part of me longs to see and touch you and realise you as tangible.'

To console myself, I concluded, I had been re-reading one of our favourite fragments from W. E. Henley's *Bric-à-Brac*:

What is to come we know not. But we know
That what has been was good – was good to show,
Better to hide, and best of all to bear.
We are the masters of the days that were:
We have lived, we have loved, we have suffered . . . even so.
Shall we not take the ebb who had the flow?
Life was our friend. Now, if it be our foe—
Dear, though it spoil and break us! – need we care
What is to come?

A day or two afterwards, Edward arrived home for a long leave which seemed likely to be his last; it was now possible, he told us with his usual serene aloofness, that the 11th Sherwood Foresters might be ordered to the Persian Gulf. 'Mother,' I noted, 'wants him and me to have a snapshot taken together – I say as a typical example of two people (one at any rate for the first time in her life) who-are-doing-just-what-other-people-think-they-ought!'

Together Edward and I looked at *The Times* History of the War, picked out a newspaper paragraph stating that the total estimate of European war casualties was already five million dead and seven million wounded, and studied with care the first official account of Neuve Chapelle.

'It is quite impossible to understand,' I commented afterwards, 'how we can be such strong individualists, so insistent on the rights and claims of every human soul, and yet at the same time countenance (and if we are English, even take quite calmly) this wholesale murder, which if it were applied to animals or birds or indeed anything except men would fill us with a sickness and repulsion greater than we could endure.'

On the last evening of his leave, we celebrated the first anniversary of the War by a long walk between the dark moorlands up the Manchester Road. Again, as in the garden at Micklem Hall, Edward expressed the haunting premonition that he himself would not survive to see the coming of peace. It wasn't, he said, as though he were a full-fledged and well-known composer; he couldn't see that his life at present was of much use to anyone, including himself. Everything, it seemed, after he had gone the next day, was being taken from me – my future, my work, my lover, and now my brother. Life was melancholy indeed. Even Roland's mother, whose brave communications, dramatically transcribed with a quill pen in gigantic jet-black caligraphy, had often heartened me to face the interminable suspense of days that we both dreaded, for once wrote sadly, commenting on the many letters of sympathy that had now so reluctantly to be sent.

In the middle of August, to conclude three miserable weeks of disappointment, and parting, and anxiety, and depression following the news of the expensive operations at Suvla Bay, the first death that I had ever witnessed occurred at the hospital. Although surprised at my own equanimity, I had not yet acquired the self-protective callousness of later days, and I put into the writing of my diary that evening an emotion comparable to the feeling of shock and impotent pity that had seized Roland when he found the first dead man from his platoon at the bottom of the trench:

'Nothing could have looked more dreadful than he did this morning, lying on his back worn just to skin and bone and a ghastly yellowish colour all over. He lay with his eyes half closed and turned up so that only the whites were showing, and kept plucking at the bed-clothes and pulling them down. It quite made me shudder to see his great bony hands at the end of his thin skeleton arms. He died from a most obscure complaint; they do not know exactly, I think, what it is. I pray that when I come to die it may not be like that. We ought to pray in our litany for deliverance from a lingering as well as from a sudden death. It is not death itself that presents such terrors to the mind but dissolution – and when that begins before death . . . It seems sad that he should die like this in the midst of strangers, with Sister beside him of all people, and no one really to care very much . . . To me it is strange that I take this death – sad as it makes me feel – so much as a matter of course when only a short time ago the idea of death made me shudder and filled me with horror and fear. From the time Nurse Olive related to me the one or two deaths she had been present at and I thought her callous to take it so much as a matter of course, to the time when I take it as a matter of course myself, I must have undergone a great revulsion of mind . . . And now that he is dead, reasonable as I try to be I cannot make myself feel that the individual, whatever it may have been, has really vanished into nothing and *is* not. I merely feel as if it had gone away into another place, and the worn-out shell that the men carried away was not Smith at all.'

10

'Never, never,' begins my diary for August 18th, 'have I been in such agitation before. He has got leave; he is in England now. This morning as I was dusting bedsteads at the hospital Mother came with a wire from Mrs L. to say: "Roland comes home to-day!"'

At midday a telegram sent off from Folkestone by Roland himself came to confirm the news. The afternoon interval of freedom was spent in the usual prolonged endeavour – inevitable owing to the distance between our homes – to get into touch by telegraph or telephone. Finally Roland wired asking if I would meet him next morning at St Pancras, and the Matron, to whose interested ears my mother had already confided the news of our unofficial relationship, gave me leave from the hospital for a long week-end.

No one, this time, suggested going with me to London; already the free-and-easy movements of girl war-workers had begun to modify convention. So I went up to town by the early train, to be at last alone with Roland for an uninterrupted day. Feverishly excited as I had been since the previous morning, I found it very difficult to realise that I was actually doing what I had dreamed of for months. To read was quite impossible, and I spent the entire four-hour journey in agitatedly wondering how much he would have altered.

During the few minutes that I had to wait at St Pancras for him to arrive from Liverpool Street, I shivered with cold in spite of the hot August noon. When at last I saw him come into the station and speak to a porter, his air of maturity and sophistication turned me stiff with alarm.

At that stage of the War it was fashionable for officers who had been at the front to look as disreputable and war-worn as possible in order to distinguish them from the brand-new sub-alterns of Kitchener's Army. Not until later, when almost every young officer except eighteen-year-old cadets had been abroad at one time or another, was it *comme il faut* to model one's self the more assiduously on a tailor's dummy the longer one had been in the trenches. Modishly shabby, noticeably thinner and looking at least thirty, Roland on leave seemed Active Service personified.

In another moment we were standing face to face, tense with that anxiety to find one another unchanged which only lovers know at its worst. Just as we had parted we shook hands without any sign of emotion, except for his usual pallor in moments of excitement. For quite a minute we looked at each other without speaking, and then broke awkwardly into polite conversation.

'What shall we do?'

'Oh, I don't know.'

'Don't you think we'd better go and have lunch somewhere?'

'All right, but isn't it a little early?'

'Oh, never mind!'

So we went once again to the Florence, and, on the way there, looked out of opposite windows in the taxi. Even when we had sat down at our table, it was difficult to begin anything – including luncheon. We started to thaw only when I told him that, half waking one morning, I seemed to hear an inner voice saying quite audibly: 'Why do you worry about him? You know he will be all right.'

This information stirred his customary conscious optimism into expression.

'All along I have felt I shan't be killed. In fact I may almost say I *know* it. I quite think I shall be wounded, but that is all.'

And when I recalled how much he had once wanted to go to the Dardanelles, where the casualties were so terrible, he rejoined with gay confidence: 'Oh, I should have come through even there!'

'Your hair's just like a bristly doormat!' I told him inconse-quently, and he endeavoured, quite unsuccessfully, to smooth his close-cropped head with his strong fingers as he remarked that after all he hadn't had such a bad time in France or ever been in specially dangerous trenches.

'In fact,' he concluded, 'in many ways it's quite a nice life!' His one regret appeared to be that his regiment had not yet taken part in even a minor action.

A good deal of that afternoon was spent in discussing how much we should be able to see of each other during my precious week-end. After prolonged argument we agreed that, as my family were expecting me and I had no luggage, he should come back to Buxton with me for the night; I could then, I said, return with him to Lowestoft from Saturday till Monday.

In these maturer years I have often reflected with amazement upon the passionate selfishness of twenty-year-old love. During that brief respite from clamorous danger Roland must have needed, above all things, rest and freedom from noise, yet without compunction I involved him in a series of tedious, clattering journeys. He must have dreamed in crowded dug-outs of the peace and privacy of his bedroom at home, yet later, when I arrived at Lowestoft, I accepted with equanimity the fact that in occupying it I had turned him out to share a room with his brother. Not once did it occur to me – nor even, I believe, to him – that my company was dearly bought at the expense of his comfort.

Into the midst of our discussion of time-tables we sandwiched a visit to Camberwell, for, in spite of the previous day's preoccupations, I had remembered to write for an appointment with the Matron of the 1st London General. A very small woman, grave and immensely dignified, the Matron seemed to me unexpectedly young for such an impressive position.

'I stood,' I recorded afterwards, 'all through the interview, and know now just how a servant feels when she is being engaged.'

'And what is your age, nurse?' the Matron inquired, after hearing the necessary details of my Devonshire Hospital experience.

'Twenty-three,' I replied, promptly but mendaciously, giving the minimum age at which I could be accepted in an Army hospital under the War Office, as distinct from the smaller hospitals run by the Red Cross and the St John Ambulance Brigade. Since I still looked, in the provincial excessiveness of my best coat and skirt, an unsophisticated seventeen, she probably did not believe me, but being a woman of the world she accepted the bold statement at its face value, and promised to apply for me in October as soon as their new huts were ready.

When telegrams had been sent to Buxton and Lowestoft, and the time for returning to St Pancras arrived with surprising suddenness, the thought of parental reactions on both sides became a little subduing. In those days, as we knew well enough, parents regarded it as a bounden duty to speak their minds at every tentative stage of a developing love-affair; they had none of that slightly intimidated respect which modern fathers and mothers feel for the private preoccupations of their self-possessed and casual children.

During dinner in the train we discussed the still critical attitude of the wartime world towards the relations of young men and women, and railed against society for its rude habit of waking one out of one's dreams. We foresaw a series of 'leaves' in which our meetings would be impeded by suspicion, and our love tormented by ceaseless expectant inquiries. After Derby, for the first time, we had the carriage to ourselves. Almost immediately he came quite close to me and asked, with a queer little smile, half cynical, half shy: 'Would it make things better if we were properly engaged?'

For the remainder of the journey to Buxton we argued on this topic almost to the point of quarrelling. I even told him, I remember, that he had spoilt everything by being so definite, for we both felt thoroughly bad-tempered over the situation into which an elderly, censorious society appeared to have manœuvred us. We did not want our relationship, with its thrilling, indefinite glamour, shaped and moulded into an acknowledged category; we disliked the possibility of its being labelled with a description regarded as 'correct' by the social editor of *The Times*. Most of all, perhaps, we hated the thought of its shy, tender, absorbing progress being 'up' for discussion by relatives and acquaintances.

'A mere boy-and-girl affair between a callow subaltern and a college student! This dreadful War, you know — it makes young people lose their heads so, doesn't it?'

I could hear some of my critical aunts and uncles revelling in the words; for this is the way in which disapproving middle-age invariably describes those young loves which thrill us most splendidly, hurt us most deeply, and remain in our memories when everything else is forgotten.

Eventually we decided to tell Roland's mother that we were engaged 'for three years or the duration of the War', but to say nothing to my family until Roland's leave was over. Exhausted and excited as I was, I felt unable to face either conventional congratulations or the raising of equally conventional obstacles. My father, I was convinced, would want to spend precious moments in asking Roland how he proposed to 'keep' me – an inquiry which I thought both irrelevant and insulting. I was already determined that, whether married or not, I would support myself, preferably by writing, and never become a financial burden to my husband. I believed even then that personal freedom and dignity in marriage were incompatible with economic dependence; I also laboured under the happy delusion that literature was a profession in which self-support was rapidly attainable.

My parents, who not unnaturally expected some explanation for the series of journeys upon which Roland and I proposed to embark together, were obviously puzzled by our silence and by the casual brusquerie with which we treated both them and one another. When, a few days later, I did tell them that we considered ourselves engaged, they received the news with calmness if not with enthusiasm, and protested only about our failure to mention the fact. This *dénouement*, after all, was hardly unexpected, and the War – as my mother by much unobtrusive co-operation had tried to make clear to me – had already begun to create a change of heart in parents brought up in the Victorian belief that the financial aspect of marriage mattered more than any other. The War has little enough to its credit, but it did break the tradition that venereal disease or sexual brutality in a husband was amply compensated by an elegant bank-balance.

Throughout our few hours in Buxton and again on the way back to London, Roland and I remained cold and rather formal with one another. We did discuss, very earnestly, the relation between love's spiritual elements and its physical basis, but in 1915 such a conversation was calculated to increase perversity and embarrassment rather than to remove them, and we almost welcomed the interruption provided by a luncheon that we had arranged with Edward and Victor at the St Pancras Hotel.

Dressed in their newest and cleanest uniforms, with sprucely brushed hair and well-polished boots, Victor and Edward, who was still marking time in the southern counties waiting for his final orders, resembled an exceptionally tall Tweedledum and Tweedledee. Roland, with his shabby tunic and worn Sam Browne belt, looked a war-scarred warrior beside them, and over a prolonged meal the two bombarded him with eager, excited questions, which he answered with the calm nonchalance of a professional instructor.

Victor, now almost recovered from the after-effects of his cerebro-spinal meningitis, told us that he, like Roland, had recently been gazetted first lieutenant.

'In my case, though,' he observed appreciatively, 'it was merely for gallant conduct in the hospital.'

Both he and Edward took our engagement entirely for granted – a fact which made their congratulations more tolerable than we had expected. Edward even appeared disappointed that we had not caused a little excitement by a secret and hasty marriage.

'After all,' he remarked, 'you're only giving a name to what has existed for quite a long time.'

11

As the train drew slowly into Lowestoft that evening, my nervousness at the prospect of meeting Roland's family was intensified by the grim strangeness of the shrouded east coast. In the vanishing light the sea was visible only as a vast grey shadow, scarcely distinguishable from smaller shadows of floating cloud in a gently wind-blown sky. Far out to sea, the tiny twinkling eyes of buoys and vessels starred the vague dimness. As we drove through the streets, the faint outlines of the buildings and the muffled stillness broken only by the smooth wash of the waves on the shore, gave the curious impression of a town wrapped in fog. Until his parents' house appeared, a warm refuge from the colourless twilight, all that I could see reminded me of the dreamy, intangible world of Pierre Loti's *Pêcheur D'Islande*.

Tall and round and turret-like, the house, Heather Cliff, had been built with an immense number of seaward-looking windows. As it stood alone near a machine-gun station at the extreme end of the town, it provided a conspicuous landmark for ships far out to sea; consequently no lights were permitted except in the few back rooms, and the whole family lived in a state of semi-preparation for departure in case Zeppelin raids and possible bombardments should prove too disturbing to literary production.

It was somewhat disconcerting to be shown into a pitch-dark house and instantly surrounded by vague, alarming figures – the vital mother, the unknown father, and, perhaps most intimidating of all, the two adolescents, Roland's seventeen-year-old sister and his fourteen-year-old naval cadet brother. These two, I felt sure, would display either exaggerated tact or youthful imperviousness to 'atmosphere'. Actually, they exhibited both in turn.

Roland's mother received me with warmth and generosity, though she was somewhat perturbed by our flippant announcement that we were engaged 'for three years or the duration of the War'. Love, for her, was something to be gloried in and acknowledged; like so many others, she had not seen enough of the War at first hand to realise how quickly romance was being replaced by bitterness and pessimism in all the young lovers whom 1914 had caught at the end of their teens. But though our sense of love's glamour seemed to her inadequate, I am still glad to remember the eager sympathy with which she so bravely helped me through months of suspense that without her unhesitating acceptance of me would have been unendurable.

In Roland's bedroom, where at last we were allowed a light, she took both my hands and kissed me impulsively.

'Why!' she exclaimed, 'what a tiny thing you are! I didn't realise you were so little. I feel as if I wanted to pick you up and carry you about!'

Roland told me that she said to him afterwards: 'Traditionally, I suppose, I ought to hate her – but I don't.'

His father, whose vigorous red hair and individualistic moustache gave him the appearance of a benevolent Swinburne, extended to me an equally kind though less definite welcome; and later I was to listen with rapt fascination to his tales of literary London and the adventurous journalistic world.

This general glowing warmth of acceptance banished in a few moments my suppressed fear of the household, though after the colourless formality of Buxton society I found somewhat embarrassing the family's habit of frankly discussing personal appearances in front of their owners. But I drank in thirstily the literary gossip which I had never heard before – except in very small snatches from Roland, who, unlike the rest of his family, was not much addicted to this agreeable form of entertainment – and listened spell-bound to his mother's stories 'of her and publishers and their annoying habits'. The whole atmosphere of the house thrilled and delighted me, and made me more than ever conscious of Buxton limitations and my young lady's upbringing.

'Alas! What I have missed,' I wrote, with intolerant regret, 'I who have had to make my spiritual and intellectual way alone! If there is a Law of Compensation perhaps one day I shall find the sweetness I never experienced in giving to a son or daughter of mine that which I myself never received.'

It was a strange week-end. Still inwardly annoyed at having to label ourselves 'engaged', Roland and I were a little angry with one another all the time; the belief that demonstrative affection was expected of us made us both reticent, restless and perverse. Roland, indeed, for the first twenty-four hours seemed to hold himself deliberately aloof from me; five months of active service had intensified in him some ruthless, baffling quality which before had only been there in embryo, and his characteristic air of regarding himself as above the ordinary appeared to have grown. Uneasily I recalled my desperate fear lest he should have changed, lest the War should come between us and thrust me out of his consciousness and his life.

Only once, on the Sunday evening, did we recapture for a few moments the lovely enchantment of New Year's Eve. Sitting together on a heather-covered cliff, looking out at the shadowy sea and the thin veil of sunset mist blotting out the brightness of the sky, we watched twilight deepen into night. Soon the faint, steady gleam of a pale moon blurred the outlines of the cliff and the gorse-bushes, and turned all the world to a luminous grey. Roland discovered that my hands were cold and put his own leather gloves on them; the gloves slipped on without the fastenings having to be undone. Afterwards I remembered so well the feeling of their intimate warmth; 'it was like having all the satisfaction of his touch without the shyness of touching him,' I recorded.

During the day, walking among the wire-entanglements and emergency trenches on the calm, sunny shore, we had discussed the callousness engendered by war both at the front and in hospital, and Roland had said that after several months in France the idea of annihilation, of ceasing to be anything at all, had come to have a great attraction for him. But that evening we spoke very little.

'If I heard you were dead,' I told him after a while, 'my first feeling would be one of absolute disbelief. I can't imagine life without you, now.'

'You'd soon forget,' he said abruptly.

I felt a little sore, and asked: 'Why do you always say that? Do you really think me one of the forgetting sort?'

'No, I'm afraid you're not.'

'I think, Roland,' I went on, 'that if you died I should deliberately set out to marry the first reasonable person that asked me.'

He looked at me questioningly, a little puzzled, so I explained more fully.

'You see, if one goes on obviously mourning someone, other people come along and insist on entering in and pitying and sympathising, and they force one's recollection into one's outward life and spoil it all. But if one seems to have forgotten, the world lets one alone and thinks one is just like everyone else, but that doesn't matter. One lives one's outer life and they see that, but below it lies the memory, unspoiled and intact. By marrying the first reasonable person that asked me, I should thereby be able to keep *you*; my remembrance would live with me always and be my very own. Do you understand a little?'

'Yes,' he replied very gravely, 'I think I understand what you mean.'

'But I won't talk about that now,' I said. 'At least, now, I have you here with me; and nothing else matters.'

And indeed nothing else did seem to matter; for the time being each of us remembered neither the past nor the future, but only the individual and the hour.

Some weeks later he wrote to me from the trenches of that evening, and sent me, copied from the *Westminster Gazette*, a poem by Kathleen Coates called 'A Year and a Day':

I shall remember miraculous things you said
  My whole life through—
Things to go unforgotten till I am dead;
  But the hundredfold, adorable ways of you,
The tilt of your chin for laughter, the turn of your head
  That I loved, that I knew—
Oh! while I fed on the dreams of them, these have fled!

Words which no time can touch are my life's refrain,
  But each picture flies.
All that was left to hold till I meet you again,
  Your mouth's deep curve, your brows where the shadow lies,
These are the things I strive to capture in vain,
  And I have forgotten your eyes,
And the way that your hair spun curls in the beating of rain.

Reminiscent as the lines were, they embodied my own failure of memory as well as his. Try as I would I could never, once we were apart, recollect his face, nor even in the silence of night hear his voice, with its deep notes and its gay, high laugh. I used to think that if, by closing my eyes or sitting in the dark, I could picture his eyes as they looked when I last saw them, or in imagination listen to him speaking, it would not be so hard to be separated. It is years now since I have been able to recall his face, and

I know that, even in dreams, I shall never hear the sound of his voice again.

Except for a few hurried moments, we did not come near to one another after that evening on the cliff. On the Monday – our last day together, for I was due back at the Devonshire Hospital on the Tuesday morning – Roland and his mother and I went up together to London, where he had arranged to spend the rest of his leave. At Heather Cliff he said good-bye to Clare and his brother, and at the station to his father; in spite of these farewells he seemed preoccupied, as though living in an inner world from which experience excluded even those whom he dearly loved.

All day I felt inordinately tired, and so, I think, did Roland. His mother and I had sat up till 3 a.m. the previous night talking about him and our possible future; we had been obliged to get up early to catch the London train, so that none of us had spent more than three hours in bed. Roland and I, weary and depressed, passed most of the day in shops, renewing his equipment for the winter. To the disappointment of his mother, who thought a ring the only true symbol of union between a man and a woman, and to the subsequent surprised incredulity of other engaged Buxton girls – who used to remove their gloves in church in order to display a diamond half-hoop on the conspicuous third finger of their left hands – we both reacted violently against the idea of an engagement ring, Roland saying that he 'detested the obvious', and I fiercely determined to exhibit no 'token of possession'. I could not endure the thought of displaying a conventional jewel in order to indicate to other men that I was 'appropriated' and to suggest to other women that I had won a long-sought prize after a successful hunt; it seemed too typical of the old inequality.

Throughout the remaining hours the shadow of the approaching end of day – and perhaps of so much more – lay heavily upon us. I made Roland go to Dunlop's and choose himself a pipe, and he bought me an extravagant bouquet of deep red roses, but despite these lover-like transactions we felt jarred and irritated by the knowledge that the little time left to us had to be spent in the noise and tantalising publicity of shops and streets. At Savory & Moore's he restocked his medical case with morphia;

I was glad, later, to remember that he had bought a good supply.

After tea – for both of us a sullen, subdued meal, at which we had joined his mother and an old novelist friend – I had to go to St Pancras to catch my train back to Buxton. I felt sadder and more listless than ever; so much that I had meant to say to him was still unsaid, and yet it seemed of no use to say anything more. He told me at last, very bitterly, that he didn't want to go back to the front; he had come to loathe its uncongenial monotony, and this glimpse of England and 'real life' had made him hate it more than before.

At St Pancras there was no empty carriage in which we could talk for the few moments left to us, so we had perforce to walk up and down the noisy platform, saying nothing of importance, and ferociously detesting the cheerful, chattering group round my carriage door.

'I wish to God there weren't other people in the world!' he exclaimed irritably.

'I agree,' I said, and remarked wearily that I should have to put up with their pleasant company in a lighted dining-car all the way to Buxton.

'Oh, *damn!*' he responded.

But when, suddenly, the shriek of the whistle cut sharply through the tumult of sound, our resolution not to kiss on a crowded platform vanished with our consciousness of the crowd's exasperating presence. Too angry and miserable to be shy any more, we clung together and kissed in forlorn desperation.

'I shan't look out of the window and wave to you,' I told him, and he replied incoherently: 'No – don't; I can't!'

To my amazement, taut and tearless as I was, I saw him hastily mop his eyes with his handkerchief, and in that moment, when it was too late to respond or to show that I understood, I realised how much more he cared for me than I had supposed or he had ever shown. I felt, too, so bitterly sorry for him because he had to fight against his tears while I had no wish to cry at all, and the intolerable longing to comfort him when there was no more time in which to do it made me furious with the frantic pain of impotent desire.

And then, all at once, the whistle sounded again and the train started. As the noisy group moved away from the door he sprang on to the footboard, clung to my hand and, drawing my face down to his, kissed my lips in a sudden vehemence of despair. And I kissed his, and just managed to whisper 'Good-bye!' The next moment he was walking rapidly down the platform, with his head bent and his face very pale. Although I had said that I would not, I stood by the door as the train left the station and watched him moving through the crowd. But he never turned again.

12

I suppose, as I took a seat in the dining-car, that I must have had some dinner that evening, but I remember nothing of the next four hours; I only became conscious of myself when I had to change into the local train at Miller's Dale station. It was getting on for midnight, and a cold moon, bland and indifferent, gleamed above the deep blue hills. As I looked dazedly at their familiar outline they seemed to say to me: 'You're changed! Everything's changed!'

At home I found an upset which I would have given, on that evening of all others, the world to avoid – an upset which reminded me that in wartime, even more than usual, life was just one damned thing after another. The parlour-maid met my train at Buxton with the news that a wire had come earlier in the day from Edward; his battalion was ordered to leave for France that night, and my parents had rushed off to Farnham to say good-bye. Cold and unutterably fatigued as I was, I entered the desolate house sick with the consciousness that fate was simultaneously sending into danger the two human beings for whom I cared most deeply. If only I had known, I thought wretchedly, I could easily have gone to Farnham too; Edward just *would* be sent to the front on the one day that I was inaccessible by telegram.

Though the three maids had been unoccupied all evening, not one of them offered to help me unpack or to get me a cup of tea, and I was far too much absorbed in my misery to ask them for anything. Shivering, and beyond description lonely, I huddled senselessly over my suitcase, too tired to cry, to unpack, or to go to bed. There seemed to be nothing left in the world, for I felt that Roland had taken with him all my future and Edward all my past. So instead of trying to sleep I sat down at my desk and began a letter to Roland.

'I can only express the feeling that this deserted house gives me to-night by the word *désolée* – it was something less passive than depression and more active than loneliness . . . I am trying to recall the warmth and strength of your hands as they held mine on the cliff at Lowestoft last night. So essentially You. It is all such a dream. Often as I have come home by the late train I have seen the moonlight shining over the mountains, but it has never looked quite the same as it did to-night . . . I should have been really thankful if I could have gone away somewhere and cried. *Mais – que voulez-vous?* One does not cry in a brightly lighted dining-car full of Philistines. One studies the menu and pretends one enjoys one's dinner. And later when the Philistines are sleepy and well fed, one gazes into the blue darkness, and dreams of the dream, and one's eyes hurt, but one is too sore by that time for tears to heal.'

The whole of the next day in hospital had the grim, mechanical vagueness of a nightmare. In the afternoon came a tiny note from Roland, which bitterly renewed the passion of impotent grief that had seized me on St Pancras Station.

'I could not look back, dear child,' it began; 'I should have cried if I had. I am writing this in a stationary taxi drawn up in a corner of Russell Square. The driver thinks I am a little mad, I think, to hire him and then only sit inside without wanting to go anywhere at all. But although it is past dinner-time I cannot bring myself to go . . . I don't know what I want to do and don't care for anything except to get you back again . . .'

That same evening my parents came home, tired and exasperated, to tell me that after all they had been to Farnham on a futile errand. Some at least of the previous night's desolation might have been avoided, for though Edward's regiment had gone to France, he himself, with eight other supernumerary subalterns – including the friend with whom he had long shared billets – had been left behind to be attached to the 13th Reserve Battalion.

Edward attributed this omission of himself to the fact that his elderly commanding officer disliked him. In a despondent letter to Roland – which Roland afterwards sent me in the hope that it might explain a little the unsatisfactory situation – he expressed in no uncertain terms his opinion of the sceptical C.O., and went on sadly: 'I suppose it is no good being depressed and I suppose the future will disclose something good in the end. As you say the difficulties the Triumvirate has had in trying to do that most ordinary thing which men call fighting for your country have been most gigantic – difficulties in getting a commission, delay caused by illness, and my insuperable difficulties in trying to get out.'

The decision to leave Edward behind – although, as he said, he was among neither the eight most junior nor the eight most incompetent officers – no doubt provided a form of humiliation very gratifying to the colonel's prejudice, for it was a bitter experience to be sent to Lichfield while the 11th Battalion, with a large number of new officers who did not know their men, went to the front. With a heavy heart Edward watched the platoon that he had commanded for nine months leave Farnham for France. On hearing the news I secretly concluded, without surprise or distress, that my musical and peace-loving brother was probably no soldier, but events were to prove me completely mistaken.

As we were all three too tired to be anything but laconic, I told my parents, without preface, of my engagement to Roland. Having accepted the fact with less perturbation than I had feared, they decided to make it public, and though I argued successfully against a *Times* announcement, I could not prevent my jealously guarded privacy of heart from being invaded during the next few weeks by the grotesque congratulatory observations of relatives and friends.

'Rowland, by everyone's account, seems a very nice sensible young fellow,' commented my grandmother, but I forgave this singular conglomeration of inaccuracies more readily than the unjustified conclusions of the aunt who wrote: 'I hear that but for this terrible War he would now be at Oxford. This explains to me your eagerness to go to college!'

'I can't help feeling rather sad,' I remarked to him, 'when I think that either very few people indeed have ever really loved, or else they have quite forgotten what they felt like when they did.'

In the meantime my letters from the 'nice young fellow' continued to be very far from 'sensible'.

'Everything now gives me a dust and ashes feeling since you are gone,' he wrote on his last day in London. 'In a way I am glad that I am going back to-morrow. If I cannot be with you I prefer to be as far away as possible . . . And not being able to, I feel an insane desire to rush back to France before I need, and leave all to memory only.'

Back again in billets, he continued in a similar strain. 'And now it seems to count for so little that I did come back after all, so little that I saw and talked with what was no longer a dream but a reality, and found in My Lady of the Letters a flesh-and-blood Princess . . . I am feeling very weary and very, very *triste* – rather like (as is said of Lyndall) "a child whom a long day's play has saddened." . . . There is sunshine on the trees in the garden and a bird is singing behind the hedge. I feel as if someone had uprooted my heart to see how it was growing.'

As August slipped imperceptibly into September, his letters dominated the days. For two or three weeks one came almost every morning or evening, and my nursing dropped into the background like Pass Moderations earlier in the year – though there were moments when I regretted a little ruefully the lost tranquillity of steady work undisturbed by passionate preoccupations.

'I could have done so well without love – before it came – I with my ambitions and life work . . .' I wrote in my diary. 'I shall never again now be able to work towards worldly triumphs with the same disinterested concentration. It was so pleasant when I had only myself to care for most instead of someone else. My peace of mind is gone for ever – it will never completely return again.'

People talked so foolishly, I thought, about the ennobling effects of suffering. 'No doubt the philosophy that tells you your soul grows through grief and sorrow is right – ultimately. But I don't think this is the case at first. At first, pain beyond a certain point merely makes you lifeless, and apathetic to everything but itself.'

This apathy eclipsed the initial eagerness with which I had set about my work in the hospital; now that Roland's leave was over and there was nothing immediate to look forward to, the endless trudging over stone floors seemed more tiring than ever. My days, I told him, had to be passed in the spirit of Alice Meynell's 'Renouncement':

> I must not think of thee; and, tired yet strong,
> I shun the thought that lurks in all delight—
> The thought of thee – and in the blue Heaven's height,
> And in the sweetest passage of a song.
> Oh, just beyond the fairest thoughts that throng
> This breast, the thought of thee waits, hidden yet bright;
> But it must never, never come in sight;
> I must stop short of thee the whole day long.
> But when sleep comes to close each difficult day,
> When night gives pause to the long watch I keep,
> And all my bonds I needs must loose apart,
> Must doff my will as raiment laid away,—
> With the first dream that comes with the first sleep,
> I run, I run, I am gathered to thy heart.

He wrote very tenderly in reply.

'Your photograph . . . is on the table now in front of me, leaning up against the lamp – such a sad two eyes, too, "as if," as Walter Pater says of Leonardo's Gioconda, "upon this little head all the ends of the earth had come." . . . Lyndall's eyes must have been like that. I wonder why I have always thought of you two together . . . It is getting very late. I have been thinking more than writing, I am afraid, and coming to life again, and finding the pen still in my hand. I am going to kiss the photograph good night, as you do the amethyst . . .'

Did my picture really look so sad, I wondered – the small photograph taken just before those Christmas days in London which now seemed such ages ago? It ought to have been, comparatively, a happy photograph, for the fear that was now an insistent anguish had then threatened only as a remote possibility.

'Thoughts and feelings like those . . . of the last few weeks, destroy the first phase of one's youth – its careless happy freshness,' I admitted to him. 'The first thing I noticed about you the other day was that that had gone – if indeed you ever really had it. And I am afraid that all the compensation in the world will not bring it back to either of us ever. When one has known, one can never be again as one was before one knew. But I suppose it's no use weeping over last year's dead leaves. All the tears in the world cannot make them green again. Perhaps when it is all over we shall find that other and better things have taken root in the mould of their dying.'

Early in September, we heard of the first casualty to happen in our family. A cousin from Ireland, we learnt, had died of wounds after the landing at Suvla Bay; the original bullet-wound behind the ear had not been serious, but he had lain untended for a week at Mudros, and was already suffering from cerebral sepsis when operated on, too late, by an overworked surgeon on the crowded *Aquitania*. I had hardly known my cousin, but it was a shock to learn that lives were being thrown away through the inadequacy of the medical services in the Mediterranean. Was it, I wondered, a repetition of Scutari, with no Florence Nightingale to save the situation?

'The shortage of doctors,' I commented, 'must be a tremendous problem – yet when the women doctors they are crying out for now began their training, every possible obstacle was put in their way.'

I did not then know that when the group of medical women who later organised the Scottish Women's Hospitals in France and Serbia had offered their services to the War Office in 1914, they had been told that all that was required of women was to go home and keep quiet. But I felt miserably conscious that, apart from the demand for doctors and nurses, women in war seemed to be at a discount except as the appendages of soldiers. It must have been about this time that I cut out and sent to Roland a remarkable notice in the 'Agony Column' of *The Times*: 'Lady, *fiancé* killed, will gladly marry officer totally blinded or otherwise incapacitated by the War.'

Was that her way of remembering while seeming to have forgotten? I wondered. Was she feeling useless and unwanted, or did she, perhaps, really wish to forget? In sudden fear that, in spite of our conversation on the cliff at Lowestoft, he might think me, too, capable of such a desire, I implored Roland to believe that, whatever happened, I should ask nothing better than remembrance.

'It will not be possible to forget you, Roland, ever, except perhaps in death. For then – about which we both admitted we could come to no conclusion – one may be obliged to forget, even against one's will. I never can understand the Nirvâna ideal – which you sometimes rather rejoice in, don't you? I would rather suffer æons of pain than be nothing . . . I keep getting moments of fierce desire to write something, I don't mind what, except that trifles wouldn't do. Could I write an autobiographical novel, I wonder? Can one make a book out of the very essence of one's self? Perhaps so, if one was left with one's gift stripped bare of all that made it worth having, and nothing else was left . . . It is a cold and cheerless . . . afternoon; the sky is as leaden as if laden with coming snow. I have had a somewhat annoying morning at the hospital, due chiefly to the Sister, who quite by chance and very much against my will heard the other day that I was engaged to you.'

Since that time, I told him, my popularity with this disapproving and vigilant spinster had not exactly increased. 'I wonder,' I concluded, 'if she really thinks me enviable?'

But his reply made me feel that, in spite of so much grief and apprehension, I was, perhaps, enviable after all.

'This afternoon is glowing with the languorous warmth of the dying summer,' he wrote from the trenches. 'The sun is a shield of burnished gold in a sea of turquoise; the bees are in the clover that overhangs the trench – and my superficial, beauty-loving self is condescending to be very conscious of the joy of living. It is a pity to kill people on a day like this. In a way, I suppose, it is a pity to kill people on any kind of day, but opinions – even my own – differ on this subject. Like Waldo I love to sit in the sun, and like him I have no Lyndall to sit with. But it was the last verse of his poem; it is only the first of mine . . . Mother has asked me once or twice lately whether I should like to go into the Regular Army as a profession . . . Now, having hitherto developed the scholastic at the expense of the active, I feel in the spirit of Rafael in Browning's poem that I would far rather win the Military Cross than the Nobel Prize, perhaps because it is the opposite to what most people would expect of me. "What of Rafael's sonnet, Dante's picture?" *Qu'en dis-tu?* . . . I wonder what I should say to you if you came along the trench now and in at the open doorway – I can imagine very well how you would step from the bright sun into the twilight, though I cannot see your face. I don't think I should say anything. I shouldn't be able to. I should probably feel rather like a very shy child at his first party; and just look at you; and you would look at me and through me with your "wet" eyes; and there would be a hopeless inadequacy about it all. I'm sure we should both forget that we had ever been so intimate in our letters. It does seem silly, though, doesn't it? When I have actually seen you intermittently for as long as 17 days!'

13

My sense of being enviable was very short-lived.

As September wore on and the Battle of Loos came nearer, an anxious stillness seemed to settle upon the country, making everyone taut and breathless. The Press and personal letters from France were alike full of anticipation and suspense. Roland wrote vaguely but significantly of movements of troops, of great changes impending, and seemed more obsessed with the idea of death than ever before. One letter describing how he had superintended the reconstruction of some old trenches, was grim with a disgust and bitterness that I had never known him put into words:

'The dug-outs have been nearly all blown in, the wire entanglements are a wreck, and in among the chaos of twisted iron and splintered timber and shapeless earth are the fleshless, blackened bones of simple men who poured out their red, sweet wine of youth unknowing, for nothing more tangible than Honour or their Country's Glory or another's Lust of Power. Let him who thinks War is a glorious, golden thing, who loves to roll forth stirring words of exhortation, invoking Honour and Praise and Valour and Love of Country with as thoughtless and fervid a faith as inspired the priests of Baal to call on their own slumbering deity, let him but look at a little pile of sodden grey rags that cover half a skull and a shin-bone and what might have been Its ribs, or at this skeleton lying on its side, resting half crouching as it fell, perfect but that it is headless, and with the tattered clothing still draped round it; and let him realise how grand and glorious a thing it is to have distilled all Youth and Joy and Life into a fœtid heap of hideous putrescence! Who is there who has known and seen who can say that Victory is worth the death of even one of these?'

Had there really been a time, I wondered, when I believed that it was?

'When I think of these things,' I told him in reply, 'I feel that that awful Abstraction, the Unknown God, must be some dread and wrathful deity before whom I can only kneel and plead for mercy, perhaps in the words of a quaint hymn of George Herbert's that we used to sing at Oxford:

> *Throw away Thy wrath!*
> *Throw away Thy rod!*
> *O my God*
> *Take the gentle path!'*

His next letter, which arrived only two or three days before the battle, spoke even more definitely of some coming cataclysm.

'Away on our left in the French area we could hear what is even at a distance the most terrifying thing on earth – the pounding of heavy guns, now fainter, now louder, but coalescing always into one dull, thundering roar . . . At night the sky was lit with the flashes and flickered strangely with a yellow, restless glow . . . A glorious day, but rather hot for much marching. Am feeling delightfully dilettante and lazy this morning. After all I do agree that it is a pity to kill people in any weather really; though there are some who deserve it. I have sometimes wondered whether I should mind being killed after all, but on days like this I cannot help wanting passionately to live. Life is very attractive, if only as a toy to play with.'

A toy to play with! And to me it appeared a giant to contend with! Waiting for that something which everyone seemed convinced would happen reduced me to a condition not far from insanity. I dreaded going to bed because of the shock of acute realisation with which I awoke every morning, yet when I came back from the hospital I was too tired to sit up. One evening, overcome with fatigue and wretchedness, I flung myself down, fully dressed, on my bedroom floor, and awoke to find myself, sore and stiff, still there at daybreak. Even sleep brought no relief, so restless and disturbed with dreams were the nights. Time – as always in the tense intervals before a great push – seemed to stop moving.

In the afternoon off duty hours of that warm, lovely September I could not sit still, but once again took to my bicycle and rode off to the quiet scenes of the spring's mental wrestlings. The whole of one hot afternoon I spent lying in the half-sleep of tormented delirium on a bank above the riverside path to Miller's Dale, listening to the gurgle of the water as anxiously as though it were the guns in France, and miserably watching the long brown grass on the opposite hillside swaying in the wind.

On Sunday, September 26th, came a brief note from Roland, written three days earlier:

'I have heard nothing definite yet, but they say that all posts will be stopped very soon. *Hinc illæ lacrimæ.* "Till life and all." . . .'

'*Hinc illæ lacrimæ*' was the short Latin sentence which we had agreed that he should use if he knew that he was going into action. Edward, who was on leave with us for the week-end, increased my agitation by telling me that posts had never been stopped since their establishment after the Retreat from Mons. Desperately conscious that he might now never read them, I hurriedly wrote and sent off a few lines to Roland:

'If this word should turn out to be a "*Te moriturum saluto*", perhaps it will brighten the dark moments a little to think how you have meant to someone more than anything ever has or ever will. What you have striven for will not end in nothing, all that you have done and been will not be wasted, for it will be a part of me as long as I live, and I shall remember, always.'

Next day the news came.

'TWO REAL VICTORIES AT LAST!'

announced the *Daily Mail* in exuberant headlines. 'German line pierced in two places! The French and British take 20,000 unwounded prisoners and 33 guns! The Allies have won two splendid victories. The British have advanced 2½ miles on a 5-mile front south of La Bassée.'

Gradually, after a few days in which the awful sluggishness of the hours seemed a specially devised torture of hell, came the usual apologetic modifications of our 'great victory', and, still later, the lists showing the price that we had paid for this sorry achievement. The country, though growing accustomed to horror, staggered at the devastating magnitude of the cost of Loos. Even now, eighteen years afterwards, September 25th remains with July 1st and March 21st, one of the three dates on which the '*In Memoriam*' notices in *The Times* fill the whole of one column and run on into the next. The usual rumour that the 6th Sherwood Foresters had been in the battle threw the whole of Buxton into a state of apprehension, and though, once again, this particular battalion had missed the worst of the fighting, news soon came of young officers killed in action who as boys had been with Edward at his Buxton day-school. But of Roland, still, there was no news at all.

'Dreams, ideals, impersonal visions bow down to-day before this terrible human love,' my diary records, 'and in this hour my heart knows only one prayer.'

And when at last, on October 1st, a letter did come from Roland, it was to tell me that the alarm over which I had agonised had been false after all, and that after twice preparing to go 'over the top', his regiment had escaped the battle.

'Oh, Roland! . . .' I responded; 'that exclamation comprises every comment I have to make on the situation. "Continuation of Allied Offensive," I keep on reading, so I suppose you *are* in it now. But I felt so sure you were in all that awful week-end fighting . . . When you are out there and know what is going on it must be quite impossible to put yourself in the place of people here, who don't know and can't get news. You have no idea what . . . these last few days have been to Mrs L. and me. Perhaps one day you will see the letters we have exchanged on the subject! For my part I have done nothing since Monday . . . but watch the gate, and follow every telegraph boy that went in the direction of our house . . . I am expecting to be called to London any day now. The wounded are beginning to come into England already and there will be a great rush soon.'

The summons, I felt, was near. Instinctively I dreaded it even though I had already recorded in my diary my longing for it to come.

'It will be a relief not to be told I look tired by someone every night. If I don't feel tired it is very annoying, and if I do it is more annoying still.'

One October afternoon I met in the town a visiting Somervillian whose comments on my prospective war-service so roused my indignation as temporarily to divert my thoughts from the still-raging battle.

'This girl,' I told Roland, 'continued to remark rather sarcastically that she supposed I had no ideas of ever going back to Somerville . . . Everyone thinks I have left because I hadn't enough stability to stick to it, and wanted . . . a little excitement. (Fancy nursing being *excitement!*) . . . My late music master actually said to Mother: 'Going down, *is* she? Well, I told you so – I knew she would get tired of it before long.' . . . Sometimes when I think . . . of the Dream-city, with its grey towers and autumn sunsets, and the little room where surrounded by books I used to read

Tess of the D'Urbervilles before a glowing fire at twelve o'clock at night, I can only cry inwardly: 'I *hate* nursing! How tired I am of this War – will it never end!' And then I think of you out there in the danger and the darkness, and the cold and the rain – most precious being, a thousand times more tired of it than I! . . . The latest people who seem to know all about the ending of the War – and they are more depressing than usual – are turning round and making most ingeniously appropriate a prophecy in the Revelation of St John about the beast with seven heads and ten horns (who is of course the Kaiser!) 'and all power was given unto him for two and forty months.' Therefore, say they, the War will end in January 1918. Sounds delightful, doesn't it!'

All that autumn Edward expected to be sent to France to join one of the numerous battalions of Sherwood Foresters already out there; in consequence his 'last leaves' were legion, and on one occasion he invited for the night his now beloved friend from the regiment, a young subaltern whom we all knew as Geoffrey. When that reticent idealist with visions of a clerical career in a slum parish first entered our house, he was so shy that his few remarks were almost inaudible. Geoffrey was too diffident, Edward told me, to be good at dealing with people, and yet his very self-depreciation caused him to be embarrassingly adored by his batmen and his men.

I was not surprised; from the first moment that I saw Geoffrey, I found in his baffling, elusive abruptness an indefinable attraction. He hated war, and though the rôle of poor curate would probably have made him as happy as anyone of his Franciscan temperament could be in a materialistic and self-seeking world, as an officer with the trenches in prospect he became uncertain of his own courage and felt profoundly miserable. Perhaps his most surprising quality was his beauty, which I cannot remember having seen equalled in any young man. Over six feet tall and proportionately broad, he had strongly marked, rather large features, deeply set grey-blue eyes with black lashes, and very thick, wavy brown hair. Owing to the appropriate sequence of his initials, he and Edward were known to the battalion as 'Brit and Gryt'.

'Public opinion has made it,' I remarked to Roland, 'a high and lofty virtue for us women to countenance the departure of such as these and you to regions where they will probably be slaughtered in a brutally degrading fashion in which we would never allow animals to be slaughtered . . . To the saner mind it seems more like a reason for shutting up half the nation in a criminal lunatic asylum!'

The very term in which I had gone up to Somerville and Edward had spent his few weeks in Oxford, Geoffrey had been due there at University College. After following the progress of the new Allied expedition to Salonika, and studying with mixed feelings the competitive journalistic outbursts over the shooting of Nurse Cavell, the three of us read, rather sadly, in *The Times* of October 15th, the customary account of the opening of the Michaelmas Term at Oxford, and speculated whether we should ever again see as students the grey walls clothed in their scarlet robes of autumn creeper. Would Roland, I wondered, read the article in France, and share both the poignancy of our regret and the bitter obstinacy of our determination to go on repudiating the life of scholarship that we had once chosen with such ardent enthusiasm?

On the following day, as if to justify my decision to remain away from college, my orders came from Devonshire House, telling me to report at the 1st London General Hospital, Camberwell, on Monday, October 18th. Simultaneously a card arrived from Betty to say that she too had received orders to go to the same unit. Twenty-four hours later, in the midst of the rapid clearing-up and packing to which I was to grow so tediously accustomed during the next three years, I walked up and down the familiar roads, bidding a hurried good-bye to all the places made dear to me, even in Buxton, by association with Roland. It might be a long time, I thought, before I saw them again, and I was not mistaken, for I have never revisited the town since that Sunday afternoon. The leaves were falling fast, and a misty twilight quenched the autumn tints into greyness. Now that the moment of departure had come, I felt melancholy and a little afraid.

The next morning, soberly equipped in my new V.A.D. uniform, I took for the last time the early train to London, and turned my back for ever upon my provincial young-ladyhood.

CHAPTER V

Camberwell versus Death

TRIOLET

There's a sob on the sea
And the Old Year is dying.
Borne on night wings to me
There's a sob on the sea,
And for what could not be
The great world-heart is sighing.
There's a sob on the sea
And the Old Year is dying.

R. A. L.

1913.

1

After the solid, old-fashioned comfort of the Buxton house, it seemed strange to be the quarter-possessor of a bare-boarded room divided into cubicles by much-washed curtains of no recognisable colour, with only a bed, a washstand and a tiny chest of drawers to represent one's earthly possessions. There was not, I noticed with dismay, so much as a shelf or a mantelpiece capable of holding two or three books; the few that I had brought with me would have to be inaccessibly stored in my big military trunk.

As soon as I had unpacked in the cold, comfortless cubicle, I sat down on my bed and wrote a short letter to Roland on an old box-lid.

'I feel a mixture of strangeness and independence and depression and apprehension and a few other things to-night. Though I am really nearer to you, you somehow feel farther away. Write to me soon,' I implored him. 'London – darkest London – sends you its love too, and wishes – oh! ever so much! – that it may soon see you again.'

Now two insignificant units at the 1st London General Hospital, Camberwell – the military extension of St Bartholomew's Hospital – Betty and I had reported to the Matron that afternoon. We were among the youngest members of the staff, we learnt later, only two of the other V.A.D.s being 'under age'. The nucleus of the hospital, a large college, red, gabled, creeper-covered, is still one of the few dignified buildings in the dismal, dreary, dirty wilderness of south-east London, with its paper-strewn pavements, its little mean streets, and its old, ugly houses tumbling into squalid decay. Formerly – and now again – a training centre for teachers, it was commandeered for use as a hospital early in the War, together with some adjacent elementary schools, the open park-space opposite, and its satellite hostel nearly two miles away on Champion Hill.

To this hostel, as soon as we had reported ourselves, Betty and I were dispatched with our belongings. Our taxicab, driving through Camberwell Green over Denmark Hill and turning off the summit of Champion Hill into a pleasant, tree-shaded by-road, deposited us before a square, solid building of dirty grey stone, with gaping uncurtained windows. Closely surrounded by elms and chestnuts, tall, ancient and sooty, it looked gloomy and smelt rather dank; we should not be surprised, we thought, to find old tombstones in the garden.

At that stage of the War the military and civilian professional nurses who had joined Queen Alexandra's Imperial Military Nursing Service or the Territorial Force Reserve were still suspicious of the young semi-trained amateurs upon whose assistance, they were beginning to realise with dismay, they would be obliged to depend for the duration of the War. Only about a dozen V.A.D.s had preceded the batch with which I was sent, and the arrangements made for our reception were typical of the spirit in which, as a nation, we muddled our way through to 'victory'.

It still seems to me incredible that medical men and women, of all people, should not have realised how much the efficiency of over-worked and under-trained young women would have been increased by the elimination of avoidable fatigue, and that, having contemplated the addition of V.A.D.s to the staff for at least six months before engaging them, they did not make the hostel completely ready for them before they arrived instead of waiting till they got there. But in those days we had no Institute of Industrial Psychology to suggest ideal standards to professional organisations, and a large proportion of our military arrangements were permeated with a similar unimaginativeness. On a small scale it undermined the health and even cost the lives of young women in hospitals; on a large scale it meant the lack of ammunition, the attempt to hold positions with insufficient numbers, and the annihilation of our infantry with our own high-explosive shells.

Each morning at 7 a.m. we were due at the hospital, where we breakfasted, and went on duty at 7.30. Theoretically we travelled down by the workmen's trams which ran over Champion Hill from Dulwich, but in practice these trams were so full that we were seldom able to use them, and were obliged to walk, frequently in pouring rain and carrying suitcases containing clean aprons and changes of shoes and stockings, the mile and a half from the hostel to the hospital. As the trams were equally full in the evenings, the journey on foot had often to be repeated at the end of the day.

Whatever the weather, we were expected to appear punctually on duty looking clean, tidy and cheerful. As the V.A.D. cloakroom was then on the top floor of the college, up four flights of stone steps, we had to allow quarter of an hour for changing, in addition to the half hour's walk, in order to be in time for breakfast. This meant leaving the hostel at 6.15, after getting up about 5.45 and washing in icy water in the dreary gloom of the ill-lit, dawn-cold cubicle. After a few grumbles from the two eldest of the room's five occupants, we accepted our unnecessary discomforts with mute, philosophical resignation. When the rain poured in torrents as we struggled up or down Denmark Hill in the blustering darkness all through that wet autumn, Betty and I encouraged each other with the thought that we were at last beginning to understand just a little what winter meant to the men in the trenches.

Many chills and other small illnesses resulted from the damp, breakfastless walk undertaken so early in the morning by tired girls not yet broken in to a life of hardship. After I left I heard that a V.A.D. living at the hostel had died of pneumonia and had thus been responsible for the establishment of morning and evening ambulances, but until then no form of transport was provided or even suggested. Neither, apparently, did it occur to the authorities who so cheerfully billeted us in a distant, ill-equipped old house, that young untried women who were continually in contact with septic wounds and sputum cups and bed-pans, and whose constantly wet feet became cumulatively sorer from the perpetual walks added to the unaccustomed hours of standing, required at least a daily bath if they were to keep in good health.

At the hostel, to meet the needs of about twenty young women, was one cold bathroom equipped with an ancient and unreliable geyser. This apparatus took about twenty minutes to half fill the bath with lukewarm water, and as supper at the hospital was not over till nearly nine o'clock, and lights at the hostel had to be out soon after ten, there was seldom time after the journey up Denmark Hill for more than two persons per evening to occupy the bathroom. So temperamental was the geyser that the old housekeeper at the hostel refused to allow anyone but herself to manipulate it. While the tepid water trickled slowly into the bath she would sit anxiously perched beside the antique cylinder, apparently under the impression that if she took her eye off it for a moment it was bound to explode.

Any gas company could probably have installed an up-to-date water-heater in half a day, but it had not occurred to anybody to order this to be done. As several Sisters also slept in the hostel the V.A.D.s had seldom much luck in appropriating the bath, so in the bitter November cold we did our shivering best to remove the odours and contacts of the day with tiny jugfuls of lukewarm water. Later a second bathroom was installed, a process which, as I told Roland a few weeks afterwards, 'for some reason or other requires the cutting off of the entire hot water supply . . . It is rather an amusing state of affairs for the middle of London.' Never, except when travelling, had I to put up with so much avoidable discomfort throughout my two subsequent years of foreign service as I endured in the centre of the civilised world in the year of enlightenment 1915.

Much subsequent reflection has never enabled me to decide who was really responsible for our cheerless reception. Probably, in the unfamiliar situation, responsibility was never formally allocated to anyone by anybody, and, human nature being incurably optimistic and fundamentally hostile to assuming any work not established as its own by long tradition, each person who might have shouldered the task of organisation hopefully supposed it to have been performed by one of the others.

Organisation and regulation of another sort existed in plenty; it was evidently felt that, without the detailed regimentation of their daily conduct, amateur intruders would never fit into the rigid framework of hospital discipline. We went on duty at 7.30 a.m., and came off at 8 p.m., our hours, including three hours' off-time and a weekly half day – all of which we gave up willingly enough whenever a convoy came in or the ward was full of unusually bad cases – thus amounted to a daily twelve and a half. We were never allowed to sit down in the wards, and our off-duty time was seldom allocated before the actual day. Night duty, from 8 p.m. to 8 a.m. over a period of two months, involved a twelve-hour stretch without off-time, though one night's break was usually allowed in the middle. For this work we received the magnificent sum of £20 a year, plus a tiny uniform allowance and the cost of our laundry. Extra mess allowance was given only on foreign service, but at Camberwell the food, though monotonous, was always sufficient.

Those of us whose careers survived the Denmark Hill conditions gradually came, through the breaking-in process of sheer routine, to find the life tolerable enough. We all acquired puffy hands, chapped faces, chilblains and swollen ankles, but we seldom actually went sick, somehow managing to remain on duty with colds, bilious attacks, neuralgia, septic fingers and incipient influenza. It never then occurred to us that we should have been happier, healthier, and altogether more competent if the hours of work had been shorter, the hostel life more private and comfortable, the daily walks between hostel and hospital eliminated, the rule against sitting down in the wards relaxed, and off-duty time known in advance when the work was normal. Far from criticising our Olympian superiors, we tackled our daily duties with a devotional enthusiasm now rare amongst young women, since a more cynical post-war generation, knowing how easily its predecessors were hoodwinked through their naïve idealism, naturally tends to regard this quality with amusement and scorn.

Every task, from the dressing of a dangerous wound to the scrubbing of a bed-mackintosh, had for us in those early days a sacred glamour which redeemed it equally from tedium and disgust. Our one fear was to be found wanting in the smallest respect; no conceivable fate seemed more humiliating than that of being returned to Devonshire House as 'unsuitable' after a month's probation. The temptation to exploit our young wartime enthusiasm must have been immense – and was not fiercely resisted by the military authorities.

2

Most of the patients at Camberwell were privates and N.C.O.s, but the existence of a small officers' section made me dream of fascinating though improbable coincidences.

'I wonder,' I wrote to Roland, 'if some fine morning I shall come on duty and hear indirectly from a friendly V.A.D. that a certain Lieutenant L. of the 7th Worcestershires came in with the convoy last night . . . But it's too good to think of. It is the kind of thing that only happens in sensational novels.'

My first ward was a long Tommies' hut in the open park, containing sixty beds of acute surgical cases. The knowledge of masculine invalid psychology that I gradually acquired in my various hospitals stopped short at the rank of quarter-master-sergeant, for throughout the War I was never posted to a British officers' ward for longer than a few hours at a time. Apparently my youth and childish chocolate-box prettiness gave every Matron under whom I served the impression that if I were sent to nurse officers I should improve the occasion in ways not officially recognised by the military authorities.

When I began to work in the long hut, my duties consisted chiefly in preparing dressing-trays and supporting limbs – a task which the orderlies seldom undertook because they were so quickly upset by the butcher's-shop appearance of the uncovered wounds. Soon after I arrived I saw one of them, who was holding a basin, faint right on the top of the patient.

'Many of the patients can't bear to see their own wounds, and I don't wonder,' I recorded.

Although the first dressing at which I assisted – a gangrenous leg wound, slimy and green and scarlet, with the bone laid bare – turned me sick and faint for a moment that I afterwards remembered with humiliation, I minded what I described to Roland as 'the general atmosphere of inhumanness' far more than the grotesque mutilations of bodies and limbs and faces. The sight of the 'Bart's' Sisters, calm, balanced, efficient, moving up and down the wards self-protected by that bright immunity from pity which the highly trained nurse seems so often to possess, filled me with a deep fear of merging my own individuality in the impersonal routine of the organisation.

'There is no provision,' I told Roland in one of my earliest letters from Camberwell, 'for any interests besides one's supposed interest in one's work. Of course I hate it. There is something so starved and dry about hospital nurses – as if they had to force all the warmth out of themselves before they could be really good nurses. But personally I would rather suffer ever so much in my work than become indifferent to pain. I don't mind anything really so long as I don't lose my personality – or even have it temporarily extinguished. And I don't think I can do that when I have You.'

It was perhaps fortunate that I did not know how inexorably the months in which I should have to do what I hated would pile themselves up into years, nor foresee how long before the end I too, from overwork and excessive experience, should become intolerant of suffering in my patients. Even without the bitterness of that knowledge I felt very desolate, and as much cut off from what philosophers call 'the like-minded group' as if I had been imprisoned in one of the less 'highbrow' circles of Dante's *Purgatorio*. My first experience of convoys – the 'Fall in' followed by long, slowly moving lines of ambulances and the sudden crowding of the surgical wards with cruelly wounded men – came as a relief because it deprived me of the opportunity for thought.

'I had no time to wonder whether I was going to do things right or not,' I noted; 'they simply *had* to be done right.'

But afterwards the baffling contrast between the ideal of service and its practical expression – a contrast that grew less as our ideals diminished with the years while our burden of remorseless activities increased – drove me to write a puzzled letter to Roland.

'It is always so strange that when you are working you never think of all the inspiring thoughts that made you take up the work in the first instance. Before I was in hospital at all I thought that because I suffered myself I should feel it a grand thing to relieve the sufferings of other people. But now, when I am actually doing something which I know relieves someone's pain, it is nothing but a matter of business. I may think lofty thoughts about the whole thing before or after but never at the time. At least, almost never. Sometimes some quite little thing makes me stop short all of a sudden and I feel a fierce desire to cry in the middle of whatever it is I am doing.'

As the wet, dreary autumn drifted on into grey winter, my letters to him became shorter and a little forlorn, though my constant awareness of his far greater discomforts made me write of mine as though they possessed a humour of which I was too seldom conscious. The week-ends seemed especially tiring, for on Saturdays and Sundays even the workmen's trams ceased to function, and the homeward evening walk through the purlieus of Camberwell was apt to become more adventurous than usual.

'I picture to myself,' I told Roland, 'Mother's absolute horror if she could have seen me at 9.15 the other night dashing about and dodging the traffic in the slums of Camberwell Green, in the pitch dark of course, incidentally getting mixed up with remnants of a recruiting meeting, munition workers and individuals drifting in and out of public houses. It is quite thrilling to be an unprotected female and feel that no one in your immediate surroundings is particularly concerned with what happens to you so long as you don't give them any bother.'

After twenty years of sheltered gentility I certainly did feel that whatever the disadvantages of my present occupation, I was at least seeing life. My parents also evidently felt that I was seeing it, and too much of it, for a letter still exists in which I replied with youthful superiority to an anxious endeavour that my father must have made to persuade me to abandon the rigours of Army hospitals and return to Buxton.

'Thank you very much for your letter, the answer to which really did not require much thinking over,' I began uncompromisingly, and continued with more determination than tact: '*Nothing* – beyond sheer necessity – would induce me to stop doing what I am doing now, and I should never respect myself again if I allowed a few slight physical hardships to make me give up what is the finest work any girl can do now. I honestly did not take it up because I thought you did not want me or could not afford to give me a comfortable home, but because I wanted to prove I could more or less keep myself by working, and partly because, not being a man and able to go to the front, I wanted to do the next best thing. I do not agree that my place is at home doing nothing or practically nothing, for I consider that the place now of anyone who is young and strong and capable is where the work that is needed is to be done. And really the work is not too hard – even if I were a little girl, which I no longer am, for I sometimes feel quite ninety nowadays.'

Fortunately most of my letters home were more human, not to say schoolgirlish, in content. Their insistent suggestions that my family should keep me supplied with sweets and biscuits, or should come up to London and take me out to tea, are reminders of the immense part played by meals in the meditations of ardent young patriots during the War.

3

Apart from all these novel experiences, my first month at Camberwell was distinguished by the one and only real quarrel that I ever had with Roland. It was purely an epistolary quarrel, but its bitterness was none the less for that, and the inevitable delay between posts prolonged and greatly added to its emotional repercussions.

On October 18th, Roland had sent a letter to Buxton excusing himself, none too gracefully, for the terseness of recent communications, and explaining how much absorbed he had become by the small intensities of life at the front. As soon as the letter was forwarded to Camberwell, I replied rather ruefully.

'Don't get *too* absorbed in your little world over there – even if it makes things easier . . . After all the War *cannot* last for ever, and when it is over we shall be glad to be what we were born again – if we can only live till then. Life – oh! life. Isn't it strange how much we used to demand of the universe, and now we ask only for what we took as a matter of course before – just to be allowed to live, to go on being.'

By November 8th no answer had come from him – not even a comment on what seemed to me the tremendous event of my transfer from Buxton into a real military hospital. The War, I began to feel, was dividing us as I had so long feared that it would, making real values seem unreal, and causing the qualities which mattered most to appear unimportant. Was it, I wondered, because Roland had lost interest in me that this anguish of drifting apart had begun – or was the explanation to be found in that terrible barrier of knowledge by which War cut off the men who possessed it from the women who, in spite of the love that they gave and received, remained in ignorance?

It is one of the many things that I shall never know.

Lonely as I was, and rather bewildered, I found the cold dignity of reciprocal silence impossible to maintain. So I tried to explain that I, too, understood just a little the inevitable barrier – the almost physical barrier of horror and dreadful experience – which had grown up between us.

'With you,' I told him, 'I can never be *quite* angry. For the more chill and depressed I feel myself in these dreary November days, the more sorry I feel for you beginning to face the acute misery of the winter after the long strain of these many months. When at six in the morning the rain is beating pitilessly against the windows and I have to go out into it to begin a day which promises nothing

pleasant, I feel that after all I should not mind very much if only
the thought of you right in it out there didn't haunt me all day
. . . I have only one wish in life now and that is for the ending
of the War. I wonder how much really all you have seen and done
has changed you. Personally, after seeing some of the dreadful things
I have to see here, I feel I shall never be the same person again,
and wonder if, when the War does end, I shall have forgotten how
to laugh. The other day I did involuntarily laugh at something
and it felt quite strange. Some of the things in our ward are so
horrible that it seems as if no merciful dispensation of the Universe
could allow them and one's consciousness to exist at the same
time. One day last week I came away from a really terrible ampu-
tation dressing I had been assisting at – it was the first after the
operation – with my hands covered with blood and my mind full
of a passionate fury at the wickedness of war, and I wished I had
never been born.'

No sudden gift of second sight showed me the future months
in which I should not only contemplate and hold, but dress
unaided and without emotion, the quivering stump of a newly
amputated limb – than which a more pitiable spectacle hardly
exists on this side of death. Nor did Roland – who by this time
had doubtless grown accustomed to seeing limbs amputated less
scientifically but more expeditiously by methods quite other than
those of modern surgery – give any indication of understanding
either my revulsion or my anger. In fact he never answered this
particular communication at all, for the next day I received from
him the long-awaited letter, which provoked me to a more
passionate expression of apprehensive wrath than anything that he
had so far said or done.

'I can scarcely realise that you are there,' he wrote, after telling
me with obvious pride that he had been made acting adjutant to
his battalion, 'there in a world of long wards and silent-footed
nurses and bitter, clean smells and an appalling whiteness in everything. I wonder if your metamorphosis has been as complete as
my own. I feel a barbarian, a wild man of the woods, stiff, narrowed,
practical, an incipient martinet perhaps – not at all the kind of
person who would be associated with prizes on Speech Day, or

poetry, or dilettante classicism. I wonder what the dons of Merton would say to me now, or if I could ever waste my time on Demosthenes again. One should go to Oxford first and see the world afterwards; when one has looked from the mountain-top it is hard to stay contentedly in the valley . . .'

'Do I seem very much of a phantom in the void to you?' another letter inquired a day or two later. 'I must. You seem to me rather like a character in a book or someone whom one has dreamt of and never seen. I suppose there exists such a place as Lowestoft, and that there was once a person called Vera Brittain who came down there with me.'

After weeks of waiting for some sign of interested sympathy, this evidence of war's dividing influence moved me to irrational fury against what I thought a too-easy capitulation to the spiritually destructive preoccupations of military service. I had not yet realised – as I was later to realise through my own mental surrender – that only a process of complete adaptation, blotting out tastes and talents and even memories, made life sufferable for someone face to face with war at its worst. I was not to discover for another year how completely the War possessed one's personality the moment that one crossed the sea, making England and all the uninitiated marooned within its narrow shores seem remote and insignificant. So I decided with angry pride that – however tolerant Roland's mother, who by his own confession had also gone letterless for longer than usual, might choose to be – I was not going to sit down meekly under contempt or neglect. The agony of love and fear with which the recollection of his constant danger always filled me quenched the first explosion of my wrath, but it was still a sore and unreasonable pen that wrote the reply to his letter.

'Most estimable, practical, unexceptional adjutant, I suppose I ought to thank you for your letter, since apparently one has to be grateful nowadays for being allowed to know you are alive. But all the same, my first impulse was to tear that letter into small shreds, since it appeared to me very much like an epistolary expression of the Quiet Voice, only with indications of an even greater sense of personal infallibility than the Quiet Voice used to contain.

My second impulse was to write an answer with a sting in it which would have touched even R. L. (modern style). But I can't do that. One cannot be angry with people at the front – a fact which I sometimes think they take advantage of – and so when I read "We go back into the trenches tomorrow" I literally dare not write you the kind of letter you perhaps deserve, for thinking that the world might end for you on that discordant note.

'No, my metamorphosis has not been as complete as yours – in fact I doubt if it has occurred at all. Perhaps it would be better if it had, for it must be very pleasant to be perfectly satisfied both with yourself and life in general. But I cannot . . . Certainly I am as practical and outwardly as narrow as even you could desire. But although in this life I render material services and get definite and usually immediate results which presumably ought therefore to be satisfying, I cannot yet feel as near to Light and Truth as I did when I was "wasting my time" on Plato and Homer. Perhaps one day when it is over I shall see that there was Light and Truth behind all, but just now, although I suppose I should be said to be "seeing the world", I can't help feeling that the despised classics taught me the finest parts of it better. And I shan't complain about being in the valley if only I can call myself a student again some day, instead of a "nurse". By the way, are you *quite* sure that you are on "the mountain-top"? You admit yourself that you are "stiff, narrowed, practical, an incipient martinet", and these characteristics hardly seem to involve the summit of ambition of the real you. But the War kills other things besides physical life, and I sometimes feel that little by little the Individuality of You is being as surely buried as the bodies are of those who lie beneath the trenches of Flanders and France. But I won't write more on this subject. In any case it is no use, and I shall probably cry if I do, which must never be done, for there is so much both personal and impersonal to cry for here that one might weep for ever and yet not shed enough tears to wash away the pitiableness of it all.'

To this unmerited outburst, though I received other letters from him, I did not get an answer for quite a long time. Just before I wrote it he was transferred to the Somerset Light Infantry for temporary duty, and could get his letters only by riding over some miles of water-logged country to the 7th Worcesters' headquarters at Hebuterne, which was not, in winter, a tempting afternoon's occupation. But when, at the end of November, the reply did come, it melted away my fear of his indifference into tears of relief, and made me, as I confessed to my diary, 'nearly mad with longing for him, I wanted him so'.

'Dearest, I do deserve it, every word of it and every sting of it,' he wrote in a red-hot surge of impetuous remorse. '"Most estimable, practicable, unexceptional adjutant." . . . Oh, damn! I have been a perfect beast, a conceited, selfish, self-satisfied beast. Just because I can claim to live half my time in a trench (in very slight, temporary and much exaggerated discomfort) and might possibly get hit by something in the process, I have felt myself justified in forgetting everything and everybody except my own Infallible Majesty . . . And instead of calling it selfishness pure and simple I call it "a metamorphosis", and expect, in consequence, consideration and letters which can go unanswered.'

He didn't deserve, he concluded, to get my letters at all, but only to be ignored as completely as he had ignored me and his family. Apparently he had found my unhappy little tirade as soon as he arrived at Hebuterne that afternoon; it made him, he told me, so furious with himself that he left the rest of his correspondence lying on the table and rode straight back.

'I don't think I have ever been so angry or despised myself so much. I feel as if I hardly dare write to you at all. And to make it worse I have given up my chance of getting any leave before Christmas in order to be with this battalion a month instead of only a week. Oh, damn!'

For the time being, at any rate, these young, inflammatory emotions had burned down whatever barrier might have existed, and once more his letters became alive and warm with all the sympathy that I could desire for the unæsthetic bleakness of days and nights in hospital. But I, too, had by then something more to write about than the grey duties of Camberwell, for in the interval between my angry letter and his repentant response I had been down again – and for the last time – to Lowestoft.

4

One strenuous evening, after a month's work at the 1st London General, I nearly fainted in the ward and had to be put to bed in a Sister's cubicle at the hospital. I was intensely surprised and humiliated by this weakness, of which I had never before been guilty and was not to repeat. Probably the grim, suppurating wounds of the men in the huge ward were partly responsible, although, as I was to learn later in France, they were by no means the worst wounds that a man could receive without immediately qualifying for the mercy of death. Nevertheless, I had found them bad enough to make me pray nightly that Roland, for whom I had once regarded a wound as a desirable experience which might enable me to see him for weeks and perhaps months, might go through the War with body unscathed even though I never saw him at all.

'From my inmost heart,' I told him, 'I have taken to cursing the War . . . and the jarringness of even healed mutilations, and the ghastly look of wounds which are never the same in different people and which one can therefore never get used to. When it is all over — if it ever is — one will have to get out of the habit of retrospect . . . Dearest, I don't want you to get wounded now — not even a little. This War means such a waste of life even when people don't die.'

I knew that I was to see the doctor next morning, and lay awake half the night in terror lest I should be found medically unfit to nurse, and returned ignominiously home like a garment vainly sent on approval. Perhaps, I thought, the quarrel with Roland and the endless waiting for an answer to my angry letter had lowered my resistance to septic infection. Perhaps even the gramophones, oppressive and persistent, had contributed to my humiliation.

'In a surgical ward,' I had told Roland a little earlier, 'the nurses hardly occupy the silent-footed, gliding rôle which they always do in story-books and on the stage. For one thing, there is too much work to be done in a great hurry. For another, the mixture of gramophones and people shouting or groaning after an operation relieves you of the necessity of being quiet as to your footsteps, for it drowns everything else.'

They were blaring, blatant gramophones, and though the men found them consoling – perhaps because they subdued more sinister noises – they seemed to me to add a strident grotesqueness to the cold, dark evenings of hurry and pain. Many a man beyond the reach of harmony or discord must have breathed his last to the tune of 'When Irish eyes are smilin''; many a diseased, feverish brain must have wondered when it returned to normality why it was ceaselessly haunted by the strains of 'If you were the only girl in the world'. One Harry Lauder ditty, of which I cannot remember the beginning or the end, was invariably turned on just before the evening washings and temperatures; it had an insistent refrain which rang in my head all that autumn and always brought Roland vividly before me:

> *Don't – forget – yer – sodjer – laddie*
> *When – he's – fightin' – at – the Wa-ar!*
> *The time draws near that I must leave ye,*
> *But I* knaw *– that – ye'll – be –* TROO—

Soon after breakfast the doctor appeared – a young, sensitive man who died of cholera in the Persian Gulf a few months later. He tested my heart and pronounced me constitutionally fit, but said that I must have an immediate rest. Although my temperature was still slightly up, and no one knew whether I had anywhere accessible to go, I was ordered to leave the hospital at once on week-end sick-leave.

As I dressed rather dizzily and went up to Denmark Hill in a chilly tram to put a few things into a suitcase, I wondered vaguely what to do with myself. Buxton seemed impossibly far away even if I had not known that my parents were already in the throes of packing up for a sudden removal. For a moment I played with the notion of St Monica's, where I knew that my aunt's solicitude would provide me with a pleasant room and breakfast in bed. But the comforts with which the school tempted my weary flesh were as nothing to the stimulus which the Lowestoft household – where Roland's mother had said that I should be welcome whenever I cared to send a telegram – offered to my desolate spirit.

So, with the incredible idiocy of twenty-one, I sent my wire and set off that afternoon on a cold, dilatory, four-hour journey to Lowestoft. I did not mention that I was supposed to be an invalid, for I was anxious not to be treated as one, and on three successive evenings Roland's mother and I sat up until long past midnight, discussing his history and character from birth to manhood.

When I returned to London my temperature, after another dark, slow journey in an unheated train, was certainly no lower than it had been at the outset. But I felt psychologically cheered, and after a few feverish days in a lighter ward I somehow worked myself back to normal. For the next three months, I continually recovered from one small chill only to begin another – the result, no doubt, of constantly turning out of the poisonous atmosphere of the wards, made still stuffier by the stoves which combated the cold draughtiness of wood and canvas – into the perpetual rain and sleet.

'I don't dream often,' I wrote to Roland, shivering over the gas fire in the Sisters' sitting-room on the day after my return from Lowestoft, 'but all last night I was dreaming about you. It was a very pleasant dream; we were doing nothing in particular but wandering together about some fields I did not know. We weren't talking much but just roaming indefinitely, and you were holding my hands to warm them as you did on the cliff that evening. And when the morning came all too soon and I found I had to go out into pouring rain and two inches of dirty slush, and get quite soaked through just when I particularly didn't want to, it relieved me to shock my fellow-sufferers greatly by saying "Damn this War!" out loud. The person who said

I slept, and dreamt that life was beauty;
I woke, and found that life was duty,

was painfully appropriate on this occasion.

'All this morning I have been seeing in my mind Heather Cliff, and the sun on the sea, and the fishing-smacks with ruddy sails. I don't think I could do without the family at Lowestoft now. I shall be glad when they are near and I can see them often. I saw some of Clare's drawings this time. I think they are quite remarkable. They are better already than my artist friend's, and she is supposed to be exceptionally good. I had no idea Clare was as gifted as that.'

The possibility of Roland's family coming nearer to London was soon, I knew, to materialise, for I had learnt on my visit that they intended to leave the Lowestoft house, which was becoming more and more dangerous and inconvenient, and look for a cottage somewhere in Sussex. At the end of November they let Heather Cliff, with all its contents, to two Army officers, and went to live in a small house at Keymer, near Hassocks, where the domestic work was done by a village charlady who 'ran in'. This cottage, with its manuscripts, its drawings, its vital, discursive inhabitants and its gorgeous, colourful disorder, provided a refuge which, almost exclusively during the next few months, bound me to life. Roland's mother announced that they were moving for only a short period; actually, they lived in Sussex for nearly four years, and never returned to Lowestoft.

At exactly the same time, my own methodical parents were sentencing themselves to weeks of cleaning and packing in preparation for their immediate departure from Buxton for a few unsettled months in Brighton hotels. The rapid march of events since August 1914 had left them breathless and a little bewildered. Edward, that autumn, was at Penkridge Bank Camp, near Stafford, drifting nearer and nearer to despair as, one after another, the supernumerary officers of the 11th Sherwood Foresters were ordered to France without him. Even the diffident and over-sensitive Geoffrey had gone to join the 10th Battalion near Ypres, and Edward did his best to forget how much he missed him by composing a little symphony called 'Sunset Clouds'. But sooner or later, in a War which now seemed destined to be interminable, he was bound to be sent to the front, while my own long-awaited orders for London had been carried out, when they did come, with perturbing expeditiousness in the eyes of my parents.

Apart from our exodus from home, a business disagreement had made my father suddenly decide to retire – all too early, for he was only just fifty – from the mills in Staffordshire. There was thus nothing to keep him near the Potteries, particularly as he was not on really intimate terms with any member of his family. My grandmother's death when I was eleven had removed the last uniting link between her numerous descendants, who were henceforth, in accordance with their austere tradition, to meet chiefly at family funerals.

'I am so glad,' I commented tersely on the parental removal, 'that they are leaving that artificial, north-country hole.' How thankful I should have been if they had only gone three years earlier! But already my débutante days in Buxton seemed to have vanished too far into the remote past to count any more.

5

At the end of my first five weeks at Camberwell, I was told, to my relief, that I was 'shaping very well', and asked to sign on for six months' service, my contract of course being renewable at the end of that time. I celebrated my satisfaction by a solitary expedition to the theatre, and afterwards wrote to Roland in a happier mood than I had known since leaving Buxton.

'Do you ever like to picture the people who write to you as they looked when they wrote? I do. At the present moment I am alone in the hostel common-room, sitting in an easy chair in front of the fire, clad precisely in blue and white striped pyjamas, a dark blue dressing-gown and a pair of black velvet bedroom slippers. It is my half-day and though only about 7.30, the opportunity of going to bed, or at least getting ready for it, moderately early is too rare to be missed. I have just been to St James's Theatre by myself to see George Alexander in *The Big Drum*.'

It was still an adventure to go about London alone, especially in the pitch blackness of the cold winter evenings. Such solitude was usually inevitable, for my favourite companions among the V.A.D.s – Betty, and one of my room-mates whom I called Marjorie, a dark, sallow girl some years my senior, the sister of a now famous dramatist – were seldom off duty at the same time as myself. But it was only among the suffering patients and the alien Sisters in the wards that I felt really lonely. I was never alone amid the dark stir of the West End streets and squares, for Roland was with me everywhere, 'all about me and nearer' than he usually seemed in the flesh.

His answer to my letter was warm and sweet with sensitive understanding.

'Through the door I can see little mounds of snow that are the parapets of trenches, a short stretch of railway line, and a very brilliant, full moon. I wonder what you are doing. Asleep, I hope – or sitting in front of a fire in blue and white striped pyjamas. I should so like to see you in blue and white pyjamas. You are always very correctly dressed when I find you, and usually somewhere near a railway station, *n'est-ce pas*? I once saw you in a dressing-gown with your hair down your back playing an accompaniment for Edward in the Buxton drawing-room. Do you remember? . . . I am often regretful that you should be at the hospital after all. I picture you getting up at the same too early hour every morning, to go out into a cold world and to a still colder and monotonous routine of fretful patients and sanguinary dressings and imperious Sisters . . . and then late to bed, to begin all over again to-morrow. It all seems such a waste of Youth, such a desiccation of all that is born for Poetry and Beauty. And if one does not even get a letter occasionally from someone who, despite his shortcomings, perhaps understands and sympathises it must make it all the worse . . . until one may possibly wonder whether it would not have been better never to have met him at all or at any rate until afterwards . . . Good night, Dear Child.'

Never to have met him till afterwards! What a poor, empty thing life would be now if he weren't right in it, I reflected, filling the whole horizon, giving purpose and justification to the abandonment of loveliness and learning, the substitution of forlorn hours of pain-tormented monotony. Oh, my darling, why don't you come home again and let me show you – as I never showed you properly last time – how much I love you, whether you are self-absorbed or remorseful, autocratic or tender?

'Sometimes,' I told him, 'I do wonder if you are not just an imagined lover that I have created in my own mind to bring a little romance into my present rather dreary existence. But when your letters are brought to my ward and the sight in the midst of disinfecting dishes of your delightful handwriting . . . reminds me that the imagined lover has a flesh-and-blood counterpart somewhere, I wish so greatly that he would materialise once more. Is there any chance of your coming over here again soon? Surely if there is very little to do, and winter being here it is not likely there can be much in the immediate future – why, then—? I *have* forgotten what you look like, though often your personality is with me still. And I want to remember again.'

And, unexpectedly, the very next day, before he could possibly have received my letter, came a tiny, thrilling note.

'I hope now to get leave about December 31st. Will you be on night-duty then? . . .'

Although my frenzied longing to see him which was the aftermath of our quarrel made me anxious for him to have leave as soon as possible, I knew that my own chance of some extra off-duty time would be better after Christmas than before, and the world brightened with the suddenness of an electric light going up in a dark room. The men in my ward, too, were recovering; the worst-wounded derelicts from Loos had by now all gone to join their comrades in the damp autumn earth, and the gay impudence of the survivors, as I told Roland, made the whole affair less tragic and more amusing.

'They say such things to me – sometimes quite embarrassing. It is never any use scolding them, as you can imagine; I have always to take it as a complete joke or else pretend not to see the point. One said yesterday, "You'll be losing yourself in your off-time one of these fine days, nurse," and the one in the next bed chimed in "Oh no! she won't. She's waiting till *he* comes back from the front, aren't you, nurse?" And I don't know that my efforts to behave as though there were no he are quite as successful as I could wish. Another one asked me to tell him what it felt like to be in love. So I said, "How should I know? You'll find out for yourself quick enough." And he said, "Oh, I bet you can tell me if you like, nurse. You've got just the right sort of face for love." I don't know what the Sisters would say if they could hear these little remarks.'

Should I find him, I wondered, even more of a stranger than before – still older, still maturer, yet treating me always with that queer mixture of a boy's ruthlessness and a man's passion?

'Eight months since you went, now,' I reminded him. 'Sometimes I daren't think of it, and certainly I never dare look back and remember what I have felt all the time . . . I am sorry your leave is not to come at present, yet, if you don't in the meantime "get hit by something" (what a cruel little wretch that small phrase of yours makes me feel!) it will probably be better as far as I am concerned for you to have it in a month or so's time, rather than now . . . It is very convenient,' I went on, after telling him that after three months in hospital I should have a chance of a week's leave out of the fortnight given every six months to V.A.D.s, 'that both our families will be quite near one another in the Brighton district. No more enforced racing from Buxton to Lowestoft! Oh, don't "get hit by something" in the meantime! When I think how all my world would go down into the abyss . . .'

6

Now that the time of waiting for him was measurable, going on night-duty early in December seemed a new and exciting experience. It also meant more privacy and less waste of time on perpetual walking, since the V.A.D. night quarters had recently been moved to some small individual huts just erected in the open park opposite the hospital. So Marjorie and Betty and I moved down from Denmark Hill with all our possessions – brown paper parcels, golf-bags full of shoes and bottles, a large package lavishly open at both ends containing Marjorie's scarlet wadded dressing-gown – and I wrote and told Roland what fun it all was.

I was lucky, too, in my ward, for I was sent to the big surgical hut in the park where I had started my day-duty. There I found, as my Sister-in-charge, the first trained nurse I had yet encountered who seemed to possess the normal characteristics of vulnerable humanity – a pretty young Scotswoman, pink-cheeked, dark-haired and dewy-eyed. As she had recently married a doctor serving with the R.A.M.C. in France and was always on tenterhooks for letters, I found myself talking to her about Roland in the semi-darkness with a freedom from shyness that I had never yet felt with anyone. It was a relief from strain that began, too, on the very first evening, for just as the last of our restless patients had suddenly fallen from groaning into sleep, and we had settled down close to the stove beneath a red-shaded lamp half enclosed in a screen, the night-orderly brought me two letters from Roland from the wind and rain outside.

'I don't think,' the first one announced defensively, 'that when one can still admire sunsets one has altogether lost the personality of pre-war days. I have been looking at a blood-red bar of sky creeping down behind the snow, and wondering whether any of the men in the trenches on the opposite hill were watching it too, and thinking, as I was, what a waste of life it is to spend it in a ditch . . . It will feel like coming to another planet to come back to England, or rather to certain people in England. My leave, of course, is not definite at all yet and may not come off for some long time. But I have hopes; and anticipation is very sweet.'

The second and shorter letter acknowledged my swift and warm response to his remorseful termination of our quarrel.

'Your sweet letter nearly made me cry . . . It reminded me of how much I really deserved the former one . . . No, it would not have been better to have thought the things and not written them, though they did hurt me, perhaps more than you thought they would. But it was very good for my Infallible Majesty; and you are very adorable when you are angry.'

It seemed strange and rather frightening, when the Sister had gone to supper, to be all alone in the long dark ward. Once, in the midst of trying to read a Strindberg play, I felt ghostly fingers gently stirring my hair, and twice mysterious footsteps walked slowly up the ward, stopped opposite my table and never returned. When the orderly officer came in on his round I almost shrieked in terror, but managed just in time to convert my alarm into a jump to attention, and to call him 'Sir' with circumspect propriety. Then, thinking how he whose grimmer ghosts were gaunt skeletons and squeaking rats might use the Quiet Voice to rebuke me a little amusedly for my fears, I made myself write to Roland in the Sister's absence, telling him that I too understood the sinister qualities of wakeful nights, which made me think of all the people who had suffered agony and died in my ward.

'The realisation *must* be better than the anticipation, this time,' I went on to urge. 'And since the hours of our meeting . . . are likely to be even briefer than the brief ones of last time, they must make up in sweetness for what they lack in duration. Must – and shall . . . It seems quite queer to think that (if you're not "hit by something" in the meantime – oh! that expression does haunt me so!) I can really count the days till I see you. Do you remember our somewhat embarrassed meeting at St Pancras? I wonder what it will be like this time – where and when. And I shall probably be in this abominable uniform . . . and you'll wonder what sort of an object you've picked up . . . I am just going out,' I concluded when the night was over, 'into a sunny, windy morning after rain. I do love my morning till 12.30 off-duty time. I never realised how lovely mornings are until I had been up all night.'

Roland, however, appeared for the moment to be less moved by my night-fears or even by the prospect of leave, than by a belated letter, describing my visit to Lowestoft, which he had found on returning to his own battalion from the Somerset Light Infantry.

'You seem,' he wrote ruefully, 'to have spent most of your time . . . in discussing me and my general goings-on. I should very much like to know what conclusions you and Mother did come to. You say that I should have been "mystified and a little astonished" if I had overheard you. I wonder whether you ultimately decided that I *was* a somewhat fickle and superficial person. I shouldn't be at all surprised, you know . . . "Well, after all, your real love was just a character in a book . . . And she whom you took to Lowestoft the first time was simply a flesh and blood approximation to Lyndall!" Is this true – or, rather, do *you* think it is true? It is quite possible to love an ideal crystallised in a person, and the person because of the ideal; and who shall say whether it is not perhaps better so in the end? Though it must be very trying to be the incarnation of an ideal – very trying. Apropos of which I may remark that the unfortunate Olive Schreiner is too often made responsible for things over which she had no control whatever. Also, that when one does not yet know one's own self, there will still be several persons who will profess an exhaustive knowledge of it and undertake intimate diagnoses from an entirely hypothetical basis . . . All of which sounds, and is, just a little bit bad-tempered. Good night, Phantom . . .'

It was disconcerting a day or two later to be sent for, together with several V.A.D.s who had joined the hospital at the same time, and be told by the Matron that we were all due (as V.A.D.s were invariably 'due' whenever the season was unpropitious and none of the Sisters wanted to go away) for a week's leave of our six-monthly fortnight. I was still enormously in awe of the Matron, whose impregnable calm gave nothing of herself away, but when the others went out I stood my ground and asked if I could speak to her alone. My cheeks turned scarlet and my hands, which suddenly seemed to have become four times their normal size, stole irresistibly towards the starched pockets of my clean apron as I explained the circumstances of Roland's leave and begged to have mine a little later.

'You see,' I stammered, 'he's been at the front nearly nine months, and I've only seen him once all that time . . .'

I fully expected, in common V.A.D. parlance, to be 'jumped on', but to my astonishment the Matron gave me a sweet smile – and wasn't it, too, most amazingly, just a tiny bit amused? – and answered benevolently: 'Certainly, nurse; I'll postpone your leave.' I nearly fell over a chair from excess of gratitude as I stumbled out of her office, and, immediately I went off-duty, rushed to my pen to tell the good news to Roland.

'To think,' I wrote ecstatically, 'that I can *really* look forward now to the end of this month! If only you are safe till then! And it will be all the time this time, instead of three and a half over-crowded days filled with railway journeys . . . Life seems quite irradiated now when I think of the sweet hours that may be ahead

– when I shall see once more "the things I strive to capture in vain". It will be worth while getting some really nice mufti for a week. I must try for once to look as well for you as I always do for people I don't care about.'

On my next half-day I occupied an entranced hour or two in taking a tram to Victoria and putting this pleasant resolution into practice. At Gorringe's in Buckingham Palace Road – already the scene of many large and satisfying off-duty teas – I spent all that was left of two months' pay, and the whole of the supplementary pocket-money sent to me at intervals by my forgiving father, upon a stimulating selection of brave new garments. After a comprehensive examination of half the contents of two or three departments, my choice fell, colourfully rather than judiciously, upon a neatly cut navy coat and skirt, a pastel-blue blouse in soft crêpe-de-Chine, an unusually becoming fawn felt hat trimmed with crimson berries, and a black taffeta dinner-dress with scarlet and mauve velvet flowers tucked into the waist. With this I decided that I could still wear the black moiré rose-trimmed hat purchased the previous winter in Manchester.

7

Certainly the stage seemed perfectly set for his leave. Now that my parents had at last migrated temporarily to the Grand Hotel at Brighton, our two families were so near; the Matron had promised yet again that my own week's holiday should coincide with his, and even Edward wrote cheerfully for once to say that as soon as the actual date was known, he and Victor would both be able to get leave at the same time.

'Very wet and muddy and many of the communication trenches are quite impassable,' ran a letter from Roland written on December 9th. 'Three men were killed the other day by a dug-out falling in on top of them and one man was drowned in a sump hole. The whole of one's world, at least of one's visible and palpable world, is mud in various stages of solidity or stickiness . . . I can be perfectly certain about the date of my leave by to-morrow morning and will let you know.'

And, when the final information did come, hurriedly written in pencil on a thin slip of paper torn from his Field Service notebook, it brought the enchanted day still nearer than I had dared to hope.

'Shall be home on leave from 24th Dec. – 31st. Land Christmas Day. R.'

Even to the unusual concession of a leave which began on Christmas morning after night-duty the Matron proved amenable, and in the encouraging quietness of the winter's war, with no Loos in prospect, no great push in the west even possible, I dared to glorify my days – or rather my nights – by looking forward. In the pleasant peace of Ward 25, where all the patients, now well on the road to health, slept soundly, the sympathetic Scottish Sister teased me a little for my irrepressible excitement.

'I suppose you won't be thinking of going off and getting married? A couple of babies like you!'

It was a new and breath-taking thought, a flame to which Roland's mother – who approved of early marriages and believed that ways and means could be left to look after themselves far better than the average materialistic parent supposed – added fuel when she hinted mysteriously, on a day off which I spent in Brighton, that *this* time Roland might not be content to leave things as they were . . . Suppose, I meditated, kneeling in the darkness beside the comforting glow of the stove in the silent ward, that during this leave we *did* marry as suddenly as, in the last one, we became 'officially' engaged? Of course it would be what the world would call – or did call before the War – a 'foolish' marriage. But now that the War seemed likely to be endless, and the chance of making a 'wise' marriage had become, for most people, so very remote, the world was growing more tolerant. No one – not even my family now, I thought – would hold out against us, even though we hadn't a penny beyond our pay. What if, after all, we did marry thus foolishly? When the War was over we could still go back to Oxford, and learn to be writers – or even lecturers; if we were determined enough about it we could return there, even though – oh, devastating, sweet speculation! – I might have had a baby.

I had never much cared for babies or had anything to do with them; before that time I had always been too ambitious, too much interested in too many projects, to become acutely conscious of a maternal instinct. But on those quiet evenings of night-duty as Christmas approached, I would come, half asleep, as near to praying as I had been at any time, even when Roland first went to France or in the days following Loos.

'Oh, God!' my half-articulate thoughts would run, 'do let us get married and let me have a baby – something that is Roland's very own, something of himself to remember him by if he goes . . . It shan't be a burden to his people or mine for a moment longer than I can help, I promise. I'll go on doing war-work and give it all my pay during the War – and as soon as ever the War's over I'll go back to Oxford and take my Finals so that I can get a job and support it. So *do* let me have a baby, dear God!'

The night before Christmas Eve, I found my ward transformed into the gay semblance of a sixpenny bazaar with Union Jacks, paper streamers, crinkled tissue lampshades and Christmas texts and greetings, all carried out in staggering shades of orange and vivid scarlet and brilliant green. In the cheerful construction of red paper bags, which I filled with crackers and sweets for the men's Christmas stockings, I found that the hours passed quickly enough. Clipping, and sewing, and opening packets, I imagined him reading the letter that I had written him a few days earlier, making various suggestions for meeting him, if he could only write or wire me beforehand, when the Folkestone train arrived at Victoria, and travelling down with him to Sussex.

'And shall I really see you again, and so soon?' it had concluded. 'And it will be the anniversary of the week which contained another New Year's Eve – and *David Copperfield*, and two unreal and wonderful days, and you standing alone in Trafalgar Square, and thinking of – well, what *were* you thinking of? When we were really both children still, and my connection with any hospital on earth was unthought-of, and your departure for the front merely the adventurous dream of some vaguely distant future date. And life was lived, at any rate for two days, in the Omar Khayyámesque spirit of

Unborn to-morrow and dead yesterday—
Why fret about them if To-day be sweet?

But we are going to better that – even that – *this* time. Au revoir.'

When I went to her office for my railway-warrant in the morning, the Matron smiled kindly at my bubbling impatience, and reminded me how lucky I was to get leave for Christmas. At Victoria I inquired what boat trains arrived on Christmas Day, and learnt that there was only one, at 7.30 in the evening. The risk, I decided, of missing him in the winter blackness of a wartime terminus was too great to be worth taking: instead, I would go straight to Brighton next morning and wait for him there.

As Christmas Eve slipped into Christmas Day, I finished tying up the paper bags, and with the Sister filled the men's stockings by the exiguous light of an electric torch. Already I could count, perhaps even on my fingers, the hours that must pass before I should see him. In spite of its tremulous eagerness of anticipation, the night again seemed short; some of the convalescent men wanted to go to early services, and that meant beginning temperatures and pulses at 3 a.m. As I took them I listened to the rain pounding on the tin roof, and wondered whether, since his leave ran from Christmas Eve, he was already on the sea in that wild, stormy darkness. When the men awoke and reached for their stockings, my whole being glowed with exultant benevolence; I delighted in their pleasure over their childish home-made presents because my own mounting joy made me feel in harmony with all creation.

At eight o'clock, as the passages were lengthy and many of the men were lame, I went along to help them to the communion service in the chapel of the college. It was two or three years since I had been to such a service, but it seemed appropriate that I should be there, for I felt, wrought up as I was to a high pitch of nervous emotion, that I ought to thank whatever God might exist for the supreme gift of Roland and the love that had arisen so swiftly between us. The music of the organ was so sweet, the sight of the wounded men who knelt and stood with such difficulty so moving, the conflict of joy and gratitude, pity and sorrow in my mind so poignant, that tears sprang to my eyes, dimming the chapel walls and the words that encircled them: 'I am the Resurrection and the Life: he that believeth in Me, though he were dead, yet shall he live: and whosoever liveth and believeth in Me shall never die.'

Directly after breakfast, sent on my way by exuberant good wishes from Betty and Marjorie and many of the others, I went down to Brighton. All day I waited there for a telephone message or a telegram, sitting drowsily in the lounge of the Grand Hotel, or walking up and down the promenade, watching the grey sea tossing rough with white surf-crested waves, and wondering still what kind of crossing he had had or was having.

When, by ten o'clock at night, no news had come, I concluded that the complications of telegraph and telephone on a combined Sunday and Christmas Day had made communication impossible. So, unable to fight sleep any longer after a night and a day of wakefulness, I went to bed a little disappointed, but still unperturbed. Roland's family, at their Keymer cottage, kept an even longer vigil; they sat up till nearly midnight over their Christmas dinner in the hope that he would join them, and, in their dramatic, impulsive fashion, they drank a toast to the Dead.

The next morning I had just finished dressing, and was putting the final touches to the pastel-blue crêpe-de-Chine blouse, when the expected message came to say that I was wanted on the telephone. Believing that I was at last to hear the voice for which I had waited for twenty-four hours, I dashed joyously into the corridor. But the message was not from Roland but from Clare; it was not to say that he had arrived home that morning, but to tell me that he had died of wounds at a Casualty Clearing Station on December 23rd.

PART II

'When the Vision dies in the dust of the market place,
When the Light is dim,
When you lift up your eyes and cannot behold his face,
When your heart is far from him,

Know this is your War; in this loneliest hour you ride
Down the roads he knew;
Though he comes no more at night he will kneel at
    your side
For comfort to dream with you.'

May Wedderburn Cannan.

CHAPTER VI

"When the Vision Dies . . ."

PERHAPS . . .
TO R. A. L.

Perhaps some day the sun will shine again,
And I shall see that still the skies are blue,
And feel once more I do not live in vain,
Although bereft of You.

Perhaps the golden meadows at my feet
Will make the sunny hours of spring seem gay,
And I shall find the white May-blossoms sweet,
Though You have passed away.

Perhaps the summer woods will shimmer bright,
And crimson roses once again be fair,
And autumn harvest fields a rich delight,
Although You are not there.

But though kind Time may many joys renew,
There is one greatest joy I shall not know
Again, because my heart for loss of You
Was broken, long ago.

V. B. 1916.
From *Verses of a V.A.D.*

1

Whenever I think of the weeks that followed the news of Roland's death, a series of pictures, disconnected but crystal clear, unroll themselves like a kaleidoscope through my mind.

A solitary cup of coffee stands before me on a hotel breakfast-table; I try to drink it, but fail ignominiously.

Outside, in front of the promenade, dismal grey waves tumble angrily over one another on the windy Brighton shore, and, like a slaughtered animal that still twists after life has been extinguished, I go on mechanically worrying because his channel-crossing must have been so rough.

In an omnibus, going to Keymer, I look fixedly at the sky; suddenly the pale light of a watery sun streams out between the dark, swollen clouds, and I think for one crazy moment that I have seen the heavens opened . . .

At Keymer a fierce gale is blowing and I am out alone on the brown winter ploughlands, where I have been driven by a desperate desire to escape from the others. Shivering violently, and convinced that I am going to be sick, I take refuge behind a wet bank of grass from the icy sea-wind that rushes, screaming, across the sodden fields.

It is late afternoon; at the organ of the small village church, Edward is improvising a haunting memorial hymn for Roland, and the words: 'God walked in the garden in the cool of the evening', flash irrelevantly into my mind.

I am back on night-duty at Camberwell after my leave; in the chapel, as the evening voluntary is played, I stare with swimming eyes at the lettered wall, and remember reading the words: 'I am the Resurrection and the Life', at the early morning communion service before going to Brighton.

I am buying some small accessories for my uniform in a big Victoria Street store, when I stop, petrified, before a vase of the tall pink roses that Roland gave me on the way to *David Copperfield*; in the warm room their melting sweetness brings back the memory of that New Year's Eve, and suddenly, to the perturbation of the shop-assistants, I burst into uncontrollable tears, and find myself, helpless and humiliated, unable to stop crying in the tram all the way back to the hospital.

It is Sunday, and I am out for a solitary walk through the dreary streets of Camberwell before going to bed after the night's work. In front of me on the frozen pavement a long red worm wriggles slimily. I remember that, after our death, worms destroy this body – however lovely, however beloved – and I run from the obscene thing in horror.

It is Wednesday, and I am walking up the Brixton Road on a mild, fresh morning of early spring. Half-consciously I am repeating a line from Rupert Brooke:

'The deep night, and birds singing, and clouds flying . . .'

For a moment I have become conscious of the old joy in rain-washed skies and scuttling, fleecy clouds, when suddenly I remember – Roland is dead and I am not keeping faith with him; it is mean and cruel, even for a second, to feel glad to be alive.

2

Gradually the circumstances of Roland's death, which at first I was totally unable to grasp, began to acquire coherence in my mind. Through letters from his colonel, his fellow-officers, the Catholic padre who had buried him, and his servant whose sympathy was extremely loquacious and illegibly expressed in pencil, we were able to piece together the details of his end – so painful, so unnecessary, so grimly devoid of that heroic limelight which Roland had always regarded as ample compensation for those who were slain, like Kingsley's *Heroes*, 'in the flower of youth on the chance of winning a noble name'. The facts, as finally gathered, were more or less these:

On the night, December 22nd, that Roland was mortally wounded, the 7th Worcesters had just taken over some new trenches. Like the company whose lethargic captain appears in the opening scene of *Journey's End*, the previous occupants of these trenches had left them dirty and dilapidated, while the wire in front was so neglected that Roland's platoon was ordered to spend the night in repairing it. Before taking the wiring party over, he went to inspect the place himself, using a concealed path which led to No Man's Land through a gap in a hedge, because the communication trench was flooded. As it happened, this trench had been flooded for a long time, and the use of the alternative path was known to the Germans. Not unnaturally, they had trained a machine gun on the gap, and were accustomed to fire a few volleys whenever the troops facing them showed signs of activity. This enemy habit was known to the Worcesters' predecessors, but they did not, apparently, think it worth mentioning to the relieving battalion.

At the time that the Worcesters took over, the moon was nearly full, and the path through the hedge must have been quite visible by night to the vigilant eyes which were only, at that point, a hundred yards away. As soon as Roland reached the gap, the usual volley was fired. Almost the first shot struck him in the stomach, penetrating his body, and he fell on his face, gesticulating wildly, in full view of the company. At the risk of their lives, his company commander and a sergeant rushed out and carried him back to the trench. Twenty minutes afterwards the doctor at the dressing-station put an end to his agony with a large dose of morphia, and from that moment Roland ceased – and ceased for ever – to be Roland.

The next morning a complicated abdominal operation was performed on him by the senior surgeon of the Casualty Clearing Station at Louvencourt, ten miles away, but the wound had caused so much internal mutilation that the doctors knew he was not likely to last longer than a few hours. The machine-gun bullet had injured, amongst other things, the base of the spine, so that if by some combined miracle of surgical skill and a first-rate constitution he had been saved from death, he would have been paralysed from the waist downwards for the rest of his life. As it was, he only came round from the operation sufficiently to receive, 'in a state of mazy contentment', Extreme Unction from the Jesuit padre who, unknown to us all, had received him into the Catholic Church early that summer. 'Lying on this hillside for six days makes me very stiff,' he told the padre cheerfully. They were his last coherent words. At eleven o'clock that night – the very hour in which I had been so happily filling the men's paper-bags with crackers – Uppingham's record prize-winner, whose whole nature fitted him for the spectacular drama of a great battle, died forlornly in a hospital bed. On the Sunday morning that we, in the Keymer cottage, were vainly trying to realise his end, his burial service was read in the village church beside the military cemetery at Louvencourt. As they brought his body from the church, the colonel told us, 'the sun came out and shone brilliantly.'

That was all. There was no more to learn. Not even a military purpose seemed to have been served by his death; the one poor consolation was that his routine assumption of responsibility had saved the wiring party.

Later, night after night at Camberwell, watching the clouds drift slowly across the stars, I dwelt upon these facts until it seemed as though my mind would never contain the anguish that they brought me. Had it been heroism or folly, I asked myself for the thousandth time, which had urged him forth to inspect the wire beneath so bright a moon? In those days it seemed a matter of life or death to know.

'All heroism,' I argued desperately in my diary, 'is to a certain extent unnecessary from a purely utilitarian point of view . . . But heroism means something infinitely greater and finer, even if less practical, than just avoiding blame, and doing one's exact, stereotyped duty and no more.'

All the same, gazing fixedly out of the ward window at a tall church spire blackly silhouetted against banks of cloud pierced by a shaft of brilliant moonshine, I would whisper like a maniac to the sombre, indifferent night: 'Oh, my love! – so proud, so confident, so contemptuous of humiliation, you who were meant to lead a forlorn hope, to fall in a great fight – just to be shot like a rat in the dark! Why did you go so boldly, so heedlessly, into No Man's Land when you knew that your leave was so near? Dearest, why did you, why did you?'

Hardest of all to bear, perhaps, was the silence which must for ever repudiate that final question. The growing certainty that he had left no message for us to remember seemed so cruel, so baffling. To-day, after one or two experiences of shattering pain, I understand the degree to which both agony and its alleviations shut out the claims of memory and thought, but at that time, in spite of six months in hospital, I did not allow for the compelling self-absorption of extreme suffering or the stupefied optimism induced by anæsthetics, and it seemed as though he had gone down to the grave consciously indifferent to all of us who loved him so much. All through the first months of 1916, my letters and diaries emphasise, again and again, the grief of having no word to cherish through the empty years. He had been coming on leave the very next day – the day after he was wounded, the day that he died – and yet he had never mentioned to anyone his mother or me, nor the fact that he expected to see us so soon.

For weeks after the news of his death I waited and waited in the hope of a message, and wrote letters to France which my correspondents must have found very childish and pitiful, for they replied with infinite patience and kindness. But when I too had heard from his colonel, and his company commander, and his servant, and the Catholic padre, and a sympathetic officer who, in order to satisfy me, made a special journey to Louvencourt and catechised the doctors, I knew I had learnt all that there was to know, and that in his last hour I had been quite forgotten.

3

When my leave, which I spent entirely at Keymer, came to an end, it was Edward who took me back to Camberwell. In the final months of intense, exclusive preoccupation with Roland, I had almost forgotten him, but now he returned quite suddenly to the chief place in my consciousness.

One evening in Sussex I came in from a lonely walk to find him and Victor almost filling the tiny sitting-room with their long, khaki-clad limbs. Together they were trying to occupy the leave which now had hardly more point for them than for myself, and Roland's mother had invited them both to tea. They looked, I remembered later in my diary, 'like courtiers without a king'. The strained sorrow which lined their faces and darkened their eyes moved me to unexpected remorse, and I remembered, with the surprise of a new discovery, that Roland had been their friend long before he became my lover.

The death of the friend that he most admired before he himself had even succeeded in getting to France, plunged Edward, as I learnt long afterwards, into bitter humiliation even less endurable than his grief for Roland's loss; he had not, he felt, the excuse of serious illness which gave Victor his right to mourn in the monotonous security of 'defending' Woolwich Arsenal. But in tenderness for my desolation he concealed from me much of his sorrow and all his bitterness, and I parted from him outside the 1st London General with a sense of leaving behind me all that life still held of strength and comfort.

My small room in the long wooden hut, uncannily silent because everyone else on night-duty was already asleep, seemed the utmost limit of miserable solitude, although Betty had put a fragrant bowl of mimosa there to welcome me. Sleep was impossible, and at supper I became wretchedly conscious of furtive glances from Sisters and V.A.D.s, intrusively curious, despite their embarrassed pity, to discover how an acquaintance was 'taking' her bereavement.

For the next few nights, I was sent on temporary duty to a variety of unknown wards. The Matron, whose humane sympathy had already extended my leave, no doubt meant to protect me from the tactless condolences of my former patients, but the experiment was not a success. With the Scottish Sister in my familiar ward – where the lively arguments about the evacuation of Gallipoli would not long have been diverted to the sorrows of a nurse over one more man 'gone west' – I might have settled down into some kind of routine, but a series of strange Sisters and patients provided me with no incentive to forget myself in work. As I was conspicuously not sleeping and must have appeared the ghost of the excited girl who went on leave – indeed, I felt as though I had gone down to death with Roland and been disinterred as somebody else – the Matron sent for me and offered to put me, with Betty, back on day-duty.

Obstinately I refused the concession, ungraciously insisting that I had 'got to get through this alone', but in the next ward to which I was sent I much regretted my stupidity, for the work was depressing beyond description. A harsh, intolerant day Sister carped at me perpetually, attributing every small mishap in her ward to my nocturnal activities, while her V.A.D., who was shortly getting married, exasperated me with her jubilant complacency and the freedom with which she shared her romance with the men – particularly as, unconsciously cruel, they persisted in discussing it with me. To complete my nervous misery, a paralytic patient required constant uninviting ministrations, and drove me half crazy with the animal noises which he emitted at intervals all through the night.

Even death was evidently better than paralysis, I reflected miserably, vainly endeavouring to defeat thought by working my way with resentful conscientiousness through the pile of correspondence that had descended upon me. At the beginning of 1916 the amount and variety of letters of sympathy were still overwhelming, for reiteration had not yet wearied the pens of the sympathisers, but out of them all only two really counted. One of these came from my English tutor, to whom also the War had brought a measure of personal sorrow. Her brief, grave note, suggesting as consolation the living beauty of the life that was gone, assumed a degree of contemplative detachment of which I was then quite incapable. But it comforted me, with its beautiful scholarly script, in a way probably unguessed by the writer, for it represented a link with the world once so rapturously chosen and now incredibly remote – the world of intellectual experiment, of youthful hope, of all the profound and lovely things that belong to the kingdom of the mind. Yet it was to the other letter, so great a contrast in its shy abruptness, that I turned still oftener.

'I'm so very, very sorry,' Geoffrey had written from the bleak perils of the Salient, vainly striving for words that would express his acute sensitiveness to another's pain. There were times, he said, when letters were but empty things, and he could not write.

By the end of January, Camberwell and its demands had come to seem unspeakably hateful. I had hardly realised how entirely it had been the eagerness to share Roland's discomforts which had made me shoulder the disagreeable tasks left over by everyone else, but now that he was dead the stultifying monotony of the rough work that I had once found so inspiring weighed upon me with growing heaviness, and the increasing consciousness of loss and frustration filled me with impotent fury and resentment.

'Everything is so exactly the same as it was before, which brings it all back so vividly,' I wrote to Edward. 'It seems unendurable that everything should be the same.'

The Sisters must have been disconcerted by the change in me, for I now evaded all but the most obvious duties, and took an infinite time to perform the simplest tasks, while the inquisitive pity of the V.A.D.s soon turned to bewildered impatience. No doubt they would have understood a sentimental, dependent sorrow, with hair-stroking at bedtime and hand-holdings in the dark, but they were not unnaturally baffled by an aloof, rigid grief, which abhorred their sympathy, detested their collective gigglings and prattlings, and hated them most of all for being alive when Roland was dead. Betty, in spite of much rough treatment, was invariably gentle, but Mina wrote two or three reproachful letters, scolding me for having become – as Betty had told her – so 'difficult'. The sooner I left that hospital, the better for everyone concerned it would be, her final effort concluded severely.

Numerous other correspondents counselled patience and endurance; time, they told me with maddening unanimity, would heal. I resented the suggestion bitterly; I could not believe it, and did not even want it to be true. If time did heal I should not have kept faith with Roland, I thought, clinging assiduously to my pain, for I did not then know that if the living are to be of any use in this world, they must always break faith with the dead.

Deliberately I turned my back upon my companions at the hospital, and except when Edward or Victor came up to town, spent all my off-duty time alone. Driven in upon myself, I sought such consolation as I could find in books and letters, and in Sunday morning visits to the Catholic church of St James's, Spanish Place. Roland, his mother told me, had often gone to this church; long before the impulse had seized him to put 'R.C.' in the space for 'Religion' in his Army papers, he had been attracted by the sybaritic mysticism of the Catholic faith. I could not follow him there, being temperamentally too much of an agnostic to become a convert even in tribute to his memory. But as I knelt, drowsy with sleeplessness, at High Mass beneath the tall, pointed arches, the lovely

Latin intonations which I could not follow flowed over me with anodyne sweetness, drugging my senses with temporary resignation to the burden of my sorrow.

In my wooden hut, by means of a folding card-table and a remnant of black satin for tablecloth, I made a small shrine for a few of the books that Roland and I had admired and read together. *The Story of an African Farm* was there and *The Poems of Paul Verlaine*, as well as *The Garden of Kama* and *Pêcheur d'Islande*. To these I added Robert Hugh Benson's Prayer Book, *Vexilla Regis*, not only in honour of Roland's Catholicism, but because my mother had sent me some lines, which I frequently read and cried over, from Benson's 'Prayer after a Crushing Bereavement':

'And lastly to me who am left to mourn his departure, grant that I may not sorrow as one without hope for my beloved who sleeps in Thee; but that, always remembering his courage, and the love that united us on earth, I may begin again with new courage to serve Thee more fervently who art the only source of true love and true fortitude; that, when I have passed a few more days in this valley of tears and in this shadow of death, supported by Thy rod and staff, I may see him again, face to face, in those pastures and amongst those waters of comfort where, I trust, he already walks with Thee. Oh Shepherd of the Sheep, have pity upon this darkened soul of mine!'

Fifteen years were to pass before Bertrand Russell, ruthlessly undeluded by beatific visions of a compensating futurity, published *The Conquest of Happiness*, with its unresigned, unpitying exhortation to the bereaved:

'A man of adequate vitality and zest will surmount all misfortunes by the emergence after each blow of an interest in life and the world which cannot be narrowed down so much as to make one loss fatal. To be defeated by one loss or even by several is not something to be admired as a proof of sensibility, but something to be deplored as a failure in vitality.

All our affections are at the mercy of death, which may
strike down those whom we love at any moment. It is therefore necessary that our lives should not have that narrow
intensity which puts the whole meaning and purpose of our
life at the mercy of accident.'

Both passages are beautiful, and Benson's has a faith and a
mysticism which Russell's lacks, but if I were to suffer the same
loss to-day, it would be in Russell, and not in Benson, that I
should find courage and comfort.

4

Whenever half-days made it possible, I escaped from London to
the family at Keymer, but in the daily three-hour intervals a new
source of consolation presented itself, unexpectedly enough, in
the person of Victor. His meningitis had apparently entitled him
to indefinite light duty combined with frequent and prolonged
periods of leave, and these he dedicated entirely to my service,
unobtrusively constituting himself the Father Confessor that he
had once been to Roland.

Towards himself his attitude was consistently humble. 'I am a
very ordinary and matter-of-fact person,' he told me once. Upon
his friends he made no demands, but continually encouraged the
staking of claims upon himself by others. On alternate Sundays,
when I was off duty in the evening, we had supper together for
several fortnights running at the Trocadero, where I was always
the talker and he the patient, untiring listener. However much I
railed, complained and lamented, his dark, considerate eyes never
lost their gentle expression of interested attention.

For the first two months after my return to Camberwell, we
seem to have corresponded every few days. His letters in their
sloping, ingenuous hand now appear pathetically childish, and yet
so maturely selfless in their obvious determination to see both sides
of every problem, and then to give exactly the advice likely to
prove most congenial to the inquirer. As the details of Roland's last
moments came through, he must have spent hours in laboriously

writing to explain how important it was that the wire should be mended even on a moonlit night, while 'the best traditions of the Regular Army' demanded that a platoon commander should inspect the damage himself even when the occasion was dangerous.

At the time – accustomed though I was by Roland's passionate vitality to quite a different manifestation of youth – I did not perceive the ingenuous childishness; I realised only the healing balm of unself-regarding sympathy, and found the long, boyish letters very comforting. His unmitigated kindness, his gift of consolation and his imaginative pity for the sorrows of others, still impress me, when I re-read his letters, as quite astonishing in a young man at an egotis-tical age.

The more I came to detest my work at Camberwell, the more I relied upon my short intervals with Roland's family to give some purpose to an existence which seemed to have become singularly pointless. Two or three weeks after Roland's death, his mother began to write, in semi-fictional form, a memoir of his life, which she finished in three months, as well as replying at length to letters of condolence from friends and readers all over the country. At the end of that time she had a short breakdown from shock and overwork, and was in bed warding off serious heart trouble for several weeks. The many occasions on which I went down to see her and discuss the publication of her memoir, filled me with longing to write a book about Roland myself, but I concluded that three months was too short a time for me to see personal events in their true perspective. I would wait, I decided, rather longer than that before contributing my own account of his brief, vivid existence. I should have been astonished indeed had anyone told me that I should wait for seventeen years.

In Sussex, by the end of January, the season was already on its upward grade; catkins hung bronze from the bare, black branches, and in the damp lanes between Hassocks and Keymer the birds sang loudly. How I hated them as I walked back to the station one late afternoon, when a red sunset turned the puddles on the road into gleaming pools of blood, and a new horror of mud and death darkened my mind with its dreadful obsession. Roland, I reflected bitterly, was now part of the corrupt clay into which war had transformed the fertile soil of France; he would never again know the smell of a wet evening in early spring.

I had arrived at the cottage that morning to find his mother and sister standing in helpless distress in the midst of his returned kit, which was lying, just opened, all over the floor. The garments sent back included the outfit that he had been wearing when he was hit. I wondered, and I wonder still, why it was thought necessary to return such relics – the tunic torn back and front by the bullet, a khaki vest dark and stiff with blood, and a pair of blood-stained breeches slit open at the top by someone obviously in a violent hurry. Those gruesome rags made me realise, as I had never realised before, all that France really meant. Eighteen months afterwards the smell of Étaples village, though fainter and more diffused, brought back to me the memory of those poor remnants of patriotism.

'Everything,' I wrote later to Edward, 'was damp and worn and simply caked with mud. And I was glad that neither you nor Victor nor anyone who may some day go to the front was there to see. If you had been, you would have been overwhelmed by the horror of war without its glory. For though he had only worn the things when living, the smell of those clothes was the smell of graveyards and the Dead. The mud of France which covered them was not ordinary mud; it had not the usual clean pure smell of earth, but it was as though it were saturated with dead bodies – dead that had been dead a long, long time . . . There was his cap, bent in and shapeless out of recognition – the soft cap he wore rakishly on the back of his head – with the badge thickly coated with mud. He must have fallen on top of it, or perhaps one of the people who fetched him in trampled on it.'

Edward wrote gently and humbly in reply, characteristically emphasising the simple, less perturbing things that I had mentioned in another part of my letter.

'I expect he had only just received the box of cigarettes and the collars and braces I gave him for Christmas and I feel glad that he did get them because he must have thought of me then.'

So oppressively at length did the charnel-house smell pervade the small sitting-room, that Roland's mother turned desperately to her husband:

'Robert, take those clothes away into the kitchen and don't let me see them again: I must either burn or bury them. They smell of death; they are not Roland; they even seem to detract from his memory and spoil his glamour. I won't have anything more to do with them!'

What actually happened to the clothes I never knew, but, incongruously enough, it was amid this heap of horror and decay that we found, surrounded by torn bills and letters, the black manuscript note-book containing his poems. On the fly-leaf he had copied a few lines written by John Masefield on the subject of patriotism:

'It is not a song in the street and a wreath on a column and a flag flying from a window and a pro-Boer under a pump. It is a thing very holy and very terrible, like life itself. It is a burden to be borne, a thing to labour for and to suffer for and to die for, a thing which gives no happiness and no pleasantness – but a hard life, an unknown grave, and the respect and bowed heads of those who follow.'

The poems were few, for he had always been infinitely dissatisfied with his own work, but 'Nachklang' was there, and 'In the Rose Garden', as well as the roundel 'I Walk Alone', and the villanelle 'Violets', which he had given me during his leave. The final entry represented what must have been the last, and was certainly the most strangely prophetic, of all his writings. It evidently belonged to the period of our quarrel, when he was away from his regiment with the Somerset Light Infantry, for it was headed by the words:

HÉDAUVILLE. *November 1915:*

> *The sunshine on the long white road*
> *That ribboned down the hill,*
> *The velvet clematis that clung*
> *Around your window-sill,*
> *Are waiting for you still.*

Again the shadowed pool shall break
In dimples round your feet,
And when the thrush sings in your wood,
Unknowing you may meet
Another stranger, Sweet.

And if he is not quite so old
As the boy you used to know,
And less proud, too, and worthier,
You may not let him go—
(And daisies are truer than passion-flowers)
It will be better so.

What did he mean, I wondered, as I read and re-read the poem, puzzled and tormented. What could he have meant?

Five years afterwards, as I motored from Amiens through the still disfigured battlefields to visit Roland's grave at Louvencourt, I passed, with a sudden shock, a white board inscribed briefly: 'HÉDAUVILLE'.

The place was then much as it must have looked after a year or two's fighting, with only the stumpy ruins of farmhouses crumbling into the tortured fields to show where once a village had been. But over the brow of a hill the shell-torn remnants of a road turned a corner and curved steeply downwards. As the car lurched drunkenly between the yawning shell-holes I looked back, and it seemed to me that perhaps in November 1915, this half-obliterated track had still retained enough character and dignity to remind Roland of the moorland road near Buxton where we had walked one spring evening before the war.

5

At the beginning of February my night-duty ended, and with tears falling into my trunk I packed up to move from my quiet hut to Denmark Hill. When I reached the hostel my dreariest apprehensions were realised, for I had to share a room with five other women, most of whom belonged to a new batch of V.A.D.s with strange accents and stranger underclothes whom Betty described as 'the second Derby's Army'.

'I wonder,' I wrote in my diary after the first afternoon under a new Charge-Sister in my old sixty-bed hut, 'if ever, ever I shall get over this feeling of blank hopelessness . . . Resistance requires an energy which I haven't any of – and to try to acquire it just to face bravely a world that has ceased to interest me . . . hardly seems worth while.'

It was just at this moment that Edward wrote to say that his orders to go to the front had come at last and he was leaving London for France on February 10th. The date was memorable for other reasons, since it brought conscription into operation in England for the first time in history, but about this I neither knew nor cared when my mother and I saw him off from Charing Cross on one of those grey, unutterably dismal afternoons in which a London February seems to specialise. With him went two other officers who were also joining the 11th Sherwood Foresters – the one, Captain H., a big, bluff, friendly man who afterwards became his company commander; the other a plump, insignificant sub-altern who lived long enough to find death and presumably glory in the final advance on the Western front.

As I dragged myself back to Camberwell my feet seemed weighted with lead, and I realised that there had still, after all, been something capable of increasing the misery of the past few weeks.

'I cannot cherish any optimistic hopes about the front now . . .' my diary recorded. 'Yet I cannot feel very acutely – I don't feel anything but an utter, utter weariness . . . It is all so unbelievable. He – to be standing in water and mud, when I can remember him in a brown holland overall, and everyone was always so careful to see that he didn't get his feet wet . . . I do not think about him in the same invariable way as I thought and think about Roland. But when I do think about him, which is very often indeed, I realise how it is to him all my hopes of the future are anchored, upon him that my chances of companionship and understanding in the future depend.'

A week later a letter came to say that he was already in the trenches.

'It is quite easy for me now,' he wrote, 'to understand how Roland was killed; it was quite ordinary but just unlucky . . . I do not hold life cheap at all and it is hard to be sufficiently brave, yet I have hardly ever felt really afraid. One has to keep up appearances at all costs even if one does.'

He did not go into dramatic details of the perils that surrounded him, but remembering the vividness of Roland's descriptions I knew only too well what they were. Over the uninspiring task of mackintosh-scrubbing in the ward-annex I moped and dawdled, trying to read between the lines of his letter and wondering whether he would ever come back.

That afternoon my new Charge-Sister, a dark, attractive young woman of perhaps thirty, sent for me to come to her in the little office attached to each ward. She was very angry, and for about five minutes scolded me for my slackness, dreaminess, and general lack of interest in my work.

'Do you realise,' she concluded, 'that you spent half an hour scrubbing that one mackintosh?'

Taken utterly aback, and perhaps sensing some human quality behind the external indignation, I suddenly sobbed out that I had indeed no interest in the ward or the work; my *fiancé* had recently been killed, my only brother had just gone to the front, and I thought, and wanted to think, about nothing else.

When I looked up a moment later, furiously scrubbing my eyes with a wet handkerchief, the Sister's face had lost its severity. Like most of the 'Bart's' nurses she was a kind, well-educated girl, who realised that, when a certain stage of desperation has been reached, neither scolding nor sympathy for the time being avail.

'I'm sorry, nurse,' she said quietly. 'I'll look at it from another point of view,' and she sent me off duty for the rest of the day. So I went up to the hostel and, angry and humiliated, wept again.

In the evening, after supper, when I was already in my dressing-gown preparing to go to bed with a splitting headache, our Matron came round with the Principal Matron on a tour of inspection of our cubicles. I had been sitting forlornly beside the shrine, on which all my books were laid out, but as the two Matrons came in I moved back into the shadow to hide my tear-stained face, wondering miserably whether in all my life I should be allowed privacy again.

The Principal Matron, a bulky, red-faced woman, stood over my books, not noticing me, and examined their titles. Suddenly she gave an exclamation of horror and pointed to Compton Mackenzie's *Carnival*, a favourite of Roland's and mine which had recently been added to the small collection.

'Who,' she demanded, 'is reading that *disgusting* book?'

Our Matron, who may or may not have noticed my glowering, reddened eyes, but who still remembered to be sorry for me, made some soothing remark about 'Nurse Brittain' having been a student, and the two passed on.

'The only conclusion of this disturbing day,' I wrote in my diary after getting, still ruffled, into bed, 'is that at all costs I must preserve my self-respect – preserve the self which he loved and I have lost . . . I only wish I could see a little light in all the depths and blackness – only wish I knew what my obvious duty was. Perhaps it is not impossible to regain one's self-respect. Even Lyndall – his ideal – had her weak times and was strong again.'

A day or two afterwards, looking anxiously as usual at the casualty list in *The Times*, I noticed with cold dismay that Geoffrey's name was among the wounded. Almost immediately my mother, who had heard from his family, wrote to tell me that he was now a patient at Fishmongers' Hall, in the City; he had escaped with shell-shock and a slight face wound from a heavy bombardment in front of Ypres, which had caused many casualties among the 10th Sherwood Foresters.

On my next afternoon off duty I went to Fishmongers' Hall, and found him, in a green dressing-gown, huddled over a gas-fire with a rug across his knees. Though the little wound on his left cheek was almost healed, he still shuddered from the deathly cold that comes after shell-shock; his face was grey with a queer, unearthly pallor, from which his haunted eyes glowed like twin points of blue flame in their sunken sockets. Ill and nightmare-ridden as he looked, I was impressed once again by his compelling, devotional beauty.

At first our conversation was slow and constrained, but as he grew accustomed to me, and I did not mention Roland, he began to talk, as though throwing off a burden of memory with painful relief. He was not, he told me, a successful officer as he knew Edward to be; in the trenches he always felt afraid, not of the danger but of completely losing his nerve with a suddenness that he had once seen overwhelm another officer.

'It's awful the way the men keep their eyes fixed on you!' he said. 'I never know whether they're afraid of what's going to happen to me, or whether they're just watching to see what I'll do.'

After the bombardment, he went on, he had stayed with his men, whom he had ordered to 'rapid fire' against hordes of advancing Germans. When they were practically surrounded he told them to retreat, but he still worried perpetually over this decision, wondering whether they should all have stayed to face certain and unavailing death. As he talked, he clasped and unclasped his hands; I had never seen any face so overshadowed with sorrow and anxiety as was his when he spoke of his brief but unforgettable weeks in Flanders.

'I think he is the kind of person who suffers more than anybody at the front,' I wrote later to Edward. 'I wonder if you mind its horrors and trials as much as he does. I expect you do, but being calmer in your nerves and more confident of your own powers you can bear it better. I wish they would send him to Egypt or Salonika, where not much is going on in the way of actual fighting: physically I should think he is quite strong; it seems to be his nerves that get quickly overstrained.'

Before I left Fishmongers' Hall, Geoffrey asked me if I would go and see him again in spite of the fact that he couldn't be charming. I did go, and gladly, for I soon came to feel a deep regard for him; I found a strange consolation in his diffident shyness and his intense consciousness of the loss of which we never spoke except in letters. He even took me, one afternoon, to a concert at the Queen's Hall, followed by tea at Fuller's in Regent Street, and almost lost the tickets in his agitation over this extremely bold and unusual adventure.

After leaving hospital he went before a succession of Medical Boards. He always told them that he 'felt quite fit', and was ready to go back to France, but they continually prolonged his period of light duty until he had been in England for nearly six months.

6

Roland's death, Edward's departure and Geoffrey's readiness to take up once more a life which he knew must break him physically or mentally in a very short time, all increased my certainty that, however long the War might last, I could not return to Somerville while those whom I loved best had sacrificed, and were sacrificing, everything that they cared for in the world. I even began to face, bitterly and reluctantly, the possibility that I might never return at all. The Germans were now hammering remorselessly at Verdun, and pessimists had already begun to discuss the chances of a ten-year war. 'The first seven years will be the worst!' was now an accepted slogan amongst the men, and even the spirit of the *Punch* cartoons, once so blithely full of exhortations to stand up 'For King and Country', had changed to a grim and dogged 'Carry On!'

So on a half-day in March, I went up to Oxford to discuss the uncertain future with the Principal of Somerville. My first-year friends, Marjorie and Theresa, met me at the station, and later gave me tea – to which they invited my Classical tutor – in their Oriel study overlooking the High Street. Perhaps it was the wandering ghosts of bygone conversations among generations of men in that old college room which broke down the normal barrier between tutors and students, for we talked of the War and those who went to it and those who died, until my tutor and I forgot our hostesses, who sat, quite silent, on either side of the blazing fire. People realised in these days, she said, how much more than physical existence a man's life meant, and how much life was gained by laying down the physical side of it.

At that stage of the War, mercifully preserved from knowledge of a world seventeen years older, in which second-rate masculine ability would struggle helplessly with almost insoluble problems because the first-rate were gone from a whole generation, we were still able to believe that a country which laid down the best of its life would somehow surely find it. Nothing thus given up, my tutor maintained, was ever lost, and those who died were not really gone but were with us always, canonised for us more truly than the saints. She was thinking, I knew, of a distinguished life which had been cut short by a bullet in Mesopotamia, and I, she knew, was thinking of Roland, whom I had dreamed of in my coachings with her when we were reading the *Iliad*, and who now was dead. Then, all at once, she was gone and we three were alone, staring at each other, shy, surprised, queerly exalted.

Later I saw the Principal, of whom I had strangely ceased to be in awe. She was so much less terrifying than most hospital Matrons, so I told her finally that I should not return to college until after the War.

Back at Camberwell, I found a notice pinned to the board in the dining-hall asking for volunteers for foreign service. Now that Roland was irretrievably gone and my decision about Oxford had finally been made, there seemed to be no reason for withholding my name. It was the logical conclusion, I thought, of service in England, though quite a number of V.A.D.s refused to sign because their parents wouldn't like it, or they were too inexperienced, or had had pneumonia when they were five years old.

Their calm readiness to admit their fears amazed me. Not being composed in even the smallest measure of the stuff of which heroines are made, I was terrified of going abroad – so much publicity was now given to the German submarine campaign that the possibility of being torpedoed was a nightmare to me – but I was even more afraid of acknowledging my cowardice to myself, let alone to others. A number of neurotic ancestors, combined with the persistent, unresolved terrors of childhood, had deprived me of the comfortable gift of natural courage; throughout the War I was warding off panic, but so long as I was able to do that, I could put up a fair show of self-control. If once I allowed myself to recognise my fear of foreign service, and especially of submarines, all kinds of alarming things that I had survived quite tolerably – such as Zeppelin raids, and pitch-black slum streets, and being alone in a large hut on night-duty – would become impossible.

So I put down my name on the active service list, and never permitted my conscious self to hear the dastardly prayer of my unconscious that when my orders came they might be for anywhere but a hospital ship or the Mediterranean.

7

The final and worst stage of my refusal to be reconciled to my world after the loss of Roland was precipitated by quite a trivial event.

When the bitter Christmas weeks were over, my parents, for the sake of economy, had moved from the Grand Hotel to a smaller one, where the service was indifferent and the wartime cooking atrocious. As the result of its cold draughtiness, its bad food, and her anxiety over Edward, my mother, in the middle of March, was overcome by an acute species of chill. Believing herself, in sudden panic, to be worse than she was, she wrote begging me to get leave and come down to Brighton and nurse her.

After much difficulty and two or three interviews, I managed to obtain the grudging and sceptical leave of absence granted to V.A.D.s who had sick relatives – always regarded as a form of shirking, since the Army was supposed to be above all but the most vital domestic obligations. When I arrived at the hotel to find that my mother, in more stoical mood, had already struggled out of bed and was in no urgent need of me, I felt that I was perpetrating exactly the deceit of which I had been suspected. Forgetting that parents who had been brought up by their own forbears to regard young women as perpetually at the disposal of husbands or fathers, could hardly be expected to realise that Army discipline – so demonstrably implacable in the case of men – now operated with the same stern rigidity for daughters as for sons, I gave way to an outburst of inconsiderate fury that plunged me back into the depths of despondency from which I had been struggling to climb.

Wretched, remorseful, and still feeling horribly guilty of obtaining leave on false pretences, I stayed in Brighton for the two days that I had demanded. But the episode had pushed my misery to the point of mental crisis, and the first time that I was off duty after returning to Camberwell, I went up to Denmark Hill to try to think out in solitude all the implications of my spasmodic angers, my furious, uncontrolled resentments.

It was a bitter, grey afternoon, and an icy wind drove flurries of snow into my face as I got off the tram and hastened into the hostel. Huddling into a coat in my cheerless cubicle, I watched the snowflakes falling, and wondered how ever I was going to get through the weary remainder of life. I was only at the beginning of my twenties; I might have another forty, perhaps even fifty, years to live. The prospect seemed appalling, and I shuddered with cold and desolation as my numbed fingers wrote in my diary an abject, incoherent confession of self-hatred and despair.

'I really am becoming quite an impossible person nowadays. I never could have dreamed of the effect Roland's death would have on me . . . Maybe one day I shall be better for having suffered, when I can get far enough away from his life and death to remember the sweetness of possessing him without the anguish of losing him, to remember the grandeur of his death when the sense of its appalling waste and pitifulness will have grown less acute . . . But at present I really am an abominable person . . . I have a bad character everywhere . . . Perhaps any place I had been in, anything I had been doing, would have had the same effect on me under the circumstances. And I begin to feel that perhaps after all I must accept defeat, and must do something to change my present conditions of life if I am going to have any personality left that is worth having. And yet all the time I know that I am not a horrid person at all inside . . . Will the Recording Angel, I wonder, put down a little to one's credit for all one meant, and yet failed, to do? . . . The last three months have been dark, confused, nightmare-like − I can barely remember what has happened in them, any more than one can properly remember a terrible illness after it is over. Everything I loved and love, everything I lived for, worked for, prayed for, seems to be slipping away . . . Oh, God! How unhappy I am!'

In April, with the first termination of my contract, I knew that I should have to decide either to leave the 1st London or to sign on again, and for the next few weeks I worked myself into a nervous frenzy because I could not make up my mind whether to stay at the hospital, or to abandon nursing and take up work at the War Office – where I imagined, quite erroneously, that such intelligence as I possessed would be more appropriately employed. I even went so far as to interview a War Office official, and to take a tiny bedroom in the Bayswater apartment occupied by Clare's ex-governess.

I had notified the Matron of my intention to leave and had even begun to pack, when I was suddenly overwhelmed by a passionate conviction that to give up the work and the place I hated would be defeat, and that Roland, and whatever in the world stood for Right and Goodness, wanted me to remain at the hospital and go on active service. I was far too deeply immersed in my obsession to speculate even for a second whether Right and Goodness, if personified, were likely to turn from the terrific task of assessing war-guilt to interest themselves in my little difficulty about the hospital and the War Office. Overcome with shame and remorse, I begged the Matron to allow me to withdraw my notice. Tolerant and understanding as always, she permitted me to sign on again, and I dropped limply back into the hospital routine, too much exhausted by the irrational conflict to resent my family's resigned conclusion that anyone so madly erratic was beyond even protest.

On April 23rd – it was Easter Sunday, and exactly four months after Roland's death – I went to St Paul's Cathedral for the morning service, and sat in a side aisle beneath G. F. Watts's picture of Hagar in the Desert. Her Gethsemane, I thought, had been even darker than that of the Man of Sorrows, who after all knew – or believed – that He was God; she was merely a human being without omnipotence, and a woman too, at the mercy, as were all women to-day, of an agonising, ruthless fate which it seemed she could do nothing to restrain. 'Watchman, will the night soon pass?' ran the inscription under the painting, and I wondered how many women in the Cathedral that morning, numbed and bewildered by blow after blow, were asking the self-same question.

'Will the night soon pass? Will it ever pass? How much longer can I endure it? What will help me to endure it, if endured it must be?'

In a Regent Street tea-shop after the service had ended, I sat over one of the innumerable cups of coffee that we drank during the War in order to get a few moments of privacy, and endeavoured, as earnestly as though humanity itself had entrusted me with the solution of its problems, to discover what was left that would help. In the small notebook that I always carried with me, I scribbled down some of the conclusions at which, in those weeks of wrestling with unseen enemies, I seemed to have arrived.

'I know that, come what may, our love will henceforth always be the ruling factor in my life. He is to me the embodiment of that ideal of heroism – that "Heroism in the Abstract" – for which he lived and died, and for which I will strive to live, and if need be, die also.

'If people say to me, "Why do you do this? It is not necessary, your duty need not take you thus far," I can only answer that in one way heroism is always unnecessary, in so far as it always lies outside the scope of one's limited, stereotyped duty. I do not know with how much or how little courage I should face dangers and perils if they came to me – I am less blindly confident than I once was, for I have been learning a truer estimate of myself, my failings and limitations, in these dark days. I have learnt to hope that if there be a Judgment Day of some kind, God will not see us with our own eyes, nor judge us as we judge ourselves.

'But perhaps – and this is my anchor in the present deep waters – self-knowledge is a surer foundation than self-exaltation, and having reached down to it, the ground which nothing can cut away from under my feet, I may achieve more than in the old days. Perhaps one can never rise to the heights until one has gone right down into the depths – such depths as I have known of late.

'Perhaps now I shall one day rise, and be worthy of him who in his life both in peace and in war and in his death on the fields of France has shown me "the way more plain". At any rate, if ever I do face danger and suffering with some measure of his heroism, it will be because I have learnt through him that love is supreme, that love is stronger than death and the fear of death.'

8

Fortunately for the mental balance of average mankind, exalted emotions of this type do not as a rule last very long, but before mine relapsed once more into despondency, respite came from an undignified but not altogether unwelcome source.

So preoccupied had I been with my griefs and problems that I had barely noticed a mild epidemic of German measles which was distributing members of the Camberwell nursing staff round various London fever hospitals. But when Betty went down with it, and a day or two later I awoke to find my arms speckled with red from wrist to elbow, I reported sick at once, and was sent off to a fever hospital in south-west London.

In this elegant institution, thankful for a few days of rest for an aching body and of release from introspective torment for a tired mind, I shared with one other V.A.D. a small ground-floor ward looking out upon a coal-heap. The 'rest' was psychological rather than physical, for the loud and continuous noises in the Fever Hospital ran to even greater variety than its infectious diseases. When I had listened for two or three days to the children crying in the next ward, the maids yelling and screaming in the kitchen opposite, coal being carted in the yard outside the window, a piano in a near-by house being execrably thumped from early morning till close upon midnight, the roaring and whistling of trains from the railway a hundred yards distant, an apparatus in an adjacent shed making an incessant sound like a hoarse threshing-machine, and the continual dropping of plates and trays with resounding crashes all over the ground floor, I began to feel acutely sorry for any patients who were seriously ill.

'I forget if I told you about morning visits here – which are the greatest trial of the day,' runs a letter written on April 30th to my mother, who by then was in Macclesfield, where she and my father, tired of the tedium of Brighton hotels, had taken a pleasant furnished house before deciding upon a final move. 'First the Matron comes round, then the house-doctor and then the visiting doctor. They all address you with fatuous, condescending remarks, to which you are expected to make a bright reply. The Matron . . . calls the smell of a rose "a delightful perfume". The doctors have a very pronounced bedside manner, and talk to you in a half-teasing way as if you were a child – the "Well, how are *we* to-day?" kind of attitude. To crown everything, on Friday afternoon we were visited by the C. of E. chaplain, a very shy, nervous young man. When he entered, I happened to be sitting up in a chair in my dressing-gown, showing a good deal of mauve-striped pyjama leg. I suppose this frightened him, for he relapsed at once into an embarrassed silence, and the whole of the conversation devolved upon me, while he wriggled in his chair and played with his cassock.'

I had not been allowed to bring my own clothes to the hospital, so as soon as I became convalescent I was presented with a selection of institution garments, and sent to take the air with the other municipal paupers. After getting into a pair of unbleached calico knickers, thick woollen socks, a bulky grey and white striped petticoat, a sage-green flannel blouse, and a huge pleated navy-blue skirt made for an old charlady six times my size, which I had to attach to my voluminous underclothes with half a dozen large safety-pins, I successfully accomplished several perambulations round the scrubby square of hospital grass without my costume disintegrating in the process. I was also permitted to take a bath, with unlocked door, in a bathroom used by patients recovering from various diseases. A dank, stuffy odour prevailed there, and enormous black beetles slithered perpetually in and out of the pipes.

During my three weeks' captivity, Victor and Geoffrey wrote to me constantly, and sent flowers and fruit which caused some of my fellow-sufferers to christen me 'the plutocrat of the workhouse table'. Edward, whose experience in the trenches had so far been uneventful, wrote also from Albert, describing the Golden Virgin of the Basilica, which had just been knocked horizontal – still holding the Child with its tiny arms outspread in benediction – by the first enemy bombardment. The French, he told me afterwards, believed that so long as the statue remained on the steeple they would never lose Albert. It actually fell in 1918 as the Germans entered the town.

When they first went to France, wrote Edward, the 11th Sherwood Foresters had been in trenches some distance from Louvencourt, but now they were not far from Roland's grave. 'The sun set last night in a red glow over him as I looked from here, giving a sense of the most perfect and enduring peace.'

Three weeks later he wrote to tell me that he had been to Louvencourt. Very carefully he described his journey, knowing how much each detail would mean to me, and drew a little diagram showing the arrangement of the graves in the cemetery.

'I walked up along the path,' he concluded, 'and stood in front of the grave . . . And I took off my cap and prayed to whatever God there may be that I might live to be worthy of the friendship of the man whose grave was before me . . . But I did not stay there long because it was so very clear that he could not come back, and though it may be that he could see me looking at his grave, yet I did not feel that he was there . . . So I went away, and first I went on into the little town; it was crowded with troops and I did not go far and did not find the hospital. There were some Worcesters about but they were not the 7th or 8th; and so I went back the way I had come.'

After the first few days at the Fever Hospital I felt perfectly well, and was kept there only by the length of the infection period. Although, during those noisy, monotonous weeks, I had at last time to read the newspapers, with their perturbing accounts of the Easter Rebellion in Ireland, and Townshend's surrender at Kut, and the first stages of Roger Casement's progress towards his execution in August, there was still more than enough opportunity for thoughts about the past. At the beginning of May a *Times* paragraph describing the ceremony on Magdalen Bridge brought back to me the cool, sweet ride through Marston just after dawn a year ago, and all at once the impulse to put what I felt into verse – a new impulse which had recently begun both to fascinate and torment me – sprang up with overwhelming compulsion. Seizing my notebook and a pencil, I retired to the beetle-infested bathroom, which, owing to the persistent loquacity of the V.A.D. who shared my room, was the only place in the building where I could be certain of peace.

Later I polished up the poem, 'May Morning', and sent it to the *Oxford Magazine*. It appeared in the next number, and was afterwards included in *Verses of a V.A.D.*:

> *The rising sun shone warmly on the tower;*
> *Into the clear pure heaven the hymn aspired,*
> *Piercingly sweet. This was the morning hour*
> *When life awoke with spring's creative power,*
> *And the old city's grey to gold was fired.*
>
> *Silently reverent stood the noisy throng;*
> *Under the bridge the boats in long array*
> *Lay motionless. The choristers' far song*
> *Faded upon the breeze in echoes long.*
> *Swiftly I left the bridge and rode away.*
>
> *Straight to a little wood's green heart I sped,*
> *Where cowslips grew, beneath whose gold withdrawn*
> *The fragrant earth peeped warm and richly red;*
> *All trace of winter's chilling touch had fled,*
> *And song-birds ushered in the year's bright morn.*
>
> *I had met Love not many days before,*
> *And as in blissful mood I listening lay,*
> *None ever had of joy so full a store.*
> *I thought that spring must last for evermore,*
> *For I was young and loved, and it was May.*
>
> ★   ★   ★
>
> *Now it is May again, and sweetly clear*
> *Perhaps once more aspires the Latin hymn*
> *From Magdalen tower, but not for me to hear.*
> *I toil far distant, for a darker year*
> *Shadows the century with menace grim.*

I walk in ways where pain and sorrow dwell,
 And ruin such as only War can bring,
 Where each lives through his individual hell,
 Fraught with remembered horror none can tell,
 And no more is there glory in the spring.

And I am worn with tears, for he I loved
 Lies cold beneath the stricken sod of France;
 Hope has forsaken me, by death removed,
 And Love that seemed so strong and gay has proved
 A poor crushed thing, the toy of cruel chance.

Often I wonder, as I grieve in vain,
 If when the long, long future years creep slow,
 And War and tears alike have ceased to reign,
 I ever shall recapture, once again,
 The mood of that May Morning, long ago.

The concluding speculation is answered now – not only for me but for all my generation. We never have recaptured that mood; and we never shall.

9

After the Fever Hospital came a blessed fortnight of sick leave in Macclesfield.

The year was now on the high road to summer, and, whenever I could forget for a few moments that warmth and fine weather meant great campaigns and peril for Edward, I was conscious of a quiet pleasure in my surroundings such as I had not known since leaving Oxford. For nearly twelve months I had had no holiday in its true sense of an interval of tranquillity, and those two weeks did a great deal to hasten the process of psychological recuperation which had begun on Easter Sunday.

The house, which my parents had taken from a local family, had a gracious little garden where lilac and laburnum and pink hawthorn were already in flower. Beneath the hot, scented bushes

I read for many hours my neglected books, and, in a warm, semi-furnished loft attached to the house, compiled a small volume of favourite quotations. When the long spring evenings grew too cold for the garden, a very tolerable piano in the drawing-room helped me both to forget and to remember.

'This afternoon,' I wrote to Edward, 'I have been playing over the slow movement from Beethoven's No. 7 Sonata, and some of the Macdowell Sea Songs which you used to play. Whenever I sit down to the piano now I can always see you playing away, absolutely unconcerned by other people's requests to you to come out, or listen a moment! If you were to die I think I should have to give up music altogether, for there would be so many things I could never bear to hear or play – just as now I cannot bear to play "*L'Envoi*", or the "*Liber scriptus proferitur*" part of Verdi's Requiem, which for some reason or other I always connected with Roland's going to the front . . .

'I am a little amused by the tone of the Uppingham magazine sent on to you. The Editorial has certainly greatly deteriorated since Roland's day. Both it and the entire magazine seem chiefly concerned with football. Exploits on the football field are related in detail, while the exploits of those on another field across the sea pass unnoticed, and such names of those who met their death there as R. A. Leighton and S. I. Mansel-Carey are hidden in a little corner marked "Died of Wounds". But one consoles one's self with the thought that their names will live on the Chapel walls long after the zealous footballers have passed out of remembrance. I noticed also that people who distinguished themselves at football while at school get biographies in the magazine, though he who surpassed the school record for prizes had no special mention at all. *Sic transit gloria mundi.*'

I returned to a London seething with bewildered excitement over the Battle of Jutland. Were we celebrating a glorious naval victory or lamenting an ignominious defeat? We hardly knew; and each fresh edition of the newspapers obscured rather than illuminated this really quite important distinction. The one indisputable fact was that hundreds of young men, many of them midshipmen only just in their teens, had gone down without hope of rescue or understanding of the issue to a cold, anonymous grave.

'I have just been to St Paul's where they closed the service by singing a hymn of thanksgiving for our "Moral" Victory! That seems to me to be going just a little too far,' a letter of mine commented to Edward on June 11th. 'We couldn't do more than that if we had given the German navy a smashing blow, instead of having ended the battle in a draw which we say was a victory to us, and they say was a victory to them.'

But before this letter was written, Edward had been home on a short, unexpected leave.

As soon as he arrived he went up to Macclesfield, with Geoffrey, for the week-end, but he and my mother came back to London for the last two days, and I was given forty-eight hours off duty to stay with them at the Grafton Hotel. Except for an intense antipathy to noise — noise in trains, in 'buses, in the street, in restaurants — he seemed unchanged.

The afternoon of his return to London stands out very clearly in my recollection, for on that day the news came through of Kitchener's death in the *Hampshire*. The words 'KITCHENER DROWNED' seemed more startling, more dreadful, than the tidings of Jutland; their incredibility may still be measured by the rumours, which so long persisted, that he was not dead, that he had escaped in another ship to Russia, that he was organising a great campaign in France, that the wreck of the *Hampshire* was only a 'blind' to conceal his real intentions, that he would return in his own good time to deliver the final blow of the War.

For a few moments during that day, almost everyone in England must have dropped his occupation to stare, blank and incredulous, into the shocked eyes of his neighbour. In the evening, Edward and our mother and I walked up and down, almost without a word, beside the river at Westminster. Sad and subdued, we stood on the terrace below St Thomas's Hospital and looked at the black silhouette of the Union Jack on the War Office, flying half-mast against the darkening red of an angry June sky. So great had been the authority over our imagination of that half-legendary figure, that we felt as dismayed as though the ship of state itself had foundered in the raging North Sea.

Edward's leave, like all short leaves, vanished in a whirl-wind of activities. Somehow he crowded into it an afternoon at Keymer, a visit to Victor, who was now at Purfleet, a concert, and one or two theatres, which inevitably included *Romance*, with Doris Keane and Owen Nares, and *Chu Chin Chow*. I seemed hardly to have seen him when it was time for him to return, but in a quiet interval, when we were alone together, he spoke in veiled but significant language of a great battle impending. It would start, he told me, somewhere near Albert, and he knew that he would be in it.

Before his train left for Folkestone, I had to go back to Camberwell, and he went with me to get my 'bus from the bottom of Regent Street. I climbed the steps of the 'bus with a sinking heart, for I knew very well how many were the chances against our meeting again. When I turned and waved to him from the upper deck, I noticed with impotent grief the sad wistfulness of his eyes as he stood where Roland had stood to watch the advent of 1915, and saluted me beside the fountain in Piccadilly Circus.

'I'm more than ever convinced,' Victor said to me afterwards, 'that it's worse for him than it was for Roland. Edward entirely lacks any primitive warring side to his character such as Roland possessed . . . I don't think that the heroic and glorious side of war appeals to him as it did to Roland and I think that this makes it much harder for him.'

Later he told me that Edward had said to him at Purfleet: 'The thought of those lines of trenches gives me a sick feeling in the stomach.'

Just after Edward's return to France, I had the first of those dreams which were to recur, in slightly different variations, at frequent intervals for nearly ten years. Sometimes, in these dreams, Roland was minus an arm or a leg, or so badly mutilated or disfigured that he did not want me to see him; sometimes he had merely grown tired of all of us and of England, and was trying to become another person in a country far away. But always he was alive, and within range of sight and touch after the conquest of some minor impediment.

'I thought that Tah and I suddenly got a letter each in Roland's handwriting,' I told Edward. 'In the dream we knew he was dead just as we do in everyday life. I opened mine with the very strange kind of feeling that one would have if such a thing happened actually. In the letter he said it was all a mistake that he was dead, and that he was really a prisoner in Germany but so badly maimed that he would never be able to get back again. I felt a sudden overwhelming feeling of relief to think he was after all alive under any circumstances whatever, and I gazed and gazed at the familiar handwriting on both Tah's letter and mine, marvelling that it was really his, and as I gazed at it, it seemed gradually to change and become more and more different, till finally it was not like his at all.'

Edward's reply closed with one or two sentences that quickened the sense of forboding anxiety which I had felt since his departure.

'I am sure you will be interested to hear that we have quite a lot of celery growing near our present position.' ('The celery is ripe' was for some obscure reason the phrase chosen by us to indicate that an attack was about to come off.) 'It is ripening quickly although it is being somewhat delayed by this cold and wet weather we are having lately, and if the weather continues better I expect it will be ready in about a week.'

At the end of June, the hospital received orders to clear out all convalescents and prepare for a great rush of wounded. We knew that already a tremendous bombardment had begun, for we could feel the vibration of the guns at Camberwell, and the family in Keymer heard them continuously. The sickening, restless apprehension of those days reminded me of the week before Loos, but now there was no riverside bank beside which to dream, no time to spare for the somnolent misery of suspense. Hour after hour, as the convalescents departed, we added to the long rows of waiting beds, so sinister in their white, expectant emptiness.

On June 30th, a tiny pencilled note came from Edward. 'The papers,' it announced tersely, 'are getting rather more interesting, but I have only time to say adieu.'

Obviously the moment that I had dreaded for a month was

imminent, and I had no choice but to face it. How much longer
was there, I wondered, to wait in this agony of fear? Had I time
to get one last message through to Edward before the attack
began? I decided to try; and sent off a letter that night.

'Your little note has made me very sad. It seems not even yet
time to cry "Will the night soon pass?" for you are very right,
all too right, about the papers; the news this morning is like the
sinister gathering of a thunderstorm just about to break overhead.
There seems to be an atmosphere of tense expectation about all
the world, and a sense of anguished foreknowledge of the sacrifice that is to be made . . . But I know you will not forget that
as long as I am alive . . . I shall always remember all the things
that both you and he meant and wished to do and be, and that
as far as I am able, they shall all be fulfilled.

'I say this because the remembrance of his death is with me
very vividly to-day; I say it too because in your little note – in
case of what may be – you say farewell. Adieu, then, if it must
be. But I still prefer to say, and believe, what I said before at
Piccadilly Circus—

"Au revoir."'

10

By the next day, July 1st, all the beds were ready, and Betty and
I were each given an afternoon off duty. Neither of us felt in the
mood for shops, or restaurants, or the proletarian *camaraderie* of
the parks in midsummer, but we had heard that Brahm's Requiem
was to be sung that afternoon at Southwark Cathedral, and we
decided to go.

'What a theme for what a day!' I thought afterwards. In the
cool darkness of the Cathedral, so quieting after the dusty, reeking
streets of Camberwell, we listened, with aching eyes, to the solemn
words in their lovely, poignant setting:

> *Lord, make me to know what the measure of my days may
> be, let me know all my frailty, ere death overtake me.
> Lord God, all my days here are but a span long to*

> *Thee, and my being naught within Thy sight . . .*
> *O Lord, who will console me? My hope is in Thee.*

When the organ had throbbed away into silence, we came out
from the dim, melodious peace to hear the shouting of raucous
voices, and to see newspaper boys with huge posters running
excitedly up and down the pavement. Involuntarily I clutched
Betty's arm, for the posters ran:

'GREAT BRITISH OFFENSIVE BEGINS.'

A boy thrust a *Star* into my hand, and, shivering with cold in
the hot sunshine, I made myself read it.

'BRITISH OFFENSIVE BEGINS – OFFICIAL

'FRONT LINE BROKEN OVER
'16 MILES

'FRENCH SHARE ADVANCE

'THE FIGHTING DEVELOPING IN
'INTENSITY

'British Headquarters, France.
'*Saturday*, 9.30 a.m.
'British Offensive. At about half-past seven o'clock this
morning a vigorous offensive was launched by the British
Army. The front extends over about 20 miles north of the
Somme.
'The assault was preceded by a terrific bombardment,
lasting about an hour and a half.
'It is too early as yet to give anything but the barest
particulars, as the fighting is developing in intensity, but
the British troops have already occupied the German front
lines.'

Two days afterwards, that singularly wasteful and ineffective orgy of slaughter which we now know as the Battle of the Somme was described by *The Times* correspondent as '90 miles of uproar':

'For nearly four whole days now the 90 miles of the lines along the British front have been 90 miles of almost continuous chaos, of uproar and desolation. Day by day our bombardment has grown in intensity, until under the dreadful hurricane whole reaches of the enemy's trenches have been battered out of existence.'

Only the mechanical habit of work which I had by now acquired enabled me to get through that evening, for the whole of my conscious mind resolved itself into one speculation: Was Edward still in the world – or not? At the hostel, after supper, I wrote to my mother; I did not know how much Edward had told her, but if he was dead it seemed better that she should share my knowledge and be forewarned. It surprises me still that I was able to write so calmly, so unemotionally. The whole of my generation seems always to have worn, for the benefit of its parents, a personality not quite its own, and I often wonder if, in days to come, my own son and daughter will assume for me the same alien disguise.

'The news in the paper, which we got at 4 0 this afternoon, is quite self-evident,' ran my letter, 'so I needn't say much about it. London was wildly excited and the papers selling madly. Of course you remember that Edward is at Albert and it is all round there that the papers say the fighting is fiercest – Montauban, Fricourt, Mametz. I have been expecting this for days, as when he was here he told me that the great offensive was to begin there and of the part his own regiment was to play in the attack.'

For the next three days I lived and worked in hourly dread of a telegram. Had it not been for the sympathy of Geoffrey and Victor, and the knowledge that they too were watching and waiting in similar anxiety, this new suspense would have been overwhelming. Geoffrey wrote from Brocton Camp, in Staffordshire, where he was once more temporarily attached to the 13th Sherwood Foresters, to tell me that nine officers were going to the front from his battalion next day; he would have been going himself were he not on a course which lasted five more weeks. He'd been thinking about us all more than usual, he said, and only hoped that Edward would be as well looked after as himself 'out there'. For many things, he concluded, he yearned to be there once more, and yet he knew that when the summons came again he would dread it – 'or, to use a balder word, funk it' – which was, he seemed to think, an awful confession to make, 'as it's absolutely the only thing now.'

On Sunday, the day after the battle, Victor came up from Purfleet to see me, for he too had had a note from Edward similar to mine. 'The remark "One can only hope they will follow" now applies. I am so busy that I have only time for material things. And so I must bid you a long, long adieu.'

Throughout the brief hour of my off-duty time we walked up and down St James's Park, staring with unseeing eyes at the ducks fluttering over what was left of the lake – which was being drained to make room for Army huts – while Victor vainly tried to convince me how excellent were Edward's chances of survival, since he was the kind of person who always kept his head in a crisis.

Next day we were told that the first rush of wounded was on its way to Camberwell.

'This afternoon,' I wrote to my mother, 'the hospital was warned to get ready for 150 patients, 50 officers and 100 men. We had not really that much accommodation for officers, so all the patients from one of the surgical wards in the College were transferred into one of the new huts and their ward made into an officers' ward. There was terrific tearing about all afternoon and everyone available was sent for to help haul mattresses, trollies and patients about . . . When I came off duty to-night the convoy had not yet arrived but was expected any hour. We were all warned by Matron to-night that very busy and strenuous days are ahead of us, and all our own arrangements must go quite on one side for the time being.'

At the usual 'break' for 9.30 biscuits and apron-changing next morning I had only a few moments' respite, as the 'Fall In' had already sounded for the first expected ambulances. But on my way to the dining-hall I went – as I had gone at every available opportunity during the past three days – to the V.A.D. sitting-room to take another fearful glance at the letter-rack, and there, high above the other letters, I saw a crushed, pencil-scrawled envelope addressed in Edward's handwriting. In a panic of relief – for at least he couldn't be dead – I pulled it down, but even then I could hardly open it, for the paper was so thin and my fingers shook so.

The little note was dated July 1st, and the written words were faint and uneven.

'DEAR VERA,' it said, 'I was wounded in the action this morning in left arm and right thigh not seriously. Hope to come to England. Don't worry. EDWARD.'

For a moment the empty room spun round; then I remembered the waiting ambulances and the Sister's injunction to 'hurry back.' In the effort of pulling myself together I recalled, too, that I could save my father and mother, whose letters arrived in Macclesfield a day later than mine, another twenty-four hours of cruel anxiety. Regardless of the indignant glances of Sisters who knew that V.A.D.s were allowed to run only in cases of hæmorrhage or fire, I dashed like a young hare down the stone corridor to the telephone and asked my uncle at the National Provincial Bank to wire to the family.

'I hope they will send him to England soon . . .' I wrote home late that night, 'but we hear hundreds and probably thousands of them are waiting to come across . . . the large number of officers we were expecting yesterday did not arrive . . . There were so many wounded the day before . . . that there were not platforms enough at Charing Cross to land them and they had to be taken round to Paddington . . . Do you see his regiment is mentioned as having done specially well in the battle by *The Times'* special correspondent to-day? It would be funny if he turned up here. I only wish he would.'

On that morning, July 4th, began the immense convoys which

came without cessation for about a fortnight, and continued at short intervals for the whole of that sultry month and the first part of August. Throughout those 'busy and strenuous days' the wards sweltered beneath their roofs of corrugated iron; the prevailing odour of wounds and stinking streets lingered perpetually in our nostrils, the red-hot hardness of paths and pavements burnt its way through the soles of our shoes. Day after day I had to fight the queer, frightening sensation – to which, throughout my years of nursing, I never became accustomed – of seeing the covered stretchers come in, one after another, without knowing, until I ran with pounding heart to look, what fearful sight or sound or stench, what problem of agony or imminent death, each brown blanket concealed.

In order to be within call at night, Betty and I were moved from Denmark Hill to a ground-floor flat in a block just outside the Brixton gate of the hospital. Every evening, after managing by the complete sacrifice of off-duty time to finish the morning dressings just before supper and leave the night people to give the afternoon and evening treatment, we limped from the chaos of the wards into the grateful privacy of our flat, and fell on to our beds feeling as though someone had dealt a series of numbing blows to all our bones and muscles from knee to shoulder. It was an effort to make our aching arms go through the movements of taking off our clothes, a triumph of resolution to force our sore feet to carry us to the bathroom.

Our daily work was complicated and increased by the new V.A.D.s who were rushed to the hospital by Devonshire House to meet the emergency. Not having been broken in to a 'push' by preceding weeks of ordinary routine, they went sick in shoals with septic fingers, heat strokes and chills. At the same time the orderlies were fast disappearing to take the place of stretcher-bearers wounded at the front, and the few that remained had constantly to answer the 'Fall In' and were never available for work in the wards.

For the first time I learnt that one could be tired to the limits of human endurance, and yet get through more work in a day than I had ever thought possible. When the groans of anæsthetised men made the ward a Bedlam, and the piteous impatience of boys in anguish demanded attention just when the rush of work was worst and the heat least endurable, I kept myself going, with the characteristic idealism of those youthful years, by murmuring under my breath two verses from Kipling's 'Dirge of Dead Sisters':

(When the days were torment and the nights were clouded terror,
 When the Powers of Darkness had dominion on our soul—
When we fled consuming through the Seven Hells of fever,
 These put out their hands to us and healed and made us
 whole.)

    ★   ★   ★   ★   ★

(Till the pain was merciful and stunned us into silence—
 When each nerve cried out on God that made the misused clay;
When the Body triumphed and the last poor shame departed—
 These abode our agonies and wiped the sweat away.)

But there were other and greater compensations than Kipling. Edward was safe and Victor and Geoffrey were still in England; for the time being I had no immediate anxiety, and physical fatigue was a small price to pay for that relief.

By the evening of July 4th, my forty-bed hut in the park was already filled beyond capacity with acute surgical cases. But across the road in the College, the long empty rows of officers' beds still waited.

11

Very early next morning, I heard the two V.A.D.s from J, the officers' ward in the College, summoned from their beds by telephone. I was then still sleeping at Denmark Hill, and in a half-dream listened to them a few minutes later hurrying down the stairs and out into the quiet yellow light of the summer dawn.

After breakfast I went to my own ward as usual, and was in the midst of preparing dressing-trays – with which, regardless of floors and lockers, the day now began – when I heard a voice agitatedly calling: 'Brittain! Brittain! Come *here*!'

I turned, and saw to my great astonishment the elder of the
two V.A.D.s from J standing in the doorway. She was panting so
much from hurry that she could hardly speak, but managed just
to gasp out: 'I say – *Do* you know your brother's in J ward?'

By pure good luck I managed to avoid the complete wreckage
of my dressing-bowls, and gasped in my turn: '*What!* Edward in
J?'

'Honestly, he is,' she answered jerkily; 'I've just been washing
him. Sorry I can't stop – only got permission to come over and
tell you!' And she rushed back across the road.

I was excitedly explaining the situation to my Charge-Sister,
when Matron – the stony-eyed and somewhat alarming successor
to the first Matron, who had left the hospital a few weeks earlier
for work in another field – rang up to say that Second-Lieutenant
E. H. Brittain had come in with the convoy that morning and
was asking for his sister. I could see him, she added, as soon as I
could be 'spared from the ward'. Overwhelmed with work though
we were, the Sister told me that I might go and need not return
at once, so, half-dazed with surging emotions, I raced over to the
College.

Such a confusion of screens and stretchers and washing-bowls
replaced the orderly beds of the previous night that for several
seconds I stood in the doorway of J and looked for Edward in
vain. Then, half way down the ward, a blue pyjama-clad arm
began to wave, and the next moment I was beside his bed.

For a minute or two we gazed at each other in tremulous
silence. One of his sleeves, I saw, was empty and the arm beneath
it stiff and bandaged, but I noticed with relief, as I looked with
an instinctively professional eye for the familiar green stain, that
the outer bandage was spotless. With his one available hand he
was endeavouring to negotiate a breakfast tray; I helped him to
eat a poached egg, and the commonplace action restored to both
of us the habit of self-control.

Even then, neither of us could say much. He seemed – to my
surprise, for I remember Geoffrey's haggard depression after a
much smaller wound – gayer and happier than he had been all
through his leave. The relief of having the great dread faced and

creditably over was uppermost in his mind just then; it was only later, as he gradually remembered all he had been through on July 1st, that Victor and Geoffrey and I realised that the Battle of the Somme had profoundly changed him and added ten years to his age.

Throughout that day, when he saw no one except myself and the uncle who again sent out a series of telegrams, the astounding coincidence of his arrival at Camberwell possessed all his thoughts. At Waterloo, he told me, the congestion had been so enormous that there was no hope of being allocated by request to special hospitals.

'I simply couldn't believe my eyes,' he concluded, 'when an orderly pinned a label on me saying "1st London General".'

That afternoon and for several successive days, I was allowed to have tea with him in his ward. Except for a brief good-night it was my only chance of seeing him, for I was on duty without a break for nearly a fortnight. Even the end-of-day ten minutes were difficult to wrest from the J Charge-Sister, a cynical old curmudgeon who could not be persuaded that I really wanted to talk to Edward, and not to flirt with the twenty other officers whose beds surrounded his in the crowded ward. She was so palpably hostile to my visits that one evening, exhausted by ten days' unremitting endeavour to save thirty or forty shattered men whose tendency to die continually threatened to defeat us, I suddenly relapsed into tears as I sat by Edward's bed, and could do nothing but try wordlessly to choke them back as he stroked my hand with his long, thin fingers.

The first gaiety of relief was by now slowly evaporating. He still remained tranquil and controlled, but his left arm was stiff and the fingers immovable; the bullet had badly damaged the central nerve, and he secretly worried about its possible effect upon his violin playing. I learnt the details of July 1st only by degrees, for whenever my mother or Victor or Geoffrey was not with him at tea-time, he was endeavouring to give such poor comfort as he could to his company commander's mother, a dignified, white-haired woman with tragic eyes. Captain H. was missing for weeks after the battle; early in the day he had been wounded in the stomach by shrapnel, but had told two of the attacking party, who stopped to pick him up, to 'get on with the job and not bother about him'. Edward privately believed that 'Bill' had been blown up by a shell, but long afterwards his body was found; he must have died as he lay there on the field.

Edward's own story, when finally pieced together, seemed a typical enough narrative, but, remembering how repeatedly he had been omitted from drafts going to France, I found myself listening to it with secret satisfaction. He told it to me at intervals in approximately these words:

'The battalion was ordered to take part in the main attack, and only about seventeen men and two officers of the attackers came through altogether. The barrage lifted at 7.30, and in the sudden silence I remember noticing what a perfect morning it was, with a cloudless blue sky. I had to lead the first wave of our company, but we didn't go over right away because other regiments were opening the attack. While we were waiting for the order to start, a whole lot of wounded from the first part of the show came crowding into the trench; that upset the men a good bit, and then just before we were supposed to go over, part of the Yorkshire regiment in front of us got into a panic – probably started by German counter-orders – and began to retreat.

'It looked like a regular rot, and I can't remember just how I got the men together and made them go over the parapet. I only know I had to go back twice to get them, and I wouldn't go through those minutes again if it meant the V.C. . . . They'd followed me across the open for about seventy yards when I got hit the first time; that was in the thigh. I fell down and got up, but fell down again; after twice trying to go on I gave it up and crawled into a shell hole. I was lying there with my arms stretched out and my head between them, as we'd been told to do, when a huge beast of a shell burst quite close to the hole. A splinter from it went through my arm; the pain was so frightful – much worse than the thigh – that I thought the arm had gone, and lost my nerve and began to scream. Then I saw it was still there and managed to pull myself together;

and after I'd been in the hole about an hour and a half, I noticed
that the hail of machine-gun bullets on the British trenches
seemed to be slackening.

'By this time there were two other men in the shell-hole
with me – one was very badly wounded, but the other wasn't
hurt at all – only in a blue funk. I did all I could to persuade
him to carry the wounded man in and send help for me, but I
soon saw he wasn't going to budge, so I decided to risk a crawl
home myself. I climbed out of the hole and started dragging
myself along between the dead and wounded to our trenches
seventy yards away; I don't remember much about it except that
about half-way across I saw the hand of a man who'd been killed
only that morning beginning to turn green and yellow. That
made me feel pretty sick and I put on a spurt; luckily two of
our stretcher-bearers saw me when I'd been in the open about
twenty minutes, and they helped me over the parapet and carried
me down to the dressing-station. When we got there, I sent
them back for the wounded man in the shell-hole. At the C.C.S.
I found crowds of officers and men that I knew; I'd quite lost
count of the time, but after a while I was put to bed and was
just dropping off to sleep when a damned orderly, thinking I
was worse hit than I was, tried to make off with my watch; I
cursed him pretty thoroughly, as you can imagine. They sent me
straight back by ambulance train, where I had to lie in a filthy
draught all the time, and across on the *Egypt*, but there were
such crowds of wounded and so many delays that the whole
journey took me five days.'

Later, when I remarked to Geoffrey how much I had been
surprised by this story, and especially by the part where Edward
rallied his men after the panic, Geoffrey announced that he wasn't
astonished at all; he'd always known, he said, that Edward was 'a
stout fellow'. Apparently other friends shared this opinion, for
long afterwards another officer told me that in the 11th Sherwood
Foresters' mess they nicknamed Edward 'the immaculate man of
the trenches'; his habit of shaving with calm regularity on the
worst days of a later and more continuous 'push' had a far more
stimulating effect on the men's morale than any number of pious

exhortations. On the Sunday, too, after Edward came to Camberwell, my mother received a letter from Richard N., a senior subaltern who had been left out of the attack to look after the remnants of the battalion, congratulating her on Edward's 'courage and splendid behaviour' on July 1st.

N. was one of Edward's best friends in France; I had already heard how he and 'Bill' had listened to the record 'God so loved the world' on Edward's portable gramophone during the tense evenings before the attack. The warmth of his letter seemed natural; we took it to be merely one friend's tribute to another, and Edward himself treated it with pleasant ridicule; as soon as he left his bed he never spoke of the Somme again except under pressure. It was only at the end of August – just after Geoffrey had abruptly thrust some red and white carnations into my hands before going back to the front – that we realised that we had attached insufficient importance both to Edward's story and N.'s letter.

At that time Edward had just begun his much-prolonged period of sick-leave; a serious injury to the nerves of his arm caused him intense pain for months, and involved a course of massage which lasted for nearly a year. One late summer evening I came off duty to find a pencilled post-card from him, telling me that he and my father had been inspecting a block of flats in Kensington, where my parents soon afterwards went to live and have remained to this day.

The rest of the post-card was brief:

'Father came up this morning . . . He brought with him a letter from France addressed to me which contains the following: "To /2nd-Lt. E. H. Brittain. The G.O.C. congratulates you on being awarded the Military Cross by the Commander-in-Chief."'

12

Already, I thought, his prayer at Roland's grave had been answered – by himself. In 1916, it should be added, the M.C. meant a good deal; it was still a comparatively rare decoration, awarded only for acts of really conspicuous courage.

'Isn't it too unspeakably splendid about Edward's Military Cross?' I wrote to my mother. 'And how like him to send you a post card, when anybody else would have wired . . . You must come down soon and see him wearing the ribbon . . . Other officers turn round and look at him and he never appears to notice it . . . Isn't it amusing to think with what reverence and awe he used to point out to us an officer who had the Military Cross. He says he will undoubtedly get promotion now – though what does it matter if you are a 2nd-Lieut. all your days, when you are an M.C.!'

At first my one regret was that Roland – always so sympathetic and yet just a little sceptical over Edward's unavailing efforts to get to France – would never know how courageously and completely he had turned the tables on the scornful senior officers who left him behind when the regiment went to the front. But almost at once I realised that it was best that Roland, dead and undecorated, could not know; his reflections would have been too bitter. He had been so definitely 'after' the Military Cross, had thought it more to be desired than the Nobel Prize, and his fellow-officers in the 7th Worcesters had shared our confidence that some high military distinction would be his fate. Yet he had gone unadorned to his grave without taking part in a single important action, while the friend who had been a mere peace loving musician wore the coveted decoration. How could he have endured, the next autumn term, to be a silent witness of Edward's clamorous reception at Uppingham? – a reception such as we had often imagined for himself, but had never even thought possible for Edward, except perhaps years and years later as a great violinist and composer.

The ironies of war, I reflected sadly, were more than strange; in terms of a rational universe they were quite inexplicable. But now the universe had become irrational, and nothing was turning out as it once seemed to have been ordained.

Edward's award was officially announced in *The Times* of October 21st, 1916, under the heading of 'Rewards for Gallantry: Short Stories of Brave Deeds':

'Temp. Sec.-Lt. EDWARD HAROLD BRITTAIN, Notts and
Derby R. – For conspicuous gallantry and leadership during
an attack. He was severely wounded, but continued to lead
his men with great bravery and coolness until a second
wound disabled him.'

But when I read this notice, I was far away from both Edward
and England.

With the coming of summer weather and increased activity
on the various fronts, small groups of Sisters and V.A.D.s had
begun to leave Camberwell for foreign service, chiefly in France.
During the rush of work after the Somme, when every London
hospital needed its full quota of nurses, the exodus had
temporarily ceased, but as soon as the convoys slackened a Sister
and two V.A.D.s were ordered, to my secret terror, to leave for
service on a hospital ship, the *Glenart Castle*. Their names had
been just above Betty's and mine on the list of active service
volunteers; from this we knew that our own summons would
not be long delayed, and each privately prayed that when it came
it might be for France.

At the beginning of September I was due for leave, which
seemed more than ever desirable after an attack by thirteen
German airships on September 2nd had deprived London of a
whole night's rest. The heavy work of July and August in the
incessant heat of that long London summer had left me limp and
jaded, and I left Euston for Macclesfield, where my parents were
still living, with a sense of profound relief.

On Macclesfield station my father met me with the news that
a telegram awaited me at the house. Hurrying there in a taxi, I
opened and read it; it announced that I was ordered on foreign
service, and recalled me to Camberwell at once.

After scrambling through a dinner which I could hardly eat
for fatigue and excitement, I caught the last train back to London.
Too tired, too apprehensive and too bitterly disappointed at losing
my leave to read or to sleep, I found the second long journey
interminable. It was almost midnight when I tramped wearily
through the silent slums between Camberwell New Road and

our flat, but Betty was lying awake in bed, waiting for my return. When she heard me at the door she called through the window that both of us were ordered east, probably to Malta.

CHAPTER VII

Tawny Island

WE SHALL COME NO MORE

So then we came to the Island,
Lissom and young, with the radiant sun in our faces;
Anchored in long quiet lines the ships were waiting,
Giants asleep in the peace of the dark-blue harbour.
Ashore we leapt, to seek the magic adventure
Up the valley at noontide,
Where shimmering lay the fields of asphodel.

O Captain of our Voyage,
What of the Dead?
Dead days, dead hopes, dead loves, dead dreams, dead sorrows—
O Captain of our Voyage,
Do the Dead walk again?

To-day we look for the Island,
Older, a little tired, our confidence waning;
On the ocean bed the shattered ships lie crumbling
Where lost men's bones gleam white in the shrouded silence.
The Island waits, but we shall never find it,
Nor see the dark-blue harbour
Where twilight falls on fields of asphodel.

V. B.
1932.

1

The memory of my sunlit months in the Mediterranean during the War's worst period of miserable stagnation still causes a strange nostalgia to descend upon my spirit. For me, as for all the world, the War was a tragedy and a vast stupidity, a waste of youth and of time; it betrayed my faith, mocked my love, and irremediably spoilt my career – yet Malta remains in my recollection as an interval of heaven, a short year of glamorous beauty and delight, in which, for the time being, I came to life again after Roland's death.

Quite why the island should have had this effect upon me I do not know, for I went to Malta in peril, I arrived there in pain, I was often lonely and homesick, and I left in the deepest depths of sorrow and abnegation. Nevertheless, the enchantment remains. The place has become for me a shrine, the object of a pilgrimage, a fairy country which I know that I must see again before I die. Looking back through the years to sun-filled memory-pictures of golden stone buildings, of turquoise and sapphire seas, of jade and topaz and amethyst skies, of long stretches of dust-white road winding seaward over jagged black rocks older than history, I am filled with yearning and regret, and I cry in my heart: Come back, magic days! I was sorrowful, anxious, frustrated, lonely – but yet how vividly alive! Take away this agreeable London life of writing, of congenial friends, of minor successes for which I fought so long and worked so hard, take away my pleasant Chelsea home that would have seemed in the Buxton days an unattainable Paradise – and give me back that lovely solitude, that enchanted obscurity, those warm shimmering mornings of light and colour, those hours of dreaming in hot scented fields of oxalis and gladioli and asphodel!

But I know that those things will never come back. I may see the rocks again, and smell the flowers, and watch the dawn sunshine chase the shadows from the old sulphur-coloured walls, but the light that sprang from the heightened consciousness of wartime, the glory seen by the enraptured ingenuous eyes of twenty-two, will be upon them no more. I am a girl no longer, and the world, for all its excitements of chosen work and individualistic play, has grown tame in comparison with Malta during those years of our anguish.

It is, I think, this glamour, this magic, this incomparable keying up of the spirit in a time of mortal conflict, which constitute the pacifist's real problem – a problem still incompletely imagined, and still quite unsolved. The causes of war are always falsely represented; its honour is dishonest and its glory meretricious, but the challenge to spiritual endurance, the intense sharpening of all the senses, the vitalising consciousness of common peril for a common end, remain to allure those boys and girls who have just reached the age when love and friendship and adventure call more persistently than at any later time. The glamour may be the mere delirium of fever, which as soon as war is over dies out and shows itself for the will-o'-the-wisp that it is, but while it lasts no emotion known to man seems as yet to have quite the compelling power of this enlarged vitality.

I do not believe that a League of Nations, or a Kellogg Pact, or any Disarmament Conference, will ever rescue our poor remnant of civilisation from the threatening forces of destruction, until we can somehow impart to the rational processes of constructive thought and experiment that element of sanctified loveliness which, like superb sunshine breaking through thunder-clouds, from time to time glorifies war.

2

On the late afternoon of Saturday, September 23rd, 1916, a large tender carried a party of excited and apprehensive young women down the glittering expanse of Southampton Water. The tender had orders to embark them on H.M. Hospital Ship *Britannic*, which was sailing next day for Mudros in order to bring home the chronically sick and wounded from various Eastern campaigns. Betty and I, by far the youngest of the group, were also the most excited and certainly not the least apprehensive, for a persistent wonder whether I should ever see Edward or Victor or Geoffrey again caused a lump in my throat and a dull ache at the pit of my stomach.

The mingled depression and exhilaration of that day still lives in the pages of my diary.

'Mother and Edward . . . spent an hour or two with me this morning before our final departure. I bade them a last *au revoir* at the corner of Brief Street, as I did not want to watch them walk away.

'We left the hospital with Miss C. in a 'bus and met Principal Matron at Waterloo. I hated Waterloo and the Southampton express; there was such a general bustle and noise and confusion which somehow seemed to intensify the feeling that we were going away . . . I felt acutely miserable, not so much at the idea of leaving England and everybody (for since Roland went the long, long journey no place in the world seems so very far away from any other place) as because everything was so unsettled and I hate things to be unsettled and not know at all what is going to happen to me . . . In spite of the depressing effect of the 'bus and Waterloo it was a great relief to me to leave Camberwell . . . So much had I grown to hate it that I felt that any change, to however much worse physical conditions, would be a welcome relief . . .

'At 4.0 we all assembled at the dock . . . As we left the harbour a transport of the R.F.C. cheered us and waved their hats. We sailed down the Solent just as the sun was setting; on either side of us the colours of the mainland were vividly beautiful. The sinking sun made a shimmering golden track on the water which seemed to link us in our tender to the England we were leaving behind, and in the evening light the aeroplanes and seaplanes which now and again flew round us looked like fairy things.'

When we came near to the Isle of Wight, the *Britannic*, anchored off Cowes, appeared in the distance like a huge white mammoth lying on its side. For a moment a sick dread had seized me when I learnt that she had been built as sister ship to the *Titanic*, but as I watched her scarlet crosses and four large funnels gleaming in the low sunshine, I consoled myself by reflecting that her conversion into a hospital ship had removed her to a different category. During the winter of 1915 she had run between England and Mudros, but her use was discontinued after the evacuation of the Dardanelles. Now that the Balkans had become active she was to start again, and this journey to Mudros, where those of us destined for Malta had to tranship, was the maiden voyage of her new series.

I had hardly begun to unpack in the luxurious inner cabin which I was to share with Betty, when we were summoned to listen to an address by the Sister-in-Charge of the Malta contingent on the behaviour expected from the V.A.D.s on board. Her injunctions involved so frequent a repetition of the words: 'They may not . . . they shall not . . .' that we should soon have become openly mutinous had not a tranquillising service on the deck next morning before we sailed reminded us how futile were little hot-headed rebellions against injudicious severity in face of the hazards that might be before us. By the time that we had sung 'Jesu, Lover of my soul', and listened to an idealistic red-haired chaplain telling us that 'for a certain high type of human nature the far and the perilous thing has always had an alluring charm', some of us were ready to confront danger and suffer martyrdom to the limit of endurance.

Martyrdom, however, though admittedly uncomfortable, might have been less exasperating than the constant humiliation to which our youthful dignity, far from enabling us to shine, in the chaplain's words, 'as lanterns of hope in the darkest hours of distress and fear', was compelled ignominiously to submit. Our Sister-in-Charge, an Amazonian individual with a harsh voice and hawk-like features, appeared to us as one of those women whose idea of discipline is to visualise every activity that her subordinates might enjoy and then issue a general prohibition. We had not been on the ship for a day before the boat deck – the best place from which to see the unfamiliar countries that we were passing – was put out of bounds. We were also forbidden to leave our cabins in pyjamas – a regulation guaranteed to prevent all those who, like ourselves, had inside cabins, from observing any passing attraction in the way of land or ships. Had I obeyed it I should have seen neither Gibraltar at midnight nor Messina at dawn.

The V.A.D. passengers were ruthlessly divided into 'sections', each under a section-leader who led a dog's life trying to keep pace with the orders issued to her. Every V.A.D. had to sit, eat and attend functions with other members of her section even though her best friend was in another – as she always was if the Sister happened to discover the friendship. Finally, as these arrangements did not separate us from the medical officers as completely as the Sister had intended, she and the Matron of the *Britannic* nursing staff – a sixty-year-old 'dug-out' with a red cape and a row of South African medals – ordered a rope to be stretched across the main deck to divide the V.A.D. sheep from the R.A.M.C. goats; by this expedient they hoped automatically to terminate the age-long predilection of men and women for each other's society. After a few days, during which the more adventurous of both sexes had edged as near to the rope as they dared, and several others had regarded one another from a distance with eyes full of cupidity, the guardians of our virtue were astonished and pained beyond measure when one or two couples, being denied the opportunity of normal conversation on deck, were found in compromising positions beneath the gangways.

Late on the Sunday afternoon, we sailed. At chapel that evening, the Sisters and V.A.D.s at the 1st London General sang on our behalf the hymn: 'Eternal Father, strong to save' – not without good reason, as later experience was to prove. Their thought 'for those in peril on the sea' was perhaps stimulated by the fact that they themselves had just emerged from peril of another kind, for, on the very evening after our departure, a fleet of raiding Zeppelins dropped bombs on Purley, Streatham Hill and Brixton, doing a good deal of damage quite near to the hospital. 'The windows of the White Horse were smashed – just where Mother and I passed that morning after saying good-bye to you,' wrote Edward later.

'Providence has tempered the wind to the shorn lamb again,' I thought a little ruefully, remembering how frightened I had been of air-raids when I first went to London, and reflecting that so close a conjunction of Zeppelins and submarines might entirely have annihilated that modicum of courage which, throughout the War, only just enabled me to keep my dignity in perilous situations.

As the great screws began to thrash and throb, Betty and I, alien in our thoughts yet very glad of one another's company, escaped to the forbidden boat deck to see the last of England. Making for the Cornish coast and the Bay of Biscay, the *Britannic* began her journey east by going west, and as we passed the Needles we seemed to sail right into the heart of a gold and purple sunset, which dazzled us with a lovely radiance too bright for human eyes. On the deck below us the R.A.M.C. orderlies were singing and dancing; we looked down upon them as though seeing a music-hall stage from the front of the dress-circle. One man who had a violin played Tosti's 'Good-bye'; the plaintive, familiar notes rang out into the mild September twilight.

> *Falling leaf and fading tree,*
> *Lines of white in a sullen sea,*
> *Shadows rising on you and me—*
> *Sha-dows rising – on you-ou and me!*
> *The swallows are making them ready to fly,*
> *Wheeling* out *– on a wind-y sky.*
> *Good-bye, Summer – Good-bye, good-bye!*
> *Good-bye,* Sum-*mer! Good-bye – go-od-bye!*

Now that the perils of the sea were really at hand, the terror that had hung over me since I volunteered for foreign service and for one grim second had gripped me by the throat when Betty told me that we were going to Malta, somehow seemed less imminent. The expensive equipment of our cabins was illogically reassuring; those polished tables and bevelled mirrors looked so inappropriate for the bottom of the sea. 'We are in danger!' I kept saying as I lay awake in the dark that night, but although we knew that our voyage was to be so much longer than we had expected, it was difficult on so warm and calm an evening to convince one's self that at any moment might come a loud explosion, followed by a cold, choky death in the smooth black water. Later, when a storm swept over the Bay of Biscay and land was far away, the gruesome possibility seemed less remote.

Six months afterwards, writing to my mother about the torpedoing of the *Asturias* with two of our most popular Malta V.A.D.s on board, I tried to describe the disintegrating fear which left me with a sick reluctance to undertake long voyages that ignominiously persists to this day.

'I feel so sorry for them to think it happened at night, for I remember the feelings of terror the dark hours used to bring us on the *Britannic* – feelings which, of course, we never mentioned to each other at the time but afterwards all admitted we had had. I used to look over the steep side of that tremendous ship and think to myself: "Perhaps now – or now –or now!" It is being on the *qui vive* for something that may happen any moment of any hour which makes the strain of a long voyage nowadays. "Betty" and I were not in a very good place for being torpedoed on the *Britannic* as having a cabin we were on a lower deck than most of the others, in fact we were only a yard or two from the place where the torpedo ultimately went through. I used to wake up at night and listen to the thresh of the screws and the whistle of the wind above the mastheads and the rushing of the water against the side, and wonder if any among the strange occasional crashes and bangs that went on all night was a torpedo or mine striking the ship.'

But even feeling so desperately afraid could not entirely quench the thrill of passing those far, enchanted lands which to a sixteen-year-old Cook's tourist had seemed so inaccessible. For the whole of one long hot evening I lay on deck, still a little sick and faint from the trials of the Bay, and watched the brick-red coast of Portugal deepen into the low grey rock of Cape St Vincent. That night Gibraltar towered above us, a black shadow studded with lights, and the next morning the arrogant peaks of the Sierra Nevada leaned over the jagged summits of the Alpujarras to see the white monster, to which over-confident men and women had entrusted their lives, slip noiselessly along the menacing blue water. One day more, and the grey and purple rocks of Sardinia greeted us before we stopped for forty-eight hours to coal at Naples in the shadow of the cloud-crowned giant Vesuvius. Messina, that narrow, tragic strait perpetually guarded by the blue sentinel Etna, slipped past us in the dawn of our ninth morning afloat, and on the tenth day the Mediterranean began to gleam with great jewels – golden islands, purple-shadowed, set in a sapphire sea.

As the sun rose, the *Britannic* lurched and swayed drunkenly through the Archipelago, leaving far behind the three cruisers which were supposed to be her escort into the perilous Ægean.

'How fast we can go when we like!' I thought admiringly, crouching in my dressing-gown with half a dozen others beside a prohibited porthole. I did not know until weeks afterwards that an enemy submarine was actually chasing us as we sat there so serenely without our lifebelts, nor realise that the beautiful ship was already doomed by a threat which was destined, in as lovely a dawn, to be cruelly fulfilled in that very place.

3

Nine hours later we lay anchored in Mudros harbour, waiting to tranship. Never before had I seen so many vessels of all kinds, great and small, old and new, British and French and Levantine. Hospital ships gleamed white and enormous above the small black cargo-boats that ran inconspicuously through the Mediterranean to take refuge in the estuaries of large rivers; gaunt Dreadnaughts lay close beside little sailing vessels, with ancient rigging so fantastic that they seemed, in the brilliant incredible light which flooded the harbour, to be no longer the property of the Levantines from the tumble-down village on the sinister shore, but the old beautiful ships of the Greeks awaiting the Persian fleet.

Behind the camps and the miserable hovels of the fishermen, range upon range of savage hills enclosed the multitude of ships within a lost, incongruous world. Above these hills, as the sun set, the distant peaks of Samothrace burst into flame, and away to the right a cone-shaped mountain summit stood out darkly against the majestic red reflected from the western sky. One of the Sisters told me that this mountain was Achi Baba, a dominant memorial to the lost gallantry wasted in the Dardanelles. 'It gave me,' my diary records, 'a queer thrill to be so near, so very near, that dreadful Unknown Land – that most unknown of all this War's unknowns – to women, at any rate.'

All afternoon and evening I stood on the deck, gazing as in a trance upon that momentous curve of Lemnos in the rich desolation of the Ægean. From this harbour, as John Masefield was even then recording, the men on the transports bound for Gallipoli had gone 'like kings in a pageant to the imminent death'. Not far away, two days before the landing at Cape Helles, Rupert Brooke had died, and had become part of some magic island in that blue, unearthly sea. With a pang I remembered my English tutor reading his sonnets at Oxford just after Roland had gone to the front, and thought how strange it was that I should be near to Rupert Brooke's 'corner of a foreign field' so long before I was likely to see Roland's.

I learnt soon afterwards that Rupert Brooke had been buried on the Island of Skyros, in an olive grove above a watercourse at the foot of Mount Khokilas. By cloudy moonlight the men of his company had carried him in his uniform up the silent hill, and over his head they placed a big wooden cross and put a smaller one at his feet. On the back of the larger cross an R.N.V.R. interpreter wrote in Greek: 'Here lies the servant of God, sub-lieutenant in the English Navy, who died for the deliverance of Constantinople from the Turks.'

That night we transhipped to another hospital boat, the small Union Castle liner *Galeka*, and under cover of the darkness slipped quietly out of the harbour. Above our heads in a deep indigo sky the great pale stars shone over us, looking so much larger and nearer than they had ever seemed in Buxton or Oxford or Camberwell. It was fortunate that we had the stars to give a lofty illumination to our adventure, for our new quarters, in contrast to the superb luxury of the *Britannic*, filled us with rueful dismay.

By one of the characteristic wartime muddles of officialdom, the *Galeka* had been ordered to take many more passengers than she was able to accommodate, with the result that a hundred V.A.D.s were obliged to occupy two big 'wards' in the hold, which all too recently had been used by convalescent Tommies suffering from dysentery and kindred ailments. These quarters, whether for men or for women, were singularly ill-suited to a semi-tropical, submarine-infested sea. Apart from tiny portholes high above our heads and one or two electric fans, there was no method of changing or moving the hot, fœtid air, and only a narrow, ladder-like staircase, difficult to negotiate except in calm weather, provided a means of exit to the upper decks. If an enemy torpedo had struck the ship, we should have been trapped as surely as rats in a sealed sewer.

Our 'beds' at night were swinging iron cots, made up with the same blankets and mattresses as the sick men had used. Sleep, owing to the stuffy heat and the persistent flies, was almost impossible. Privacy, however great our need of it – and a few of us had begun inexplicably to suffer from headaches and acute diarrhœa – proved equally inaccessible, for each ward had only one washhouse, a rough annex containing several tin basins in a row, and one privy, with five tin commodes side by side and sociably free from partitions. To young women delicately brought up in fastidious homes, it was a perturbing demonstration of life as lived in the publicity of the slums. Several girls solved the ablution problem by not washing at all, but the other difficulty was less easily remedied. We began by using the five-seated privy one at a time, but the waiting queues became so lengthy that this form of individualism soon proved impracticable.

However, I was not long in a condition to be oppressed by such inconveniences. On the third morning in the new ship, a feverish discomfort that I had endured for two days turned suddenly to shivering fits and a stiffening of the limbs. Shamefaced but rather alarmed, I reported sick, and was greeted with the words: 'What? Another!' and sent to my cot in the sweltering hold. Sixteen V.A.D.s altogether retired there that day, smitten by a mysterious disease which later caused quite a mild sensation, followed by an epidemic of research amongst the medical officers in Malta.

Indescribably hot, aching in every limb and semi-delirious, I was hardly conscious of anxious visits from the Matron and the chief Medical Officer, but lay listening to the groans of my fellow-sufferers, and watching the legions of indeterminate insects crawling along the wooden flooring above my head, until I fell feverishly asleep. When I did have to visit the communal lavatory, my soaring temperature rendered me equally indifferent to the altruistic friends who helped me there, and the strangers already in occupation. During the stuporous night the drowsiness of fever at last quenched my terror of torpedoes, although the danger was far from over. Throughout our journey from Mudros to Malta, an enemy submarine which no boat could locate lurked unmolested in the

Mediterranean; it sank the Cunarder *Franconia* on October 4th, and the same day torpedoed a French transport, the *Gallia*, quite close to us, with a loss of six hundred lives. Altogether, the situation seemed a curious comment on my father's fear, two or three years earlier, that if I went to a finishing school in Paris I might develop appendicitis.

When the *Galeka* at last docked in the Grand Harbour at Valletta on October 7th, I awoke to find the Principal Matron of Malta standing by my side, looking down at me. A handsome woman of classic proportions, she seemed somehow to restore their lost heroic quality to our vicissitudes, and I grinned apologetically at her from my lowly cot.

'*This* one can smile, at any rate!' I heard her remark in a singularly gracious voice to the Matron of the *Galeka*.

In the afternoon I was carried off the boat on a stretcher, and pushed into one of the ambulances which were taking the convoy of sick nurses to Imtarfa Hospital, seven miles away in the centre of the island. I dozed fitfully throughout the ride, and realised Malta only as a waking dream of brilliant white buildings against a bright blue sky. The scintillating air seemed to echo with the clang and clatter of half the bells in the world; I believed them to be imaginary noises ringing in my head until a Sister in the hospital told me that the day was a *festa*.

'There seem to be so many saints,' I explained later to my mother, 'and so many things that happen to them, and every time there is a *festa*, which is always on the day that you want to go to Valletta. I think saints are a very good idea if you are fond of holidays.'

At Imtarfa occurred an uncomfortable delay upon which I commented with some feeling in a subsequent letter to Edward. 'When we arrived at the hospital we were left waiting for at least twenty minutes with the hot afternoon sun pouring right in to the ambulance; several A.S.C. men came and gazed in with great interest, but no one attempted to move us. Finally the Matron came out and asked indignantly why we weren't brought in, and one of the men said it was the orderlies' work, not theirs, and the orderlies were having their tea! Typical, *n'est-ce pas*? When I think of the number of meals I have postponed or cut short or missed altogether in order to help with convoys – and in other people's wards too, I think how unduly altruistic women are!'

For some reason my anonymous germ behaved more malignantly than anyone else's; I had left England for Malta without having had a day's rest since the beginning of the rush after the Somme, and the invader probably took advantage of my need for a holiday. Days passed in the drowsy discomfort of fever, with large doses of castor oil as the only interruption to the monotony of burning head and aching limbs. Almost the end of October had come before I was able to drag myself to a chair on the stone balcony outside my ward, and look across a deep, rocky valley to the domes and towers of Città Vecchia, the old Maltese capital, drowsing in a heat more radiant and profound than the warmest English midsummer.

In those first normal hours I fell in love with the island; a secret rapture which the years have not dimmed made me thank heaven that I had defied the nightmare sea and bidden farewell to melancholy, tragic England. It was all so different from Buxton, and so infinitely different from Camberwell! At the end of the summer the grass all over the island was parched and withered; from a distance the surface of the uplands resembled the stretched skin of a great tawny lion. A macabre fascination, such as I had realised in Mudros, seemed to radiate from the dazzling light which drenched this treeless barrenness, making black and sharp-edged the tiny shadows cast by the clumps of tropical shrubs – cactus and prickly pear and eucalyptus – that fringed the dusty white roads or leaned against the ubiquitous stone walls. In the hospital garden immediately below the balcony, pastel-blue plumbago and pink geranium foamed with luscious generosity over sulphur-hued balustrades.

It's just like the illustrations to Omar Khayyám, I thought.

> *They say the lion and the lizard keep*
> *The Courts where Jamshyd gloried and drank deep.*

That's what it reminds me of. But it's like the Bible too. That rough track dipping steeply down into the valley and then winding up to walled Città Vecchia might be the road from Bethany to Capernaum.

Whenever I could escape from my fellow-patients in the stone-floored ward with its wide-open doors and windows, I sat alone on the balcony, happy and at peace in this strange, new country as I had never been since the War began. Occasionally, as strength returned to insecure legs, another patient and I made expeditions in a *carrozza* to Città Vecchia across the valley, where we encountered the characteristic Maltese odour of unwashed humanity, centuries-old mud, and goats. We debated quite hotly which were the more numerous and which smelt worse, the monks or the goats, without coming to any permanent conclusion.

Never before had I realised the sense of spiritual freedom which comes with southern warmth and colour and beauty. Night after night the sun set exuberantly all over the sky. Beneath its glories of orange and violet, of emerald and coral and aquamarine, the dusty flats surrounding Imtarfa turned into purple moorlands. I began to understand why Roland, hating the grey abnegations of Protestantism, had turned from mud and horror and desolation to the rich, colourful glamour of the Catholic Church.

For Imtarfa, and indeed for the whole of Malta, the sick V.A.D.s remained interesting patients even when the last of them – myself – was up and about, and Lord Methuen himself, the Governor of the Island, came up to pay us an official visit.

'Everyone here is trying to trace the origin of our disease,' runs a letter to Edward written at Imtarfa. 'We have had quite twelve doctors in here, sometimes five at once. Three of them are lady doctors, all very charming too, in khaki tussore coats and skirts, dark blue ties and solar topees. I am getting quite tired of giving my name (and wish it was Jones so that I didn't have to spell it every time), my age, my detachment number, particulars of what I had to eat lately, etc., etc. They have taken blood tests of various kinds from us, for malaria, dysentery, etc., from our ears, fingers and wrists. They still don't seem able to decide whether we have been poisoned by something we had to eat or whether we just picked up some unoccupied germ that was wandering about the Mediterranean.'

Food poisoning of an obscure type was the final tentative

verdict, and the *Britannic* and the *Galeka* were both detained for several days in their respective harbours while investigations were made. The Principal Matron professed herself 'very unhappy' about the quarters allotted to the V.A.D.s between Mudros and Malta, and the *Galeka* had to undergo a thorough disinfection before leaving Valletta. It was a work of supererogation on the part of the sanitary squad, for she was torpedoed and sunk in the Channel on her next voyage home.

After nearly three weeks of treatment I was passed fit for light duty, and sent across the island to join Betty at St George's Hospital on a lovely peninsula of grey rock and red sand almost encircled by the sea.

4

I was still at Imtarfa when I received my first letters from England.

In Malta the arrival of the mail – which was often held up so long by storms, submarines and the censors at various ports that letters dispatched on widely different dates overtook one another on the way out – became the chief event of the week. We awaited the P. & O. liner that brought it with a perturbing mixture of pleasant anticipation and sick dread, for owing to casualties at the front, and air-raids and other troubles at home, neither life nor happiness nor peace of mind could be counted on for more than a few days at a time.

My worst fears now were for Geoffrey in France; he had grown into a very dear friend whose intelligent understanding never failed the most exacting demands, and my admiration for his determined endurance of a life that he detested was only enhanced by his shy self-depreciation and his frequent asseverations of cowardice. In letters it was possible to get behind the defences of this abrupt young man to a sensitive mind as responsive to beauty as it was considerate towards human pain and fatigue.

'Promise me faithfully this one thing,' I urged Edward in reply to his first letter from home; 'if anything important happens to either you, Geoffrey or Victor, will you cable to me at once? You have no idea what one feels out here when one realises it is

October 20th and the last one heard of anyone was October 9th ... It gives me a queer feeling to read Geoffrey's letter of October 9th and remembering that "out here we are here to-day and gone to-morrow", to think that he has had time to die a thousand deaths between then and to-day. The other day I got hold of a weekly *Times* of October 13th and looked down the casualty list in absolute terror, fearing to see Geoffrey's name.'

'I never thought,' I added, 'that there was Tah's to look for too' – for Edward's letter had contained the surprising news that Victor had gone unexpectedly to the front by transferring from the Royal Sussex Regiment into the King's Royal Rifle Corps. 'On the Monday after you left,' he wrote, 'a wild telegram from Tah announced that he was going to France. I met him in town, helped him with all his shopping (and you can imagine he needed some help) – it was an awful business as he didn't like most things and knew nothing about anything; occasionally he would suddenly take a violent dislike to a most necessary article of clothing and refuse to have it until I had wasted about ½ an hour conjuring up an imaginary situation in which he couldn't possibly do without the thing in question.'

My mother, after describing the move from Macclesfield to Kensington, told me that they were having a portrait of Edward in uniform painted by a Chelsea artist, Mr Graham Glen. Even my work-driven uncle at the bank wrote a long letter, enclosing a fragment of philosophy which had recently come to England from the French trenches:

'When you are a soldier you are one of two things, either at the front or behind the lines. If you are behind the lines you need not worry. If you are at the front you are one of two things. You are either in a danger zone or in a zone which is not dangerous. If you are in a zone which is not dangerous you need not worry. If you are in a danger zone you are one of two things; either you are wounded or you are not. If you are not wounded you need not worry. If you are wounded you are one of two things, either seriously wounded or slightly wounded. If you are slightly wounded

you need not worry. If you are seriously wounded one of
two things is certain – either you get well or you die. If
you get well you needn't worry. If you die you cannot worry,
so there is no need to worry about anything at all.'

This uncle, who was never a strong man, died in 1925 after a
long illness caused by incessant overwork throughout the War.
The numerous letters that he wrote me while I was in Malta –
all emphasising the difficulty of carrying on the business of a bank
from which men were constantly joining up – are typical of the
more heroic civilian to whom, at that time, patriotism was the
genuine and indeed the sole inspiration of a hard and disappointing life. In 1916 he was only thirty-five and still miserably
anxious to enlist – a step that, as an 'indispensable', he was never
permitted to take by the various authorities which now directed
the occupations of 'eligible' men.

'I am getting more and more ashamed of my civilian togs,' he
wrote unhappily to me about the beginning of 1917, 'and I shrink
from meeting or speaking to soldiers or soldiers' relatives, and to
take an ordinary walk on a Sunday is abominable. I cannot do
anything to alter matters, for even if I walked out of the bank
and joined up, I should in all probability be fetched back at once,
as the Government are now making entirely their own decision
as to which of us go and which stay, but the net result is real
misery and the contemplation of the future if one has to confess
never to have fought at all is altogether impossible.'

Though the future was to prove so much more indifferent to
war records than my uncle imagined, such letters as his – which
must have been reduplicated hundreds of times – do suggest that
the men officially tied to civilian posts should either have been
allowed to wear military uniform, or else have been enlisted into
a recognised corps with a uniform of its own. Only a gross failure
of psychological understanding in high places compelled men who
were working themselves to death by simultaneously doing two
or three full-time jobs to wear garments which in popular opinion
branded them as 'shirkers', while 'dug-outs' engaged upon very
light and perfectly safe garrison duty were eulogised as heroes.

The War cost my uncle his life as surely as if he had been in the trenches, yet, far from sharing in the 'glory' of sacrifice, he was not permitted even to discard the trappings which brought him humiliation.

5

After a week at St George's Hospital I decided that, although lonely, I was really quite happy. My loneliness was due to the speedy drifting away of Betty, who, having so far neither loved nor lost, did not share my depressing predilection for solitary meditations on the rocks or wanderings *à deux* about the uninhabited parts of the island. Her more normal instincts, intensified by the social bias of her upbringing, led her to prefer the naval society of Valletta, and, fortified by introductions from home, she was quickly absorbed into its tennis-parties and teas.

I did not much miss her as soon as I grew stronger, and began to enjoy the work which just after my illness had seemed so exhausting. The hospital, like Imtarfa, was an ex-barracks built entirely of stone, with marquees for extra beds, and the nursing staff was posted not to wards but to 'blocks', which were long, narrow, two-storied buildings, with open verandahs above and below. Half a dozen or more small wards, each containing from ten to twenty beds, opened off each verandah. In nearly all the blocks the V.A.D. was left on duty alone – a responsibility never permitted her at the 1st London General – for either the afternoon or the evening, and was often in charge of over a hundred patients.

After the fatiguing stuffiness of the hot wards in Camberwell, this open-air life in the warm sun beside a sparkling sea sent me tripping up and down the blocks with a renewed youthful vigour which even intervals of remorseful grief could not permanently quench. There was a definite pleasure in the limitation of discipline to essentials, as well as in the relaxed uniform regulations, which allowed the addition of a white drill coat and skirt, white shoes, panama hat and blue crêpe-de-Chine mess dress to our ugly outdoor uniform. At night came a final joy, when I stood on the verandah outside the stone-floored room shared with only one other V.A.D., and looked across the silver streak of St George's Bay between black rocks to the moonlit expanse of sea and the dark shadows of occasional ships passing close to the shore. The notes of 'The Last Post', as they died away over the water each evening, sounded so poignant that I never could hear them without a pricking of the eyes.

'I continue to like the whole place immensely,' runs a letter written to my mother on November 6th. 'They even give lectures – good ones – on nursing to V.A.D.s here, which they would never do at Camberwell – chiefly, so I always imagined, because they were afraid of V.A.D.s getting to know too much. In fact they used to say we were there to be useful and not to be taught things, which seems rather a contradictory point of view.'

This 1st London General attitude to V.A.D.s was typical of the nursing profession as a whole, especially in England, where the introduction of semi-trained Red Cross probationers into military hospitals had pushed to a crisis the thirty-year-old struggle for the registration of nurses. The Matron at Camberwell was always scrupulously just to us in practice, but we must have been bogies to her in theory, for she and other promoters of state registration evidently visualised a post-war professional chaos in which hundreds of experienced V.A.D.s would undercut and supplant the fully qualified nurses. Actually, this fear was groundless; all but a very few V.A.D.s were only too thankful when the War was over to quit a singularly backward profession for their own occupations and interests, but many 'trained women', having no such interests themselves, could not believe that others were attracted by them. The presence of Red Cross nurses drove some of them almost frantic with jealousy and suspicion, which grew in intensity as the V.A.D.s increased in competence.

With November began the rainy season, when nights of thunder and fierce lightning followed copper-red sunsets, and tremendous gales left the sea with a swept and garnished appearance which filled us with dread for the ships in the Mediterranean. The furious wind blew the rain with such violence into the open verandah that water ricocheted off the stone walls and floors in a constant splash, and we were obliged to go on duty clad in black mack-intoshes, gum-boots and sou'-westers.

'The doors and shutters are always blowing open and letting in a chill blast heavy with rain,' I wrote to my mother. 'One often wakes at night to hear the wind howling, the sea raging and the rain coming down with the sound of an express train rushing past. Having one's meals in the mess tent . . . is like sitting under a wet umbrella; the rain rattles on the canvas above, occasionally leaking through on to your head; tent poles and lights sway together till one feels confused and sleepy, and the water comes in at the sides of the tent and runs under the tables.'

About the middle of the month Edward's sick-leave ended, and he returned to light duty with the 3rd Sherwood Foresters at Cleadon Hutments, near Sunderland. A letter came from him, mentioning a new British attack against the German front line at Thiepval and Beaumont Hamel, just after I had been to Pietà Cemetery, the military burial-ground on the road from Valletta to Hamrun, to find the grave of one of the Buxton boys who had been buried among the purple bougainvillæa and the little stiff cypresses after dying at Cottonera Hospital from typhoid contracted in Gallipoli. To his mother in Buxton I sent a care-fully wrapped pink geranium picked from his grave before I opened Edward's sad little note briefly describing the end of the two friends who had been with him on the Somme.

'Captain H.'s body was found quite close to the old front line of July 1st. E. of Authuille Wood as far as I know but I should think it was hardly recognisable . . . N. was hit in the head by a sniper after capturing the German front line at Le Sars on Oct. 1st; he is buried in Peake Wood near Contalmaison.'

In the midst of the fear-inspiring gales, it was hard to believe that I should see my beloved three again before they had joined those friends in the crowded earth.

'It is such a wild, stormy night, and the sea is beating the rocks like anything,' I wrote to him in reply one desolate evening. 'On this island, the land seems to shrink as one knows it better, and the miles and miles of sea between here and home to get longer and longer . . . One begins to understand a little the significance

of the Revelation – "And there was no more sea." For here sea
is the very symbol of separation.'

We were certainly surrounded by a sea which held terrors never
contemplated even by the prophetic author of the Revelation, for
Malta from 1916 to 1917 was in the very centre of submarine
warfare. Our daily life was dominated by maritime disasters; our
conversation turned perpetually upon the dangers that threatened
our letters, our parcels and our supplies. For meat, milk, jam and
fish we were dependent upon tinned and dried foods from
England, as fresh fish was unobtainable, goat's milk unsafe, and the
water undrinkable until it had been chlorinated.

'Our extreme care at home to have nothing tinned amuses me
now,' I commented in one letter. Even the fruit and vegetables so
plentiful upon the island could not be eaten raw on account of
dysentery germs. Our systems, stimulated by energetic work and
an outdoor life, never seemed to get as much sugar as they required,
and whenever we were off duty we gorged ourselves with incredible avidity upon biscuits and sweets supplied by friends from
home, who must have been horrified by our constant demands
at a time when sugar was becoming the housekeeper's nightmare.

My letters from Malta are full of wrecks and drownings; the
sinking of ships provided much the same drama for us as a great
battle for the hospitals of England and France. The *Arabia* was torpedoed a month after I landed, and constant rumours of submarine
damage or alleged threats of bombardment by Austrian vessels kept
our excitement up to fever pitch. Each new wreck was followed
by an influx of half-drowned patients suffering from shock; having
lost everything but the clothes that they arrived in, they bought up
half the garments in Valletta. During the winter of 1916 the shops
could hardly cope with the demands of stranded sailors and passengers, for their own supplies frequently went to the bottom, together
with the tea and sugar intended for the hospitals.

'If Malta existed solely for the reception of torpedoed people
it would have fulfilled its mission in life,' I wrote to my family.

In the third week of November, three hospital ships were sunk
almost simultaneously. A few hours before the Anglican chaplain
told us of the death of the Emperor Francis Joseph, we learnt that

the *Britannic* had gone down in the Ægean. The news of her loss galvanised the island like an electric shock. A week later, the rescued members of her staff came on to Malta after spending some days in nursing their own sick and wounded at the Russian hospital in Athens, and were distributed among the various hospitals. As the clothing stores in Valletta were now temporarily depleted, we supplied the refugees with our own pyjamas and undergarments and hot-water bottles until they could return to England and re-equip. Boy-Scout hats from the Serbian Relief Fund picturesquely crowned the miscellaneous garments in which they were arrayed.

Among the sick was a young, cheerful Sister who had made friends with Betty and myself on the voyage to Mudros. We went to see her at Floriana Hospital, in Valletta, and found her completely changed – nervous, distressed and all the time on the verge of crying. But to talk of the disaster seemed to bring her relief, and from her conversation we learnt the story of the ship's last hours.

The explosion, she told us, occurred during breakfast; it blew up the bottom of the main staircase, together with an orderly who happened to be there at the time. The nursing staff marched quietly out of the dining-saloon; they were told to fetch any valuables that they could get quickly and reassemble at once on the boat deck. The 'valuables' taken illustrated the strange workings of a mind trying to control its own panic; one girl seized her fountain pen and left £30 in notes under her pillow.

The old Matron, motionless as a rock, sat on the boat deck and counted the Sisters and nurses as they filed past her into the boats, refusing to leave until all were assembled. None of the women were lost; but a number of casualties occurred among the orderlies through the smashing of the last two boats by the huge propeller as the ship lurched over on her side. The medical officers, remaining to the end, climbed down the wire ropes – which almost cut their hands to pieces – dropped into the sea in their lifebelts, and struggled to the boats already afloat. Two of them disappeared and were never accounted for.

In one of the boats sat the Matron, looking towards the doomed *Britannic* while the rest of its occupants, with our friend amongst them, anxiously scanned the empty horizon. She saw the propeller cut a boat in half and fling its mutilated victims into the air, but, for the sake of the young women for whom she was responsible, she never uttered a sound nor moved a muscle of her grim old face. What a pity it is, I meditated as I listened, remembering the rope across the deck, that outstanding heroism seems so often to be associated with such unmitigated limitations! How seldom it is that this type of courage goes with an imaginative heart, a sensitive, intelligent mind!

They had spent three hours in the boats, concluded the Sister, before they saw two rescuing destroyers racing over the edge of the calm, sunny sea. Among those saved was a stewardess who had been on the *Titanic*, two medical officers from the torpedoed *Galeka*, and a released officer-prisoner from Würtemberg who was suffering from nerve-strain and had been ordered a sea voyage for the benefit of his health. At first their rescuers had looked, not for the boats, but for the *Britannic* herself, never dreaming, in spite of the fate of the *Lusitania*, that so great a ship could have gone down so soon.

Actually, she sank in three-quarters of an hour, and for many of the survivors, already sick with shock, the worst part of their ordeal was the sight of her disappearance. Incredulously horrified, they watched porthole after porthole slide under the water, until at length she heeled right over and went down in a pitiless whirlpool. The dreadful cry of the last siren, 'All hands off the ship!' just before she sank, would haunt their nights, our friend said, for the rest of their lives.

6

In England the sinking of the hospital ships and the gravity of the news from Roumania intensified the growing popular belief that our failure to beat the Germans months ago, and thus forestall these disasters, must be somehow due to inefficient political leadership. So Mr Asquith and his unwieldy Cabinet became the whipping-boys of emotional chagrin, and a letter from my uncle, after mentioning the probable appointment of a Food Dictator and the establishment of 'meatless days', discussed the Government crisis and the possibility of 'the lethargic 23' being replaced by a War Cabinet of five.

'Either Mr Lloyd George or Sir Edward Carson are fancied for the Premiership and I think we should do well with either. Undoubtedly where warfare is concerned we want business men rather than politicians to direct affairs, and certainly the only man in the Government of the present who shows real power and the strength of mind to use it is Mr Lloyd George. He has consistently from the outbreak of War shown himself a strong man in every sense of the word.'

The enormous prestige of Mr Lloyd George and his Government in the eyes of the 'plain man' at this time is reflected in later letters, written when the War Cabinet had been in existence for two or three weeks. Apparently their popularity reached its height when they loftily rejected the idea of a 'negotiated peace'; no one, it seemed, wanted to discuss anything so academic – except a strange little society which I had just seen mentioned in the newspapers, called the Union of Democratic Control. This amazingly optimistic organisation, I read, had actually held a meeting at Walthamstow to urge rational consideration of the peace proposals – and had of course had it broken up for their pains.

'The new Government is going strong,' wrote my uncle enthusiastically, 'and already has effected more in a fortnight than the old one did in two years. We now have control of Shipping, Coal, Wines and Food, and in addition every man between 16 and 60 is now to be taken entirely in hand . . . The German Peace inquiries have left us quite cold; they were so evidently an attempt to get a German (in the strongest sense of the word) peace. But today President Wilson has stepped boldly into the arena and had the consummate effrontery to tell us that both sides are evidently fighting for the protection of small States (what price Belgium and Serbia?) and therefore the Allies should try to discuss peace terms with Germany. The newspaper comments are amusing and very instructive and even the American papers in some cases have taken Mr Wilson to task pretty severely . . .

'Lloyd George is quite marvellous – his insight and powers of

perception of the important features of this most complex situation border upon the uncanny at times and one almost feels afraid
when one realises to what an extent the Nation is leaning upon
the energy and brains of one man through this awful crisis . . .
We are up against it with a vengeance this time but there is no
panic and we are all prepared to carry the thing through and
damn the consequences. Even though we know they will be hard
enough to bear in the very near future . . . I feel a worm of
course, and quite naturally, but when I look on and watch my
fellow men and women carrying on and doing it with grim determination but withal everlasting cheerfulness and modesty, I cannot
help feeling a very proud worm. It is something to know from
what a nation one is bred.'

Shortly before Christmas, Geoffrey, who had been very much
'in the War' all that autumn, wrote to assure me that he was still
alive. He evidently felt less confidence than my uncle in the
Nation, and none whatever in himself, and his letters made trench
life sound as boring and monotonous as the peace-loving student-
temperament invariably found it. Victor, on the contrary, lived in
a state of permanent enthusiasm for the military standards of the
K.R.R.C. in comparison with those of the 'old men' with whom,
on account of his prolonged light duty, he had had so much
contact for nearly two years. After describing the discovery of a
certain happiness in trench warfare through the attainment of
a surface efficiency, he wrote to me on December 6th half apologising for his new militaristic mood.

One could not, he said, continually reflect upon the material
and spiritual waste involved whenever that highly trained product,
a man in the prime of life, was instantaneously killed by a stray
bullet, or life at the front would be one long misery. Yet nothing,
he curiously concluded, had depressed him so much in France as
the Crucifixes which were occasionally to be seen still standing
in desolate shell-swept areas. The horror of the one intensified a
hundred-fold that of the other, and the image of the tortured
Christ struck him as 'an appalling monument to the personifica-
tion of Utter Failure'.

Three weeks afterwards he wrote again to tell me that he had 'not yet seen War'. He was perpetually haunted, he added, by the fear of not coming up to scratch in an emergency. 'I tell you it is a positive curse to have a temperament out here. The ideal thing to be is a typical Englishman.'

As Christmas approached I was moved from the eye and malaria block, in which I had worked since October amongst semi-convalescent patients, to the Sisters' quarters, where I became a combination of assistant housekeeper and head parlourmaid. This work, which every V.A.D. had to do for a month, was even less congenial to me than nursing, and I found the supervision of the Maltese maids no light occupation. 'If you don't keep *everything* – even half a jug of diluted milk – either locked up or directly under your eyes,' I recorded, 'you needn't inquire where it has gone when you can't find it.'

There was compensation, however, in the New Year flowers – golden oxalis and white arabis and red campions and miniature celandines – which were already springing up on the patch of rocky ground in front of the Sisters' quarters. Here, I noticed, the lords-and-ladies were striped brown and terra-cotta, 'like one curly petal of a tiger lily'. More frequent visits to Valletta, too, were possible, and were always potentially exciting, for Malta, that little dumping-ground of the nations, was full of unexpected meetings. I nearly ran into a boy from Buxton one afternoon as I was hurrying to take the ferry from Valletta back to Sliema, and the very V.A.D. who now shared my room was the daughter of the 'little' greengrocer with whom we used to deal in Macclesfield during my childhood.

The Indian and Egyptian markets in Valletta, with their silk shawls, embroidered kimonos, Maltese lace, grass-lawn tablecloths, rich crêpe-de-Chines, Chinese embroideries, sandalwood boxes, painted fans and black cigarette-cases inlaid with gold, had already tempted me to spend all the pay and allowances that I could rake together upon Christmas presents of every kind, and with these I sent home two small water-colours purchased in Naples.

'They are for my study at Oxford if ever I get there again,' I told my mother, 'and even if I don't I can't imagine myself without a study if I am alive. I would rather do without a bedroom and sleep on the sofa in the drawing-room than without a room to myself where I can have a fire of my own and not be interrupted by anyone . . . Your remark about the War lasting five (more) years makes me wonder if I shall ever go there at all. If it really does . . . I should think we should all be dead by then, but if I am not I shall only be twenty-seven, and it would still be worth while . . . It seems very hard that we should be the generation to suffer the War, though I suppose it is very splendid too, and is making us better and wiser and deeper men and women than our ancestors ever were or our descendants ever will be. It seems to me that the War will make a big division of "before" and "after" in the history of the world, almost if not quite as big as the "B.C." and "A.D." division made by the birth of Christ . . . Sorry you see me in spirit in my V.A.D. hat; can't you try to think of me in something more becoming? I am always glad Roland never saw me in it, so that if he has taken any memory of me into the next world, it isn't of me in that hat . . . Tell me more about Oliver Lodge's *Raymond*.'

When Christmas preparations began in earnest, and I was set to decorate the mess-tent with palms and streamers, and to make jellies and huge fruit salads for the men's special teas, the memory of the previous year, with its similar activities so blindly and cheerfully performed in the very hour of Roland's death, came back like the dull ache of an old shattering wound. In the middle of the bright, noisy kitchen, with the Home Sister issuing orders in her harsh, melancholy voice, and the Maltese maids around her chattering like monkeys, it was sometimes difficult to prevent an inconvenient tear from falling into the pail of fruit salad.

'I wonder where he is – and if he is at all,' I soliloquised in my diary, for there was now no one within several hundred miles to whom such personal speculations could be expressed. 'I wonder if he sees me writing this now. It's absurd to say time makes one forget; I miss him as much as ever I did. One recovers from the shock, just as one gradually would get used to managing with one's left hand if one had lost one's right, but one never gets over the loss, for one is never the same after it. I have got used to facing the long empty years ahead of me if I survive the War, but

The Brittain family outside their Macclesfield home, Glen Bank, 1905. From left to right: Thomas Arthur Brittain, Vera, Miss Newby (the governess), Edward and Edith Brittain

Vera outside Melrose, Buxton, circa 1912

House photograph, The Lodge, Uppingham School, 1914. Roland Leighton (second row from front, first left); Victor Richardson (third row from front, first left); Edward Brittain (third from left)

Geoffrey Thurlow

Victor Richardson

Roland Leighton

Vera and Edward
with their parents,
Buxton, 1915

Vera at the First London General Hospital, Camberwell, 1915

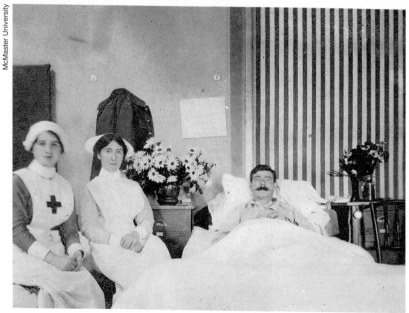

Vera and a nursing sister with a patient at Camberwell, 1915

MALTA . 1916

Vera and patients at St George's Hospital, Malta, 1916

Vera outside the night quarters,
St George's Hospital, 1917

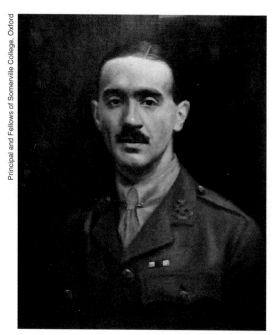

Captain Edward Brittain, MC, a portrait
by Graham Glen

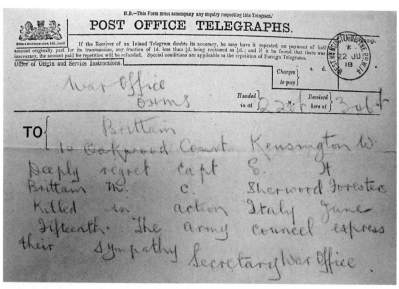

The telegram received by the Brittain family in June 1918, informing them of
Edward's death in action

Vera, circa 1924

Vera and George Catlin's wedding day, June 1925. From left to right:
Edith Brittain, the Revd Catlin, George Catlin, Vera Brittain, Thomas Arthur
Brittain, Winifred Holtby

Vera with her children, John and Shirley. A publicity photograph for
Testament of Youth, 1933

I have always before me the realisation of how empty they are and will be, since he will never be there again.'

A letter from Edward which came just after Christmas told me that I had not really been alone during those days of recollection; as usual, he had shared my thoughts with that peculiar intimacy which is supposed to exist only between twins. He began, however, by describing his investiture at Buckingham Palace on December 17th.

'There were 3 C.M.G.s, about 72 D.S.O.s and about 30 M.C.s, so it was a fairly small investiture. We were instructed what to do by a colonel who I believe is the King's special private secretary and then the show started. One by one we walked into an adjoining room about 6 paces – halt – left turn – bow – 2 paces forward – King pins on Cross – shake hands – pace back – bow – right turn and slope off by another door . . . The King spoke to a few of us, including me; he said, "I hope you have quite recovered from your wound," to which I replied "Very nearly, thank you, Sir" and then went out with the Cross in my pocket in a case. I met Mother just outside and we went off towards Victoria thinking we had quite escaped all the photographers, but unfortunately one beast from the *Daily Mirror* saw us and took us.'

He concluded with a paragraph which showed that no Military Cross, no Royal congratulations, no uproarious welcome from his successors at Uppingham, could alter his estimate of Roland as a lost leader whose value to the world was so far in excess of his own.

'I know it is just a year and you are thinking of him and his terrible death, and of what might have been, even as I am too. This year has, I think, made him seem very far off but yet all the more unforgettable. His life was like a guiding star which left this firmament when he died and went to some other one where it still shines as brightly, but so very far away. I know you will in a way live through last year's tragedy again, but may it bring still greater hopes for "the last and brightest Easter day" which you and I can barely conceive, let alone understand . . . How happy I could be to see you meet again.'

In my reply, just after the New Year, I told him, alone amongst my correspondents, of a small but strange happening that occurred just after I had written my diary on the anniversary of Roland's death.

'It seems rather curious that on the night of December 23rd I was kneeling by my bed in the dark thinking about him and that night last year when suddenly, just before 11.0, at the very hour of his death, the whole sky was lighted up and everything outside became queerly and startlingly visible. At first I thought it was just lightning, which is very frequent at night here, but when the light remained and did not flash away again I felt quite uncanny and afraid and hid my face in my hands for two or three minutes. When I looked up again the light had gone; I went to the window but could see nothing at all to account for the sudden brilliant glow. A day or two after I heard that there had been a most extraordinary shooting star, which had lit up the whole sky for two or three minutes before it had fallen . . . (Someone suggested it was the Star of Bethlehem fallen to earth because it could no longer shine in the dark hour of War.) Just coincidence, of course, but strange from my point of view that it should have happened at that hour. I remember one day last winter how Clare pointed out to me a star, which shone very brightly among the others, and said "Wouldn't it be strange if that star were Roland?"'

7

As 1917 came in, bringing warmer winds to Malta and a riot of brilliant flowers to the rocks, I realised that, for the time being, I was certainly having the best of things. One after another, my mails from home emphasised the shortage of food, of money, of domestic help, the cost of eggs and butter and the difficulty of buying them, the struggle to disregard minor illnesses and keep on at work. Each letter was grey with growing depression, but grim with the determination to 'carry on', 'keep a stiff upper lip', or whatever special aphorism appealed to the writer. The winter, too, was excessively cold in England and France, and its bitter discomforts added to the general gloom and the sense of endurance strained beyond its limit.

'My work in town is daily getting heavier,' wrote my uncle in the midst of an attack of bronchitis, 'and last weekend and this I have felt more like a beaten dog than anything else. Just at present of course the War Loan is giving us an enormous amount of work ... The past fortnight has been intensely cold, 18 and 20 degrees of frost in Purley and as much as 36 degrees in other parts of England. Coal is of course very short and very expensive but there is some to be had at round about 40s. a ton and gas is plentiful though the price of that has gone up 50 per cent since the War.'

In his first letter after January 19th, he dropped the sombre tale of domestic misery to give me an account of the Silver-town explosion.

'On Friday evening we were working quietly away in the office when there was a most appalling bang, and the whole building shook visibly and windows were shattered. We first thought a Zeppelin was overhead and had just missed us, but there was no repetition so we went out to investigate. There was not much news that evening – but we since learnt it was a great explosion about 10–12 miles way east of London ... I should think it is the worst accident we have had at all on munitions work.'

Years afterwards a journalist friend told me that on the evening of this disaster she was working in her room in Bayswater when the drawn blind suddenly lifted without a sound, remained horizontal in the air for a moment or two, and then slowly dropped. There was no wind and she had heard no noise. She said it was the most terrifying experience that she had ever been through.

In Malta the nursing was now very light; most of our patients were convalescent, and off-duty time was plentiful. Many of the V.A.D.s and the younger Sisters, whose work on the blocks no longer exhausted their vitality, began to find scope for superfluous energy in circumventing the Army regulations which, even in the atmosphere of comparative reasonableness that prevailed on the island, forbade the nursing and medical staffs to mix except after elaborate permission had been obtained, and chaperonage, which was hopefully supposed to be effective, provided. Whispered conversations and outbursts of giggling all over the Sisters' quarters proclaimed the existence of numerous minor intrigues. At many of these I could guess, but I did not join them, for my one experience, so far, of mixed parties had not tempted me to desire a repetition.

On Boxing Day night, fortified by permission from the Matron, I went to the opera, *Madame Butterfly*, in Valletta with two medical officers and a Sister, who was not young and very far from beautiful. Even during the War quite tolerable performances were given, though most of the choruses had a Maltese tang and the progress of the opera was liable to be interrupted by 'incidents'. On this very evening, the baritone in the midst of a passionate declamation was loudly challenged to a duel by an off-stage rival. He immediately interrupted his love-plaint to arrange time and place with the challenger, and returned amid the enthusiastic plaudits of the audience to resume his song exactly where he had broken it off.

As soon as the opera with its emotional music and heroic disturbance was over, the Sister, who had been confidently appointed my chaperon, and one of the medical officers – an ill-mannered individual remotely resembling the Kaiser, of whom I knew her to be hopelessly and inexplicably enamoured – disappeared completely for the rest of the evening. I was left to go home with the other M.O., a moustachioed middle-aged Scotsman whose presence was emphasised by a permanent aroma of whisky. He was evidently inspired – or had always intended – to emulate his colleague's good fortune, for as we drove back in the *carrozza* along the dark road from Sliema to St George's Bay, I found myself suddenly enfolded in a noxious embrace. I demonstrated my objection to this treatment with more vehemence than tact, and we arrived back in St George's compound about 1 a.m., both of us sullen and speechless.

Long walks across the island, sometimes alone, sometimes with one of the older V.A.D.s who had not yet been stirred to indiscreet emotion by the coming of spring, seemed infinitely preferable to such unattractive company. Two of these women, one of whom came from Oxford and for years had played the violin in the Bach Choir Orchestra, went with me on half-day expeditions to Musta, to Dingli, to the V-shaped sandy beach at Ghain Tuffieha, to the crumbling megalithic temple at silent Hagiar Kim and to the far point of Melleha, where we looked across a dark-blue channel to the steep golden-brown rocks of Gozo rising sheer out of the water. At St Paul's Bay we rowed in a hazardous green tub to the inhospitable rock on which the much-travelled Apostle was said to have been wrecked, and afterwards walked the six miles homeward along the stony road over the rocks, with the brilliant glow of the sunset behind us, and before us the swift star-studded darkness rising over the sea. I never felt quite at ease among those rocks; a strange silence pervaded them and a sense of being observed, as though age-old presences were watching our sacrilegious invasion with hostile, inhuman eyes.

Wherever we went the spring flowers, lovely and benevolent, mitigated the invisible antagonism of the rocks. Their colours, so clear, so delicate, so generous, smote our eyes with their candid beauty. I still remember the exquisite pang with which, after crossing a field carpeted golden and orange with oxalis and single wild marigolds, I suddenly saw for the first time the silvery pink of tall asphodels lifting their heads from the deep grass of a half-hidden glade. Between the boulders beside the road, giant irises waved their purple flags, and among the rocks a deep scarlet vetch grew from so shallow a soil that it seemed to spring from the very face of the stone, and created, quite startlingly, an illusion of spilt blood.

After describing the flowers in my letters home, I mentioned how much our comfort had lately been increased by the rather public erection of three bath huts on the high road running in front of St George's and St Andrew's Hospitals. No longer would it be necessary, I told my father, to rely for our major ablutions upon the tin foot-baths filled once a week from a stone vat in the yard.

'Real hot water,' I boasted, 'comes out of a tap; it is worked by a geyser on a Primus stove . . . When the tents were first put up someone . . . made slits in the sides to peep through, but the damage has now been replaced and the scandal has died down! Of course you have to keep getting out of the bath to pump the Primus, which would otherwise go out, but that is a detail!'

As the bath orderly was above suspicion, and in any case had as many opportunities as he could wish of seeing the nurses standing in the main road awaiting their turn in the tent with their dressing-gowns blowing round their necks, we concluded that some of the numerous roaming Maltese males must for quite a long time have substituted for their usual evening amusements the entertainment of watching the English Sisters take their baths.

At the beginning of February I was moved from my domestic occupations in the Sisters' quarters to the one surgical block, where none of the patients were seriously ill. Most of them had slight wounds, originally received in the campaign on the Struma, which owing to peculiarities of constitution or climate had obstinately refused to heal.

'Our methods here . . . would cause the M.O.s and Sisters at the 1st London to hold up their professional hands in horror,' runs one letter home. 'It makes me smile to remember how there we had hot water that came sterilised out of the tap and so many annexes and wash-places carefully separate from one another – one sink for the dressing-bowls, one for the patients' crocks, another for the Sisters' tea-things, etc., etc. Here there is one (cold) tap and one sink, down which everything goes – lysol, dirty water, tealeaves, etc., and in which everything is washed up, from the dressing-bowls and soiled towels and bandages to our biscuit-tin and our soiled tea-cups! (Of course we don't wash them all up together; we do draw the line at that!)

'Edward and I both have recollections of the pride they took at the 1st London – not always to the comfort of the patient – in spotless, unruffled beds and beautiful white blankets. I wonder what they would think if they had to try and make comfortable beds out of rough brown Army blankets and mattresses of three 'biscuits' – which will never lie properly together – and counterpanes invariably dirty. Here of course you may dust and clean and shake, and shake and dust and clean till you are tired without ever making much impression, as the whole place is so dusty, and one warm gust of sirocco will undo half an hour's work in half a minute.

'Yesterday one man couldn't have his bed made and had to lie between blankets half the morning, because it was the day for changing sheets and not quite the right number had come up (we only have the *exact* number). It is very complimentary to call them sheets, too; some are of the consistency of muslin curtains and others are more hole than sheet. However, Army equipment *is* Army equipment, and you have to hang on to the last thread of a sheet and the last prong of a fork, lest when the day of reckoning comes you should be found wanting. Equipment day is the bane of one's life in the Army; it is a sort of periodic stocktaking, in which you have to produce everything (or the remains of everything) that has been issued to you in the equipment line. So if you break a cup or tear a sheet or burn a duster you have carefully to keep the fragments, partly to show that you really did have them, partly to prove that you have not absconded with them and put them to some illegitimate use, but chiefly because it is Red Tape, which is the most binding thing in this world and far more binding, it is to be hoped, than anything in the next.'

The leisurely life on this surgical block left plenty of time for reading the various newspapers sent to me from England. From one of these I learnt that the new President of the Board of Education, Mr H. A. L. Fisher, had lately written to the Principal of Somerville deprecating the departure of Oxford women students on war-service. The information left me unperturbed; it belonged to a life which seemed too remote and irrelevant to concern me any more. Some of the dons, I reflected, were doubtless glad to fortify unquiet consciences with such a pronouncement; if patriotic hankerings after war-service drove even the women out of Oxford, Othello's occupation would indeed be gone, and his – or her – excuse for continuing a pleasant academic life in wartime would no longer exist.

My Classical tutor, I felt sure, would not be influenced by the Fisher declaration. At heart she was always a pioneer, an adventurer, who never accepted the limitations imposed by donnish standards, and later in the spring of 1917 she went to Salonika to act as orderly at one of the Scottish Women's Hospitals. Her boat, she wrote to me after landing, had anchored for twelve hours outside Valletta, but she had not been allowed to communicate with me or to go ashore. She stayed in Salonika for some months, fighting summer heat and disease with her usual gallantry, and was there during the great fire which devastated half the town.

8

By the same mail as the newspaper from which I learnt that patriotism amongst Oxford women was now a discredited virtue, came a long communication from Edward, who described one of the characteristic problems of an acting company commander.

'I . . . spent some time this morning writing a letter on the usual difficult subject: – I had a letter from an innkeeper in B—— the other day saying that a certain Corporal S—— in my company had an illegitimate child by a Miss J——, who is the innkeeper's ward, and was not paying for its upkeep. Under such circumstances a man's pay is compulsorily stopped to the extent of 4*d.* a day, as I expect you know. I interviewed the corporal, who is a very decent boy not yet nineteen and found that he was quite willing to marry the girl but couldn't get his parents' consent and didn't want to quarrel with them and so get out of any inheritance there might be, etc. Of course he cannot get out to France until he is nineteen and I explained to him and he clearly understood where his duty lay, especially in the event of his being killed, because his parents will allow the marriage after the War. S—— wrote to his father again for consent on Friday and got a negative answer and so asked me to write to him this morning, which I did . . . It is the old, old story, as old as the hills, but these things take up a company commander's time.

'Do you know, dear child,' he went on, 'that women are a great problem to me. I meet very few, of these I dislike almost all, and I don't think I understand any of them. Of course I am speaking about girls of my own age. Most other officers of my age seem to know any number of fairly decent girls; now and again of course they seem to get hold of a rotten one and sometimes even a prostitute, but I never seem to meet any. Can you throw any light on the matter and do you think I shall ever meet the right one, because at present I can't conceive the possibility? . . . I am inclined to think that my lack of knowledge of women is due to an incomplete upbringing. What do you think?'

On the island, as the work became still lighter and the weather still warmer, we too had our sex-incidents, and some of them were as crude, and as time-worn, as the one described by Edward. Only a few days before I received his letter, a V.A.D. and a naval officer had been surprised late at night in a disused tent beside St George's Bay, but had managed to escape before the identity of either was discovered. The episode was followed at our hospital by a series of interviews in which every V.A.D. was individually catechised by the Matron, a gaunt, shy, benevolent woman to whom the whole affair must have been purgatory. These interviews, being 'strictly private', were naturally discussed afterwards with mutual enjoyment by all the interviewed, whose interrogations appeared very similar to my own.

'I am asking you to tell me the truth, nurse.'

'Yes, Matron; of course.'

'We know it must have been someone either from this hospital or St Andrew's.'

'Yes, Matron.' I resisted the temptation to ask how she knew, since all V.A.D. uniforms looked identical in the dark, and if any girl wanted to commit what was technically a misdemeanour, common sense would not seem to suggest a spot within a hundred yards of her own hospital.

'I am putting you on your honour, nurse.'

'Yes, Matron.'

'You were not the person?'

'No, Matron.'

I went out. So far as I know, her two hours of embarrassed questioning did not succeed in their object. I was not the culprit, for I was still too deeply and romantically in love with a memory to have any appetite for sexual unorthodoxies, but I am not sure that I should have owned up if I had been. To confess guilt would have meant being sent home under a cloud certain to eclipse the chances of further war-work, at a time when every intelligent person who had acquired the efficiency and staying-power only attainable after long experience was a strong link in the forged chain of active endurance.

In Malta we often envied the women doctors, whose complete freedom to associate with their male colleagues appeared to result mainly in the most determined chastity. At St George's the staff included quite a number of medical women, since the War Office, having at last decided to employ them, evidently regarded Malta – where there was now so little serious illness – as a suitable place for such a desperate experiment.

One of these women, an elderly spinster whom everyone called 'Auntie', showed her determination to make herself felt by putting her patients on so many medicines that the V.A.D. who carried the medicine-basket round the block had a back-breaking half-hour after every meal. Another, a small brunette known to the nursing staff as 'Kitty', cultivated a flirtatious femininity, and appeared on her round as orderly officer in frilly evening dresses reminiscent of a four-year-old at a juvenile party. But most of them apparently belonged to the coat-and-skirt species, with an official manner and the traditional belief – which is fast being abandoned by more recently qualified women – that their wisest course was to model themselves upon their male predecessors, thus tending to repeat some of men's oldest mistakes and to reproduce their lop-sided values.

My reply to Edward's letter described accurately enough the limitations characteristic of most middle-class girls before and during the War.

'So many people are attracted by the opposite sex simply because it *is* the opposite sex – the average officer and the average "nice" girl demand, I am sure, little else but this. But where you and I are concerned, sex by itself doesn't interest us unless it is united with brains and personality; in fact we tend to think of the latter first and the person's sex afterwards. This is quite enough to put you off the average "nice" girl, who would neither give you what you want nor make the effort herself to try and understand you when other men, who can give her what *she* wants, are so much easier to understand . . .

'I think the old saw about young women being so much older than young men for their age, has always been very untrue and since the War is more so than ever. Women "grow up" in a certain sense (that of finishing their education just when they ought to begin it) much sooner than men and so get a sort of superficial "grown-upness" due to mixing with people and going out in a way the boy of the same age doesn't. But in the things that really count it is the boy who is grown up; he has had responsibilities which under the present benighted system of educating women she has never had the fringe of . . . The boy of eighteen or nineteen has probably – and since the War certainly – had to cope with questions of morality and immorality whose seriousness would astound her if she understood it, and deal with subjects of whose very existence she is probably ignorant. Of course a man doesn't mind the superficiality of inexperience if all he asks of her is her sex, but you . . . are different . . . I have noticed occasionally a slight suspicion of patronage in your dealings with women; I don't really think this is because you think their sex inferior so much as you realise their inferiority (as it probably is) to you in personality and brain. I, conversely, feel the same, with many men! But it is necessary to be rather more careful in dealing with women, as if a man patronises a woman she always thinks it is because of her sex, whereas if a woman patronises a man, he (if he is cute enough to notice it, which he generally isn't) never puts it down to *his*! I think there's every hope for you in time to come from some woman several years older than you are now.'

9

By the middle of March the sunny afternoons had become as hot and sleepy as an English July. In Gargar Ravine, a deep valley where the greenest grass in Malta was strewn with grey boulders of incalculable age, scarlet anemones and a dozen varieties of vetch – yellow and mauve and cerise and orange and purple – sprang up beneath the old stumpy trees, with their dry, hollow trunks and dark, smooth leaves. The ravine must have been an ancient watercourse, for maidenhair fern grew in the damp crevices of the rocks and between the stones of the steps leading upwards to cultivated fields. The asphodels and oxalis were now over, but heavy masses of magenta clover, four times the size of the English variety, covered the ground, and mauve and pink gladioli held their slender, spiky heads erect in the warm, scented air.

Now that Edward, who had been ordered to take two successive officers' courses, was safely in England for a few more months, I should have been drugged into comfortable peace by the calm, drowsy weather and the lovely, serene flowers, had not my letters from France continually sounded a note of apprehension, a warning yet again of approaching calamity. Geoffrey wrote ruefully that leave was remote, and a course for which he had hoped to be sent to the Base had been cancelled, while Victor deplored his lack of a consoling religious philosophy, and regretfully described himself as 'an awful atheist'. He only wished, he confessed, that he were not, for in the New Army soldiers were made, not born, and with the knowledge of a coming ordeal in the near future, a man required something more to fall back upon than self-manufactured ideals. Not only, he said, were those ideals liable to be insufficient and unpractical, but even so they were hard enough for 'unsoldierly natures' like his to live up to. 'If I only had a tenth of such a personality as Roland's, I should have no anxieties about the future.'

Towards the end of the month I was put on night-duty in the eye and malaria block where I had started work at St George's. Here I was in sole charge except for the occasional visits of the night-superintendent and the 'co-operation' of an orderly, who slept soundly for about ten hours out of the twelve. He explained to me his own theory of night-duty the first evening that I appeared on the block.

'What I always says is, Sister, when a man asks you for a drink in the middle of the night and you gives it 'im, you wakes 'im up thoroughly. If you don't take no notice, 'e just goes off to sleep agen.'

During my first week I came in for a new series of stormy nights, and had to walk up and down the verandah continually because the voice of any patient who called to me was drowned by the noise of the sea crashing on the rocks below.

'There are no moon or stars, so it is pitch dark,' I told my mother on March 19th. 'There are occasional gusts of rain, distant rumbles of thunder and frequent flashes of lightning . . . It is eerie and very lonely to stand on the open verandah with the rain blowing against you, looking into absolute pitch darkness and listening to the sea roaring . . . with a hurricane lamp which the wind keeps blowing out. (Have just been round the block to see if any of them are frightened of the storm.) Do you remember how afraid I used to be of thunder when I was little? Now I feel quite a "Lady of the Lamp" marching along with the thunder crashing and the lightning – such lightning as you never see in England – flashing around us, to see if other people are afraid.'

After the coldest of cold blue dawns had leapt into sudden flame each morning with the swift up-rushing of the sun from behind a low turret-crowned hill, we retired to bed in our lovely night-quarters at the far end of the compound. The stone-floored room which I shared with Betty and another young nurse was only a few yards from the sea. Outside our windows the far purple distance – in which, on the clearest days, the snow-capped summit of Etna appeared as dimly as the dream of a white cloud – blended through shades of cobalt and sapphire into the brilliant turquoise of sea and sky. The door opened on to a fringe of short green grass; beyond this the golden rocks met the white crests of miniature waves which swung rather than broke against the shore. Before going to sleep in the early morning we usually read or talked for an hour, sitting in dressing-gowns and pyjamas on the grass or the rocks. From my bed I could watch through the open door the white-sailed Gozo boats floating with spread wings a hundred yards out to sea, and the tiny painted *dhaisas* passing like lethargic green and red beetles along the water's edge.

Although we were at the opposite end of the compound from the Sisters' quarters, the medical officers' block was next to ours on the extreme point of the peninsula. This convenient contiguity made pleasantly possible some unofficial afternoons of tennis and conversation without much likelihood of discovery by the Matron. Now that the warm weather was really beginning, long walks had become less attractive; the best of the flowers were over, and fleas and mosquitoes had taken their place. So Betty and I and our room companion, with an appearance of great virtue, went to our beds directly after breakfast. About three in the afternoon we hurriedly dressed ourselves in the white blouses and skirts and panama hats which were the nearest approach to mufti that we could devise, and cautiously crept over with our racquets to the officers' quarters.

Agreeable teas, with vermouths and whiskies at the officers' mess, followed these stolen games. Quite what would have happened had we been found so blatantly breaking the sacred rule of segregation, I never troubled to inquire. The medical officers were not, upon closer acquaintance, a collection of earth-shaking personalities, but the pleasant, normal afternoons that we spent with them saved us from the neuroses that spring from months of conventual life, and gave us a vitality which was well worth the sacrifice of our afternoon sleep.

The brief hours in bed seemed sufficient because the nights were so placid. On C Block I had nothing to do but dress a few eyes four-hourly, make half a dozen beds, and give hot drinks to wakeful patients. Only once was this smooth serenity interrupted, when a twenty-year-old orderly, who had been isolated in an empty ward, died from convulsions in the early hours of the morning. As an infectious case he had been under the care of an R.A.M.C. 'special', and I had merely to report progress to the Night Superintendent.

One evening I came on duty to find him rolling his eyes and choking in continuous grotesque paroxysms, with 'Auntie', a dignified embodiment of superb inactivity, supervising his death-bed. The young man suffered, I was told – though never straight-forwardly – from venereal disease, and had been precipitated into this convulsive condition by a hypodermic injection. Soon after midnight a final paroxysm finished him off, and when the order-lies had removed him I had to spend several hours in disinfecting the ward.

'There was a brilliant moon that night,' I wrote home after-wards, 'and it was very solemn and impressive to watch the order-lies carry him across the compound on a stretcher to the mortuary, with the Union Jack over him and the moonlight shining on all – it is a queer moonlight in these places, very black shadows and startling outlines; everything is transfigured. The orderlies marched in that special slow order – I don't know what its name is – that they always use when carrying a corpse.'

Less eventful nights slipped away in the laborious creation of a scarlet kimono from a length of vivid silk purchased in Valletta. Often, when my incompetent needle refused, as it has always refused throughout my life, to collaborate with my intentions, the kimono was abandoned for such scanty literature as I had collected from home – Thomas Hardy's poems, John Masefield's *Gallipoli*, numerous copies of *Blackwood's Magazine*, and the recently published Report of the Commission on the Dardanelles.

'It makes very tragical reading, but is extraordinarily interesting in conjunction with the colour and romance of Masefield's *Gallipoli*,' I told Edward one evening. 'The latter makes you feel, in spite of the condemnatory language of the report, and the sense one has all through that the campaign was an utter failure with nothing in its result large enough to justify it, that it must have been a very fine and wonderful thing to have been one of that small army that fought so gallantly for such a forlorn hope. Since Roland had to die . . . I have often wondered whether really I would not have been glad for him to have been to Gallipoli . . . He was such a person for a forlorn hope. And nothing more could have happened to him than to be dead. We might not then have known the place of his grave, but after all that doesn't matter much. I cannot see that one gets much more satisfaction out of a wooden cross on a mound of grass than out of an unknown gully or ravine on the Gallipoli peninsula. But no wonder poor Jerry . . . got enteric and came here to die.'

That day's mail had been depressing, I admitted, and not least because I had learnt from it that his arm was now quite healed and could hardly keep him in England any longer as soon as the officers' courses were finished.

'As well as your news about being passed fit, there was a letter from Father . . . – German retirement at the wrong time for us and therefore anything but an advantage, Russia internally rotten and likely to sue for a separate peace – conditions dreadful at home, end no nearer in sight, etc., etc. . . . Victor too sends me a letter half cynical, half hopelessly resigned; apparently he was on the verge of an attack . . . This too leaves me anxiously . . . wondering how long it will be before I hear any more of him and what it will be when I do. I think I would rather have had an attitude of open resentment and rebellion in the face of death than this sort of stifled bitterness.'

10

Victor's long letter had been written on March 24th from a sector near Arras. To-day, as I re-read his realistic phrases, they seem to me to be less infused with bitterness than with a completely adult and slightly sardonic philosophy. Accustomed though I was by 1917 to the sudden tragic maturities of trench life, the speed with which he had grown up moved me to intolerable pity.

The letter began with a keen criticism of Robert Service's *Rhymes of a Red Cross Man*, which had just been sent out to him from England. He particularly resented, it seemed, a line in the poem called 'Pilgrims' which described death as 'the splendid release'. That, he commented, was the phrase of 'a Red Cross Man', and not of a member of a fighting unit.

As Roland had done so often two years earlier, Victor went on to speculate why they were all out there; it was a meditation then very characteristic of the more thoughtful young officer, who found himself committed to months of cold and fear and discomfort by the quick warmth of a moment's elusive impulse. Like Victor he usually concluded that, although the invasion of Belgium, and the example set by friends, and perhaps even 'Heroism in the Abstract', had a share in it all, the only true explanation that could be given by ninety per cent of the British Expeditionary Force was to be found in the words of an Army marching song to the tune of 'Auld Lang Syne':

> *We're here because*
> *We're here because*
> *We're here because*
> *We're here . . .*

The acutely conscious and purposeful soldier such as Donald Hankey, the author of *A Student in Arms*, was, according to Victor, quite exceptional; a recent *Punch* essay in the Watch Dogs series on 'a little word of six letters' represented far more truthfully the Army's view of the War. If taken literally it was, he said, 'no exaggeration – "it is a shorter word than sanguinary" – and figuratively it really expressed the whole situation, but my one fear in case of my safe return is that I may be perpetually uttering it in the drawing-room.'

The letter closed with a final grave paragraph which told me that at the end of March the situation in France had been still unchanged, but was likely 'on the day of the hunt' to alter a good deal. 'Well, Vera,' ran its concluding words, 'I may not write again – one can never tell – and so, as Edward wrote to me, it is time to take a long, long adieu.'

Such valedictory resignation seemed almost to have pushed him over the border of the tangible world already, I thought unhappily, reflecting that even if events failed to justify his pessimism, the submarines were steadily reducing my chance of seeing either him or Geoffrey before that indeterminate Mafeking which we called the end of the War. Civilians had now been forbidden to leave Malta, and for the time being no women either civilian or military were allowed on the *Isonzo*, the ex-destroyer mail-boat running between Malta and Sicily. Rumours that we should all be sent to Salonika because the submarine campaign was making Malta impracticable as a hospital base buzzed continually round the island. Unsettled and restless, we waited impatiently for something to happen.

Outside our few square miles of expectation, a good deal was happening. The taking of Baghdad, the Russian Revolution, and America's entry into the War penetrated even the surprised pages of the *Daily Malta Chronicle*, though they failed to interrupt for long its assiduous preoccupation with events nearer home.

'I do not remember if I remarked last week upon the sudden cessation of all news from Petrograd,' ran a letter written by my uncle on March 18th, 'but people were at great pains to imagine what was the cause of the curious silence. There have been suggestions of a revolution in Russia for months past, and everyone hoped and prayed that a catastrophe might be averted, as people here naturally feared the effect not only upon Russia but upon the whole Grand Alliance. And now when the curtain is raised again we find this most wonderful upheaval has taken place with comparatively no bloodshed and certainly no interruption of war operations.'

The last sentence appears a somewhat curious comment on the subsequent history of the Revolution, but at this stage the Allies were busily taking both Russians and Americans to their bosoms with fervent impartiality. A newspaper cutting preserved from this time – unnamed and undated, though the style seems familiar – represents the mood of enthusiastic self-congratulation then indulged in by the responsible but sadly misguided Press.

'Unless Isaiah were an editor, with the minor prophets for a staff, how should any newspaper hope to deal adequately with a time when new marvels and portents are added to things already on a scale so far beyond ordinary human grasp? Weeks ago, in an interpretation and a forecast, which seemed bold, but have been verified almost to the letter, we explained the real America, the real Mr Wilson. Anticipating the entrance of the United States into the struggle we dwelt on the vast meaning of the sign. In this War full idealism is the only common sense for all the people who intend to count. Those who are still of little faith, despite all that has happened, are of no further use to God or man in an age when there is less fear, physical or moral, than ever before since the earth was. Prudence that mimicked sagacity is discovered to be a wiseacre, the sharpest cynic known to be no more than a man with a hatpin.'

For me the splendour so obvious to the papers had turned a little pallid in the light of the news from France. Despite the curt-ness of telegrams, the discretion of letter-writers and the vague optimism of official *communiqués*, the uproar of the Battle of Arras had somehow echoed across the Mediterranean. The wind that churned the sand into eddies, filling our eyes with grit, seemed heavy with a universal uneasiness, as though it had once carried the sound of great guns bludgeoning the battered remnants of men and trenches into ghoulish anonymity.

'The sirocco is blowing to-night in a hateful way, rushing down the stone verandah, and making the doors and shutters creak and groan,' I wrote anxiously to Geoffrey, in a kind of superstitious belief that I could hold him to life by my letters: 'To me this particular wind always seems fraught with sinister things; it hides the stars, so that the night is as black as ink, and makes the men peevish and sends their temperatures up.'

All that week the sirocco blew, ominous with apprehension, driving me to confess my misery of suspense to correspondents who would, I knew, have suffered or escaped the pains and griefs of hell weeks before the mail could reach them.

'I have to keep on writing letters because the vague bits of news from France that filter through to us make me so anxious to receive them,' I admitted to Edward on April 17th. 'From the long list of names that appear in the telegrams there seems to be a vast battle going on along the whole of our front and the French one too, but it is very difficult to make out at all what is happening. *Is* Geoffrey anywhere in the Bapaume direction? The longer the War goes on, the more one's concern in the whole immense business seems to centre itself upon the few beings still left that one cares about, and the less upon the general issue of the struggle.

'One's personal interest wears one's patriotism rather threadbare by this time,' I continued, ignominiously forgetting that in editorial eyes the expression of these sentiments would automatically relegate me to the ranks of those 'of little faith', who were 'of no further use to God or man'. 'After all, it is a garment one has had to wear for a very long time, so there's not much wonder if it is beginning to get a little shabby . . . The last two nights have been horribly windy, but at 4 a.m. yesterday there was one of the most impressive skies I have ever seen – deep indigo blue, with long torn cloud-wracks stretched all across, the spaces between them studded with big brilliant stars, and, on the horizon just above the sea, a little red crescent of moon shining beneath a very black cloud.'

Yet another night's red moon, I thought, looking up after finishing Edward's letter at the ominous glow in the unquiet sky. Another night, and still no news. Is Victor still alive? Is Geoffrey? Oh, God – it's intolerable to be out here, knowing nothing till ages afterwards, but just wondering and wondering what has happened!

11

I had good reason to wonder.

The next night, just after I had gone on duty and was making the usual tour of the wards, an orderly brought me a cablegram. Standing between the beds of two patients, I opened it and read the words:

'Victor dangerously wounded; serious.'

'I hope it isn't bad news, Sister?' exclaimed one of the men, who must have gathered from my face that it certainly was.

'A great friend of mine's been dangerously wounded in France,' I replied, surprised to find that I could speak quite quietly. 'He's been dangerously wounded – and it doesn't say how!'

It didn't say how. Now that I knew so much about wounds, that vagueness seemed the telegram's worst infliction. After the Somme I had seen men without faces, without eyes, without limbs, men almost disembowelled, men with hideous truncated stumps of bodies, and few certainties could have been less endurable than my gruesome speculations. Long afterwards I learnt that the cable had been sent by my father, who, with the kindest possible intentions, had believed that he was letting me down gently by suppressing the exact truth.

I could not, I knew, send off a demand for more precise information until the morning, and if I was to preserve sufficient sanity for the responsibilities of the night, I must somehow put a stop to this mental reconstruction of appalling mutilations. I didn't feel inclined, just then, to talk about Victor to Betty or any of the other night V.A.D.s, who would not have understood why I should mind so much about someone who was not a *fiancé* or a brother or one of the other standard relationships. It was futile to write further letters until I knew more, so the only remaining resource was my now intermittent diary. I fetched it from the night-quarters, and poured into it the chaotic wretchedness which had, as so often before, no other outlet.

'He has "made good" now,' the entry concluded, 'and won through to the bridging of the gulf which he always felt lay between himself on the one hand and Roland and Edward on the other. Is he able to realise this – or has he, like Roland, departed hence without the consciousness of his supreme glory? Did he fight and conquer Death in his dreadful illness of 1915, only to die of dreadful wounds? For these answers too I must wait. Waiting, watching, suspense, mourning – will there never be anything else in life? I am so weary of it all – but I bow my head before the storm now, I don't try to fight it any more. I no longer expect things to go well for me; I don't know that I even ask that they shall. All I ask is that I may fulfil my own small weary part in this War in such a way as to be worthy of Them, who die and suffer pain.'

It all sounded, like most of my youthful diary, very earnest and sentimental; only an experienced writer can put aspirations and prayers and resolutions into words without appearing a sententious prig. From the patients' point of view, at any rate, it was probably better for me to be priggish than hysterical, which was the other alternative.

I had to wait four days before a reply came from Edward, to whom I had cabled because I knew that I could trust him to spare me nothing.

'Eyesight probably gone. May live.'

So that's it, I thought. He's blind. His eyes are gone. I wonder if his face is gone too? No, not that; if it had been, Edward would have told me.

'I don't know whether to hope he will live or not,' I wrote that night to my mother. '"Betty" says what a good thing he has not got a mother, thinking, I suppose, how upset his mother would be, but I think he is all the more to be pitied on that account, especially as he has no sister either . . . Poor dear "Three Musketeers", it doesn't seem fair that Roland should be dead and Victor blind, to say nothing of Edward's bad arm. What a good thing we had no knowledge of what was in store for them in the future to spoil that last Speech Day.'

I learnt from the next two mails that Victor had been wounded on April 9th at Arras, first in the arm – which he had disregarded – and then in the head, while leading his platoon to attack the inexorable redoubt known as 'The Harp'. At Rouen a hospital Matron had summoned his father, thinking that he could only last a few days. But unexpectedly he had rallied, and was sent home to the optical ward in the 2nd London General Hospital, Chelsea, where the care of the best eye specialists in England or France represented his only chance of sight.

The reports from France had been so conflicting that Edward, who sent me these details from Stafford, had vetoed all cables until nine days after the battle.

'It has been bad enough for me in this out-of-the-way hole,' he explained, 'waiting a day and a half for letters from London and waiting in intolerable suspense the whole time, but it would be worse for you.'

He had been able, he told me, to get two leaves from Brocton Camp to go to London; even the first time Victor had recognised his voice, and on the second occasion he had talked quite rationally.

'I don't think he will die suddenly,' the letter concluded, 'but of course the brain must be injured and it depends upon how bad the injury is. I am inclined to think that it would be better that he should die; I would far rather die myself than live entirely without sight . . . You and I know how to lose all that we have most dearly loved but I think we hardly bargained for this. Sight is really a more precious gift than life . . . As he lies on his bed with bandages round his left eye and head and the right eyelid closed, he looks just like a picture of the Christ – the familiar expression seen on the Cross.

'If only that right eye might have its sight!'

Immediately after the battle, the Colonel of the 9th K.R.R.C. had written to tell Victor's father that he had recommended him for the Military Cross; 'he did exceedingly well that day and . . . I have no doubt he will get it.'

The M.C. was in fact awarded to Victor a few weeks later, but this tribute did little more than intensify the stricken confusion into which his family had been plunged since the telegram from Rouen. After living in Sussex for many years, peacefully indifferent to foreign affairs, and politics, and all the other sources from which irrelevant calamity can descend upon the unprepared heads of inoffensive citizens, they found it almost as difficult to credit Victor with a supreme act of military courage as to grasp the overwhelming fact of his blindness.

To Edward also the prospect of Victor's Military Cross brought no consolation; he had worn the purple and white ribbon himself for nearly a year, and knew that the attractions of being a hero were apt to lose their staying power when they were expected to compensate for severe physical damage.

'Victor got a bullet right through the head behind the eyes,' he wrote miserably on April 22nd to Geoffrey, who was waiting for dawn in the trenches on the Scarpe. 'I'm afraid the sight has gone entirely; the left eye had to be removed in France and a specialist here thinks there is no hope for the right eye; the optic nerve is severed. It is a tragedy which leaves one stupefied and he had such beautiful eyes.'

But Geoffrey, the only person who could have comforted him, never read the letter, for on April 23rd he was killed in action at Monchy-le-Preux.

12

I had just got into bed on May Morning and was drifting into sleep, when the cable came from Edward to say that Geoffrey was dead.

When I had read it I got up and went down to the shore in my dressing-gown and pyjamas. All day I sat on the rocks by the sea with the cable in my hand. I hardly noticed how the beautiful morning, golden and calm as an August in Devon, turned slowly into gorgeous afternoon, but I remembered afterwards that the rocks were covered with tiny cobalt-blue irises, about the size of an English wood violet.

For hours I remained in that state of suspended physical animation when neither heat nor cold, hunger nor thirst, fatigue nor pain, appear to have any power over the body, but the mind seems exceptionally logical and clear. My emotions, however, in so far as they existed, were not logical at all, for they led me to a conviction that Geoffrey's presence was somewhere with me on the rocks. I even felt that if I turned my head quickly I might see him behind me, standing there with his deep-set grey-blue eyes, his finely chiselled lips and the thick light-brown hair that waved a little over his high, candid forehead.

And all at once, as I gazed out to sea, the words of the 'Agony Column' advertisement, that I had cut out and sent to Roland nearly two years before, struggled back into my mind.

'Lady, *fiancé* killed, will gladly marry officer totally blinded or otherwise incapacitated by the War.'

I even remembered vaguely the letter in which I had commented on this notice at the time.

'At first sight it is a little startling. Afterwards the tragedy of it dawns on you. The lady (probably more than a girl or she would have called herself "young lady"; they always do) doubtless has no particular gift or qualification, and does not want to face the dreariness of an unoccupied and unattached old-maidenhood. But the only person she loved is dead; all men are alike to her and it is a matter of indifference whom she marries, so she thinks she may as well marry someone who really needs her. The man, she thinks, being blind or maimed for life, will not have much opportunity of falling in love with anyone, and even if he does will not be able to say so. But he will need a perpetual nurse, and she if married to him can do more for him than an ordinary nurse and will perhaps find relief for her sorrow in devoting her life to him. Hence the advertisement; I wonder if anyone will answer it? It is purely a business arrangement, with an element of self-sacrifice which redeems it from utter sordidness. Quite an idea, isn't it?'

I was still, I reflected, a girl and not yet a 'lady', and I had certainly never meant to go through life with 'no particular gift or qualification'. But – 'quite an idea, isn't it?' Was it, Geoffrey? Wasn't it? There was nothing left in life now but Edward and the wreckage of Victor – Victor who had stood by me so often in my blackest hours. If he wanted me, surely I could stand by him in his.

If he wanted me? I decided, quite suddenly, that I would go home and see. It would not, I knew, be difficult to get permission, for though the renewal of my contract was overdue and I had said that I would sign on again, I had not yet done so. Work was slack in Malta; several hospitals were closing and the rest were overstaffed. Much as I liked my hospital and loved the island, I knew that I was not really needed there any more; any one – or no one – could take my place. If I could not do anything immediate for Victor I would join up again; if I could – well, time and the extent of his injuries would decide when that should be.

That night – quiet as all nights were now that so few sick and wounded were coming from Salonika – I tried to keep my mind from thoughts and my eyes from tears by assiduously pasting photographs of Malta into a cardboard album. The scent of a vase of sweet-peas on the ward table reminded me of Roland's study on Speech Day, centuries ago. Although I had been up for a day and two nights, I felt no inclination to sleep.

I was not, as it happened, very successful in stifling thought. By one of those curious chances which occurred during the War with such poignant frequency, a mail came in that evening with a letter from Geoffrey. It had been written in pencil three days before the attack; reading it with the knowledge that he had been so soon to die, I found its simple nobility even less bearable than the shock of the cablegram.

As I took in its contents with a slow, dull pain, the silent, shadowy verandah outside the door seemed to vanish from my eyes, and I saw the April evening in France which Geoffrey's words were to paint upon my mind for ever – the battened-out line of German trenches winding away into shell-torn trees, the ant-like contingent of men marching across a derelict plain to billets in the large town outlined against the pale yellow sky, the setting sun beneath purple clouds reflected in the still water at the bottom of many 'crump-holes'. How he wished, he said, that Edward could have been with him to see this beauty if it were any other place, but though the future seemed very vague it was none the less certain. He only hoped that he would not fail at the critical moment, as he was indeed 'a horrible coward'; for his school's sake, where so often he had watched the splendours of the sunset from the school field, he would especially like to do well. 'But all this will be boring you.'

Characteristically he concluded his letter with the haunting lines that must have nerved many a reluctant young soldier to brave the death from which body and spirit shrank so pitifully.

> *War knows no power. Safe shall be my going . . .*
> *Safe though all safety's lost; safe where men fall;*
> *And, if these poor limbs die, safest of all.*

'Rupert Brooke,' he added, 'is great and his faith also great. If destiny is willing I will write later.'

Well, I thought, destiny was not willing, and I shall not see that graceful, generous handwriting on an envelope any more. I wonder why it is that both Victor and Geoffrey were fired to such articulateness by the imminence of death, while Edward and Roland, who had the habit of self-expression, both became so curtly monosyllabic? Oh, Geoffrey, I shall never know anyone quite like you again, so true, so straight, such an unashamed idealist! It's another case of 'whom the Gods love'; the people we care for all seem too fine for this world, so we lose them . . . Surely, surely there must be somewhere in which the sweet intimacies begun here may be continued and the hearts broken by this War may be healed!

13

I had to wait for nearly a month before I received permission 'to proceed to the United Kingdom' by the overland route. Since the beginning of 'unrestricted submarine warfare' on February 1st, and the subsequent endless story of torpedoed transports and hospital ships, we were no longer allowed to travel by sea; passenger boats were infrequent, and the Mediterranean had become so perilous that even the six-hour journey from Malta to Sicily offered possibilities which did not bear contemplation.

In the interval I received news from Edward of both Victor's progress and Geoffrey's end. 'Tah,' he told me, 'is perfectly sensible in every way and I don't think there is the very least doubt that he will live. He said that the last few days had been rather bitter. He hasn't given up hope himself about his sight and occasionally says, "If I get better."'

On April 30th, when Edward wrote from Brocton Camp, he had heard only that morning of Geoffrey's death, and did not yet know that he had been killed by a sniper while endeavouring to get into touch with the battalion on his left some hours after the attack on the Scarpe began. Shot through the chest, he died speechless, gazing intently at his orderly. The place where he lay was carefully marked, but when the action was over his body had disappeared and was never afterwards found.

'I have been afraid for him for so long,' ran Edward's small, precise handwriting – an incongruous medium for such abysmal grief, 'and yet now that he has gone it is so very hard – that prince among men with so fine an appreciation of all that was worth appreciating . . . Always a splendid friend with a splendid heart and a man who won't be forgotten by you or me however long or short a time we may live. Dear child, there is no more to say; we have lost almost all there was to lose and what have we gained? Truly as you say has patriotism worn very very thread-bare . . . This is an unlucky place – I was here when Roland died of wounds, when Tah was blinded and when Geoffrey was killed.'

If only I could comfort him a little, I thought, and I felt more than ever glad that I was going home.

'I dare not think much about Geoffrey,' I told him in reply. 'As I work there is a shadow over everything; I know it is there but I try not to think why it is there or to analyse it too much . . . I used to write to him a great deal. I sent him cigarettes quite a few days ago; I am glad I sent them although he never received them.'

In the same letter I tried to indicate to him the decision to which I felt that I had come, but which I couldn't put into definite words until I knew how far Victor had recovered and what shape his plans were taking for the future.

'No one could realise better than I our responsibility towards him – not only because of our love for him, but because of his love for us, and the love felt for him by the one we loved and lost. I am not sure that this doesn't apply more to me than to any of you. I at any rate know this, that I should be more glad than I can say to offer him a very close and life-long devotion if he would accept it, and I cannot imagine that Roland, if he had known what was to be – if he knows – would be anything but glad too. Those two are beyond any aid of ours – they who have died; and the only way to pay even one little bit of the debt to them is through the one who remains.'

On May 22nd, with a small party of home-going Sisters and V.A.D.s, I began my long, dirty and uncomfortable journey to an England that seemed, at the outset, curiously improbable and remote. We had to send our heavy luggage by sea – it arrived home, very typically, the day after I had once again departed on active service and had been obliged to purchase a complete new outfit – and were allowed to carry only one package, into which, disregarding uniform and equipment, I stuffed the silks, laces, pale blue kimono and other treasures acquired in Valletta. We were told to carry food for six days, and filled our haversacks with bread, butter, tinned milk and potted meat, all of which had become repulsively languid by the end of the second outrageously hot day. Somehow I found a corner for my diary; the last few entries describe what I still remember, for all my sorrow and anxiety, as one of the queerest and most exciting adventures of the War. I do not know why I omitted an incident which I recalled long after other details of the journey were forgotten – the melancholy sadness of listening, at sunset in Syracuse harbour, to the 'Last Post' being sounded for a Japanese sailor who had been washed overboard from the destroyer that had acted as our convoy across the turbulent Mediterranean.

'*May 22nd, 1917.* – Left Malta with Sisters L. and N. and V.A.D.s K., M——n, M——n, and M——y. I hated to go, for I had been very happy there, and it was a real pain to say good-bye to Betty, with whom I have been for so long.

'We were taken by transport to Grand Harbour, and after

waiting on docks for about an hour, put on the *Isonzo*. Lady Methuen and party were on board and we had a Japanese destroyer "Q" as escort. It was a rough, wet and stormy day, and as there were no chairs we had to sit on deck on our piled-up luggage. Then began about the worst five hours I have ever experienced. Outside the harbour the seas were terrible; I have never known anything so rough, not even in the Bay of Biscay. The people on the *Isonzo* said it was one of the worst days they had ever been out, and probably they would not have gone on such a day were it not that on a very rough day the danger from submarines is less. We had not been long out of the harbour when the waves seemed mountains high and the ship pitched and rolled to an angle, as they afterwards told us, of 42 degrees. All the luggage piled up at the back, to say nothing of ourselves, rolled down the deck right as far as the rails. Mrs M., M——y and M——n kept up wonderfully; Sister N. and K. were being sick, and Sister L. and I felt terrible though we were not so sick as the others. Sister L. lay on a rug on the deck and I on the top of a pile of luggage, both of us incapable of moving. The waves broke not only over the deck but over the tarpaulin covering it, and dripped down in streams; the deck got covered with dirty sea-water, which rolled over us in a turgid stream every time the boat lurched upward. However, we were quite incapable of caring how much water we sat in till finally one terrific roll dispersed all the luggage and sent me slipping down the deck. This happened three times; the last time I sat in about two inches of dirty water and slid in it nearly down to the rails, which effectually ruined all the clothes I had on.

'Reached Syracuse at last; pretty harbour of small warm-coloured buildings and mountains rolling away into distance behind. Not allowed on shore; had good dinner on ship, of which we were more than in need.

'Spent night squashed together on mattresses on deck with tarpaulin stretched in front; no chance of undressing or washing. Very noisy and stuffy, but slept fairly well.

'*May 23rd.* – Roused at 4.0, breakfasted hastily at 5.0. At 6.0 got in Messina train on quay. Lovely scenery all along the line;

rich in flowers (poppies, mauve columbine, etc.), orange and lemon groves and corn. Large and rugged mountains; deep clefts and gorges on edges of which tiny villages were perched. Saw Etna all the way, finally passed the foot of it. Day calm and beautiful. Reached Messina about 12.0. Just outside saw group of black crosses by railway line – evidently graves of unknown people who perished in earthquake. Stayed outside station an hour, then got out of train and crossed strait on big ferry-boat. Ferry took a train over but not ours . . . Messina strangely desolate; half ruins, half new unfinished buildings. Rush for Rome express; porters gesticulating, everything very hot and dirty. Got only second-class carriage; various odours, chiefly smoke, dust and "Retirata" prevailed. Dinner on train. Dreadful night, hardly slept; very cold at dawn. Mrs M. very selfish and trying; took up my seat as well as hers. Lay on holdall on floor with head on seat. Very dirty and uncomfortable.

'*May 24th.* – Roused up at 5.0, attempted a little tidying; though without any water or space this was a little difficult. (Had to take most of our food with us from Malta, so seldom got anything to drink.) Went along edge of Apennines; quite beautiful in light of early morning.

'Reached Rome at 8.30. Bundled out of train into Hotel Continental, luggage and all. Luggage piled up in entrance; hotel people slightly disturbed. Our six straightened up in a room we shared for the day with 3 others and had a bath (found by me). Had lovely coffee, rolls and syrup brought up to our room. Went out and sent telegram home. Then went out in small carriages to see sights. Thought Rome very majestic – grand rather than beautiful. Age seems to have touched it not to mellow but to render it the more austere . . . Had tea in an English restaurant; after tea drove to English quarter and wandered around curio shops. Bought Roman pearl brooches and crucifix. Met an English woman friend of one of the Sisters, who told M——n and me we looked very young to be in the Red Cross! Had dinner at hotel; after dinner fell asleep on bed for an hour through sheer fatigue.

Roll-call in hotel hall at 9.0; then went to station, collected luggage together and sat on it on dark dimly-lighted platform for about ½ an hour. When train came struggled in all together into comf. 1st class carriage and slept well all night.

'*Friday, May 25th.* – Woke to find we were all among mountains, just going into Pisa. Saw Leaning Tower of Pisa from train. Glorious mountain scenery; mountain-sides covered with thick trees, cypresses and pines standing out among them . . . Went through 98 tunnels between Spezzio and Genoa. Reached Genoa about 11.30. On learning we had 20 mins. to wait, dashed out of train and into buffet just as we were, I in blue motor veil, dirty blouse and bedroom slippers; others in similar state. Restaurant very perturbed; regular turmoil ensued. Had omelette and coffee, bought oranges and dashed back to train with them . . . Stopped at Alessandria and Turin, where we expected to change but did not. Scenery after Turin very lovely; we passed all through the Southern Alps . . . Air very cold and pure; great relief after the stuffiness and heat between Genoa and Turin. Stopped at many small stations where there were pumps; we held out our enamel mugs and the porters filled them for us with the water. The water was beautiful; this way we gradually quenched our thirst for about first time since journey began. Passed quite close to Mt Cenis. Went through very long tunnel just before reaching Modane, on the Franco-Italian frontier. Here we changed, passed through Customs, and got into Paris express. Most splendid train I have ever been in; seats very large and comfortable; got a corner. Had a most excellent dinner. Could feel we were travelling very swiftly and hardly stopped at all; had water in lavatory, too, for first time. Excellent night.

'*May 26th.* – Were approaching Paris when we woke up; typical French scenery so often described by Roland – thin sentinel trees and straight white roads. Thought very much about Roland and Geoffrey, for this was their country, now.

'Arrived at Paris about 10.0, St Lazare. Met by Red X doctors (not R.A.M.C.) from the Hôtel Asturia, now an officers' hospital under the Franco-British Red X, where we were to be put up for the day. Drove there in a large motor wagon; Paris seemed fairly familiar, even after 4 years. Found Hôtel Asturia in Champs-Élysées, close to Arc de Triomphe. Most of the party by now were very nearly fainting and collapsed, and after breakfast proceeded to lie down at once somewhere in the two rooms allotted to us. Nurses there were very kind and lent their rooms to the illest people . . .

'They have luxurious suites of rooms and when off duty, which seems to be often, go out in gorgeous Paris mufti; it hardly seems pukka nursing to us.

'Fortunately M———n, K. and I didn't feel at all collapsed, so after lunch, as neither of them had seen Paris before, I took them round to look at some of the sights. Took them to Notre-Dame, the Madeleine and along the most important streets – Rue de Rivoli, Avenue de l'Opéra, Place de l'Opéra, Boulevards, Place de la Concorde, etc. . . . . Had delightful coffee and *pâté de foie gras* sandwiches at Kardoma Restaurant in Rue de Rivoli.

'Afterwards did a little shopping; bought a cigarette-case and some handkerchiefs. Returned to hotel for dinner and went to station for train about 10.0. Mrs M. very trying, espec. when the only seats we could get turned out to be a second-class carriage and we had to have 8 in it. However we didn't mind much as we learnt we were crossing from Boulogne instead of Havre, and this was the last night. Night somewhat uncomfortable but slept a little.

'*May 27th.* – Woke up at 5.0 when train stopped at Amiens. Seething crowd of British and French officers and soldiers, most of them in a trench-state. Thought of Roland, Edward and Geoffrey as having been here; don't think Victor ever was. Felt very near the War. Left Amiens at last and went through Abbeville and Étaples. Étaples seemed one enormous and very dirty camp; we were much cheered by Tommies in a troop train that we passed, and cheered and waved to by the soldiers in the camps along both sides of the railway. Made me very glad I had elected to be a nurse and remain one, instead of doing something else. Sat outside Boulogne for about 2 hours. Could see it just in front; could easily have got out and walked to it. Got very bored; however we moved at last, got out and had breakfast – a good and pleasant breakfast – at the Hôtel de Louvre (familiar of course to Edward).

'Boat left at 1.0; we were on deck at 12.0 and all had to wear lifebelts. Boat was a leave-boat – mostly officers and nurses but some Tommies; another boat crammed with Tommies followed in our wake. Were escorted by 6 destroyers. Met another transport going towards Boulogne; men all waved to us and cheered. Crossing very good and smooth; seemed a very little way after the many hours I had spent on the sea. Found a pleasant 8th Sherwood Foresters officer to talk to. The white cliffs seemed to appear very quickly; it seemed like a dream to be seeing them again, or else a dream that I had ever left them.

'Soon luggage had to be collected and we were hastened across the gangways. It was Whit-Sunday, the day after the big air-raid at Folkestone, but I saw no traces of it. Great crush at Folkestone Station; only three trains for two boat-loads. Should never have found a seat and my luggage had not two very charming officers, a staff lieutenant and a R.F.A. colonel, helped K. and me. They talked to us hard all the way to London. It seemed very strange to be at Victoria again; same old crowd round barriers, same old tea-rooms, same old everything. One began to believe one hadn't really been away.'

Twenty minutes after leaving the two officers – K. and I had tea with them at Victoria, I remember, and we all sentimentally wondered whether we should meet again, which of course we never did – I was standing, a little bewildered, outside my parents' flat in Kensington. I had never seen the flat before, and because I knew that my mother ran it – incredible thought! – with only one maid, I had expected to find it small and compact. So much overawed was I by the imposing block of buildings, the numerous entrances, the red-carpeted staircase and the lift, and so conscious did I suddenly become of my battered straw hat and dirty, sea-stained uniform, that I quite forgot to impress the elderly porter who took me up to the top floor with the information that I had just returned from service overseas.

The inside of the flat was as spotlessly immaculate as any dwelling-place that my parents have inhabited, and my mother, though indubitably relieved that I had not been stranded in the Alps or torpedoed in the Channel, was most immediately concerned to disposses me of the accumulated grime of Malta,

Sicily, Italy and France. Supper was not yet ready, so, pausing only to learn that Victor was still alive and still progressing, I threw off my dilapidated garments and jumped into a hot bath, while my mother hurried my holdall and my much-travelled uniform out of the newly decorated flat.

'I thought the best thing was to take them up to the roof — because of fleas,' she explained.

I laughed at her, and did not tell her that she had guessed right about the fleas. Two or three had been wandering pertinaciously under my vest ever since the night in Syracuse harbour, and a peculiarly big brown one had walked in circles round my hat all the way from Paris. It was delicious after the bath to slip into clean underclothes, and to appear before my family gorgeously wrapped in the scarlet silk kimono that I had made so perseveringly on night-duty. In spite of six days of dirt and heat, of interrupted uncomfortable nights and two crowded afternoons of sight-seeing of which the mere memory now fills me with exhaustion, I did not really feel tired.

After supper I settled down luxuriously to smoke — a new habit originally acquired as a means of defence against the insect life in Malta — and to talk to my father about the hazards and adventures of my journey home. My parents took a gratifying pleasure in my assumption of worldly wisdom and the sophistication of the lighted cigarette; after twenty continuous months of Army service I was almost a stranger to them. Sitting before the open French windows of the big drawing-room, I looked out upon the peaceful, darkening square with a sense of unbelievable repose. Between the flats and the turmoil of London lay a long unspoilt area of wooded parkland; the great trees stretched eastwards as far as I could see. Hidden by the cool green of their new spring foliage, innumerable birds twittered softly on their topmost branches. The War with its guns and submarines, its death and grief and cruel mutilations, might have been as innocuous and unreal as time and the smooth, patriotic selections of school history-books had made the Napoleonic campaigns of a century ago.

That night I slept without thinking or dreaming, but the next day the glamour of scarlet kimonos and idle cigarettes had firmly to be put aside. I had come home for a purpose and must now face up to it.

14

The 2nd London General Hospital opened out of a short street in the Chelsea half of the monotonous and dreary buildings which run almost continuously from the public house appropriately known as World's End to Fulham and Hammersmith. Two schools formed part of the building, and their joint play-grounds made a large open space which held quite comfortably the collection of huts and tents that sprang up wherever a few hundred mangled heroes were gathered together. It was not nearly so big as the 1st London General, and had several wards exclusively devoted to head wounds and eye cases.

I found Victor in bed in the garden, his pale fingers lethargically exploring a big book of braille. His head was still copiously bandaged, and one brown eye, impotently open, stared glassily into fathomless blackness. If I had not been looking for him I should not have known him; his face seemed to have emptied and diminished until what was visible of it was almost devoid of expression. 'Hallo, Tah!' I said, as casually as I could, self-consciously anxious to keep the shock of his appearance out of my voice.

He did not answer, but stiffened all over like a dog suddenly hearing its master's call in the distance; the drooping lethargy disappeared, and his mouth curved into the old listening look of half-cynical intelligence. 'Do you know who it is, Tah?' I asked him, putting my hand on his.

'Tah!' he repeated, hesitating, expectant – and then all at once, with a ring of unmistakable joy in his voice, 'Why – it's Vera!'

All that afternoon we sat and talked. The world had closed in around him; he definitely discouraged the description of loveliness that he could no longer see, of activities that he could never again share, and at first seemed interested only in discussing the visits of his friends and the hospital detail of every day. But of his complete rationality there could be no question, and with time and the miraculous adaptability of the blind, the wider outlook would certainly return.

I saw no trace on that day, nor any of the successive afternoons on which I visited him, of the bitterness that Edward had mentioned; he seemed to have accepted his fate, to have embarked upon the conquest of braille, and to have compared, with a slight bias in favour of the former, the merits of an East End curacy with schoolmastering as a career for a blinded man. Captain Ian Fraser of St Dunstan's – then also recently blinded – came several times to visit him, and told him of the work that had already been done in making other sightless officers independent and self-supporting. The news of these experiments gradually stimulated his own determination, and he was ready, as soon as his curiously obstinate head wound had healed, to divert the energy with which he had made himself into a soldier to the reconstruction of his future.

I did not see Edward until he appeared on June 1st for a week-end leave. When he did come he was an unfamiliar, frightening Edward, who never smiled nor spoke except about trivial things, who seemed to have nothing to say to me and indeed hardly appeared to notice my return. More than his first weeks in the trenches, more even than the Battle of the Somme, the death of Geoffrey and the blinding of Victor had changed him. Silent, uncommunicative, thrust in upon himself, he sat all day at the piano, improvising plaintive melodies, and playing Elgar's 'Lament for the Fallen'.

Only a week later – the day after a strange early morning shock like an earthquake had shaken southern England with its sinister intimation of the terrific mine-explosion at Messines Ridge – my mother and I went to Chelsea to find the usually cheerful, encouraging Matron with a face grown suddenly grave and personal. There was an unexpected change, she said, in Victor that morning. He had told his nurse that during the night something had 'clicked' in his head, like a miniature explosion; since then he had gradually grown vaguer and stranger, and had begun to wander a little . . . She thought that perhaps it would be wise to send for his people.

We sent for them at once; and later that afternoon, when his father and aunt had come up from Brighton, we returned with them to the hospital. Physically, Victor was there as usual, but the real Victor, no longer restrained by rational probabilities, had meandered off through the grotesque bypaths of delirium. He was quite oblivious of our presence, and when for a moment we turned away from him to talk to his nurse, he plucked the clothes one by one from his bed with gentle deliberation.

We were sent away while he was tidied up and his bed was remade, and when we came back he seemed once more himself, courteous as ever and apologetic for having been so 'queer'. Left alone with him for a few moments while the others went to see the Matron and the doctor, I looked down at his quiet, passive paleness with a sense of heavy finality. So much human wreckage had passed through my hands, but this . . . well, this was different.

'Tah – dear Tah!' I whispered, in sudden pitying anguish, and I took his fingers in mine and caressed and kissed them as though he had been a child. Suddenly strong, he gripped my hand, pressed it against his mouth and kissed it convulsively in return. His fingers, I noticed, were damp, and his lips very cold.

That night Victor's relatives stayed with us in Kensington; the doctor had advised them not to risk returning to Sussex. Next day, just before breakfast, his father was summoned to the public telephone on the ground floor of the flats; my parents had not yet had a private telephone installed. The message was from the hospital, to say that Victor had died in the early hours of the morning. The Matron had tried to call us during the night, but could get no reply; apparently the night-porter's attitude towards his duty was similar to that of my orderly in Malta.

I still remember that silent, self-imposed breakfast, and the dull stoicism with which we all tried to eat fried bread and bacon. Immediately afterwards we went down to Chelsea; on the way there the aunt and I bought a sheaf of lilies and white roses, for our minds were still too numbed to operate in any but the conventional grooves.

Victor's body had already been taken to the mortuary chapel; although the June sunshine outside shone brilliant and cheerful, the tiny place was ice-cold, and grey as a tomb. Indifferently, but with the mechanical decorum of habit, the orderly lifted the sheet from the motionless figure, so familiar, but in its silent unfamiliarity so terrible an indictment of the inept humanity which condemned its own noblest types to such a fate. I had seen death so often . . . and yet I felt that I had never seen it before, for I appeared to be looking at the petrified defencelessness of a child, to whose carven features suffering and experience had once lent the strange illusion of adulthood. With an overwhelming impulse to soften that alien rigidity, I laid my fragrant tribute of roses on the bier, and went quickly away.

Back at home, the aunt, kind, controlled, too sensitive to the sorrows of others to remember her own, turned to me with an affectionate warmth of intimacy which had not been possible before and would never, we both knew, be possible again.

'My dear, I understand what you meant to do for Victor. I know you'd have married him. I do wish you could have . . .'

'Yes,' I said, 'I wish I could have,' but I did not tell her that the husband of my imagination was always Roland, and could never now be Victor. The psychological combats and defeats of the past two years, I thought, no longer mattered to anyone but myself, for death had made them all unsubstantial, as if they had never been. But though speech could be stifled, thought was less easy to tame; I could not cease from dwelling upon the superfluous torture of Victor's long agony, the cruel waste of his brave efforts at vital readjustment.

As for myself, I felt that I had been malevolently frustrated in the one serious attempt I had ever made to serve a fellow-creature. Only long afterwards, when time had taught me the limits of my own magnanimity, did I realise that his death had probably saved us both from a relationship of which the serenity might have proved increasingly difficult to maintain, and that I had always been too egotistical, too ambitious, too impatient, to carry through any experiment which depended for its success upon the complete abnegation of individual claims.

When Victor's young brother had been sent for from school and the family had gone back to Sussex, I wandered about the flat like a desolate ghost, unable to decide where to go or what to do next. Only when twilight came could I summon sufficient resolution to write to Edward in the dim drawing-room, and to copy into my quotation-book Rupert Brooke's sonnet 'Suggested by some of the Proceedings of the Society for Psychical Research':

> *Not with vain tears, when we're beyond the sun,*
> *We'll beat on the substantial doors, nor tread*
> *Those dusty high-roads of the aimless dead,*
> *Plaintive for Earth; but rather turn and run*
> *Down some close-covered by-way of the air,*
> *Some low sweet alley between wind and wind,*
> *Stoop under faint gleams, thread the shadows, find*
> *Some whispering, ghost-forgotten nook, and there*
> *Spend in pure converse our eternal day;*
> *Think each in each, immediately wise;*
> *Learn all we lacked before; hear, know and say*
> *What this tumultuous body now denies;*
> *And feel, who have laid our groping hands away;*
> *And see, no longer blinded by our eyes.*

15

Five days afterwards Victor was buried at Hove. No place on earth could have been more ironically inappropriate for a military funeral than that secure, residential town, I reflected, as I listened with rebellious anger to the calm voice of the local clergyman intoning the prayers:

'Grant, we beseech Thee, O Lord, Thine Eternal Rest to all those who have died for their country, as this our brother hath; and grant that we may so follow his good example that we may be united with him in Thine Everlasting Kingdom.'

Eternal Rest, I reflected, had been the last thing that Victor wanted; he had told me so himself. But if, thus prematurely, he had to take it, how much I wished that fate had allowed him to lie, with other winners of the Military Cross, in one of the simple graveyards of France. I felt relieved, as I listened to the plaintive sobbing of the 'Last Post' rising incongruously from amid the conventional civilian tombstones, that Edward had not been able to come to the funeral. The uncomprehending remoteness of England from the tragic, profound freemasonry of those who accepted death together overseas would have intensified beyond endurance the incommunicable grief which had thrust us apart.

But when, back in Kensington, I re-read the letter that he had written in reply to mine telling him of Victor's death, I knew that he had never really changed towards me, and that each of us represented to the other such consolation as the future still held:

'I suppose it is better to have had such splendid friends as those three were rather than not to have had any particular friends at all, but yet, now that all are gone, it seems that whatever was of value in life has all tumbled down like a house of cards. Yet in Tah's case I will not, I cannot say that I wished from the bottom of my heart that he should live; I have a horror of blindness, and if I were blinded myself I think I should wish to die . . . I am so very glad that you were near him and saw him so nearly at the end; in a way too I am glad not to have been there; it is good to remember the cheerfulness with which he faced the living of a new life fettered by the greatest misfortune known to man.

'Yes, I do say "Thank God he didn't have to live it." We started alone, dear child, and here we are alone again; you find me changed, I expect, more than I find you; that is perhaps the way of Life. But we share a memory which is worth all the rest of the world, and the sun of that memory never sets. And you know that I love you, that I would do anything in the world in my power if you should ask it, and that I am your servant as well as your brother.

                                                          'EDWARD.'

CHAPTER VIII

Between the Sandhills
and the Sea

THE LAST POST

The stars are shining bright above the camps,
The bugle calls float skyward, faintly clear;
Over the hill the mist-veiled motor lamps
Dwindle and disappear.

The notes of day's goodbye arise and blend
With the low murmurous hum from tree and sod,
And swell into that question at the end
They ask each night of God—

Whether the dead within the burial ground
Will ever overthrow their crosses grey,
And rise triumphant from each lowly mound
To greet the dawning day.

Whether the eyes which battle sealed in sleep
Will open to réveille once again,
And forms, once mangled, into rapture leap,
Forgetful of their pain.

But still the stars above the camp shine on,
Giving no answer for our sorrow's ease,
And one more day with the Last Post has gone,
Dying upon the breeze.

V. B., Étaples, 1917.
From *Verses of a V.A.D.*

1

When Edward went back to France in the last week of June 1917, I did not go with him to Victoria, for I had come superstitiously to believe that a railway station farewell was fatal to the prospect of meeting again.

Instead, I waved to him from the window as his taxi rounded the corner of the square, and then helped my mother to wrap up his violin and put it away once more. In the dining-room hung his portrait by Graham Glen; painted while his wound was still painful, the face above the Military Cross ribbon looked pale and sad and retrospective, as it had been for many months after the Somme.

It was not an auspicious return. At Boulogne his valise, with its newly purchased trench equipment, unaccountably disappeared and was never recovered, and he was obliged to go on without even a revolver to protect him during the miserable process of getting re-acclimatised to the War. For the next two months his lack of possessions, and the exasperating endeavour to replace them through correspondence while the postal communications between England and France grew steadily worse, added immeasurably to the wretched discomfort of that menacing summer.

At the Base, to his bitter disappointment, he was ordered to join the 2nd (Regular) Sherwood Foresters at Lens instead of his own 11th Battalion. When he returned to the line on June 30th, a year, less one day, after he had left it, he found the unfamiliar regiment on the verge of going into action. All too soon, my habitual suspense was renewed by a melancholy letter telling me that he was 'in for another July 1st. If it should be that "Ere the sun swings his noonday sword" I must say good-bye to all of this – then good-bye. You know that, as I promised, I will try to come back if I am killed. It is all very sudden and it is bad luck that I am here in time, but still it must be.'

I had to wait nearly a week before learning that he was still alive and unhurt. A letter dated July 3rd, and written with quite uncharacteristic indignation, describes how he was sent into an attack the moment that he arrived, without knowing officers or men or the ground itself. It reveals how 'magnificently' some of our actions were organised, and how wastefully courageous lives were placed in jeopardy, and often thrown away, as the result of the crudest and most elementary failures of intelligence.

'When I reported my arrival on Saturday night, having only left Étaples in the morning, I was told that I was to go up with the company and that they were going to attack in the early morning. The whole thing was a complete fiasco; first of all the guide who was to lead us to our position went wrong and lost the way completely. I must tell you that the battalion had never been in the sector before and nobody knew the way at all. Then my company commander got lost and so there was only one other officer besides myself and he didn't know the way. The organisation of the whole thing was shocking as of course the position ought to have been reconnoitred before and it is obviously impossible for anyone who has never seen the ground before to attack in the dark. After wandering through interminable trenches I eventually found myself with only five men in an unknown place at the time when our barrage opened. It was clearly no use attempting to do anything and I found a small bit of trench and waited there till it got light. Then I found one of our front posts (there was no proper front line) and there we had to stop till we were relieved last night. As you can imagine, we had a pretty rotten time altogether. I don't think that I and the other officer who reported with me ought to have been rushed into the show like that after a tiring two days' travelling and not knowing the map.'

Had this incident found its way into the official *communiqué*, an admiring nation would no doubt have been told (especially in view of Edward's record on the Somme) that 'this gallant officer held the trench for two days with the help of only five men.' Many similar 'acts of heroism' probably originated in equally crass incompetence at Staff Headquarters. 'The C.O. said he was very pleased with the way we carried on in the line,' Edward's next communication reported, but the whole experience upset him so much that for nearly a month his letters were scrappy and impersonal. He only began to recover towards the end of July, when he was sent back to the 11th Battalion and rejoined it as second in command of his old company.

All this agitation made me very anxious to get back to the midst of things, especially as inactivity led to brooding, and brooding was, of all futile occupations, the most important to avoid. Although three out of the four persons were gone who had made all the world that I knew, the War seemed no nearer a conclusion than it had been in 1914. It was everywhere now; even before Victor was buried, the daylight air-raid of June 13th 'brought it home', as the newspapers remarked, with such force that I perceived danger to be infinitely preferable when I went after it, instead of waiting for it to come after me.

I was just reaching home after a morning's shopping in Kensington High Street when the uproar began, and, looking immediately at the sky, I saw the sinister group of giant mosquitoes sweeping in close formation over London. My mother, whose temperamental fatalism had always enabled her to sleep peacefully through the usual night-time raids, was anxious to watch the show from the roof of the flats, but when I reached the doorway my father had just succeeded in hurrying her down to the basement; he did not share her belief that destiny remained unaffected by caution, and himself derived moral support in air-raids from putting on his collar and patrolling the passages.

The three of us listened glumly to the shrapnel raining down like a thunder-shower upon the trees in the park – those quiet trees which on the night of my return from Malta had made death and horror seem so unbelievably remote. As soon as the banging and crashing had given way to the breathless, apprehensive silence which always followed a big raid, I made a complicated journey to the City to see if my uncle had been added to the family's growing collection of casualties.

When at last, after much negotiation of the crowds in Cornhill and Bishopsgate, I succeeded in getting to the National Provincial Bank, I found him safe and quite composed, but as pale as a corpse; indeed, the whole staff of men and women resembled a morose consignment of dumb spectres newly transported across the Styx. The streets round the Bank were terrifyingly quiet, and in some places so thickly covered with broken glass that I seemed to be wading ankle-deep in huge unmelted hailstones. I saw no

dead nor wounded, though numerous police-supervised barri-
cades concealed a variety of gruesome probabilities. Others were
only too clearly suggested by a crimson-splashed horse lying indifferently on its side, and by several derelict tradesman's carts bloodily
denuded of their drivers.

These things, I concluded, seemed less inappropriate when they
happened in France, though no doubt the French thought otherwise. At St Monica's, one July afternoon, I became aware of a
periodic thumping, like a tremendous heart-beat, which made one
parched corner of the games-field quiver; the sound might have
been a reaping-machine two hundred yards away down the valley,
but I knew it for the echo of the guns across the Channel,
summoning me back to the War. 'Oh, guns of France,' Rose
Macaulay has written of that same summer in 'Picnic, July 1917':

> *Oh, guns of France,*
> *Be still, you crash in vain . . .*
> *Heavily up the south wind throb*
> *Dull dreams of pain . . .*
>
> *Be still, be still, south wind, lest your*
> *Blowing should bring the rain . . .*
> *We'll lie very quiet on Hurt Hill*
> *And sleep once again.*
>
> *Oh, we'll lie quite still, nor listen nor look,*
> *While the earth's bounds reel and shake,*
> *Lest, battered too long, our walls and we*
> *Should break . . . should break.*

There was no way of escaping that echo; I belonged to an
accursed generation which had to listen and look whether it
wanted to do so or not, and it was useless, at this late hour, to
try to resist my fate. So, drowning compunction in determination, I ignored my parents' anxious entreaties to me to stay with
them a little longer and, a week or two after Edward had gone,
I went to Devonshire House.

I was interviewed by a middle-aged woman with a grave face and an 'official' manner, who sat before a desk frowning over a folder containing my record. She motioned me to sit down, and I told her that I wanted to join up again.

'And why,' she asked peremptorily, 'did you leave Malta?'

I trembled a little at the sharp inquiry. Breaches of contract were not, I knew, regarded with favour at Red Cross Headquarters, and were pardoned only on condition of a really good excuse. My own reason, which could not help sounding sentimental, was not, I felt certain, a 'good excuse' at all. But I could think of no plausible alternative to the simple truth, so I told it.

'I came home meaning to marry a man who was blinded at Arras,' I said, 'but he died just after I got back.'

To my surprise, for I had long given up expecting humanity in officials, a mask seemed to drop from the tired face before me. I was suddenly looking into benevolent eyes dim with comprehension, and the voice that had addressed me so abruptly was very gentle when it spoke again.

'I'm so sorry . . . You've had a sad time. Is there anywhere special you want to go?'

I hated England, I confessed, and did so want to serve abroad again, where there was heaps to do and no time to think. I had an only brother on the Western Front; was it possible to go to France?

'There are two drafts going quite soon,' said the kind voice. 'Only a few vacancies are left, but I'll do my best for you.'

She smiled at me as I got up to go, and, rather wanly, I smiled back. Outside her room, I asked a V.A.D. clerk who it was that had interviewed me. I have never been quite sure of the name that she gave me, but it sounded like 'Mrs Keynes'.

2

On the wet afternoon of August 3rd, feeling rather sick after a rough crossing and a hasty second inoculation against typhoid done only the day before, I sat in the stuffy *salon* of the Hôtel du Louvre at Boulogne, writing out endless 'particulars'.

The rest of the draft were similarly engaged; most of them were new to foreign service, and I had felt all the veteran's superiority towards their awkwardness over their life-belts, and their light, nervous conversation about submarines. It had seemed a little strange starting off without Betty, but familiarity with the routine was a very fair compensation for solitude.

When the forms were filled in, a Sister from Headquarters ordered me to go to No. 24 General Hospital at Étaples; I was told to 'proceed' the next day, and to spend the night in Boulogne. So I wired to Edward that I had arrived in France, and shared a room for the night with S., a talkative, red-haired V.A.D. some years older than myself. By the time that Edward replied to my telegram the 11th Battalion had moved up to the Salient, to take part in the series of offensives round Ypres which began on July 31st and continued, futile and expensive, till the middle of November.

Our train next day did not leave until the afternoon, so I spent the morning in the English Church at Boulogne commemorating the Third Anniversary of the War. The Chaplain-General to the Forces, once Bishop of Pretoria, preached to the packed congregation of officers and nurses a sermon to which I only half listened, but I paid more attention to the prayers and the collects:

'Remember not, Lord, our offences, nor the offences of our forefathers; neither take Thou vengeance of our sins; spare us, good Lord, spare Thy people, whom Thou hast redeemed with Thy most precious blood, and be not angry with us for ever.'

A phrase from my Pass Mods. days at Oxford slipped into my mind; I had quoted it not long ago to Edward in a letter from Malta:

'The gods are not angry for ever . . .'

It came, I thought, from the *Iliad* and those quiet evenings spent with my Classical tutor in reading of the battles for sorrowful Troy. How like we were to the fighters of those old wars, trusting to the irresponsible caprices of an importuned God to deliver us from blunders and barbarisms for which we only were responsible, and from which we alone could deliver ourselves and our rocking civilisation!

But I did not, at the moment, allow my thoughts to pursue the subject thus far. Dreaming in the soft light that filtered through the high, stained-glass windows, I saw the congregation as a sombre rainbow, navy-blue and khaki, scarlet and grey, and by the time that the 'Last Post' – with its final questioning note which now always seemed to me to express the soul's ceaseless inquiry of the Unseen regarding its ultimate destiny – had sounded over us as we stood in honour of the dead who could neither protest nor complain, I was as ready for sacrifices and hardships as I had ever been in the early idealistic days. This sense of renewed resolution went with me as I stepped from the shadowed quiet of the church into the wet, noisy streets of Boulogne. The dead might lie beneath their crosses on a hundred wind-swept hillsides, but for us the difficult business of continuing the War must go on in spite of their departure; the sirens would still sound as the ships brought their drafts to the harbour, and the wind would flap the pennons on the tall mast-heads.

Since those years it has often been said by pacifists – as in a brave, lop-sided pamphlet which I read only the other day – that war creates more criminals than heroes; that, far from developing noble qualities in those who take part in it, it brings out only the worst. If this were altogether true, the pacifist's aim would be, I think, much nearer of attainment than it is. Looking back upon the psychological processes of us who were very young sixteen years ago, it seems to me that his task – our task – is infinitely complicated by the fact that war, while it lasts, does produce heroism to a far greater extent than it brutalises.

Between 1914 and 1919 young men and women, disastrously pure in heart and unsuspicious of elderly self-interest and cynical exploitation, were continually re-dedicating themselves – as I did that morning in Boulogne – to an end that they believed, and went on trying to believe, lofty and ideal. When patriotism 'wore threadbare', when suspicion and doubt began to creep in, the more ardent and frequent was the periodic re-dedication, the more deliberate the self-induced conviction that our efforts were disinterested and our cause was just. Undoubtedly this state of mind was what anti-war propagandists call it – 'hysterical exaltation', 'quasi-mystical, idealistic hysteria' – but it had concrete results in stupendous patience, in superhuman endurance, in the constant re-affirmation of incredible courage. To refuse to acknowledge this is to underrate the power of those white angels which fight so naïvely on the side of destruction.

3

A heavy shower had only just ceased when I arrived at Étaples with three other V.A.D.s ordered to the same hospital, and the roads were liquid with such mud as only wartime France could produce after a few days of rain.

Leaving our camp-kit to be picked up by an ambulance, we squelched through the littered, grimy square and along a narrow, straggling street where the sole repositories for household rubbish appeared to be the pavement and the gutter. We finally emerged into open country and the huge area of camps, in which, at one time or another, practically every soldier in the British Army was dumped to await further orders for a still less agreeable destination. The main railway line from Boulogne to Paris ran between the hospitals and the distant sea, and amongst the camps, and along the sides of the road to Camiers, the humped sandhills bristled with tufts of spiky grass.

To-day, when I go on holiday along this railway line, I have to look carefully for the place in which I once lived so intensely. After a dozen almost yearly journeys, I am not sure that I could find it, for the last of the scars has disappeared from the fields where the camps were spread; the turnips and potatoes and mangel-wurzels of a mild agricultural country cover the soil that held so much agony. Even the weather-beaten crosses, with their bright gardens of pansies and stocks and marigolds, in the big cemetery below the pinewoods at the top of the hill have been replaced by the stone architecture of our post-war frenzy for memorials – as though we could somehow compensate the dead by remembering them regardless of expense. Only the sandhills and the sea remain unchanged.

Between rows and rows of long wooden huts splashed with

the scarlet and yellow of nasturtiums, we found the white placard:
No. 24 GENERAL HOSPITAL. The camp, which I had noticed from
the train only a few weeks before, seemed quite familiar, and in
spite of Betty's absence I did not feel lonely in the boarded mess-
room with its green and red chintz curtains, and its vivid dahlias
standing in pickle-jars upon the scrubbed trestle tables. Although
I had been such a short time in England, with its diminishing
rations, it was quite strange to see unlimited butter and sugar
again.

That evening, when I had unpacked in the small wood and
canvas shanty – known as an Alwyn hut – which had to be shared
between the red-haired S. and myself, I sat down to rest on the
grass of the Sisters' compound, where some allotment enthusiast
had succeeded in growing a row of strong-smelling cabbages. S.
was not a soothing companion; her active service kit seemed a
mystery to her, and like most novices she had brought too many
possessions, including an array of boots and shoes worthy of a
débutante at her first house-party. Since offers of help only
rendered her the more voluble, I left her struggling to adapt her
belongings to half a dozen nails and a few square feet of space,
and surrendered myself to the spell – unspoilt even by the perva-
siveness of the cabbages in the damp, warm air – that France had
already cast upon me.

The noise of the distant guns was a sense rather than a sound;
sometimes a quiver shook the earth, a vibration trembled upon
the wind, when I could actually hear nothing. But that sense made
any feeling of complete peace impossible; in the atmosphere was
always the tenseness, the restlessness, the slight rustling, that comes
before an earthquake or with imminent thunder. The glamour of
the place was even more compelling, though less delirious, than
the enchantment of Malta's beauty; it could not be banished
though one feared and resisted it, knowing that it had to be bought
at the cost of loss and frustration. France was the scene of titanic,
illimitable death, and for this very reason it had become the heart
of the fiercest living ever known to any generation. Nothing was
permanent; everyone and everything was always on the move;
friendships were temporary, appointments were temporary, life

itself was the most temporary of all. Never, in any time or place, had been so appropriate the lament of 'James Lee's Wife':

> *To draw one beauty into our hearts' core,*
> *And keep it changeless! such our claim;*
> *So answered, – Never more!*

Whenever I think of the War to-day, it is not as summer but always as winter; always as cold and darkness and discomfort, and an intermittent warmth of exhilarating excitement which made us irrationally exult in all three. Its permanent symbol, for me, is a candle stuck in the neck of a bottle, the tiny flame flickering in an ice-cold draught, yet creating a miniature illusion of light against an opaque infinity of blackness.

4

The next morning saw me begin an experience which I remember as vividly as anything that happened in my various hospitals.

Soon after our arrival the Matron, a beautiful, stately woman who looked unbelievably young for her South African ribbons, had questioned us all on our previous experience. I was now the owner of an 'efficiency stripe' – a length of scarlet braid which V.A.D.s were entitled to wear on their sleeve if they had served for more than a year in military hospitals and had reached what their particular authority regarded as a high standard of competence – and when I told the Matron of my work in Malta, she remarked with an amused, friendly smile that I was 'quite an old soldier'. This pleasant welcome confirmed a rumour heard in Boulogne that the hospital was very busy and every pair of practised hands likely to count. I was glad to be once more where the work was strenuous, but though I knew that 24 General had a special section for prisoners, I was hardly prepared for the shock of being posted, on the strength of my Malta experience, to the acute and alarming German ward.

The hospital was unusually cosmopolitan, as in addition to German prisoners it took Portuguese officers, but I can recall nothing about these except their habit of jumping off the tram and publicly relieving themselves on the way to Le Touquet. Most of the prisoners were housed – if the word can be justified – in large marquees, but one hut was reserved for very serious cases. In August 1917 its occupants – the heritage of Messines and the Yser – were soon to be replenished by the new battles in the Salient which have given their sombre immortality to the Menin Road and Passchendaele Ridge.

Although we still, I believe, congratulate ourselves on our impartial care of our prisoners, the marquees were often damp, and the ward was under-staffed whenever there happened to be a push – which seemed to be always – and the number of badly wounded and captured Germans became in consequence excessive. One of the things I like best to remember about the War is the nonchalance with which the Sisters and V.A.D.s in the German ward took for granted that it was they who must be overworked, rather than the prisoners neglected. At the time that I went there the ward staff had passed a self-denying ordinance with regard to half days, and only took an hour or two off when the work temporarily slackened.

Before the War I had never been in Germany and had hardly met any Germans apart from the succession of German mistresses at St Monica's, every one of whom I had hated with a provincial schoolgirl's pitiless distaste for foreigners. So it was somewhat disconcerting to be pitch-forked, all alone – since V.A.D.s went on duty half an hour before Sisters – into the midst of thirty representatives of the nation which, as I had repeatedly been told, had crucified Canadians, cut off the hands of babies, and subjected pure and stainless females to unmentionable 'atrocities'. I didn't think I had really believed all those stories, but I wasn't quite sure. I half expected that one or two of the patients would get out of bed and try to rape me, but I soon discovered that none of them were in a position to rape anybody, or indeed to do anything but cling with stupendous exertion to a life in which the scales were already weighted heavily against them.

At least a third of the men were dying; their daily dressings were not a mere matter of changing huge wads of stained gauze and wool, but of stopping hæmorrhages, replacing intestines and draining and re-inserting innumerable rubber tubes. Attached to the ward was a small theatre, in which acute operations were performed all day by a medical officer with a swarthy skin and a rolling brown eye; he could speak German, and before the War had been in charge, I was told, of a German hospital in some tropical region of South America. During the first two weeks, he and I and the easy-going Charge-Sister worked together pleasantly enough. I often wonder how we were able to drink tea and eat cake in the theatre – as we did all day at frequent intervals – in that fœtid stench, with the thermometer about 90 degrees in the shade, and the saturated dressings and yet more gruesome human remnants heaped on the floor. After the 'light medicals' that I had nursed in Malta, the German ward might justly have been described as a regular baptism of blood and pus.

While the operations went on I was usually left alone in the ward with the two German orderlies, Zeppel and Fritz, to dress as best I could the worst wounds that I had ever seen or imagined.

'I would have written yesterday . . . but I was much too busy,' runs a typical letter to my mother. 'I did not get off duty at all, and all afternoon and evening I had the entire ward to myself, as Sister was in the operating theatre from 1.30 to 8.0; we had fifteen operations. Some of the things I have to do would make your hair stand on end!'

Soon after my arrival, the first Sister-in-charge was replaced by one of the most remarkable members of the nursing profession in France or anywhere else. In an unpublished novel into which, a few weeks after leaving Étaples, I introduced a good many scenes from 24 General, I drew her portrait as that of its chief character, Hope Milroy, and it is by this name, rather than her own, that I always remember her. Sister Milroy was a highbrow in active revolt against highbrows; connected on one side with a famous family of clerics, and on the other with an equally celebrated household of actors and actresses, she had deliberately chosen a hospital training in preference to the university education for which heredity seemed to have designed her, though no one ever suffered fools less gladly than she. When she first came to the ward her furious re-organisations were devastating, and she treated the German orderlies and myself with impartial contempt. On behalf of the patients she displayed determination and efficiency but never compassion; to her they were all 'Huns', though she dressed their wounds with gentleness and skill.

'Nurse!' she would call to me in her high disdainful voice, pointing to an unfortunate patient whose wound unduly advertised itself. 'For heaven's sake get the iodoform powder and scatter it over that filthy Hun!'

The staff of 24 General described her as 'mental', not realising that she used her reputation for eccentricity and the uncompromising candour which it was supposed to excuse as a means of demanding more work from her subordinates than other Sisters were able to exact. At first I detested her dark attractiveness and sarcastic, relentless youth, but when I recognised her for what she was − by far the cleverest woman in the hospital, even if potentially the most alarming, and temperamentally as fitful as a weathercock − we became constant companions off duty. After the conscientious stupidity of so many nurses, a Sister with unlimited intelligence and deliberately limited altruism was pleasantly stimulating, though she was so incalculable, and such a baffling mixture of convention and independence, that a long spell of her society demanded a good deal of reciprocal energy.

The desire for 'heaps to do and no time to think' that I had expressed at Devonshire House was certainly being fulfilled, though I still did think occasionally, and more especially, perhaps, when I was nursing the German officers, who seemed more bitterly conscious of their position as prisoners than the men. There were about half a dozen of these officers, separated by a green curtain from the rest of the ward, and I found their punctilious manner of accepting my ministrations disconcerting long after I had grown accustomed to the other patients.

One tall, bearded captain would invariably stand to attention when I had re-bandaged his arm, click his spurred heels together, and bow with ceremonious gravity. Another badly wounded boy − a Prussian lieutenant who was being transferred to England −

held out an emaciated hand to me as he lay on the stretcher waiting to go, and murmured: 'I tank you, Sister.' After barely a second's hesitation I took the pale fingers in mine, thinking how ridiculous it was that I should be holding this man's hand in friendship when perhaps, only a week or two earlier, Edward up at Ypres had been doing his best to kill him. The world was mad and we were all victims; that was the only way to look at it. These shattered, dying boys and I were paying alike for a situation that none of us had desired or done anything to bring about. Somewhere, I remembered, I had seen a poem called 'To Germany', which put into words this struggling new idea; it was written, I discovered afterwards, by Charles Hamilton Sorley, who was killed in action in 1915:

> *You only saw your future bigly planned,*
> *And we, the tapering paths of our own mind,*
> *And in each other's dearest ways we stand,*
> *And hiss and hate. And the blind fight the blind.*

'It is very strange that you should be nursing Hun prisoners,' wrote Edward from the uproar in the Salient, 'and it does show how absurd the whole thing is; I am afraid leave is out of the question for the present; I am going to be very busy as I shall almost certainly have to command the coy. in the next show . . . Belgium is a beastly country, at least this part of it is; it seems to breathe little-mindedness, and all the people are on the make or else spies. I will do my best to write you a decent letter soon if possible; I know I haven't done so yet since I came out – but I am feeling rather worried because I hate the thought of shouldering big responsibilities with the doubtful assistance of ex-N.C.O. subalterns. Things are much more difficult than they used to be, because nowadays you never know where you are in the line and it is neither open warfare nor trench warfare.'

A few days afterwards he was promoted, as he had expected, to be acting captain, and a letter at the end of August told me that he had just completed his course of instruction for the forthcoming 'strafe'.

'Captain B.,' he concluded, 'is now in a small dug-out with our old friend Wipers on the left front, and though he has got the wind up because he is in command of the company and may have to go up the line at any moment, all is well for the present.'

5

In the German ward we knew only too certainly when 'the next show' began. With September the 'Fall In' resumed its embarrassing habit of repetition, and when we had no more beds available for prisoners, stretchers holding angry-eyed men in filthy brown blankets occupied an inconvenient proportion of the floor. Many of our patients arrived within twenty-four hours of being wounded; it seemed strange to be talking amicably to a German officer about the '*Putsch*' he had been in the previous morning on the opposite side to our own.

Nearly all the prisoners bore their dreadful dressings with stoical fortitude, and one or two waited phlegmatically for death. A doomed twenty-year-old boy, beautiful as the young Hyacinth in spite of the flush on his concave cheeks and the restless, agonised biting of his lips, asked me one evening in a courteous whisper how long he had to wait before he died. It was not very long; the screens were round his bed by the next afternoon.

Although this almost unbearable stoicism seemed to be an understood discipline which the men imposed upon themselves, the ward atmosphere was anything but peaceful. The cries of the many delirious patients combined with the ravings of the five or six that we always had coming round from an anæsthetic to turn the hut into pandemonium; cries of '*Schwester!*' and '*Kamerad!*' sounded all day. But only one prisoner – a nineteen-year-old Saxon boy with saucer-like blue eyes and a pink-and-white complexion, whose name I never knew because everybody called him 'the Fish' – demanded constant attention. He was, he took care to tell us, '*ein einziger Knabe*'. Being a case of acute empyema as the result of a penetrating chest wound, he was only allowed a milk diet, but continually besieged the orderlies for '*Fleisch, viel Brot, Kartoffeln!*'

'*Nicht so viel schreien, Fisch!*' I scolded him. '*Die anderen sind auch krank, nicht Sie allein!*'

But I felt quite melancholy when I came on duty one morning to learn that he had died in the night.

There was no time, however, for regrets, since I had to spend half that day sitting beside a small, middle-aged Bavarian who was slowly bleeding to death from the subclavian artery. The hæmorrhage was too deep-seated to be checked, and Hope Milroy went vehemently through the dressings with her petrified cavalcade of orderlies while I gave the dying man water, and wiped the perspiration from his face. On the other side of the bed a German-speaking Non-conformist padre murmured the Lord's Prayer; the sombre resonance of its conclusion sounded like the rolling of some distant organ:

'*Und vergieb uns unsere Schulden, wie wir unsern Schuldigern vergeben. Und führe uns nicht in Versuchung, sondern erlöse uns von dem Übel. Denn Dein ist das Reich und die Kraft und die Herrlichkeit in Ewigkeit, Amen.*'

But the dying patient was not much interested in the forgive-ness of his sins; the evil from which neither friends nor enemies could deliver him prevailed all too obviously.

'*Schwester, liebe Schwester!*' he whispered, clutching at my hand. '*Ich bin schwach − so schwach!*'

When I came back from luncheon he too had died, and Hope Milroy was sitting exhausted at the table.

'I've just laid that man out,' she said; 'and now I want some tea. I don't care about watching a man bleed to death under my very eyes, even if he is a Hun.'

Before making the tea, I went behind the screens to take a last look at the wax doll on the bed. Now that the lids had closed over the anxious, pleading eyes, the small bearded face was devoid of expression. The window above the body happened to be closed, and Hope called to me to open it.

'I always open the windows when they die − so as to let their souls go out,' she explained.

Plenty of fresh air was, of course, desirable for many other reasons. September that year was as hot and damp as August had been, and after several weeks in an atmosphere heavy with sepsis, we were both suffering from an uncomfortable variety of those inconveniences known to hospitals as 'd. and v.' which we called 'Étaplitis'.

Such was my life in the German ward. In the middle of September it ended abruptly with a bewildering rumpus, of which I appeared to be the victim rather than the culprit. Although I had been two years with the Army, I was still very innocent; I may be mistaken in supposing that I am less so now, but I am no more certain to-day than I was then of the reason for my sudden transfer to an English surgical ward.

Amongst the prisoners was a twenty-two-year-old medical student whom we called Alfred; he often helped with the operations, and being a natural intriguer, was apt to gossip and cause trouble. One morning I discovered Hope Milroy involved in an acrimonious dispute with both him and the M.O.; all day she strenuously kept me out of the theatre, and after tea I found myself, unaccountably, in the Matron's office.

'I'm very sorry indeed, nurse, that you've been so much annoyed by that dreadful man,' the Matron amazingly began. 'I do hope it hasn't upset you very much. I've arranged for you to go to another ward to-morrow morning.'

Completely unaware whether the 'dreadful man' was Alfred or the M.O., and entirely ignorant of what the one or the other was supposed to have done, I protested quite truthfully that I had not been annoyed at all, that I liked my work in the German ward, and would much rather remain there than be moved. But this, I was told, kindly but very definitely, was out of the question. I still wonder whether the whole upset was not a figment of Hope Milroy's picturesque imagination – or whether some unperceived menace was really threatening my guileless head.

6

Off duty in France, I was less lonely than I had been in either London or Malta. Since I was not new to active service, the agreeable staff of 24 General treated me as a 'veteran' like themselves, and I had a pleasant choice of companions on country walks or shopping expeditions to Paris-Plage.

The area, too, as I came to know it better, seemed anything but the mere dust-heap that it had appeared to me on my journey from Malta. I remember mornings when exiguous wraiths of cloud scudded unsubstantially over the sandhills, crowned always by their tall clumps of thin, dark pines; and afternoons in which the blue shadows lengthened across the vast expanse of coast where the estuary met the distant sea. Towards Paris-Plage the ruddy sails of brown fishing-smacks caught the brief flame of sunset; along the shore irregular patches of emerald seaweed made a futurist pattern upon a golden-brown carpet. Close to the sea a delicate scattering of pink and purple shells began a new design; other cone-shaped varieties, curiously striped in black and yellow, might have been miniature models of the fashionable millinery in the Rue de la Paix.

No seascape in England quite resembles that coast, but the three miles of Romney Marsh between Rye and the sandhill-guarded shore of Camber-on-Sea have at least a family likeness. The same vivid light, due to the perpetual sweeping away of the mists by the wind, lies upon the Marsh and the flat water-logged meadows on either side of the white sentinel road running from Étaples to the woods surrounding Le Touquet. In summer and autumn this light becomes golden-yellow, but in winter it is always a dazzling green.

Along that straight road, Hope Milroy and I walked together one late evening in early September. So close a companionship between a Sister and a V.A.D. would have been frowned upon severely by the portentous Territorials at the 1st London General, but in France, though necessary discipline was maintained in the wards, the Q. A. Reserve Sisters had no such feeling of professional exclusiveness towards the girls who had helped them to fight so many forms of death since almost the beginning of the War. I had had a bitter disappointment that week, for Edward had put in for local leave to come and see me, but though I waited expectantly about the camp for two or three days, he never appeared. To divert my mind from gloomy speculations as to why leave was unobtainable, Hope invited me to one of those stray meals by means of which the insistent appetite of wartime could sometimes successfully challenge a disconsolate mood.

As we crossed the bridge which spanned the river Canche just before it branched into its shallow estuary, we saw two medical officers from 24 General walking a hundred yards in front of us, with backs stiff and shoulders hunched, pretending not to know that we were behind them.

'They're going Paris-Plaging,' observed Hope dispassionately; it was a euphemism that we both understood. Like most of us she suffered from the strained atmosphere created by segregation, but she was among the few who despised surreptitious breaches of a rule that she could not alter. It made the men so conceited, she said, to think themselves worth any amount of risk to women who stood the chance of dismissal while they would get off scot-free whatever happened.

That evening, deep in the woods, we drank coffee and ate omelettes in a cottage garden carved out of a sunlit clearing. The tall, intertwined trees cast their growing shadows over us, and the evening sunlight, glancing through the boughs, made a quivering leafy pattern on the grass. Columbines and pansies framed the narrow garden path with pink and purple borders; the scent from a bush of sweetbriar in the corner hung like the lightest incense upon the quiet air. It seemed impossible that this untouched serenity and the German ward could exist within a few miles of each other; except for the occasional soft thumping of anti-aircraft guns at a distant gunnery school, the War had disappeared. From the depths of the wood a feathery line of blue smoke curled lazily upward; some peasants were making a fire of dry sticks, which recalled to my senses the friendly smell of a thousand bonfires that drifts across England in the early autumn. A verse from Thomas Hardy's 'In Time of the Breaking of Nations' floated into my mind from the volume of his poems that Edward had sent me in Malta:

> *Only thin smoke without flame*
> *From the heaps of couch grass:*
> *Yet this will go onward the same*
> *Though Dynasties pass.*

We sat in the garden till twilight, talking about Oxford, and Hope's reaction against the academic traditions of her family. By the time that we reached the village again, long indigo shadows lay dark upon the fields, and the harvest moon hung like a Chinese lantern in the pale green sky.

7

Through my new surgical hut in the 'front line' of the hospital passed a ceaseless stream of Tommies from the Salient. The ward was less of a strain than the German ward only because it was more adequately staffed; my letters home tell the same story of perpetual convoys, of hæmorrhages, of delirium, of gas-gangrene cases doomed from the start who watched our movements with staring, fear-darkened eyes, afraid to ask the questions whose answers would confirm that which they already knew.

By the time that the new Battle of Ypres had blundered round those costly ridges for six unbroken weeks the whole staff of 24 General was jaded, and in spite of Passchendaele the Matron insisted upon the temporary re-establishment of 'days off'. I spent mine with one of the senior V.A.D.s, who had been in France since 1915: at twenty-six, Norah had made up her mind that intellectual pretensions were not for her, but a large endowment of humorous common sense made her a pleasing companion for the sixteen-mile walk to Hardelot and back which proved the fatigue of the past weeks to have been nervous rather than physical.

I was now quite hardened to living and working on my feet; only a very exceptional 'push' made bones and muscles ache as they had ached after the Somme. As for the wounds, I was growing accustomed to them; most of us, at that stage, possessed a kind of psychological shutter which we firmly closed down upon our recollection of the daily agony whenever there was time to think. We never dreamed that, in the years of renewed sensitiveness after the War, the convenient shutter would simply refuse to operate, or even to allow us to romanticise – as I who tried to write poetry romanticised in 1917 – the everlasting dirt and gruesomeness.

'Have just been writing a poem on the German ward,' I told

my mother on September 15th; 'was composing it this morning while watching a patient who was rather sick come round from an operation.'

The poem was published later in *Verses of a V.A.D.* As anyone who can visualise the circumstances of its composition will imagine, it was not a good poem, and would not be worth mentioning but for the fact that it produced a letter of congratulation from Lady Ampthill – who had succeeded Dame Katharine Furse as Chairman of the Joint Women's V.A.D. Committee – on its irreproachable sentiments. The sentiments were, of course, irreproachable only from the standpoint of a society whose motto was '*Inter Arma Caritas*'; that first flicker of genuine if slightly patronising internationalism would hardly have commended itself to the 'Fight to a Finish' enthusiasts.

Beneath the drifting clouds of a warm September morning, Norah and I walked through sandhills and meadows and pine-woods on our way to Hardelot. At a searchlight depôt on a lonely hillside two Tommies hailed us with delight when we asked them thirstily for water; they said they had not seen an English woman for over three months. We arrived at Hardelot a little before lunch-time; after hesitating outside the Pré Catalan, an old château with a beautiful garden which had been converted into an expensive restaurant 'for officers and nurses', we decided that it would be cheaper, if not quite so pleasant, to eat at the small hotel at Hardelot-Plage.

So we went on for the extra mile, and were about to order a meal in the hotel salon, when a car drove up and an Australian officer stalked through the door with a Q. A. Reserve Sister sidling in behind him. The officer had begun to make some inquiries in very bad French about a room for the night when he noticed Norah and me. He turned and glared at us with a degree of malevolence that I have seldom seen on any human countenance; the worst language in the world could not have told us more plainly how unutterably *de trop* we were.

Norah and I concluded that if the Sister liked to spend part of her leave in this manner it was no business of ours; we rather deplored her choice of officer, but perhaps the selection was limited. The hotel, we decided, was obviously not large enough to hold both ourselves and them, so we walked back again to Hardelot, and lunched in sylvan chastity at the Pré Catalan.

The incident made a good tale to tell over the supper-party that we held in Norah's hut when we got back. Those evening parties – not so dissimilar from the cocoa-drinkings at Oxford, except that instead of essays and dons and Napoleon we discussed operations and Sisters and lumbar punctures – made life in France much more sociable than in Camberwell or Malta, where we had never forgathered in the same way. At Étaples the supervision in 'quarters' was slight and infrequent; the privacy of the V.A.D.s was respected and they were credited with responsible behaviour off duty as well as on – a policy which made for good discipline, though in English hospitals no one appeared to understand this elementary fact of psychology.

8

I returned to my ward for another six weeks without a half day – a deprivation due not only to the perpetual rush of operations and dressings, but to the local mutiny afterwards described by the men as the 'Battle of Eetapps'. At the time, this somewhat disreputable interruption to a Holy War was wrapped in a fog which the years have deepened, for we were not allowed to mention it in our letters home, and it appears, not unnaturally, to have been omitted from standard histories by their patriotic authors.[1]

We were told that the disturbance began by a half-drunken 'Jock' shooting the military policeman who had tried to prevent him from taking his girl into a prohibited café. In some of the stories the girl was a young Frenchwoman from the village, in others she had turned into one of the newly arrived W.A.A.C.s; no doubt in the W.A.A.C.

[1] Since writing the description of the mutiny at Étaples I have learnt from 'Songs and Slang of the British Soldier, 1914–1918', by John Brophy and Eric Partridge (Eric Partridge Ltd.), that the only account of it hitherto published appeared in the *Manchester Guardian* on several dates during February, 1930. The mutiny was due to repressive conditions in the Étaples camps and was provoked by the military police.

camp she was said to be a V.A.D. Whatever the origin of the outbreak, by the end of September Étaples was in an uproar. A number of Australians and New Zealanders, always ready for trouble, joined in the fray; rumour related that numerous highly placed officials had resigned from the control of the camp, and a young officer with the M.C. was said to have shot himself on the Bull Ring.

Quite who was against whom I never clearly gathered, but one party was said to be holding the bridge over the Canche and the others to be trying to take it from them. Obviously the village was no place for females, so for over a fortnight we were shut up within our hospitals, to meditate on the effect of three years of war upon the splendid morale of our noble troops. As though the ceaseless convoys did not provide us with sufficient occupation, numerous drunken and dilapidated warriors from the village battle were sent to such spare beds as we had for slight repairs. They were euphemistically known as 'local sick'.

It was mid-October before the 'Battle of Eetapps' ended and the Sisters and V.A.D.s were at last allowed to leave their respective camps. Fortunately the mutiny had not prevented the arrival of letters, from which I learnt that, throughout the latter fortnight of September, Edward had been in the worst of the 'strafe' perpetually roaring round Passchendaele. On the 19th a note came from him to say that his company had already suffered many casualties, though he himself was so far unhurt.

'Here,' I wrote to my mother, exactly two years after the Battle of Loos, and in language not so different from that used by Roland to describe the preparations for the first of those large-scale massacres which appeared to be the only method of escape from trench warfare conceivable to the brilliant imagination of the Higher Command, 'there has been the usual restless atmosphere of a great push – trains going backwards and forwards all day bringing wounded from the line or taking reinforcements to it; convoys coming in all night, evacuations to England and bugles going all the time; busy wards and a great moving of the staff from one ward to another . . . I hope I shall hear something of Edward soon; I seemed to be thinking of him and listening to the bugles going through the whole of last night.'

Four days later, I learnt that his company had left the front line on September 24th, after being in the 'show' without a break since the 14th. 'We came out last night,' he told me, 'though perhaps "came out" scarcely expresses it; had about 50 casualties, including 1 officer in the company – the best officer of course. I ought to have been slain myself heaps of times but I seem to be here still.'

It was during this offensive that he came to be known as 'the immaculate man of the trenches'. In addition to his daily shave, he wrote most considerately whenever he could to let me know that he was still 'quite alright'. 'In the second half of September,' he finally summed up the position on October 2nd, 'we only had 3½ days out of the line, which is heavy work for the Salient when straffing.'

This was war in real earnest, yet to my tense anxiety he did seem to bear the proverbial charmed life. So long as he remained, even though the others were dead, hope remained, and there was something to live for; without him – well, I didn't know, and blankly refused to think. But between mid-September and mid-October his activities so distressed me that I seldom wrote to him at all, superstitiously believing that if I did he would certainly be dead before the letter arrived. With his usual tolerance he only protested very mildly about this unexpected treatment.

'I quite understand why you didn't write during the interval but, if possible, please don't do so again or else I shan't tell you when I am about to face anything unpleasant, and then you will not be able to help me face it.'

By October 9th, though I had heard from him that he had come safely, and, as he thought, finally, out of 'the strafe', the rush at 24 General had increased rather than slackened.

'Someday, perhaps,' I wrote home on October 12th, 'I will try to tell you what this first half of October has been like . . . Three times this week we have taken in convoys and evacuated to England, and the fourth came in this morning. On one occasion sixteen stretcher cases came into our ward all at the same time. Every day since this day last week has been one long doing of the impossible – or what seemed the impossible before you started. We have four of our thirty-five patients on the D.I.L.

(dangerously ill list) . . . and any one of them would keep a nurse occupied all day, but when there are only two of you for the whole lot you simply have to do the best you can . . . No one realises the meaning of emergencies who has not been in France . . . I am at the moment sitting in an extremely cold bath-hut waiting for the hot water to be turned on . . . This is going to be a dreadfully cold winter, and every day the rain teems down, very cold and heavy . . . Every night and morning I make up my mind that any money I can save here will go towards buying stores of coal, so that for the rest of my natural life when the War is over (if there is anything left of me by then) I can have a fire in my bedroom for ever and ever! . . . I didn't have a bath after all, as the water was only tepid.'

On the same day, Edward sent me a characteristic picture of life in the Salient during that saturating autumn:

'We are in another lot of wet tents surrounded by mud and it is very cold as usual; consequently our servants, with the customary incorrigibleness of the British soldier, are singing lustily and joyfully. A new draft has just arrived wet through and are sitting on wet ground under wet bivouac sheets. The next man due for leave has been out 16 months and the next dozen have been out 14 or 15, and the order has just come round that all men must wash their feet in hot water – presumably in the dixies in which their tea is made or else in the canteens out of which they eat and drink, as there is no other receptacle; I suppose the A.D.M.S. thinks we carry portable baths in the forward areas – and the intelligence officer has managed to procure us 2 bottles of whisky, the first we have had for quite 3 months, and the bombing officer – a gentleman of forgetful disposition about 7 feet by 4 and clumsy in proportion and belonging to our company – has gone to the field cashier miles away and has probably got lost as he started about noon and it has now been dark an hour, and the C.O. has cursed most people during the day, and I observe that this tent is not as waterproof as it may have been once upon a time, and there is our old friend miserably holding on to the eastern slopes of the ridges from which he has been driven but still demanding our presence in this sorrowful land; of such is daily life.'

He had been mistaken in supposing that his share in the Ypres *mêlée* was over. In the latter half of October, A and C Companies of the 11th Sherwood Foresters lost nearly all their officers, and Edward, who had been given a respite as 'O.C. Details' after being in so many 'shows', was urgently sent for to go up to A Company, where only one officer was left. There he was nearly killed while changing from one support line to another, yet once again he arrived back unwounded at Battalion Headquarters.

'We might have come off worse considering that we were in the most pronounced salient just E. of Polygon Wood – one of the worst bits of the whole front during the whole War. However I am told that I am going on leave in 3 or 4 days . . . We have at last a gramophone and a very fine song by a man named Sherrington, "Sweet Early Violets" . . . You have no idea how bitter life is at times.'

How much of its bitterness was due, I wonder, to his knowledge that three months of incessant anguish had produced a total insecure advance of less than five miles? How fully did he realise the utter failure of the long offensive which had absorbed half the gallantry and chivalry, not only of the 11th Sherwood Foresters, but of the whole Fifth Army? Tired and discouraged as he and the surviving remnant of the battalion had become, the terrific gales and whipping rains of the late autumn, which turned the shell-gashed flats of Flanders into an ocean of marshy mud that made death by drowning almost as difficult to avoid as death from gun-fire, must have added the last intolerable straw to their burden of misery.

At Étaples the wind from the sea, heavy and cold and menacing, turned the camp into a dizzy panorama of rocking wood and flapping canvas. One afternoon I came off duty to find my Alwyn hut blown into a collapsed heap of rags and planks on the top of all my possessions. It was past hope of repair, so after grubbily collecting our belongings from beneath the débris, S. and I, without undue reluctance, parted company and were sent to occupy vacant beds in the two-to-a-room winter quarters.

9

At the end of October came the Italian collapse at Caporetto. As von Bülow pursued his demoralised opponents to the River Piave, and one by one captured the heights between the Piave and the Brenta which protected the Venetian plain, there was much speculation in France over the fate of Venice. For the moment I took little interest in these discussions, never dreaming that the rout of an Italian Army in a remote mountain village could concern me for the rest of my life, nor that a time would come when I should not be able to look at a map of the Italian front without a tightening of the throat.

But on November 3rd, when the Flanders offensive was subsiding dismally into the mud and Edward was daily expected home on leave, a brief, mysterious note came from him, written in the vaguely remembered Latin of the Sixth Form at Uppingham:

'Hanc epistolam in lingua Latina male conscripta – nam multorum sum oblitus – quasi experimentiam tibi mitto. Si plurimos dies litteras a me non accipis, nole perturbari; ut in fossis sim ne credideris. Non tamen dies decimos domum redibo, utrumque ad locum aliquem propinquum ei quo parum ante Kalendas Junias revenisti necne eamus haud certe scio. Ut plurimos menses vel etiam annos te videre non possim maxime timeo; sed "vale" priusquam dixi et me vixurum esse ut rursus te videam semper spero. Spem aeternam ad laetitas in futuro tibi etiam tradent di immortales.'

Calling desperately upon the elusive shades of Pass Mods., I managed to gather from this letter that Edward's battalion had been ordered to join the British and French Divisions being sent from France under Lord Plumer and General Fayolle to reinforce the Italian Army. When I had recovered a little from the shock, I took his note to the C. of E. padre, a burly, rubicund individual whose manner to V.A.D.s was that of the family butler engaging the youngest between-maid, and with innocent eyes asked him to translate. As I had suspected, he had not the remotest idea where to begin, and after much protest about the thinness of the notepaper, and the illegibility of Edward's clear handwriting, he was obliged, to my secret triumph, to confess his ignorance.

Although I was glad that Edward had left the Salient, I couldn't help being disappointed that he was going so far away after I had manœuvred myself, as I had hoped, permanently near him for the duration of our wartime lives.

'Half the point of being in France seems to be gone,' I told my family, 'and I didn't realise until I heard he was going how much I had . . . looked forward to seeing him walk up this road one day to see me. But I want you to try and not worry about him more because he is there . . . no one who has not been out here has any idea how fed-up everyone is with France and with the same few miles of ground that have been solidly fought over for three years. There is a more sporting chance anywhere than here. Of course there has been great talk about the migration . . . and all the men whose units are going are very pleased.'

It was certainly a change to get picture-postcards of bright-looking villages in the remote north of Italy after the mud-stained letters from Passchendaele, though the move did not appear, as yet, to have eradicated the pessimism that had seeped into Edward's spirit in melancholy Flanders.

'We have been accorded a most hearty reception all the way and been presented with anything from bottles of so-called phiz. to manifestoes issued by mayors of towns . . .' he wrote on November 15th from Mantua. 'We have got a very hard job to do here and during the next few weeks the uninitiated may think we have failed in it but I trust we shall not really have done so; everything is going to be very different to what we have been used to before . . . We have got the gramophone all this way all right – but I am afraid we may have to throw it away any time now. These plains are so boring; it is impossible to see more than 100 yards for vines. Sorry – I am wandering to-night being rather tired.'

That same evening I was sent on night-duty to an acute medical ward. Since each of my previous night-duties had become a sharp, painful memory of telegrams and death and brooding grief, I did not welcome the change, and wrote to my mother in a sudden

fit of despondency, deepened by the renewed recollection that
Edward, my fellow-survivor, was far away and depressed:

'I feel very old and sad these days, though Sister "Milroy" . . .
tells me she feels like my mother when she goes out with me,
though she's only eight years older. I wonder if I shall ever be
eight years older, and if the next eight could possibly be as long
as the last three. I suppose I am saturated with War, and getting
thoroughly war-weary, like everyone else.'

10

The acute medical ward was under the night supervision of a
Sister whom I soon came to address off-duty as 'Mary', for she
was the trained-nurse elder sister of the V.A.D. with whom I had
walked to Hardelot. Still in her twenties, tall, buxom and
immensely strong, Mary, who had just come down from a Casualty
Clearing Station, at first provoked me to antagonism as she moved
calmly about the ward, interested, half smiling, a little complacent. But very soon we became friends and allies, and I put a
poem about her into the small volume called *Verses of a V.A.D.*
which I published in 1918.

'I always follow the work – or else it follows me,' I thought,
looking apprehensively at the gasping pneumonias, the puffy, inar-
ticulate nephritics and the groaning, blanket-swathed rheumatic
fevers. Nights would go by, I knew, before I should have time to
write to Betty or to Clare, whose brave, infrequent letters,
describing the struggles of a would-be artist to acquire an adequate
training at the Brighton Art School, revealed between the lines
a prolonged battle against increasing domestic depression. Betty
was now back in London, as there was 'nothing doing' in Malta
– Malta which for me belonged already to a past life in another
era. She didn't want to leave home again, she wrote, and proposed
to take a course of training as a masseuse.

Her dutiful readiness to abandon adventure perhaps made my
own family restless, for they wrote with increasing perturbation
about servant difficulties, towards which, with the nightly responsibility for thirty lives on my shoulders, I felt patronisingly

unsympathetic. At twenty-three, having been consistently well fed on a rough but ample Army diet since 1915, I realised only dimly the state of acute neurasthenia into which poor food, constant anxiety, frequent air-raids and the shortage of all necessities were steadily driving middle-aged London.

'I am sorry you have so much trouble about servants,' runs a letter to my mother after a fortnight of night-duty: 'it all seems such a waste of energy when energy is so precious. I really think that soon people will have no choice but either to live in hotels or else do their own work entirely. Personally I would not be in England now for anything; I only wish there were some job that would bring you out here, for people at home seem to be having a pretty bad time.'

I had not underrated the strenuousness of my ward; indeed, it contained possibilities hitherto unrealised – as I knew one night after I had been chased up and down the hut by a stark naked six-foot-four New Zealander in the fighting stage of delirium. Two orderlies, hastily summoned from adjacent wards by one of my few convalescent patients, finally rescued my five-foot-three from its predicament, and as they strapped the insane giant into bed I sat by my table with a beating heart, listening to his fury exploding in a torrent of such expressive language as had not yet assailed my innocent ears even in two and a half years of Army life. When at last he had subsided under the quietening prick of Mary's hypodermic syringe, the elderly Cockney dying of pneumonia in the corner began his permanent refrain: 'Give me me trousers, I want to go to Trouville – want to go to Trouville – to Trouville!'

These acute medical cases were a disturbing contrast to the sane, courageous surgicals. Wounded men kept their personalities even after a serious operation, whereas those of the sick became so quickly impaired; the tiny, virulent microbe that attacked the body seemed to dominate the spirit as well. Why was personality so vulnerable, why did it succumb to such small, humiliating assailants? I mused perturbedly, as I hurried with the bed-pans along the frozen paths between the huts under the bright December stars.

'Never in my life have I been so absolutely filthy as I get on duty here,' I wrote to my mother on December 5th in answer to her request for a description of my work.

'Sister A. has six wards and there is no V.A.D. in the next-door one, only an orderly, so neither she nor he spend very much time in here. Consequently I am Sister, V.A.D. and orderly all in one (somebody said the other day that no one less than God Almighty could give a correct definition of the job of a V.A.D.!) and after, quite apart from the nursing, I have stoked the stove all night, done two or three rounds of bed-pans and kept the kettles going and prepared feeds on exceedingly black Beatrice oil-stoves and refilled them from the steam kettles, literally wallowing in paraffin all the time, I feel as if I had been dragged through the gutter! Possibly acute surgical is the heaviest kind of work there is, but acute medical is, I think, more wearing than anything else on earth. You are kept on the go the whole time and in the end there seems nothing definite to show for it − except that one or two people are still alive who might otherwise have been dead.'

The rest of my letter referred to the effect, upon ourselves, of the new offensive at Cambrai.

'The hospital is very heavy now − as heavy as when I came; the fighting is continuing very long this year, and the convoys keep coming down, two or three a night . . . Sometimes in the middle of the night we have to turn people out of bed and make them sleep on the floor to make room for more seriously ill ones that have come down from the line. We have heaps of gassed cases at present who came in a day or two ago; there are 10 in this ward alone. I wish those people who write so glibly about this being a holy War, and the orators who talk so much about going on no matter how long the War lasts and what it may mean, could see a case − to say nothing of 10 cases − of mustard gas in its early stages − could see the poor things burnt and blistered all over with great mustard-coloured suppurating blisters, with blind eyes − sometimes temporally [*sic*], sometimes permanently − all sticky and stuck together, and always fighting for breath, with voices a mere whisper, saying that their throats are closing and they know they will choke. The only thing one can say is that such severe cases don't last long; either they die soon or else improve – usually the former; they certainly never reach England in the state we have them here, and yet people persist in saying that God made the War, when there are such inventions of the Devil about . . .

'Morning work – i.e. beds, T.P.R.s (temperatures, pulses, respirations), washings, medicines, etc., which in Malta I started at 6.0, start here at 3.30! The other morning there were no less than 17 people to wash! . . . Cold is terrific; the windows of the ward are all covered with icicles and the taps outside frozen. I am going about the ward in a jersey and long coat.'

The extreme cold had begun very early that winter. By the middle of December our kettles and hot-water bottles and sponges were all frozen hard when we came off duty if we had not carefully emptied and squeezed them the night before – which in our hasty, last-minute toilettes we seldom did, for getting up to go on duty in the icy darkness was a shuddering misery almost as exacting as an illness. Our vests, if we hung them over a chair, went stiff, and we could keep them soft only by sleeping in them. All the taps froze; water for the patients had to be cut down to a minimum, and any spilt in the hut passage between our rooms turned in a few seconds to ice.

Except for the weather it didn't seem much like Christmas, with no Roland or Victor or Geoffrey to buy presents for, and Edward so far away that the chance of anything reaching him within a week of the proper time was discouragingly remote. Wartime Christmases anyhow had long lost their novelty, but Mary and I got up early all the same and made shopping expeditions to the village, walking back in pitch darkness through the frozen mud laden with fruit and sweets and gaudy decorations. Christmas Day itself was less unhappy than I had expected, for after a tea-party with the men in my ward, I spent the evening warmly and sleepily at a concert given by the convalescents from the two next-door huts, of which Hope Milroy was now in charge by day.

My own tea-party had to be brief because of another Corporal Smith – though of a type very different from that of the first mortally ill man that I had seen at the Devonshire Hospital – who was rapidly dying of phthisis. The traditional only son of a widow, who had been sent for from England, he was one of those grateful, sweet-tempered patients whom it was torture to be unable to save. As he and 1917 ebbed away together, I couldn't rest even though the surviving gassed cases had gone to England and the convoys had suddenly ceased, but hovered all night between the stove and the foot of his bed, waiting for the inevitable dawn which would steal greyly around the folded screens. Only once, for ten minutes, did I forsake the self-imposed futility of watching the losing struggle, when Edward's Christmas letter, written on December 22nd, came out of a snowstorm to remind me that love still existed, quick and warm, in a world dominated by winter and death.

'To-night I owe you a long letter; I have written nothing but the shortest of notes since we started from Mantova over a month ago. I am so thankful for your letters – they are now as before the greatest help in the whole world . . . I don't know whether I am glad to be here or not – it sounds strange but it's quite true; I was glad to leave the unpleasant region we were in not far from you and the novelty was good for a time but yet in a way it is all the same because there is no known future and the end is not yet, though, on the face of things at present, there is perhaps more chance of return. Why do you want me to get married – a most improbable occurrence? Anyhow there will be no chance for a very long time. It is wonderful that you manage to write a play in spite of all your work; I never have time to do anything . . . and I dream of things and never do them. It is partly the fault of the Army itself . . . this sort of routine is so deadening; it is a life of thinking about little details the whole time and especially thinking about the right one at the right time; the brain must be essentially a machine of memory and after that the rule of life is expediency . . . I can't get on with this because of the number of messages, orders, etc., which are continually arriving; the same happens every evening only it is more usual for them to come in the middle of dinner. I am rather a grumbler.

'Those 2 poems of Masefield's are very good . . . Poetry counteracts the deadening influence a good deal ... I am reading *The Loom of Youth* in bits ... It is very good and it is very true even if slightly exaggerated ... My own experience is that the language and morals generally are not so blatant as he depicts them ...

'We are only half in the mountains here; we face them and the Austrian sits on them; they look very beautiful at times, sometimes near sometimes far off, and there is generally snow on the higher ones ... We were all very short of anything to smoke until just lately when some cigarettes came for me from home; it is an absurd country for supplies though canteens are coming now ... The gramophone returned last night with the spare kit from the base; great joy – "Sweet Early Violets" and "Down in the Forest" again ... I wish I could see you again; it is so long since I did that we shouldn't be able to talk properly for about ½ hour. It seems so much more than two years ago since Roland was killed – to-morrow and Monday I will think of you whenever I can and our love of him may lessen the miles between us. What a long war this is! It seems wonderful to have lived so long through it when everyone else is dead.

'Good night, dear dear child.'

It must have been very soon afterwards that Corporal Smith died. His mother, a little woman in rusty black, wept quietly and controlledly beside him when the final struggle for breath began, she gave us no trouble even when Mary replied 'Yes, quite sure,' to her final piteous inquiry. After I had taken her through the bitter, snowy darkness to the night superintendent's bunk, Mary and I laid out the boy's wasted body. His rapid death had been due, we were told, to an over-conscientious determination to endure; he had refused to complain until too late.

When the orderlies had carried him away, we sat shivering over the stove and discussed in whispers the prospect of a future life; that old discussion, the answer to which three of the four with whom I had most often shared it had now discovered for themselves – or not, as the case might be. But on night-duty many things appeared possible which were quite improbable by day; there seemed, that midnight, to be strange whispers in the snow-laden silence, and the beating of invisible wings about us in the dimly lighted ward.

11

As the winter grew colder and colder I spent the deep trough of the early hours in a huddled heap beside the stove, drinking sample bottles of liqueur from Paris-Plage out of a tin egg-cup, and reading an impressive poem called 'The City of Fear' by a certain Captain Gilbert Frankau, who had not then begun to dissipate his rather exciting talents upon the romances of cigar merchants:

> . . . *the steel has stripped*
> *And ravished the splendours of graven stone, the ruby*
> *glory of glass,*
> *Till apse and gargoyle, buttress and nave,*
> *Reredos, pillar and crypt,*
> *Lie tumbled and crumbled to monstrous ruins of splintering granite-*
> *blocks* . . .
> *Over the grave*
> *Of the work that was spared for the sake of the work*
> *by the Vandals of elder wars,*
> *Only one tattered pinnacle leers to the calm of the*
> *outraged stars.*

I had seen the volume of poems reviewed in a magazine, and had asked for it as an unusual alternative to the perpetual demand for sweets, which were now preferred before newspapers, and certainly before books, since we never felt really warm and our primary need was to combat the eternal cold. To me most books had ceased to seem desirable even in theory, for my recurrent hopes had at last died of ever fulfilling those ambitions which had inspired the long-ago passionate fight to go to Oxford.

It had been, as Edward wrote on New Year's Eve, such 'a rotten year in many ways – Geoffrey and Tah dead and we've seen each other about a week all told . . . F. is in hospital at present so the C.O. and I are the only officers who joined the Bn in 1914.' The War had gone on for such centuries; its end seemed as distant as ever, and the chances of still being young enough, when it did finish, to start life all over again, grew more and more improbable.

By 1918 I had already begun to have uncomfortable, contending dreams of the future. Sometimes I had returned, conscience-stricken and restless, to civilian life while the War was still on, and, as in its first year, was vainly struggling to give my mind to learning. In other dreams I was still a V.A.D., at thirty, at forty, at fifty, running round the wards at the beck and call of others, and each year growing slower, more footsore, more weary.

For the first time, during that night-duty, I definitely gave up – except for occasional poetry – the attempt to read anything more exacting than magazines, which did not recall the bitter desire for intellectual work and the aspirations that had grown so old in waiting upon events. My Classical tutor, when she heard that Edward had gone to Italy, sent me a copy of *Garibaldi's Defence of the Roman Republic* by G. M. Trevelyan. I looked at the attractive red volume with yearning and fear, and the fear conquered; though my nights had become comparatively peaceful by the time that the book arrived, I did not open it until I was studying the history of the *Risorgimento* long after the War. Even novels had ceased to be a refuge; most of them took me so far from everyday wartime life that coming back to it was a shock and a sorrow for which no temporary distraction could compensate.

The magazines, when more demanding than the *Tatler*, still belonged to the Conservative variety, such as the weekly *Times*, the *Spectator* and *Blackwood's*, so that my impression of the winter's most significant events – the Bolshevik November *coup d'état* two months after the proclamation of the Russian Republic, and the final act at Brest Litovsk on March 2nd, 1918, following the complete collapse of the Russian armies – was inevitably somewhat onesided. My upbringing had been so typical of my parents' class that I did not become clearly aware of the existence and influence of such periodicals as the *Manchester Guardian*, the *Nation* and the *New Statesman* until I had left college and was nearing the end of my twenties. Before the War I had heard, academically, of Socialism – it was one of the subjects discussed at Sir John Marriott's Buxton lectures, though his attitude towards it may be imagined – but the existence of the Labour Party, though

I must have known of it, made no impression upon my political consciousness.

Meanwhile, as anticipation grew grey and hopes withered, my letters from home became more and more miserable.

'Conditions . . . certainly seem very bad,' I wrote to my family on January 10th; 'from everyone's people come exactly the same sort of letters as I get from you. Everyone is servantless, no one visits anyone else or goes away, and the food seems as hard to get hold of in other places as in London now. But do if you càn,' I implored, 'try to carry on without being too despondent and make other people do the same . . . for the great fear in the Army and all its appurtenances out here is not that it will ever give up itself, but that the civil population at home will fail us by losing heart – and so of course morale – just at the most critical time. The most critical time is of course now, before America can really come in and the hardships of the winter are not yet over. It wouldn't be so bad if the discomfort and incon-venience and trouble were confined to one or two towns or one or two families, but it seems to be general.'

This despondency at home was certainly making many of us in France quite alarmed: because we were women we feared perpetually that, just as our work was reaching its climax, our families would need our youth and vitality for their own support. One of my cousins, the daughter of an aunt, had already been summoned home from her canteen work in Boulogne; she was only one of many, for as the War continued to wear out strength and spirits, the middle-aged generation, having irrevocably yielded up its sons, began to lean with increasing weight upon its daugh-ters. Thus the desperate choice between incompatible claims – by which the women of my generation, with their carefully trained consciences, have always been tormented – showed signs of afflicting us with new pertinacity.

On January 12th, a hard, bitter morning, a telegram suddenly arrived from Edward: 'Just got leave. Can you get it too?' I went at once to the humane Scottish 'Redcape' who had succeeded the Matron of the autumn; I had been in France for nearly six months, and she told me that she would put in for my leave immediately. In a day or two my orders came through, and I packed up and started for England.

As I was too late for that afternoon's boat I had to spend the night in Boulogne, where I scarcely slept for a burning head and a dull ache all over my body. Next morning a very rough and prolonged crossing made me feel so ill that I hardly knew how to bear it, and as the freezing train from Folkestone did nothing to aid my recovery, I reached Kensington in a state of collapse very different from the triumphant return from Malta. Edward, who had arrived from Italy four days earlier, had gone to Victoria to meet me, but in the crowd and the dark confusion we had somehow missed each other.

Fortified by a large dose of aspirin from Edward's medical case, I went to bed at once, but woke next morning with a temperature of 103 degrees, and for several days had such high fever that the London doctor thought I should be obliged to overstay my leave. The particular 'bug' that had assailed me was difficult to locate, but was obviously a form of 'P.U.O.' or trench fever not dissimilar from the Malta disease in 1916. Perhaps, indeed, that old enemy was reasserting itself, stimulated by overwork or by my fatigued failure to dry my bedclothes sufficiently one recent morning when I had come off duty to find them saturated by a snowstorm which had blown open my hut window during the night.

After a week of feverish misery I was thankful to find myself beginning to feel better. The aches and pains had been bad enough, but worst of all was the conscience-stricken sense that I had spoiled Edward's leave and overburdened my mother. Her health was certainly none too good; with one indifferent maid she had felt her powers taxed to their limit by the care of the flat, and must have been driven nearly frantic by the simultaneous appearance of a sick daughter who needed quite careful nursing, and a vigorous son who continually demanded her society at concerts or urged her to accompany him in a newly acquired selection of violin sonatas.

As soon as my temperature went down it seemed like a pleasant dream to have Edward once more beside me, telling me stories of the journey to Italy, and describing the grey rocks and dark pine forests of the Asiago Plateau. But by the time that I was able to go out, rather shakily holding his arm, only three days of his leave were left, and all that we could manage to achieve alone were two theatres and a few hours of Bach and Beethoven.

Our short time together, so long anticipated and so much discussed in letters, had been completely upset by my absurd illness, and on January 25th, almost before we had talked of anything, he was obliged to go back. I had missed so much of his society that I broke my resolution to avoid stations and saw him into the return leave-train for Italy at Waterloo; I compromised with superstition by leaving the platform before the train went out. At the flower-stall on the station he bought me a large bunch of the year's first Parma violets, and though we did not mention it, we both thought of a verse in the song 'Sweet Early Violets', which he had bought for his gramophone in Italy and played over to me at home:

> *Farewell! Farewell!*
> *Tho' I may never see your face again,*
> *Since now we say 'good-bye!'*
> *Love still will live, altho' it live in vain,*
> *Tho' these, tho' these, my gift, will die!*

How handsome he is now, I thought, but so grave and mature; it's obviously an ageing business to become a company commander at twenty-one. Dear Edward, shall we ever be young again, you and I? It doesn't seem much like it; the best years are gone already, and we've lost too much to stop being old, automatically, when the War stops – if it ever does.

If it ever does! The journey back from Waterloo, in a chilly Tube train, had a quality of wretchedness that no words can convey, though I had now said good-bye at stations so often that I had long outgrown the disintegrating paralysis which followed the first farewell to Roland in March 1915. I couldn't help asking myself for the hundredth time if I should ever see Edward again, but the sorrow of parting had become almost a mechanical sorrow; like the superhuman achievements of ward rushes after convoys, it was an abnormality which had been woven into the fabric of daily life. I no longer even wondered when the War would end, for I had grown incapable of visualising the world or my own existence without it.

At home a flat dejection pervaded everything now that Edward was gone, and I firmly resisted the suggestion that I should use my semi-invalid weakness as an excuse to apply for extension of leave. The universal topics of maids and ration-cards now so completely dominated the conversation in every household that I felt quite glad when my own fortnight was up four days later, and I could return from food-obsessed England to France.

Remembering the eager feminism of my pre-war girlhood, and the effervescent fierceness with which I was to wage post-war literary battles in the cause of women, it seems incredible to me now that I should have gone back to hospital completely unaware that, only a few days before my leave began, the Representation of the People Bill, which gave votes to women over thirty, had been passed by the House of Lords. I had been equally ignorant of its passage through the Commons the previous June, when my thoughts were occupied with Victor's death and the daylight air-raid, but my indifference to the fact that, on February 6th, 1918, woman suffrage became a part of English law only reflected the changed attitude of the war-absorbed Pankhursts themselves. With an incongruous irony seldom equalled in the history of revolutions, the spectacular pageant of the woman's movement, vital and colourful with adventure, with initiative, with sacrificial emotion, crept to its quiet, unadvertised triumph in the deepest night of wartime depression.

12

When I arrived at Boulogne I half expected to be sent to another unit, as movement orders were often the consequence of leave, but no such instructions awaited me, and I returned thankfully to 24 General and my friends.

I reached Étaples just before midnight; my crossing had been velvet-smooth, and the night was still and calm. Overhead in an indigo sky a brilliant moon shone frostily above the camps, casting sharply defined black shadows along the iron paths. At Sisters' quarters I learnt that Hope Milroy had just gone on night-duty – a typically annoying coincidence, since I had just come off – so I crept between the silent huts to her ward, and sat beside its glowing stove drowsily drinking coffee until half way through the night.

In the light medical ward to which I was posted next day, I soon recovered from the heavy-footed aftermath of my illness. A fortnight later the hut was reserved for gassed cases, and I had once again the task of attending to the blinded eyes and scorched throats and blistered bodies which made the struggle for life such a half-hearted affair. One of the dying men had his wife beside him for two or three days; she didn't much enjoy her vigil, and had already begun to flirt with the orderly sergeant before he came to superintend the removal of her husband's body. I wondered whether she knew that the dead man had been syphilitic as well as gassed.

About this time I had a strange little adventure on one of my shopping expeditions into Étaples. I usually walked there with Norah or Mary, but that evening I happened to be alone, and was turning away from the small, somnolent harbour into the muddy stretch of road between the village and the camps, when a young officer planted himself in front of me. Instinctively I stopped; in the waning light I could see that he was shaking all over like a sick man seized with a rigor. Wild blue eyes stared at me from a pinched, pallid face, and at first he had great difficulty in speaking.

'I say!' he burst out at last, 'I d-do want you to forgive me for the way I insulted you yesterday!'

'Insulted me?' I repeated vaguely, for to my certain knowledge I had never seen the young man before.

'Yes – insulted you! I do apologise!' he reiterated passionately.

'But you haven't insulted me!' I reassured him in the most soothing tones that my surprise could assume. 'I don't even know who you are. You must have mistaken me for somebody else.'

He glared at me bitterly, as though I were making an intolerable task even worse than it need have been.

'Oh, no, I haven't!' he insisted. 'It was you all right. I insulted you horribly and I beg you to forgive me.'

Obviously there was no way of getting rid of him but to accept the apology.

'Oh, well!' I capitulated, 'I can't imagine what you're apologising for, but whatever it was I forgive you if it makes you any happier.'

'Thank you – thank you!' he gasped, as though at the end of his endurance, and, saluting desperately, disappeared into the darkness. I walked back to the hospital feeling as mystified as I had been over 'Alfred' and the German ward. France was certainly a queer, haunted country in 1918, peopled by ghosts and bogies and insane sex-obsessions.

'We are beginning now to feel the deprivations of the War a little more out here,' I wrote home on March 3rd; 'no more cakes or biscuits can be bought at the French shops or the E.F. canteen or chocolates or sweets after the present stock is sold out and you can only get meals at restaurants between the hours of twelve and two or after six.'

That same week Edward himself was taken ill with a form of P.U.O. similar to mine; it was not serious, he wrote to me from hospital, and by the middle of the month he was back with the battalion, ruefully describing the joys of billets in the mountains of the Trentino.

'We have had an awful lot of trouble with the civilians on whom we are billeted; the places are very small farms for the most part, very dirty, and with an average of 6 to 10 small, screaming children in each; several families, some being refugees, live in each house. The day we got here 4 teaspoons disappeared and the next day most of the sugar ration went, and then a knife and 3 plates and several cigarettes out of the room where I sleep. Consequently I sent for an interpreter this afternoon, and there was a great wailing and chattering for about ¾ hour – one of the stolen articles made its appearance every 5 minutes except 3 teaspoons and a knife for which we eventually accepted 9 lire; I was rather sorry to take the money off them, but there was nothing else to do if the business was going to be stopped.'

By this time I had been moved from the 'gassed' ward to take charge of a light medical hut. Although I had no Sister I was not very busy, and was often able to stand at the door in the softening air of early spring, listening to the unintelligible sing-song chatter of a Chinese Labour Company putting up some new huts close by, or watching the German Taube 'planes that now seemed to appear so frequently above the camp. It became quite a familiar sight – the pretty silver-white bird with the cotton-wool puff-balls of smoke from our anti-aircraft guns surrounding but never quite reaching it in the clear blue sky.

Idly I supposed that the enemy were reconnoitring and would one day bomb us. Rumour, as busy as usual, reported that on one of their visits 'the Huns' had dropped a message: 'Move your railway-line or move your hospitals', and a lethargic effort to dig trenches near the camps had been started in consequence. Although I had not realised before how conveniently the main line from Boulogne to Paris was safeguarded by the guileless Red Cross, I felt no particular apprehension, for I had grown accustomed to air raids that didn't come off. The roar of bombs dropping on Camiers soon after I arrived had awakened me to the petrifying realisation that there were no cellars in a camp, but since then the lights had gone out in the wards on numerous winter evenings when nothing had happened except 'wind-up' on the part of shell-shocked patients.

On March 20th, Hope Milroy came off night-duty; the next day, Thursday the 21st, she had the usual day off before going to a new ward, and we arranged to spend the afternoon and evening together. At lunch-time, before we started, the staff were discussing a disturbing report that had come, no one knew whence, of a terrific enemy onslaught on the now too far-extended British lines. I felt reluctant to leave the hospital, but the Sister who supervised my hut persuaded me to go.

'It'll probably be the last half-day you'll have for some time,' she said. 'And no convoys can possibly be here before to-night.'

So Hope and I set off together towards Camiers across the muddy fields. At a village *estaminet* we divided the usual enormous omelette, sitting before the fire in an old kitchen which shone with pewter and polished saucepans. The air was strangely still that evening; long wraiths of mist hung like white veils over the sodden meadows, and as we worked our way back to the coast we lost ourselves continually among the darkening sand-hills. Close to the shore, the high, black windows of a deserted watch-tower seemed to leer at us like a wicked eye; try as we would to escape from the encircling sand-dunes, we found ourselves again and again within sight of the grim little ruin. I remembered once, years before, when I was a child of thirteen, listening in half-fascinated terror to a mistress at St Monica's reading 'Childe Roland to the Dark Tower Came':

> *What in the midst lay but the Tower itself?*
> *The round squat turret, blind as the fool's heart,*
> *Built of brown stone, without a counterpart*
> *In the whole world.*

I clutched Hope's arm in sudden agitation.

'Do let's get away from that tower!' I implored her. 'I'd rather go back all the way we've come than pass it again.'

'Don't be absurd!' expostulated Hope. 'There's nothing to be frightened of in an old watch-tower!'

But I seized her and dragged her away until at last, after much struggling through wet sand and thin prickly grass, we reached the shore. She protested that I had hurried her to the point of exhaustion, but as we stood, breathless, beside the muffled sea, the queer menace of that evening startled us both into silence. A sinister stillness hung like heavy fog upon the air; even the waves lapping the shore appeared to make no sound. The setting sun, an angry ball of copper looming through a heavy battalion of thunderous clouds, reminded me of the lurid suns that had set over England in the July before the War, and the belief of the superstitious that they had seen blood upon the sun and moon. Once again, everything seemed waiting, waiting.

'Doesn't it all look ominous!' said Hope at last.

Almost without speaking, we walked back to the camp. There we learned that the rumours of the morning were confirmed, and the great German offensive had begun.

13

I went on duty the next day to find that my light medical hut had been hastily 'converted' into a surgical ward during the night. The harassed and bewildered V.A.D. who had taken in the convoy gave me the report. Ten patients, she explained, were for immediate operation; a dozen more were for X-ray; several were likely to hæmorrhage at any moment, and others were marked down for visits by specialists. No, she was afraid she didn't know who had had breakfast and who had not, as the orderly was away on picket-duty. Then she departed, leaving me in sole charge of forty desperately wounded men.

Only a short time ago, sitting in the elegant offices of the British Red Cross Society in Grosvenor Crescent, I read in the official *Report by the Joint War Committee of the British Red Cross Society and Order of St John* the following words – a little pompous, perhaps, like the report itself, but doubtless written with the laudable intention of reassuring the anxious nursing profession:

'The V.A.D. members were not . . . trained nurses; nor were they entrusted with trained nurses' work except on occasions when the emergency was so great that no other course was open.'

And there, in that secure, well-equipped room, the incongruous picture came back to me of myself standing alone in a newly created circle of hell during the 'emergency' of March 22nd, 1918, and gazing, half hypnotised, at the dishevelled beds, the stretchers on the floor, the scattered boots and piles of muddy khaki, the brown blankets turned back from smashed limbs bound to splints by filthy blood-stained bandages. Beneath each stinking wad of sodden wool and gauze an obscene horror waited for me – and all the equipment that I had for attacking it in this ex-medical ward was one pair of forceps standing in a potted-meat glass half full of methylated spirit.

For a moment my sword of Damocles, the ever-brooding panic, came perilously near to descending on my head. And then, unexpectedly, I laughed, and the danger disappeared. Triumphantly elated by the realisation that I had once again done it in, I began to indent quite gaily for surgical instruments, tourniquets, bandages, splints, wool, gauze, peroxide, eusol and saline. But I had to bombard the half-frantic dispensary for nearly an hour before I could get my stores, and without them it was impossible even to begin on the dressings. When I returned I found to my relief that a Sister had been sent to help me. Though only recently out from England she was level-headed and competent, and together we started on the daily battle against time and death which was to continue, uninterrupted, for what seemed an eternity.

However long I may be destined to survive my friends who went down in the Flood, I shall never forget the crushing tension of those extreme days. Nothing had ever quite equalled them before – not the Somme, not Arras, not Passchendaele – for into our minds had crept for the first time the secret, incredible fear that we might lose the War. Each convoy of men that we took in – to be dispatched, a few hours later, to England after a hasty wash and change of dressing, or to the cemetery after a laying-out too hurried to be reverent – gave way to a discouragement that none of us had met with in a great battle before.

'There's only a handful of us, Sister, and there seem to be thousands of them!' was the perpetual cry whether the patient came from Bapaume or Péronne or St Quentin, where the enemy hordes, released from the Eastern Front, were trying to smash the Allied resistance before the rescuing Americans arrived in force. Day after day, while civilian refugees fled panic-stricken into Étaples from threatened villages further up the line, and the wounded, often unattended, came down in anything that would carry them – returning lorries, A.S.C. ambulances and even cattle-trucks – some fresh enemy conquest was first incredulously whispered and then published tentatively abroad. One after another, Péronne, Bapaume, Beaumont Hamel, were gone, and on March 27th Albert itself was taken. Even Paris, we learnt, had been shelled by a long-range gun from seventy-five miles away. Gradually we became conscious that we were in the midst of what a War historian afterwards called 'the most formidable offensive in the history of the world'.

On the 4th of April, after a fortnight of fourteen-hour days, with the operating theatres going day and night, the 'Fall-In' sounding continuously, and the day staff taking it in turns to be called up to help with night convoys, we limped wearily into the Mess for supper to hear a new and yet more hair-raising rumour.

'The Germans are in the suburbs of Amiens!' it ran round the tables.

We looked at each other, speechless, with blanched faces; I was probably as pale as the rest, for I felt as though cold fingers were exploring my viscera. We were already becoming a Casualty Clearing Station, with only the advance units at Abbeville between ourselves and the line; how much longer should we be able to remain where we were? How long until we too fled before the grey uniforms advancing down the road from Camiers? This horror . . . monstrous, undreamed of, incredible . . . this was defeat. That night we began to pack our boxes. Each evening when we came off duty, we wondered whether the morning would find us still at our posts.

For nearly a month the camp resembled a Gustave Doré illustration to Dante's *Inferno*. Sisters flying from the captured Casualty Clearing Stations crowded into our quarters; often completely without belongings, they took possession of our rooms, our beds, and all our spare uniform. By day a thudding crescendo in the distance, by night sharp flashes of fire in the sky, told us that the War was already close upon their heels.

Nearer at hand, a ceaseless and deafening roar filled the air. Motor lorries and ammunition waggons crashed endlessly along the road; trains with reinforcements thundered all day up the line, or lumbered down more slowly with their heavy freight of wounded. Even the stretcher cases came to us in their trench-stained khaki, with only the clothing round the wound roughly torn away; often their congealed blood fastened them firmly to the canvas, and we had to cut it before we could get them free. The wards were never tidied and the work was never finished; each convoy after staying its few hours was immediately replaced by another, and the business of dressing wounds began all over again. I was glad to be no longer nursing German prisoners; social tact, I felt, would now have become altogether too difficult on either side.

'I won't talk about your push as you will have too much to do with it already,' considerately wrote Edward on Easter Sunday, when the offensive was ten days old, 'but I am glad we have recaptured Albert if only for memory's sake; if the Hun cannot break our line, and I don't think he can, I should think that the end of the War is fairly near. We are in the line with snow all about us – a great change as it is very cold but we are just getting used to it. There have been wonderful sights to see – huge peaks covered with tall pine trees – marvellous roads with hairpin bends and everything solid rock where the snow lies until June . . . Early this morning we had a most extraordinary communion service about 300 yards behind the front line behind a knoll – a most original performance.'

He would forgive me, I knew, for my sudden apparent neglect; 'I imagine you to be so busy that you have no time for anything and I quite understand why you haven't written,' he assured me on April 10th. Why did I leave him letterless ever? I ask myself now. Why didn't I send him Field Postcards, or brief two-line pencil scrawls, as he always found time to send to me even during a push?

'It is most pathetic,' he went on, 'to think that the old places where we were 2 years ago are now in the hands of the Hun as also are the graves of many people we know. As far as I can tell Louvencourt is still behind our lines though fighting in Aveluy Wood doesn't sound far away. I was talking to a Major who was attached to us yesterday about making some dug-outs in a stony piece of ground and he was very particular about wire goggles being worn by men working or living there because of splinters caused by shells bursting on the stone "because," he said, "I can imagine nothing worse than being blinded for the rest of your life." It seemed rather strange that he should say this on the anniversary of the day on which Tah was blinded.'

14

As the German offensive rolled heavily on without appearing to slacken, the men who came into hospital after two or three weeks

of continuous fighting no longer seemed to be weighed down
with the sombre depression of the first batches of wounded;
instead, they were light-headed and often strangely *exaltés*. After
the first shock of defeat, certain units of the British Army began
to suffer from a curious masochism, and, as in 1914, turned from
their usual dogged reliance upon their own strength to the consolations of superstition and the illusions of fatigue.

There was little chance to get to know patients who arrived
in the morning and left before the evening, and in the daily
rush of dressings and convoys I had not much time for talking,
but once or twice I became aware of strange discussions being
carried on by the men. On one occasion I stopped to listen,
and was impelled to remain; I wrote down the conversation a
few weeks afterwards, and though it cannot have been verbally
exact, I reproduce it as it appeared in my 1918 'novel' of nursing
in France:

'‘Ave yer come down from Albert way?' inquired a sergeant of
a corporal in the next bed, who, like himself, wore a 1914 ribbon.

'Yus,' was the reply, 'I have. There's some mighty queer things
happenin' on the Somme just now, ain't there, mate?'

'That there be,' said the sergeant. 'I can tell yer of one rum
thing that 'appened to me, meself.'

'Git on then, chum, let's hear it.'

'Well, when the old regiment first came out in '16, we had a
Captain with us – O.C. of our company, 'e was – a mighty fine
chap. One day at the beginning of the Somme battle some of the
boys got into a tight place – a bit foolish-like, maybe, some of
them was – and 'e comes along and pulls 'em out of it. One or
two of 'em had got the wind up a bit, and 'e tells 'em then not
to lose 'eart if they gets into difficulties, for 'e sorter knows, 'e
says, when the boys 'as need of 'im, and wherever 'e is, 'e says,
'e'll do 'is best to be there. Well, 'e was killed, 'elpin' the boys as
usual, at the end of the fightin' on the Somme, and we mourned
for 'im like a brother, as you might say . . . 'E were a tall fine
chap, no mistakin' 'im, there wasn't. Well, the other day, just before
the Boches got into Albert, we was in a bit of a fix, and I was
doin' all I knew to get us out. Suddenly I turns round, and there

I sees 'im with 'is bright eyes and 'is old smile, bringin' up the rear.

'"Well, Willis, it's been a narrow shave this time," 'e says. "But I think we've pulled it off."

'An' forgettin' 'ow it was, I makes as if to answer 'im, and all of a sudden 'e ain't there at all. Struck me all of a heap for a bit, like. What do you make of it, mate?'

'It's more nor I can tell,' answered the corporal. ' 'Cos another very queer thing happened to some chaps in our company. In the old days on the Somme we had a tophole party of stretcher-bearers, and one day a coal-box comes and wipes out the lot. But last week some of our chaps sees 'em again, carrying the wounded down the communication trench. And I met a chum in the train who swears he was carried out by two of 'em.'

A Lancashire boy from an opposite bed leaned forward eagerly.

'I can tell yer summat that'll beat that,' he said. 'T'other day when we was gettin' clear of Péronne, I found a chap beside me lookin' very white and done-up, like, as if 'e could scarcely walk; fair clemmed, 'e seemed to me. I found I'd got one or two of them 'ard biscuits in me pocket, an' I pulls one out and hands it to 'im. " 'Ave a biscuit, mate," sez I.

' "Thank you, chum," 'e sez, "I don't mind if I do."

'And 'e takes the biscuit and gives it a bite. As 'e puts out 'is 'and for it I sees 'e's got one o' them swanky identity-disks on 'is wrist, and I reads 'is number as plain as anythink. Then 'e gets mixed up wi' t'others, and I don't see 'im no more. And it's not till I gets back to billets that I remembers.

' "Lawks," I sez to meself, "if that ain't the chap I 'elped Jim to bury more'n a week agone, my name ain't Bill Bennett."

'An' sure enough, mates, I remember takin' the silver identity-disk off 'is wrist, an' readin' the number on it as plain as plain. An' it were the number of the man I gave the biscuit.'

There was an awed silence in the ward, and I turned from the dressing I was doing to ask rather breathlessly:

'Do you really mean that in the middle of the battle you met those men again whom you'd thought were dead?'

The sergeant's reply was insistent.

'Aye, Sister, they're dead right enough. They're our mates as was knocked out on the Somme in '16. And it's our belief they're fightin' with us still.'

Not long afterwards I was reminded of this conversation by some lines from E. A. Mackintosh's 'Cha Till Maccruimein', in his volume of poems *A Highland Regiment*, which Roland's mother and sister had sent me for Christmas:

> *And there in front of the men were marching,*
> *With feet that made no mark,*
> *The grey old ghosts of the ancient fighters*
> *Come back again from the dark . . .*

But at the time I merely felt cold and rather sick, and when I had finished the dressing I put down my tray and stood for a moment at the open door of the hut. I saw the Sisters in their white overalls hurrying between the wards, the tired orderlies toiling along the paths with their loaded stretchers, the usual crowd of Red Cross ambulances outside the reception hut, and I recognised my world for a kingdom of death, in which the poor ghosts of the victims had no power to help their comrades by breaking nature's laws.

Angels of Mons still roaming about, I thought. Well, let them roam, if it cheers the men to believe in them! No doubt the Germans, too, had their Angels of Mons; I have often wondered what happened when the celestial backers of one Army encountered their angelic opponents in the nocturnal neutrality of No Man's Land. Michael's war in heaven was nothing, I feel certain, to what happened then.

Certainly no Angels of Mons were watching over Étaples, or they would not have allowed mutilated men and exhausted women to be further oppressed by the series of nocturnal air-raids which for over a month supplied the camps beside the railway with periodic intimations of the less pleasing characteristics of a front-line trench. The offensive seemed to have lasted since the beginning of creation, but must actually have been on for less than a fortnight, when the lights suddenly went out one evening as the daystaff was finishing its belated supper. Instead of the usual interval of silence followed by the return of the lights, an almost immediate series of crashes showed this alarm to be real.

After days of continuous heavy duty and scamped, inadequate meals, our nerves were none too reliable, and I don't suppose I was the only member of the staff whose teeth chattered with sheer terror as we groped our way to our individual huts in response to the order to scatter. Hope Milroy and I, thinking that we might as well be killed together, sat glassy-eyed in her small, pitch-black room. Suddenly, intermittent flashes half blinded us, and we listened frantically in the deafening din for the bugle-call which we knew would summon us to join the night-staff in the wards if bombs began to fall on the hospital.

One young Sister, who had previously been shelled at a Casualty Clearing Station, lost her nerve and rushed screaming through the Mess; two others seized her and forcibly put her to bed, holding her down while the raid lasted to prevent her from causing a panic. I knew that I was more frightened than I had ever been in my life, yet all the time a tense, triumphant pride that I was not revealing my fear to the others held me to the semblance of self-control.

When a momentary lull came in the booms and the flashes, Hope, who had also been under fire at a C.C.S., gave way to the sudden bravado of rushing into the open to see whether the raiders had gone; she was still wearing her white cap, and a dozen trembling hands instantly pulled her indoors again, a dozen shakily shrill voices scolded her indiscretion. Gradually, after another brief burst of firing, the camp became quiet, though the lights were not turned on again that night. Next day we were told that most of the bombs had fallen on the village; the bridge over the Canche, it was reported, had been smashed, and the train service had to be suspended while the engineers performed the exciting feat of mending it in twelve hours.

For a day or two after the raid I felt curiously light-hearted; like the hero of Hugh Walpole's *The Dark Forest* – one of the few novels that I read that winter – 'I was happy . . . with a strange exultation that was unlike any emotion that I had known before. It was

. . . something of the happiness of danger or pain that one has dreaded and finds, in actual truth, give way before one's resolution.'

But that vital sense of self-conquest soon vanished, for within the next few weeks a good night's rest proved impossible for most of us. The liability to be called up for late convoys had already induced a habit of light, restless dozing, and the knowledge that the raiders meant business and might return at any moment after sunset did not help us to settle down quietly and confidently during the hours of darkness. Whenever a particularly tiring day had battered our exhausted nerves into indifference, the lights went out as the result of alarming reports from Abbeville or Camiers and revived our apprehensions. Rumour declared that we were all to be issued with steel helmets, and further spasmodic efforts were made to provide us with trenches in case of emergency.

Three weeks of such days and nights, lived without respite or off-duty time under the permanent fear of defeat and flight, reduced the staffs of the Étaples hospitals to the negative conviction that nothing mattered except to end the strain. England, panic-stricken, was frantically raising the military age to fifty and agreeing to the appointment of Foch as Commander-in-Chief, but to us with our blistered feet, our swollen hands, our wakeful, reddened eyes, victory and defeat began – as indeed they were afterwards to prove – to seem very much the same thing. On April 11th, after a dizzying rush of wounded from the new German offensive at Armentières, I stumbled up to the Sisters' quarters for lunch with the certainty that I could not go on – and saw, pinned up on the notice-board in the Mess, Sir Douglas Haig's 'Special Order of the Day'. Standing there spellbound, with fatigue and despair forgotten, I read the words which put courage into so many men and women whose need of endurance was far greater than my own:

'TO ALL RANKS OF THE BRITISH ARMY IN FRANCE
AND FLANDERS

'Three weeks ago to-day the enemy began his terrific attacks against us on a fifty-mile front. His objects are to separate us from the French, to take the Channel Ports and destroy the British Army.

'In spite of throwing already 106 Divisions into the battle and enduring the most reckless sacrifice of human life, he has as yet made little progress towards his goals.

'We owe this to the determined fighting and self-sacrifice of our troops. Words fail me to express the admiration which I feel for the splendid resistance offered by all ranks of our Army under the most trying circumstances.

'Many amongst us now are tired. To those I would say that Victory will belong to the side which holds out the longest. The French Army is moving rapidly and in great force to our support.

'There is no course open to us but to fight it out. Every position must be held to the last man: there must be no retirement. With our backs to the wall and believing in the justice of our cause each one of us must fight on to the end. The safety of our homes and the Freedom of mankind alike depend upon the conduct of each one of us at this critical moment.

'D. HAIG, F.M.,
'General Headquarters,   'Commander-in-Chief
'*Thursday, April 11th*, 1918.'   'British Armies in France.

Although, since that date, the publication of official 'revelations' has stripped from the Haig myth much of its glory, I have never been able to visualise Lord Haig as the colossal blunderer, the self-deceived optimist, of the Somme massacre in 1916. I can think of him only as the author of that Special Order, for after I had read it I knew that I should go on, whether I could or not. There was a braver spirit in the hospital that afternoon, and though we only referred briefly and brusquely to Haig's message, each one of us had made up her mind that, though enemy airmen blew up our huts and the Germans advanced upon us from Abbeville, so long as wounded men remained in Étaples, there would be 'no retirement'.

Only a day or two afterwards I was leaving quarters to go back to my ward, when I had to wait to let a large contingent of troops march past me along the main road that ran through our camp. They were swinging rapidly towards Camiers, and though the sight of soldiers marching was now too familiar to arouse curiosity, an unusual quality of bold vigour in their swift stride caused me to stare at them with puzzled interest.

They looked larger than ordinary men; their tall, straight figures were in vivid contrast to the under-sized armies of pale recruits to which we had grown accustomed. At first I thought their spruce, clean uniforms were those of officers, yet obviously they could not be officers, for there were too many of them; they seemed, as it were, Tommies in heaven. Had yet another regiment been conjured out of our depleted Dominions? I wondered, watching them move with such rhythm, such dignity, such serene conscious-ness of self-respect. But I knew the colonial troops so well, and these were different; they were assured where the Australians were aggres-sive, self-possessed where the New Zealanders were turbulent.

Then I heard an excited exclamation from a group of Sisters behind me.

'Look! Look! Here are the Americans!'

I pressed forward with the others to watch the United States physically entering the War, so god-like, so magnificent, so splen-didly unimpaired in comparison with the tired, nerve-racked men of the British Army. So these were our deliverers at last, marching up the road to Camiers in the spring sunshine! There seemed to be hundreds of them, and in the fearless swagger of their proud strength they looked a formidable bulwark against the peril looming from Amiens.

Somehow the necessity of packing up in a hurry, the igno-minious flight to the coast so long imagined, seemed to move further away. An uncontrollable emotion seized me – as such emotions often seized us in those days of insufficient sleep; my eyeballs pricked, my throat ached, and a mist swam over the confi-dent Americans going to the front. The coming of relief made me realise all at once how long and how intolerable had been tension, and with the knowledge that we were not, after all, ated, I found myself beginning to cry.

15

Just when the Retreat had reduced the strip of coast between the line and the sea to its narrowest dimensions, the summons came that I had subconsciously dreaded ever since my uncomfortable leave.

Early in April a letter arrived from my father to say that my mother had 'crocked up' and had been obliged, owing to the inefficiency of the domestic help then available, to go into a nursing-home. What exactly was wrong remained unspecified, though phrases referred to 'toxic heart' and 'complete general breakdown'. My father had temporarily closed the flat and moved into an hotel, but he did not, he told me, wish to remain there. 'As your mother and I can no longer manage without you,' he concluded, 'it is now your duty to leave France immediately and return to Kensington.'

I read these words with real dismay, for my father's interpretation of my duty was not, I knew only too well, in the least likely to agree with that of the Army, which had always been singularly unmoved by the worries of relatives. What was I to do? I wondered desperately. There was my family, confidently demanding my presence, and here was the offensive, which made every pair of experienced hands worth ten pairs under normal conditions. I remembered how the hastily imported V.A.D.s had gone sick at the 1st London during the rush after the Somme; a great push was no time in which to teach a tyro her job. How much of my mother's breakdown was physical and how much psychological – the cumulative result of pessimism at home? It did not then occur to me that my father's sense of emergency was probably heightened by a subconscious determination to get me back to London before the Germans reached the Channel ports, as everyone in England felt certain they would. I only knew that no one in France would believe a domestic difficulty to be so insoluble; if I were dead, or a male, it would have to be settled without me. I should merely be thought to have 'wind-up', to be using my mother's health as an excuse to escape the advancing enemy or the threatening air-raids.

Half-frantic with the misery of conflicting obligations, I envied Edward his complete powerlessness to leave the Army whatever happened at home. To-day, remembering the violent clash between family and profession, between 'duty' and ambition, between conscience and achievement, which has always harassed the women now in their thirties and forties, I find myself still hoping that if the efforts of various interested parties succeed in destroying the fragile international structure built up since the Armistice, and war breaks out on a scale comparable to that of 1914, the organisers of the machine will not hesitate to conscript all women under fifty for service at home or abroad. In the long run, an irrevocable allegiance in a time of emergency makes decision easier for the older as well as for the younger generation. What exhausts women in wartime is not the strenuous and unfamiliar tasks that fall upon them, nor even the hourly dread of death for husbands or lovers or brothers or sons; it is the incessant conflict between personal and national claims which wears out their energy and breaks their spirit.

That night, dizzy from work and indecision, I sat up in bed listening for an air-raid and gazing stupidly at the flickering shadows cast by the candle-lantern which was all the illumination that we were now allowed. Through my brain ran perpetually a short sentence which – having become, like the men, liable to sudden light-headed intervals – I could not immediately identify with anything that I had read.

"'The strain all along,'" I repeated dully, "'is very great . . . very great.'" What exactly did those words describe? The enemy within shelling distance – refugee Sisters crowding in with nerves all awry – bright moonlight, and aeroplanes carrying machine-guns – ambulance trains jolting noisily into the siding, all day, all night – gassed men on stretchers, clawing the air – dying men, reeking with mud and foul green-stained bandages, shrieking and writhing in a grotesque travesty of manhood – dead men with fixed, empty eyes and shiny, yellow faces . . . Yes, perhaps the strain all along *had* been very great . . .

hen I remembered; the phrase came out of my father's letter,
t described, not the offensive in France, but the troubles at

home. The next day I went to the Matron's office and interviewed the successor to the friendly Scottish Matron who had
sent me on leave, and whose health had obliged her to leave
Étaples and return to the calmer conditions of home service. The
new Matron was old and charitable, but she naturally did not
welcome my problem with enthusiasm. The application for long
leave which I had hoped to put in would have, she said, no chance
at all while this push was on; the only possibility was to break
my contract, which I might be allowed to do if I made conditions at home sound serious enough.

'I'm giving you this advice against my will,' she added. 'I'm
already short of staff and I can't hope to replace you.'

So, with a sinking heart, I asked for leave to break my contract
owing to 'special circumstances', and returned to my ward feeling
a cowardly deserter. Only to Edward could I express the explosive misery caused by my dilemma, and he replied with his usual
comprehending sympathy.

'I can well understand how exasperating it must be for you to
have to go home now . . . when you have just been in the eddying
backwater of the sternest fight this War has known; it is one of
those little ironies which life has ready to offer at a most inop-
portune moment. I suppose that the Armentières push will have
affected you more nearly still as it is not so very far away . . .
There was a rumour yesterday here that Ypres had gone at last
but there is nothing official about it. It is quite surprising that we
are still here but if we all came back these people would probably give up the War, and "the last state of that man . . ."'

I was glad that my orders did not come through until almost
the end of April, when the offensive against the British had slackened, and we knew for certain that we had not yet lost the War.

Early one morning I bade a forlorn farewell to my friends and
went down alone in an ambulance to the station. From Hope
Milroy I parted with special reluctance, though I should not have
had her companionship much longer in any case, for a few weeks
afterwards she was transferred from Étaples to Havre. In spite of
her unconventionality she was awarded the Royal Red Cross at
the end of the War, and is now Matron of a hospital abroad. Apart

from our periodic correspondence, nothing remains of my days
in France but the crowded cemetery at Étaples and a host of
memories.

I was supposed to be catching the 8.20 for Boulogne that
morning, but when, about 8.30, I endeavoured to board the train
that came in, I was firmly prevented by the military officials at
the station. The new arrival, they told me, was not the 8.20 but
the night train from Paris, which should have appeared about 2
a.m.; since my orders were for the 8.20, by the 8.20 I must go,
whatever time it arrived at Étaples. So I spent the rest of that
interminable morning walking up and down the draughty station
and hoping that the 8.20 would not be quite so late as its predecessor, though I knew that the push and the air-raids between
them had so disorganised the railways that they probably wouldn't
recover for weeks.

When a sleet-shower came down and drove me into the cheerless waiting-room, I found my melancholy vigil shared by two
officers, an American airman in the Canadian Air Force and a
distracted infantry officer who was even more impatient than
myself. He was getting married the next day, he told us, and everything depended on his catching the afternoon boat. The three of
us pooled our agitation, joined up for luncheon in the small cold
buffet, and once again paced the platform, with the knowledge
that the boat was already missed driving the would-be husband
almost to tears.

Eventually the young airman and I agreed to become philosophical; we would spend the night in Boulogne, we decided –
I going as usual to the Louvre, and he, with extreme propriety,
to the R.A.F. Club round the corner – and cross peacefully
together the next morning. But no philosophy ever invented could
console the infantry officer, and when we did reach Boulogne at
dusk he hurriedly left us, saying he had heard that a hospital ship
was going over by night, and he thought he knew someone on
it who could 'wangle' him across. The 'wangle' evidently
succeeded, for we never saw him again.

It was after 2 p.m. before the 8.20 arrived at Étaples, and we
were able to rest our tired legs and cold feet in the comparative

warmth of a first-class carriage. We talked spasmodically for a time, but the long wait had exhausted the few conversational topics that we all had in common, and I began to feel unusually sympathetic towards the familiar notice above the door: 'Taisez-vous! Méfiez-vous! Les oreilles ennemies vous écoutent!' So I left the two officers to carry on a duologue, and looked out of the window at the tormented, hag-ridden country in which I had worked so fiercely for nine months, and was now obliged, by force of circumstance, to leave to the War.

As the train passed through Hardelot, I noticed that the woods on either side of the line were vivid with a golden-green lattice-work of delicate leaves. For a whole month in which off-duty time had been impossible, I had ceased to be aware of the visible world of the French countryside; my eyes had seen nothing but the wards and the dying, the dirt and dried blood, the obscene wounds of mangled men and the lotions and lint with which I had dressed them. Looking, now, at the pregnant buds, the green veil flung over the trees and the spilt cream of primroses in the bright, wet grass, I realised with a pang of astonishment that the spring had come.

CHAPTER IX

"This Loneliest Hour"

ROUNDEL

I walk alone, although the way is long,
And with gaunt briars and nettles overgrown;
Though little feet are frail, in purpose strong
 I walk alone.

Around me press, unknowing and unknown,
In lampless longing the insensate throng,
Seeing but the shadow that my star has thrown.

Across the sundering seas my heart's wild song
Wakes in you joy for my joy, moan for moan.
What if, when Life on Love can wreak no wrong,
 I walk alone?

R. A. L.
August, 1914.

1

From Victoria the young airman, still cheerful and irrepressible after a choppy crossing, drove me straight to the Mayfair nursing-home, where I found my mother certainly ill, but even more worried and distressed.

It seemed to me then, with my crude judgments and black-and-white values, quite inexplicable that the older generation, which had merely looked on at the War, should break under the strain so much more quickly than those of us who had faced death or horror at first hand for months on end. To-day, with middle-age just round the corner, and children who tug my anxious thoughts relentlessly back to them whenever I have to leave them for a week, I realise how completely I under-estimated the effect upon the civilian population of year upon year of diminishing hope, diminishing food, diminishing light, diminishing heat, of waiting and waiting for news which was nearly always bad when it came. Those older men and women who, by good fortune or artful ingenuity, escaped the dreariness of passive submission to wartime circumstances, the colonels, senior to my father, who commanded home battalions, the Matrons and Red Cross Commandants, senior to my mother, who ran hospitals in towns or convalescent homes in the country, had a far better chance of surviving with nerves unimpaired than those who played exclusively the apprehensive rôle of parents.

Having driven direct from the station to see my mother at the home I was still wearing my uniform, which gave the Matron, whom I encountered just as I was leaving, an excuse to treat me with a brisk peremptoriness not usually accorded to nursing-home visitors.

'Be quiet!' she commanded sharply, though I was not making a noise. 'There's an operation patient coming round in that room by the door!'

As I had grown accustomed, for over a month, to doing the day's work in the midst of ten or more operation patients coming round simultaneously, this information did not particularly impress me, but I made a mental resolve never again to appear officially dressed as a V.A.D. within a hundred yards of any non-military trained nurse.

The home, I decided, with its gloomy, airless, expensive rooms, was certainly not calculated to restore the spirits of a sick parent suffering also from nervous prostration, and the Matron's brusqueness had done nothing to remove my initial prejudice. I have often since thought that nothing so clearly illustrates the cautious, unenterprising conservatism that hampers the medical profession as the affection with which it clings, for its own convenience, to the tradition-steeped 'doctor's mile' in the West End. How the invalids who pay so lavishly for their accommodation in the heavy, sunless purlieus of Harley Street ever recover from anything at all remains to me a perpetual mystery. Nor can I understand why, in these days of quick transport, a newly planned area of modern hospitals, with gardens, balconies, vita-glass windows and beds for 'paying' patients, is not started by an enterprising group of younger men and women upon the wind-swept heights of Hampstead or around the sun-drenched open spaces near the river in Chelsea.

As soon, therefore, as I had re-established my father in the flat, I brought my mother back from the costly ground-floor dreariness of Mayfair to her own high bedroom, where she could at least look upon the wooded park with its vivid, blossoming trees, which alone of all creation seemed unaffected by the grey, life-draining economy of 1918. Throughout the hot, dusty months of that comfortless summer, I proceeded to 'run' the flat with a series of ever-changing, inefficient maids, varied by servantless intervals in which I played the part of nurse, cook and maid-of-all-work.

To begin with, the maids were chosen by my mother from the rag-tag and bob-tail selection of girls who for some reason, usually none too creditable, had not been absorbed by munitions or the Service organisations. The first turned out to be several months pregnant, and, as soon as we discovered the fact, left us in wrath to take refuge upon the capacious bosom of the Salvation Army; the second was an amateur prostitute who painted her face ten years before lipstick began to acquire its present fashionable respectability, and smoked pungent cigarettes which, to my father's intense indignation, continually permeated the flat from her bedroom. It was not until late in the summer, while my mother was away in the country, that I happened by chance upon a black-haired, beetle-browed girl whose quick-tempered abruptness concealed an honest disposition and a real capacity for hard work. After I had engaged her, comparative peace descended upon our household for over a year.

I can look back more readily, I think, upon the War's tragedies – which at least had dignity – than upon those miserable weeks that followed my return from France. From a world in which life or death, victory or defeat, national survival or national extinction, had been the sole issues, I returned to a society where no one discussed anything but the price of butter and the incompetence of the latest 'temporary' – matters which, in the eyes of Kensington and of various acquaintances who dropped in to tea, seemingly far out-weighed in importance the operations at Zeebrugge, or even such topical controversies as those which raged round Major-General Maurice's letter to *The Times*, and the Pemberton-Billing case.

Keyed up as I had been by the month-long strain of daily rushing to and fro in attendance on the dying, and nightly waiting for the death which hovered darkly in the sky overhead, I found it excruciating to maintain even an appearance of interest and sympathy. Probably I did not succeed, for the triviality of everything drove me to despair. The old feeling of frustration that I had known in Buxton came back a thousand times intensified; while disasters smashed up the world around me I seemed to be marooned in a kind of death-in-life, with the three years' experience that now made me of some use to the Army all thrown away.

There I had definitely counted; here I seemed merely the incompetent target for justifiable criticism, since a knowledge of surgical nursing did not qualify me for housekeeping, which I had never attempted even in peacetime, and which baffled me completely when I was suddenly faced with its intricacies under wartime restrictions to which people at home had at least grown accustomed gradually. Most bitterly of all I resented the constant dissipation of energy on what appeared to me to be non-essentials. My youth and health had mattered so much when the task was that of dragging wounded men back to life; I believed that the vitality which kept me going had helped others who had lost their own to live, and it seemed rather thrown away when it was all exploded upon persuading the grocer to give us a pot of jam. The agony of the last few weeks in France appeared not to interest London in comparison with the struggle to obtain sugar; the latter was discussed incessantly, but no one wanted even to hear about the former.

Still sore and indignant, I happened one day to read some verses by Sir Owen Seaman which I found in a copy of *Punch* dated April 3rd, 1918 – the very week in which our old strongholds had fallen and the camp at Étaples had been a struggling pandemonium of ambulances, stretchers and refugee nurses:

'THE SOUL OF A NATION'

The little things of which we lately chattered—
  The dearth of taxis or the dawn of spring;
Themes we discussed as though they really mattered,
  Like rationed meat or raiders on the wing;—

How thin it seems to-day, this vacant prattle,
  Drowned by the thunder rolling in the West,
Voice of the great arbitrament of battle
  That puts our temper to the final test.

Thither our eyes are turned, our hearts are straining,
  Where those we love, whose courage laughs at fear,
Amid the storm of steel around them raining,
  Go to their death for all we hold most dear.

New-born of this supremest hour of trial,
  In quiet confidence shall be our strength,
Fixed on a faith that will not take denial
  Nor doubt that we have found our soul at length.

O England, staunch of nerve and strong of sinew,
  Best when you face the odds and stand at bay,
Now show a watching world what stuff is in you!
  Now make your soldiers proud of you to-day!

Sir Owen had been mistaken, I reflected sorrowfully; representing the finer type of non-combatant whose mind was concerned with the larger aspects of the situation, he had ignored – perhaps intentionally – the less disinterested crowd to whom the 'little things' went on mattering more than the Army's anguish. The thunder might roll in the west as loud as it could, but in spite of his noble verses, it would still be drowned in England by the chatter about meat and milk.

The sole consolation of those antagonistic weeks was the young

American airman, to whom I shall always be grateful for the sunny imperturbability which never seemed in the least shaken by my irritable impatience, my moods of black depression. Almost every day for a month or so he 'blew in' to the flat like a rush of wind from the wings of his own 'plane, and extravagantly insisted upon taking me to the Savoy Grill and numerous theatres – which were at least a pleasant contrast to the back of the Western Front – in the intervals of escorting Gaiety girls to less obvious but doubtless more enthralling entertainments. He also, with characteristic generosity, presented me with innumerable meat coupons, which by that time had become far more precious than all the winking diamonds in the empty luxury shops of deserted Bond Street.

2

I was no better reconciled to staying at home when I read in *The Times* a few weeks after my return that the persistent German raiders had at last succeeded in their intention of smashing up the Étaples hospitals, which, with the aid of the prisoner-patients, had so satisfactorily protected the railway line for three years without further trouble or expense to the military authorities.

It was clear from the guarded *communiqué* that this time the bombs had dropped on the hospitals themselves, causing many casualties and far more damage than the breaking of the bridge over the Canche in the first big raid. Hope Milroy, I was thankful to remember, had been moved to Havre a fortnight earlier, but a few days later a letter from Norah filled in the gaps of the official report. The hospital next door, she told me, had suffered the worst, and several Canadian Sisters had been killed. At 24 General one of the death-dealing bombs had fallen on Ward 17, where I had nursed the pneumonias on night-duty; it had shattered the hut, together with several patients, and wounded the V.A.D. in charge, who was in hospital with a fractured skull. The Sisters' quarters were no longer safe after dark, she concluded, and they all had to spend their nights in trenches in the woods.

More than ever, as I finished her letter, I felt myself a deserter, a coward, a traitor to my patients and the other nurses.

How could I have played with the idea – as I had, once or twice lately – of returning to Oxford before the end of the War? What did the waste of an immature intellect matter, when such things could happen to one's friends? My comrades of the push had been frightened, hurt, smashed up – and I was not there with them, skulking safely in England. Why, oh why, had I listened to home demands when my job was out there?

A brief note that came just afterwards from Edward seemed an appropriate – and fear-provoking – comment on the news from Étaples.

'*Ma chère,*' he had written just before midnight on May 12th, '*la vie est brève* – usually too short for me to write adequate letters, and likely to be shorter still.'

For some time now, my apprehensions for his safety had been lulled by the long quiescence of the Italian front, which had seemed a haven of peace in contrast to our own raging vortex. Repeatedly, during the German offensive, I had thanked God and the Italians who fled at Caporetto that Edward was out of it, and rejoiced that the worst I had to fear from this particular push was the comparatively trivial danger that threatened myself. But now I felt the familiar stirrings of the old tense fear which had been such a persistent companion throughout the War, and my alarm was increased when Edward asked me a week or two later to send him 'a funny cat from Liberty's . . . to alleviate tragedy with comedy'.

'This evening,' he added wistfully, 'I should like to hear Dr Farmer play the same Bach Prelude and Fugue which he played in Magdalen chapel on the evening of November 15th, 1914.'

We had perhaps gone to Magdalen together that evening, I thought; it had been just before he left the O.T.C. to join the 11th Sherwood Foresters at Sandgate.

I procured the 'funny cat' and sent it off; was he in for yet another July 1st? I wondered. And because the original July 1st was so nearly approaching its second anniversary, I felt moved to write him a poem that would tell him, as I could never quite tell him in words or in letters, how greatly I esteemed him for the brave endurance which he had shown on that day and so many times since. So I wrote the poem, purchased a copy of the newly published war-poets' anthology, *The Muse in Arms*, and sent the book to Italy with my own verses inscribed on the fly-leaf:

TO MY BROTHER
(In Memory of July 1st, 1916)

Your battle-wounds are scars upon my heart,
Received when in that grand and tragic 'show'
*   You played your part*
*   Two years ago,*

And silver in the summer morning sun
I see the symbol of your courage glow—
*   That Cross you won*
*   Two years ago.*

Though now again you watch the shrapnel fly,
And hear the guns that daily louder grow,
*   As in July*
*   Two years ago,*

May you endure to lead the Last Advance,
And with your men pursue the flying foe,
*   As once in France*
*   Two years ago.*

In the meantime my sudden dread had somewhat diminished, for the newspapers, though they had plenty to say about the new German advance on the Aisne, remained persistently silent about Italy, and instead of further hints of imminent peril, a present came for me from Edward of a khaki silk scarf, and a letter, begun on May 30th and finished on June 3rd, which told me that he was again in hospital.

'Thanks awfully for sending off the cat though of course it hasn't arrived as parcels take so long now. However there isn't as much hurry for it now as there was ... It so happens, quite unexpectedly too, that the time when I wanted it particularly is not

yet . . . If the War goes on much longer nobody will go back to
Oxford in spite of the concessions; I often think I am too old
now to go back.'

On June 3rd he continued in pencil.

'I am now in hospital and oddly enough not so bored as before
because it is rather a relief to be down in the foothills again and
not to have anything to do for a change. It is just a form of P.U.O.
which everybody is having just now but fortunately not all at
quite the same time. I shall be back again in a few days. I have
now finished *Fortitude* and find it excellent . . . I rather think leave
has been reopened while I have been away, but of course I am
about 20th on the list.'

Temporarily reassured about his safety, I went on grieving for
the friendly, exhausting, peril-threatened existence that I had left
behind at Étaples. To my last day I shall not forget the aching
bitterness, the conscience-stricken resentment, with which during
that hot, weary June, when every day brought gloomier news
from France, I read Press paragraphs stating that more and more
V.A.D.s were wanted, or passed the challenging posters in Trafalgar
Square, proclaiming that my King and Country needed me to
join the W.A.A.C., or the W.R.N.S., or the W.R.A.F.

And it was just then, a few days before midsummer, that the
Austrians, instigated by their German masters, decided to attack
the Allies on the Asiago Plateau.

3

On Sunday morning, June 16th, I opened the *Observer*, which
appeared to be chiefly concerned with the new offensive – for
the moment at a standstill – in the Noyon-Montdidier sector of
the Western Front, and instantly saw at the head of a column the
paragraph for which I had looked so long and so fearfully:

'ITALIAN FRONT ABLAZE
GUN DUELS FROM MOUNTAIN TO SEA
BAD OPENING OF AN OFFENSIVE

'The following Italian official *communiqué* was issued yesterday:

'From dawn this morning the fire of the enemy's artillery,
strongly countered by our own, was intensified from the
Lagerina Valley to the sea. On the Asiago Plateau, to the east
of the Brenta and on the middle Piave, the artillery struggle
has assumed and maintains a character of extreme violence.'

There followed a quotation from the correspondent of the
Corriere della Sera, who described 'the Austrian attack on the Italian
positions in the neighbourhood of the Tonale Pass.' 'Possibly,' he
suggested,

'this is the prelude of the great attack which the Austrian
Army has been preparing for so long a time . . . the employment of heavy forces proves that this is not a merely isolated
and local action, but the first move in a great offensive plan.
The Austrian infantry and the *Feldjäger* have not passed. The
Italian defenders met them in their first onslaught and immediately retook the few small positions that had been lost in
the first moments of the fighting. This success on the part
of the Italian defence is a good augury for the future.'

'I'm afraid,' I thought, feeling suddenly cold in spite of the
warm June sunlight that streamed through the dining-room
window. True, the *communiqué* didn't specifically mention the
British, but then there was always a polite pretence on the part
of the Press that the Italians were defending the heights above
Vicenza entirely on their own. The loss of a 'few small positions',
however quickly recaptured, meant – as it always did in dispatches
– that the defenders were taken by surprise and the enemy offensive had temporarily succeeded. Could I hope that Edward had
missed it through being still in hospital? I hardly thought so; he
had said as long ago as June 3rd that he expected to be 'back
again in a few days'.

However, there was nothing to do in the midst of one's family
but practise that concealment of fear which the long years of war

had instilled, thrusting it inward until one's subconscious became a regular prison-house of apprehensions and inhibitions which were later to take their revenge. My mother had arranged to stay with my grandmother at Purley that week in order to get a few days' change from the flat; it was the first time that she had felt well enough since her breakdown to think of going away, and I did not want the news from Italy to make her change her plans. At length, though with instinctive reluctance, she allowed herself to be prevailed upon to go, but a profound depression hung over our parting at Charing Cross.

A day or two later, more details were published of the fighting in Italy, and I learnt that the Sherwood Foresters had been involved in the 'show' on the Plateau. After that I made no pretence at doing anything but wander restlessly round Kensington or up and down the flat, and, though my father retired glumly to bed every evening at nine o'clock, I gave up writing the semi-fictitious record which I had begun of my life in France. Somehow I couldn't bring myself even to wrap up the *Spectator* and *Saturday Review* that I sent every week to Italy, and they remained in my bedroom, silent yet eloquent witnesses to the dread which my father and I, determinedly conversing on commonplace topics, each refused to put into words.

By the following Saturday we had still heard nothing of Edward. The interval usually allowed for news of casualties after a battle was seldom so long as this, and I began, with an artificial sense of lightness unaccompanied by real conviction, to think that there was perhaps, after all, no news to come. I had just announced to my father, as we sat over tea in the dining-room, that I really must do up Edward's papers and take them to the post office before it closed for the week-end, when there came the sudden loud clattering at the front-door knocker that always meant a telegram.

For a moment I thought that my legs would not carry me, but they behaved quite normally as I got up and went to the door. I knew what was in the telegram – I had known for a week – but because the persistent hopefulness of the human heart refuses to allow intuitive certainty to persuade the reason of that which it knows, I opened and read it in a tearing anguish of suspense.

'Regret to inform you Captain E. H. Brittain M.C. killed in action Italy June 15th.'

'No answer,' I told the boy mechanically, and handed the telegram to my father, who had followed me into the hall. As we went back into the dining-room I saw, as though I had never seen them before, the bowl of blue delphiniums on the table; their intense colour, vivid, ethereal, seemed too radiant for earthly flowers.

Then I remembered that we should have to go down to Purley and tell the news to my mother.

Late that evening, my uncle brought us all back to an empty flat. Edward's death and our sudden departure had offered the maid – at that time the amateur prostitute – an agreeable opportunity for a few hours' freedom of which she had taken immediate advantage. She had not even finished the household handkerchiefs, which I had washed that morning and intended to iron after tea; when I went into the kitchen I found them still hanging, stiff as boards, over the clothes-horse near the fire where I had left them to dry.

Long after the family had gone to bed and the world had grown silent, I crept into the dining-room to be alone with Edward's portrait. Carefully closing the door, I turned on the light and looked at the pale, pictured face, so dignified, so steadfast, so tragically mature. He had been through so much – far, far more than those beloved friends who had died at an earlier stage of the interminable War, leaving him alone to mourn their loss. Fate might have allowed him the little, sorry compensation of survival, the chance to make his lovely music in honour of their memory. It seemed indeed the last irony that he should have been killed by the countrymen of Fritz Kreisler, the violinist whom of all others he had most greatly admired.

And suddenly, as I remembered all the dear afternoons and evenings when I had followed him on the piano as he played his violin, the sad, searching eyes of the portrait were more than I could bear, and falling on my knees before it I began to cry 'Edward! Oh, Edward!' in dazed repetition, as though my persistent crying and calling would somehow bring him back.

4

After Edward was killed no wealth of affectionate detail flowed in to Kensington, such as had at least provided occupation for Roland's family at the end of 1915. Roland had been one of the first of his regimental mess to suffer wounds and death, but the many fellow-officers who would have written of Edward with knowledge and admiration had 'gone west' before him in previous offensives – the Somme, Arras, the Scarpe, Messines, Passchendaele – that he had either missed or survived. Of the men with whom he had lived and worked in Italy before the Asiago Battle, I hardly knew even the names.

As time went on, however, we did get three letters – from the officer who was second in command of his company, from his servant, and from a non-combatant acquaintance working with the Red Cross – which told us that Edward's part in withstanding the Austrian offensive had been just what we might have expected from his record of coolness and fortitude on the Somme and throughout the 1917 Battles of Ypres. Of these letters, that from the private was the most direct and vivid.

'I was out on Trench Duty with Capt. Brittain about 3 a.m. on the morning of the 15th June when we were caught in a terrific Barrage; we managed to get back to our Headquarters safely. About 8 a.m. the enemy launched a very heavy attack and penetrated the left flank of our Company and began to consolidate. Seeing that the position was getting critical Captain Brittain with a little help from the French led a party of men over driving the enemy out again. Shortly after the trench was regained Capt. Brittain who was keeping a sharp look out on the enemy was shot through the Head by an enemy sniper, he only lived a few minutes. He has been buried in a British Cemetery behind our lines . . . Allow me to express my deepest sympathy, Captain Brittain was a very gallant officer and feared nothing.'

The cemetery, so the Red Cross friend told us, was in the mountains, 5,000 feet up; he hadn't seen it himself, but Edward's burial the day after the battle was attended by his second in command and the quartermaster of the 11th, who described it to him; they were the only officers out of the line.

"'Brit.',' said the quartermaster, 'was buried in his blanket with 4 other officers, he was placed lying at the head of the grave upon which a cross "In loving memory" with the names, etc., was placed.'

This seemed to be as much as any of our correspondents, who had not themselves taken part in the battle, were likely to tell us, but long before we received their brief information, I saw by the casualty list which contained Edward's name that his twenty-six-year-old colonel had been wounded, obviously in the same action. Knowing that he, the only surviving officer who had been in the battalion with Edward since 1914, could tell me, if he chose, more than anybody else, I visited Harrington House – then the head-quarters for information about the wounded and missing – until I tracked him down to a luxurious officers' hospital in the region of Park Lane.

I had heard, from time to time, a good deal from Edward about his youthful C.O., for whom he seemed to have great respect without much affection. Ambitious and intrepid, the son of a Regular Army officer who could not afford to equip him for a peacetime commission, the young man had found in the War the fulfilment of his baffled longing for military distinction. Since 1914 he had been the regiment's 'professional survivor', fighting unscathed through every action from the Somme to Asiago, and picking up out of each battle another 'pip' and a new decoration. When the 11th Sherwood Foresters were ordered to Italy he went there in command of the battalion; at the time of the Austrian offensive he had already been awarded the D.S.O., M.C., Croix de Guerre and several minor decorations, and from Asiago – which disabled him just sufficiently to keep him in England until almost the end of the War – he gathered the crowning laurels of the V.C.

I did not, of course, know that he was destined for this superlative glory when in stoical desperation I went straight from Harrington House to his hospital. My mother, who had not yet received the letters from Italy, had said emphatically that she did not want to hear any details, but though I dreaded more than

death whatever I might be self-condemned to learn, I was driven
and impelled by a remorseless determination to find out as much
as I could. All the same, I did wish that I had someone other
than the colonel from whom to demand it, and half hoped, half
feared, that he might be too ill to be interviewed by a stranger.
But when I heard that he was severely but not dangerously
wounded in the leg, I sent a message by a nurse to ask if Captain
Brittain's sister might see him for a moment. She returned almost
immediately to fetch me, and, feeling half suffocated, I followed
her up the stairs.

I found the colonel propped up in bed, with a large 'cradle'
over his leg; his features looked pale and drawn, and his dark eyes
burned intently from their sunken sockets as I came into the
room. Quite obviously he did not want to see me, but this I
understood; no wounded man ever did want to see the female
relatives of a friend who had been killed; he always expected them
to break down, or make a scene, or ask awkward questions. It was
a hard young face, I decided; the luminous, vulnerable eyes were
probably some accident of heredity. I resolved to be as brusque
and brief as possible, and found in the colonel's sister – a girl
somewhat older than himself, with gentler features and the same
surprisingly tender expression, who sat beside his bed – an unexpected ally in both the asking and the answering of questions.

'I should have known you were Brittain's sister – you've got
the same eyes,' he began abruptly, and then gave me a brief, matter-
of-fact account of the battle without saying very much about
Edward's part in it. But the moment for describing his death had
to come; he was 'sniped', the colonel said, by an Austrian officer
just after the counter-attack which he had organised and led had
regained the lost positions.

'Where was he shot?' I inquired, as steadily as I could.

Again the young man cast over me his keen, searching glance,
as though I were a subaltern whose ability to go calmly 'over the
top' he was trying to estimate; then he answered curtly: 'Through
the head.'

I looked at him in silent reproach, for I frankly did not believe
him. At that late stage of the War – as I had realised only too

well from the agitated efforts of Army Sisters to mitigate truth with compassion in letters describing the last moments of men who had died in hospital – the colonels and company commanders on the various fronts were so weary of writing gruesome details to sorrowing relatives, that the number of officers who were instantaneously and painlessly shot through the head or the heart passed far beyond the bounds of probability. But when, a few days later, the quite independent letters from Italy confirmed the colonel's statement, I realised that he had not been trying to spare my feelings, and that Edward had escaped Victor's fate only by the sudden death which he himself had repeatedly said that he would prefer to blindness.

Throughout his protracted convalescence I haunted the colonel quite shamelessly, for I still felt convinced that he knew far more than he chose to reveal. Later in the year an acquaintance of mine reported a conversation which she had heard in a railway carriage between a group of Sherwood Foresters who had been in the battle of 15th June. One of them remarked that he had had 'a real good officer, a slim dark chap . . . and a regular *nut*. You'd have thought that he hadn't an ounce of ginger in him, but Lord! miss, he didn't know what fear was.' This officer's name, the man said, was 'Brittain', and he'd deserved the V.C. for pushing back the enemy 'by sheer force' in that 'do' on the Plateau.

This type of appreciative judgment from a private who admired his officer was, of course, common enough, but an inward certainty possessed me that it was not unfounded; I could bear, I felt, the colonel's superior claim to the V.C. if only I knew why the men had thought that Edward deserved it too. So, still passionately determined to learn whatever of the truth remained undisclosed, I accepted the colonel's occasional polite but reluctant invitations to luncheon or tea, tried to make him talk though I always felt embarrassed in his presence, and even forced myself to go to Buckingham Palace to watch him receive his Victoria Cross.

But it was all quite useless. Since adding the V.C. to his collection of decorations, the colonel appeared to have become nervously afraid that every young woman he met might want to marry him, and his fears were not altogether unnatural, for with his long row of ribbons, his premature seniority, his painful limp, and his pale, dark-eyed air of a weary Crusader, the tall young man was an attractive and conspicuous figure wherever he went. In those weeks when he sat so securely upon the pinnacle of his martial ambitions, he could hardly have been expected to realise that no decoration could make him appear to me other than a stiff young disciplinarian, impregnated with all the military virtues but limited in imagination and benevolence, or to believe that I was not fascinated by his medals, but merely anxious for information.

The more assiduously I pursued him in the hope of learning the details that I sought, the more resolutely he faded out of my existence until, after the Armistice, I lost sight of him altogether.

Before he went back to the front just in time for the ending of the War, the 11th Sherwood Foresters and several other British regiments had left the demoralised Austrians to the mercy of the now jubilant Italians and returned to France, where the surviving officers from Edward's company had been killed in the last great push. So whether Edward's part in the vital counter-attack on the Plateau really involved some special act of heroism, I shall now never know.

5

Even if I had found out, it would have made little difference at the time, for as the sudden closing-down of silence upon our four years' correspondence gradually forced on my stunned consciousness the bare fact that Edward was dead, I became progressively unable to take in other facts, or to estimate their value.

So incredible was our final separation that it made life itself seem unreal. I had never believed that I could actually go on living without that lovely companionship which had been at my service since childhood, that perfect relation which had involved no jealousy and no agitation, but only the profoundest confidence, the most devoted understanding, on either side. Yet here I was, in a world emptied of that unfailing consolation, most persistently, most unwillingly alive. I was even alive enough to unpack his possessions when they were returned to us from Italy, and to find amongst them *The Muse in Arms*, which had arrived just after the battle, with my poem inside, unopened and unread. I knew then that he had died without even being aware of my last endeavour to show him how deeply I loved and admired him.

The return of the poem began a period of isolation more bleak, more complete and far more prolonged than the desperate months in 1916 which had followed the death of Roland. My early diaries had been full of the importance of 'standing alone', 'being sufficient unto one's self', and I sometimes re-read them with sombre cynicism during the time that, for nearly two years after Edward's death, I had to be 'sufficient unto myself' whether I liked it or not. However deep our devotion may be to parents, or to children, it is our contemporaries alone with whom understanding is instinctive and entire, and from June 1918 until about April 1920, I knew no one in the world to whom I could speak spontaneously, or utter one sentence completely expressive of what I really thought or felt. I 'stood alone' in very truth – and I hope profoundly that I may never repeat the experience. It lasted so long, perhaps, because I decided in the first few weeks after his loss that nothing would ever really console me for Edward's death or make his memory less poignant; and in this I was quite correct, for nothing ever has.

During this period, one or two sympathetic friends wrote earnestly to me of the experimental compensations of Spiritualism. As always in wartime, the long casualty lists had created throughout England a terrible interest in the idea of personal survival, and many wives and mothers and sisters had turned to *séances* and mediums in the hope of finding some indication, however elusive, of a future reunion 'beyond the sun'.

But I knew that this short cut to convictions which I longed to feel held no comfort for me. I remember walking down the shimmering Sunday emptiness of Kensington High Street on the hot summer morning after the telegram came, intoxicated, strangely *exaltée*, lifted into incongruous ecstasy by a sense that Edward's invisible presence was walking there beside me. After that, everything relapsed into paralysis. I did not want to speak or even to think much about him, and I could find no relief, as after Roland's death, by translating my grief into long replies to letters of sympathy. There was no rush to poems now, no black quotation book, no little library of consecrated volumes; we never had a late meal, nor changed one item of our dull routine. I felt enormously, interminably tired; that was all. One had to go on living because it was less trouble than finding a way out, but the early ideals of the War were all shattered, trampled into the mud which covered the bodies of those with whom I had shared them. What was the use of hypocritically seeking out exalted consolations for death, when I knew so well that there were none?

One day I remembered how Edward had told me that Geoffrey's last letter, written two days before he was killed at Monchy-le-Preux, had ended with the words: 'Till we meet again, Here or in the Hereafter.' Had they met now in the hereafter, I wondered? On the whole I could not believe that they had. Edward, like Roland, had promised me that if a life existed beyond the grave, he would somehow come back and make me know of it. I had thought that, of the two, Roland, with his reckless determination, would be the more likely to trespass from the infinite across the boundaries of the tangible, and incur any penalties that might be imposed. But he had sent no sign and Edward sent none; nor did I expect one. I knew now that death was the end and that I was quite alone. There was no hereafter, no Easter morning, no meeting again; I walked in a darkness, a dumbness, a silence, which no beloved voice would penetrate, no fond hope illumine. Only, as I went mechanically about my daily occupations, three lines from Sir Walter Raleigh's farewell verses kept beating through my brain:

> *Even such is Time, that takes in trust*
> *Our youth, our joys, our all we have,*
> *And pays us but with earth and dust.*

6

In July we closed the flat, and went for a 'holiday' in Cornwall through a melancholy country now extensively parcelled into allotments.

It was already the middle of the month; the Bolsheviks were busy murdering the Czar, and his allied avengers, after sending a hopeful expedition to Vladivostock, were completing their preparations for the landing at Archangel, when Foch's great counter-attacking blow of July 18th, followed by Haig's offensive on the Avre, turned the German advance for the first time into a retreat. But I had ceased to care what happened to the War; having now no hope, and therefore no fear, I did not open *The Times* even to read the casualty lists, and for weeks remained blankly unaware that the Germans had already begun to travel along the great road between Amiens and St Quentin in the opposite direction to that in which they had thundered in March.

I remember that July as a dry, bright month, reflecting in its external brassiness the dry, bright-eyed stoicism of those human automata upon whose love life could wreak no more wrong. Above the crisp Cornish turf the milk-blue harebells, hot in the sun, hung unswayed by the windless air. As I sat below two poppy-flecked fields of oats on the rocky coast of West Pentyre, and watched the camouflaged ships gliding across the smooth sea with the unreality of ships in a dream, my reflections grew so painful that I decided to stampede thought by continuing my wild novel of the War in France. But the plot became so lurid, and the characters and places so easily recognisable, that Roland's father, to whom I showed the manuscript after it was completed, advised me to make no attempt to publish it if I wanted to keep out of the Law Courts. I was really quite safe; no publisher would have dreamed of accepting so crude a piece of semi-fiction, but I took his advice and put the manuscript away in a cupboard, where it has remained ever since.

On some utterly forgotten date, however, during those empty weeks, my small volume of war-poems, *Verses of a V.A.D.*, was unobtrusively ushered into an indifferent world. Roland's mother had arranged for its publication and wrote a short introduction, but my verses, naturally enough, caused not a second's ripple upon the much-bestrewn waters of contemporary war literature. Only, in the 'Shorter Notices' section of *The Times Literary Supplement* – now known to the initiated as 'the paupers' burial-ground' – a minute but surprisingly gracious review appeared, and even to-day I correspond at intervals with a Queensland sheep-farmer, who by chance came across the book while he was still in England with the Australian Expeditionary Force, and for some obscure reason found comfort in the raw little verses.

By mid-September, after Bessie, the hard-working maid, had been engaged, there seemed no longer any real reason why I should remain at home. I couldn't feel much interest now in any kind of military service, but Edward's death had made a wartime return to Oxford more than ever impossible, and the Army had become a habit which only the end of the War could break. Although the Turks in their thousands were surrendering to Allenby in Palestine, and the new British offensive between Arras and Albert had gained ground held by the Germans since 1914, it still did not occur to me that anything unusual was happening, and even the collapse of Bulgaria at the end of September seemed only to have a remote significance.

So, for the third time, I went like a returning somnambulist to Devonshire House, and was interviewed by Lady Oliver. I had hoped that foreign service might restore me, as it had done twice before, to some kind of clear-headed vitality, but I found that, for me, foreign service was no longer available. There was now, I was told, 'a rule' – Heaven knew in whose bright brain it had origi-nated – that V.A.D.s who had broken their contracts for any reason whatsoever while on active service might not go abroad again until they had been once more through the 'grounding' in home hospitals that they would have required had they never served at all.

I could not, I learnt, be posted to any place in which my long practice in dressing wounds under active service conditions would be of the least use to anyone – though every month numbers of 'green' V.A.D.s were being sent abroad whose knowledge of emer-gency nursing had to be acquired at the expense of long-suffering Sisters and patients. Instead, the Red Cross authorities went to the other extreme; they sent me to a big civilian hospital which had a few military wards, and for the purposes of this volume shall be known as St Jude's.

7

My surgical experience might just as well have been taken to the Devonshire Hospital in Buxton; it would have been quite as useful there, and some awareness might even have emerged of the fact that I possessed it. At St Jude's I came across nothing, and no one, that could have restored in any wounded spirit the will to do and endure. 'All hope abandon, ye who enter here', might appropriately have been inscribed for me above its grim, gloomy doors. Even to-day I cannot pass without a shudder those uninviting acres of brown brick with their Victorian elaborations of worn grey stone.

A number of us, including myself, were housed a short distance from the hospital in a large ecclesiastical mansion, where we occupied part of the servants' quarters. Here the small, single rooms at least allowed reasonable privacy, but one dark basement bathroom with a limited supply of hot water was again, as at Denmark Hill, thought sufficient for a number of us, in spite of the infectious diseases or the septic dressings with which we were in contact all day.

Not one V.A.D., I think, would have raised any objection to the servants' quarters or even to our drab apology for a bathroom, had the rest of the mansion been full. Accommodation in wartime London was, as we all knew, by now expensive and difficult to find, but the inescapable supposition that we were not thought good enough to sleep in the empty bedrooms or important enough to wash our cold and weary persons in the unused bathrooms on the upper floors of the great house was not calculated to produce in us that gay, affirmative spirit which causes a young woman to fall in love with her work.

From time to time, when our clercial host was in residence, an invitation which was practically a command would come for a few of the V.A.D.s to take coffee with him and his wife. I found my own invitation one Sunday evening when I was off duty and had already arranged to go to Kensington, and though I knew that the elderly cleric merely intended a gesture of ecclesiastical goodwill towards the 'War Office tweenies' who occupied the humbler quarters of his establishment, this indication of benevolent despotism filled me with irrational fury.

At that stage of the War, I decided indignantly, I did not propose to submit to pious dissertations on my duty to God, King and Country. That voracious trio had already deprived me of all that I valued most in life, and if the interminable process of attrition lasted much longer, the poor surviving remnants of the writer's career that I once prepared for so fiercely would vanish into limbo with the men whom I had loved. My only hope now was to become the complete automaton, working mechanically and no longer even pretending to be animated by ideals. Thought was too dangerous; if once I began to think out exactly why my friends had died and I was working, quite dreadful things might suddenly happen. Without the discipline of faith and courage, disillusion and ferocious resentment would ravage unchecked; I might even murder my Ward-Sister, or assault the distinguished ecclesiastic. On the whole it seemed safer to go on being a machine, so, none too respectfully, I declined the invitation to coffee and took refuge in Kensington.

This minor discourtesy gave me a childish, triumphant feeling that I had scored off the Church, but the hospital in general, and my Ward-Sister in particular, presented a tougher proposition. Like other civilian nurses, the Sisters at St Jude's hated the necessity of using V.A.D.s, but I never came across any institution where they showed it so plainly.

Whatever training or experience a Red Cross nurse might have had before going there, they were determined that she should not be permitted to imagine, even for a moment, that this entitled her to any kind of status. The longer a V.A.D. had performed the responsible work that fell to her on active service, the more resolutely her Ward-Sister appeared to relegate her to the most menial and elementary tasks. At St Jude's I was never allowed so much as to attempt the simplest of the dressings: I was not permitted even to remember the experience in nursing malaria and pneumonia which I had acquired in Malta and in the medical wards at Étaples.

Instead I was set, together with the rest of the V.A.D.s and the ordinary probationers, to that multitude of soul-killing, time-wasting tasks so dear to civilian hospital tradition, and so infinitely destructive of young energy and enthusiasm. Not even in the first ignorant days of nursing in Buxton had the years deliberately stolen from Oxford been so unintelligently spent. My ward at St Jude's seemed to be a regular ironmonger's shop of metal rails, brass sterilisers and instruments which required perpetual polishing. No one, I felt, would have suffered had the brass sterilisers been replaced by white enamel, the metal rails by polished wood and the instruments – except for the sharpest – by stainless steel, but probationers were cheap, and it never seemed to occur to anyone that the dissipation of their bright-eyed keenness and their youthful idealism upon monotonous, unconstructive and completely valueless duties mattered in the least.

The drabness of this stultifying, wasteful routine was made yet more discouraging by a cast-iron, unimaginative discipline which could hardly have been better qualified to replace the positiveness of eager initiative by the negativeness of submissive resignation. For me this discipline, with its determined inculcation of that type of inferiority complex which undermines self-confidence for ever, came to be particularly associated with meal-times.

When first I sat down to the hospital supper and remembered the rough and ready plentifulness of Army meals, I realised with dismay the lower valuation of equally hard-worked civilian women both by the Food Ministry which estimated their requirements, and the hospital authorities who apparently witnessed without perturbation the maltreatment of the meagre rations permitted them. But I should have remained quite indifferent to what I regarded as a daily massacre of common-place food had it not been for the ceremony of disapproving vigilance which turned each unappetising repast into a nightmare.

The medical ward in which I worked at one end of the huge building was several minutes' walk from the dining-room at the other end, but 'etiquette' and my Ward-Sister alike forbade me to leave it until the exact hour appointed for luncheon, and we were sternly reprimanded if we were ever seen running or even conspicuously hurrying through the long ground-floor passage. In the dining-room the Assistant Matron stood censoriously over the luncheon-table with watch in hand, ready to pour a volume of sarcastic reprimand over any V.A.D. or probationer who was even half a minute late.

Inevitably, for me, each luncheon-hour became an ignominious tussle with my Ward-Sister and an apprehensive scuttle along the corridor, followed by another and worse tussle with the Assistant Matron. Had the miserable meal been ten times more attractive than it was, I should never have been able to reach it inconspicuously or to eat it with enjoyment. In consequence I welcomed with passionate relief the occasional days on which my time off happened to come in the morning.

In France and in Malta, except during a push, off-duty time had followed a pre-arranged schedule, but at St Jude's, as in Camberwell, it was seldom allotted until the actual day. The three-hour afternoons and evenings made it possible to go to Kensington for tea or supper without prearrangement, but 'mornings off' only lasted for about two hours, and as my Sister seldom told me that I was free until ten or more minutes after I ought to have gone, they were usually, in practice, shorter still.

Plans for spending such brief and sudden off-times obviously could not be made, but the opportunity that they gave for having luncheon away from the hospital was sufficient compensation for their solitude. Once again I became familiar with the restaurant at Gorringe's, which had supplied me with such large and satisfying teas in my early days at the 1st London General. I can still remember the profound satisfaction with which I lingered over the attenuated egg-cutlets and cups of coffee which were all that my ludicrous salary would now run to at wartime prices, far from the sight of critical eyes and the sound of scolding voices.

8

One evening at prayers I remembered reading somewhere a passage which had referred in impressive terms to the sanctity of the nursing profession.

That's just the trouble, I thought, as the others devoutly

murmured the Lord's Prayer; it's considered so holy that its organisers forget that nurses are just human beings, with human failings and human needs. Its regulations and its values are still so Victorian that we even have to do our work in fancy dress, struggling perpetually with an exasperating seven-piece uniform, always changing caps, collars, aprons, cuffs and waist-belts that accumulate germs and get lost in the laundry, or collecting the innumerable studs, clips and safety-pins required to hold the cumbrous outfit together, instead of wearing one loose-necked, short-sleeved overall that could be renewed every day.

Had I been able, in 1918, to imagine that anything so remote as 1933 could possibly arrive, I should never have believed that even in so distant a future nearly all hospitals and nursery training schools would still be clinging with pathetic conservatism to their mediæval trappings. But in the long interval between that year and this, I have often thought, as I thought then, that the 'holiness' of the nursing profession is easily its worst handicap; a profession, it seems, has only to be called a 'vocation' for irresponsible authority to be left free to indulge in a type of exploitation which is not excused by its habitual camouflage as 'discipline'. It is true – it has to be true – that most of the women who choose this harsh, exacting life are urged by semi-conscious idealism, but idealists, being eager and sensitive, are often more liable to nervous strain than the less altruistic who take care of themselves before they think of others.

Four impressionable years spent in a number of very different hospitals convinced me once for all that nursing, if it is to be done efficiently, requires, more than any other occupation, abundant leisure in colourful surroundings, sufficient money to spend on amusements, agreeable food to re-establish the energy expended, and the removal of anxiety about illness and old age; yet of all skilled professions, it is still the least vitalised by these advantages, still the most oppressed by unnecessary worries, cruelties, hardships and regulations. St Jude's to-day may be, and probably is, quite different from the hospital of fifteen years ago, but the recent Report of the *Lancet* Commission on Nursing has shown the unimaginative stupidities which then oppressed me to be still only too prevalent in a large number of training schools.

As I gradually realised, during that autumn of 1918, how St Jude's, because of its great tradition, collected within its walls some of the best nursing material in the country, and then, by its unillumined routine and its rigid sectarian orthodoxy, crushed the gaiety and independence out of the young women who went there so hopefully, I developed a ferocious hatred of all civilian hospital authorities from Florence Nightingale onwards. For years I continued to detest the founder of modern nursing and all that she stood for – a state of mind which persisted until, quite recently, I read her essay 'Cassandra' in the Appendix to Ray Strachey's *The Cause*, and realised the contrast between her rebellious spirit, her administrator's grasp of essentials, and the bigoted narrowness of some of her successors.

My wrathful consciousness of inhuman idiocy reached its height one October evening, after an unusually exhausting round of bed-making, bed-pans and bowl-washing, all of which had fallen to my unaided share because the beginning of the ferocious influenza epidemic was already making us short of staff. By means of sustained and violent energy I managed to complete these enthralling tasks a few moments before the night people were due, and, in accordance with custom, reported the fact to the staff-nurse in charge of the ward that evening.

'I've finished, Sister,' I informed her.

There was not a Ward-Sister in France or Malta or even at the 1st London who would not have told me that after such a hard day's work I could go off duty, but the staff-nurse, from beneath her starched cap, regarded me critically with bright, hard brown eyes.

'It isn't eight o'clock yet, nurse,' she said. 'You can go into the annex and polish the wheel chairs.'

An obscure rage burned in my tired brain as I obeyed her, and this, by the next morning, had translated itself into a determination to leave at once.

'I won't stay here for six months even if it means a row with Devonshire House that finishes me for good,' I told myself grimly, but I didn't intend to remain at the mercy of chance, and before putting my resolve into practice, I took the precaution to discover a reasonable alternative.

On one of my solitary morning perambulations round Westminster, I happened to pass Queen Alexandra's Military Hospital, in Millbank, and remembered hearing that its new Matron was my January friend at 24 General. I had not forgotten her kind eyes when she agreed to put in for my leave, and on my next free afternoon I called at the hospital and asked if I might see her. I was shown up at once, and after reminding her that she had enabled me to share his last fortnight at home with Edward, who now was dead, and explaining my determination to quit St Jude's, I inquired whether there chanced to be a vacancy at Millbank.

'I'm glad,' she said, quite simply, 'that I helped you to see your brother again.'

She had room, she told me, for another V.A.D.; being herself a 'Red Cape', she obviously sympathised with my distaste for the narrow rigidity of civilian discipline, and promised to ask for me from Devonshire House as soon as I obtained permission to transfer from St Jude's.

A day or two later, after an acrimonious interview with the Assistant Matron, I found myself once more in Devonshire House, interviewing a young official with a round face and bright, chubby cheeks, whose name I never discovered. She sat with the usual folder containing my record in front of her; quite good reports, I felt, might once have been sent in from Malta, or from France, but my stock must now have fallen so low that whatever I said or did could hardly matter.

'I've come to say I can't stop at St Jude's,' I began aggressively. 'If I can't go somewhere else, I just shan't sign on again.'

But the wrath that I awaited did not descend. Instead, my young *vis-à-vis* merely looked melancholy.

'You're not the first,' she said with a sigh, gazing pensively at the blue active-service stripes on my sleeve. 'What exactly is your objection to St Jude's?'

'It's rather difficult to put into words,' I answered, completely mollified by her air of lugubrious resignation. 'It just isn't a place for V.A.D.s, except very new ones. One might as well never have served at all.'

'I know,' she assented, sighing again – and then inquired, more cheerfully: 'Well, is there anywhere special you *would* like to go? I'm sorry I can't send you back to France.'

And, without further delay, we completed to my entire satisfaction the arrangements already begun with the Scottish Matron.

9

So at the end of October I joined the staff at Queen Alexandra's Hospital, Millbank, on the Westminster side of the river. In those days it seemed quite an imposing block of buildings, but now, dwarf-like and apologetic, it cowers behind the flat white immensity of Thames House and Imperial Chemicals. The black corrugated iron hut opposite the main entrance, in which I worked for the greater part of my time there, still remains shabbily standing – a very poor relation to the splendid giants erected around it – as an annex to the Ministry of Pensions.

Thankful to have returned to a military atmosphere from the lampless conventionality of civilian nursing, I settled down to a humdrum but tolerable routine. Throughout the new Sisters' quarters reigned the peace which is always present in a hospital where the controlling authority is benevolent and reasonable. On the whole I was very fortunate in my Matrons all through the War; at the Devonshire Hospital, at the 1st London, in Malta, in France and at Millbank, they were all humane, conscientious women, genuinely anxious to do their best for their subordinates in a profession as cluttered with outworn traditions and vexatious restrictions as an old farmyard with disused tin cans and rusty fragments of barbed wire.

Mechanical contentment, however, is one thing, and vital contact with life quite another. Of the five months that I spent at Millbank, hardly a memory now remains. Dimly I recall my frequent crossings of the road between the hospital and my ward, always with a sideways glance towards the Embankment at the end and the funnels of the barges slipping across that narrow glimpse of the river; vaguely I remember the winter creeping on – a mild, muggy winter, so different from the biting cold in France a year ago – and my mother coming into my flag-decked ward for a party to the men on Christmas Day. I have faint recollections, too, of scurryings back from the West End down Great Smith Street on an 88 or 32 'bus at the close of off-duty time in the early months of 1919 – less rapid and conscientious scurryings than those back to Camberwell three years before, since I was by now indifferent to reprimand and had nothing to lose by being late. My whole attention was concentrated on surviving until my six months' contract expired and brought release from the suddenly unbearable monotony of nursing – though I feared my freedom, too, for reasons that I could not then quite explain even to myself.

Finally, and most clearly of all, I remember a young medical officer scolding my Ward-Sister for making me day-time 'special' to a hopeless and peculiarly revolting case of syphilitic cancer; it wasn't a job for a girl, he said, and one of the older nurses ought to have taken it on. He seemed surprised that I hadn't protested, but it never occurred to me to do so; I no longer thought of myself as younger or less experienced than the Sisters with whom I worked, and I couldn't see that it mattered to myself or anyone else if I caught and even died from one of my patient's dire diseases, when so many beautiful bodies of young men were rotting in the mud of France and the pine forests of Italy.

Having become, at last, the complete automaton, moving like a sleep-walker through the calm atmosphere of Millbank, I was no longer capable of either enthusiasm or fear. Once an ecstatic idealist who had tripped down the steep Buxton hill in a golden glow of self-dedication to my elementary duties at the Devonshire Hospital, I had now passed – like the rest of my contemporaries who had survived thus far – into a permanent state of numb disillusion. Whatever part of my brief adulthood I chose to look back upon – the restless pre-war months at home, the naïve activities of a college student, the tutelage to horror and death as a V.A.D. nurse, the ever-deepening night of fear and suspense and agony in a provincial town, in a university city, in London, in the

Mediterranean, in France – it all seemed to have meant one thing, and one thing only, 'a striving, and a striving, and an ending in nothing'.

And now there were no more disasters to dread and no friends left to wait for; with the ending of apprehension had come a deep, nullifying blankness, a sense of walking in a thick mist which hid all sights and muffled all sounds. I had no further experience to gain from the War; nothing remained except to endure it.

It had not, however, to be endured much longer. I had only been at Millbank for a few days when it became obvious even to me that something unusual and important was happening all over Europe. For a long time, although I read spasmodically about the German retreat, my mind refused to take in its significance; I had ceased to think of the War as ever ending, and much less as ending in victory. But now the growing crescendo of triumphant battle, the rapid withdrawal of the Germans on the Western Front to the Hindenburg line and beyond while Turkey and Austria were collapsing in the East, penetrated even my torpid consciousness, and I awoke with a fearful start to the astonishing fact that, up at Ypres, the Allies had required only one day to gain as much territory as had been taken in three months during the costly and all too bitterly memorable offensive round Passchendaele in 1917.

After November 3rd, when the Germans were left alone to face the united strength of their old enemies reinforced by the exultant, inexhaustible Americans, when Valenciennes fell and the British Army struck its ultimate blow on the Sambre, I realised that the end had become a matter of days. But I could still call up only a languid interest when I read that the Canadians, by capturing Mons, had picturesquely finished the War where it began, and I neither knew nor cared that a day or two afterwards a section of the recovered territory was occupied by a new battalion of the London Rifle Brigade, which had crossed the Channel just in time to see the fighting reach its incredible conclusion.

Among these newly arrived troops marched a speculative young rifleman whose acceptance for military service had been delayed by ill health and the devastations of personal grief until the final spring of the War; in his pack, side by side with the *De Rerum Natura* of Lucretius, he carried a bulky manuscript note-book containing highly philosophical disquisitions on the causes of military conflict and the ethics of its elimination from the body politic, which would have amazed and mystified his fellow privates. But even in that heavy day of harsh surprises, that conclusive hour which dragged me back unwillingly to the sharp remorselessness of continuing life, nothing would have astounded me so much as the suggestion that those weighty manuscripts and their youthful writer might have some possible significance for myself in the time to come.

10

When the sound of victorious guns burst over London at 11 a.m. on November 11th, 1918, the men and women who looked incredulously into each other's faces did not cry jubilantly: 'We've won the War!' They only said: 'The War is over.'

From Millbank I heard the maroons crash with terrifying clearness, and, like a sleeper who is determined to go on dreaming after being told to wake up, I went on automatically washing the dressing bowls in the annex outside my hut. Deeply buried beneath my consciousness there stirred the vague memory of a letter that I had written to Roland in those legendary days when I was still at Oxford, and could spend my Sundays in thinking of him while the organ echoed grandly through New College Chapel. It had been a warm May evening, when all the city was sweet with the scent of wallflowers and lilac, and I had walked back to Micklem Hall after hearing an Occasional Oratorio by Handel, which described the mustering of troops for battle, the lament for the fallen and the triumphant return of the victors.

'As I listened,' I told him, 'to the organ swelling forth into a final triumphant burst in the song of victory, after the solemn and mournful dirge over the dead, I thought with what mockery and irony the jubilant celebrations which will hail the coming of peace will fall upon the ears of those to whom their best will never return, upon whose sorrow victory is built, who have paid with their mourning for the others' joy. I wonder if I shall be one of those who take a happy part in the triumph – or if I shall listen to the merriment with a heart that breaks and ears that try to keep out the mirthful sounds.'

And as I dried the bowls I thought: 'It's come too late for me. Somehow I knew, even at Oxford, that it would. Why couldn't it have ended rationally, as it might have ended, in 1916, instead of all that trumpet-blowing against a negotiated peace, and the ferocious talk of secure civilians about marching to Berlin? It's come five months too late – or is it three years? It might have ended last June, and let Edward, at least, be saved! Only five months – it's such a little time, when Roland died nearly three years ago.'

But on Armistice Day not even a lonely survivor drowning in black waves of memory could be left alone with her thoughts. A moment after the guns had subsided into sudden, palpitating silence, the other V.A.D. from my ward dashed excitedly into the annex.

'Brittain! Brittain! Did you hear the maroons? It's over – it's all over! Do let's come out and see what's happening!'

Mechanically I followed her into the road. As I stood there, stupidly rigid, long after the triumphant explosions from Westminster had turned into a distant crescendo of shouting, I saw a taxicab turn swiftly in from the Embankment towards the hospital. The next moment there was a cry for doctors and nurses from passers-by, for in rounding the corner the taxi had knocked down a small elderly woman who in listening, like myself, to the wild noise of a world released from nightmare, had failed to observe its approach.

As I hurried to her side I realised that she was all but dead and already past speech. Like Victor in the mortuary chapel, she seemed to have shrunk to the dimensions of a child with the sharp features of age, but on the tiny chalk-white face an expression of shocked surprise still lingered, and she stared hard at me as Geoffrey had stared at his orderly in those last moments of conscious silence beside the Scarpe. Had she been thinking, I wondered, when the taxi struck her, of her sons at the front, now safe? The next moment a medical officer and some orderlies came up, and I went back to my ward.

But I remembered her at intervals throughout that afternoon, during which, with a half-masochistic notion of 'seeing the sights,' I made a circular tour to Kensington by way of the intoxicated West End. With aching persistence my thoughts went back to the dead and the strange irony of their fates – to Roland, gifted, ardent, ambitious, who had died without glory in the conscientious performance of a routine job; to Victor and Geoffrey, gentle and diffident, who, conquering nature by resolution, had each gone down bravely in a big 'show'; and finally to Edward, musical, serene, a lover of peace, who had fought courageously through so many battles and at last had been killed while leading a vital counter-attack in one of the few decisive actions of the War. As I struggled through the waving, shrieking crowds in Piccadilly and Regent Street on the overloaded top of a 'bus, some witty enthusiast for contemporary history symbolically turned upside down the sign-board 'Seven Kings'.

Late that evening, when supper was over, a group of elated V.A.D.s who were anxious to walk through Westminster and Whitehall to Buckingham Palace prevailed upon me to join them. Outside the Admiralty a crazy group of convalescent Tommies were collecting specimens of different uniforms and bundling their wearers into flag-strewn taxis; with a shout they seized two of my companions and disappeared into the clamorous crowd, waving flags and shaking rattles. Wherever we went a burst of enthusiastic cheering greeted our Red Cross uniform, and complete strangers adorned with wound stripes rushed up and shook me warmly by the hand. After the long, long blackness, it seemed like a fairy-tale to see the street lamps shining through the chill November gloom.

I detached myself from the others and walked slowly up Whitehall, with my heart sinking in a sudden cold dismay. Already this was a different world from the one that I had known during four life-long years, a world in which people would be light-hearted and forgetful, in which themselves and their careers and their amusements would blot out political ideals and great national issues. And in that brightly lit, alien world I should have no part. All those with whom I had really been intimate were gone; not one remained to share with me the heights and the depths of my memories. As the years went by and youth departed and remembrance grew dim, a deeper and ever deeper darkness would cover the young men who were once my contemporaries.

For the first time I realised, with all that full realisation meant, how completely everything that had hitherto made up my life had vanished with Edward and Roland, with Victor and Geoffrey. The War was over; a new age was beginning; but the dead were dead and would never return.

PART III

'Longumque illud tempus, quum non ero, magis me movet quam hoc exiguum.'

Cicero, *Ad Atticum*, Book 12, Letter 18.

CHAPTER X

Survivors Not Wanted

THE LAMENT OF THE DEMOBILISED

'Four years,' some say consolingly. 'Oh well,
What's that? You're young. And then it must have been
A very fine experience for you!'
And they forget
How others stayed behind and just got on—
Got on the better since we were away.
And we came home and found
They had achieved, and men revered their names,
But never mentioned ours;
And no one talked heroics now, and we
Must just go back and start again once more.
'You threw four years into the melting-pot—
Did you indeed!' these others cry. 'Oh well,
The more fool you!'
And we're beginning to agree with them.

V. B.

From *Oxford Poetry* 1920.

1

Early in April 1919, I said good-bye to Millbank and the War, taking home with me a legacy of rough hands and swollen ankles, and a fine collection of exotic oaths. Just as Victor had foreseen for himself if he survived, I found considerable difficulty during the next twelve months in avoiding these expressions in Oxford lecture-halls and Kensington drawing-rooms, to both of which they seemed to me peculiarly appropriate.

To-day, as we look back, 1919 seems a horrid year, dominated by a thoroughly nasty Peace. But when it came in, it appeared to an exhausted world as divine normality, the spring of life after the winter of death, the stepping-stone to a new era, the gateway to an infinite future – a future not without its dreads and discomforts, but one in whose promise we had to believe, since it was all that some of us had left to believe in. At that time, too, various authorities were busy being grateful to us who had once been young and were apparently, amazing as it seemed, still so regarded. Only two days after the Armistice, Sir Douglas Haig, in the special Order expressing his gratitude to 'all ranks of the Army and the non-combatant and auxiliary services', had actually included 'the many thousands of women who by devoted work in so many capacities have assisted in the victory of our arms', and no doubt many of these felt quite elated at being told – for as long as they were able to believe it – that 'generations of free people, both of your own race and of all countries, will thank you for what you have done . . . your gallantry never failing, your courage most resolute, your devotion to duty unquestioning.' Even the Army Council had expressed its thanks by the end of April to the V.A.D. nurses for 'the keenness, self-sacrifice and devotion . . . so unstintingly given during,' as they somewhat modestly expressed it, 'the long and trying period through which the country has passed.'

Nevertheless, the year did not seem to have begun very auspiciously for those who still clung to the ingenuous notion that by their sacrifices they had created a world of sweetness and light for their descendants to inhabit. During the weeks immediately after the Armistice, my automatic existence at Millbank virtually obliterated for me the fact that, all over the country, eloquent platform heroes were busily engaged in Making Germany Pay and Hanging The Kaiser. But while I was making up my mind to go back to Oxford – not because I particularly wanted to go back, for I was not conscious of wanting to do anything, but because college seemed the one thing left out of the utter wreckage of the past, and I had a prejudice against leaving unfinished something that I had begun – I could not remain blind to the hectic reactions of my generation, frantically dancing night after night in the Grafton Galleries, while pictures of the Canadian soldiers' wartime agony hung accusingly on the walls. Shocked by the spectacle, Mr Alfred Noyes described these nocturnal orgies:

> *The cymbals crash,*
> *   And the dancers walk;*
> *With long silk stockings,*
> *   And arms of chalk,*
> *Butterfly skirts*
> *   And white breasts bare;*
> *And shadows of dead men*
> *   Watching 'em there—*

and the older generation held up outraged hands in horror at such sacrilege, not understanding that reckless sense of combined release and anti-climax which set my contemporaries, who had lived a lifetime of love and toil and suffering and yet were only in their early twenties, dancing in the vain hope of recapturing the lost youth that the War had stolen.

Not having anyone left with whom to dance, I spent most of the blank and rather frightening days between leaving Millbank and returning to Somerville in roaming about London with a demobilised and erratically jubilant Hope Milroy, and in meditating, as the differences between our war and peace-time preoccupations forced themselves upon my mind, on the problems of an uncompanioned civilian life. How would the War ultimately have affected me? I wondered, looking with dull eyes into a singularly empty future, which seemed capable of being filled only by individual efforts that I did not feel in the least inclined to make. The immediate result of peace – the cessation of direct threats to one's personal safety – was at first almost imperceptible, just as a prolonged physical pain which has turned from acuteness into an habitual dull ache can cease altogether without the victim noticing that it has gone. Only gradually did I realise that the War had condemned me to live to the end of my days in a world without confidence or security, a world in which every dear personal relationship would be fearfully cherished under the shadow of apprehension; in which love would seem threatened perpetually by death, and happiness appear a house without duration, built upon the shifting sands of chance. I might, perhaps, have it again, but never again should I hold it.

Meanwhile in Paris, the nucleus of a wild, international, pleasure-crazy crowd, the Big Four were making a desert and calling it peace. When I thought about these negotiations at all – which was only when I could not avoid hearing them discussed by Oxford dons or Kensington visitors – they did not seem to me to represent at all the kind of 'victory' that the young men whom I had loved would have regarded as sufficient justification for their lost lives. Although they would no doubt have welcomed the idea of a League of Nations, Roland and Edward certainly had not died in order that Clemenceau should outwit Lloyd George, and both of them bamboozle President Wilson, and all three combine to make the beaten, blockaded enemy pay the cost of the War. For me the 'Huns' were then, and always, the patient, stoical Germans whom I had nursed in France, and I did not like to read of them being deprived of their Navy, and their Colonies, and their coal-fields in Alsace-Lorraine and the Saar Valley, while their children starved and froze for lack of food and fuel. So, when the text of the Treaty of Versailles was published in May, after I had returned to Oxford, I deliberately refrained from reading it; I was beginning already to suspect that my generation had been deceived, its young courage cynically exploited, its idealism betrayed, and I did not want to know the details of that betrayal. At an inter-collegiate debate a Hindu student remarked that here, at any rate, was 'the Peace that passeth all understanding' – and I left it at that.

I was not, of course, so clearly conscious of these anxieties and revulsions and suspicions as to-day, with full awareness of the direction in which I was about to move, I sometimes seem to myself to have been. Letters and articles written at the time show that my mind groped in a dark, foggy confusion, uncertain of what had happened to it or what was going to happen. Still partly dominated by old ideals, timeworn respectabilities and spasms of rebellious bitterness, it sometimes seized fleetingly the tail of an idea upon whose wings it was later to ascend into a clearer heaven of new convictions.

One of these half-found inspirations translated itself, trivially enough, into a determination to read History at Oxford instead of English, but the motive behind this superficial change of School was not really trivial. After the first dismayed sense of isolation in an alien peace-time world, such rationality as I still possessed reasserted itself in a desire to understand how the whole calamity had happened, to know why it had been possible for me and my contemporaries, through our own ignorance and others' ingenuity, to be used, hypnotised and slaughtered. I had begun, I thought, by feeling exasperated about the War, and I went on by ignoring it; then I had to accept it as a fact, and at last was forced to take part in it, to endure the fear and sorrow and fatigue that it brought me, and to witness in impotent anguish the deaths, not only of those who had made my personal life, but of the many brave, uncomplaining men whom I had nursed and could not save. But even that isn't enough. It's my job, now, to find out all about it, and try to prevent it, in so far as one person can, from happening to other people in the days to come. Perhaps the careful study of man's past will explain to me much that seems inexplicable in his disconcerting present. Perhaps the means of salvation are already there, implicit in history, unadvertised, carefully concealed by the war-mongers, only awaiting rediscovery to be acknowledged with enthusiasm by all thinking men and women.

When I was a girl at St Monica's and in Buxton, I remembered, I imagined that life was individual, one's own affair; that the events happening in the world outside were important enough in their own way, but were personally quite irrelevant. Now, like the rest of my generation, I have had to learn again and again the terrible truth of George Eliot's words about the invasion of personal preoccupations by the larger destinies of mankind, and at last to recognise that no life is really private, or isolated, or self-sufficient. People's lives were entirely their own, perhaps – and more justifiably – when the world seemed enormous, and all its comings and goings were slow and deliberate. But this is so no longer, and never will be again, since man's inventions have eliminated so much of distance and time; for better, for worse, we are now each of us part of the surge and swell of great economic and political movements, and whatever we do, as individuals or as nations, deeply affects everyone else. We were bound up together like this before we realised it; if only the comfortable prosperity of the Victorian age hadn't lulled us into a false conviction of individual security and made us believe that what was going on outside our homes didn't matter to us, the Great War might never have happened. And though a few isolated persons may be better for having been in the War, the world as a whole will be worse; lacking first-rate ability and social order and economic equilibrium, it will go spinning down into chaos as fast as it can – unless some of us try to prevent it.

Henceforward, my thought struggled on, following the faint gleam through the darkness, people will count only in so far as they realise their background and help to create and to change it. We should never be at the mercy of Providence if only we understood that we ourselves *are* Providence; our lives, and our children's lives, will be rational, balanced, well-proportioned, to exactly the extent that we recognise this fundamental truth. It may be that our generation will go down in history as the first to understand that not a single man or woman can now live in disregarding isolation from his or her world. I don't know yet what I can do, I concluded, to help all this to happen, but at least I can begin by trying to understand where humanity failed and civilisation went wrong. If only I and a few other people succeed in this, it may be worth while that our lives have been lived; it may even be worth while that the lives of the others have been laid down. Perhaps that's really why, when they died, I was left behind.

So, thus portentously, I decided to read History, and then, when I had gone down from Oxford, to get into touch with some organisation which thought and tried to act along these lines. I had heard, as yet, very little of the bitter tale of pacifism during the War – the Union of Democratic Control, with its interrupted meetings and police-raided offices; the imprisonment of E. D. Morel; the removal of Bertrand Russell from his post at

Cambridge; the persecution and humiliation of conscientious objectors – but I had already started on the road which was ultimately to lead me to association with the group that accepted internationalism as a creed.

At Somerville the news of my intention to change my School was received without enthusiasm; in English I had been regarded as a probable First, but in the field of History I had forgotten even such information as I had once derived from Miss Heath Jones's political and religious teaching, and a student's ingenuous anxiety to remedy the errors of the ages could hardly be expected to count with an Oxford college in comparison with the possibility of increasing its list of Firsts. But although the hazy ignorance from which I set out to read the newly chosen subject was a permanent handicap throughout my university life, I never regretted the decision, for in studying international relations, and the great diplomatic agreements of the nineteenth century, I discovered that human nature does change, does learn to hate oppression, to deprecate the spirit of revenge, to be revolted by acts of cruelty, and at last to embody these changes of heart and mind in treaties – those chronological records of a game of skill played by accomplished technicians who can hardly, in any time or place, be described as leading the van of progressive opinion. Even after the Franco-Prussian War – one of the bitterest campaigns in history – the dead were remembered and soldiers' graves were mentioned, for the first time in any international agreement, by the treaty of 1871. The more widely I read, the more clearly I seemed to discover that nobler prospects existed for humanity than had appeared possible when the Peace of Versailles was reluctantly signed by Germany in the Galerie des Glaces on June 28th, 1919 – and what was the sacrifice of a possible First compared to that knowledge?

2

Two days before the League of Nations came into existence at the end of April by the adoption of the revised Covenant at the Fifth Plenary Session of the Peace Conference, I returned to

Oxford to find Somerville in the last term of its long occupation of Oriel. My parents, like myself, took my reincarnation as a student entirely for granted; my father, indeed, so strongly approved of college in comparison with the perturbations of hospitals and foreign service that he was now as ready to send me there as any modern father who considers the safeguard of a profession to be as much the right of a daughter as of a son.

Going back felt disturbingly like a return to school after a life-time of adult experience; nevertheless, I pinned to Oxford – having nothing else to which to pin them – such hopes for the future as I still possessed. The dons, I believed, would recognise and concede to me the privileges of maturity; time had obliterated in my mind the various differences between the average academic and my adventurous Classical tutor, who had urged me after Edward's death to keep to my plan of coming back to Somerville – especially because at college, more than anywhere else, one was likely to make the friendships that supported one through life.

She was quite right, as she always was; had I not taken her advice I should never have known either of the persons who now share my home, but at the time I scarcely bargained for the period of forlorn isolation that would have to be endured before the fulfilment of her prophecy. My own 'Year' had gone down long ago, but the unknown students would be, I felt confident, quite different from Kensington calling acquaintances or some of my relatives, who only wanted to be told how splendid our dear boys had been at the front, and how uplifting it was to be on active service in hospital, and how edifying to have had a lover and a brother who had died for their country. These young Somervillians were bound, I thought hopefully, to feel an interest in someone who had had first-hand experience of the greatest event of their generation, and, being interested, perhaps they would be kind. At the moment I felt as though kindness, provided it were intelli-gent kindness, mattered more than anything else. I was sore and angry and bitter, and I wanted desperately to be comforted and restored; the still rational remnants of my mind recognised anger and bitterness as crippling things which made for inefficiency, and I could not afford to be inefficient; it was more than time, if I were ever to accomplish it, to get on with the job of becoming a writer.

My confidence in this sympathetic, congenial future was considerably shaken by my first interview with the Principal of Somerville. When I had last seen her, between my periods of service in Malta and in France, she had been cordial and benevolent, but now her face wore an inscrutable and rather grim expression. 'This is going to be a difficult term – a very difficult term,' it seemed to say. 'If we're not careful these wild young men and women back from the War will get out of hand!' Her greeting, at any rate, was as brief and laconic as though she had taken leave of me the previous Easter.

'How do you do, Miss Brittain?'

'Quite well, thank you,' I answered conventionally, being as yet unaware that the War's repressions were already preparing their strange, neurotic revenge. 'I'm so glad to be back – at last,' I added, unable to resist that injudicious, emotional plea for one word of welcome, of encouragement, from the university which had become, for me, the last refuge of hope and sanity. But the disturbing hint was quietly disregarded, and any suggestion that my interview represented more than an ordinary beginning-of-term routine visit was discreetly tidied out of the atmosphere by the Principal's next words.

'You are living in King Edward Street this term, I think?'

I agreed that this was so. I had gone down four years ago from Micklem Hall and now I was living in King Edward Street; that was, apparently, the only change in my circumstances of which the university was prepared to take cognisance.

Looking back, after fourteen years, upon the spiritual jar of that rebuff, I realise now that the college authorities had been, according to their lights, thoroughly generous. (Had I been an ex-service man, their concessions would have seemed obvious enough, and were, indeed, granted to every male who wanted to take advantage of them, but Oxford women, after Mr H. A. L. Fisher's pronouncement, were never officially regarded as 'patriots' whatever their service might have been.) They had kept my exhibition for me for four years; they had undertaken, since I was

so excessively 'over-standing' for Honours, a special procedure on
my behalf to enable me to take an Honours Degree at all; they
had even tolerated my inauspicious change of School. But they
could not add the final graciousness and make me feel welcome.

It would have been, perhaps, more remarkable than I was then
able to perceive if I had been welcome. The few other female
rebels from Somerville had nearly all conveniently failed to come
back; they had married, or found jobs, or merely become bored
at the thought of re-curling themselves into the chrysalis stage of
development. Except, the following term, for Winifred Holtby,
who had only been down for a year and had not come into direct
contact with the War until it was almost over, I was the only
woman returning, bringing with me, no doubt – terrifying
thought! – the psychological fruit of my embarrassing experiences. During the War the tales of immorality among V.A.D.s, as
among W.A.A.C.s, had been consumed with voracious horror by
readers at home; who knew in what cesspools of iniquity I had
not wallowed? Who could calculate the awful extent to which I
might corrupt the morals of my innocent juniors?

Undoubtedly the Senior Common Room, like other Senior
Common Rooms, was nervous. All over Oxford, university and
college authorities were quaking in their carpet slippers at the
prospective invasion of war-hardened, cynical, sophisticated youth;
their attitude vacillated between elaborate preparations against
ruthless presumption, and an ostentatious unawareness that there
had been a war at all. One undergraduate, an ex-officer with three
years' service and a wound stripe, who returned the same term
as myself, told me later that at his first interview the President of
his college had addressed him thus: 'Let me see, Mr X., you've
been away a long time, I think; a very long time? It's a pity – a
great pity; you'll have to work very hard to catch up with the
others!'

Those first eight weeks of renewed contact with a once familiar
world proved, in many minor ways, to be curiously disconcerting.
I found that I had completely forgotten the daily detail of a
student's life; I innocently disregarded – until surprisedly called
to order – most of the regulations involved in being *in statu pupil-*

lari, and could not even recollect the trivial procedure for getting books out of the library. Each person whom I asked for information on these points appeared astonished and almost affronted. 'Whatever's come over her, she's as bad as a fresher!' their looks seemed to imply. But on the whole I marked time that term, feeling like a ship waiting in harbour before starting out on a new and strenuous voyage to an unknown port.

3

Once again, as in 1915, Oxford from Carfax to Summertown was warm and sweet with lilac and wallflowers and may; it seemed unbearable that everything should be exactly the same when all my life was so much changed. Living quietly among the six seniors in the rooms in King Edward Street, I found it easy – and preferable – to avoid contact with the other students, whose very names I hardly knew. Occasionally at lectures I met a girl who was then in her last term, waiting to take her History Finals; I never spoke to her, but I carried away a definite impression of a green scarf, and dark felt hat negligently shading a narrow, brooding face with arrogant nose and stormily reserved blue eyes; it was Margaret Kennedy. One of the seniors in my rooms, Nina Ruffer, an anthropology student with a hard, good mind and an incongruously pale, diffident exterior, was the daughter of Sir Armand Ruffer, the medical chief of the British Red Cross Society in Egypt; he had been drowned in the Mediterranean on the torpedoed *Arcadian* in the spring of 1917, when I was in Malta, and this link with the War drew Nina and myself together. As the term went on I came to depend more and more upon her eager, intelligent society, for it quickly became clear that some of the more obvious alleviations to memory and nervous fatigue on which I had counted were not to materialise.

One of the pleasantest recollections of my previous Oxford summer had been, for my athletic disposition, the vigorous games of tennis and the closely fought matches on the green, sunny lawns; I had hoped to take part in them again, but these expectations were hardly of a type to commend themselves warmly to the second-year tennis captain. As I had played for Somerville in 1915 and thus interfered rather inconveniently with the calculations of more recent candidates, I had to be tried for the six although I had never handled a racket since the stolen games in Malta on night-duty. Testing me early in the term before I had had much opportunity to practise, the young captain must have been greatly relieved when I fell far below team standard, and felt – and indeed had – no compulsion to test me a second time at a later stage. In consequence I never again had a first-class game; only the second-rate were prepared to play with the universal stranger whose sudden appearance out of a remote and unknown world was a little embarrassing for everyone, and from that time onwards my tennis steadily descended from bad to execrable.

Nor, to begin with, did my prospects in the Honours School of Modern History appear much more promising. Fully conscious of my limitations in this unfamiliar field, I had hoped to be allowed, that extra term, to work alone, studying world history in outline, and afterwards fitting modern European history into its place in the story of the world, and English history into the story of Europe. But the rest of the second-year History School were in process of studying Tudors and Stuarts, and for Tudors and Stuarts, detached from their past and their future and completely unrelated to anything whatever in time or space, I had to whip up some kind of enthusiasm. With my conjectural essays on the vicissitudes of these momentous monarchs, I combined a few miscellaneous lectures which were intended to prepare me for the carefully selected period of European history – 1789 to 1878 – that I was to begin the next term. At one of these lectures – the second or third of a course by Mr J. A. R. Marriott on the Eastern Question, to which I had asked to go as much for the sake of old memories as for the purpose of studying nineteenth-century Europe – an incident occurred which I related to my mother in one of the few animated letters of that term:

'Yesterday when at Mr Marriott's lecture I was sitting near the front, and after it was over and I was putting up my books he came up to me and said: "Don't I know you? Weren't you up here before?" So then I explained who I was and what I had been doing away so long. He remembered me perfectly, also that I had been doing English; shook hands, said he was very pleased to see me again and was so glad I was doing History as he was sure it would interest me more. He certainly has a wonderful memory; do you remember him saying he never forgot a face? It was nice of him to come and speak to me too; he is a very great person in Oxford now he is M.P.'

What a coincidence it seemed, I thought, that he, the person mainly responsible for getting me to college, should be almost the only one to take the slightest interest in my return! The small, human act of recognition warmed my chill stagnation for several days.

Apart from lectures, and walks with Nina, the suspended existence of that summer was enlivened chiefly by what was, for the university, a most daring innovation, in the form of inter-collegiate debates between the men and the women. Somerville's programme included debates with New College, Oriel and Queen's – 'so we are coming on!' I told my mother triumphantly – and at each of these I plunged recklessly into speeches as halting and unpractised as my tennis. To the New College debate – on the economic consequences, so far as I remember, of the peace then raging on the Franco-German frontier – came the young rifleman who had spent the previous winter at Mons; he was back in Oxford now, taking up the New College exhibition that he had won in 1914, but I never spoke to him there nor even consciously saw him. If the War had not happened, he and Edward would have been college contemporaries, but the cataclysm of Europe, as I learnt long afterwards, caused each to remain unknown to the other. Even the New College Roll of Honour did not, and does not, contain Edward's name – presumably because he was never in residence as an undergraduate, though he gave up his university 'years to be' as deliberately as any first-year student.

The ex-rifleman had more time now for writing in the unwieldy manuscript volume that had once weighed down his pack, and a little group of intelligent friends, chosen with unerring judgment, gave him innumerable opportunities of discussing the foundation of a Science of Politics and the future elimination of war, but though he was destined to achieve academic reputation and to occupy a distinguished position in an American university, limited parental resources and a temperament naturally mystical and religious caused him to live quietly and without notoriety amongst his Oxford contemporaries. Occasionally, in the intervals of endeavouring to maintain himself upon his exhibition, reinforced by scholarships from St Paul's School and the London County Council, he permitted himself ambitions both more worldly and more romantic than his contemplated plan of becoming a Dominican friar. These led him to read, and become unduly interested in, the poems and controversial articles contributed to the *Oxford Chronicle* and the *Oxford Outlook* by a Somerville student who signed herself Vera Brittain. In the hope of meeting her he attended the inter-collegiate debates, but he was too shy to ask her fellow-students to introduce him, and it was not until four years afterwards that she first heard his name.

The *Oxford Outlook* was a new undergraduate production of that summer term; it provided self-expression for a group of remarkable young men who believed themselves to be the creators of a post-war university Renaissance, and had begun, amongst numerous other literary activities, the passionate reviewing of each other's early works. Their names included those of P. H. B. Lyon, the present Headmaster of Rugby; Leslie Hore-Belisha, now Liberal M.P. for Devonport; V. de S. Pinto; P. P. S. Sastri, and Charles Morgan, the author of *The Fountain*. To the second number of this magazine Charles Morgan contributed a romantic poem, which represented the spirit of the surviving soldier-undergraduate at its most idealistic; it described the miracle of life, the wonder of love and the enhanced value of common possessions for those to whom death no longer beckoned with the urgent insistence of the past four years.

The founders and editors of the *Oxford Outlook* were two young Balliol men, N. A. Beechman and Beverley Nichols, the latter a nineteen-year-old Marlburian, who had just returned from serving as secretary to the British Universities Mission to the United States. The presence of so many mature undergraduates provided him with a first-rate background for the professional youth that, with the help of his chubby cheeks and his curly hair, he had already begun to cultivate; I used to think it odd that his rising reputation should be one of the results of the War for Democracy, though it seems less odd to-day. 'Daddy, what did YOU do in the Great War?' I would mentally inquire in the words of the familiar poster; and always the experimental answer would come: 'I made the world safe for Beverley Nichols, my son.' And then I would reflect, rather remorsefully: 'That's too bitter! That's unfair! It isn't his fault that he was too young for the War.'

At any rate, he had manœuvred himself into an influential position in the new Oxford − which seemed more than I, for all the battering of the years, was ever likely to do − so I sent him an article for his *Outlook*. It was accepted with flattering promptitude, and published in the same number as Charles Morgan's poem and a characteristic dissertation by the ex-Somervillian, Dorothy L. Sayers, called 'Eros in Academe'. Isolated, as none of the men were isolated, from contemporaries who had shared the common experiences of wartime, I could not achieve the philosophical appreciations of Charles Morgan; instead I contributed, less loftily and more critically, an analysis of Oxford as seen after four years by a returning woman student, who found in her own colleagues little of the 'Renaissance' attitude so noticeable among the men released from death. Nevertheless, I concluded, the ex-war-worker had her special function to perform in the life of the post-war Oxford woman (a reflection with which the rest of Somerville was not, apparently, then inclined to agree):

'The woman student is now in a stage of transition, and this is the conclusion of the whole matter. With the signing of the Armistice she passed from the all-important to the negligible. She has been the slender bridge over which university life has crept from the brilliant superficiality of the years immediately preceding 1914 to the sober but splendid revival of the present. This in itself has led her, if not to exaggerate the value of her own position, at any rate to see it in the wrong perspective. Her sudden relegation to her old corner in the university has shaken her into confusion, but time will prove that she can survive the shock of peace as surely as she has weathered the storms of war.

'Finally, she will both claim and deserve the right to grow out of her corner till, side by side with Oxford's new manhood, she will inherit that wider future which the university owes both to its living and its dead. And in this gradual renaissance the woman student who felt the claims of war upon her, and departed thence, and after many days came back again, will find her place at last. Because she is the connecting link between the women who remained and the men who have returned, she too will play her own momentous part.'

Just then, however, the part that I personally was playing seemed anything but momentous, for I was about to complete those inquiries into the excursions of St Paul which had begun in Malta by doing Divinity Moderations (more commonly known as 'Divvers', and now abolished). At the end of the term, when the Germans were sinking their fleet in Scapa Flow and Convocation at Oxford was wrangling hotly on the subject of compulsory Greek, I took this belated examination – a feat which had to be accomplished, since my own 'compulsory Greek' was now completely forgotten, by learning the translation by heart with the assistance of a 'crib' and hoping to recognise the first line of the text on the question-paper. Being more fortunate than the undergraduate who translated 'δ γέγραφα, γέγραφα' ('What I have written, I have written') as 'O Jerusalem, Jerusalem!' and ran completely off the rails in consequence, I did not have to take the tedious papers again.

I went down quite cheerfully, for I had arranged to join Nina at Girton, where a vacation Summer School was being held on 'Italian History and Art'. During my Malta adventure I had only spent a few hours in Naples and Rome, and I wanted to know more about the country for which – perhaps not untruly – I thought of Edward as having died; already I had begun to save up for a few weeks' pilgrimage some day to that lovely and sorrowful land which had swallowed up my earliest memories and my last surviving hopes. Meanwhile Girton, incongruously enough, might supply some of the deficiencies of my experience; but when I arrived there a vague message greeted me, to the effect that Nina was ill and could not come. No longer tolerant of the shabby teachers and the gawky youths who had once so much impressed me – was it six years ago or six hundred? – at a similar Summer School, I fled in shuddering distaste from the shrill, garrulous crowd, and took spontaneous refuge with Mary and Norah, my hospitable friends from 24 General, who lived in a village some twenty miles from Cambridge.

A day or two later a letter came to say that Nina, who had a weak heart, had died quite suddenly from pneumonia, the result of a chill presumably caught from sitting on damp grass. I pushed the thought of her away and flung myself furiously into Mary's tennis-parties, for I was sick beyond description of death and loss. But before I left the village to go home, I looked one evening into my bedroom glass and thought, with a sense of incommunicable horror, that I detected in my face the signs of some sinister and peculiar change. A dark shadow seemed to lie across my chin; was I beginning to grow a beard, like a witch? Thereafter my hand began, at regular intervals, to steal towards my face; and it had quite definitely acquired this habit when I went down to Cornwall in the middle of July to spend a fortnight with Hope Milroy and escape the Peace Celebrations.

4

My real return to Oxford seemed to come the next term, when I found myself, lost and bewildered, amid a crowd of unfamiliar ex-schoolgirls in a semi-familiar Somerville, which had now been restored, considerably the worse for wear, to its original owners. Nobody knew or appeared to want to know me; one or two stared with half-insolent curiosity at my alien face, and my Classical tutor, though she was no longer responsible for my work, invited me occasionally to tea in her study, but the majority disregarded me completely, and I thanked my seniority and the Principal for the fact that I was living out of college. But now there was no Nina to share the solitude of my cold little room in Keble Road, and though the term had its humours (it was, I think, this autumn that the Bishop of London, at a special service for women students, told us that we were all destined to become the wives of 'some good man' – a polygamous suggestion which delighted Somerville), I spent many hours of it in lonely walks and in 'cutting' college dinner.

On Boar's Hill, where I wandered alone very often, the cherry-trees were turning to flame against the lowering greyness of the stormy October clouds. Had I actually walked there with Edward when for a few weeks we had both been in Oxford during that first autumn term so long ago, or had he accompanied me only in spirit? With Roland, I knew, I had never been on the Hill, and yet it was as vivid with memories of him as though we had often seen it together. The two of them seemed to fuse in my mind into a kind of composite lost companion, an elusive ghost which embodied all intimacy, all comradeship, all joy, which included everything that was the past and should have been the future. Incessantly I tramped across the Hill, subconsciously pursuing this symbolic figure like a lost spirit seeking for its mate, and one dark afternoon, when I came back from a long walk to a solitary tea, followed by a lonely evening in the chill room at whose door nobody ever knocked, I endeavoured to crystallise the mood of that search in a poem which later, in *Oxford Poetry*, 1920, I called 'Boar's Hill, October 1919':

Tall slender beech-trees, whispering, touched with fire,
Swaying at even beneath a desolate sky;
Smouldering embers aflame where the clouds hurry by
At the wind's desire.

Dark sombre woodlands, rain-drenched by the scattering shower,
Spindle that quivers and drops its dim berries to earth—
Mourning, perhaps, as I mourn here alone for the dearth
Of a happier hour.

Can you still see them, who always delighted to roam
Over the Hill where so often together we trod,
When winds of wild autumn strewed summer's dead leaves on
the sod,
Ere your steps turned home?

Only occasionally was I driven by loneliness to seek the companionship of students in one of the numerous 'Years' to which I did not belong; even less frequently it was thrust upon me, but in neither event did the experiment appear particularly successful. It seemed, indeed, doomed with unusual certainty to failure in the case of the girl with whom I had to share my coachings in modern European history with the Dean of Hertford College. Miss Holtby, my tutor told me, was anxious, like myself, to study the nineteenth century; she had also been down from college for a year serving in the W.A.A.C., so perhaps that too would form a link between us. Quite sure that it would not, and wishing that I could have had the Dean to myself, I sauntered lugubriously down to Hertford, where I was to meet both him and this stranger towards whom I felt so unaccountably antagonistic.

At Hertford I found the Dean waiting for me; I had some confidence in the prospect of his teaching, for I had attended his lectures the previous term on 'Nationality and Self-Determination', and though I had hardly understood a word of them, their dynamic picturesqueness had lighted one or two minute candles of interest in the dark chaos of ignorance and confusion that called itself my mind. The unknown ex-W.A.A.C. had not arrived, so we sat on either side of the Dean's hearth and waited for her, he puffing at a pipe and wearing carpet slippers. I had a bad cold, caught the previous week while seeing Hope Milroy off to India; my last friend, my final contact with the War, and all that it meant, had vanished into space, I reflected, and my much-enduring nose was indubitably turning red from the heat of the fire. I certainly did not feel as though I were awaiting so much of my destiny.

I was staring gloomily at the Oxford engravings and photographs of the Dolomites which clustered together so companionably upon the Dean's study wall, when Winifred Holtby burst suddenly in upon this morose atmosphere of ruminant lethargy. Superbly tall, and vigorous as the young Diana with her long straight limbs and her golden hair, her vitality smote with the effect of a blow upon my jaded nerves. Only too well aware that I had lost that youth and energy for ever, I found myself furiously resenting its possessor. Obstinately disregarding the strong-featured, sensitive face and the eager, shining blue eyes, I felt quite triumphant because – having returned from France less than a month before – she didn't appear to have read any of the books which the Dean had suggested as indispensable introductions to our Period.

He 'put her off', she told me long afterwards, for he had been in the War and looked like a colonel, and she expected him to treat her as all colonels treated all W.A.A.C.s, who weren't supposed to be ladies. Not, she explained, that she pretended to be a lady; she was accustomed good-humouredly to boast that, as a prospective journalist, she had a great advantage over me because she was a Yorkshire farmer's daughter, whereas I, a descendant of the Staffordshire *bourgeoisie*, was merely 'genteel'.

In the autumn of 1919, however, the social and intellectual differences between agriculture and industry contributed less towards thrusting Winifred and myself apart than the sanguinary drama of the French Revolution. For some obscure reason, the Dean approved of my essays, and at our joint coachings I sat, doubtless with an exasperatingly superior air, and listened while he, with no more intuitive vision of Winifred's distinguished future as novelist and journalist than I had insight into the essential nobility of her generous spirit, proclaimed her style laborious, her sentences involved, her subject-matter confused and her spelling abominable. When the end of the term came, I was able to write triumphantly home of a really stimulating report from the Dean – and took care to add, with patronising blindness, that 'he didn't give a bit of a good report to the girl I coach with, and yet she always strikes me as being quite good.'

5

That Michaelmas saw the birth of a new Somerville debating society, which organised periodic discussions on topical subjects, and about the middle of the term, Winifred, as its secretary, invited me to propose the motion 'That four years' travel are a better education than four years at a university'. It was a subject upon which, in my hostile isolation, I felt able to express myself with vehemence; university life, it now seemed to me, conduced neither to adult manners nor mature values, and I agreed to do as she asked.

I revive this incident, of which I have already given a substantially correct version in my novel *The Dark Tide*, only because it illustrates so clearly the many possibilities of acute misunderstanding which embittered the relations of the War generation and its immediate juniors – a type of misunderstanding that is perhaps inevitable whenever one group has been through some profound experience which another has missed. That Winifred and I, for example, could have been so completely at cross purposes as we were that evening seems to me now quite incredible, yet even though its ultimate consequences were to prove my redemption from the lethargy of post-war despair, the memory of that debate is still able to reawaken the bitter sense of having outlived my day which possessed me when it was over. For years I believed that it had been deliberately planned with a view to my humiliation; to-day it seems to me far more probable that the whole situation developed spontaneously and unintentionally, though it was of course rooted in the fundamental antagonism which persists to this day between those who suffered deeply from the War, and the others who escaped its most violent impacts.

When the evening came I made what I had already described to my mother as 'a most revolutionary speech, ardently supporting travel and . . . attacking the university'. Undoubtedly it turned into a sharper criticism of academic limitations than I had really intended, coupled with a recommendation – which I was far from feeling – of 'experience' as worth more than anything else, including its own heavy cost. In dialectical retaliation, Winifred's

speech, which was one of the first on the opposition side, eagerly
defended her young comrades against that 'superiority' in myself
which led me, she believed, to disdain their society; many of them,
she knew, envied me for 'adventures' of which they felt themselves deprived, while I, on the other hand, had long ceased to
imagine that anyone in their senses could really covet war-work
and war-experience. Her witty indictment provided a trenchant
foretaste of those qualities for which, in after years, her addresses
were to be so much in demand at public meetings, and concluded
with a quotation from *As You Like It* which appropriately indi-
cated the depressing effect of my superfluous presence upon my
fellow-students: 'I had rather have a fool to make me merry, than
experience to make me sad; and to travel for it, too!'

This speech was followed by several others which, because they
lacked Winifred's poise and wit, made the numerous claims to
imaginary war-work which were put forward in a very fair imita-
tion of my own manner less amusing – at any rate to myself –
than their makers intended, for though my youthful critics were
perhaps a little crude and unimaginative, they were certainly not
sadistic by nature. I didn't really care what they said or thought,
my pride insisted, as the voting went unanimously against me and
I watched the crowd of my opposers go triumphantly from the
hall, but afterwards, alone in my cheerless lodging, I realised that
I had minded dreadfully. Too miserable to light the fire or even
to get into bed, I lay on the cold floor and wept with childish
abandonment.

'Why couldn't I have died in the War with the others?' I
lamented, uncertain whom I detested most, myself, or the exultant debaters. 'Why couldn't a torpedo have finished me, or an
aerial bomb, or one of those annoying illnesses? I'm nothing but
a piece of wartime wreckage, living on ingloriously in a world
that doesn't want me!'

Obviously it wasn't a popular thing to have been close to the
War; patriots, especially of the female variety, were as much discredited in 1919 as in 1914 they had been honoured, I reflected, making
no effort to shut out the series of pictures that passed insistently
through my mind – the dark, blurred spire of a Camberwell church

at midnight – the *Britannic* lurching drunkenly through the golden, treacherous Archipelago – sun-drenched rocks and a telegram on a gorgeous May morning – Syracuse harbour and the plaintive notes of the 'Last Post' testifying to heaven of the ravage of a storm – the German ward and the sharp grey features of a harmless little 'enemy' dying in the sticky morass of his own blood – the Great Push and a gassed procession of burned, gruesome faces – the long stone corridor of St Jude's where walked a ghost too dazed to feel the full fury of her own resentment – Millbank and the shattering guns announcing the Armistice. On the whole the 'experience' of those four years didn't seem exactly conducive to the development of a sense of humour – but perhaps I was prejudiced. No doubt the post-war generation was wise in its assumption that patriotism had 'nothing to it', and we pre-war lot were just poor boobs for letting ourselves be kidded into thinking that it had. The smashing-up of one's youth seemed rather a heavy price to pay for making the mistake, but fools always did come in for a worse punishment than knaves; we knew that now.

Some time or other during the next few days, I wrote the poem entitled 'The Lament of the Demobilised' which Louis Golding, in his *Oxford Chronicle* review of *Oxford Poetry*, 1920, afterwards remarked might have been produced 'by Godfrey Elton out of Siegfried Sassoon'. But even those angry lines did not eradicate the resentment from my system, and on the Sunday evening after the debate I went to see Winifred, whom, as secretary of the Debating Society, I regarded as technically, if not actually, responsible for the bitter episode. I even took the precaution of making an appointment, for she was so popular that, although she was only just twenty-one, her room was always thronged with impetuous young creatures demanding sympathy and advice for their hopes and problems. Finding her alone, puzzled and a little perturbed by my visit, I reminded her of the debate, and then gave her a *résumé* of those 'experiences' which, all unknowing, my fellow-students seemed to me to have derided with so little compunction.

'If you're going to make the proposer's chair a stool of repentance for people whose histories you know nothing about,' I concluded, with harsh intolerance, 'you'd much better abolish your debating society before it does any more harm.'

It never occurred to me that I was being either severe or ridiculous; not until weeks later did I learn that Winifred, like myself, had known that *via dolorosa*, the road to Camiers, and had lived beside the same historic railway-line, and heard the same rattling engines go shrieking through the night. The War had not been for her, as for most of the others, a calamity as impersonal as a storm rumbling in the distance; within her memory lived the authentic recollection of the Base in the last and most anxious year of the fighting – a recollection which took shape only in 1931, when after a night journey back to London from the Riviera she published in *Time and Tide* her poem 'Trains in France':

> All through the night among the unseen hills
> The trains,
> The fire-eyed trains,
> Call to each other their wild seeking cry,
> And I,
> Who thought I had forgotten all the War
> Remember now a night in Camiers,
> When, through the darkness, as I wakeful lay,
>   I heard the trains,
>   The savage, shrieking trains,
> Call to each other their fierce hunting-cry,
> Ruthless, inevitable, as the beasts
>   After their prey.
> Made for this end by their creators, they,
> Whose business was to capture and devour
> Flesh of our flesh, bone of our very bone.
>   Hour after hour,
> Angry and impotent I lay alone
> Hearing them hunt you down, my dear, and you,
> Hearing them carry you away to die,
> Trying to warn you of the beasts, the beasts!
> Then, no, thought I;
> So foul a dream as this cannot be true,

And calmed myself, hearing their cry no more.
Till, from the silence, broke a trembling roar,
And I heard, far away,
The growling thunder of their joyless feasts—
The beasts had got you then, the beasts, the beasts—
    And knew
    The nightmare true.

That Sunday evening, however, trains in France were merely, for Winifred, a distant echo, while the wrathful presence of their self-constituted representative was all too verbally apparent. I have often amusedly thought how profoundly, that evening, she must have disliked me, with my absurd conviction of her malicious intentions, but she received my complaint with determined charity, murmured a few words of bewildered regret, and afterwards made the Debating Society president send me an 'official' apology. To the president, a serious, preoccupied Greats student, the attacks of the opposers had represented nothing more than 'a little mild chaff'; my insistent memories would not allow me to think of them as that, but I eventually accepted her assurance that my hurt had been 'unintentional'.

Nevertheless, I did not forget the debate, for it had taught me a salutary lesson. In the eyes of these realistic ex–High-School girls, who had sat out the War in classrooms, I was now aware that I represented neither a respect-worthy volunteer in a national cause nor a surviving victim of history's cruellest catastrophe; I was merely a figure of fun, ludicrously boasting of her experiences in an already *démodé* conflict. I had been, I suspected, largely to blame for my own isolation. I could not throw off the War, nor the pride and the grief of it; rooted and immersed in memory, I had appeared self-absorbed, contemptuous and 'stand-offish' to my ruthless and critical juniors.

'That's the worst of sorrow,' I decided, with less surprise than I had accepted the same conclusion after Roland's death. 'It's always a vicious circle. It makes one tense and hard and disagreeable, and this means that one repels and antagonises people, and then they dislike and avoid one – and that means more isolation and still more sorrow.'

After that, until I left college, I never publicly mentioned the War again.

6

Except at coachings I saw no more of Winifred Holtby that term, and during the vacation I completely forgot her, for my father nearly died from an operation suddenly rendered necessary by the unsuccessful experiments of the Staffordshire surgeons with his appendix a quarter of a century before. This new disaster not only effectually prevented me from noticing either the fresh epidemic of outrages in Ireland or the introduction of Prohibition into the United States, but rendered almost impossible the requisite concentration upon the Congress of Vienna or J. H. Round's exacting volume on the economics of the reign of Stephen, *Geoffrey de Mandeville*.

Thus sadly unprepared either mentally or physically for the icy rigours of the Easter term, I succumbed almost immediately to a chill, and was lying mournfully in bed one afternoon in my desolate room when Winifred appeared quite suddenly, laid a bunch of grapes beside me, and immediately vanished. But she came back the next day, and to our mutual astonishment we found ourselves discussing her camps at Abbeville and Camiers, and the plot of her projected story of a Yorkshire farm which afterwards became her first novel, *Anderby Wold*. As soon as I was better she took me over to tea in her room, and introduced me to her friend Hilda Reid, the pale, whimsical second-year student who has since become, as H. S. Reid, the author of exquisite historical novels, delicately etched with the fine pen of a literary drypoint artist.

After the interminable loneliness of the previous months, I felt like an icicle beginning to melt in the gathering warmth of the pale spring sunshine. My work, too, suddenly seemed more prom-ising; encouraging whispers began to circulate that, even in History, I was a possible First, and though, as I admitted to my father, 'Sometimes I get a great desire to go on the bust – one has to be so terribly respectable and economical as a woman student!', I was also able to inform him proudly that, after my change of

'coaches' at the end of the term, 'I am going to all the best people
... The Master of Balliol is one; it is supposed to be a great privilege even for a man to go to him. One would never think so
either, as he is a funny-looking old ruffian of about seventy with
wild tufts of grey hair and a sense of humour.' Winifred and I
actually had a coaching from the Master – then Dr A. L. Smith
– on his seventieth birthday the following Michaelmas term.
Twirling round and round on a swivel chair, he shook contemptuously the first of our long, earnest essays, and muttering, 'I don't
want *pamphlets!*' forbade us to waste any more of his time with
our literary efforts.

During the remainder of the Easter term, I found Winifred's
large first-floor room in the West Building at Somerville a pleasant
alternative to Keble Road. Accompanied by Hilda Reid, we went
to see the O.U.D.S. performance of Hardy's *The Dynasts*, and
decided to spend part of the vacation together at rooms in
Holywell, reading at the Radcliffe Camera. With this arrangement, though I realised it only dimly at the time, my personal
life was renewed.

The friendship into which, from such ironically inauspicious
beginnings, I had drifted with Winifred Holtby began an association that in thirteen years has never been broken and never spoilt,
and to-day remains as intimate as ever. Although I am still, comparatively speaking, a young woman, I feel, looking back upon the
past, that it has been immeasurably long, for in the twenty years
that have vanished since I left school, I have had – like many, I
suspect, of my War generation contemporaries – two quite separate lives, two sets of circumstances and of personal relationships.

Between the first life that ended with Edward's death in 1918,
and the second that began with Winifred's companionship in 1920,
no links remain except Roland's family and my parents; they alone
can remember the world that revolved for me round Edward,
round Roland, round Victor and Geoffrey. Of those others upon
whom my deepest affections now rest – Winifred, my husband,
my children – not one knew even by name a single contemporary who counted for me in the life before 1918. For a time I felt
forlorn, even bitter, because they could not share my memories,

but now I have grown accustomed to revisiting that past world alone.

Only the permanence of my fondest ambitions, and the strange and growing likeness of my son to Edward, reminds me that I am still the individual who went to Uppingham Speech Day in July 1914, for although I was a student at Oxford in both my lives, it was not the same Oxford and I was not the same student. The fact that, within ten years, I lost one world, and after a time rose again, as it were, from spiritual death to find another, seems to me one of the strongest arguments against suicide that life can provide. There may not be – I believe that there is not – resurrection after death, but nothing could prove more conclusively than my own brief but eventful history the fact that resurrection is possible within our limited span of earthly time.

It is not, however, possible for everyone. I was fortunate. Too many victims of the Great War have not risen again and will never rise, while there appear to be quite a number of that younger generation which swings between jazz and unemployment in a world denuded of prospects and left arid and pointless, who have never risen at all. Even for me, the new life took long enough to begin, for, try as I would to conceal my memories, the War obstinately refused to be forgotten; and by the end of the Easter term, 1920, its extraordinary aftermath had taken full possession of my warped and floundering mind. When I left Millbank, I had never contemplated any alternative other than an immediate return to Oxford; the idea of a long holiday did not occur to me, and I had no one to go with had the suggestion been made. Although persistent dreams recurred of Roland and Edward – the one missing and purposely hiding his identity because facially mutilated, the other suffering some odd psychological complex which made him turn against us all and keep silence – I endured none of those nightmare recapitulations of hospital sounds and sights of which other wartime nurses complained for two or three years. Only the horrible delusion, first experienced after the flight from Girton, that my face was changing, persisted until it became a permanent, fixed obsession.

I have since been told that hallucinations and dreams and

insomnia are normal symptoms of over-fatigue and excessive strain, and that, had I consulted an intelligent doctor immediately after the War, I might have been spared the exhausting battle against nervous breakdown which I waged for eighteen months. But no one, least of all myself, realised how near I had drifted to the borderland of craziness. I was ashamed, to the point of agony, of the sinister transformation which seemed, every time I looked in the glass, to be impending in my face, and I could not bring myself to mention it even to Winifred, who would probably have dispelled the illusion by a sane reassurance that I was neither developing a beard nor turning into a witch. Nothing has ever made me realise more clearly the thinness of the barrier between normality and insanity than the persistent growth, like an obscene, overshadowing fungus, of these dark hallucinations throughout 1920.

7

The strained and hectic atmosphere of that summer term was hardly calculated to restore to sanity any man or woman driven to the edge of neurosis by the War. It was the first summer in which the university had its full complement of men after demobilisation, and the now almost successful struggle for Degrees for women contributed to a strange biological excitement in which the eagerness of the women students to associate with young men after so many years of war was intensified by the chaperon rules which not only made it difficult to do so, but appeared specially important to female dons anxious to create a good impression in the university.

The swarming male undergraduates varied in type from the ex-officers – mainly Colonials – on shortened courses who were determined to have a good time and forget, to the small but very articulate group of young writers such as Edmund Blunden, Charles Morgan, Louis Golding, Robert Graves, L. A. G. Strong, Robert Nichols and Edgell Rickword, who were seriously analysing the effect of the War upon themselves and their world. Between these two extremes, large numbers of exhausted ex-soldiers pursued their

War Degrees with the dull-eyed determination of tired brains, while the normal contingent of nineteen-year-old boys just up from Public Schools oscillated between a profound inferiority complex in the presence of the ex-officers, and a noisy determination to make their youthful presence felt in this abnormal university. A few of the latter found the intense post-war atmosphere a first-rate forcing house for the talents of those whose vitality had not been impaired by four years of strain.

Whatever their type, one and all combined to create that 'eat-drink-and-be-merry-for-to-morrow-we-die' atmosphere which seemed to have drifted from the trenches *via* Paris hotels and London night-clubs into the Oxford colleges. The War generation was forcibly coming back to life, but continued to be possessed by the desperate feeling that life was short. An inexplicable sense of urgency led, as in wartime leaves, to a greedy grasping after the second-rate lest the first-rate should never materialise. For a time the normal interest in Final Schools became almost as unfashionable at Somerville as it usually was at Magdalen or Exeter; reaction against the sex-stagnation of the War meant that for the first time in their ascetic history, the women's colleges were obsessed by those values – so familiar to provincial towns – in which success is measured in terms of sex-attraction rather than by intellectual achievement.

This phase passed quickly enough with the departure, in 1920 and 1921, of the undergraduates who had returned from the War. As far as the women were concerned, it had to pass, for the intense competition for vacancies at their four colleges had made the conditions of residence almost as inexorable as death; there was literally no room for students who did not intend to work all or most of the time, and tutors had always a rod in pickle for the backs of the would-be frivolous. The post-war outbreak was sufficiently rare to be satirised in the 1920 Somerville Going-Down play in a song which was sung to the then popular tune of 'O Hel—, O Hel—':

> *Oh pen—, oh pen—, oh penetrating eye!*
> *Why do you gaze so coldly from the High?*

Say, is the cause which makes your glances freeze
Our men——, our men——, our many 'unchapped' teas?

Ostensibly, that term, I was working once again at the recurrent Tudors and Stuarts, and studying the portentous topic of political science; actually, my mind was in a condition of heated chaos which I managed to camouflage only by dividing with another student the Somerville Coombs Prize for 'the best work in History' done during the year. Perpetually through my head, interfering with the detached contemplation of Hobbes's *Leviathan* and Mill on *Liberty*, ran a sentence from one of the Elizabethan documents: 'The Queen of Scots is the mother of a gallant son, but I am a barren stock.'

What follies they drove some of us into, the biological needs of that tense, turbulent year! I myself even became argumentatively engaged for a few weeks to an undergraduate taking a 'shortened course' at one of the less conspicuous colleges – an error of judgment which, in the light of the sorrowful but dignified past, soon filled me with deep humiliation. As soon as I went down with Winifred, in July, to the Cornwall house that I had shared the previous summer with Hope Milroy, I put a speedy end to an intolerable situation which no neurotic metamorphosis seemed by then to excuse. That evening I breathed again in grateful freedom, with a sense of emerging into normal daylight after a night of delirium, yet the next day I wrote one more bitter poem, which was almost the last of my post-war efforts. I did not send it to any of the Oxford magazines, and it certainly would not have found favour in the eyes of my feminist friends of a year or two later, for it was called 'The Superfluous Woman'.

Back at Oxford after a vacation spent in reading Grotius and Machiavelli and Treitschke in preparation for my special subject, 'International Relations', I was more than ever a victim of delusions. My lodging in Keble Road had now been changed for a supposedly superior room in a Bevington Road house where Winifred was also living; it contained five large mirrors and for this reason had been selected for me by the Bursar, who was amusedly aware of that vain interest in clothes for which my fellow-seniors were accustomed good-humouredly to tease me. This ground-floor habitation, which faced due north and was invaded at night by armies of large, fat mice, soon became for me a place of horror; I avoided it from breakfast till bed-time, and if ever I had to go in to change my clothes or fetch a book, I pressed my hands desperately against my eyes lest five identical witches' faces should suddenly stare at me from the cold, remorseless mirrors. Because of the mice, and the constant watch on the impending witch's beard, I became progressively unable to sleep; the old inability to put the secret dread into words prevented me from asking the Bursar to change my room, and I took to spending the nights on a couch in Winifred's attic. The next term, though the sleeplessness persisted, the hallucinations began at last slowly to die away; and for the fact that they did not quite conquer me, *Oxford Poetry*, 1920, and the objective, triumphant struggle for women's Degrees were probably, together with Winifred's eager and patient understanding, jointly responsible.

8

The term after I had published my article, 'The Point of View of a Woman Student', in the second number of the *Oxford Outlook*, the editor of the weekly *Oxford Chronicle*, a competently managed local newspaper which represented both Town and Gown, sent for me and asked if I would care to undertake a small piece of journalistic work. Could I contribute a weekly column of half a dozen paragraphs describing the activities of the women's colleges, similar to that habitually sent in by the men? He offered me 10*s.* 6*d.* for each contribution and I accepted with enthusiasm; not only would the four guineas more than cover my book bill for each term, but I should really have started to tread the path of authentic, remunerated journalism. I had lately begun to imagine, quite correctly, that I should not for years be able to live on the proceeds of any book that I might write, and free-lance journalism, if only I could push my way into that charmed circle which seemed to exclude everyone who had not already – God knew how – made a reputation, seemed by far the most agreeable and appropriate method of supplementing an elusive income. Consequently, when my History tutor of the previous summer had contemptuously described the vivacious but utterly uninformed essays on 'The Great Discoverers' and 'The Divine Right of Kings' which I inflicted upon her, as 'mere journalism', I did not feel so ashamed of the criticism as she evidently expected.

'I may make a little money,' I wrote triumphantly of the *Chronicle* suggestion to my mother, 'unless the Principals of the women's colleges interfere; I hear they are afraid of topical articles for fear anything will reflect on them.' The desire of Degree-seeking Principals, during a difficult period of post-war excitement, to represent their students as meek, chaste little angels, who would never under any circumstances criticise the university nor incur the wrath of the proctors, did indeed create an obstacle upon which the *Chronicle* editor had not reckoned, for as soon as I began to demand from the other colleges those simple details about debates and hockey-matches which I required for my column, I found my contemporaries, especially at Lady Margaret Hall, timidly unwilling to supply them. So I went again to the editor and explained to him that, at a time when every woman don was waiting in nervous trepidation for Convocation's verdict on Degrees, it would probably be wise to ask official permission for any activity which could possibly be construed as an innovation.

The editor, being a reasonable man, grasped the position and wrote to the Principal of Somerville, asking if I might contribute the paragraphs and even offering to submit them to her before publication. No immediate answer was forthcoming to this request, and when, after several days' delay, I inquired from the Somerville senior student if she knew what was happening, I was told that the five Principals of the women's societies were sitting in solemn conclave over the editor's letter. Eventually the verdict came through; the Principals had decided that I was not to be permitted to write the paragraphs, the Head of Lady Margaret Hall especially insisting that 'she did not consider it suitable for a student to do such work'.

There was no court of appeal to which I could protest that,

for a student who intended to become a journalist, it could hardly be 'unsuitable' to practise journalism, and that the men had contributed a similar column from time immemorial. I had perforce to accept the absurd decision and tell the editor that I could not do the work. He received the news with ludicrous dismay, but asked me to let him have as many general articles and poems as I cared to publish. In the winter of 1919–20 I found the *Oxford Chronicle* a convenient stamping-ground for a good deal of wrathful self-expression, and through this and other minor literary activities I came to know Basil Blackwell, then partner with his father in the famous bookselling and publishing business in Broad Street.

Throughout 1920 I spent many agreeable evenings at the Blackwells' house in North Oxford; even for this innocent amusement I had elaborately to obtain permission, stating exactly where I was going and undertaking to return at a specified hour. Early in the summer, Basil Blackwell asked me if I would act as one of the three editors of his annual publication, *Oxford Poetry*; the 1920 edition would be, he thought, unusually interesting, for it would represent the literary gleanings of no less than seven years. I agreed to interrupt still further my tattered and torn work for the History School by this singularly congenial task, and was shortly afterwards invited to one of the Blackwells' literary 'socials' to meet my co-editors, the fair and immaculate C. H. B. Kitchin, of Exeter College, and the swarthy Alan Porter, of Queen's.

Throughout that summer term and vacation, the three of us ploughed through oceans of MSS., enthusiastically submitted to us by literary aspirants of all ages from eighteen to twenty-eight. We also laboured, not unnaturally, to produce some contributions of our own which we felt that we could justifiably include in the volume. C. H. B. Kitchin's poems were long and persevering, while those submitted to his own inspection by Alan Porter – for whom Clifford Kitchin and myself, especially myself, were so much birdseed – ran to nudity and prostitution. The chief merit of my own disillusioned productions lay in their brevity.

Eventually the selections were made and the book was ready for publication; at the beginning of the Michaelmas term the *Oxford Chronicle* reported a remark by Basil Blackwell to the effect that it would be 'the best single volume I have turned out'. '*Oxford Poetry*, 1920,' continued the reporter, 'will be a notable little volume. Mr Alan Porter (Queen's), Mr Louis Golding (Queen's), Mr Robert Graves (St John's), Mr Edmund Blunden (Queen's), Mr L. A. G. Strong (Wadham), Mr C. H. B. Kitchin (Exeter), Mr Edgell Rickword (Pembroke), Mr L. P. Hartley (Balliol), Miss Vera M. Brittain (Somerville), and Mr Eric Dickinson (Exeter) are among the contributors . . .'

In view of the reputation now attached to some of these names, Mr Blackwell's estimate of the book's value may perhaps be regarded as justified and our editorial selections as endorsed, particularly as they also included poems by Roy Campbell, Richard Hughes, Winifred Holtby, W. Force Stead and Hilda Reid. Viola Garvin, who was then in her third year at Somerville, dreamily impressive with her dark loveliness like that of some mediæval saint, did not send us an example of her sensitive poetry; to her, who had known from childhood the finest writers and journalists of the day, our earnest activities must have seemed amateurish and irrelevant.

Nevertheless, young literary Oxford was beginning to make itself felt in the wider world; in the winter of 1920 the eternal controversy eddying round the *Autobiography* of Margot Asquith sometimes gave way to a discussion of Louis Golding's first novel, *Forward from Babylon*, while the youthful Beverley Nichols was said to have his second novel, *Patchwork*, ready for publication in the autumn. Like Winifred Holtby, I had already begun to make notes for my own first novel, but in the winter of 1920–21, I contented myself with writing a short story, 'All Souls' Day', for the *Oxford Outlook*. The fiercest polemic that I ever contributed to that shining organ of undergraduate opinion had already appeared in the late autumn of 1919 under the title of 'The Degree and *The Times*'.

9

The fight for Degrees for Women at Oxford had always been closely connected with the feminist movement as a whole, and in 1919 it shared in the impetus given everywhere to the women's cause by the ending of the War. Except for Lord Curzon, Lord Birkenhead and Mrs Humphry Ward, no anti-feminists of any importance appeared to be left in the country, and on July 22nd, 1919, while a regular chorus of praise of women's war-work was accompanying their gradual replacement by men in every type of occupation, the House of Commons passed the Second Reading of the Sex Disqualification (Removal) Bill, with its comprehensive opening words: 'A person shall not be disqualified by sex or marriage from the exercise of any public function, or from being appointed to or holding any civil or judicial office or post, or from entering or assuming or carrying on any civil profession or vocation.'

This Act, which became law on December 23rd, 1919, also stated in its 'permissive' Clause III that nothing in the statutes or charter of any university should be deemed to preclude the authorities of such university from admitting women to its membership, and at Oxford the advocates of Degrees for Women acted upon this clause so promptly that by November 27th of that year, the day before Lady Astor was first returned as Member of Parliament for the Sutton Division of Plymouth, I was able to write to my mother: 'The statute for Degrees for Women has just been published; in it they give us absolutely everything we ask for and it will be discussed at the beginning of next term. If they pass it – and everyone seems to think they will – it will come into force on October 9th next year, which means that when I do my Finals I shall also get my Degree and you will see me going about in a mortar-board and gown . . . before I go down.'

To a *Times* leader-writer, however, the publication of the statute merely suggested that women at Oxford were seeking an extension of their 'present advantages' without corresponding obligations, and if admitted to full membership of the university, must undergo 'stricter discipline than is at present in force'. Raging with partisan fury, I took up my pen; the *Oxford Outlook*, I had heard, was now occasionally read by persons of discrimination in London, and whether this was so or not, it certainly represented the only medium in which I was likely to be given the chance to express my indignation. My article, 'The Degree and *The Times*', disputed with meticulous fierceness the major premisses of the solemn leader:

> 'We would ask for a more exact definition of that "stricter discipline" to which *The Times* writer refers. We should like to know from what rules and regulations, written or unwritten, we are supposed to be so conspicuously exempt. Is it generally presumed outside the precincts of this university that, whereas undergraduates are induced by the vigilance of authority to enter their college gates at a reasonable hour of the night, the women students are free to wander whithersoever they will from darkness to dawn? Do our critics really think so ill of us as to imagine that we always arrive late, or not at all, at the lectures we are not officially entitled to attend? Or are we pictured as Mænads dancing before the Martyr's Memorial, or as Bacchantes revelling in the open spaces of Carfax and the High? If such notions as these really do exist abroad, we can but protest that we are law-abiding citizens, keeping the rule of those whose work we share in full and whose privileges we enjoy in part, perhaps more religiously than those for whom it was first made.'

But the university and *The Times* alike proceeded majestically along their dignified paths, completely unaffected for good or for ill by the explosive ebullitions of feminine wrath. In the Hilary term, when Congregation was to discuss the proposed new statute, Winifred and I slipped into the Divinity School at the tail of a group of Somerville dons; we were evidently regarded by the ushers as belonging to them, for no one challenged our occupation of the limited space available to non-disputants. Almost the only women students present, we listened, our hearts surging warm with hero-worship, to Professor Geldart and young Dr Moberly – who had come back from the War with a D.S.O. and two mentions in dispatches – putting in their plea for the women, and realised from the small opposition encountered by their speeches that the battle was almost won. The statute was actually passed on May 11th,

1920; before it came into force on October 7th, the universal tide then flowing so strongly towards feminism throughout the world had swung woman suffrage into the American Constitution.

That Michaelmas term saw both the largest number of under-graduates ever known in Oxford – there were 4,181 men and 549 women – and the greatest change that had taken place in the constitution of the university. One of the first duties of Dr Farnell, the Rector of Exeter, who began that term his adven-turous Vice-Chancellorship, was the matriculation of nearly a thousand women. Winifred and I were among the number, together with several headmistresses, whose hair had grown grey in the process of training generations of girls to educate and work for their still handicapped sex.

'One is a little puzzled,' the *Oxford Chronicle* remarked compla-cently, 'to know why what Oxford did with such graceful unanimity is still a matter for hesitation and controversy at Cambridge.' Nevertheless I felt afraid – not, as time has proved, without justi-fication – that the university might feel too proud of itself, too sure that it had done everything which could be done to put women undergraduates on an equal footing with men; 'if freedom at Oxford broadens down from precedent to precedent a little less slowly than at Cambridge, this is the utmost that can be said for it,' I protested, in a *Chronicle* article advocating (then very daringly) the amalgamation of the Women's Dramatic Society with O.U.D.S.

On October 14th, I joined the crowds of young women in the Sheldonian Theatre to see the first Degree-giving in which women had taken part. It was a warm, scintillating autumn day, and the crimson hoods of the M.A.s rivalled the wine-red amphilopsis which hung with decorative dignity over walls and quadrangles. Within the Sheldonian, rows of eager childish faces looked down, awed and marvelling, upon the complicated cere-mony in the arena below; the excited atmosphere was tense with the consciousness of a dream fulfilled which had first been dreamt, years before these feminine Masters and Bachelors were born, by women long dead – women who did not care whether they saw the end so long as they had contributed to the means. Everyone pretended to ignore this atmosphere – the men assumed an attitude of determined conviction that nothing special was happening, the women wore an expression of demure severity, as though Degrees were commonplace to them – but there was no gainsaying the nervous tension of the hour, and after much robing and unrobing and clicking of Press cameras, the harassed Vice-Chancellor, in dignified confusion, tapped one candidate on the head with his mortar-board instead of with the Testament.

Before the usual ceremony began, the five Principals of the women's societies – now all vanished from the Oxford limelight – became M.A.s by order of Convocation, and the theatre vibrated with youthful applause as they put on their robes and sat down behind the Vice-Chancellor – a ceremony which the Principal of Somerville had practised with other Degree-taking Somervillians for nearly an hour the previous day. What a consummation of her life-work this was for her! I reflected, with a feeling of partisan warmth towards the intellectually arrogant college whose Principal, more than any other Oxford woman, had been responsible for the symbolic celebrations of that morning. Brought up in the nineteenth-century educational tradition, she was an academic Metternich of an older régime – but it was a Metternich that the War and post-war periods had required. Her task, during those complicated years, of reconciling college and university, don and student, man and woman, war-service and academic work, conscience and discretion, had been colossal in its demands upon tact and ingenuity, and probably no woman living would have done it so well. The wide gulf fixed during her period of authority between the Senior and Junior Common Rooms at Somerville had been largely of her own creation, as a means to an end; she herself for thirteen years had reigned above them both, a lonely Olympian, secure in the legend of her purpose, her omnipotence and her inhumanity. Who knew what Spartan ideal of justice, endurance and self-sacrifice had inspired the ruthless impartiality of that splendid isolation?

When the men, in turn, had received their Degrees, renewed cheers echoed wildly to the vaulted roof as the first women stood before the Vice-Chancellor; among them were Dr Ivy Williams, Dorothy L. Sayers, and D. K. Broster, once at St Hilda's. Even the unchanging passivity of Oxford beneath the hand of the centuries must surely, I thought, be a little stirred by the sight of the women's gowns and caps – those soft, black pseudo-mortar-boards with their deplorable habit of slipping over one eye – which were nevertheless the visible signs of a profound revolution.

For the rest of the term, at any rate, the male undergraduates were very much stirred indeed. 'I realised with a pang,' wrote one typical humorist in an Oxford journal after describing the 'strange vision' of a woman in cap and gown descending from a bicycle, 'that I was in the presence of my equal, and Schools assumed a new terror for me. The woman undergraduate stood revealed. Two senile, placid dons passed me. "*Monstrum horrendum informe*," I heard one murmur. I wonder how the charming ladies will enjoy their new status . . . Shall we behold them in white ties when the last dread moment comes?'

And so on. Quite soon, we all got used to it and didn't read it, but the men – no doubt hopefully supposing that we did – still continued to write it.

10

By November the excitement of these triumphs was dying down, and I read – with a feeling that by going back to Oxford I had strayed away from the life that really mattered into a world of small things – about the burial in Westminster Abbey on the third Armistice Day of the Unknown Warrior who might so well have been Geoffrey, and the opening of the first League of Nations Assembly by M. Hymans on November 15th, while Convocation was discursively making up its mind to establish, a fortnight later, the new School of 'Modern Greats'. But when, in December, Olive Schreiner died in Capetown, early memories of *Woman and Labour* and *The Story of an African Farm* put the women's movement back into perspective in my mind, and my feminist enthusiasm had completely revived by the time that Queen Mary came up to Oxford to receive the Honorary Degree of D.C.L., and to visit Somerville and Lady Margaret Hall.

A few of us were divided that day into groups of 'distinguished students' – scholars and exhibitioners, Colonials, games captains, 'notable old students', and war-workers. I preferred the last of these groups to the first, and stood rather self-consciously between Winifred and a First-Year who had been quartermaster in a Surrey Red Cross hospital. Among the 'distinguished students' who awaited the Queen there was naturally no group – though even then its nucleus might have been collected – which described itself, in accordance with the label afterwards bestowed upon it by the popular Press, as 'the Somerville School of Novelists'. I cannot remember whether, among the Somervillians from previous 'Years', Rose Macaulay or Dorothy Sayers or Margaret Kennedy or Doreen Wallace was present in the hall that day, but Winifred Holtby and Hilda Reid appeared there as Third-Years, while among the new students who had come up the previous term was Sylvia Thompson, whose *Hounds of Spring* was to carry her so early in life into the ranks of the best-sellers. Sylvia, at eighteen, already possessed the luscious beauty of a ripened grape; her elaborate clothes were carefully selected, and she wore large drooping hats and coloured shoes when these were still a daring and unusual fashion. But her reputation for schoolgirl precocity had not the same interest for us who were mature undergraduates with literary ambitions as the rising star of Rose Macaulay, who after pressing slowly towards fame before and during the War with several novels, had suddenly achieved it in 1920 with the brilliant and cynical *Potterism*. To Winifred and myself she was a portent, a symbol, an encouraging witness to the fact that a university education could produce writers of a non-academic yet first-rate calibre; and we collected all the tales of her, both authentic and apocryphal, that we could gather together from dons and old students.

On the afternoon of the royal visit, those of us – namely, Winifred and myself – who were entitled to active-service ribbons had been ordered to wear them, and as the Queen, followed by Princess Mary and tall, gracious Lady Ampthill, whose appreciative letter about *Verses of a V.A.D.* I still secretly treasured, moved solemnly up the large oak-panelled dining-hall, I reflected with a slightly bitter satisfaction that, for the first time since returning to Oxford, I hadn't to feel ashamed of the War.

Noticing the ribbons, the Queen and Princess Mary both stopped in front of me; had I enjoyed my war-work? the Princess inquired. I compromised with truth by saying that I had preferred nursing to anything else while the War was on, and had just begun an enthusiastic conversation with Lady Ampthill about 24 General, when I noticed, as I subsequently related to my mother, that the Queen had 'suddenly turned round to Winifred who was standing beside me. She had on her blue coat frock and a high white blouse collar; her hair was very nicely brushed and waved and the light was shining on it. She really looked quite beautiful and Mary was evidently rather struck with her appearance. She said to Winifred, "I see you were abroad too – where were you?" and Winifred said, "I was at Abbeville, your Majesty." The Queen then asked, "Were you nursing too?" and I was terrified she was going to say, "I was in the Waacs," which would hardly be tactful to the Queen, but fortunately Miss P. came up and said, "This is Miss Holtby, who was in Queen Mary's Army Auxiliary Corps." . . . Winifred by this time was scarlet all over, but I wasn't so much impressed by the Queen as she had been, because her manner is so exactly like Aunt F.'s that it seemed quite familiar. She looked stiff but really very impressive; she is almost as tall as Winifred so no wonder she makes the King look small.'

11

The weeks immediately preceding Schools in the summer of 1921 were as inauspicious for me as for the whole country, which after the evanescent post-war boom was already beginning its long descent into trade depression and unemployment. By the end of the Easter term my sinister hallucinations were practically gone, but I had fought so long against threatening, indefinite neuroses that I fell an easy victim to a sharp attack of influenza. The college nurse for whose institution Winifred and I had contended gave me an efficient care very different from the perfunctory attention meted out to me during the uncomfortable illness of 1915, but I returned to London considerably devitalised, only to find my mother stricken down by the same exasperating disease.

Nearly all my vacations had been – as was perhaps inevitable during those disturbed and difficult years of transition – to some extent interrupted by family illnesses or domestic crises. After the hard-working Bessie had left to get married, efficient single-handed maids appeared, in spite of the general demobilisation, to be almost as difficult to find as they were during the War; the multitudinous obligations of domesticity seemed overwhelming, and I was involved in a perpetual struggle between my clamant reading and my remorseful conscience. Trained nurses were not popular at home owing to the strong probability that a starched, bustling presence would completely demolish the tottering edifice of household organisation; so I nursed my mother by day for about a fortnight, and at night plunged from 10 p.m. until 1 a.m. into a course of belated, frantic revision which quite extinguished my now eager interest in the developing problem of Reparations and Greece's new war with Turkey. By the time that I went back to Oxford for my final term, the intermittent insomnia of the spring had become chronic, and throughout the weeks before Schools I rarely slept until 5 a.m.

The May and June which began that long, radiant summer had nevertheless their compensations, of which the most spectacular centred round Eights Week. I had by now a good many undisturbing acquaintances among the men undergraduates, and I watched the upward progress of New College from bump to bump in the sociable atmosphere of the college barges. 'I wore the yellow dress and blue hat on Thursday and Hilda said it was a vision of beauty,' I told my mother on May 19th; 'to-day I shall wear the patterned voile dress and the black hat with the feather.'

New College ended as head of the river that summer, but the ex-rifleman was no longer there to watch the races; he had gone down the previous year with a wartime History Degree, with Distinction, in order to become a lecturer in a northern university. I took little interest then in university prizes, which had not been open to women students before Michaelmas, 1920, and did not know until long afterwards that he had broken Oxford's prize record by winning three of these prizes in eighteen months, as well as being placed *proxime accessit* for a fourth before he went down to begin a career which was later to include the practice as well as the theory of politics.

On the long, hot evenings which followed Eights, Winifred and I occasionally rested from the race against time of our last-moment revision by taking a punt up the river with Hilda Reid or Grace Desmond (daughter of G. G. Desmond of the *Daily News*, who later stood as Labour candidate for Bath, and in 1923 introduced us to our first Labour rally after Robert Smillie had been elected as M.P. for Morpeth). The placid reaches around the Cherwell Hotel provided an ideal atmosphere for the composition of the Going-Down play, which Winifred and another inventive Third-Year were writing, with the assistance of parodies contributed chiefly by Hilda and myself. It was called *Bolshevism in Baghdad*, and was based upon the performance by O.U.D.S., the previous term, of *Antony and Cleopatra*, with C. B. Ramage and Cathleen Nesbitt in the title-rôles. Having seen the two of them walking up and down the garden at Somerville, where Cathleen Nesbitt knew one of the dons, we had drawn conclusions not dissimilar from those arrived at by other junior members of the university, and in November of that year, when we were undergraduates no longer and were about to take our B.A. Degrees, I was able to write triumphantly to Winifred: 'What a swiz for all the people who swore that there was nothing in it between Ramage and Cathleen Nesbitt . . . If only it weren't the day we go to Oxford, I would go to the wedding.'

In June 1921, however, the rumours of an impending marriage were still being vigorously denied, and in the Going-Down play I had merely to act the part of the not-yet-attached heroine, Cleopatra O'Nesbitt, a romantic combination of the Queen of Egypt with our Irish History tutor, who as a young Oxford don was being sent to convert the Baghdad Bolsheviks to political sanity.

'Do you know if my old white satin frock is about anywhere?' I inquired anxiously of my mother. 'I have got to try and look like Cathleen Nesbitt as Cleopatra in the scene where she wore white and a feather sticking up on her head.'

Whenever we felt too tired even to manufacture the ribald

witticisms of the Going-Down play, we took it in turns to read Professor A. F. Pollard's ironic *History of England* or Lytton Strachey's newly published *Queen Victoria* aloud to each other, while the sun sank splendidly behind the willows. These two books still bring back to me the strange, half-waking dream of that summer term, in which I always felt so sleepy and yet could never sleep.

Some weeks afterwards my young tutor, once optimistic but now regretfully kind, remarked to me of my Schools papers: 'They represent, I take it, the best you can do when your energy and intellect are at their nadir. I feel sure that for some reason or other the edge of your mind was blunted' – and perhaps the excuse was as true as any that our compassionate friends make for us when we fail to come up to their expectations. Certainly, as my Finals approached, I began to feel more and more ill and apprehensive; the enormous cumulative tiredness of the past seven years seemed to gather itself up into a crushing weight which lay like a clod upon my brain. The week of the examination itself was a feverish torment, and two of the papers completely annihilated such flickering powers as I still possessed. One of the subjects, Early English History, had always bored me to the limit of impatience. Are Vinagradoff on *The Growth of the Manor* and J. H. Round on *Scutage* still the authorities for this remote and difficult period, I wonder, or has some incisive and lucid writer at last let in light on its tangled obscurity? The other subject, Political Science, I was supposed to have studied during the hectic term of my ludicrous little engagement; the 'γ+' – a very poor mark – that I received for it was the price of that unbalanced excursion into spurious romance.

Waiting with Winifred in the Examination Schools for our Viva Voce a month later, after recapitulating the papers in my head for nights on end and dwelling lugubriously upon tutorial expectations, I doubtless looked unduly pale and extinguished, for a benevolent fellow-student who had brought a flask insisted upon fortifying me with a large dose of brandy. I was not accustomed to spirits, and as my name, amongst the women, came first in alphabetical order, I went almost immediately before the examiners feeling very cheerful but completely intoxicated.

To the benevolent and helpful questions on the Political Science
Schools of the eighteenth and nineteenth centuries by means of
which one of them, Mr G. W. Wakeling, endeavoured to make
me redeem my deplorable paper, I replied with confident equanimity that I had never heard of any political scientist later than
Hobbes – although I had spent several afternoons with J.-J.
Rousseau, and had studied Treitschke and the *Testament Politique*
of Frederick the Great as part of my Special Subject. I saw the
faces of the examiners only as an agreeable blur, though I
remember the amused smile that spread over the large pale countenance of Professor C. K. Webster as I gave my ridiculous answers,
and the saturnine expression of the chairman, Professor H. W. C.
Davis, whose alleged conviction that women students were
second-rate simpletons who should never have been given Degrees
on the same terms as men must certainly have been confirmed
by my self-possessed idiocy. I often wondered afterwards if the
young university don who had admired my articles in the *Oxford
Outlook* would have maintained his respect for me and my writings had he listened in to that rag-time performance.

Immediately after the Viva, Winifred and I returned together
to Yorkshire, where her parents had taken a house after retiring
from their farm. There, a few days later, we learnt that we had
both got Seconds – a catastrophe for which I personally ought
to have been thankful, since a Third would more accurately have
represented the amount of history that I knew. I was never, I
think, even within jumping distance of the First of which
Somerville had hopefully believed me to be capable, but Winifred
came so near to that desirable goal that, under a different chairman
of examiners, and in any other but that crowded year in which
five hundred undergraduates took History and the usual number
of examiners was doubled, she would certainly have reached it.
As it was, she was viva-ed for a First for forty-five minutes; and
for days the ten examiners carried her papers about with them,
unable to make up their minds. After the Viva the anti-feminist
chairman gave his casting vote against her, and she still maintains
that she lost her First by a facetious remark about the domestic
idiosyncrasies of Henry VIII.

The day after the results came out, my name – the only one beginning with 'B' amongst the women – was accidentally omitted from the official list published by *The Times*, and my mother, who was staying with one of her sisters, had some perturbing speculations to go through before an exchange of telegrams cleared up the mistake. Too disgusted by my failure to get a First to send in a correction to *The Times*, I had the bitter amusement during the next few days of replying to several letters tactfully condoling with me on having 'ploughed'. The men and women tutors who had hoped that I might achieve the highest academic honours did not seriously believe that I had not even 'satisfied the examiners', but many of them, away on vacation, depended for their information upon *The Times*, and a good deal of agitated correspondence ensued before everyone interested realised that I was not the heroine of a dramatic *débâcle*.

'Miss P.,' I wrote to my mother, 'sent Miss F. post-haste down to the Schools to see what had happened to me. So I managed to be conspicuous by my absence, at any rate! . . . I specialised too much on European history and diplomacy to be able to be good all round,' I went on to explain, hoping to mitigate her disappointment. 'However, I am glad I did specialise as the European history interested me much more and it is what is going to be useful to me in the future and it is after all the future that counts. Firsts are sometimes dangerous because they make you rest on your oars and we shan't do that now at any rate . . . After all, one's general reputation and the opinion of half a dozen different people is a better guide than the production of one week's highly strung nerves! You'll see!'

But actually it was a bitter blow, and when I was not writing letters home, I didn't even pretend to be philosophical.

12

Fortunately for Winifred and myself, it did not take us many months to drift into the retrospective, amused detachment with which the average ex-student comes later to regard the results of Schools – so desperately tragic at the time, so completely forgotten within a year by everyone concerned. Our ambitions were not academic, and our Seconds released us from the temptation to make them so which was occasionally offered to us by well-intentioned dons.

Winifred, for a short time, suffered from a feeling of moral obligation to become a school-teacher which she had inherited from the example-setting traditions of her hostel-forewoman days in the W.A.A.C., but the project soon collapsed before the more congenial notion of sharing a tiny flat with me in London and trying to write, while my own intentions were too long established to be shaken by the most flattering tutorial encouragements to take up research. We succumbed to academic pressure only to the extent of contemplating, for a short time, a joint history-book dealing with the relations between Alexander I of Russia and Metternich, the Austrian Chancellor – a scheme much encouraged by Somerville, which we thankfully abandoned as soon as Professor C. K. Webster, to whom we had naïvely written for advice, reminded us, very gently and kindly, that this was his field and it would hardly be profitable for us to enter into competition.

Throughout the vacations from Easter, 1920, onwards, the two of us had corresponded regularly on literary projects, planned articles and short stories, and exchanged fragments of dialogue and descriptions intended for *Anderby Wold* and *The Dark Tide*. At that time Roland's father, who took a benevolent interest in the future of us both, helped us considerably with criticism and advice. During my two post-war years at college, he and his family had moved from Keymer and now occupied a small Noah's Ark of a house in St John's Wood, where the undaunted Clare succeeded in combining a good deal of domestic activity with studying at the Slade and teaching drawing and painting at a school in Southwark.

From time to time Winifred sent me short stories and articles to submit to Roland's father; humbly and resolutely she struggled with the style which the Dean of Hertford had criticised so adversely, until at last she made of it an instrument of simplicity and beauty seldom forged by those born with a natural facility of expression. One of the first stories that she wrote shocked Roland's father into a revised conception of the modern realistic young woman; it was called *The Amateur*, and described the adventures of a vicar's daughter who took to prostitution in the hope of making £50, but actually received only 2*s*. 6*d*.

'Why does one write beastly things?' she inquired of me with regard to this unvarnished story. 'I want to write happy, jolly songs and I write "The Dead Man". I want to write clean, spacious stories like *Anderby Wold*, and I've just finished *The Amateur*.'

In spite of his scandalised objection to the theme of Winifred's story, Roland's father conscientiously reported to me that 'she writes well, with pleasantly unexpected little turns of phrase . . . and her psychology is unusually good.' In my own case both he and Roland's mother seemed to fear the influence of university traditions and standards. 'He's terribly afraid,' I told Winifred, 'that I am going to forsake fiction for Academe. Why is it that all my university mentors want me to do research-work at the expense of fiction, and my literary mentors fiction at the expense of history? I wish I hadn't both tendencies; it makes things so complicated . . . He says I mustn't forget that fiction is always greater than scholarship because it is entirely creative, whereas scholarship is synthetic. On the other hand one has people like M. [our tutor] urging one on to the ideal of historical truth and the world's need of more and more enlightenment. How is one to reconcile the two ideals?'

But as the summer moved on from the Viva Voce into August, the problem appeared less a question of philosophical reconciliation than one of physical and psychological recuperation. Staying for a fortnight with Miss Heath Jones in Cornwall – where I read aloud to her a large selection of the works of Bernard Shaw, including the newly published *Back to Methuselah*, but otherwise had plenty of time for reminiscent meditation – I realised that the past two years at Oxford were going to take a good deal of getting over; they had meant an effort so great that I had not calculated its cost until it was finished. Not overwork, nor sleepless nights, nor undergraduate journalism, nor Degrees for women, nor domestic crises, nor getting engaged to the wrong person, nor even the prolonged battle with nervous delusions, accounted, in themselves, for that sense of stupendous fatigue; I only knew that at the time of the Armistice I had touched the bottom of a spiritual gulf, and that everything in me that mattered had had to climb out of it or die. Somehow or other I *had* climbed out of it, and at the age, already, of twenty-seven, having at last ceased to be either a 'nurse' or a 'student', I was now free – supposing I had sufficient energy left – to begin my career. But had I the energy? After a day's tortured and unsuccessful endeavour to plan to my own satisfaction a new chapter of *The Dark Tide* – the theme of which was, appropriately enough, the conquest of 'that despair which lies waiting to storm the defences of every human soul' – I wrote to Winifred expressing my doubts.

She replied at once, urging me not to give up the struggle at the last fence; she had been discussing, she said, examples of my work with her mother, who, regarding herself as 'the average reader', had always been one of her own keenest critics.

'Mother thinks you are going to write . . . Any suffering that you have borne, from the really big things down to a Second in Schools . . . is only the penalty to be paid . . . And you don't pay just in the way of compensation. You pay because you can't write until you've paid. Mother quoted Frances Ridley Havergal, who said to the child trying to write poetry:

> *'Tis not stringing rhymes together—*
> *With your heart's blood you must write it,*
> *Though your cheek grows pale, none knowing.*
> *So the song becomes worth singing.*

She said . . . you have already paid a high price, and in the end, in life as well as in business, we get our "money's worth". It may not lie in a transitory or even a lasting fame; but it will lie in a power that only suffering can give – a courage and understanding and inspiration, that is a greater gift to the world than anything – even greater than joy.'

Well, I supposed, Winifred might be right; perhaps 'experience', hampering as it seemed at present, would count for something in the end, even though its value to one's work didn't become apparent for years and years. At any rate, there was nothing left but to make the experiment. Feeling old and tired, as though my life were half done before it was well begun, I must now fight my way into the sceptical, indifferent world of London journalism.

But before this new battle began in earnest, there came a blessed interval of invigoration and peace.

13

At the beginning of September, Winifred and I found ourselves in Milan on the way to Venice. It was the first stage of a six weeks' holiday together which still remains in my mind as a treasured memory of warmth and beauty and perfect companionship, deepened and intensified by two days of poignant sorrow.

By the summer of 1921, the fund for going to Italy, which I had begun to save directly after the War, had swollen to satisfactory proportions. I had always meant to spend it, first of all, upon finding and climbing to the mountain-top where Edward was buried; afterwards, I thought, I would look at some of the lovely, vivid towns that he had occasionally mentioned in his letters, and on the way home I could stop at Amiens and visit that other grave in Louvencourt, beside which he had prayed for courage to acquit himself worthily of his friend in the coming battle on the Somme. I knew of no one with whom I would rather share this pilgrimage than Winifred, who had identified herself so closely in imagination with Edward and Roland that they almost seemed to be her dead as well as my own; and as her parents – more enlightened and reasonable than many high-brows for all their agricultural history – felt that six weeks abroad would renew her vitality after the strain and disappointment of our Final Schools, we set out together on the first of many journeys into post-war Europe.

We did not stay long in Milan, where we wanted only to see Leonardo da Vinci's 'Last Supper' on the refectory wall in the Convent of Santa Marie delle Gracie.

'If you really were as Leonardo saw you,' I thought, looking at the faded, tragic face of the Redeemer with its background of remote blue hills, 'You'd be able to tell me why Edward died on

the Asiago Plateau and yet I'm still left alive to look for his grave.'
But if any answer existed to this question, it was not to be found
even in the sad, pictured eyes which looked as though they had
seen so far into the depths of human grief and disappointment;
and the next day we pushed on to Venice.

My determination to find the Plateau had been keyed up to
ultimate decision by a curious coincidence that had happened just
before the Viva.

'What do you think?' I had written to Winifred on July 12th.
'Here, in this flat, we have the cross that's been standing on Edward's
grave in Italy for the last three years. When they wrote to us . . .
to ask permission to remove the wooden cross his battalion put
up to him, and put the regulation stone one, Mother said of course,
but as we couldn't bear the idea of the battalion's cross being
thrown on some Italian scrap-heap we asked that it should be sent
to us. Mother would like to have it put in a church some day . . .
or possibly in his old school chapel . . . It's such a queer feeling
to have it here, when it's been above him all that time . . . I am
sorry in a way that they have removed it, but . . . glad I shall see
the grave as it is to remain . . . It's a strange world – where the
symbols of people count so much because they're all one has left.'

The ultimate destination of the cross was the chapel of Mark
XIV., a Toc H hostel in Manchester, where a Lancashire relative
interested in the movement asked our permission to have it
erected. But when it came, wrapped up in canvas, to Kensington,
it seemed like a message urging me to go at once to Edward's
grave, and the very fact that work had recently been in progress
in the Italian cemeteries suggested that those distant battlefields
would not, perhaps, be so difficult to locate as I had supposed.
So, full of confidence, I went with Winifred to the offices of
Thomas Cook & Son in Venice, believing that they would have
arranged similar expeditions and be quite familiar with the route
to Asiago. To our dismay, they told us that no such request had
ever been made to them; they had never heard of the little cemetery called Granezza in the pine-woods, and their vagueness with
regard to the exact position of the Plateau seemed almost to equal
our own.

We had only planned to spend four days in Venice; there was no time to get into touch with the Imperial Graves Commission or with ex-officers from the Sherwood Foresters, so we had perforce to accept Cooks' suggestion that they should wire for information to the proprietor of a small touring club hotel in the village of Bassano, on the edge of the mountains. The proprietor telegraphed back that he knew the way to the battlefields and could supply a car. With only this guarantee, we set off for the day to Bassano upon one of the strangest, saddest and most memorable of all my adventures.

Sitting side by side in a gondola at five o'clock in the morning, we glided smoothly to the station over the rippling grey silk of the Grand Canal. With melancholy possessiveness I looked upon those enchanted waters, those carven palaces, those fairy lagoons, incredible as a gorgeous mirage in the muffled silence. Edward had died in saving this beauty from the fate of Ypres, yet its luscious magnificence seemed very far removed from the austere integrity of himself and his violin. But remembering the descriptions in his letters, I thought perhaps I should find that in the mountains.

At Bassano the proprietor of the small hotel – entitled, somewhat excessively, Hotel Mondo – welcomed us with sympathetic enthusiasm, and offered to show us the position of the battlefields while his cook prepared an early luncheon. From the village we looked across the sweeping Brenta Valley, with its dark cypresses, its sun-drenched, shuttered houses and its sulphur-hued spires, to Monte Grappa and the Asiago Plateau, that huge grey shadow of a mountain with its abruptly flattened summit, as though, after the Creation, some Titan had taken a gigantic sword and sliced off the top. The characteristic silhouette of that truncated peak still has a shattering effect upon me after all these years. Only the other day I discovered that the husband of a novelist friend at whose house I was dining had been for a time *liaison* officer with the French on the Italian front; at my request he showed me some of his war maps and pictures, and when he turned up a photograph depicting the familiar outline, I found myself as near tears as I was when I first saw the Plateau twelve years ago.

By the time that we had finished our luncheon the car was

ready. We looked, no doubt, younger than we felt, for the hotel proprietor – one of the most truly courteous gentlemen that I have ever met in any country – decided that he couldn't allow two such youthful Englishwomen to go off alone into the mountains with an unknown and rather fierce-looking chauffeur (though it had never occurred to either of us to feel any anxiety on that account). Moreover, he explained, in the erratic mixture of Italian and broken French of which our mutual conversation was composed, the roads were steep and rather frightening, perhaps, to strangers; just to show that there wasn't any real danger, might he bring his little son as well? The *bambino* would enjoy the ride, and there was plenty of room in the car.

So we started together for the Plateau with the red-moustachioed chauffeur in the powerful Fiat – Winifred and myself, the kindly, plump hotel-keeper, and the brown six-year-old child, who resembled a tiny, dark-eyed Jesus wearing a beret. Villages that grew thinner as the ascent became steeper clustered at intervals round the first few miles of the route; at length the sheer mountain-side towered above the car, and my heart jumped at every hair-pin bend of the unwalled road. At each corner we seemed about to drive straight over the edge into the deepening precipice; thousands of feet below us, Venetia and the Brenta Valley lay unrolled like a map, with the river – a streak of silver in a blue-green mist – flowing in a great curve towards Venice.

After a climb that seemed to have lasted for hours, the road became more level. Villages and vineyards had long disappeared; the air was cold, and the narrow track began to wind between granite rocks and pine-forests that seemed to stretch to infinity, very dark and strangely sombre in contrast to the sunny, fertile plain below. We saw no heather and very few flowers; the whole world was green and grey, and still as a lost country fathoms deep below the waters of the sea. Suddenly, in the midst of the forest, we came upon the rusty ruins of tin cans and barbed-wire entanglements, stretched across the fallen entrances of dug-outs and the half-obliterated remains of shallow trenches. We were now driving, said the chauffeur, through the old Austrian lines, to which the enemy had advanced after the victory at Caporetto in 1917.

It was not at all the kind of 'devastated area' so characteristic of Flanders and France; the shells had merely deepened the curves of the hillsides, splitting the rocks into sharp stones and adding a few more scars to those already made by time and weather. Once they had evidently torn screaming through the pine-woods, as the thin broken tree-trunks piled in hundreds beside the road bore witness, but the pines could still have been counted only by that omniscient Mathematician who alone can number the hairs of a man's head. Now and again a rough tangle of barbed wire climbed like an alien plant over the rocks, or the gleaming surface of a mountain tarn disguised the rude disfigurement of a shell-hole, or a trail of Austrian trenches wound serpent-wise across a distant hill. But those incongruous traces of strife seemed only to emphasise the silent scorn of the Plateau for war's feverish folly; they did not detract from the grim, imperturbable grandeur which guns could not annihilate nor the tramp of armies deface.

As we crossed the former No Man's Land and reached the old British lines, the pine-woods became darker and thicker, and the ground more like that of a battlefield; could this, I wondered, with thumping heart, be the scene of Edward's final hour on June 15th? The road, torn with shell-holes, presented a baffling problem to the car, and we lurched dizzily from side to side as we sought vainly for Granezza. None of the scattered gangs of workmen still gathering together the broken pine-trunks seemed to know where it was, and we stopped first at a tiny cemetery which we afterwards learnt was called Balfaconte. In it a number of missing found during the clearing of the battlefields must have been buried, for it seemed to be half full of stones inscribed: 'Here lies a British soldier – known unto God.'

At last, in the depths of the forest, past a rough track marked 'To Asiago', we came upon Granezza; not even a village shared the name with the cemetery, which seemed to be near no human habitation except a mountain inn about a mile away. The little graveyard, half hidden by rocks, stood high above the road at the foot of a green hill covered with pines; so much did its white stones seem a part of the grey and white Plateau that at twilight it would have been indistinguishable. Going through the small gate fastened with a leathern thong, I found only sixty graves enclosed within a white wall; through the middle of them a straight green path ran to the foot of a cenotaph surmounted by a cross. In front of each stone a miniature fern was growing; only wild flowers, hardy and sparse, pushed themselves through the barren ground, but the cemetery looked well kept and the grass path was mown. The afternoon sun, dipping westward above the low hills opposite, shone direct upon the graves; had they faced east they would have looked straight into the pine-wood and never had the sun upon their carved inscriptions.

'How strange, how strange it is,' I reflected, as I looked, with an indefinable pain stabbing my chest, for Edward's name among those neat rows of oblong stones, 'that all my past years – the childhood of which I have no one, now, to share the remembrance, the bright fields at Uppingham, the restless months in Buxton, the hopes and ambitions of Oxford, the losses and long-drawn agonies of the War – should be buried in this grave on the top of a mountain, in the lofty silence, the singing unearthly stillness, of these remote forests! At every turn of every future road I shall want to ask him questions, to recall to him memories, and he will not be there. Who could have dreamed that the little boy born in such uneventful security to an ordinary provincial family would end his brief days in a battle among the high pine-woods of an unknown Italian plateau?'

Close to the wall, in the midst of a group of privates from the Sherwood Foresters who had all died on June 15th, I found his name: 'Captain E. H. Brittain, M.C., 11th Notts. and Derby Regt. Killed in action June 15th, 1918. Aged 22.' In Venice I had bought some rosebuds and a small asparagus fern in a pot; the shopkeeper had told me that it would last a long time, and I planted it in the rough grass beside the grave.

'How trivial my life has been since the War!' I thought, as I smoothed the earth over the fern. 'How mean they are, these little strivings, these petty ambitions of us who are left, now that all of you are gone! How can the future achieve, through us, the sombre majesty of the past? Oh, Edward, you're so lonely up here; why can't I stay for ever and keep your grave company, far from the world and its vain endeavours to rebuild civilisation, on this Plateau where alone there is dignity and peace?'

But when at last I came from the cemetery, the child, who had been playing with his father near the car, ran up to me holding out a bunch of scabious and white clover that he had picked by the roadside.

'For the little signorina,' he said.

14

Four days later, *en route* for Florence, a pandemonium at Bologna, where we had to change, demonstrated to us the rapidity with which, in Latin countries, the sublime is apt to descend into the ridiculous.

Nobody seemed to know why the station was so crowded and everybody so excited, but foreigners had the worst of it in that struggling uproar, and we should have had little chance to escape from one train and find the other, had not an agreeable young Italian helped us to transfer our luggage. Having completed his service to us he noticed an elderly American lady staggering up the platform with an enormous hat-box; standing before her he bowed, took off his hat, and, knowing no English, gently laid his hand upon the strap.

The lady, no doubt well-primed by warnings from Middle Western neighbours, turned furiously upon the would-be cavalier.

'If you try to take my things I'll knock you down!' she exclaimed.

The Italian, nonplussed, turned to us with hands outspread, and we shook with helpless laughter as we took the places that he had found for us. Our neighbours in the carriage – also, I regret to say, Americans, but the pure accident of their not being English was probably designed by Providence to preserve our self-respect – conceived an immediate antipathy to us, for there had been a rush for seats and they objected to our occupation of the corners pre-empted by our rescuer. But they detested the Italian railway officials even more.

'Animals!' chattered one of the elderly ladies to her crushed-looking companion-secretary. 'Nothing but animals! No order on the station! No porters, no station-master, nobody who could even speak English!'

No doubt, I remarked *sotto voce* to Winifred, she would have been equally scandalised had a Florentine countess arrived at one of her own junction towns – Buffalo or Columbus or Kansas City – and complained bitterly that no one spoke Italian!

We liked Florence so much that we stayed in that incomparable city in our *pension* beside the Arno for ten divine days.

'Venice is all sea and sculpture,' I wrote to my mother, 'and this is mountains and fir-trees and white houses with red roofs . . . Somehow Venice is like a great mausoleum; there is plenty of life in it but the life is not the life of Venice, which one feels to have died ages ago. Whereas in this place the spirit of the Renaissance seems to have lived on; it is more of a personality and less of a museum.'

So we walked around the town and did not spend much time in the picture-galleries; I never had expected to find any spiritual affinity with the placid Rafael Madonnas in the Uffizi, but I fell in love, in the Pitti, with the little Murillo Madonna holding the brown curly-haired Baby with the big dark eyes. Seven years afterwards Miss Heath Jones sent me a post-card of this picture, for she thought that my son, then a few months old, was the image of Murillo's painted Child. But in September 1921 the surface of my mind was not at all concerned with the possibility of future sons, or husbands; it was pleasantly preoccupied with the preparations for the Dante Festival.

This celebration of the sexcentenary of the poet's death transformed the city into a mediæval bazaar, although on the day that we saw the King of Italy, grandiosely attended by General Diaz and Baron Sonnino, being officially received by the Signoria at the Palazzo Vecchio, a note of incongruous modernity was introduced by an aeroplane which dropped coloured leaflets on our heads. It had disappeared, however, by the next day, when we watched the Dante pageant from the upper window of a flower shop near the Piazza del Duomo, and found ourselves able, by half-closing our eyes, to imagine that we were witnessing the Florentine Army – with Dante marching in it as a young officer – returning in 1269 from the Battle of Campaldino after its victory over the Imperial troops. Had the Austrians at Caporetto, I wondered – having learnt now that seven hundred years was not too long for the working out of time's inscrutable purposes – been inspired by a subconscious impulse to avenge that defeat? Had Edward's death lain so long ago in the logic of history?

Meditating thus, I found myself able to speak to Winifred of Asiago and my sudden desire to remain there, secluded from the tumultuous pettiness of these post-war days—

> *. . . the multitude below*
> *Live, for they can, there:*
>
> .   .   .   .
>
> *Here – here's his place, where meteors shoot, clouds form,*
> *Lightnings are loosed,*
> *Stars come and go! . . .*

But Winifred told me that the voice of the pine-trees had seemed to her to hold a promise of tranquillity and peace even among 'the multitude below'; they reminded her more, she said, of some lines by Walter de la Mare:

> *Not a wave breaks,*
> *Not a bird calls,*
> *My heart, like a sea,*
> *Silent after a storm that hath died,*
> *Sleeps within me.*
>
> *All the night's dews,*
> *All the world's leaves,*
> *All winter's snow*
> *Seem with their quiet to have stilled in life's dream*
> *All sorrowing now.*

A day or two later we left Florence for the hill towns. Strangely enough, my first contact with the swiftly gathering momentum of Fascism occurred in the drowsy semi-darkness of an evening motor-'bus between Florence and Siena. In the course of that four-hour journey over the Apennines we got into conversation – in bad French on both sides – with our next-door neighbour, a student from the University of Florence. He was very young, and resembled, with his cherubic and transparently innocent countenance, an Italian version of Beverley Nichols; his name, he told us, was Oswaldo Giacomo. Hailing us enthusiastically as fellow-students, he talked to us earnestly about 'Fascismo', a word then unknown to us and rather puzzling. His political diatribes were enlivened at intervals by outbursts of protesting cackles from the hens in the basket of an old peasant woman on the opposite side of the 'bus; disregarding these irreverent interruptions, he spoke excitedly of a coming revolution, in which we felt too lazy to believe. There certainly weren't many signs of it at present, we thought; nobody in Italy appeared to want a change of circumstance, and none of the trains started on time.

The next day, at Siena, we returned from exploring the black and white cathedral and counting the familiar names of the Popes whose sculptured heads looked down over the arches like faces gazing from a balcony, to find Oswaldo, who was staying with an uncle in an adjacent village, waiting for us at our *pension*. He insisted upon taking us that afternoon to the top of the tower of the Palazzo Communale – which swayed alarmingly in a howling wind that nearly blew me off altogether when the huge clock just over our heads suddenly struck two and I jumped about three feet into the air – and afterwards gave us ices at a café. Over these ices, constituting himself the protector of our maidenhood, he warned us with all the solemnity of his eighteen years against making chance acquaintances.

'Signorine,' he began, 'the soul of the Italian is as clear as crystal!' – but the designs of this noble-minded national upon unprotected young females were not, apparently, always so innocuous. In spite of this moral homily, Oswaldo himself did not appear in the least interested in our sex; no doubt, like a good little Black Shirt, he was merely fulfilling instructions to 'put over' Fascist propaganda to foreigners at every possible opportunity. After we had gone to Perugia, where a stormy autumn gale blew down from the heights across the wide Umbrian plain to Assisi nestling beneath the gaunt curve of Monte Subasio, he sent us a picture post-card of Dante meeting Beatrice; with discreet impartiality it was addressed to us both.

At Assisi we found a Festival of St Francis in progress and the ground floor of our hotel was crowded with 'pilgrims', amongst whom the proprietor gesticulated in helpless frenzy. About them hovered an affluvia which lingered on to remind visitors of their insistent presence even when they had departed. In a walk across the hills to the Carceri, a small monastery in the ilex-grove where St Francis used to pray, we temporarily forgot them, but they reappeared on the long journey to Rome, crowding us into the third-class corridor with their bundles and their baskets and the crumby exuberance of their garlic-scented repasts. Rome seemed a very different city from the tense, austere capital of 1917; so completely was my week there eclipsed by the subsequent days in Paris and the melancholy journey from Amiens through the battlefields, that I remember now only the red, sweet-scented roses blooming against the grey ruins of the Forum, and the tall pomposity of Trajan's Column, the enclosure of which, judging from the number of its vociferous occupants, had apparently become a maternity home for cats.

At Amiens, with a sense of having strayed into the heart of an old, tragic legend, we stood in the dimness of the once threatened Cathedral; everything had deliberately been left, we were told, as it was just after the 1918 offensive, and we looked up with reminiscent melancholy at the still-boarded stained-glass windows smashed by German shells. How long will this bitter hatred continue? I wondered, thinking what æons ago seemed the Retreat in which that damage was done, and realising with sudden surprise that in my own mind the anger and resentment had died long ago, leaving only an everlasting sorrow, and a passionate pity which I did not yet know quite how to use or to express. But then, I reflected, I have only a personal and not an historical memory; the Germans didn't really mean to kill Roland or Victor or Geoffrey, but they did intend to hold on to Alsace-Lorraine.

To-day, tours of the battlefields in France are arranged by numerous agencies; graves are visited in parties, and a regular trade has been established in wreaths and photographs and cemeteries. But that level of civilisation had not been reached in 1921, so Winifred and I hired a car in Amiens, and plunged through a series of shell-racked roads between the grotesque trunks of skeleton trees, with their stripped, shattered branches still pointing to heaven in grim protest against man's ruthless cruelty to nature as well as man. Along the road, at intervals, white placards were erected in front of tumbledown groups of roofless, windowless houses; were these really the places that we had mentioned with gasping breath at Étaples three and a half years ago? I asked myself incredulously, as with chill excitement I read their names: BAPAUME – CLÉRY – VILLERS-BRÉTONNEUX – PÉRONNE – GRIVESNES – HÉDAUVILLE. At Albert a circumspect row of Army huts, occupied by reconstruction workers, stood side by side with the humped ruin which had once been the ornate Basilica, crowned by its golden Virgin holding her Child aloft from the steeple. Was this, I wondered, apart from the huts, the place as Edward had known it?

But the day's real purpose was my visit to Louvencourt – as the words of the dead American poet, Alan Seeger, restlessly hammering in my head against the grinding of the car's sorely tried gears, had reminded me at intervals all afternoon:

> *I have a rendezvous with Death*
> *On some scarred slope of battered hill . . .*

As the car drove through the village to the cemetery, I realised with a shock, from its resemblance to a photograph in my possession, that the grey château half hidden by tall, drooping trees had once been the Casualty Clearing Station where Roland had drifted forlornly and unconsciously into death. We found the cemetery, as Edward had described it, on the top of a hill where two roads joined; the afternoon was bright and sunny, and just beyond the encircling wall a thin row of elms made a delicate pattern against the tranquil sky. The graves, each with its little garden in front, resembled a number of flower-beds planted at intervals in the smooth, wide lawn, which lay so placidly beneath the long shadow of the slender memorial cross. As I walked up the paved path where Edward had stood in April 1916, and looked at the trim, ordered burial-ground and the open, urbane country, I thought how different it all was from the grey twilight of the Asiago Plateau, with its deep, sinister silence. The strange irony which had determined the fates of Roland and Edward seemed to persist even after death: the impetuous warrior slept calmly in this peaceful, complacent earth with its suave covering of velvet lawn; the serene musician lay on the dark summit of a grim, far-off mountain.

I left Louvencourt, as I thought, unperturbed; I had read the inscription on Roland's grave and gathered a bronze marigold to keep in my diary without any conscious feeling of emotion. Whatever, I decided, might be true of 1918, I was beginning to forget the early years of the War and to recover from the anguish of its second Christmas.

But late that night, back in the Paris hotel, I picked a quarrel with Winifred over some futile trifle, and went to bed in a fury of tears.

CHAPTER XI

Piping for Peace

THE SUPERFLUOUS WOMAN

Ghosts crying down the vistas of the years,
Recalling words
Whose echoes long have died,
And kind moss grown
Over the sharp and blood-bespattered stones
Which cut our feet upon the ancient ways.
  ★   ★   ★   ★   ★   ★   ★   ★
But who will look for my coming?

Long busy days where many meet and part;
Crowded aside
Remembered hours of hope;
And city streets
Grown dark and hot with eager multitudes
Hurrying homeward whither respite waits.
  ★   ★   ★   ★   ★   ★   ★   ★
But who will seek me at nightfall?

Light fading where the chimneys cut the sky;
Footsteps that pass,
Nor tarry at my door.
And far away,
Behind the row of crosses, shadows black
Stretch out long arms before the smouldering sun.
  ★   ★   ★   ★   ★   ★   ★   ★
But who will give me my children?

V. B.
July, 1920.

1

Soon after we returned from Italy I became ill with jaundice, which kept me in bed for nearly three weeks. It was probably due, said my doctor, to a revival of the mysterious Malta germ which had remained latent since my leave in 1918, and might never completely vanish. But though this particular disease involves a good deal of discomfort and is supposed to be accompanied by colossal depression, I lay in bed after the first few days in saffronhued contentment, happily drafting the middle chapters of *The Dark Tide*, which was then often referred to by Winifred and myself as 'Daphne', the name of the character who shared the rôle of heroine with another called 'Virginia Dennison'. Italy, with its new scenes and experiences, had made all the difference; in spite of Asiago, in spite of Louvencourt, those weeks abroad had somehow healed the acutest soreness of the War's deep hurt. After them, apart from occasional dreams, I had no more hallucinations nor night terrors nor insomnia, and by the time that I joined Winifred at the end of the year in the Bloomsbury studio which we had taken as the result of our determination to live independently together, I was nearly a normal person.

From the moment that the War ended I had always known, and my parents had always tolerantly taken for granted, that after three years at Oxford and four of wartime adventure, my return to a position of subservient dependence at home would be tolerable neither for them nor for me. They understood now that freedom, however uncomfortable, and self-support, however hard to achieve, were the only conditions in which a feminist of the War generation — and, indeed, a post-Victorian woman of any generation — could do her work and maintain self-respect. After the Armistice my father, with characteristic generosity, had made over to me a few of his shares in the family business, in order that I might pay my own college bills and be spared the ignominy of asking him for every sixpence after so long a period of financial self-sufficiency.

Although I could not live upon this tiny income and a growing

accumulation of rejection-slips, it enabled me to give more attention to writing and politics than would otherwise have been
possible, and less to the part-time lecturing and teaching which
Winifred and I had alike decided were the most accessible and
least exacting methods of earning our living until journalism could
be made to pay.

As both our families expressed a desire for a few weeks of our
company before we finally left them for good, we postponed our
joint migration to the end of 1921, and spent the interval after
our return from Italy in planning future work and acquiring
enough small 'money-making' jobs to occupy about three days a
week. Almost daily I wrote long letters to Winifred, coloured by
that curious mixture of maturity and childishness which was so
long characteristic of our dislocated generation; they palpitated
with schemes for writing and lecturing and travelling, and for the
dissemination of those internationalist ideas the teaching of which,
I still felt, alone justified my survival of the War. In this ingenuous eagerness for every kind of new experiment and reform I
resembled many other contemporaries who were at last recovering from the numbing shocks of the wartime years; our hopefulness was due to a belief that the War was really over, and to a
failure as yet to understand completely how deep-rooted and far-
reaching its ultimate consequences must be.

The prospects of interesting and suitable work seemed unexpectedly promising; I had already been offered some part-time
teaching at a school in South Kensington, my aunt had invited
me to give a course of six lectures on 'International Relations' at
St Monica's, and two pupils presented themselves to be coached
for Oxford examinations while I was still at home. The elder of
these, a nervous and propitiatory graduate from the University of
Wales, lived in Anerley, completely lacked the most elementary
rudiments of a literary style, and had incongruous aspirations after
Lady Margaret Hall which, greatly to my own surprise, I actually
helped her to fulfil.

'I do wish her appearance didn't depress me so,' I confessed
to Winifred. 'I have only seen the blue velours hat and long
tweed coat twice, but am tired of them already. I have the

feeling, too, that I shall never see anything else. Next time I will invite her to take the coat off – that will at least make a change . . . I am so glad I used to put on my best clothes for . . . Mr C . . . What a difference it makes to have something nice to look at!'

After speaking often at college debates and hearing a number of Oxford dons lecture in that inimitable fashion which scorns the base vulgarity of mere technical competence, the prospect of becoming a lecturer who could give a tolerable discourse from a platform no longer seemed so wildly unattainable as it had appeared in 1913. Not only, before going to Italy, did I boldly accept the St Monica's invitation, but I wrote still more daringly to the newly established headquarters of the League of Nations Union in Grosvenor Crescent and offered myself as a speaker on the League of Nations, that international experiment in the maintenance of peace and security which I felt, in common with many other students of modern history, to be the one element of hope and progress contained in the peace treaties. In reply I was asked to come to Grosvenor Crescent and be inspected by the secretary. The interview was arranged for me by Elizabeth Murray, my dazzling Somerville predecessor, now haughtily beautiful with her exquisite, adventurous clothes, her imperious figure and her short, waving dark hair.

When I first saw the secretary, I felt that his handsome, melancholy face and reticent, dreaming eyes would have been more appropriate to a stained-glass window than to that rather turbulent office of emphatic young men and women, who waged a gallant, perpetual battle against shortage of funds, the lethargy of the public, and the well-meaning inefficiency of untrained volunteers. But his gentle courtesy was almost immediately over-shadowed by the startling presence of an anonymous, impressive individual in morning coat, spats, and monocle, who suddenly burst through an adjacent glass door into the middle of my interview, and without ceremony inquired of me in a sceptical drawl: 'What makes you think you can speak?'

I never learnt this intruder's name, nor do I recall what explanation I gave for the incongruous juxtaposition of mature claims and an immature appearance, but I left the secretary's office with a suitcase full of informative literature, and the encouraging impression that I should be invited to take meetings for the Union in the winter if he was satisfied with the specimen lecture that he had asked me to prepare.

Upon this lecture and the series for St Monica's I spent many hours that autumn, spurred to gigantic efforts by the deliberations of the Washington Conference and the unexpected success of the League in settling the dispute between Serbia and Albania. I felt my responsibility very keenly; already, I thought, I had begun to take part in that campaign for enlightenment which must inevitably lead a bewildered, suffering world into the serene paths of rational understanding.

'You would have been amused,' I told Winifred, who was herself preparing a course of lectures on 'Personalities of Pre-Renaissance Italy' to succeed my own series at St Monica's, 'if you could have seen me last night, dressed up in a hat and a fur, declaiming in front of the looking-glass! I am going to do it every day once, till I know the thing by heart and stop feeling a fool . . . I'm so glad I did "International Relations", glad I am lecturing on them now, though in ever such a small way, glad to do anything, however small, to make people care for the peace of the world. It may be Utopian, but it's constructive. It's better than railing at the present state of Europe, or always weeping in darkness for the dead.'

The half-realised onset of jaundice spoilt my first St Monica's lecture, making me oppressively aware how trivial this event, so momentous to me, had appeared to everyone else. 'How good it is for us,' I recorded disconsolately, 'to be mere business units . . . people whose colossal edifice of life means nothing more than an interrupted half-hour of preparation.' But during my convalescence the reading of a newly published selection of internationalist essays, entitled 'The Evolution of World Peace', restored to me that sense of the cause's momentous dignity which for the next few years was to drive me in pursuit of small, reluctant audiences conscientiously shivering in draughty town halls, in dusty clubs, in dimly lighted schoolrooms, or beneath the gaunt roofs of whitewashed Wesleyan chapels which continually eluded my frantic search for them through the wintry darkness of unknown streets. Joyously recognising, clearly and convincingly expressed, the motive which had set me reading History at Oxford, I copied from Mr F. S. Marvin's editorial Introduction to the essays a paragraph which embodied, and still embodies, the inspiration of hopeful humanity's quest after international harmony, although the eager confidence which illumined the minds of reason's postwar exponents was so soon to fade into the dun stoicism of baffled yet persistent endeavour:

'If we desire peace and co-operation in the world, and can find in history clear indications that co-operation is a growing quantity, then our desires become a reasonable ideal, we are fighting to enlighten mankind as to their true destiny and to hasten its realisation . . . It is the broad view and the long vision which alone can cure our fearfulness and fortify our steps . . . A longer vista lies before us than even anthropology can offer of the past. "*Magis me movet illud longum tempus quum non ero, quam hoc exiguum.*"'

2

As soon as I had recovered sufficiently to go out again, I sent, with much trepidation, my specimen lecture to the League of Nations Union. It was long, persevering and dogmatic, and my inexperienced rehearsals before the looking-glass had failed to indicate to me the quite important fact that as it stood it would have taken at least three hours to deliver, and was indigestibly packed with enough information to keep a class of graduates busy for twelve or more study circles. My kindest friend could hardly have called it an attractive piece of popular propaganda, but the patient secretary signified his approval, and day after day I nervously anticipated a summons from the Union to address a large, critical and terrifying audience in some unfamiliar and remote part of England.

But even in those days that cautious organisation never yielded to the temptation of impetuous action, and it proceeded to forget my existence until the early spring of 1922. My first invitation, therefore, to address an adult audience came not from Grosvenor Crescent, but from a clerical friend of Miss Heath Jones, who wanted to experiment with one or two lectures in his large, poor parish midway between London and Windsor, and had asked her to recommend a speaker. Could I, he inquired, give them addresses on the Russian Revolution and the League of Nations – the former to be as impartial as possible owing to the strength of Socialist influence in the parish?

I didn't know whether I could, but I said that I would, and plunged into a series of anxious days spent in reading up Bolshevism in the British Museum. To my dismay I discovered that this task was by no means as straightforward as it sounded, for in 1921 the entire resources of the Museum Library seemed unable to yield one document which gave an unbiased account of developments in Russia since 1917.

'The Russian Revolution is almost driving me mad,' I complained gloomily to Winifred. 'Each book one picks up flatly contradicts the last. No one writes about it sanely – in one the Bolsheviks can do no right and in the others no wrong . . . I look wildly for facts and I can only find arguments . . . Some of the works on communal kitchens and nationalisation of women have none of the qualities of historians unless you count fury to be one.'

With my letter I enclosed a list of inquiries about elementary facts to which, after looking through all the available material, I had failed to discover satisfactory replies:

(1) What are the main events of the Revolution, with approximate dates, from 1917 till to-day?

(2) When did the Allied blockade begin and who led it?

(3) Has it ended yet, and if so when did it, and why?

(4) What parts of Russia are Red and what parts are White?

(5) What has been happening in Russia this year?

(6) What is happening at the moment?

These innocent questions led to a furious correspondence between London and Yorkshire which raged for several days on the subject of Bolshevism. At that time Winifred was strongly anti-Bolshevik, for a very close friend of hers, a young Russian who had been left parentless when still a schoolboy and brought up by her family as an adopted son, had been captured by brigands and presumably murdered in Georgia in 1919 while serving as an interpreter to one of the British contingents attached to Deniken's army. To the numerous details that she sent, in reply to my letter, about the long tale of famine and typhus which was then as much a part of Russian history as its political reorganisation, she added a series of fierce arguments against the growing sympathy with Bolshevism which my reading had unexpectedly given me, until I was moved to protest that 'if I gave a Socialistic parish a violently anti-Bolshevik lecture I should do as much harm as I should with an equally violent lecture in favour of Bolshevism . . . They are the only body in Russia to-day with any common ideas, any constructive policy, any power of organisation . . . In your notes you keep on saying that so-and-so is "in German pay". It sounds very damning but that's not the point . . . Germany did not make the Revolution, she only took advantage with her usual skill (which we call "diabolical" because it is hers, but which we should call "incomparable" if it was our own) of a situation which had already arisen.

'You will be bored stiff with me and my Russian Revolution,' I concluded with some reason, 'but I feel rather oppressively the responsibility of an educated person who has to lecture to and probably influence considerably a whole crowd of the ignorant . . . It will be a desperate matter if the Socialists throw eggs at my new black gabardine and satin frock.'

With my long-established reverence for lectures and their givers, I was still far from realising how many speeches have to be made on any subject before a normal English audience remembers a week later even what it was, let alone anything that has been said about it. Needless to say, my carefully prepared lecture – which I read, word for word, with laborious conscientiousness for fear that I should forget to maintain my determined impartiality – made not a stir upon the lethargic surface of Y—— parish; its chief effect was that of clearing my own brain on an acute political topic. 'It would have been as useful to lecture on a turnip at Y——,' I remarked ruefully to Winifred, but my disappointment was over-shadowed by the B.A. Degrees which had been conferred upon us both in the academic splendour of the Sheldonian Theatre four days earlier, and by the London bazaar in aid of Somerville finances two days later, at which we both assisted with jubilant eagerness at a bookstall presided over by Rose Macaulay.

In January 1921, the Oxford women's colleges had begun their three years' special appeal for financial aid. Poorly endowed, and frequented chiefly by students who were obliged to earn their living and had no money to give, the women's colleges, as I had realised with such dismay in 1914, had none of the resources which made Oxford a comparatively luxurious university for men. After the War, the economic outlook seemed darker than ever, and the funds of Somerville especially were depleted by the return to a building in which everything had deteriorated. The War Office 'compensation' by no means compensated in full for the numerous structural alterations that had to be made, and sufficient spare cash was not even available for the cleaning and repairing of the numerous college clocks which had remained untouched during the War.

Reluctantly Somerville was obliged to descend to appeals and bazaars, and immediately after our return from Italy, a letter asking me to help Miss Macaulay to sell books offered that prospect of a temporary acquaintanceship with a really famous writer which had hitherto seemed utterly unattainable by a struggling journalist whose persistent onslaughts on London newspapers remained lamentably fruitless. Enthusiastically I attended one or two of the bazaar committees at the University Women's Club; 'the meeting lasted 1½ hours,' I related to the envious Winifred, whose co-operation had not then been invited; 'I promised desperately to try and collect books; it's a great bore, but I think that to run the bookstall with Rose Macaulay is worth the price.'

The collection of books had perforce to continue during the period of jaundice, and *The Dark Tide* was frequently abandoned for the bedside opening of colossal parcels, and the half-excited, half-apprehensive reading of novels and articles by my eminent stallholder.

'I *must* send you this review by Rose Macaulay out of *Time and Tide*,' ran one perturbed letter to Yorkshire, written when the bazaar's near approach had rendered me even more conscious than usual of my literary shortcomings. 'Let us, oh! let us both remain for ever silent if we are going to deserve such a review. Let us at least not deserve it, even if we get it. I have just finished *Dangerous Ages*. It is not a story but one of the most brilliant and cruel satires I have ever read . . . Winifred, I am terrified of that woman – terrified of meeting her on the 7th of Dec. . . . I feel tempted to scrap "Daphne"; it's as bad to add to the stacks of literary sloppiness as to add to the number of potential unemployed.'

In the end the bazaar proved much less alarming than I had feared, and, painstakingly and elaborately dressed in brown marocain and a brown velvet picture hat with a flame-coloured 'glycerine' feather trailing over the edge, I stood entranced and watched Rose Macaulay, far more appropriately clad in a neat blue coat-frock, casually conversing with the half-legendary gods of literary London. John Buchan was there, brisk and unpretentious, and the bluff and cordial Hugh Walpole, over whose new novel, *The Cathedral*, I was to laugh and weep so rapturously in the next few months. It was too wonderful, too incredible, actually to stand within speaking distance of these Olympian presences. But best of all, perhaps, was the quiet, fatigued moment in which, as we were clearing up the stall, Miss Macaulay asked me what I meant to do with myself now that I'd gone down from Oxford, and I answered, breathlessly daring, that I was trying to be a writer and was half-way through an Oxford novel entitled *The Dark Tide*.

3

By the end of the year, after three months in Kensington, I had had more than enough of being the unmarried daughter at home. It was not, certainly, as exasperating an experience as it would have been in Buxton, where my mother's acquaintances would

have expressed an endless patronising solicitude for my failure
to achieve marriage ten years after 'coming out', combined with
charitable references to the fortunate compensation of my literary
interests. But I was clearly enough aware that parents brought
up in the nineteenth-century tradition would have preferred,
not unnaturally, a happily married daughter producing grand-
children to a none-too-triumphant Oxford graduate floundering
unsuccessfully in that slough of despond which lies just inside
the gateway of every path to the literary life. So I welcomed
the late December day when I could remove my disappointing
spinsterhood, together with my typewriter and rejected manuscripts, to the penurious but unhumiliating independence of
Bloomsbury.

The Doughty Street studio, chosen for its nearness to the British
Museum at a time when we still expected to put in months of
research on Metternich and Alexander, consisted of one large high
room lighted only by windows in the roof, and divided by thin
matchboard partitions into two tiny bedrooms, a minute sitting-
room, and a 'kitchen' so small that two of us and the gas-cooker
could not comfortably inhabit it at the same moment. As the
partitions reached only just above our heads, every sound made
in one 'room' was completely audible in all the others, so that
when I coached my Welsh graduate in the sitting-room, Winifred,
temporarily banished to her bedroom, had to sit perfectly still for
an hour without rustling her papers, sneezing or coughing. As
the roof was so high, and the sunless rooms were fitted only with
infinitesimal penny-in-the-slot gas-stoves, the studio was always
freezingly cold unless we lighted a fire in the huge 'passage' grate,
which consumed a sackful of coal in an afternoon, and emitted
volumes of smoke that covered ourselves and everything else with
a black layer of sooty dust.

Each morning a scanty breakfast was brought to us on a tray
by the blowsy, henna-haired housekeeper from the lodging-house
off which the studio was built, and for an hour, directly afterwards, we conscientiously cleaned and tidied our rooms. Luncheon
was always 'eaten out' in a restaurant in Theobald's Road, but we
bought and prepared our own tea and supper. Every moment not

required for meals or cleaning was strenuously devoted to work, and hour after hour, for weeks on end, we crouched with cold feet and red noses on either side of the flickering sitting-room gas-fire, drafting the final sections of our novels, getting up speeches, preparing classes, correcting childish essays, and writing scores of permanently homeless articles.

Superficially it was a supremely uncomfortable existence – and yet I felt that I had never known before what comfort was. For the first time, I knew the luxury of privacy, the tranquil happiness of being able to come and go just as I wished without interference or supervision. There had been no privacy in Victorian or Edwardian childhood, and from the age of thirteen to that of twenty-seven, I seemed to have lived in public. At school I had gone to bed and got up in dormitories, walked in 'crocodiles', read and worked in the company of others; nothing, perhaps, is still so oppressive in traditional boarding-school life as the inability of a boy or girl ever to be quite alone. Buxton, no doubt, could hardly have been called community life, for I had the physical seclusion of a bedroom to myself, but it certainly did not allow privacy of any other kind; no member of that pre-war provincial 'set' could hope to live to herself even if adult, and local and family searchlights had played continuously upon the dearest hopes, the most intimate relationships, of every 'young person'. As for the next seven years, four in the Army and three in college, they had represented community life at its most complete. Astounded relatives who occasionally dropped in to see me wondered 'how on earth I could stand' such 'Bohemian' discomfort, but to me it was Paradise.

We both felt quite guilty, sometimes, for revelling in the uninterrupted companionship of those crowded days, so busy and yet so free, so stimulating and yet so dignified with their deep undercurrent of memory, when so many of our Somerville contemporaries were going through purgatory and humiliation in their first teaching posts. Letters from twenty-two-year-old girls, gay and confident and irresponsible less than twelve months ago, telling us of the 'awful time' that they were having with rigid, domineering headmistresses in conventional schools, arrived so often that Winifred, who had once thought it her duty to share their fate, was filled with melancholy compunction because she could afford the risk of becoming a writer.

'People like you and me . . . possessed of sufficient means to choose the form of expression their intellectuality shall take, are very few and far between and yet very much needed,' I had portentously urged her just before Christmas, in terror lest her social conscience should persuade her to abandon, just because she so much enjoyed it, the literary life for which she was best fitted. 'Aristotle was so right that the work of a citizen . . . needs at any rate sufficient leisure to enable one to think. I think it would be wrong not to take advantage of the fact that fate has made one such a person. I don't think the B.s and J.s do more good to the world just *because* they have an awful time. I think they are victims of a system which exploits women as much in some schools as in some hospitals. We should do no good by voluntarily joining those victims. It is much more our job to remain outside and if possible acquire a standing which may enable us one day to combat that system . . . I think that where the compensation comes in for the victims of the system is that they do not have to leave so much to chance as we do. People like us may work for years and then find it's all in vain – that no one wants to read the book or learn the lesson. Whereas those others do get some direct return for every hour's work they put in.'

When, as soon as we had settled in Bloomsbury, I began my one-morning-a-week expedition to the fashionable little South Kensington school with which I had been in negotiation the previous autumn, I realised clearly enough that this comfortable money-making expedient had no relation to the gruelling experiences in which some of my fellow Somervillians were so miserably immersed. I had only to give one lecture or class to each of the three higher forms in this polite, unexacting academy for wealthy Society girls, and the headmistress, a small humane woman with a sense of humour who always treated me with respect and kindness, realised at least as keenly as I did the intellectual limitations of her pupils.

Each Tuesday morning began with a quiet and reasonably

intelligent Sixth Form, continued with an uproarious and unmanageable Fifth which exhibited at their worst the characteristics of pampered, uncontrolled adolescence, and concluded in the cheerful company of a pleasantly naughty Fourth to which I taught Greek and Roman history, incidentally learning it myself in the process. To this class of twelve- and thirteen-year-olds came an earl's daughter of fifteen, accompanied by an elderly, spectacled governess who looked as though she had walked straight out of Miss Pinkerton's Female Academy.

My ex-pupil is now one of the much-photographed Bright Young Things of London Society, but in those days it was difficult to believe that she would ever be bright, or even young; her large, timid eyes blinked at me behind her shining, old-fashioned glasses, and I wrestled perpetually with the problem of finding some truthful criticism for her smudgy, infantile essays which would not get my kind employer into trouble with the parental earl and countess. Why this aristocratic little rabbit was sent to my classes I could never understand, but perhaps her parents thought it would be an 'experience' for her (as indeed it was, and judging from her worried expression, a very painful experience) to be taught a safe minimum of history by an Oxford graduate. She never appeared at my classes without the governess, who clung to her like a burr – presumably as a safeguard against the risk that I might mention the Hetairai, or discuss the less repeatable irregularities of Alcibiades.

The term after I began this visiting work in South Kensington, my St Monica's aunt invited me to spend a similar weekly day at Kingswood, where one of the forms was taking the Higher Certificate examination and wanted some special coaching in history. I agreed to undertake this coaching, and on the same day to give four or five classes to other forms, as well as correcting a large number of essays and exercises. The standard of scholarship in the school had improved beyond recognition since my own day; public examinations in both English and French were now taken and passed in triumph, and although, in too many cases, I still felt that it would all end at St Paul's, Knightsbridge, or Holy Trinity, Sloane Street, I enjoyed the endeavours that I made for

nearly three years to interest my youthful successors in the idea
of self-supporting professional work which would not necessarily
terminate with marriage.

My classes, I knew, were never first-rate; I was too anxious to
write myself, and to take part in political movements, to feel any
great enthusiasm for teaching children about the writers and politicians of the past. But at least, through my work at Oxford and
my subsequent reading of F. S. Marvin and Gilbert Murray and
H. G. Wells, I had come to realise history as the whole story of
man's development from the cave to comparative civilisation, with
his constructive experiments in science and art and government,
and his blind, tentative efforts at international co-operation,
demanding the limelight that had once been exclusively shed by
teachers upon his destructive wars and his insignificant monarchs.
And, strangely enough, in my efforts to render humanity's complicated story vivid and interesting to the girls at St Monica's, I
found myself associated with no less a colleague than Sir John
Marriott himself.

Sir John and my aunt, it seemed, had remained acquaintances
ever since the pre-war Summer School at St Hilda's, and he now
visited Kingswood two or three times a term to give Extension
Lectures to the girls on European History. Thus unexpectedly I
came into contact for the third time with the dignified arbiter of
my destiny; as usual he recognised me, expressing pleasure at the
re-encounter, and I went to one or two of his lectures to get new
stimulus for my own strenuous classes. Again I was impressed by
the enormous vitality of this remarkable man, who after a long
life of university teaching was still lecturing to the immature in
1922 with as much verve and inspiration as he had expended
upon his apathetic Buxton audience in 1913. I have heard many
other extension lecturers who as age crept over them began to
seem tired and indifferent, but Sir John never wearied, and never
failed to illuminate both past and present by bringing them into
close relationship with one another.

It was certainly a complex and fateful Europe before which
Sir John and I endeavoured to hold the mirror of historical
perspective. The numerous conferences – Cannes, Washington,

Genoa, Lausanne – which took place three or four years after the War were singularly reminiscent of the post-Napoleonic Congress period which I was taking with my intelligent Upper Fifth, and seemed likely, as I was beginning reluctantly to realise, to be just about as effective in the creation of a new heaven and a new earth. Dr Nansen, lecturing in London that spring, vainly endeavoured to instil pity for the victims of the Russian famine in the hearts of a sceptical and unimaginative Government, complacently satisfied with itself for having voted £50,000 the year before in aid of the campaign against typhus in Poland. In March, exactly a month before Germany signed the Treaty of Rapallo with the Bolsheviks, the independence of Egypt was proclaimed; Austria, under the new Seipel Cabinet founded in May, tottered nearer and nearer to financial ruin, and growing disorder in Germany led to the murder of Dr Ruthenau on the very June day that a great Hyde Park demonstration proclaimed enthusiastic national support for the League of Nations.

None of these political topics were as popular with my pupils as the summer exploits of the Everest expedition and the opening of Tutankhamen's tomb at the end of the year, but no event caused more temporary excitement than the culmination of the Irish troubles, which had revived after the establishment of the Free State at the end of 1921, in the murder of Sir Henry Wilson on June 22nd.

This former Chief of the Imperial General Staff, who had been returned unopposed as M.P. for North Down the previous February, was shot in broad daylight on the doorstep of his London house as a result of his anti-Sinn Fein policy, and for over a week a somewhat confused popular imagination endowed him with the halo of a great national hero and martyr. One chill, rainy morning at the end of June, Winifred and I pushed our way through half-hysterical crowds to the Blackfriars end of Fleet Street, and there watched Sir Henry's funeral procession majestically mount the curve of Ludgate Hill. As the bier crept upwards to St Paul's, the divine wailing of Chopin's Funeral March – swelling, at the steps of the Cathedral, into its final outburst of triumphant sorrow:

– lent an inappropriate sanctity to the exit of that hard-bitten warrior, who in his own heyday had played off generals and statesmen against one another with singularly little compunction.

Of this and other symptoms of the world's distress I tried to give impartial descriptions to my pupils; although I belonged as yet to no political Party, and had not reached the age at which women were then permitted to vote, I sometimes ventured audaciously to differ from Sir John Marriott's interpretations of current events. On the whole – though I chafed perpetually to get back from them to my writing – I was agreeably happy at both my schools, and felt grateful to fate for allowing me to finance the work I really cared for at the cost of such tolerable employment. My aunt and the South Kensington headmistress were both willing, it seemed, to accept my standard of values; they employed me less for the subjects I taught or the way that I taught them, than for the life of literature and politics that I was trying to live. To the girls, at any rate, I appeared to represent a breath of vital wind blowing through their circumscribed classrooms from a thrilling world of public affairs, and they never tired of listening to the exciting, humorous, humiliating or triumphant stories of my varied adventures on League of Nations Union platforms.

4

Early in February 1922, when I had begun to regard the Union's continued forgetfulness of my existence as one of the disappointing but inevitable facts of everyday life, a telephone message suddenly inquired whether I would take the place of a speaker who had succumbed to influenza. The meeting, my informant said, was a large affair on the following evening at a Baptist chapel in Watford, capable of holding an audience of two thousand; did I think that I could tackle so formidable a gathering? On my now established principle of never refusing anything, I replied as usual that I would, and in consequence spent a night and day of apprehensive anguish. There was no time to get up a new speech, and my few weeks of teaching had already shown me that the lengthy 'specimen lecture' could not possibly be delivered in full, so I reduced myself almost to delirium by the endeavour to make a digestible summary of all the chief points.

The next evening, after rehearsing the lecture before the looking-glass until my head was ready to split with nervous tension, I went down to Watford. When I arrived at the Baptist chapel after a shuddering search through dim, half-lighted streets, fifteen elderly females huddled in tweed coats awaited me in the vestry. The great hall next door was empty and dark, and I realised, to my crestfallen relief, that this was the meeting. Being then quite incapable of a hasty, informal speech, I breathlessly delivered the whole of my portentous discourse, but the long-suffering audience did not appear to mind, and even looked quite humanly amused. The local secretary must have given a tolerant report to Grosvenor Crescent, for twenty-four hours later I was again sent out, through a snowstorm, to act as substitute speaker at a meeting in Fulham, where the sceptical Cockney chairwoman introduced me to the audience as 'the young person sent down by 'ead-quarters to tell us about the League o' Nytions'.

After that, for the greater part of the next three years and some-times as often as four times a week, I made speeches or led discus-sions on the League in almost every London suburb and in numerous small towns and villages all over the South of England and the Midlands. Such names as Hounslow and Bromley, Fleet and Broadstairs, King's Lynn and Norwich, remain in my mind without reviving any particular impression. One of my most successful lectures was given at University College, Nottingham, on the historical development of the peace ideal. Another, addressed to a garden meeting near Beaconsfield, followed an authoritative discourse by Mr H. A. L. Fisher, once Minister of Education and now warden of that Oxford college which has entered with such persistence into my private life; when it was over, he and his wife charitably took me home in their car, though the frivolous garments that I had selected for the occasion could hardly have conformed to their academic standards of suitability. At Southwell, the tiny cathedral city on the edge of Sherwood Forest where I spoke to a selection of the local congregation, I stayed at the comfortable house of Archdeacon Conybeare, a keen-faced and stimulating cousin of Rose Macaulay. After an hour's conversation when the meeting was over, I felt as though I had known this sardonic and benevolent clergyman all my life. The next day he showed me, in the Cathedral, some records of fallen Sherwood Foresters which included Edward's name, and charac-teristically refrained from intrusive condolences when I blew my nose fiercely and became temporarily speechless.

All through the autumn of 1922, the chief subjects asked for by audiences were the Greco-Turkish conflict which had sent thousands of refugees flying in terror from devastated Smyrna, and the League scheme for the reconstruction of Austria. I had to deal with both these topics at a curious open-air gathering in Penge, where I spoke from the same platform as two Members of Parliament and a Liberal candidate. This meeting, described in the pink advance leaflets as 'A Grand Open-Air Rally', was held on a small three-cornered piece of public ground known as the Triangle – 'the usual sort of thing,' I wrote to my mother, who was then in Cornwall; 'grass and one or two trees enclosed with a railing in the middle of some wide cross roads in a very slummy district. 'Buses, trams, etc., were going by all the time. We had a big platform erected on this triangle against the railings and facing it on the opposite side of the road was a large pub. Just at the back of it and going under the triangle, was a big "Gentleman's Lavatory" of the underground variety. Consequently our audience mainly consisted of the gentlemen who patronised both the pub and the lavatory. The former variety was inclined to be argu-mentative and one particularly truculent gentleman had to be removed by a policeman.'

By 1923 I had been promoted from isolated speeches to giving 'courses' of four or six lectures, and with one of these series, given to a village audience at Mere, in Wiltshire, I combined an almost identical set delivered in the Parish Hall at Gillingham, in Dorset. For four weeks in succession I was entertained to luncheon by the Clergy House at Gillingham, where half a dozen raw, cheerful young curates consumed enormous platefuls of cold beef and boiled potatoes. The cleric then presiding over this animated table was the Rev. R. C. Abbott, a courteous and intelligent man with a strong sense of humour, who afterwards became, for two years, Bishop of Sherbourne. Although a Scholar of Trinity and the Seventh Wrangler of his year, he was accustomed to keep his youthful curates in a good humour by regaling them with ludicrous parish anecdotes or simple schoolboy 'howlers' of a Scriptural variety. ('So they brought Him a penny. And Jesus said: "Whose is this miserable subscription?" They say unto Him: "Cæsar's." So He said: "Return it to Cæsar."')

In retrospect I am still grateful to the organisers of my lectures at Gillingham and Mere for always appearing to take me seriously, and treating me as the mature woman and competent lecturer that I sometimes felt but never succeeded in looking. Photographs of the time now show me that I still gave the impression, at most, of a juvenile twenty-three; it seemed strange and a little humiliating that so many storms should have passed over my head without leaving any apparent trace upon my external personality. Organisers and secretaries were apt to greet me at stations with fallen faces and the irrepressibly spontaneous exclamation: 'Are *you* the speaker? I was looking for somebody *older*!' and on one deplorable occasion the disappointed words emerged: 'You don't mean to say that *you're* Miss Brittain? I thought headquarters was sending us a *proper* lecturer!'

In spite of such crushing criticisms, the Union continued to urge me forth upon long hot journeys in trains, or long cold journeys in trams, until the halls and chapels at which I spoke, and the houses and vicarages at which I stayed while thus carrying out the resolution made before taking History at Oxford, gradually merged into a vague kaleidoscopic dream of swaying lights and upturned faces; of sparsely furnished clerical drawing-rooms with leather-backed books, horsehair sofas and crochet antimacassars; of high teas in complacent Nonconformist parlours; of chilly bedrooms of all denominations, with semi-carpeted floors, white tomb-like jugs filled with cold water on marble-topped washstands, and black grates camouflaged with newspaper or coloured crinkled tissue. Sometimes – especially in the households of Anglican clergymen, where almost without exception the level of hospitality was far higher than that attempted by the laity – a bright, consoling fire burned in the alien hearth, but this was almost as rare as a bathroom or really hot water. So seldom, indeed, was even tepid water supplied to me at night after the longest and dustiest journey, that I was driven to conclude that most English families are still in the habit of retiring to bed with the day's grime deposited on their persons. It was all one vast demonstration-lesson in those homes of England which are so widely regarded as the backbone of our national morality, one prolonged personal experience of the great British middle class with its universal standards of respectable discomfort.

5

Each League of Nations Union speaker who could afford the cost of a short holiday in Switzerland was accustomed to visit Geneva every September for the meeting of the League Assembly, in order to revive with direct contacts and 'local colour' the material for next year's speeches.

The Assemblies of those early years were worth attending, for the Foreign Ministers of the Great Powers had not yet realised how easily, by means of a little tact and some elegant camouflage, the League might be used as a stage on which they could play the skilled game of the Old Diplomacy circumspectly dressed up in international costume. Before 1925, perhaps as many as fifty per cent of the delegates who went to Geneva honestly believed that the organisation of international peace was a workable proposition – as indeed it might be, although for the past half-dozen years it has never been permitted to become anything of the kind – and thus entered with enthusiasm into the work of debates and committees. Only a few individual representatives amongst the Great Powers – Lord Cecil, for instance, and M. Herriot, and Mrs Swanwick – could be reliably included amongst the fifty per cent, but at that time certain delegates from the smaller Powers, such as Dr Nansen of Norway, Count Mensdorff of Austria, M. Motta of Switzerland, M. Branting and Madame Bugge-Wicksell of Sweden, determinedly created an Assembly 'atmosphere', and kept in check the insolent nationalism of their more aggressive colleagues.

But when I first saw Geneva, in August 1922, the Third Assembly had not yet begun, and I joined a League of Nations Union Summer School which happened to coincide with an early meeting of the Mandates Commission. Winifred, who was now also a speaker for the Union, went with me to Geneva, and together we heard Sir Joseph Cook, my Newcastle predecessor who had become High Commissioner for Australia the previous January, wrathfully endeavouring to answer satisfactorily some awkward questions asked by the Commissioners on the subject of Nauru, a phosphates-producing island which, as a 'C' Mandate, had recently been allocated to Australian supervision. Whenever I was not zealously occupied in collecting material for my first commissioned article, for *Time and Tide*, on 'Women at Geneva', I joined my fellow thirsters for knowledge in the sultry lecture rooms at the Palais des Nations to hear the words of wisdom that fell from the inspired lips of Secretariat speakers.

We returned to England to read, in an evening paper bought at Folkestone, of the death of Lord Northcliffe, but a week later another death occurred which seemed, to us who went frequently to the Union Office, far more untimely and incongruous. In Geneva the members of the staff who were attending the Summer School had anxiously waited, day by day, for news of their brilliant colleague, Elizabeth Murray, who had accompanied some of them to a conference in South-Eastern Europe, and was now lying dangerously ill in France. On August 23rd I sent Winifred, who had gone to Yorkshire, the brief *Times* notice of her death from appendicitis in Auvergne.

'I had quite made up my mind,' I wrote, 'that she was going

to get better,' for even after the ruthless, inappropriate deaths of the War, I could not visualise the cold darkness of a premature grave closing over the meteoric radiance which had flashed through my first year at Somerville. Characteristically crowding into a few spectacular years the adventures and experiments and emotions of a lifetime, Agnes Elizabeth Murray, it seemed, had broken beneath the combined over-intensity of work and play. 'It's the plain truth,' my letter regretfully concluded, 'that if one does a great deal of both, either one's work gives up the ghost or one gives it up one's self. All honour to Agnes Murray for letting it be herself and not her work if she chose a short life and a gay one – which, in so far as I know her, I am sure would have been her choice if she had made a conscious choice at all.'

My first Assembly, in the following September of 1923, was memorable for many reasons, and not least because on this occasion I was actually the official representative of *Time and Tide*, with a green card which entitled me to sit in the crowded Press gallery in the Salle de la Reformation, and gather information for my series of articles on 'Personalities at the Fourth Assembly'. Indescribably moved by that sense of a common purpose which had given its deceptive glamour to the War, and now, struggling through the anti-social hostilities of competitive nationalism, seemed almost to have reached a point where it could be mobilised in the cause of peace, I looked down over the struggling human contingent of journalists and visitors and diplomats' wives in the galleries to the rows of grave delegates listening with dark-browed reticence to the new president giving his opening address.

The president of that year, M. Cosme de la Torriente y Peraza, was an impressive-looking Cuban whose brave but bewildering French accent represented his sole disadvantage. The attempts of some of the non-European delegates to express themselves in one of the two official languages of the League made me realise vividly Geneva's linguistic complications, and I felt considerable sympathy with a Belgian journalist who was obliged to desert his seat in front of me because he knew no English and could not understand Cuban French.

Among the delegates, seated at their desks in accordance with the French alphabetical order of the nations, the chief place belonged, as always, to Dr Nansen, once the intrepid explorer and hero of every schoolchild, but now, in his vigorous old age, the friend of prisoners and the hope of refugees. The indefinable quality which set him above his fellows seemed to belong less to his tall, conspicuous figure, with its lean, melancholy face beneath the broad-brimmed hat of grey felt, than to his long swift step and the air of untrammelled freedom which an English woman journalist described to me as 'the sleigh-dog manner'. The Scandinavian women who often accompanied him to committees, the dark, moustachioed Bulgarians and Yugo-Slavs from the Balkan peninsula, the olive-skinned South Americans from the Spanish Republics, the yellow, impassive little Japanese and Chinamen from farthest Asia, together provided sufficient racial contrasts to stock an international personalities exhibition; but even among them the leader of the newly admitted Abyssinian delegation, Dedjazinatch Nadeon, challenged journalistic attention with his flowing fur-trimmed cloak covering a white satin tunic and his long thin legs encased in white satin pyjama-like trousers, the whole being crowned with a very small grey Homburg hat.

That year's Assembly, having ritualistically admitted the Irish Free State to its membership as well as Abyssinia, prepared as usual to discuss Opium, Slavery, Refugees, Health, and Minorities, for never had there been a situation since the League was founded in which humanitarian questions provided a safer refuge from burning political controversies. Because, for the moment, even the prolonged tragedy of the Ruhr occupation, begun the previous January, had been eclipsed by the gladiatorial attitude of Italy towards Greece, the Geneva scene which stands out most clearly from the memories of that brilliant, warm September is not the ponderous pageant in the Salle de la Reformation, but a meeting of the Council at the Palais des Nations to discuss the bombardment of Corfu.

6

On August 27th, General Tellini and his four companions of the Italian Boundary Commission had been assassinated at Janina, in Greek territory. A stern Italian Note to Greece on the 29th was followed on September 1st by the bombardment and occupation of Corfu, a demonstration of 'frightfulness' which cost the lives of fifteen defenceless Greek civilians. Greece at once appealed to the League, and on September 3rd the Fourth Assembly opened in an atmosphere of strained excitement even greater, according to Secretariat observers, than that in which the problem of Upper Silesia had been discussed two years before. The Council, which had met on August 31st for its twenty-sixth session, was sitting concurrently with the Assembly; I succeeded in getting into a public meeting which it held on September 5th to consider Italy's declaration that the League was 'incompetent' to intervene in the dispute, and at once that remote official body which I had mentioned so often in my lectures sprang for me into tense and turbulent life.

The fate of the League and the peace of the world seemed to lie that day in the hands of eleven men – Greece being added to the then normal ten as one of the parties to the dispute – but the eyes of delegates and journalists were fixed especially upon the representatives of Great Britain, France, Japan, Belgium, Italy and Greece. The other five countries played the part of onlookers at this particular quarrel; Mr Tang Tsai-Fou of China, dark and phlegmatic, listened in silence to the harsh competition of argument; Señor Guani, of Uruguay, contented himself with a grunt of approval whenever someone defended the rights of the lesser Powers, and Señor Raul de Rio Branco of Brazil, a very large man with a very small voice, maintained a serene detachment by smoking a series of enormous cigars.

More closely concerned with the quarrel than these distant countries, the representatives of Spain and Sweden brooded anxiously over the Council table, the one looking for any chance of conciliation that offered itself, the other permanently ready to voice the fears and anxieties of the smaller nations. As those anxieties increased, M. Branting, the tall, dignified Swede, with his white head and flowing moustache, came more and more to resemble a lost Viking chief inadvertently strayed into the wordy councils of the New Diplomacy, where the simple and obvious solution of an international problem disappeared into the depths of verbosity as a diamond might vanish in a reedy whirlpool. In rotund contrast was the Spanish Ambassador from Paris, Señor Quinones de Léon. Large, expansive and calm, his inward perturbations seemed as incapable of changing his countenance as of ruffling the scanty hairs upon his big, round head. Probably he was meditating upon the coming Spanish Revolution – which exactly a week later was to put General Primo de Rivera at the head of the Directory in Madrid – instead of giving an unburdened mind to the troubles of Greece.

The hostile stab and clash of the chief verbal duel inevitably passed between Professor Salandra of Italy and M. Nicolas Politis, the Greek representative, but the issue was joined continually by M. Gabriel Hanotaux of France, M. Paul Hymans of Belgium, and the chief British delegate, Lord Robert Cecil, whose inclusion in the new Baldwin Government, which had succeeded that of Mr Bonar Law on May 22nd, was said to indicate a recognition of the importance of the League to British foreign policy. Viscount Ishii of Japan had also a leading part to play as President of the Council, but the bombardment of Corfu and the loss of fifteen Greek lives cannot have seemed a great matter to one whose country staggered under its death roll of half a million in the tremendous earthquake which had destroyed Tokio and Yokohama on September 1st. A small elderly man with melancholy eyes and a dark, kindly face as deeply lined as old parchment, he presided over the stormy Council with shoulders bent beneath the weight of overwhelming calamity. As the sufferings of Japan penetrated even through the solemn impassivity of the oriental demeanour, the burning discords of Europe seemed to dwindle into insignificance beneath the shadow of a great and dignified sorrow.

To the eyes of the casual observer, Dr Salandra, once Prime Minister of Italy but now representative of the unbending

Mussolini, seemed incongruously unsuited to either his own fierce statements or the sinister designs attributed to Italy by sections of the international Press. With short, thick-set figure, brown face and dark twinkling eyes, he resembled the humorous uncle in a stage comedy rather than the menacing diplomat; his double chin and large bald head with its fringe of white hair lent him an air of benevolence quite out of harmony with his uncompromising language. Still on the active side of middle age, his slender, spectacled opponent, M. Politis, seemed the incarnation of modern Greece laying its appeal before the League. In a clear, unhesitating voice, solemn as a doctor's diagnosis, he presented his country's case without anger or fear, laying bare the essentials of the situation with a skill even more conspicuous than that of the Italian in covering them up.

Of the three remaining Powers who heard him, the attitude of only one was unmistakable. So this really *is* open diplomacy, we thought excitedly, as in the packed committee room with its glass walls, through which we could see the spiky palms and the scarlet salvia in the Palais garden vivid with light in the ecstatic autumn sunshine, Lord Robert Cecil rose to demand the public reading of Articles 10, 12 and 15 of the Treaty of Versailles. In the tense, expectant silence the chief interpreter began to read, in English and in French, those three articles from the first twenty-six of the treaty which formed the Covenant of the League of Nations. The air was electric with a dramatic sense of testing and of crisis as the familiar words brought home – probably, to most of that audience, for the first time – the full significance of the League in the international relationships of a tortured post-war world:

> 'The Members of the League undertake to respect and preserve as against external aggression the territorial integrity and existing political independence of all Members of the League. In the case of any such aggression or in case of any threat or danger of such aggression the Council shall advise upon the means by which this obligation shall be fulfilled . . .'

A breathless moment followed, and then Lord Robert, his sprawling shoulders suddenly erect, stood up again and put into words the essential, unpalatable truth which streams of diplomatic eloquence had done their best to submerge: 'If these articles are disregarded, the whole foundation of new Europe will be shaken!'

As I listened there came to me, with a dark dismay and yet with the deep thrill of a worth-while contest, the suddenly complete realisation of all that the original post-war decision to range my insignificant self on the side of the forces working for peace and understanding was to mean in reluctant awareness of diplomatic tradition and intrigue, as well as in a growing bitter knowledge that men deliberately refused to perceive the obvious even when such perception was to their own advantage. Still optimistic in spite of the War, I had believed that statesmen needed only to realise the mistakes of the past in order to avoid them, only to be shown the path of peace in order to tread it; now, in spite of that momentary sense of a common purpose in the Assembly, I knew that most of them were too cynical, too suicidally wedded to expediency, to adopt the pure, lucid policy of simple wisdom. All too clearly, the conflict for internationalism as a creed was going to be longer and sterner than we had imagined in the first vigour of anti-war reaction.

And yet those great nineteenth-century treaties remained to show that progress had happened, had occurred in despite – and perhaps even because – of men like these, I reflected, contemplating the nervous face and hard, restless eyes of M. Hanotaux, the small non-committal Frenchman with the perpetual frown and the little, grey, pointed beard which gave an appearance of crafty slyness to his lined countenance. He would have been glad, we all realised, to support the uncompromising Salandra, whose country's occupation of Corfu could hardly have been uninfluenced by the predicament of the resentful Ruhr, but he feared to antagonise the Little Entente with its definite views on the rights of small States. It was less discouraging to watch the volatile movements of M. Hymans, the fragile, graceful Belgian with the abundant white hair and keen expressive eyes beneath black brows, who was so frequently in consultation with Lord Robert Cecil.

In a gathering of individuals whose beauty was the last consideration which had brought them together, his romantic appearance provided an agreeable momentary diversion from the antagonisms of Europe.

During those early days, the habit of treating the League as negligible had not reached its present stage of propagandist efficiency even in those newspapers which were later to find its perpetual disparagement a remunerative 'stunt', and the world really seemed to care that the Council should emerge with credit from the Greek-Italian crisis. Although Corfu was soon afterwards evacuated, and the question of the League's competence to intervene in the dispute was avoided with sufficient deftness to prevent Italy from carrying out her threat to leave it, the confident hopes which had rested on Geneva were cruelly disappointed when the final settlement was handed over to the Conference of Ambassadors and Greece was made to pay £500,000 to Italy. Winifred and I had to return to England for her sister's wedding before the crisis was over; at home we read numerous attacks upon Lord Robert Cecil for his bold disregard of diplomatic circumlocution, and on September 15th I wrote to tell Winifred that an eminent don whom we both knew had just sent a letter to *The Times*, 'all about members of the L.N.U. having to "reconsider" their attitude towards the League and not being likely to be willing in the future to give their time and money to an organisation which is only capable of coming to "lame and lamentable" conclusions! He does think his time is valuable, that man! I suppose a little thing like Gilbert Murray's time is of no account!'

By November the Greek-Italian dispute was still provoking such inveterate enemies of Geneva as the Duke of Northumberland and Mr J. L. Maxse to make furious attacks on the League, but during that autumn the limelight of publicity shifted from South-Eastern Europe to the Franco-German boundary owing to the new menace of separatist movements in Bavaria and Saxony. Although the cessation of passive resistance in the Ruhr and the new committees created by the Reparations Commission had now relieved the fierce tension which followed the Essen riots in March, every country was paying in loss of trade and falling

exchanges for the French occupation. The fear of complete political disruption and economic collapse in Germany diverted
Europe's interest even from the new experimental republicanism
of Mustapha Kemal in Turkey, and caused Lord Birkenhead's
expressed approval of 'glittering swords' in his Rectorial address
at Glasgow to be received somewhat coldly by an anxious England
which would gladly have seen them all turned into ploughshares.
Even quite moderate left-wing French opinion was now, it
appeared, shocked and disturbed by the consequences of the Ruhr
invasion; 'France,' M. Guyot had written in *L'Ère Nouvelle* in
December 1923,

> 'is isolated in a system of thought which Europe refuses to
> share. Poincaré prides himself on his immobility, whilst the
> tide of facts mounts further around him every day ... Reason
> applauds the rock-like stand of this Lorraine attorney, but
> "our nerves and our blood, everything in us that makes us
> live, revolt against the feeling that we are remaining stationary
> while the whole world around us is moving." Shall France
> move on up the high road along which all is life and move-
> ment, or shall she stand fast – and perish?'

When, exactly a month after the trial of Hitler and Ludendorff
for leading the separatist movement in Bavaria had begun in
Munich, I went north at the beginning of April 1924, to carry
out a lecture tour for the League of Nations Union among the
small towns on the Scottish Border, practically every audience
asked for an address on the Ruhr occupation, although both
Council and Assembly had hitherto carefully avoided the subject.
The situation in Germany seemed a curious comment, I thought,
as I moved from town to town between the snow-covered Cheviot
and Lammermuir Hills in the bitter cold of that pipe-freezing
spring, on the Centenary Debate which had just been held by
the Union at Oxford: 'That civilisation has advanced since this
society first met.'

By the time that I had lectured at Ayton and Duns and Norham
and Coldstream on Reparations, and passive resistance, and the

similar 'incidents' in the Saar Valley under the pro-French Governing Commission, and the trial of the Krupp directors, and the epidemic of unavailing Notes between the Allies and Germany, and the collapsing mark which had descended, in September 1923, to 800 million to the £, I began to feel that I should never really speak effectively on these complicated topics until I had been in the occupied areas, sensed their bitter psychology, and seen at least the external aspect of post-war hostilities for myself. Winifred, as it happened, was spontaneously coming in her own lectures to the same conclusion, for though she was speaking that year for feminist organisations as well as for the League of Nations Union, her attention had been diverted from such topical events as the Second Reading, on Leap Year's Day, of Mr Adamson's Equal Franchise Bill, and the Six Point Group's mass meeting in March to demand Widows' Pensions, by a correspondence with Gerda von Gerlach, the daughter of a conspicuous Berlin Socialist who had been the first German girl to go to Somerville after the War.

'One [letter] from the von Gerlach girl,' Winifred wrote to me from Yorkshire on April 16th, while I was still in the north, 'to say that her father has got safely out of Germany, and that if the elections go right he may not be tried for high treason even now. Poor things! What a hell of a time most European countries give their best citizens – the Liberals in Hungary, the anti-Fascisti in Italy, the pacifists in Germany, the liberty-loving in Russia – and all for what? I can still see the little von Gerlach girl leaning across the table at Pinoli's with her big tear-filled eyes and her fierce little voice. "Oh, you in England don't know what Europe is! How can you? You're so *safe!*" I thought of her as I came up in the train yesterday riding along the side of a tranquil sunset over this dull, placid, strangely untroubled country that lies from London to the Humber—

> *And much it grieved my heart to think*
> *What man has made of man!*

'Am I growing hysterical? Sometimes I look into the sunset and see only the blood spilt from bodies that might have been godlike and wept from hearts that have at least potential divinity. We could be so happy. There is such beauty, and such kindness . . . even in this unbeautiful place the crocuses, late flowering this year, and the very small buds upon the hawthorns have an almost disquieting loveliness. If only the birds would sing loud enough to drown the cry that rises from the folly, folly of people in this stupid planet!'

But we knew, with our heavy memories of the past ten years, that for us no beauty of spring flowers could blind us to the tears of the bereaved, no song of melodious birds extinguish the heart-broken mourning of the conquered, and when we both returned to London at the end of April, the opening of the Wembley exhibition, with its meretricious architecture and its exploited workers, seemed a vulgar display of national self-satisfaction when contrasted with the sorrows of prostrate Germany. So we decided to pool our savings and go that autumn to the occupied areas and bankrupt countries of Central Europe, in order to learn for ourselves what the War had meant to those peoples whose agony had been even more cruel and more prolonged than our own.

7

Between 1922 and 1925, my numerous meetings for the League of Nations Union gave me acquaintances belonging to every social class from earls to dustmen, every shade of religious conviction from Roman Catholicism to Christian Science, and every type of political opinion from true-blue Diehard Toryism to blood-red Bolshevist Communism. Among the many and varied men and women who acted as my chairmen, one of the few with whom my connection outlasted the occasion of the meeting was Mr – now Sir – Percy Harris, an industrious member of the London County Council, a former M.P. for the Harborough Division of Leicestershire, and at that time Liberal candidate for South-West Bethnal Green.

Before I went down to the Party headquarters in the Bethnal Green Road to address his small gathering of poverty-stricken but extremely vital and intelligent Liberal women, Mr Harris invited me to supper at his flat in Westminster, and shared with me, in the belief that I should speak more effectively for the knowledge, some of his earnest hopes and anxieties for the crowded working-class constituency which he had represented on the L.C.C. for fifteen years. This first expedition of mine to Bethnal Green occurred in the autumn of 1922, only a short time before the famous meeting of the Carlton Club engineered the long-anticipated downfall of the Coalition Government. A few days after I had heard the secretary of the Six Point Group breathlessly announce the resignation of Mr Lloyd George to the small audience of feminists which assembled at the Group's office for fortnightly lectures, Mr Harris wrote to ask me if I would act as his secretary during the coming election.

At that time I still belonged to no political Party, for my interest in politics was chiefly international; I knew that I was not a Conservative, but beyond this somewhat elementary certainty my Party loyalties remained undefined. I had, however, been agreeably impressed by Mr Harris's disinterested and benevolent understanding of the poor people in Bethnal Green; it seemed unlikely that they would find another Parliamentary representative who combined so long an experience of their needs with such human and intelligent sensitiveness to their psychology, so I agreed to give all my spare time for the next few weeks to helping him in his election campaign. I could not actually become his secretary because at that time my two weekly days of teaching prevented the acceptance of full-time work, and in the end Winifred, whose own engagements were for the moment less rigid, took over the secretaryship and spent the greater part of the next month in the crowded and dusty office half-way down the Bethnal Green Road.

As October slipped into chill, murky November, the excitement of the first General Election in which I had taken an active part excluded all other interests, and every evening found me rushing for the first 'bus that would take me from Bloomsbury to join the dramatic, turbulent contest in the East End. Mr Harris, who was being opposed by a conventional Conservative and an equally typical Communist, described himself as the Liberal and

Labour candidate, and on his behalf I acquired a new facility in the rapid composition of enthusiastic arguments and speeches with a vague Radical-Socialist bias. Long, damp afternoons of canvassing, attended by strident platoons of small boys, in the mazy darkness of unlighted winter slums, culminated each evening in an adventurous walk down the vivacious Bethnal Green Road, with its open-air stalls, its flaring gas-jets, its coster cries and its thronging, voluble population of Cockneys, Jews and Poles, to some riotous meeting in an elementary-school room or municipal hall.

From confused memories of earnest, conscientious speeches made by Mr Harris and Winifred and myself in determined resistance to Tory and Communist interrupters amid the concentrated fumes of Cockney tobacco, one large eve-of-the-poll meeting emerges at which the chair was taken by the Rev Stewart Headlam, the veteran Fabian who shared with Mr Harris the representation of South-West Bethnal Green on the L.C.C. The sitting-and-standing crowds in the hall, largely drawn from opposing Parties and now almost beside themselves with partisan excitement, were waiting to heckle the candidate, and had little patience to spare for a portly and somewhat prosy speaker sent down by Liberal headquarters. It was some moments before he could take advantage of a brief interval of comparative silence to open his speech.

'My friends,' he began sententiously, 'each one of us here is his brother's keeper, and—'

But the rest of the sentence was drowned by a chorus of jeers and cat-calls. Twice or three times the speaker endeavoured to make himself heard, but even the intrepid old chairman, with his noble white head and his long history of service in unpopular causes, could not succeed in quelling the tumult. Finally Mr Harris leaned across to me and whispered: 'Could you just get up and try to say something? They're decent fellows on the whole – if a woman gets up they'll probably quieten down a bit.'

So the sententious one was induced for the moment to give me his place, and I struggled to my feet, inwardly scared almost to the point of extinction, but determined somehow or other to penetrate the clamour.

''Oo's *your* keeper?' immediately demanded a voice from the back of the hall with decisive irony.

At this the long-suffering candidate sprang to his feet, his benevolent dark eyes blazing with outraged indignation. He was prepared to tolerate any number of innuendos against his past, his future, his fine public record and his own impeccable character, but this insult to a young feminine supporter was more than the Harrow and Trinity tradition could endure.

'You're a cad, sir; you're a cad!' he shouted, shaking his fist at the unseen interrupter. 'It doesn't matter about me, I can look after myself, but—'

I could not, however, allow him to go on. By an active feminist this protective line, though I recognised the generous chivalry of its intention, was not to be borne. Still standing at my corner of the platform, I bellowed above the din: 'So can I!'

The audience rocked with applause and laughter. When the noise had died down they gave me a tolerable hearing while I made the time-worn plea for fair play to opponents. After that evening, Bethnal Green always listened to me with good-humoured tolerance, though my persevering arguments in favour of Free Trade and a pro-League policy must have been far too academic and generalised to appeal to their racy notions of an entertaining address.

Mr Harris won the election with a comfortable majority, and has remained ever since the Member of Parliament for South-West Bethnal Green, keeping by means of his personal popularity that small corner of the East End faithful to Liberalism through election after election, while almost the whole of London has now divided its allegiance between Conservatism and Labour. When the poll closed and the count began, Winifred and I and the small band of canvassers went to Trafalgar Square to watch the sky-sign results of that significant election, which left the Conservatives in power but doubled the number of Labour representatives, and returned such ex-conscientious objectors as Ramsay Macdonald and Philip Snowden to become leaders of the second largest Party in the House of Commons.

My recollection of the scene in Trafalgar Square in November

1922 merges into that which followed the General Election of December 1923, for on each occasion I worked for Mr Harris, saw him elected, went to the same democratic spot to learn the results, and realised, with a half conscious feeling of triumph, the growth of Socialist influence in an electorate which now numbered over twenty million. If I close my eyes I can still see the dark massed humanity in that midnight square, flooded like a stage crowd with purple light from the sky-sign apparatus, while the brilliant letters and figures flashed intermittently between heavy banks of rolling fog. With half-blinded eyes straining through the mist, I watched for the results of our own election, and fought hard for my foothold in the jostling, excited crowd. All around me, ragged men and women with shrunken faces, livid in the unreal, fog-obscured light, frantically cheered each Labour victory as though the millennium had come. One of the earliest results on each occasion arrived from the Sutton Division of Plymouth; 'NANCY IN', read the shrieking sky-sign, momentarily clear against the turgid night.

8

Throughout 1923 we often went to Bethnal Green with Mr Harris to make speeches or attend 'socials', and he in turn, after an evening spent in his constituency, sometimes called on his way back to Westminster at the small top-floor Doughty Street flat into which we had now moved from the draughty studio. His modest demands on our hospitality never exceeded half an hour's conversation and a glass of milk, but as these visits, and those of one or two other political friends who spoke at our request to the Bethnal Green Liberals, usually occurred round about midnight, the suspicions of the aggressively respectable charlady who 'did' for us were very soon militantly aroused. In her view, young women whose activities did not terminate at 10 p.m. sharp required careful watching by them that valued their good name, but we remained sublimely unaware of this prolonged vigilance until one chilly October morning soon after our return from the 1923 Assembly.

On this occasion Winifred had given a League of Nations Union lecture at a distant town; she decided to go back to London by the midnight train, and appeared at the flat with the morning milk still wearing her platform garments of the night before. That same evening I had gone to dinner with my parents in Kensington; as I had a bad cold my mother persuaded me to stay the night, and I returned to Bloomsbury soon after breakfast in the evening clothes in which I had set out. At tea-time that day a scrawled note on a screwed up piece of paper was pushed through our letterbox; Winifred picked it up and read it, and then passed it on to me with an amused, rueful countenance. It was from our charlady, giving us notice. 'I've always been respectable myself,' it concluded, 'and I don't care to work for them that arnt.'

To our unmitigated astonishment our landlady, to whom we protested about this baseless accusation, appeared to sympathise with the charlady and even to regard us as undesirable tenants for her impeccable property. For some time we had talked vaguely of moving, as our earnings were now sufficient for a full-time housekeeper, and being no longer restricted by the hypothetical requirements of 'Metternich and Alexander', we set out to look through numerous inexpensive districts for a flat, large enough to hold three females, which we could afford. Eventually we found the cheapness and space that we required in a block of 'mansions' off a Maida Vale thoroughfare. Had our landlady's suspicions been correct we could not have moved to a district more likely to confirm them, but we were less interested in a 'good address' than in the ability to accommodate Winifred's old nurse, who had agreed to come from Yorkshire to look after us. Nevertheless, our enforced exodus from Bloomsbury to Maida Vale was not one of the contingencies which we had foreseen as a probable consequence of our incursion into politics.

A more typical result of this Liberal phase was our brief membership of a famous political club to which Mr Harris introduced us. This long-established and highly respectable Liberal organisation had been for many years exclusively male, but after the War, in deference to the then fashionable conciliation of the newly enfranchised voters, a limited number of females were admitted as members, and in 1922 four women were even elected to its committee. Notwithstanding these hotly contested concessions, its attitude and outlook remained predominantly masculine, and its solemn periodic meetings at the National Liberal Club were marked by all the pompous ritual and the slightly suspicious personal exclusiveness so characteristic of male social gatherings.

When we joined the club we hardly knew any of the other members, and most of the younger men and women who belonged appeared to be in a similar position, yet no effort was made at the meetings to introduce the members to one another or to mitigate their somewhat militant attitude towards everybody else. After a few moments of awkward standing about, we each sat down, alone or with the friend with whom we had come, at small green-baize tables, and drank an isolated cup of tepid coffee while the chairman prepared to introduce the speaker. Most of the speakers were political or semi-political officials of various types, and I never heard an address from a woman throughout the two years during which I was a member. When the speech ended, the meeting was thrown open for discussion, and one male after another would rise and harangue the smoke-laden room in five-minute speeches as solemn as though the continued existence of the Government itself were at stake. After these masculine contributions had followed one another for nearly an hour, the president of the club, a benevolent elderly peer belonging to the old school of politics, would rise and remark, with a deprecating smile: 'Now perhaps one of the *ladies* would like to give us her views?'

This invitation was invariably the signal for a fresh lighting of cigarettes, a new round of coffee-cups, and a general sense of the members leaning back in their armchairs with the restful conviction that no lady's views could possibly be worth hearing. On one occasion, suddenly provoked into defending my sane, good-humoured East-Enders against an allegation of irrational revolutionary behaviour, I anticipated the benign invitation, and was immediately conscious of a rustle of scandalised astonishment at my temerity.

About the end of 1924, Winifred and I left this organisation;

it was obvious that some years would have to elapse before 'the ladies' acquired anything like equal debating conditions, and our growing bias towards Labour had been so much increased by our tour of Central Europe that autumn that membership of a Liberal club was no longer really compatible with our convictions. When we resigned we wrote a long letter to the secretary, a young Oxford man with perfect manners and no initiative, giving in full our reasons for abandoning Liberalism, and making – as we frequently and hopefully made to the League of Nations Union – all kinds of suggestions for increasing the club's efficiency. In those days we were still naïve enough to believe that suggestions need only be bright in order to be enthusiastically accepted, and had still to learn that in clubs and societies, as in Foreign Offices, the one thing that really terrifies officials is the prospect of any alteration in the *status quo*.

It had been, ironically enough, as much Bethnal Green as Central Europe which was responsible for our decision to quit the Liberal Party. For the first time, during those General Elections of 1922 and 1923, I came into intimate contact with the homes of the poor, and learnt, as my provincial middle-class upbringing had never permitted me to learn, the semi-barbarous conditions – intensified beyond calculation by the War and its consequences – under which four-fifths of the population are obliged to live in a confused and suffering world. I saw the men fighting one losing battle against economic depression and increasing unemployment, while the women waged another against excessive procreation combined with an accumulation of wasteful, interminable domestic detail, and the babies fought yet a third against under-nourishment, over-clothing, perpetual dirt and inadequate fresh air and sunshine. At the same time I realised, with a shock of poignant revelation, the kinship between the men and women in these wretched homes, and the Tommies whom I had nursed for four calamitous years. The same brave, uncomplaining endurance was there, the same humour, the same rough, compassionate kindness to one another in circumstances under which a complete absence of courage and humour and compassion might well have been understood and forgiven.

This new knowledge did not make me philanthropically minded – the attempt to alleviate such anxious misery with soup and blankets seemed to me a mere self-deception, an endeavour to delude one's intelligence into a sense of having done one's duty and being thenceforth absolved from further responsibility. But it made me politically minded once and for all; I knew that for the rest of my life I could never again feel free from the obligation of working with those who were trying to change the social system that made this grim chaos possible, and I began to turn more definitely towards the Party which represented the spirit as well as the substance of that democracy to whose future I was for ever bound by the common experiences of the War.

9

During both General Elections, a good deal of space was given by nearly all newspapers to the demands of the recently enfranchised woman voter. Women, as such, had always possessed for the Press a peculiar fascination in which the opposite sex seemed inexplicably lacking, and though their publicity stock had fallen during the wartime preoccupation with 'heroes', it rose again directly after the War owing to the fact that, unlike men, they had inconsiderately failed to die in large numbers. The reason universally given for limiting the vote to women over thirty was that the complete enfranchisement of adult women would have meant a preponderant feminine vote.

This excessive female population was habitually described, none too flatteringly, as 'superfluous', although the teachers, nurses, doctors and Civil Servants of whom it was largely composed were far more socially valuable than many childless wives and numerous irresponsible married mothers. An agitation over the mere existence of so many unmated women began with the census revelations in the late summer of 1921, and during the 'Silly Season' of that year their position became a favourite topic with the stunt Press, which published innumerable articles on Equal Pay, Marriage *versus* Career, and the Right to Motherhood. In a letter to Winifred, dated August 25th, 1921, I included, as one superfluous woman

to another, some reflections upon a leader which had appeared
on this subject in no less an organ than *The Times* itself.

'Did you see or hear anything of the disaster to R.38 yesterday?'
my letter began. (Winifred was then in Yorkshire, and had not
only seen the airship as it passed above her village, but had heard
the explosion over the Humber a few minutes afterwards.) 'One
seems to have got over the feeling that one had during the War
that these calamities are a matter of course – which I think is a
good thing; we were all getting so callous. *The Times* is exciting
itself over the surplus women, as revealed by the census – 101
per 1,000, I believe, to be exact! They were quite nice to us in
a leading article to-day, and said that women who had lost their
husbands or lovers in the War couldn't be expected on that account
to relegate themselves to perpetual widowhood or spinsterhood.
But they suggested that women who were willing to seek work
abroad would not only obtain for themselves a better chance of
getting a husband but would be doing their country a service! It
never seems to occur to anybody that some women may not want
husbands; the article even talked about "finding the domesticity
they desire"! Personally I haven't the least objection to being
superfluous so long as I am allowed to be useful, and though I
shall be delighted for any work I may do to take me abroad, it
will not be because I shall thereby be enabled the better to capture
the elusive male.'

As the months went by, however, I had to decide how far it
was really possible for us who were 'surplus' to make into a reality
that boasted power of sublimation. As a generation of women we
were now sophisticated to an extent which was revolutionary
when compared with the romantic ignorance of 1914. Where we
had once spoken with polite evasion of 'a certain condition', 'a
certain profession', we now unblushingly used the words 'preg-
nancy' and 'prostitution'. Amongst our friends we discussed
sodomy and lesbianism with as little hesitation as we compared
the merits of different contraceptives, and were theoretically
familiar with varieties of homosexuality and venereal disease of
which the very existence was unknown to our grandparents. We
had not quite lost – and perhaps never shall lose – a self-conscious

feeling of boldness in our candour; not all our experience could change us from the earnest, idealistic War generation into our flippant juniors the post-war youth, who had never been taught to think the terms of sex indecent and to see its facts, if at all, through a glass darkly. But we were now capable of the frank analysis of our own natures, and the stoical, if reluctant, acceptance of realistic conclusions.

One Sunday soon after Winifred and I had gone to live in Maida Vale, I went down to see Betty, who had recently been married, in her new Essex home. She was expecting a baby and seemed wrapped in physiological contentment, but this evidence of a still almost universal assumption that the interests of a husband and children provided sufficient occupation for an adult woman's entire personality did not reconcile me to the idea of marriage with any type of man which the War seemed to have left available for those of us who were approaching the rubicon of thirty.

In spite of the feminine family tradition and the relentless social pressure which had placed an artificial emphasis on marriage for all the women born, like myself, in the eighteen-nineties, I had always held and still believed it to be irrelevant to the main purpose of life. For a woman as for a man, marriage might enormously help or devastatingly hinder the growth of her power to contribute something impersonally valuable to the community in which she lived, but it was not that power, and could not be regarded as an end in itself. Nor, even, were children ends in themselves; it was useless to go on producing human beings merely in order that they, in their sequence, might produce others, and never turn from this business of continuous procreation to the accomplishment of some definite and lasting piece of work.

I was not, therefore, in the least attracted by the idea of marriage divorced from love – by which I no longer meant the invading passion that for me had burnt itself out, once for all, in 1915, but the loyal, friendly emotion which arises between mutually respectful equals of opposite sex who are working side by side for some worth-while end. But my experience had made love in all its aspects seem an essentially youthful quality; at school and in Buxton I had grown up in contact with a general supposition that the girl who does not marry early is unlikely to marry at all, and so much living and loving had been crowded into the few succeeding years that now, when I was nearing the end of my twenties, it all appeared to have happened very long ago, and made me feel that I was already growing old. Not only because, through the wholesale annihilation of my masculine contemporaries, I seemed likely to prove, in Queen Elizabeth's phrase, 'a barren stock', but because the intense emotional relationships of the War had left an emptiness which not even the most intimate friendships could fill, I still felt that I was a haphazard survivor from another life, with no place in society, and no foothold on any permanent ladder except that which my own determination could construct for itself in a post-war world tormented with needs and problems.

So, during those three years of lecturing and teaching, and very partially successful writing, I gradually acquired, faced and accepted the settled conviction that I was destined for permanent spinsterhood. My poem, 'The Superfluous Woman', written in Cornwall after the anæmic Oxford love-affair had died of inanition, represented the last bitter protest against the non-fulfilment of one part of my human potentialities to which the War appeared to have condemned me and so many other women whose natural completion had been frustrated by the withering frost of grief and loss. Marriage, I definitely decided, was not for me, nor ever, for me, were the tender joys of maternal patience and pity and understanding; those romantic hopes of late flowering, of postponed fulfilment, to which some of my contemporaries clung so pathetically, were merely a form of cowardly self-delusion in which women who had seen the destructive realities of War should know better than to indulge. Very deliberately, with an aching regret that I had been born, physiologically, so normal, I pushed into the deepest recesses of my mind the old haunting memories, the once confident dreams, the sweet anticipated comfort of warm responsive flesh, the visionary children for whom, during strange dark nights in Camberwell, I had planned to work and achieve, and resolutely turned upon this too poignantly equipped storehouse the firm key of purposeful ambition.

10

In any case, it was impossible to remain very long preoccupied with the effect of the War upon one's own position when the opportunity of changing the position of all women, whether super-fluous or otherwise, was there to be seized for the first time in history. Directly after the Armistice numerous women's organisa-tions, slightly altered since pre-war days in name and constitu-tion, began to emerge from the all-pervading military fog which between 1914 and 1918 had enveloped all movements for social reform, and though their resources were low, and they had to rely upon such ignominious expedients as jumble sales for raising funds, they all had definite and intelligent political plans for the pursuit of such objects as the retention of the wartime women police, the introduction of women establishment officers into Civil Service departments, pensions for widows, and the extension of the franchise to all adult women. Under their auspices a series of long-postponed measures, such as the Criminal Law Amendment Bill, the Guardianship of Infants Bill, the Illegitimacy and Bastardy Bills and the Matrimonial Causes Bill – always strangely regarded by men as 'women's' questions in spite of the fact that men, just as much as women, are born, get married and become parents – were introduced into the House of Commons and reached the Statute Book within the next three or four years.

Much of this activity was due to the fear that the Government which had passed the Sex Disqualification (Removal) Act on a surge of sentimental post-war gratitude did not really intend to keep faith with the women who were no longer supposed to be handicapped by sex or marriage. The abolition of women police patrols had been recommended by the Geddes Committee and numerous policewomen were in process of being 'axed'; Cambridge, steadily refusing to give Degrees to women, had its female students limited to five hundred by the Royal Universities Commission; while the London Hospital refused to take any more women students at all, using the now time-worn argument about the difficulties of teaching 'certain unpleasant subjects of medi-cine' to mixed audiences. (Simultaneously, owing to the shortage of nurses, the age of admission was being lowered by the same hospital, and girls under twenty-one were accepted for training without questions of 'delicacy' being raised.)

Finally, as though to confirm the suspicions of organised women that a conspiracy existed to make the Sex Disqualification (Removal) Act a dead letter, the Glasgow and St Pancras Corporations, as well as the Education Committees in eighty-seven areas, went out of their way to dismiss or recommend the dismissal of the married women in their employment, apparently under a curious impression that the marriage and motherhood of the healthiest and most intelligent women would somehow be furthered if these normal human relationships had to be paid for by the loss of a good job. As the Viscountess Rhondda, then in the midst of her historic contest with the House of Lords, remarked at a Six Point Group meeting during the summer of 1922, the word '(Removal)' in the title of the Act had never managed to get outside its brackets.

This feeble functioning of the Sex Disqualification (Removal) Act was typical of all post-war reaction, in which war neurosis had been transformed into fear – fear especially of incalculable results following from unforseen causes; fear of the loss of power by those in possession of it; fear, therefore, of women. It all formed part of what Rebecca West, in a *Time and Tide* review of *Jailed for Freedom* by the American feminist, Doris Stevens, called 'the disappointing aftermath of our suffragist movement'.

'When we read,' she added, 'of such achievements of character as this' (the American women's endurance in prison), 'the belittling attitude towards the militant suffrage movement, which is common to-day among the younger intellectuals, appears as the mean ingratitude, the computation so grudging that it arrives at falsehood, which it is' – a comment still as appropriate in these days as in those.

In 1922 the soundest hopes for the future liberation of women from traditional restrictions and burdens appeared to lie with two widely different organisations which had both been formed the year before. With a barrister-cousin from the Temple, I went to some of the earliest Essex Hall meetings of the Society for

Constructive Birth Control, started by Dr Marie Stopes, and expressed to him my surprise at the young face, the soft voice and the youthful garments of the movement's confident and dauntless founder. The other organisation, the Six Point Group, had been inaugurated in February 1921, under the chairmanship of Viscountess Rhondda, to work for six closely connected objects – pensions for widows, equal right of guardianship for married parents, the improvement of the laws dealing with child-assault and the position of the unmarried mother, equal pay for teachers, and equal opportunities for men and women in the Civil Service.

Soon after our establishment at the Doughty Street studio in the early spring of 1922, Winifred saw in the recently founded *Time and Tide* the announcement of a mass meeting to be held by the Six Point Group in the Queen's Hall on March 14th. Chiefly attracted by the fact that Clemence Dane, whose *A Bill of Divorcement* we had seen soon after it began its long run at St Martin's Theatre in March 1921, was billed as one of the speakers, we decided to go.

As it happened, we looked vainly for Miss Dane among the distinguished women – Lady Astor, Lady Rhondda, Mrs Pethick-Lawrence, Miss Agnes Dawson and Mrs Chalmers Watson, all of them then unknown to us by sight – on the Queen's Hall platform, for she had not been able to attend, but this disappointment was compensated by the surprised interest with which we listened to Lady Rhondda's speech.

She had, we knew, the reputation of a harsh and pitiless feminist, chiefly – and quite unreasonably – because, five days after the first Degree-giving for women at Oxford, she had begun her struggle for permission to enter the House of Lords as a peeress in her own right by a petition to the King for a writ of summons to Parliament. On March 2nd the Committee for Privileges of the House of Lords had decided in favour of her petition, but their decision had still to be discussed by the House itself on March 30th. I was astonished beyond measure at the deprecating sweetness of her expression, the mild earnestness of her hesitating voice, as she spoke rather shyly on the subject of child-assault, which was said to have increased owing to the widespread mental and moral instability that had followed the War. My surprise was exceeded only on the solitary occasion that I saw Mrs Pankhurst – back in England after working for the Canadian Society of Mental Hygiene in Toronto – speaking not long before her death in Lady Rhondda's own drawing-room, and observed the wistful and faded but still potent beauty of that small, attractive figure.

Three months after the Queen's Hall rally, at a summer afternoon meeting of the Six Point Group, for which we had now begun to work and occasionally to speak, we saw a very different aspect of Lady Rhondda. By that time the House of Lords Committee for Privileges – owing to Lord Birkenhead's energetic opposition to feminine claims, and to the replacement as Attorney-General of Sir Gordon Hewart (who had become Lord Chief Justice) by Sir Ernest Pollock – had given its final vote against the admission of peeresses, and Lady Rhondda, no longer mild or deprecating, expressed to the small, select audience of women her opinion of a so-called Sex Disqualification (Removal) Act which exercised no restraint upon injustice and prejudice. With her flushed face and indignant blue eyes she looked very young and determined; as she spoke the combs fell out of her soft, exuberant hair and clattered to the floor, but she treated them with as much contemptuous indifference as if they had been the insolent witticisms of Lord Birkenhead.

When her speech was over, Winifred and I, intimidated but resolutely bold, went up to her and proclaimed our regret for the misdoings of the peers; the cordiality with which she received us revived both our courage and our determination to go on working with the Group. That meeting, especially for Winifred, was the beginning of many things. Four years later, on her return from a lecture-tour in South Africa, she was to find herself the youngest director on the Board of *Time and Tide*, while I was to join its staff of reviewers for a time when I came back from America in 1926.

The first and immediate result of this contact with post-war feminism was to send us into the crowded publicity of summer-time Hyde Park, there to advocate, from a platform lent to the Six Point Group by the London Council for Promoting Public

Morality, the early passage by the Government of the Criminal Law Amendment Bill. This Bill, which was chiefly concerned to raise the 'age of consent' in cases of indecent assault from thirteen to sixteen, and to remove from the defence permitted to the assaulter the plea of 'reasonable cause to believe' that the child was over sixteen, had been wrecked and dropped the previous August. After a good deal of Press agitation the Government reintroduced it in 1922; on June 14th its opponents deliberately 'talked out' the Second Reading by prolonging the discussion on the previous Summer Time Bill, but although they did their best to create an atmosphere of sex-antagonism during the debate, the Bill did pass its Third Reading on July 25th.

For complete novices to open-air speaking, the advocacy of such a measure offered a good many pitfalls, but in Hyde Park the necessity of resolute vocal competition with taxi-horns, thunderous 'buses and Salvation Army hymns soon overcame our surviving remnants of pre-war squeamishness over such very public discussion of assault and prostitution. One warm June evening, no longer nervous, but flushed and a little excited after a tussle with some good-humoured hecklers, I was walking dreamily back to Bloomsbury along Oxford Street, when a middle-aged man planted himself ingratiatingly in my path. Such a charming young lady, he began without preamble, oughtn't to have to go home by herself; would I allow him to call a taxi and accompany me wherever I should like to be driven? A little disconcerted at being taken in the half-light for exactly the social type against whose existence I had just been arguing, I stammered that I was going home to work, and preferred walking alone. What would the London Council for Promoting Public Morality have thought of this ironic encounter? I asked myself, as I resumed, rather more rapidly, my meditative progress towards Doughty Street.

On the oppressive July night that the Criminal Law Amendment Bill passed its Third Reading, I went with Winifred to the House of Commons, and listened from the Strangers' Gallery to that curious debate, which lasted from 10 p.m. until nearly 2.30 a.m. At an earlier hour of that same day, Mr Justice Lawrence, in giving evidence on the Guardianship of Infants Bill before a Joint

Committee of the two Houses of Parliament, had remarked that the effect of this measure was to offer an insult to God Almighty and to the father whom He had appointed; and the opposition against the Criminal Law Amendment Bill was conducted by Mr Macquisten, Sir George Hamilton and Colonel Moore-Brabazon on similar if somewhat less elevated lines. Sitting in the pale, drowsy light of the midnight House, I remembered my long-ago molestation in the train going to Buxton, and felt a little sick as I listened to the facetious gibes about pigtails and effeminate men. Was this really the heart of that conveyor of civilisation to primitive peoples, the British Empire, in the post-war summer of 1922, or had we inadvertently strayed into the time of Martin Luther, with his robust views on the uses of women?

When the Third Reading was finally passed we looked down from our seats in the gallery at Lady Astor, who had fought so fearlessly for the measure against such distasteful opposition. Slight, black-robed, persistent, she had, like ourselves, sat out the hot, stuffy debate; elatedly we believed that she smiled up at us from the floor of the House. As we went out into the cool freshness of the dark streets just before dawn, I was conscious of quite a ferocious satisfaction because the plea made by a few gallant Englishmen that our liberties would be curtailed if the opportunities for attacking female children were made more difficult had not succeeded.

11

Soon after we came back from Geneva that autumn, the General Election of 1922 broke like a storm from the threatening political skies, and at once diverted England's attention from such trivial events on 'the Continent' as the Fascist march on Rome and the opening of the Lausanne Conference. Even the picturesque erection, on the fourth Armistice Day, of a memorial in the clearing of the Forest of Compiègne where the Armistice was signed passed almost unnoticed by a country already beginning to forget its dead and to meditate upon the possibilities of 'the next war'.

As soon as the Coalition fell, the Six Point Group announced its inspired and disconcerting expedient of publishing Black and White Lists. The Black List contained the names of those Members of Parliament, including the jocular opponents of the Criminal Law Amendment Bill, who had hampered the various reforms demanded by organised women, and members of the Group were urged to work and vote against them. The White List represented those men and women who had been especially helpful to the women's cause in Parliament. Its twenty-two names included those of Lord Robert Cecil, Lady Astor, Sir Robert Newman, Mrs Wintringham and Colonel Josiah Wedgwood, and members of the Group were asked to work and vote on their behalf.

In the intervals of my work in Bethnal Green, I kept in touch with the Six Point Group campaign, which reached its most spectacular moment on November 1st with a big meeting at the Central Hall, Westminster, to demand the amendment of the Sex Disqualification (Removal) Act. It was at this meeting, where she was one of the speakers, that I first saw Rebecca West, whose novel *The Judge*, which had recently been published, I had read with a disturbed and passionate interest. Dark, courageous, still in her rebellious twenties, she gave, with her incisive voice and proud head with brushed-back hair, the impression of some intrepid young thoroughbred, destined to win all contests because completely undaunted by every obstacle conceivable to mortal imagination.

'The Houses of Parliament,' she said, 'seem to me the most romantic buildings in the world . . . They . . . are the symbol of a real miracle, a real mixture of ramshackleness and nobility. There has developed there a system of government which bears witness to the extraordinary nature of the human soul, and the hopefulness of the prospects that are before human society. There again and again assemblies have gathered in all honesty, have matured to power, have fallen into corruption, have miraculously reassembled again, glorious with the honesty of a new generation and a new movement. There men of all sorts who seemed utterly selfish and corrupt have to an extraordinary extent, that the most cynical interpretation of history cannot dispute, showed that they cared a little for the common good.'[1]

As she spoke she seemed the embodiment of the modern woman's movement, so old in its aspirations but so young in achievement, and some at least of her audience began to visualise the House of Commons, not as the place which thwarted their hopes and hampered their participation in the forward-looking work of their day, but as a genuine part of the work itself, as the actual scene in time to come of their own finer struggles and efforts. It was still many years before I was to know Rebecca as a friend, but from that moment she became to me a personal symbol of the feminist cause which had thrilled me ever since my naïve adolescence, the twentieth-century successor of Mary Wollstonecraft and Olive Schreiner.

The Six Point Group was only one of many active women's organisations that autumn, for these were now able for the first time to use a measure of power instead of merely to agitate for it. Even past and future Ministers began in alarm to remember that all but the youngest women had votes and could no longer be disregarded, and Mr Bonar Law addressed a mass meeting of women voters at Drury Lane Theatre. It was the first time that a Prime Minister had addressed an audience composed solely of enfranchised women, and many of the more prescient feminists – foreseeing deplorable consequences if the new voters came to be regarded in politics as a class apart – sincerely hoped that it would be the last. Whatever their Party, the election addresses of the thirty-three women candidates supported the League of Nations and urged the need for measures to benefit health and education, but though women had already introduced a new element of compassion, of perceptiveness, of imagination, into politics, there appeared to be no reason, other than the established tendency of certain males to look upon 'the ladies' as a sub-species of humanity, for treating them as a specialised category.

So, refusing to be pushed out of the main political stream even by a Prime Minister, a large number of the women voters went

[1] Recorded verbatim by *Time and Tide*, November 10th, 1922.

on serenely demanding equal political and economic rights, an equal moral standard, and equal status for married women in relation to employment, nationality and the guardianship of children. To many male candidates it came as a disagreeable shock to realise that women's desire – so long complacently taken for granted by anti-feminists – to assume such inconvenient responsibilities could now be attained by them as the result of persistence. When these reforms, too, were obtained by the women, what would become of their opponents? It was indeed a horrid speculation, which caused a spontaneous revision of election addresses all over the country. The over-active Six Point Group had already published a selection of quotations from the speeches of Black List M.P.s which their makers would have been thankful to forget; who knew where such detestable expedients would end?

When the election results were published, it was found that sixteen of the twenty-two White List M.P.s had been returned to Parliament, and only twelve of the twenty-three on the Black List. In spite of this encouraging portent, the twelve untouchables consistently withstood, with a united determination worthy of a better cause, the growing influence of the women's vote, and among them one of the most conspicuous was Mr – now Sir – Dennis Herbert, the Conservative M P, for the Watford Division of Hertfordshire.

During the debates on the Criminal Law Amendment Bill, Mr Herbert displayed,[1] in the eyes of the Six Point Group, a distinct tendency to defend the double standard of morality as a convenient museum-piece of English social tradition, and in the discussions on one of the most revolutionary measures of 1923, Major Entwistle's Matrimonial Causes Bill, this inclination reappeared. 'Is there any man in this House who is the father of a son and a daughter,' Mr Herbert dramatically demanded in opposing the measure, 'who would regard the sin of adultery on the part of his son as being as serious as the sin of adultery on the part of his daughter?'[2]

[1] Hansard, Second Reading, July 5th, 1922; Standing Committee D., July 13th, 1922.
[2] Hansard, Second Reading, March 2nd, 1923.

In spite of such archaic criticism, Major Entwistle's Bill had passed both Houses of Parliament by the middle of July 1923, and for the first time in England the rights of men and women were equal with regard to divorce. As usual in matrimonial legislation, adultery was over-emphasised as a wrecking factor in marriage, and conditions far more disastrous to marital relations – such as habitual drunkenness, insanity and excessive incompatibility – remained inadmissible as causes for their dissolution. 'Civilised man,' as a *Time and Tide* leader-writer expressed it, 'recognises that sexual intercourse is not the only thing that matters in married life, and he knows that there are other things besides physical unfaithfulness which can make married life impossible.' Still, it was at least an advance towards the far-off ideal of equal companionship when even the law, with its former pompous wink at masculine irregularities, began to expect the same standard of conduct from husbands as from wives, and the Six Point Group felt a strong political reluctance to forgive Mr Herbert for his endeavours to prevent the introduction of even so small a measure of civilisation into marriage.

So on July 12th the Group took a large hall in Watford and organised a protest meeting against the attitude displayed by the Member for that division towards the Criminal Law Amendment and Matrimonial Causes Bills. Numerous local clerics appeared on the platform, although one of them had included Mr Herbert amongst his churchwardens, and the hall was, irrelevantly but not unnaturally, packed with jubilant members of the local Liberal and Labour Parties. As it happened, the meeting coincided with the end of a nine days' heat wave; only three nights before, London had been kept awake until dawn by one of the most prolonged and violent thunderstorms within English memory, and the hot passions in the hall were inflamed by the sultriness of the still summer air.

It was one of the most terrifying evenings of my life. With my usual rashness I had agreed to be first on the list of speakers, and the knowledge that Mr Herbert, courageous and unrepentant, was in the hall ready to meet his critics did not exactly give me the feeling that this was a pleasant party. My first novel was about to be published after a series of agitating vicissitudes, and only the previous week my mother's mother had died after a serious operation which for a fortnight had thrown the whole family into a condition of grieved perturbation. Neither of these occurrences was conducive to that robust state of mind best suited to a political fight, but I endeavoured to pretend that I possessed it as I rose to attack this arch-anti-feminist with such eloquence as I could still command. I dared not use my notes, for I knew that the hands that held them would tremble and give me away. Later, in an interview with the local Press, Mr Herbert referred contemptuously to me as 'a sulky child', and suggested that the Six Point Group must indeed be hard up for supporters if they allowed so young and foolish a creature to advocate their cause. But even he was not so conscious as myself of the defects of my qualities. Never had I longed more passionately for a 'presence' and a dignified manner; if only, I thought, the harsh experiences of the past ten years could have been inscribed on my countenance or reproduced in my gestures! Was I always to remain this youthful, unimpressive figure, suggestive of the nursery rather than the platform?

As I had foreseen all too clearly, Mr Herbert heckled me furiously in the middle of my speech and challenged the accuracy of my statements, but the clerical chairman, who sympathised with the Group, persuaded him to allow me to continue by offering him a later opportunity to put his own case to the audience. As soon as I had finished, Lady Rhondda herself continued the indictment; flourishing several copies of Hansard, she flung Mr Herbert's own utterances back at him with fearless indignation. I have never heard her make a better fighting speech; its effect was to convert the meeting, which passed the Six Point Group resolution, 'specially deploring' Mr Herbert's attitude towards the two Bills, and urging him to bear in mind 'the effect of his utterances upon the young people of the neighbourhood', by a majority of about four to one.

The campaign was continued by the Group in Watford during the 1923 election, which not only put the first minority Labour Government into office on the day following the death of Lenin in Russia, but by giving seats to eight women M.P.s carried the hopes of political women to a point which, ten years previously, had seemed likely to remain unwarranted for centuries. In Conservative Watford the activities of the Six Point Group, rather than the left swing of the pendulum, were probably responsible for the drop of nearly 500 votes in Mr Herbert's large majority, and for several weeks after the first Watford meeting an acrimonious correspondence raged in the columns of the *West Herts Post and Watford Newsletter*. In the letters contributed by Mr Herbert's supporters my name and personality were treated with that uncompromising frankness which always characterises political controversy, and I was obliged to attempt to defend myself. But the agitation caused me by this continuous polemic was soon swallowed up in the far greater perturbations which accompanied the publication of my novel *The Dark Tide*.

12

For the first two or three years of my onslaught upon editorial offices, my journalism, like Winifred's, remained persistent and hopeful rather than progressive. It might, indeed, have perished altogether from sheer lack of encouragement as soon as I left the flattering undergraduate atmosphere of Oxford, had I not been haunted by the memory of a ride through Fleet Street with my St Monica's aunt on the top of a No. 13 'bus while I was still at school.

We were going back to London Bridge in the early twilight of a late autumn evening; against the smouldering red of the November sunset, the roofs of the tall newspaper buildings were silhouetted with black, challenging sharpness. Clenching my hands in the earnest ecstasy of seventeen, I vowed to win for myself the right to enter those offices as a respected contributor. The War came and went; love and life came and went; but the dream remained. It was with me when, in the early days of *Time and Tide*, I took my first tentative notes and articles to the former Fleet Street office. It is with me still; though for years now I have passed on numerous professional errands along that narrow thoroughfare, I never see the name 'Fleet Street' without a profound, absurd renewal of the old childish emotion.

From time to time during the months in Bloomsbury, Roland's father, who maintained his benevolent interest in our literary prospects, discussed our work with us, and deplored 'the fume and fret' of our London activities. Actually, as he came later to realise, we could hardly have had a better preparation for the free-lance political journalism to which we were both growing more and more attracted than that turbulent, kaleidoscopic life of journeys and meetings, platforms and debates and speeches. Under its influence our articles, from being the colourless, anecdotal productions which every newspaper office receives by the thousand, gradually acquired those provocative qualities which alone bring the era of rejection-slips to a close. Even when lectures and pacifist controversies were new and nerve-racking experiences, the delightful sense that I now had something else to write about but the memories which were then still too painful to be reconstructed with detachment caused me to send Winifred an unusually optimistic letter.

'I sometimes envy the Huxley family, with its swarm of distinguished relatives and hereditary niche in literature,' I told her in November 1921. 'And yet, I think, if one can only do it, it's really more exciting to rise "from obscurity", as Machiavelli would put it.'

For book-writing our swift, eager days did not, perhaps, provide the best possible atmosphere, although they did supply a wealth of material for that future time when some change in political or personal circumstances would bring the opportunity for recapitulating their complicated emotions and experiences. But book-writing of a sort was carried on with fervour; and in spite of lectures, and teaching, and propaganda, and persevering much-travelled articles, our first novels were both finished by the spring of 1922. Roland's father, after reading and approving of *The Dark Tide*, decided to take it to Putnams', where a leading member of the firm was an old friend of his, while Winifred, also by his advice, approached Cassells' with *Anderby Wold*, her story of Yorkshire farm life.

Putnams' reaction to *The Dark Tide* – a dramatic tale of Oxford women students, with black and white values quite unrelieved by half-tones – was much, and perhaps even more than, what might have been expected. Frankly, they said, they did not recommend publication, and though they thought the author should go on writing, they suggested that perhaps it would not be a bad idea for her to wait until she had settled down and had a little more experience of life before attempting another novel.

I wrote rather bitterly in response to the letter from Roland's father which enclosed this communication, for I felt that I had had quite as much experience of life (to say nothing of death) as I wanted for the present. After giving him my opinion of Putnams' perspicacity, I begged him not to involve himself in any more of my failures; would he please return the manuscript and let me shoulder the burden of possible future rejections myself? In sending back the book, he suggested that I should try John Murray, so I called, greatly intimidated, at the offices of that impressive and decorous firm. There I saw Mr Leonard Huxley, who received me with gracious benevolence; I was standing, he told me, in the place where Byron had stood, and I was a young author aspiring to fame. His publishing house, however, soon repudiated the responsibility of helping me to achieve that aspiration, and for the second time *The Dark Tide* returned to Doughty Street, where *Anderby Wold*, back from Cassells', very soon joined it.

At this moment I happened to read a Press paragraph stating that the *Femina Vie-Heureuse* Prize for 1921–22 had been awarded to Rose Macaulay for her novel *Dangerous Ages*. Tentatively I wrote to congratulate her without the slightest hope that she would remember me, but she replied almost at once, concluding with an inquiry after the progress of the novel that I had mentioned at the Somerville Bazaar. Nothing, had I but known it, could have been more profoundly self-sacrificing than this inquiry by an established writer of a junior Somervillian, for all successful authors are accustomed to receive so many requests from complete strangers for assistance with publishers, and so many unsolicited manuscripts with confident demands for free criticism, that the mere mention of somebody who has an unpublished novel and wants advice might well be enough to send any one of them out of town for a week.

Innocently regarding myself as quite a special case, I poured out to Miss Macaulay the tale of my disappointment over *The Dark Tide*, and in another letter of which the generous kindness was quite unspoilt by condescension, she suggested that I should send the book to Collins, her own publishers, offering at the same time to write to their chief reader, Mr J. D. Beresford, on my behalf. When the book, despite her intervention, came back once more, with a detailed letter of criticism upon which Mr Beresford must have spent several hours of precious time, she asked me to tea to talk it over. What she really thought of the raw crudities which even a cursory glance revealed, I now shudder to imagine, but she was too considerate, and too wise, to suggest those fundamental reconstructions which maturity and literary experience alone can make. Her advice enabled me to make numerous improvements in such details of style and syntax as were capable of amendment, and I carried away a glowing memory of hot crumpets and brisk, incisive conversation upon which I relied exclusively for stimulus in the disheartening months that followed.

During the remainder of that year I sent *The Dark Tide* to almost every publisher in London and elsewhere. It came back, on each occasion a little grimier and more dog-eared, from Constable, and Blackwell, and Chatto & Windus, and Martin Secker, and Sidgwick & Jackson; after that my memory loses count. Most publishers contented themselves with rejection-slips, but quite a number of eminent 'readers' wrote letters of advice, suggesting that I should rewrite the beginning, or the end, or the middle, or counselling a different form of dialogue, or urging me to change the story's melancholy conclusion to a 'happy ending'.

One thing, at any rate, this prolonged period of rebuff did teach me, and that was the enormous, unfailing patience of the established author with the novice. After each new rejection the untiring Miss Macaulay was ready with her inexhaustible supply of suggestions and encouragement, and to-day, when unsolicited manuscripts arrive at my house from unfamiliar sources with requests for criticism at my busiest moments, I remember her generosity to me when I was an unutterable nuisance myself, and wish that I could feel or show to my importunate correspondents a quarter of her persistent goodwill. Her periodic letters were the lamps which lighted that unprofitable year of 1922, so black in its continual discouragement, so empty, after the small comparative triumphs at Oxford, of any sign of ultimate literary success. But for Rose Macaulay I might well have given up, and although in the past ten years I have done so little of all that I hoped to do, and have advanced so short a distance along that humble path to achievement which so dimly resembles the shining highroad of my early confident dreams, I have never ceased to be glad that I did go on.

Meanwhile, the vicissitudes of Winifred's novel, *Anderby Wold*, were proving much briefer and far less harassing. When we called at the Doughty Street studio before going to our respective families for a holiday after the Geneva Summer School of 1922, Winifred opened a letter from the firm of John Lane which made, to her humble astonishment, an offer for her book. To me also this event was something of a psychological crisis; Winifred was considerably my junior, at Oxford she had followed modestly in my literary wake, and it had simply never occurred to me that her work could be preferred and published before my own. In Kensington, alone in my bedroom, I made myself face and acknowledge the hard fact that *Anderby Wold* was a better book than *The Dark Tide*. Inwardly I knew it to be more balanced and mature than my own novel in spite of the fact that Winifred had planned and begun it when barely twenty-two, and at last I wrote her the appreciation which I had dumbfoundedly withheld in Bloomsbury.

'I am trying to make myself believe that a book of yours will really exist, with your name on the cover, and we shall perhaps stand outside Bumpus's and look at it on the shelf of new novels . . . I know the reviews will be nice – it is a kind book as well as a clever one and has always inspired me with a secret envy . . . You make me feel very humble – one who talks but never achieves while you quietly achieve and don't talk. You will be quite famous by the time you are my age – and one rare thing will make your success the more distinguished, and that is that you cannot get any success so great as the success you deserve ... I shall be glad really to know someone intimately who succeeds – just because all my best friends so far have either died before they could achieve anything or else are held up for lack of funds. One needs a change to prove that just occasionally life does repay one for living ... Somehow the whole world seems subtly changed by your book getting taken. I suppose it's like what I said ... about crossing the gulf between aspiration and achievement; once people have done it they are never quite the same again.'

By the end of 1922, I had come to the sad but resigned conclusion that *The Dark Tide* was never likely to find a home, and in desperation had begun to draft my second novel, 'The Man on the Crucifix', which was afterwards published under the title *Not Without Honour*. In spite of this new experiment, the hope of becoming a writer of any kind was flickering very low; apart from Rose Macaulay, the literary world of London seemed to have made it very clear that they did not want me and my ingenuous efforts, and I began once again to feel that I could justify my survival of the War only by piping for peace upon an indefinite series of platforms. And yet, notwithstanding the lack of external evidence from publishers and editors, I could not quite slay an inward conviction that it was not really upon platforms that I could best plead either that or any other unpopular cause.

'As Vera Brittain, lecturer and speaker for the League of Nations Union, etc.,' I wrote on Christmas Eve to Winifred, who was again in Yorkshire with a family rejoicing over the imminent publication of *Anderby Wold*, 'I feel quite able to hold my own with Winifred Holtby – and to tell you the honest truth, I don't care a damn if I can't; I don't really care for anything but writing, and making up my mind to stop doing it would never prevent me from going on ... Not that writing isn't a bitter business. Yesterday I read bits of Barbellion, whose life seemed to be filled, like mine, with rejected manuscripts. Then I made up my mind that even though our flat was choked with the returned manuscripts ... I would nevertheless put all I knew into the "Man on the Crucifix" ... So I set to yesterday evening and wrote the first draft of the difficult first page of the first chapter. I immediately hated it. I wanted to produce on myself the same effect as Hugh Walpole and "Elizabeth" produce on me, and I found I couldn't do it. Then I cursed myself because I couldn't write . . . I can't remember, but I believe that a year ago I had a sort of idea that I'd only got to finish a book to get it published; Mr L.'s . . . encouragement after all did rather suggest that, didn't it? – and wasted years had shut out any other means of knowledge. At any rate perhaps hating what I do, being at least a new method, may produce a different result.'

Unfortunately the prospects of a different result, while I was only at the beginning of a new book whose predecessor was still a pariah, were too remote to provide an immediate stimulus, and the next day found me writing to Winifred more gloomily than ever.

'I am depressed this morning . . . because it is Christmas, and cold and damp, and because I ache for beauty and joy, and because there is no sun, and by no stretch of imagination can I pretend it is spring at Siena. I am bogy-ridden by ghosts of individuals and of manuscripts, and also by the dim figure of "The Man on the Crucifix", which I can't attack because my feet are too cold for inspiration. I feel like Hilda [Reid], from whom I have had a card briefly stating: "I have been chasing wild geese."'

When *Anderby Wold* appeared a few weeks later, it deservedly gained an agreeable number of interested reviews. Its agricultural theme was based upon a paragraph from Hobbes's *Leviathan*: 'Felicity is a continual progresse of the desire from one object to another, the attaining of the former being still but the way to the later . . . so that, in the first place, I put for a general inclination of all mankind, a perpetual and restlesse desire of power after power which ceaseth only after death . . . and there shall be no content-ment but proceeding.' The tolerant, imaginative treatment of so large a topic by so young a writer caused Winifred to be care-fully watched from that time onwards by the more discerning editors and critics, and put an end once for all to her occasional ludicrous misgivings about becoming a writer rather than a teacher.

While the reviews of *Anderby Wold* were coming in, *The Dark*

Tide was still lugubriously circulating, but, tattered and dirty as the manuscript now was, it had almost reached the end of its tedious travels.

13

In the late spring of 1923, my tired and dishevelled novel strayed into the hands of Mr Grant Richards, who was then enjoying one of his most elegant periods of publishing. I had almost completed 'The Man on the Crucifix' when the entire complexion of my world was changed by a note from him asking me to call. The book, he said, had certain obvious faults which would make the risk of publication considerable, but he was nevertheless attracted by its atmosphere of youth and freshness.

'What with all this youthful freshness, and needing more experience of life, and so on, I must be suffering from arrested development,' I thought ruefully to myself. 'Well, perhaps being a War Office tweeny for so long *was* rather bad for the intellect, to say nothing of the stultifying effect of suspense and sorrow. Crowded living and a great rush of events probably do retard development in some ways as much as they hasten it in others; after all, one of the chief factors in mental growth is time to think and leisure to give one's thoughts some kind of expression. Those of us who got caught up into the War and its emotions before our brains had become mature were rather like Joseph II of Austria – we had to take the second step before we took the first. I daresay if I'd stopped at Oxford, instead of becoming a V.A.D., I should be more intelligent by now; I might even have published a book or two which would have been remembered, whereas my four years with the Army seem quite forgotten by everyone except myself. Oh, well—!'

And that, after all, was the only comment now to be made on the War; it couldn't be helped that one had to make it so often.

In the end Mr Richards made a proposal on behalf of my book which probably represented more or less what it was worth. I was comparatively hard up in 1923, and the contract that I made over *The Dark Tide* meant several months of very light suppers and only the briefest of visits to Geneva when travel was a dominating passion. Nevertheless, if I were to have the choice over again and still retain my subsequent knowledge of the literary world, I should probably agree to the same arrangement, since no sacrifices, for unforeseen as well as for obvious reasons, were ever endured with more worth-while results.

The auspicious aspect of their profound and far-reaching consequences was not, however, immediately in evidence. Beautifully produced and printed in a rather blank July, the book was for a few weeks a best seller and received seventy-three notices headed by a serious and favourable review of three-quarters of a column in *The Times Literary Supplement*, but its first appearance was celebrated by a series of sharp and angry Press attacks upon my treatment of my theme. The usual attempt – then extremely surprising to me – was made by the usual type of newspaper to present the story as a 'revelation' of life as lived at an Oxford women's college – though nothing could have been more ingenuously complete than the guileless moral innocence of all the female characters – and a young man, now a reputable author, who ought to have known better but was probably in need of cash, produced an article in a large-circulation daily which began thus: 'Once upon a time an Oxford don kissed a woman student, and Miss Vera Brittain immediately sat down and wrote a book about it.'

But even this unforeseen reception was not so disintegrating as one or two acid letters that I received from individuals in Oxford who believed themselves to be portrayed by the composite characters in the story, many of whom had models quite unrelated to the university in any way. My lugubrious bursar, I was told long afterwards, had caused a good deal of purposeless heart-burning, since she represented the combined portrait of two of my own extremely unacademic relatives. No one, I suppose, who is not himself a novelist ever quite understands the process through which his characters pass in the fiction-writer's mind. With the exception of the mass-producers, few authors venture upon the dubious expedient of 'inventing' their men and women without relation to any known model, but they do not, on the other hand, put themselves into the shoes of the Court photographer. The study of a real individual leaves with the author the impression of a type; he uses this type as the basis for his fictitious creation, and from this foundation grows a character in many important respects quite unlike the actual subject of observation – a character which takes more and more control of its own personality as the story proceeds, and ends as something poles apart from the original. It is only rarely, when drawing minor characters which provide colour and background but are not required to develop psychologically, that the imaginative novelist permits himself the short cut of a direct portrait.

In 1923 I was quite unacquainted with the more malevolent aspects of publicity, and in spite of the long series of respectful, if critical, reviews that followed the opening attacks, I was unable for weeks to collect my letters after each post without trembling all over, while the sight of a bundle of press-cuttings reduced me to a condition of nervous prostration even when they contained such notices as that by Gerald Gould in the *Saturday Review* – an astringent but immensely vitalising criticism upon the concluding words of which I was so often to meditate in the months that followed with a glowing sense of infinite hope:

'*The Dark Tide* is a remarkable book, though crude. It starts off with a somewhat lurid picture of Oxford life . . . and the author displays, in the interests of the wicked tutor's subsequent career as a diplomat, an engaging disregard of the distinction between the Civil Servant who is *in* a Government department, and the politician who aims at being the temporary head of it. But she has the root of the matter in her. She knows how to communicate sympathy. She has spiritual understanding of character. Some day she may write a good book.'

That summer and autumn, Winifred took an unusually long holiday in Yorkshire owing to her sister's forthcoming marriage, and day after day I poured out to her much-enduring sympathy a series of anguished letters, describing the terrors of an inexperienced author marooned with a family which she was anxious to protect from her own perturbations while endeavouring to give a harassed mind to the conclusion of her second novel.

'This flat seems peaceful after ours,' I told her, 'though something still rises up and chokes me every time the post comes. The wallpapers and the challenging bell at 58 had rather got on my nerves . . . I am most pleased and touched by your mother's letter and yours this morning. I feel so grateful that anyone can feel like that towards my book; I only hope that others will do so; for, if they do, it cannot possibly do harm. It's the feeling I wanted people to have – that of weakness being able to rise to great heights of character when strengthened by "the dark tide" of suffering . . . If only some of the Oxford people would see it like that . . . It's because it was intended to be idealistic that the mud-throwing hurts so . . . At present all I want is to hide my head in the country and stay there without making speeches or meeting anybody.'

One of Winifred's unfailingly patient replies might with good reason be reproduced as a pamphlet and presented to every nervous young author who finds himself for the first time in contact with the critical harshness of a world which, being sensitive and susceptible, is sometimes ruthless and vindictive as well.

'I have only now come in,' she wrote, 'from having lunch with J. E. B[uckrose]. She has heard of you, and that your book has been "an unusual success for a first novel", though she has not yet read it . . . She says that she has never yet written a book without making an enemy . . . and even for her mildest has had anonymous letters and frequently people whom she has never heard of write indignantly to protest against being "charactatured". I told her a few of our troubles and she laughed and said – "Never mind. It's worth it. Whatever you do, write what you think and not what people want you to think," and she said that she had ruined herself as an artist by trying to write books that would offend no one, for she has an invalid husband, whom she most dearly loves, to support.'

Not until long afterwards did I realise that the worries and miseries of that summer had swept me across the rubicon which lies between amateur and professional status. But I had, in

September, the satisfaction of knowing that Mr Grant Richards had accepted 'The Man on the Crucifix' for publication as *Not Without Honour* on much more favourable terms than he gave *The Dark Tide*, while that winter my rejection-slips from editors began to diminish and in another two or three years had practically ceased.

To-day, if a young man or woman fresh from college brought me a first-novel manuscript, and asked for instructions with regard to publication, in the light of my own experience I should probably give without a qualm of remorse some such unorthodox advice as this: 'By all means go to a first-class agent and get good terms from a publisher if you can. But if you can't, absolve your agent and put up with the best you can get from any firm with a reputation to maintain. Don't think too optimistically in terms of profits, for any publisher who launches you, an unknown beginner, upon a world that doesn't want you, is taking a very great financial risk. But get published somehow. The only thing that matters to you at this stage is to get published and talked about, to be able to refer the editors who find your adolescent bombardments intolerably tedious to a printed work of your own. Later, when you have a following and something of a name, you can begin to think about being a good business man or woman and making watertight contracts. Before that, just concentrate on getting published, and if there is anything in you, sooner or later the rest will follow. If there is nothing in you, you will have learnt without further waste of time that a writer's calling is not for you.'

Because *The Dark Tide* made more difference to my personal and professional life than the most ardently self-deceived optimist could have expected from a first novel with ten times its merits, I should like here to place on record my gratitude to Mr Grant Richards for publishing it on his own experimental terms instead of condemning it to oblivion by a dignified refusal. His decision launched me on a career of writing which, though quite unspectacular, is tolerably remunerative, and above all has brought me a great deal of happiness – the most permanent and reliable happiness that I know, for it is not at the mercy of accident to the extent that personal relationships always are and always must be. Finally, by bringing out the book just when he did, Mr Richards set the stage for an event, of considerable importance to myself, which was probably the last result that either he or I expected from its publication.

CHAPTER XII

"Another Stranger"

HÉDAUVILLE. *November 1915.*

The sunshine on the long white road
That ribboned down the hill,
The velvet clematis that clung
Around your window-sill,
Are waiting for you still.

Again the shadowed pool shall break
In dimples round your feet,
And when the thrush sings in your wood,
Unknowing you may meet
Another stranger, Sweet.

And if he is not quite so old
As the boy you used to know,
And less proud, too, and worthier,
You may not let him go—
(And daisies are truer than passion-flowers)
It will be better so.

R. A. L.

1

In the middle of June 1923, a few weeks before *The Dark Tide* appeared, I went to Oxford with Winifred for the Somerville *Gaude*, the periodic after-term celebration for old students.

We had only just returned to London, when a minute envelope addressed to me in microscopic handwriting was forwarded by Somerville to the Bloomsbury flat. It contained a man's visiting-card, on the back of which was written, in effect, the following brief letter:

'DEAR MISS BRITTAIN, – I am almost sure I saw you when I was in the Camera on Wednesday. You probably won't remember me but I used to see you at Somerville debates. Won't you have tea with me one afternoon or come on the river?'

I turned the card over; the address on its face was certainly 'New College, Oxford', but the name of the letter-writer was one of which I had no recollection.

'Whoever's this impertinent young man?' I inquired of Winifred, passing over the card, and when she assured me that she had never heard of him, I tore up the intrusive piece of pasteboard, and, to my everlasting regret, threw the scraps of handwriting away.

The silence which I thus imposed upon the 'impertinent young man' would probably never have been broken had not my book been opportunely published a month or so later. In August, completely exhausted after the attacks on it by dons and reviewers, I gave way to the desire to hide my head in the country which I had expressed to Winifred, and was staying in one of the Kingswood houses attached to the ever-growing St Monica's, now empty for the holidays, when a small package arrived for me from Grant Richards's office with the usual sheaf of press-cuttings. As I did not recognise the handwriting in which it had originally been addressed to me care of the office, I opened it with trembling, reluctant fingers, for every strange calligraphy now suggested to me a new and furious onslaught on my novel. From the wrappings a slender book emerged, out of which fell a note written from New College, Oxford, in the same precise, beautiful characters that I had seen on the back of the visiting-card.

The note announced, a little defiantly, that the writer had read, 'with the utmost pleasure', my novel *The Dark Tide*, and asked me in return to accept 'the enclosed' – which, it said, there was no necessity to acknowledge. 'The enclosed' proved to be a short monograph on one of the seventeenth-century philosophers; its fly-leaf informed me that the author had been a New College Exhibitioner, and was now a lecturer in a northern university.

For some unaccountable reason, I felt curiously disturbed by the persistence of this determined young scholar. Why, I wondered, as I sat with his book on my knee beneath a luxurious arch of pink rambler roses in the peaceful garden, had the letter and the little academic monograph made such an impression upon me? Letters, and manuscripts, and unsolicited gifts were, I already knew, quite usual consequences of a book's publication; they were normal manifestations of that strange glamour which inexplicably surrounded the personalities of writers, murderers, musicians, boxers, tennis-champions and film-stars, yet most unjustly failed to lend a similar enchantment to teachers, magistrates, engineers, solicitors, shopkeepers and county councillors. This youthful don's letter was only an incident more trivial than many others; for the past two years, for all their comparative emotional security, had not been altogether without their incidents.

The various men, I thought bitterly, with whom I had come into contact since the War – men who were married already but enjoyed making use of my company for a little romantic diversion, men who imagined that I could be tempted by wealth and promises of financial support in politics, middle-aged men who were fussy and futile, elderly men whose avid eyes looked upon me with a narrow, appraising stare, young men who were ardent but ineffectual, men of all ages who wallowed in nauseating sentimentality and hadn't the brains of an earwig – simply provided one proof after another that the best of their sex had disappeared from a whole generation.

Quite definitely, now, I felt sure that I did not want to marry. The men I had cared for were all dead; I loved my uninterrupted independence, and believed that I had outgrown all possibility of including children in my scheme of life. At long last I had achieved the way of living that I had always desired; I rejoiced in my work, and had no desire to adapt my habits to those of a stranger. Why, then, had I put up, even agreeably, with the insufferable second-rateness of these men whose intellectual values and conversational standards I should not have tolerated for a moment if they had been women? What was happening to me that my life, for all its exciting occupations and eventful days, sometimes seemed so stale and unprofitable? The trouble about men's and women's relationships, I concluded self-contemptuously, was never so much adultery as adulteration; love that had once been a torrent flood had meandered through mediocre plains until it had run dry, and lost itself in a limitless desert of sand.

Sadly I recalled two lines of doggerel that the Tommies, ruthless and realistic, used to sing at their concert-parties in France:

> *Hug me, kiss me, call me Gertie,*
> *Marry me quick, I'm nearly thirty! . . .*

In those days, with the predicament of 'Gertie' still years ahead, her importunity had seemed incredibly ludicrous; nevertheless the years, heavy with events, had moved relentlessly on, and the time had almost come. Was only that the matter – that I was nearly thirty? Was complete sublimation never possible when once the human organism had been wrought up to a high pitch of emotion?

In spite of this unflattering conclusion, I answered the letter from Oxford. But when the reply to my answer came, I found that it had been written from very far away; my correspondent was, in fact, passing the coast of Labrador in S.S. *Regina* at the time, accompanied by the strains of 'We have no bananas to-day', though his long communication was posted from a small town in the United States, where he had gone, he told me, to take up new work for a year at a great American university.

By all the rules of common sense, these overwhelming considerations of time and space ought to have put an end to the correspondence then and there. But somehow, they didn't. The detailed and appreciative criticisms of *The Dark Tide* which came across the Atlantic were too stimulating to be lightly disregarded by so new an author as myself, and by the time that I was answering his third letter, we had already plunged into a prolonged argument upon the social conditions and consequences of marriage for the independent post-war woman.

It was a problem that I now very often discussed, and endeavoured – with a detachment which I believed complete – to solve in articles and on the public platforms of feminist organisations. Could marriage and motherhood be combined with real success in an art or profession? If it couldn't, which was to suffer – the profession or the human race? Surely, since the finest flowers of English manhood had been plucked from a whole generation, women were needed as never before to maintain the national standard of literature, of art, of music, of politics, of teaching, of medicine? Yet surely, too, a nation from which the men who excelled in mind and body were mostly vanished into oblivion had never so much required its more vigorous and intelligent women to be the mothers of the generation to come?

All the restrictions which forbade professional work to women after marriage were so anti-biological, I felt, as almost to constitute a form of race suicide; for in spite of the sentimental aphorisms still uttered by most men about woman's predominant desire for husband and home, I knew a growing number of women who would refuse marriage rather than give themselves up to years of exclusive domesticity and throw away their training and experience. The reorganisation of society in such a fashion that its best women could be both mothers and professional workers seemed to be one of the most acute problems which my generation – and to a lesser but still important extent all subsequent generations – had now to face. To find a man who appeared able to see this for himself was a novel experience in my post-war life.

2

So it was not, perhaps, so very remarkable that throughout the autumn and winter of 1923 this strange correspondence continued to gather momentum, with myself keeping up my own end of it in a rage of self-detesting, resentful regularity. After Somerville's boycott of *The Dark Tide*, I found it difficult to believe that the author of prize essays and academic monographs had really been impressed by that melodramatic if lively performance, and for a long time I read his letters suspiciously lest a subtle and humiliating mockery should be concealed beneath their apparent admiration.

But gradually I felt bound to conclude that his approbation was quite sincere; he even, to my surprise, appeared unmoved by the donnish disapproval which had caused me so much ingenuous anguish.

'A novelist has considerable latitude . . . in the interests of her art – or shall we say that individuals are only justified so far as they subserve the universal? If Somerville complains, so did St Paul's about Compton Mackenzie's *Sinister Street* – and with far better reason,' he wrote, with the assurance of one who had himself been at St Paul's School when *Sinister Street* appeared.

By the Christmas of 1923 I was already writing to Winifred: 'You know, I feel vaguely uneasy and rather miserable. I do hope that, after this lovely period of peace, some devastating male is not going to push into my life and upset it again. Just when things look so promising, too! . . . I haven't really anything to feel uneasy about – what after all are a letter from America and a box of cigarettes? – and yet I do feel it. Please write and laugh me to scorn.'

From occasional brief sections of autobiography introduced casually and without emphasis into his letters – since to their writer ideas had always been of more importance than facts – I gathered that my correspondent's Oxford career had followed a period of military service which had been postponed by ill health to the spring of 1918. Three years of war-work in the Civil Service had given him, he decided, no right to assume responsibility for other men's lives in the Army, so he went into the ranks as a rifleman in the London Rifle Brigade, and was sent to France just in time for the Armistice. The somewhat unorthodox variety of Catholicism to which he confessed stirred in me the memory of Roland's private conversion in France, while his political theories involved acceptance of the Socialism towards which I was already impelled by my experience of Bethnal Green. Later I learnt that the first vote he ever cast, as a twenty-two-year-old soldier in occupation of Mons during the 'Khaki Election', had been given to Labour, although this Party, with its tabooed group of conscientious objectors, was then at the nadir of its popularity. Even in those days, I discovered, he was a deeply absorbed student of the science of politics, and his migration to America had been due to a desire to continue his researches in a New World less harassed by political failure than the Old.

'For the moment,' he wrote, 'my hand is set to the plough of the Theory of Politics . . . I do it chiefly because the War has left me with the feeling that nothing is more imperative than to clear up these conflicting political dogmata.'

Well, I thought, whatever he might be like otherwise, we were there emphatically at one; it was certainly, if disturbing, not a little intriguing. But when, one day, a letter came which mentioned, amongst other college contemporaries of his, 'dear Henry M. Andrews of Uppingham and New College', I realised, with an almost physical shock, that my correspondent and I might have even more in common than our political ideals. But for the War, I now knew, he and Edward must have been New College contemporaries; perhaps they had even sat for the same scholarship examination in the spring of 1914. I wrote and asked him whether by any chance the two of them had met, and received a reply which seemed, I thought, to have some strange kinship with the high austerity of the mountains above Vicenza.

'I did not meet him; I should have come up next year . . . I should like to die that way For us who live on there is the feeling of death, but for those *qui pro patria dimicantes pulchre occubuerunt* (do you know the New Coll. inscription?) the music of the pæan is at one with and without break passes straight over into the requiem . . . I don't see that it matters whether it was Thermopylæ or the Asiago Plateau.'

In January he wrote to me that he had been offered an academic post at his American university, which would enable him to carry on the work of a famous English publicist who had lately returned thence to Oxford. While he was debating whether to accept this or to return to England, he sent me, somewhat tentatively, a copy of the notorious *Paradoxes* of the young reprobate John Donne. To show that I did not misunderstand this experiment in frankness, I responded with a presentation copy of my own newly published *Not Without Honour*, and received several pages of astringent criticism in reply. By the time that I returned from my

Scottish Border tour in the April of 1924 we had exchanged photographs, and I sent Winifred, who was in Yorkshire for Easter, a description of his.

'Nice-looking,' I concluded, very reluctantly, for a new, unwanted agitation had crept into life as soon as I learnt that he was coming to England in June for the Long Vacation, which made it impossible to concentrate on writing articles, or even on reading Rose Macaulay's absorbing *Told by an Idiot*, which had appeared the previous November.

'As for writing anything but letters, why, how can I?' I complained perturbedly to Winifred, 'For all life seems suddenly to be tumbling about my ears ... If only I had not this strange feeling that life is somehow or other going to blow up!' And she replied with a wise, perceptive resignation: 'My dear, it seems that one must choose between stagnation and agitation in this world – and that for some people the choice is taken out of their hands.'

After April, when I heard from him that he had accepted the post in America, a more purposeful note appeared in the letters of the young don whom I now thought of as 'G.'. Might he call on me, he inquired, as soon as he arrived in England? And I, wishing that I really wanted to say 'No', tried desperately to find some flaw in either his photograph or his philosophy.

'There is an abiding beauty,' he had written to me, 'which may be appreciated by those who will see things as they are, and who will ask for no reward except to see. There is a high æsthetic pleasure in seeing the truth clear-eyed, and in not being afraid of things ... Two campaigns seem to me at the present momentous and worth-while – that for the equalisation of the position of women, and that for economic security for the worker. Whoever puts his hand to the plough of the first will be told he is furthering immorality and the break-up of the family; whoever puts his hand to the second will be told he is a Bolshevik.'

Well, I decided apprehensively, I couldn't find much wrong with that; and a critical inspection of the photograph repaid me no better. At last, a fortnight before his boat was due to sail, a letter came which left the meaning of his correspondence no longer in doubt. A certain Oxford undergraduate, it said, had had an admiration for somebody, distant because he was not interested in women in those days and had another plan, but none the less sincere. Long after they had both gone down, he thought one day in Oxford that he saw her again at the end of a period of doubt and isolation, and the idea of writing to her suddenly occurred – an idea reaffirmed and strengthened by the publication of a novel containing just those beliefs which he had hoped that the admired person would have, and written, apparently, by someone who had known sorrow and despair but had nevertheless decided that the contest was worth continuing . . . 'On the day that I read *The Dark Tide*,' he told me later, 'I determined that I would win Virginia Dennison, and that if you were Virginia I would win you.'

Did he do wrong in writing this? his letter inquired in conclusion; it was a 'simple and naïf tale' enough. And at least it was now possible for me to tell him that I did not want to see him in June.

It certainly *was* possible, I thought, now thoroughly alarmed, and it seemed, moreover, not only possible but definitely advisable. I knew that I was 'in for it' again, and I felt reluctant and afraid; I did not wish to live, emotionally, any more, for I was still too tired; I wanted only to stand aside from life and write. I had more than enough, God knew, to remember and write about; why should I add, thus belatedly, marriage and all its consequences? But much as I longed to tell him just this, the time when I might have been capable of doing so had completely gone by. Behind all my work that year – the General Election, the conclusion of *Not Without Honour*, my lectures and articles and the Scottish Border tour – the music of his letters had sounded like the rolling of some distant organ, the tones of which became gradually deeper and the melody more sweet. Could I sharply terminate this profound and intimate correspondence, as death had once sharply terminated the dear and intimate correspondences of the War? I knew that I could not; and to my emotional inability was added the sharp salt of intense curiosity. So at last, feeling as though I were signing the warrant for my own execution, I took up my pen and wrote:

'I do realise that after all we shall not meet on an equal footing.

You, in spite of your letters which say so much (I will not, as yet, put "too much"), are still more or less of a stranger to me, whereas to you, apparently, I am both so much more than a stranger and so much less . . . How can I tell until I have seen you whether I want you to come or not? You cannot expect too much discretion from a woman's curiosity. Moreover, the "simple and naïf tale" that you have outlined . . . does interest me as a story – and I want to know how it ends. No, I think on the whole that I will not tell you not to come . . .'

3

G. arrived in England on June 10th, having previously informed me of the date by wireless cable. It happened to be the day on which the murder of Matteotti began a wave of anti-Fascist feeling in post-war Europe, but for the moment I was less troubled by atrocities in Italy than by the sudden panic which drove me out of the flat for the afternoon. My only clear purpose amid the hectic confusion of my thoughts was the determination to postpone the uncomfortable decision whether to marry or not. In Roland's case the choice had made itself; in this one, numerous incompatible claims would have to be weighed, and contending issues faced. How much easier never to be asked and therefore never to have to choose!

So I deliberately fixed an interview with Lady Rhondda at the Six Point Group office, and attended a conference at the League of Nations Union in Grosvenor Crescent, where G., after vainly telephoning to our flat, attempted without success to ring me up. At last he returned – with how much chagrin I never learnt – to his father's rooms in Oxford, and from there telephoned asking if he might call to see me on Friday, June 13th. It was hardly an auspicious date for a first meeting, and the unfamiliar voice which persuaded me over the telephone to agree to it alarmed me a good deal, but in my secret heart I knew that I had always regarded thirteen as my lucky number. Later, an amused letter described to me, without criticism or resentment, his fruitless endeavour to find me at the Union headquarters.

'To the inquiry whether you happened to be about in the office I received the reply in a super-Oxford accent: "What is your name?" "I want to see Miss Brittain if she happens to be about and is not engaged at some meeting." "Are you Miss Brittain?" "No, I am not Miss Brittain – I want to see her. But I do not want to interrupt her if she is engaged." "Oh, is she?" I gave it up; the diplomacy of the L. of N. . . . is too much for me. I took the next train.'

On the Friday he came to tea and escorted me that evening to Bernard Shaw's *Saint Joan*; we also spent the Saturday together, walking about Richmond Park and Kew Gardens beneath a sunny sky softly shadowed by nebulous clouds. I knew that marriage would be suggested during the weekend, and it was; I knew that I should repudiate the suggestion, and I did, for I had not yet completely identified this stranger with the writer of the letters. But the day happened to be Sunday, June 15th, and the sixth anniversary of Edward's death, a coincidence which seemed to emphasise the curious link that already existed between my dead brother and this new, persistent companion, whose determination appeared during the next three weeks to be in no wise damped by rejection.

Ten days after his first appearance, he came up to town again for the afternoon to persuade me to spend a week-end at Oxford and let him take me on the river – an invitation which I at first resisted, for I was well aware that Oxford and the river, with their sad, lovely memories, would fight on G.'s side against my resolution. But as we sat together in the dark church in Abercorn Place and listened to the solemn thunder of the organ – with its sudden reminder of the emptiness left in my life by the music that I had abandoned in self-defence after Edward's death – I was already reflecting how different was the peaceful independence of a post-war courtship from the struggle against intrusive observation which had harassed Roland and myself in 1914; and at last, after a day or two's meditation, I wrote and said that I would go to Oxford. I knew then that my resistance was done for, and I was right, for I returned to London engaged, once more, to be married.

'At twenty-eight you ought to be courting a girl of twenty-one instead of trying to marry a woman of thirty,' I told him without compunction, but he only answered gravely:

'I am not interested in immaturity.'

He was at any rate, I thought, of the War generation, and that was all that really mattered. Had he been post-war I could not under any circumstances have married him, for within the range of my contemporaries a gulf wider than any decade divides those who experienced the War as adults from their juniors by only a year or two who grew up immediately afterwards. Even as it was, I announced my engagement with every symptom of scepticism to the much-enduring Winifred, who had never attempted to influence my decision although at that time my marriage seemed likely to involve considerable disruption in her own existence.

There were too many potential slips between a betrothal and a wedding – as I of all people ought to know, I thought sadly. Marriage perhaps a year hence, with all the possibilities of death and accident and disagreement that twelve months contained, seemed almost equivalent, just then, to no marriage at all. Anyhow, I felt, it was quite absurd to marry so late in the day, after I'd turned thirty, when I had been in love for the first time such years and years ago. But eventually I was to realise that half my generation of women seemed to be marrying as late as I was, or even later, and their children and mine would be contemporaries – still babies when we were reaching the end of our thirties. This belated maternity, as I now admit, has had its compensations; small children have a habit of conferring persistent youth upon their parents, and by their eager vitality postpone the unenterprising cautions and timidities of middle age.

'There is indeed no second best in life,' I wrote to G., not untruthfully, at the end of June. 'One can assuredly say that one thing will be different from another, but one must not – indeed one cannot – say that it will never be as good, or better. You rightly said that there can be no such assessment of experience . . . I had forgotten that I am still quite young – the world of sorrow and experience seemed so old.'

After my inordinate encounters with a large and disputatious family, I felt thankful that G. appeared to have no relatives in the world apart from his retired cleric of a father, though I was sorry that I should never know his dead, courageous mother, a fierce advocate of woman suffrage who had found in the movement for the vote the chief inspiration of her brief, turbulent life. In type and in temperament he resembled her, I gathered; the rampageous feminism of *The Dark Tide* had certainly struck a responsive note. My own parents accepted G. with resolute benevolence, and took very well this apparently precipitate arrangement; they were hardened by now to my singular preference for highly intelligent young men with no money except that which they could make by their brains. Quite suddenly, too, I realised – for I was now old enough to realise – that the inevitable clash between the generations diminishes, also inevitably, with the passing of the years.

For a short time, G. and I discussed getting married very soon, but I did not, as yet, feel quite ready for this, nor wish temporarily to adjust my life and work to the unknown conditions of the New World until I had fulfilled my determination to discover, by an expedition through Central Europe, the after-effects of the War upon the Old. Eventually we agreed to postpone our marriage until his return for the Long Vacation in June 1925 – though I never concurred in this 'sensible' decision with the full consent of my will. Apprehension was too familiar and weary a companion to be suffered patiently for nearly another year, and its persistence was not banished by the inward conviction, inherited from the War, that for me the love of men was for ever destined to be inconclusive and impermanent. By allowing myself to become engaged to G., I knew that I had once more put myself into the hands of fate, towards which, since Edward's death, I had done my best to remain, in personal matters, cautiously on the defensive.

'All happiness to me is incredible,' I wrote to G. in July. 'The supreme moments of the War did not bring happiness; how should they, lived as they were under the shadow of death? . . . My obstinate diffidence arises partly . . . because I am afraid of giving life the means wherewith to deal me another of its major blows . . .

So like me to get engaged to someone who has to go abroad
even when there is no war.'

4

For the time being, however, I determined to forget the ten
months of suspense that were still several weeks away, and gave
myself up to a summer of week-ends spent in G.'s company alternately in London and Oxford, with long mellow evenings on the
river above the Cherwell Hotel or below Magdalen Bridge, and
week-day intervals in which daily letters, added to the normal
routine of writing and lecturing, made being engaged almost an
occupation in itself. But other and more public happenings also
brought an eventful summer, and with my journey through Central
Europe in front of me, even the most absorbing personal preoccupations could not blind me to those international changes which
appeared possible now that Socialist Governments, for the first
time since the War, flourished simultaneously in both England
and France.

At the end of July the Inter-Allied Conference in London
opened its discussions on the best method of getting the Dawes
Plan to work in Germany, and the arrival of the German delegation at this conference began, as one weekly paper remarked,
a 'peace after the War' phase which the Treaty of Versailles should
have inaugurated but did not.

'To-day,' I wrote to G. on August 4th, 'ends the black decade
that began with August 4th, 1914; perhaps if life is not too unkind
. . . it also begins a very different ten years which, though they
can never efface the memory of the others, will remove the bitterness from experience and leave only the triumph and the glory.'

With growing excitement I read that the French had agreed,
as part of the Dawes Plan, to withdraw from the Ruhr within
one year; Appenweier and Offenburg were evacuated, in token
of good faith, before the end of August, though both Nationalists
and Communists, strong in Germany after the May elections held
in the fierce atmosphere of the Ruhr occupation, criticised the
Conference for not insisting upon the immediate departure of

the French. In England the Conference decisions were received favourably enough by all political Parties, since Russia had long replaced Germany as international bogy; the real sources of Tory perturbation were the Anglo-Soviet Conference in August, and the arrest and discharge of Mr Campbell, the Communist editor of the *Workers' Weekly*, which was to lead in two months' time to the 'Scarlet Letter Election' of 1924.

At Oxford, during my week-ends, I found these political events reflected in a number of Summer Schools; once or twice, with ironic memories of my enthusiasm at St Hilda's eleven years before, I dropped in to listen, with the critical ears of a speaker, to Professor A. E. Zimmern brilliantly expounding his views on America to the League of Nations Union, and Messrs C. F. G. Masterman and H. D. Henderson, then editor of the *Nation*, telling Young Liberals what they ought to think of the international situation. This politically conscious atmosphere was emphasised, for me, by the presence in Oxford of a number of G.'s college friends, each one of whom was destined, nearly a decade later, to occupy some prominent niche in the world of affairs; they included a future newspaper leader-writer, the editor-to-be of an intellectual monthly, and the subsequent holder of a professorial Chair at a university in the north of England.

Early in September we spent our last week in England at G.'s North Oxford rooms; nothing, I told him, remembering Edward at Waterloo, would persuade me to watch him sail for America, so we agreed to part in Oxford on September 10th. His boat was due to leave Liverpool on the 12th, and I arranged to start on the same date with Winifred for Geneva. The tormenting psychological readjustments which the process of getting to know someone intimately always involves had united with the agitating prospect of re-adapting my aims and activities to marriage to impart to that summer a sense of prolonged conflict, but those final days in each other's company, with their mornings of work, their afternoon walks, and their quiet meals together, seemed to resemble a happy married life more completely, and more encouragingly, than I had thought possible. The imminent parting, however, stirred me to familiar meditations on the subject of separation and loss, which were rendered the more poignant by the sudden death, in Yorkshire, of an old friend of Winifred's – a naval officer whom I also had known.

'I don't think victory over death,' I wrote to her, 'is anything so superficial as a person fulfilling their normal span of life. It can be twofold; a victory over death by the man who faces it for himself without fear, and a victory by those who, loving him, know that death is but a little thing compared with the fact that he lived and was the kind of person he was . . . That's why those war victories with which I was specially associated are still incomplete. That the people faced their own deaths without fear I have no doubt. It is through me that the victory is incomplete, because I cannot always quite feel that their deaths matter less to me than the fact that they lived, nor reconcile their departure, with all their aspirations unfulfilled, with my own scheme of life.'

On our last afternoon, G. and I had tea together in the Trout Inn at Godstow; outside the window a sudden shower of rain beat in thin silver spears upon the flaming snapdragons in the garden, until the steaming mist from the ground intensified their colour with the soft, unearthly radiance which flowers have always worn for me in moments of heightened emotion. That night, Oxford station was chill and heavy with the gloom of a wet September evening as we waited for the last train to London; its ill-lighted darkness and the consciousness of coming separation renewed the feeling of sick inertia that came when wartime leave had ended and someone was returning to the front. In the depths of memory I knew that, for those of us who were now experienced and disillusioned, no parting would ever again have quite that quality of desolation and finality which overwhelms the moment of farewell to one's first love in early youth, but I shivered so much with cold that G. took off the scarf he was wearing and wrapped it round me as we sat together on a draughty seat, wishing that the train would come, yet dreading it as though it were death.

When it finally arrived, the once familiar necessity of keeping up an appearance of self-possession while saying good-bye brought back the atmosphere of the War more profoundly than ever, and I spent the journey to London huddled into a corner in the half-sleep of sorrowful dejection. The next morning but one, after an exhausting day of packing enough books, clothes and papers to last us for three months, Winifred and I set out for Geneva on the first stage of that journey which was to show us the aftermath of war in those countries that our own had once so expensively defeated.

5

We found Geneva convulsed with excitement over the birth of the Protocol, a new international agreement which was intended to fill the gaps left in the Covenant of the League of Nations, and to make future war more than ever improbable.

In the opening days of the Assembly, Mr MacDonald and M. Herriot – whose France had certainly seemed an easier and more courteous France to travel through than the brusque Poincaréan territory of the year before – had made 'Arbitration, Security and Disarmament' the triple slogan of the hour; they had wrung one another's hands in public, had been photographed together, and now had left Geneva to simmer pleasantly in a consoling atmosphere of peace and goodwill very different from the hectic antagonism aroused by the Corfu dispute of the previous September. Even the idea of Germany's admission to the League was being benevolently discussed, and although in the view of the League of Nations Union group at the Hôtel Richmond there was far too much wooing of America, who ought to be shown quite plainly that Geneva could manage without her, the prospects of ultimate co-operation by the United States looked more promising than they had appeared since the War.

'I sometimes wonder which will happen first,' I wrote to G., after a somewhat less dove-like note than was customary that autumn had been introduced by the discussions of the Committee of Intellectual Co-operation over an offer to the League by the ingenious French of an Institute in Paris, 'the shattering of the League in a great explosion between Teutonic reason and Latin logic, or the entry of America to hold the balance between English idealism and French realism.'

In those days our eyes were still held Europewards by the political and social aftermath of the War, and few prophets foresaw the possibility of an even more profound clash nearly ten years later between oriental aggressiveness and occidental timidity.

One afternoon, in the hall of the Palais des Nations, I encountered the representative of the *Daily News*, whom I had met once or twice at the League of Nations Union. On hearing that I was going on to Germany and Austria he promised me some useful introductions, but added immediately: 'What are you doing wandering about Central Europe after that notice I saw in *The Times*?'

'Oh, I don't allow such personal things to affect my work,' I replied, with a nonchalant bravado that I was far from feeling, for now that G. had gone, and the compelling influence of his presence no longer absorbed and flattered me week after week, the conflict between work and personal relationships which marriage would bring had begun to perplex and harass my thoughts more than ever. To escape for the moment from this perturbation, I plunged furiously into the activities of Geneva, which for me, that chilly September, were by no means light; I was again representing *Time and Tide*, and had undertaken, with Winifred, to do the Press and publicity work for the Union, which involved sending continual small articles to headquarters in London for distribution to the provincial Press. Several of these described the Mosul boundary dispute, which Fehdi Bey had just brought before the Council. 'The Turks are here,' I told G., 'discussing Iraq, and politely but fundamentally disagreeing with Lord Parmoor.' One or two of these Council meetings threatened to leave politeness very far behind, and an electrical outburst was once only just averted by the error of a translator, who in the heated controversial confusion inadvertently described the debated territory as '*le Vilayet de Parmoor*'.

On one of our last days in Geneva we heard the Third Committee of the Assembly, with M. Politis as chairman and Dr Beneš as *rapporteur*, discussing the Protocol, in evening dress, until long after midnight, and it seemed to me deeply significant that a conference in which several Great Powers were taking part should have been dominated by Greece and Czechoslovakia.

'To-morrow may or may not be a memorable day,' ran a letter to G., in which I endeavoured to season hope by the stern salt of a realism that was to prove prophetic; 'the Protocol is to be presented to the Assembly, but one can never be sure whether these League things are going to make history or not . . . There is such immense enthusiasm here; then the delegates return, to be soused with cold water in their own countries.'

In the end the completion of the Protocol was delayed by a Japanese amendment which nearly wrecked the proceedings. We had left Geneva on our way to the Saar Valley before Mrs H. M. Swanwick, as one of the British delegates, delivered the final speech summing up the progress made by the Assembly towards Arbitration, Security and Disarmament, and thus broke the tradition which had hitherto insisted that 'lady speakers' and 'lady delegates', however expert their knowledge of other subjects, must interest themselves first and foremost in the humanitarian activities of the League.

From Geneva we journeyed to Bâle through the sudden mellow warmth of a perfect autumn afternoon; 'sunlit woods splashed with orange and yellow ochre,' I described to G., in a letter written in the train; 'the lake blue-green and smooth as glass; mountains like giant shadows crowding to the shore; the summit of Mt Blanc glowing like a pink topaz in the misty sky. Wonderful world; only wish you were here with me and could see it.'

In a hand-case we carried impressive introductions from the International Federation of League of Nations Societies to the French authorities in the Ruhr and the Quakers at Essen. The League officials had been less helpful – 'everyone on the Secretariat pretends they know nothing about the Ruhr,' I had complained to G.; 'I suppose they still feel injured because Reparations have not been referred to the League' – but they had given us one or two letters for presentation in the Saar Valley, and Miss Sara Wambaugh, the American expert on plebiscites whom we had met at one of the committees, had advised us to enter the Ruhr from Düsseldorf, which, as one of the first sanctions provided for by the Treaty of Versailles, was itself neither in the Ruhr nor the Rhineland.

On the whole our experimental journey had aroused sympathetic interest in Geneva, and we had been presented, as we had hoped, with a good deal of useful advice from various international experts. Among these were an eminent professor and his French wife, who invited me, on my last evening, to a small dinner-party at the International Club, which included the secretary of the American Foreign Policy Association and a Jugoslav member of the Secretariat. Conversation had turned, inevitably, upon national characteristics; the English, it seemed to be generally agreed, found more difficulty than any nation in getting on to friendly terms with others on the Continent, for while Latins, and even Americans, could reach the subject of politics, or their own souls, in five minutes, the English thought it bad taste to discuss religion, or politics, or their feelings, or themselves, or other people; and after all, inquired the Frenchwoman pertinently, 'what else is left?'

When he was in London, announced the Jugoslav, he began an important conversation with a distinguished Englishman, and twenty minutes later found himself still discussing the weather. But after all, I thought – though I was too shy to say so – there *are* other things besides the weather that we do discuss publicly in England – our health, for instance, and our friends' health, and sea-sickness, and babies' illnesses, all of which are really much less suited to polite conversation than politics or religion.

Another expert, a well-known international lawyer who afterwards became a Liberal M.P., invited us both to luncheon, and sent us away forewarned and forearmed with the results of his experience in various European countries. But even his advice with regard to the occupied territories concerned me less than my discovery that he had been in the British Intelligence Service in Italy during the War. He had known the headquarters of the 11th Sherwood Foresters very well, he told me, and had even seen Edward's grave at Granezza, which he had visited the year after Winifred and I went to the Plateau. From him I gathered that it had been a regiment largely composed of Hungarians – always braver and fiercer fighters than the Austrians – which had broken through the British lines on June 15th. Neither the Austrians nor the Italians, he said, had ever really wanted to get on with the War; they not unnaturally preferred 'sitting on the top of a mountain and making sketches'.

6

At Bâle I collapsed suddenly and ignominiously from the stress and agitation of the preceding weeks – which had been increased by an accidental delay in G.'s telegram telling me that he had arrived safely at Quebec on the way to his American university – and had to spend a day in bed at a small station hotel before going on to the Saar through Alsace-Lorraine. 'Of us one has gone East and the other West,' G. had written in a letter which was then on its way to me from the United States, and for the rest of that autumn, in Germany, in Austria, in Czechoslovakia, in Hungary, there echoed continually through my mind the sad appropriateness of Coventry Patmore's lines:

> Go thou to East, I West.
> We will not say
> There's any hope, it is so far away.

Next morning I started off with Winifred through Alsace-Lorraine, feeling light in the head and very uncertain about the feet. In the train between Bâle and Strasbourg an Alsatian banker, red-bearded and keen-faced, with light, sensual eyes, instructed me, in return for my tolerant acceptance of the pressure of his hand upon my knee, about the economics of Mulhouse and the geography of the Vosges. He had been obliged to serve against his will, he told me, with the German Army in the War; Alsace-Lorraine was a tragic land in those days, with its families divided between the two Armies, and near relatives often fighting against one another.

'Over there,' he explained in his soft, cultured French, waving his hand towards the blue-green curve of the Vosges, which sloped away to the horizon from the rich fields below the left-hand window of our carriage, 'is a summit where no less than thirty thousand men were killed in the War, because the Germans and the French kept entrenching themselves beneath one another and setting off mines. And very soon we shall pass the Castle of Sélestat, which before the War was a thirteenth-century ruin, inhabited long ago by one of the great barons. Since the ruin was beginning to fall to pieces the people of Sélestat wished to restore it, but as they could not afford to do so themselves they conceived the bright idea of giving it as a present to the Kaiser, so that he might restore it for them. The Kaiser graciously accepted the gift, but instead of restoring the castle he rebuilt it in the best Prussian style, thereby turning a mediæval ruin into a modern German atrocity. And he made Sélestat pay for it too, by levying an income tax on the town!'

In the afternoon we reached Saarbrück without trouble at the frontier, and found it to be a large commercial town of the type of Leicester or Nottingham. The Saar Valley, we had been told, was now virtually a department of the French Foreign Office. The collieries had been handed over to France for fifteen years by the Treaty of Versailles as compensation for the Lens coal-fields destroyed during the War, and were controlled by the Minister of Public Works in Paris, but the League's clear intention that the chairman of the Governing Commission should be changed periodically had never been fulfilled, and France dominated not only the economic but the political life of the valley. Though Saarbrück was the centre of sixty-seven coal-pits, it appeared less black than the Pottery districts familiar to me in childhood; no powdering of soot spoiled the autumn-tinted plane-trees which fringed the wide streets. The Saar, a grimy-looking river about the size of the Trent, carried its traffic of coal-barges straight through the middle of the town.

Immediately after tea we started out to look for the Canadian member of the Saar Governing Commission, to whom the Administrative Section of the League Secretariat, and the secretary of the Canadian League of Nations Union, whom we had met in Geneva, had given us introductions. After much seeking we located him in the Uhlankasern, a spacious barracks which before the War had been the headquarters of a crack Uhlan regiment, and was now used for Government offices. To our surprise he gave us an interview at once, and told us, with a benevolent confidence which seemed to regard as irrelevant both our sex and our youthful appearance, more about the Saar administration in an hour than we had been able to learn in two years from lectures and pamphlets.

The treaty had indeed created an impossible situation, I gathered, for the five unfortunate Commissioners who, in the name of the much-abused League, had somehow to control the territory until the plebiscite of 1935. What would have happened if Northumberland, for instance, had been isolated from the rest of England, deprived of her collieries by a foreign Power, surrounded by a ring of alien officials, and administered by five Commissioners of different nationality who knew neither the population nor one another? These Commissioners, it seemed, were regarded by the inhabitants as their oppressors, but they themselves appeared less certain whether they were the oppressors or the oppressed. Local prophets had intimated to them on their arrival that within a month they would find a watery grave in the dirty depths of the Saar, and though they had mustered sufficient tolerance and tact to defend themselves against this undesirable fate for nearly five years, the barge-covered river flowing past the main Government building provided a constant reminder that life was short and the fate of man uncertain.

Behind the officially oppressed, on the other hand, there was obviously power. The treaty that divided the Saar territory from Germany proper by an artificial barrier could not thereby prevent something more than telepathy from existing between the five political Parties in Berlin and their counterparts in Saarbrück; nor was it to be expected that a population of which six-sevenths practised Roman Catholicism would forget, or be forgotten by, their religious princes across the border at Speyer and Trier. The coal strike of January 1923, which coincided with the occupation of the Ruhr, had been officially settled by the Governing Commission and the Saar Labour leaders on the night before it was supposed to take place; but next morning it occurred just the same, and the Saar had not yet completely recovered from the effects of those hundred days.

In Germany proper, as we later discovered, there was no attempt to disguise the extent of the power behind the Saar Valley; the antagonism aroused by the occupation of the Ruhr seemed only a drop in the ocean of bitterness directed against the Saar provisions, which so unhappily made the League of Nations the scapegoat of the treaty. The League, the Germans complained to us incessantly, would listen to protests from the natives of mandated territories, but would not hear petitions from the inhabitants of the Saar Gebiet, who apparently seized, instead, every trivial opportunity that presented itself to make their disapproval of the situation unmistakable to the French. At the station bookstalls, we found, French newspapers were unobtainable, and though the language had been compulsory in all the schools up to 1914, no one would admit that he could speak it. When Winifred, one afternoon, inquired in French at a grocer's shop for methylated spirit, the shopkeeper brusquely replied that he had none.

'Where can I get some?' she demanded, producing her empty bottle; and the man, examining the label, exclaimed, 'Why, this bottle comes from England!'

'Yes,' she replied, 'I *am* English'; and he answered immediately, 'Wait one moment and I will find you some spirit at the back of the shop.'

The morning after our interview with the friendly, white-haired Canadian, a car, complete with Government official, arrived at our hotel from the Commissioners to take us for a tour round the valley. Remembering my native Black Country, I had never dreamed that the rural districts between the small colliery towns – Saarlouis, and Brebach, and Volklingen with its immense slag-heaps and soaring skeleton-like structures of steel – would be unsurpassed for sombre loveliness by any other part of Germany. From the scattered pits and villages, dark feathers of smoke drifted across mile upon mile of flaming hills, where every tall tree was afire with the burnt-sienna and scarlet of autumn. The disputed earth, so rich with coal below, was thick with forest above – a terrifying, unbroken forest of giant beeches and firs and pines, where the narrow road between the upright tree-trunks plunged into a twilight so deep that our driver had to turn on the lamps of the car.

What a pity it seemed that the next meeting between the Governing Commission and the Saar inhabitants could not take place in this acacia-bordered forest! The stately trees, looking down with their brooding contempt upon the pigmies who possessed them, would surely suggest a quiet permanence, a grave reality, beside which Europe's political quarrels would seem but a little whirl of angry dust. Man, the most destructive of animals, might approach those dominant trees with his axe, but a hundred years hence the forest would still survive his commercial aspirations, and scorn his international disputes.

7

At the frontier between the Saar Valley and the wooded Rhineland with its deep rose-red earth through which we were travelling north to Cologne, a conversation occurred which illustrated once more the unpopularity of the French language in Occupied Germany. As soon as we reached Merzig, the frontier station, a German official burst into our carriage and attacked us with a stream of voluble instructions, of which every sentence appeared to end in '*absteigen*'.

'*Ich verstehe nicht!*' I reiterated helplessly; and the official inquired malevolently, '*Sind Sie französisch?*'

'*Nein, englisch,*' I responded promptly. '*Parlez-vous français?*'

'*Oui, mademoiselle,*' he replied at once, having apparently no objection to speaking the prohibited language with someone who was not a Frenchwoman, and he inquired of Winifred what one of her cases contained.

'*Seulement des vieilles chapeaux,*' she informed him cheerfully, forgetting such trifles as foreign genders in her relief at having overcome the obvious dislike which our appearance had originally inspired in the Customs officer.

'*Chapeaux sont toujours vieux, mademoiselle, jamais vieilles!*' exclaimed the official delightedly, and as an appreciative tribute to our imperfect French, he released us from the obligation of unfastening our boxes at all.

At Trier, with its soaring spires of a dozen churches, we were joined by a plump, voluminous pastor who was soon telling us, in slow but comprehensible English, that he acted as chaplain to Krupps' workmen in Essen. Before the War, he said, Krupps' had employed a hundred and twenty thousand men, but now that they were obliged by the treaty to make agricultural implements and railway machinery instead of armaments, they had dismissed nearly a third of their workers and there were about forty thousand unemployed in Essen alone. When we reached Cologne we should have been glad, for all our experience of independence, to retain the pastor's benevolent company a little longer, for we immediately encountered, in the demeanour of porters and taxi-drivers and hotel servants, a hostility which reminded us that we, the self-righteous British, had become to Cologne exactly what the French were to the Rhineland and the Saar.

By the time that we reached this British-occupied territory, our collection of introductions had already acquired that snowball-like tendency which later, in Czechoslovakia and Austria, developed the proportions of an avalanche and threatened to overwhelm us. Life in Germany had by now become one rapid and exhausting sequence of journeys, interrupted by incessant, head-racking conversations, usually in bad French or worse German, with strangers excitedly teeming with political information, which had to be immediately recorded in the form of diaries or memoranda, and which reached its final metamorphosis in the shape of articles forwarded to the League of Nations Union or direct to newspapers.

Pastors and professors seemed especially anxious to impress our inquiring minds with interviews and demonstrations; one Lutheran cleric from a poor parish took us over the slums of Cologne, and told us as we passed between the dark, decaying houses that even the once wealthy parishes were no longer able to maintain their clergy, who had often to become workmen or harbour-hands in order to support their families. A second pastor from St Goar in the Rhineland – a small, bearded man with an emaciated, saint-like countenance which reminded me strangely of the Bavarian whose death from hæmorrhage I had watched in the German ward at Étaples – wept piteously as he related stories of the French oppressions in his parish. Yet a third, who was attending a Church conference in Cologne, induced us to take a tedious train and tram journey to his parish near Solingen, the Sheffield of Germany, and talk about the League of Nations to a friendly but critical audience of razor-makers at his shabby, spacious house. There he introduced us to his patient, beautiful wife, who seemed almost exhausted by the constant battle with stringent economy and the care of three thin but riotous little sons. Her eldest child, a daughter, she told me, had died during the blockade; she had been a delicate baby and it had not been possible to obtain sufficient milk.

Finally, an English-speaking woman professor from Cologne University took us militantly in hand, and treated us to a long and bitter dissertation on the blind incredulity of our country during the War. England's propaganda, she insisted – quite correctly – had had to be far more malevolent than that of France and Germany, the conscription countries, because Englishmen would never have been persuaded to change their habits and join the Army without some exceptionally strong appeal to their senti mental emotions.

Battered and exhausted by the open criticism, the latent hostil-ities and the unmistakable sufferings of this fierce, unhappy city, we managed to rescue from the turmoil of activities one quiet Sunday for observation and thought. At morning Mass in Cologne Cathedral we stood unobserved beneath the high, pallid windows amid the packed congregation of shabby, heavy-eyed men and women, their sunken faces stoically devoid of emotion as they sang in harmony with the exquisite music which rolled through the vibrating arches above our heads. As I stood in that pale crowd of Germans, all singing, it seemed incredible that the world could have been as it was ten years ago; whatever evil was here, I wondered, that Edward and Roland had died to destroy? What enemy could there have been whose annihilation justified the loss of even one soldier? It was best, after all, that our dead who were so much part of us, yet were debarred from our knowledge of the post-war world and never even realised that we 'won', could not come back and see, upon the scarred face of Europe, the final consequences of their young pursuit of 'heroism in the abstract'. How futile it had all been, that superhuman gallantry! It had amounted, in the end, to nothing but a passionate gesture of negation – the negation of all that the centuries had taught themselves through long æons of pain.

When night came to end that melancholy Sunday, the Hohestrasse was filled with a moving crowd, steadily walking and talking but never laughing, like a troupe of shades newly released from some Teutonic inferno. The cloud of depression upon the city seemed heavier even than in daytime, but the street at least was free, and the unlimited exercise of one's own feet seemed the only luxury that had not to be paid for at a famine price in this new era of the *Rentenmark*. No lights illumined the opaque darkness of byways and alleys; even in the Hohestrasse the lamps were few and dim, and the Cathedral loomed, a black, immense shadow, against the starless night. The atmosphere in which these oppressed men and women moved so quietly to and fro was the apprehensive, unilluminated atmosphere of London during the War; only upon the great steel bridges across the Rhine, a hundred lights gleamed like jewels against the deep cobalt of sky and water. Along the Embankment passed a little company of girls from the League of Youth, marching and singing; they glanced at us with that half-defensive malevolence which we had learnt to expect, as though they were sure of being insulted and had made up their minds to get in the insult first.

'I wonder how we should like being a conquered people,' I wrote the next day in my diary. 'It makes me miserable to be in the midst of a whole population who feel bitterly towards me . . . War, especially if one is the winner, is such bad form. There is a strange lack of dignity in conquest; the dull, uncomplaining endurance of defeat appears more worthy of congratulation. Modern war is nothing but a temporary – though how disastrous! – forgetfulness by neighbours that they are gentlemen; its only result must be the long reaping in sorrow of that which was sown in pride.'

8

From Düsseldorf, a bright, clean town adorned with golden dahlias and purple asters, where the depression that crushed the great German cities seemed to weigh more lightly and it was a relief once again to be less ferociously hated than our fellow-conquerors, we went into the Ruhr and spent a dark, rainy day in Essen.

After so much lecturing and writing about this tormented industrial area, to enter it in the flesh renewed the queer, painful elation of adventure that had sprung from foreign service in wartime. Its family resemblance to our own Black Country was far more striking than that of the Saar Valley, I thought, as we passed through Grossenbaum and Duisburg and Mülheim, with their huge factories of iron and steel, and their stacks of tall, grey chimneys standing erect against the dull yellow sky.

At Essen the American Quakers received us enthusiastically, and regaled us for over an hour with grim details of unemployment and inflation, and the bitter poverty of the stricken middle classes. Since the inflation period neither professional nor industrial workers had had any savings with which to face unemployment, and now they lived more simply than anyone from England would believe possible, with scarcely any meat or butter, and potatoes as their staple diet. It was true, said the Quakers, that the black apprehension of the previous year, with its fear of bread riots and revolution, had diminished since the London Conference; the long tale of expulsions and arrests and imprisonments was almost over, but the small irritations and indignities, which were so much more characteristic of the day-by-day occupation than its occasional terrors, continued to oppress the Ruhr population, and though the evacuation of Dortmund had been proclaimed, the French were still in possession of the town.

Would we care, the Quakers finally inquired, to be taken over Krupps' Works before we left? Receiving our surprised and eager assent, they dispatched us through the damp, sombre streets with a young German who introduced us to one of the Krupp directors, and left us, expectant but a little intimidated, at the door of his office. The director, a saturnine, unfriendly man with an arm paralysed as the result of a war-wound, abruptly bade us follow him, and led us through a series of long, dark passages to the doorway of a lift.

As he pushed back the gates with his uninjured hand I looked nervously at his stiff figure, his useless arm, his grim, implacable face. Hostile and resentful, he quite obviously regarded us with hatred. Here were these inquisitive, officious, domineering English again, and this time, what was worse, merely two young women; and yet, to please those Quakers from America – the only country left on earth which was still rich and still generous – he was required to waste his time in showing them round the Works! The silence in the slowly ascending lift was like an ultimatum.

Just before we reached the top, the director spoke to me.

'You have been in Germany before?' he inquired contemptuously.

'No-o,' I stammered, 'I haven't,' and then, desperately impelled to seek for some human response beneath that official frigidity, I suddenly added: 'But I nursed some German soldiers in the War.'

'German soldiers!' he exclaimed. 'You mean – prisoners?'

'Yes,' I replied, 'at Étaples. Very badly wounded ones, mostly.'

This experimental information had been the mere impulse of shamed nervous tension, but had it been most carefully calculated, it could not have proved more effective. As we stood in the observation tower above the administrative offices, and looked down upon the vast area of dark, smoky factories, five miles long and one mile wide, with their myriad chimneys sharply black against a lowering sunset sky, the alarming director became positively communicative, and pointed out to us the square where the Essen riots had broken out, and the tree-shaded park which had once been used for testing munitions, and the immense dining-hall which during the War had fed forty thousand employees each day. Later, he took us through the spacious workrooms that had once been used for the manufacture of field artillery, and showed us how swords were now, literally, being turned into ploughshares in their modern guise of typewriters and surgical instruments and household pipes and cinematograph machines.

Two days afterwards, on October 11th, we went on to Berlin, without as yet knowing that twelve hours earlier, in London, the dissolution of Parliament had followed the carrying of the Liberal amendment to the Conservative vote of censure on the Labour Government for its management of the Campbell case. We found Berlin very cold; a bitter wind was blowing and the pale leaves were falling fast.

That we felt particularly sensitive to the cold was not surprising, for owing to the complications of the French Régie – the railway system in the occupied territories, where the military authorities had a disconcerting habit of annoying the population by changing the times of trains without making any alteration in the official time-tables – we arrived in Berlin with only a rug, a typewriter and a very small tea-kettle. Since none of these possessions was particularly useful in helping us to dress, wash or get warm in the cheap and chilly *Pension* to which our diminishing funds had now reduced us after the expensive inconvenience of the occupied areas, our feelings of sympathy towards the long-suffering inhabitants of the Ruhr surpassed even the emotions stirred by the melancholy recital of the Quakers at Essen.

Next day, after much expenditure of time and money, we managed, with the assistance of the English teacher who had found us our *Pension*, to get into touch with Dortmund, the last station in the Ruhr territory, and recover our boxes. We unpacked them thankfully and wrapped ourselves up in the warmest garments we possessed, for through our *Pension* in the Kaiserallee – the West Kensington of Berlin – seeped a profound, passive gloom which challenged vitality even more effectively than the cold October wind racing along the half-lit evening streets. This *Pension* must once have been an ornate private house; for its great rooms were impressive with heavy furniture and richly embossed ceilings, but now the elaborate stonework on the outside was falling, unchecked, into decay, while a Bloomsbury boarding-house atmosphere at its worst reigned within. Meals, as I told G., had to be eaten at a general table 'with elderly derelict German ladies who talk only grumpy German', and were dominated by a food-obsession which revived in my memory our rationed days in the summer of 1918. At each of the main meals we were instructed by the maid-servant whether to take one portion of meat or two; considerable agitation occurred if, being allowed two, we took only one, and whenever we went out to supper, our portions of meat and cheese were brought next morning to our bedroom on the supposition that we should eat them with our breakfast. Returning to the *Pension* at night involved a process similar to that of entering a triple-guarded prison; we were given one key for the courtyard door, another for the front door of the building, and yet a third for the door of our bedroom, and each keyhole had to be found and fitted in utter darkness. Such elaborate precautions, we soon discovered, were due to the outbreak of petty pilfering which had followed the period of inflation.

Here, we thought, as in Cologne, we had gone back to wartime conditions, but our English friend told us that we could not now imagine what war had meant to Berlin. All through it, she said, she had worked in a Berlin office, and during the later years had been obliged to go straight to bed when she came home on winter evenings, as there had been no heat, no light, no candles, and nothing to eat. To-day, though demoralisation had followed poverty and inflation, and a people accustomed to spending in billions had lost the habit of saving and tended to squander the stabilised mark, Germany's distress and bitterness were psychological rather than economic.

'This country frightens me,' I thought, remembering how, on the journey from Düsseldorf, we had got into conversation over tea with a young German officer who had served on the Russian Front during the War. He seemed quite surprised to learn that England and France had suffered at all, and expressed his hatred of the French with a cold cynicism more dreadful than passion. England, he confessed, had been regarded as the chief enemy in 1914 ('because Sir Edward Grey made war upon us without any reason!'), but now France was the object of revenge.

'One day,' he exclaimed exultantly, 'we will make war upon them and treat them as they have treated us! I am longing for that war!' And we couldn't persuade him that we were not Quakers when we said that we thought the world had had enough of destruction and death.

'Oh, life!' I silently petitioned the future, as we crossed the silver sword-sweep of the Elbe in the gathering twilight. 'Oh, life, if I do finally decide to marry G. and have a family – and I'm not absolutely certain, yet, that I really want to do either – please grant that I have only daughters; I'm afraid, in the world as it is, to have a son. Our generation is condemned, condemned, and the League, and all that it stands for, is only a brittle toy in the hands of ruthless, primæval forces!'

It was, of course, a futile prayer, based upon the supposition that another war would resemble the colossal infantry-massacre of the last. I did not then realise that the menacing future, which was to make my first-born the son that I had dreaded, would dedicate its diminishing resources and its keenest scientific brains to developing even more maniacal forms of aerial warfare, which, if employed, would descend with annihilating impartiality upon the innocent heads of sons and daughters alike.

From our *Pension*, in the persevering quest for material with which to combat those militaristic tendencies, we went forth through the grim streets of dilapidated buildings to a new series of interviews – interviews with the secretary of the *Deutsche Liga für Völkerbund*; with the Socialist von Gerlach; with the great Bernstein, whose grave, bearded face reminded me of Leonardo da Vinci's portrait of himself in old age; with the Matron of a women's hospital in the northern quarter of the city, which had been obliged through loss of endowments to close a wing once used for permanently crippled children.

Throughout Germany, we were told, the Conservative Parties were declining in power except in Bavaria; the Nationalists and Communists were losing favour, and Stresemann was trying to get the pro-Dawes Plan Nationalists into his Party. The worst period of the economic and financial crisis was past; the more intelligent Germans were ceasing to wish for a war of revenge, and desired only peace and stability; one year of 'sensible' politics among the *Entente* countries would destroy in a weary and broken people the desire for retaliation. A war-psychology had continued for so long because of the Saar provisions and the Ruhr occupation, combined with the 'war-guilt' clauses of the treaty, but now Germany was ready to accept the idea of international arbitration through a League of Nations, though her attitude towards the existing League was warped, not unnaturally, by scepticism and fear.

One afternoon I walked with Winifred through the length of the Tiergarten to the Reichstag and Unter den Linden; along the empty, wooded park the yellow leaves whirled and eddied in the persistent wind, falling like showers of paper coins upon the sculptured monarchs in the Siegesallee. Looking down the Allee to the Victory Column of 1870 with its aggressively gilded goddess, and beyond it to the wide steps of the Reichstag dominated by the statue of Bismarck, it was possible – as it was now possible nowhere else in Berlin – to understand how the upstart vainglory of pre-war Germany had infuriated other nations; a vainglory, as I wrote to G., 'now cold and empty; the mere shell of that which once, if not great, was at least impressive'.

We stopped for a moment before the statue of Frederick the Great of Prussia, that arch-Nationalist, with the thin lips and protruding eyes, whose *Testament Politique* – which embodied his belief that 'Reason of State' should overrule law and international obligations – I had read while studying my Special Subject at Oxford.

'I have just put down the *Testament Politique*,' G. was writing to me, as though by telepathy, only a week later, 'and I turn to think . . . of you reading it to enlighten you on the War, of you telling me of it in the punt on that day down stream on the Cher.'

This letter reached me in Vienna, where I was still observing, even more realistically than I had gathered from the academic study of international relations, the desolation into which Central Europe had descended through following too blindly the theories of Frederick. The logic of history lay, I now realised, upon the side of internationalism all the time. Could the new generation be taught to perceive that logic before the hatreds and passions generated by the last war led a tired and tormented world into yet another?

9

The next few weeks, in Czechoslovakia and Austria and Hungary, passed swiftly and busily away. In Prague we found the pursuit of political truth – almost a contradiction in terms, it seemed, as soon as one reached the disintegrated units of the old Hapsburg Empire – continually complicated by the grievances of the German minority, and afterwards clearly remembered only that we had stood on the bridge over the Vltava, and followed the funeral procession of Henryk Sienkiewicz, the author of *Quo Vadis?* who had died in Switzerland during the War, through the streets of the city on its way to Poland.

Ruined but unresentful Vienna – that 'great wheel turning in the air', as C. A. Macartney was shortly to describe it – received us with such open and friendly arms that we had to spend only the night hours of our month there in the cold and economical *Pension* in the Dorotheergasse, where a quarrel between landlord and tenants as to who should put in central heating resulted in the virtual absence of warmth during that bright and freezing November. But Vienna so much preferred our literary to our political selves that even the downfall of the British Labour Party in the Zinoviev Letter Election hardly entered into one conversation, and seemed less important to our cultured, agreeable entertainers than the publication of Winifred's second novel, *The Crowded Street*, just before we went on to Budapest. Here, at last, where the Danube, slow-flowing and pompous, ran darkly grey between banks powdered with snow, we found the League of Nations popular on account of its financial reconstruction scheme and the Hungarian loan.

At the end of November, with our money and energy alike exhausted, we went back to London. What, I wondered, as the express from Vienna began its journey to Ostend by a route only just reopened after the Ruhr occupation, had really emerged from the three months spent in the sorrowful region that we were now re-crossing? What was the true value of the huge collection of 'facts' that we had amassed? Wherever, from Paris to Budapest, our investigations had taken us, the unanswerable case of one country was immediately contradicted in the next; the minority population which constituted the oppressed of one State became the oppressor as soon as it crossed the border. How near, in that fog of grievances, resentments, conflicting statements, selected statistics, 'logical' arguments and furious propaganda, had we ever come to anything approaching reality?

'If Jesting Pilate were to return to-day and to visit Central Europe,' I wrote later in an article accepted by the *Nation*, 'he would be moved to ask his unanswerable question not once but many times. In the occupied territories . . . sincerity is unavailing, and conscience loses its power as a guide. You may go into Germany filled with a lofty zeal to discover and to tell the truth, but you will come out again sorrowfully realising that this is the one thing you cannot do. You will seek and you will not find; you will ask, and much will be given unto you, but never that which you demanded. The proverbial well is too shallow a hiding-place in which to look for the imprisoned Truth. In the Saar Valley, at least, she is buried in nothing more accessible than the bottom of a coal-pit.'

It was of those occupied territories especially that I found myself thinking as twilight shrouded the melancholy land of our former enemies, and at midnight I awoke from a brief doze to see, once more, the lights reflected in the black expanse of the Rhine at Cologne, and the Hohenzollern Bridge, like the skeleton of some immense prehistoric beast, darkly astride across the river. In earnest, energetic, self-satisfied Czechoslovakia, in vivacious, passionate Hungary, in resigned, easy-going Austria, where every political conversation at the numerous and agreeable tea-parties to which we were invited had glided by imperceptible but rapid stages back to the all-absorbing topics of books and music, there appeared to be literally no answer to Pilate's question, but in Germany the after-effects of war were visible and tangible; its misery and humiliation existed in grim independence of dogmatic opinions ingeniously expressed.

Once or twice, in Cologne and in the Ruhr and in Berlin, the same momentary but profound despair had come over me that I had felt beside Edward's grave on the Asiago Plateau.

'This, this! – ruin, cruelty, injustice, destruction – is what they fought and died for,' I had thought. 'All that expenditure of noble emotion, that laying down of life and youth, of hope and achievement and paternity, in order that German men and women might suffer indignity and loss, that German children might die of starvation, that the conquerors might stride triumphant over the stoical, enduring conquered. I don't want to see any more of these results, but only to go back to that past in which abstract heroism was all that mattered, and men acted finely and bravely, believing that the end would be quite other than this.'

But gradually, as the autumn weeks passed over Germany, and Austria, and Hungary, I had realised that it was not the courage and generosity of the dead which had brought about this chaos of disaster, but the failure of courage and generosity on the part of the survivors. How terrible our responsibility is! I meditated, dimly understanding that for me this journey had been the rounding off of a decade of experience which had shown, beyond all possibility of contention, the ruin and devastation wrought by international conflict in a world of mutually dependent nations. How much there was to be done for this suffering Europe, this stricken humanity; we could not, even if we would, leave it to its agony and live in the past! To find some guiding principle of action, some philosophy of life, some constructive hope upon whose wings this crippled age might swing forward into a fairer future – that at least remained and always would remain, for us who had experienced in our own souls those incalculable depths into which Germany had fallen.

It did not seem, perhaps, as though we, the War generation, would be able to do all that we had once hoped for the actual rebuilding of civilisation. I understood now that the results of the War would last longer than ourselves; it was obvious, in Central Europe, that its consequences were deeper rooted, and farther reaching, than any of us, with our lack of experience, had believed just after it was over. In any case, the men who might, in co-operation with the women who were not too badly impaired by shock and anxiety, have contributed most to its recovery, the first-rate, courageous men with initiative and imagination, had themselves

gone down in the Flood, and their absence now meant failure
and calamity in every department of human life. Perhaps, after all,
the best that we who were left could do was to refuse to forget,
and to teach our successors what we remembered in the hope
that they, when their own day came, would have more power to
change the state of the world than this bankrupt, shattered generation. If only, somehow, the nobility which in us had been turned
towards destruction could be used in them for creation, if the
courage which we had dedicated to war could be employed, by
them, on behalf of peace, then the future might indeed see the
redemption of man instead of his further descent into chaos.

10

We returned to an England politically very different from that
which we had left, for Mr Baldwin had replaced Mr MacDonald
as Prime Minister, and the Conservative Party, numbering over
four hundred in contrast to the hundred and fifty-two of discredited Socialism, were comfortably settled in office for another five
years.

In spite of this *débâcle*, I definitely became, for the first time, a
member of the Labour Party when I had been in England for
two or three weeks. My first vague realisation that poverty was
the result of humanity's incompetence, and not an inviolable law
of nature, had come with the sixteen-year-old reading of Carlyle's
Past and Present, and though, during the War, my consciousness
of political programmes and antagonisms was dim, I had seen the
poor, the meek and the modest, the young, the brave and the
idealistic – all those, in fact, who always are too easily enchanted
by high-sounding phrases – giving their lives and their futures in
order that the powerful might have more power, the rich grow
richer, the old remain in comparative security.

For years now, since the War, I had been to Geneva and worked
hopefully in the cause of the League; I had heard statesmen at the
Assembly giving lip-service to peace and then going back to their
own countries to support preparations for war; I had seen the delegates who really cared for peace ideals – Nansen of Norway,

Branting of Sweden, Lord Cecil, Arthur Henderson, Mrs Swanwick – always in a minority; I had watched protocols and pacts brought forward, piously applauded and in practice turned down. I had heard disarmament lauded to the skies while everywhere countries were increasing their armaments, and had realised that few were better and a great many were worse than ourselves, who annually spent nearly five hundred million pounds upon the causes and consequences of war, and then declared that we couldn't afford a national maternity service. I had now travelled through Germany and Austria and Czechoslovakia and Hungary; I had been in the occupied areas, and had talked to the Quakers in Essen and Vienna, and although a League of Nations existed, and French statesmen, like British and Japanese and Italian, sang hymns of praise to Geneva, I had found everywhere oppression, the conqueror grinding down the conquered by hunger and humiliation, the Conference of Ambassadors deciding against the evacuation of Cologne, hatred and fear dominant in a Europe vowed to charity and co-operation, and everywhere countries casting resentful or envious eyes upon their neighbours' territories. I had witnessed all this until there seemed to be no words in which to describe the situation but the sad, disillusioned words of Ecclesiastes: 'So I returned, and considered all the oppressions that are done under the sun: and behold the tears of such as were oppressed, and they had no comforter; and on the side of their oppressors there was power; but they had no comforter.'

And at last I had come to believe that, although men did change slowly, and left the evidence of their progressive modifications in statutes and treaties, no change would come soon enough to save the next generation from the grief and ruin that had engulfed my own so long as the world that I knew endured – the world of haves and have-nots; of owners and owned; of rich and poor; of Great Powers and little nations, always at the mercy of the wealthy and strong; of influential persons whose interests were served by war, and who had sufficient authority to compel politicians to precipitate on behalf of a few the wholesale destruction of millions. So it was that I became a Socialist, in the belief that membership of the Labour Party would help me to work for a new order based upon the discipline of man's strongest instinct – his instinct for possession.

By the time that I reached this decision we were both once more absorbed in the familiar London life of writing articles and making speeches. Winifred had already begun to collect material for an historical novel on the life of Wycliffe which has so far proved abortive, but I was now too much preoccupied by the psychological stress of approaching marriage, and too uncertain whether I was glad about it or not, to give my mind for the time being to the construction of another book.

'I am encouraged,' I wrote to G., after going to a No More War Conference in Westminster through a black December fog which preceded a Christmas of gales and floods, 'to continue my researches on the League by such remarks as that of Lord H., who in giving an inaugural address to the ... Conference informed his audience that "Jaworsina was on the boundary line between Poland and Jugoslavia"! And by that of no less an authority than Miss R., who in a recent lecture asserted that Widows' Pensions had been discussed in "both the Slovakias – Czechoslovakia and Jugoslovakia"! This poor Europe – what crimes are committed in its name!'

In the course of my subsequent wanderings in and out of newspaper offices during the early months of 1925, I heard what purported to be the true story of the death of the Geneva Protocol, and shortly before the downfall of the Herriot Government in France, I passed on to G., for what it was worth, this certainly apocryphal tale.

'Austen Chamberlain and the Cabinet,' I told him, 'looked at the Protocol and decided that they could not and never would read it. They therefore sent it to Lord Balfour, asking for a statement of his philosophical objections, and to the Ministerial departments asking for their comments. Lord Balfour produced a series of admirable philosophical objections rather drastically stated for the sake of clearness. The departments also produced their objections, and Lord Balfour was asked to work these into his own statement. Thinking that he was merely providing a memorandum for the Government at Geneva, Lord Balfour proceeded to do so, still being drastic for the sake of clearness. Austen Chamberlain went to Geneva with the memorandum in his pocket, and instead of using it as the guide Lord B. had intended it to be, read it aloud in its original form as the British contribution to the discussion! After he had finished there was a dead, affronted silence, in the midst of which M. Briand . . . was heard saying loudly: "Anybody would think that the Assembly, after being in labour for five months, had given birth to a mental defective!"'

Nevertheless, in spite of lethargy, and oppression, and unillumined conscientiousness in both high and low places, and a persistent backwoods influence which showed itself in a new defeat of the Peeresses' Bill in England, and reached its maximum during the Scopes prosecution in Tennessee, the world did seem as though it were slowly beginning to reawaken after the long winter of war. In Austria and Hungary the nightmare currency was at last successfully stabilised; conversations were taking place in Düsseldorf between the coal, iron and steel magnates of France and Germany with a view to the conclusion of a commercial treaty between the two nations; by August the last of the French troops would have left the Ruhr, and with its freedom the acutest phase of war-hatred would surely have ended. Best of all, as one standard reference-book optimistically remarked, 'during 1925 the prestige and influence of the League of Nations increased even more than it had done in 1924.'

That spring, too, looked more personally hopeful for ourselves than had any previous year. Winifred was now contributing notes and occasional leaders to *Time and Tide*, while I had begun to write for the *Nation and Athenæum*, for though our second novels – as is the habit of second novels – had not been so well reviewed as the first, they had nevertheless pushed a little wider apart those adamant gates to journalism which had begun to open after *Anderby Wold* and *The Dark Tide*. If only, I thought, as I wrote and spoke of the problems of Central Europe, if only, all over the world – at Geneva, at The Hague, in the voluntary peace organisations of every country – we who in various ways had been through the War could get hold of the management of affairs before our minds had gone rusty and we'd forgotten too much!

If only now, *now*, while we were still young, we could oust the old men and women, the worshippers of precedent, privilege and property, whose minds had been hard set before the War! We might not, perhaps, know much about procedure; we should not be patient with counter-amendments and points of order and references back, but we would at least make things move.

Such were the hopeful impressions of my conscious mind, but – as though my subconscious were determined to make one final protest against my belief that the worst phase of the War was all but over – I had just about this time the last of those dreams with which, for ten years, the griefs and losses of the past had haunted my nights. It confronted me, I told G., with an 'Enoch Arden' problem on this occasion, for I dreamed that while he was in America, regarding me as his future wife, news came that Roland had never really died, but had only been missing with a lost memory, and now, after indescribable suffering, had returned to England. In the dream his family invited me to their house to meet him; I went, and found him changed beyond recognition by cruel experience but unchanged towards myself, anxious to marry me and knowing nothing of G. in America. So sharp was the anguish of the decision to be made that I woke up quite suddenly, with the words of a familiar text sounding as clearly in my head as though someone had spoken them close beside me: 'And whose shall she be at the Resurrection?'

And then I remembered, with a startling sense of relief, that there was no resurrection to complicate the changing relationships forced upon men and women by the sheer passage of earthly time. There was only a brief interval between darkness and darkness in which to fulfil obligations, both to individuals and society, which could not be postponed to the comfortable futurity of a compensating heaven.

11

As spring matured slowly into summer, the imminence of those personal obligations, so much desired and yet so deeply dreaded, possessed more and more of my thoughts. Never before had I seemed to wait so long for May, with its warm winds and blossoming shrubs, yet when the lilac buds began to swell beneath the windows of our flat, and a chestnut-tree in Regent's Park burst prematurely into crumpled, delicate leaves, I realised that the ultimate uncertainty about my marriage had still to be faced and overcome.

So long, I knew, as I remained unmarried I was merely a survivor from the past – that wartime past into which all those whom I loved best had disappeared. To marry would be to dissociate myself from that past, for marriage inevitably brought with it a future; a new future of intimate relationships such as I once believed I had permanently renounced. I might, perhaps, even have the children that years ago I had longed for – children who would know and care nothing of the life that had been mine before I met their father, and who would certainly never ask me: 'Mother, what did YOU do in the Great War?' because the War itself would be to them less than a memory. It would not even convey as much to their minds as the South African War had conveyed to mine, for had I not heard the barrel-organs playing 'We're soldiers of the Queen, me lads!' and seen the bonfires on Mafeking Night? For them it would merely possess the thin remoteness of a legend, the story-book unreality of an event in long-past history; it would be a bodiless something, taking shape only in words upon the lips of the middle-aged and the old.

Should I, then, submit myself to the pain of a future so completely out of tune with the past? Should I, who had once dedicated myself to the dead, assume yet further responsibilities towards the living? Could I, a wartime veteran, transform myself into a young wife and mother, and thereby give fate once more the power to hurt me, to destroy my vitality and my creative ability as it had destroyed them in the years which followed 1914? If life chose to deal me a new series of blows through G. and his children, should I have the strength to survive them and go on working? I doubted it, and often felt that it would be better to avoid the risk altogether. Yet always, after a tumult of thought, I was forced to conclude that it is only by grasping this nettle, danger, that we pluck this flower, safety; that those who flee from emotion, from intimacy, from the shocks and perils attendant upon all close human relationships, end in being attacked by unseen Furies in the ultimate stronghold of their spirit.

'You fear marriage, and America, and the cost of marriage, and me because I stand for these things,' G. had written with intuitive comprehension of my hesitations only a few weeks before. 'Of course you do . . . Marriage is a great risk properly faced with fear, and we all so face it . . . Marriage is not, as it is made out conventionally, sheer joy. It is, like all life's valuable things, new pain. The best hope for us . . . is that we both recognise that . . . I offer you, I think, as free a marriage as it lies in the power of a man to offer a woman . . . I ask you to give what you want to give, no more . . . I hope you will never be condemned to regard marriage as in any sense an impoverishment . . . If it is, you should give it up. There are sacred duties one owes oneself and others through oneself . . . If when I die I shall have destroyed a few shams, done a very little for the better understanding of that social system which we must master as we have mastered Nature . . . I shall die satisfied . . . I know that your work is more to you than I am . . . for love . . . is good but it is long after our own work, the work the War imposed on us, the task imposed on us by our knowledge; a knowledge gained in bitter experience.'

Yes, I thought, that was really the point; whatever might be true for our successors, for us love and marriage must be subordinate to work. Yet surely to sacrifice them completely, and in fear of their burdens to give them up, was to deny the vital principle which insisted that ideas and philosophies, like life itself, must be carried on?

'For me,' I told G., 'the feminist problem ranks with your economic problem. Just as you want to discover how a man can maintain a decent standard of culture on a small income, so I want to solve the problem of how a married woman, without being inordinately rich, can have children and yet maintain her intellectual and spiritual independence as well as having . . . time for the pursuit of her own career. For the unmarried woman there is now no problem provided that she has the will to work. For a married woman without children there is only a psychological problem – a problem of prejudice – which can be overcome by determination. But the other problem – that of the woman with children – remains the most vital. I am not sure that by refusing to have children one even solves the problem for one's self; and one certainly does not solve it for the coming womanhood of the race. But the need to solve it is so urgent that it is raised to the level of those cases where it is expedient that one man – and more than one man – should die for the people.'

For weeks on end we exchanged similar letters, discussing how best I could combine writing and political work with temporary residence in America and the production of a family, and how we could help and not hinder each other's ambitions and occupations. Never before had I realised so forcibly as in meditating upon this problem – a problem by no means mine alone, but intimately bound up with the sociology of the future – how time had moved on for the world and myself since 1915. When I sat before the stove in the dark hut at Camberwell and considered marrying Roland, the personal difficulties of the situation had not occurred to me as fundamental, and, indeed, hardly as difficulties. In those days the War, with its dreadful and constant intimations of human mortality, made life itself infinitely more important than any way of living; in comparison with the tense anxieties of that moment, that remote post-war future had seemed curiously simple. In any case, a college first-year student temporarily transformed into a V.A.D. probationer could hardly be said to have a career to defend, but after six years of learning, and writing, and lecturing, the proposition appeared very different. Its solution was one which went far beyond both the person and the hour; the future of women, like the future of peace, could be influenced by individual decisions in a way that had never seemed possible when all individuality was quenched and drowned in the dark tide of the War.

Marriage, for any woman who considered all its implications both for herself and her contemporaries, could never, I now knew, mean a 'living happily ever after'; on the contrary it would involve another protracted struggle, a new fight against the tradition which identified wifehood with the imprisoning limitations of a kitchen and four walls, against the prejudices and regulations which still made success in any field more difficult for the married woman than for the spinster, and penalised motherhood by demanding from it the surrender of disinterested intelligence, the sacrifice of that vitalising experience only to be found in the pursuit of an independent profession. But tired as I was of conflict, I felt that I must not shrink from that fight, nor abandon in cowardice the attempt to prove, as no theories could ever satisfactorily prove without examples, that marriage and motherhood need never tame the mind, nor swamp and undermine ability and training, nor trammel and domesticise political perception and social judgment. To-day, as never before, it was urgent for individual women to show that life was enriched, mentally and spiritually as well as physically and socially, by marriage and children; that these experiences rendered the woman who accepted them the more and not the less able to take the world's pulse, to estimate its tendencies, to play some definite, hard-headed, hard-working part in furthering the constructive ends of a political civilisation.

The demonstration would not, I was well aware, be easy; for me and my contemporaries our old enemies – the Victorian tradition of womanhood, a carefully trained conscience, a sheltered youth, an imperfect education, lost time, blasted years – were still there and always would be; we seemed to be for ever slaying them, and they to be for ever rising again. Yet even these handicaps I no longer resented, for I was ceasing at last to feel bitterness against the obstacles that had impeded for half a lifetime my fight for freedom to work and to create. Dimly I perceived that it was these very handicaps and my struggle against them which had lifted life out of mediocrity, given it glamour, made it worth while; that the individuals from whom destiny demands too much are infinitely more vital than those of whom it asks too little. In one sense I was my war; my war was I; without it I should do nothing and be nothing. If marriage made the whole fight harder, so much the better; it would become part of my war and as this I would face it, and show that, however stubborn any domestic problem, a lasting solution could be found if only men and women would seek it together.

There remained now only the final and acute question of loyalty to the dead; of how far I and the other women of my generation who deliberately accepted a new series of emotional relationships thereby destroyed yet again the men who had once uncomplainingly died for them in the flesh. Up and down the narrow, solitary roads through Regent's Park, or round and round the proletarian paths of Paddington Recreation Ground, I walked pondering this ultimate uncertainty. In spite of myself and the grief for their unfulfilled lives that no time could diminish, a gulf had stretched between my spirit and theirs; the world in which at the Armistice I seemed to have no part had closed in and absorbed me – or was it, rather, that my own view of my destiny had widened to the dimensions of its needs?

If the dead could come back, I wondered, what would they say to me? Roland – you who wrote in wartime France of 'another stranger' – would you think me, because I marry him, forgetful and unfaithful? Edward, Victor, Geoffrey, would you have me only remember you, only dwell in those days that we shared so long ago – or would you wish my life to go on? In spite of the War, which destroyed so much hope, so much beauty, so much promise, life is still here to be lived; so long as I am in the world, how can I ignore the obligation to be part of it, cope with its problems, suffer claims and interruptions? The surge and swell of its movements, its changes, its tendencies, still mould me and the surviving remnant of my generation whether we wish it or not, and no one now living will ever understand so clearly as ourselves, whose lives have been darkened by the universal breakdown of reason in 1914, how completely the future of civilised humanity depends upon the success of our present halting endeavours to control our political and social passions, and to substitute for our destructive impulses the vitalising authority of constructive thought. To rescue mankind from that domination by the irrational which leads to war could surely be a more exultant fight than war itself, a fight capable of enlarging the souls of men and women with the same heightened consciousness of living, and uniting them in one dedicated community whose common purpose transcends the individual. Only the purpose itself would be different, for its achievement would mean, not death, but life.

To look forward, I concluded, and to have courage – the courage of adventure, of challenge, of initiation, as well as the courage of endurance – that was surely part of fidelity. The lover, the brother, the friends whom I had lost, had all in their different ways possessed this courage, and it would not be utterly wasted if only, through those who were left, it could influence the generation, still to be, and convince them that, so long as the spirit of man remained undefeatable, life was worth having and worth giving. If somehow I could make my contemporaries, and especially those who, like myself, had once lost heart, share this belief; if perhaps, too, I could have children, and pass on to them the desire for this courage and the impulse to redeem the tragic mistakes of the generation which gave them birth, then Roland and Edward and Victor and Geoffrey would not have died vainly after all. It was only the past that they had taken to their graves, and with them, although I should always remember, I must let it go.

> . . . *Under the sway*
> *Of death the past's enormous disarray*
> *Lies hushed and dark.*

So Henley had written: and so, with my eyes on the future, I must now resolve.

12

At last the June weather, golden and benign, had come; the Ruhr was all but free of its invaders, and the days, busy with preparations of a kind that could not be delayed until G.'s return and the final week before our marriage, rushed past with the sudden alarming rapidity of an express train. The planning of a honeymoon in South-Eastern Europe – not Germany this time, I told him; it was too harsh and bitter a country for a newly married husband and wife with their own problems to discuss – involved getting a new passport, even though, with G.'s ready co-operation, I had decided to keep and use my own name after marriage.

'Really,' I complained to him, after discovering that all the visas expensively obtained for travelling as a spinster in 1924 would have to be acquired again if I wished to revisit Austria and Hungary as a married woman in 1925, 'the legal disadvantages of being your mistress would be small compared with those of being your wife.' But I determined to have my passport made out in my maiden name; and after a brief contest it was, and still is.

We had arranged to spend the first year of our marriage together in America, a new world which would symbolise for me the breaking away from my thraldom to the sorrows of the old. After that some expedient, we both knew, would have to be thought out by which partial residence in England, where my real field of work lay, would be possible for me; an experiment in that type of arrangement which I later described in books and articles as 'semi-detached marriage', and which rendered feasible a profession for both partners even when one had a post abroad. To Winifred, in the midst of other plans to round off appropriately the years which had bound me to Oxford by taking my M.A. at a Degree-giving two days before my marriage – an intention in which I had been confirmed by the immediate response of the first family acquaintance to whom I mentioned it: 'How *can* you find time to think about a thing like *that* in the week you're going to be MARRIED!' – I outlined schemes and suggestions to which, while making her own plans for a long lecture-tour in South Africa, she listened with a half-amused, half-sad incredulity.

'Dear Winifred, I shall never be parted from you for very long,' I mentally insisted, undeterred by her scepticism; 'I never can be. You represent in my life the same element of tender, undistressing permanence that Edward represented, and in the end, when passion is spent and adventures are over, this is the thing that comes out on top.'

Our wedding-day was fixed for June 27th – the same date on which, ten years earlier, I had gone, untried and young and hopeful, as a new V.A.D. to take my part in the War. I had long intended, if I ever did marry, to go to a register office, but when G. explained to me that civil marriages were not recognised by the Catholic community, a memory suddenly came to me of Sunday mornings early in 1916, when I had knelt grieving beneath the tall, pointed arches of a Catholic church while the half-comprehended music of the Mass drugged my senses with anodyne sweetness. And I thought: 'We'll be married at St James's, Spanish Place, and I'll carry, not lilies nor white heather, but the tall pink roses with a touch of orange in their colouring and the sweetest scent in the world, that Roland gave me one New Year's Eve a lifetime ago. When the wedding is over, I'll give them to Roland's mother; I know G. will understand why.'

And the letter which crossed the Atlantic agreeing with my plans showed me how truly he had indeed understood. 'That it is I,' he wrote, 'who shall stand there is but the end of a long story.'

On June 16th, when G. was due to arrive home in the *Aquitania*, I went down to Southampton to meet his boat. It was one of the warmest days of that dry, sunny month, and I dressed myself with particular elegance in a new trousseau garment because he had told me that, in order to save towards our European honeymoon, he intended to travel third class. But I became, quite suddenly, so deeply apprehensive lest the companion whom I had not seen for ten months should prove after all to be a stranger in whose quality I had been mistaken, that Winifred characteristically decided to go with me to Southampton.

'If he's just as he was,' she said, 'I can easily disappear, but if you find you don't like him, perhaps it will be useful to have me there.'

Being then unacquainted with the vagaries of Atlantic steamships, we took for granted that the probable time of arrival given us the previous day by the Cunard office could be implicitly relied upon, but as our train slid smoothly past the harbour, I saw with a pang of unspeakable disappointment the four scarlet funnels of the *Aquitania* already towering motionless in the docks. To our dismay we learnt at the station that she had arrived nearly two hours before, but the faint possibility that steerage passengers were disembarked long after their moneyed but completely uninteresting superiors persuaded me to make a hasty expedition to the boat before taking the first train back to London. A sympathetic taxicab driver, grasping our predicament, offered to drive us rapidly to the docks, and we were skidding dizzily round corners and over level crossings when I saw, for the moment stationary on a stretch of line close to the road, a long and impressive train indubitably labelled 'SOUTHAMPTON-WATERLOO BOAT EXPRESS'.

It was, as I learnt later, the last of the three boat-trains, and there didn't seem to be much chance of finding G. on it even though he was not one of those elevated beings whose class entitled them to arrive in London at the earliest possible moment. But at least, I thought, I might get to Waterloo by it before he had collected his luggage, and thus mitigate the bewildered distress that he must certainly have felt when I apparently broke, without warning, my promise to meet him. So I ordered the taxi to stop as near to the line as it could go, and the driver, appreciating our change of plan, drew up immediately below the lofty carriages.

Just as we reached it the train began gently to move, and with Winifred propelling me vigorously from behind I scrambled, regardless of the dove-coloured coat-frock and new terra-cotta hat, up the steep step from the dirty siding. Completely ruining my pale suède gloves with the coal-dust on the grimy handle, I opened the nearest door and fell into the corridor, while Winifred, panting at my heels, was herself pushed up by the taxi-driver – to whom, with great presence of mind, she flung a ten-shilling note from the window as we were wafted away. A scandalised porter shouted at us, but I waved my ticket and harbour permit, and as the wheels were now moving quite fast, he relinquished his conscientious endeavour to prevent this unorthodox method of boarding a boat-train. I gave one swift glance round to see that Winifred was safe, and then, climbing desperately over trunks and packing-cases and junctions of carriages, I began a frantic and none too confident search for G.

I was half-way up the train and had almost abandoned hope, when I came upon him in the process, like myself, of exploring the corridor – very tall, very thin, a little dishevelled, and forgetful, in his urgent seeking, of the haughty air worn by young dons who deliberately go steerage. Quite suddenly he saw me and started eagerly forward, his hands outstretched and his face a radiance of recognition beneath his wide-brimmed hat. And as I went up to him and took his hands, I felt that I had made no mistake; and although I knew that, in a sense which could never be true of him, I was linked with the past that I had yielded up, inextricably and for ever, I found it not inappropriate that the years of frustration and grief and loss, of work and conflict and painful resurrection, should have led me through their dark and devious ways to this new beginning.